NISSAN DATSUN 200SX/510/610/710/810/MAXIMA
1973-84 REPAIR MANUAL

Vice President–Finance   Barry L. Beck
Vice President–Sales   Glenn D. Potere
Vice President & Publisher   Dean F. Morgantini, S.A.E.
Manager–Consumer Print   Kevin M. G. Maher
Project Managers   Will Kessler, A.S.E., Richard Schwartz
Editor   Jaffer A. Ahmad

CHILTON *Automotive Books*
PUBLISHED BY **W. G. NICHOLS, INC.**

Manufactured in USA
© 1997 W. G. Nichols
Chilton Way, Radnor, PA 19089
ISBN 0-8019-9070-X
Library of Congress Catalog Card No. 97-67983
1234567890 6543210987

Contents

Contents

DRIVE TRAIN   **7**

SUSPENSION AND STEERING   **8**

BRAKES   **9**

BODY   **10**

GLOSSARY

MASTER INDEX

SAFETY NOTICE

Proper service and repair procedures are vital to the safe, reliable operation of all motor vehicles, as well as the personal safety of those performing repairs. This manual outlines procedures for servicing and repairing vehicles using safe, effective methods. The procedures contain many NOTES, CAUTIONS and WARNINGS which should be followed along with standard procedures to eliminate the possibility of personal injury or improper service which could damage the vehicle or compromise its safety.

It is important to note that the repair procedures and techniques, tools and parts for servicing motor vehicles, as well as the skill and experience of the individual performing the work vary widely. It is not possible to anticipate all of the conceivable ways or conditions under which vehicles may be serviced, or to provide cautions as to all of the possible hazards that may result. Standard and accepted safety precautions and equipment should be used when handling toxic or flammable fluids, and safety goggles or other protection should be used during cutting, grinding, chiseling, prying, or any other process that can cause material removal or projectiles.

Some procedures require the use of tools specially designed for a specific purpose. Before substituting another tool or procedure, you must be completely satisfied that neither your personal safety, nor the performance of the vehicle will be endangered.

Although information in this manual is based on industry sources and is complete as possible at the time of publication, the possibility exists that some vehicle manufacturers made later changes which could not be included here. While striving for total accuracy, W. G. Nichols, Inc. cannot assume responsibility for any errors, changes or omissions that may occur in the compilation of this data.

PART NUMBERS

Part numbers listed in this reference are not recommendations by Chilton for any product by brand name. They are references that can be used with interchange manuals and aftermarket supplier catalogs to locate each brand supplier's discrete part number.

SPECIAL TOOLS

Special tools are recommended by the vehicle manufacturer to perform their specific job. Use has been kept to a minimum, but where absolutely necessary, they are referred to in the text by the part number of the tool manufacturer. These tools can be purchased, under the appropriate part number, from your local dealer or regional distributor, or an equivalent tool can be purchased locally from a tool supplier or parts outlet. Before substituting any tool for the one recommended, read the SAFETY NOTICE at the top of this page.

ACKNOWLEDGMENTS

W. G. Nichols, Inc. expresses appreciation to Nissan Motor Company for their generous assistance.

1

GENERAL INFORMATION AND MAINTENANCE

HOW TO USE THIS BOOK

Chilton's Total Car Care manual is intended to help you learn more about the inner workings of your vehicle while saving you money on its upkeep and operation.

The beginning of the book will likely be referred to the most, since that is where you will find information for maintenance and tune-up. The other sections deal with the more complex systems of your vehicle. Operating systems from engine through brakes are covered to the extent that the average do-it-yourselfer becomes mechanically involved. This book will not explain such things as rebuilding a differential for the simple reason that the expertise required and the investment in special tools make this task uneconomical. It will, however, give you detailed instructions to help you change your own brake pads and shoes, replace spark plugs, and perform many more jobs that can save you money, give you personal satisfaction and help you avoid expensive problems.

A secondary purpose of this book is a reference for owners who want to understand their vehicle and/or their mechanics better. In this case, no tools at all are required.

Where to Begin

Before removing any bolts, read through the entire procedure. This will give you the overall view of what tools and supplies will be required. There is nothing more frustrating than having to walk to the bus stop on Monday morning because you were short one bolt on Sunday afternoon. So read ahead and plan ahead. Each operation should be approached logically and all procedures thoroughly understood before attempting any work.

All sections contain adjustments, maintenance, removal and installation procedures, and in some cases, repair or overhaul procedures. When repair is not considered practical, we tell you how to remove the part and then how to install the new or rebuilt replacement. In this way, you at least save the labor costs. Backyard repair of some components is just not practical.

Avoiding Trouble

Many procedures in this book require you to "label and disconnect . . ." a group of lines, hoses or wires. Don't be lulled into thinking you can remember where everything goes—you won't. If you hook up vacuum or fuel lines incorrectly, the vehicle will run poorly, if at all. If you hook up electrical wiring incorrectly, you may instantly learn a very expensive lesson.

You don't need to know the official or engineering name for each hose or line. A piece of masking tape on the hose and a piece on its fitting will allow you to assign your own label such as the letter A or a short name. As long as you remember your own code, the lines can be reconnected by matching similar letters or names. Do remember that tape will dissolve in gasoline or other fluids; if a component is to be washed or cleaned, use another method of identification. A permanent felt-tipped marker can be very handy for marking metal parts. Remove any tape or paper labels after assembly.

Maintenance or Repair?

It's necessary to mention the difference between maintenance and repair. Maintenance includes routine inspections, adjustments, and replacement of parts which show signs of normal wear. Maintenance compensates for wear or deterioration. Repair implies that something has broken or is not working. A need for repair is often caused by lack of maintenance. Example: draining and refilling the automatic transmission fluid is maintenance recommended by the manufacturer at specific mileage intervals. Failure to do this can ruin the transmission/transaxle, requiring very expensive repairs. While no maintenance program can prevent items from breaking or wearing out, a general rule can be stated: MAINTENANCE IS CHEAPER THAN REPAIR.

Two basic mechanic's rules should be mentioned here. First, whenever the left side of the vehicle or engine is referred to, it is meant to specify the driver's side. Conversely, the right side of the vehicle means the passenger's side. Second, most screws and bolts are removed by turning counterclockwise, and tightened by turning clockwise.

Safety is always the most important rule. Constantly be aware of the dangers involved in working on an automobile and take the proper precautions. See the information in this section regarding SERVICING YOUR VEHICLE SAFELY and the SAFETY NOTICE on the acknowledgment page.

Avoiding the Most Common Mistakes

Pay attention to the instructions provided. There are 3 common mistakes in mechanical work:

1. **Incorrect order of assembly, disassembly or adjustment.** When taking something apart or putting it together, performing steps in the wrong order usually just costs you extra time; however, it CAN break something. Read the entire procedure before beginning disassembly. Perform everything in the order in which the instructions say you should, even if you can't immediately see a reason for it. When you're taking apart something that is very intricate, you might want to draw a picture of how it looks when assembled at one point in order to make sure you get everything back in its proper position. We will supply exploded views whenever possible. When making adjustments, perform them in the proper order; often, one adjustment affects another, and you cannot expect even satisfactory results unless each adjustment is made only when it cannot be changed by any other.

2. **Overtorquing (or undertorquing).** While it is more common for overtorquing to cause damage, undertorquing may allow a fastener to vibrate loose causing serious damage. Especially when dealing with aluminum parts, pay attention to torque specifications and utilize a torque wrench in assembly. If a torque figure is not available, remember that if you are using the right tool to perform the job, you will probably not have to strain yourself to get a fastener tight enough. The pitch of most threads is so slight that the tension you put on the wrench will be multiplied many times in actual force on what you are tightening. A good example of how critical torque is can be seen in the case of spark plug installation, especially where you are putting the plug into an alumi-

num cylinder head. Too little torque can fail to crush the gasket, causing leakage of combustion gases and consequent overheating of the plug and engine parts. Too much torque can damage the threads or distort the plug, changing the spark gap.

There are many commercial products available for ensuring that fasteners won't come loose, even if they are not torqued just right (a very common brand is Loctite®). If you're worried about getting something together tight enough to hold, but loose enough to avoid mechanical damage during assembly, one of these products might offer substantial insurance. Before choosing a threadlocking compound, read the label on the package and make sure the product is compatible with the materials, fluids, etc. involved.

3. **Crossthreading.** This occurs when a part such as a bolt is screwed into a nut or casting at the wrong angle and forced. Crossthreading is more likely to occur if access is difficult. It helps to clean and lubricate fasteners, then to start threading with the part to be installed positioned straight in. Then, start the bolt, spark plug, etc. with your fingers. If you encounter resistance, unscrew the part and start over again at a different angle until it can be inserted and turned several times without much effort. Keep in mind that many parts, especially spark plugs, have tapered threads, so that gentle turning will automatically bring the part you're threading to the proper angle, but only if you don't force it or resist a change in angle. Don't put a wrench on the part until it's been tightened a couple of turns by hand. If you suddenly encounter resistance, and the part has not seated fully, don't force it. Pull it back out to make sure it's clean and threading properly.

Always take your time and be patient; once you have some experience, working on your vehicle may well become an enjoyable hobby.

TOOLS AND EQUIPMENT

Naturally, without the proper tools and equipment it is impossible to properly service your vehicle. It would also be virtually impossible to catalog every tool that you would need to perform all of the operations in this book. Of course, It would be unwise for the amateur to rush out and buy an expensive set of tools on the theory that he/she may need one or more of them at some time.

The best approach is to proceed slowly, gathering a good quality set of those tools that are used most frequently. Don't be misled by the low cost of bargain tools. It is far better to spend a little more for better quality. Forged wrenches, 6 or 12-point sockets and fine tooth ratchets are by far preferable to their less expensive counterparts. As any good mechanic can tell you, there are few worse experiences than trying to work on a vehicle with bad tools. Your monetary savings will be far outweighed by frustration and mangled knuckles.

Begin accumulating those tools that are used most frequently: those associated with routine maintenance and tune-up. In addition to the normal assortment of screwdrivers and pliers, you should have the following tools:

• Wrenches/sockets and combination open end/box end wrenches in sizes from ⅛–¾ in. or 3mm–19mm (depending on whether your vehicle uses standard or metric fasteners) and a 13⁄16 in. or ⅝ in. spark plug socket (depending on plug type).

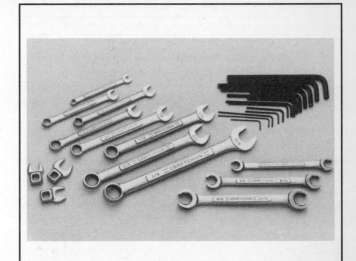

In addition to ratchets, a good set of wrenches and hex keys will be necessary

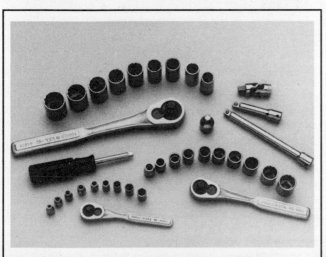

All but the most basic procedures will require an assortment of ratchets and sockets

A hydraulic floor jack and a set of jackstands are essential for lifting and supporting the vehicle

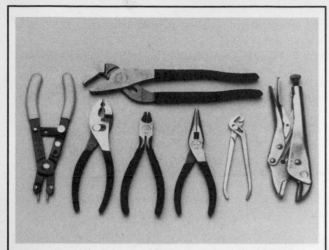

An assortment of pliers, grippers and cutters will be handy for old rusted parts and stripped bolt heads

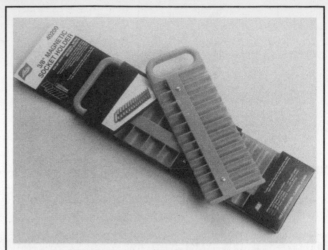

Tools from specialty manufacturers such as Lisle® are designed to make your job easier . . .

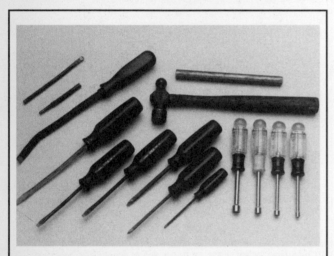

Various drivers, chisels and prybars are great tools to have in your toolbox

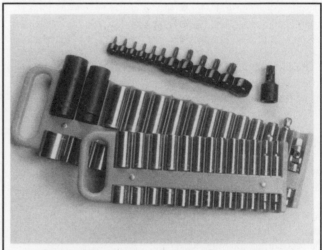

. . . these Torx® drivers and magnetic socket holders are just 2 examples of their handy products

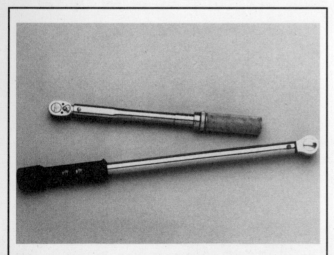

Many repairs will require the use of a torque wrench to assure the components are properly fastened

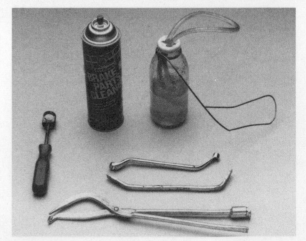

Although not always necessary, using specialized brake tools will save time

A few inexpensive lubrication tools will make maintenance easier

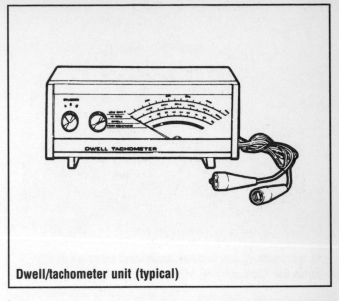

Dwell/tachometer unit (typical)

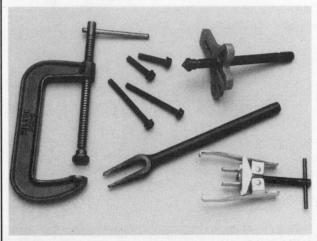

Various pullers, clamps and separator tools are needed for many larger, more complicated repairs

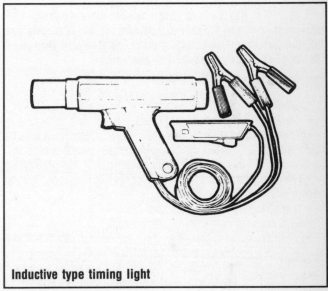

Inductive type timing light

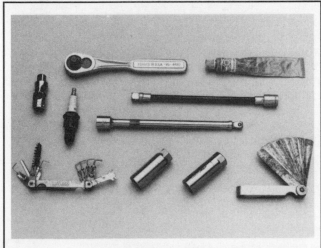

A variety of tools and gauges should be used for spark plug gapping and installation

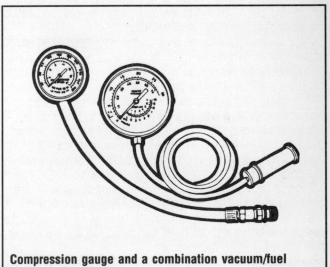

Compression gauge and a combination vacuum/fuel pressure test gauge

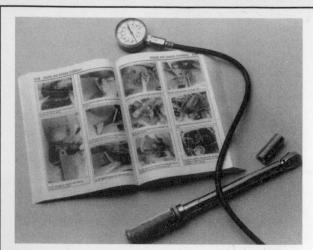

Proper information is vital, so always have a Chilton Total Car Care manual handy

➡️**If possible, buy various length socket drive extensions. Universal-joint and wobble extensions can be extremely useful, but be careful when using them, as they can change the amount of torque applied to the socket.**

• Jackstands for support.
• Oil filter wrench.
• Spout or funnel for pouring fluids.
• Grease gun for chassis lubrication (unless your vehicle is not equipped with any grease fittings—for details, please refer to information on Fluids and Lubricants found later in this section).
• Hydrometer for checking the battery (unless equipped with a sealed, maintenance-free battery).
• A container for draining oil and other fluids.
• Rags for wiping up the inevitable mess.

In addition to the above items there are several others that are not absolutely necessary, but handy to have around. These include Oil Dry® (or an equivalent oil absorbent gravel—such as cat litter) and the usual supply of lubricants, antifreeze and fluids, although these can be purchased as needed. This is a basic list for routine maintenance, but only your personal needs and desire can accurately determine your list of tools.

After performing a few projects on the vehicle, you'll be amazed at the other tools and non-tools on your workbench. Some useful household items are: a large turkey baster or siphon, empty coffee cans and ice trays (to store parts), ball of twine, electrical tape for wiring, small rolls of colored tape for tagging lines or hoses, markers and pens, a note pad, golf tees (for plugging vacuum lines), metal coat hangers or a roll of mechanics's wire (to hold things out of the way), dental pick or similar long, pointed probe, a strong magnet, and a small mirror (to see into recesses and under manifolds).

A more advanced set of tools, suitable for tune-up work, can be drawn up easily. While the tools are slightly more sophisticated, they need not be outrageously expensive. There are several inexpensive tach/dwell meters on the market that are every bit as good for the average mechanic as a professional model. Just be sure that it goes to a least 1200–1500 rpm on the tach scale and that it works on 4, 6 and 8-cylinder engines. (If you own one or

more vehicles with a diesel engine, a special tachometer is required since diesels don't use spark plug ignition systems). The key to these purchases is to make them with an eye towards adaptability and wide range. A basic list of tune-up tools could include:
• Tach/dwell meter.
• Spark plug wrench and gapping tool.
• Feeler gauges for valve or point adjustment. (Even if your vehicle does not use points or require valve adjustments, a feeler gauge is helpful for many repair/overhaul procedures).

A tachometer/dwell meter will ensure accurate tune-up work on vehicles without electronic ignition. The choice of a timing light should be made carefully. A light which works on the DC current supplied by the vehicle's battery is the best choice; it should have a xenon tube for brightness. On any vehicle with an electronic ignition system, a timing light with an inductive pickup that clamps around the No. 1 spark plug cable is preferred.

In addition to these basic tools, there are several other tools and gauges you may find useful. These include:
• Compression gauge. The screw-in type is slower to use, but eliminates the possibility of a faulty reading due to escaping pressure.
• Manifold vacuum gauge.
• 12V test light.
• A combination volt/ohmmeter
• Induction Ammeter. This is used for determining whether or not there is current in a wire. These are handy for use if a wire is broken somewhere in a wiring harness.

As a final note, you will probably find a torque wrench necessary for all but the most basic work. The beam type models are perfectly adequate, although the newer click types (breakaway) are easier to use. The click type torque wrenches tend to be more expensive. Also keep in mind that all types of torque wrenches should be periodically checked and/or recalibrated. You will have to decide for yourself which better fits your purpose.

Special Tools

▶ **See Figure 1**

Normally, the use of special factory tools is avoided for repair procedures, since these are not readily available for the do-it-yourself mechanic. When it is possible to perform the job with more commonly available tools, it will be pointed out, but occasionally, a special tool was designed to perform a specific function and should be used. Before substituting another tool, you should be convinced that neither your safety nor the performance of the vehicle will be compromised.

Special tools can usually be purchased from an automotive parts store or from your dealer. In some cases special tools may be available directly from the tool manufacturer, such as:
Kent-Moore Corporation
29784 Little Mack
Roseville, Michigan 48066

In Canada:
Kent-Moore of Canada, Ltd.,
2395 Cawthra
Mississauga, Ontario
Canada L5A 3P2

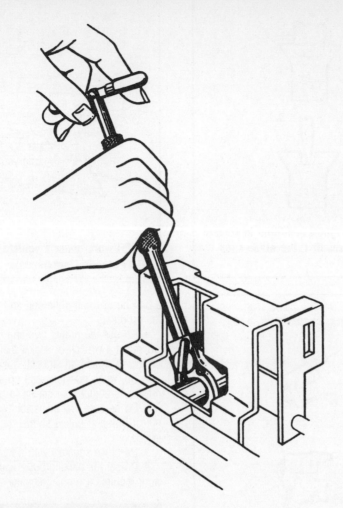

Fig. 1 It may be necessary to acquire special tools for certain jobs

SERVICING YOUR VEHICLE SAFELY

It is virtually impossible to anticipate all of the hazards involved with automotive maintenance and service, but care and common sense will prevent most accidents.

The rules of safety for mechanics range from "don't smoke around gasoline," to "use the proper tool(s) for the job." The trick to avoiding injuries is to develop safe work habits and to take every possible precaution.

Do's

• Do keep a fire extinguisher and first aid kit handy.

• Do wear safety glasses or goggles when cutting, drilling, grinding or prying, even if you have 20–20 vision. If you wear glasses for the sake of vision, wear safety goggles over your regular glasses.

• Do shield your eyes whenever you work around the battery. Batteries contain sulfuric acid. In case of contact with the eyes or skin, flush the area with water or a mixture of water and baking soda, then seek immediate medical attention.

• Do use safety stands (jackstands) for any undervehicle ser-

vice. Jacks are for raising vehicles; jackstands are for making sure the vehicle stays raised until you want it to come down. Whenever the vehicle is raised, block the wheels remaining on the ground and set the parking brake.

• Do use adequate ventilation when working with any chemicals or hazardous materials. Like carbon monoxide, the asbestos dust resulting from some brake lining wear can be hazardous in sufficient quantities.

• Do disconnect the negative battery cable when working on the electrical system. The secondary ignition system contains EXTREMELY HIGH VOLTAGE. In some cases it can even exceed 50,000 volts.

• Do follow manufacturer's directions whenever working with potentially hazardous materials. Most chemicals and fluids are poisonous if taken internally.

• Do properly maintain your tools. Loose hammerheads, mushroomed punches and chisels, frayed or poorly grounded electrical cords, excessively worn screwdrivers, spread wrenches (open end), cracked sockets, slipping ratchets, or faulty droplight sockets can cause accidents.

• Likewise, keep your tools clean; a greasy wrench can slip off

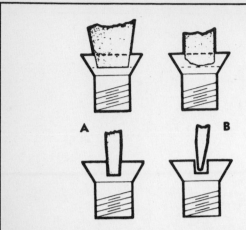

Screwdrivers should be kept in good condition to prevent injury or damage which could result if the blade slips from the screw

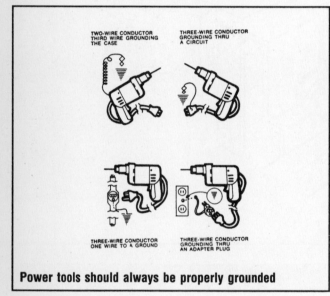

TWO-WIRE CONDUCTOR THIRD WIRE GROUNDING THE CASE

THREE-WIRE CONDUCTOR GROUNDING THRU A CIRCUIT

THREE-WIRE CONDUCTOR ONE WIRE TO A GROUND

THREE-WIRE CONDUCTOR GROUNDING THRU AN ADAPTER PLUG

Power tools should always be properly grounded

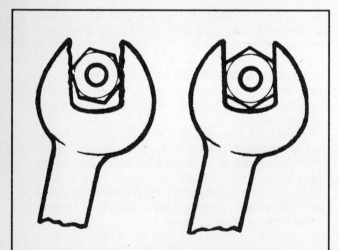

Using the correct size wrench will help prevent the possibility of rounding off a nut

NEVER work under a vehicle unless it is supported using safety stands (jackstands)

a bolt head, ruining the bolt and often harming your knuckles in the process.

• Do use the proper size and type of tool for the job at hand. Do select a wrench or socket that fits the nut or bolt. The wrench or socket should sit straight, not cocked.

• Do, when possible, pull on a wrench handle rather than push on it, and adjust your stance to prevent a fall.

• Do be sure that adjustable wrenches are tightly closed on the nut or bolt and pulled so that the force is on the side of the fixed jaw.

• Do strike squarely with a hammer; avoid glancing blows.

• Do set the parking brake and block the drive wheels if the work requires a running engine.

Don'ts

♦ See Figure 2

• Don't run the engine in a garage or anywhere else without proper ventilation—EVER! Carbon monoxide is poisonous; it takes a long time to leave the human body and you can build up a deadly supply of it in your system by simply breathing in a little every day. You may not realize you are slowly poisoning yourself. Always use power vents, windows, fans and/or open the garage door.

• Don't work around moving parts while wearing loose clothing. Short sleeves are much safer than long, loose sleeves. Hard-toed shoes with neoprene soles protect your toes and give a better grip on slippery surfaces. Jewelry such as watches, fancy belt buckles, beads or body adornment of any kind is not safe working around a vehicle. Long hair should be tied back under a hat or cap.

• Don't use pockets for toolboxes. A fall or bump can drive a screwdriver deep into your body. Even a rag hanging from your back pocket can wrap around a spinning shaft or fan.

• Don't smoke when working around gasoline, cleaning solvent or other flammable material.

• Don't smoke when working around the battery. When the battery is being charged, it gives off explosive hydrogen gas.

• Don't use gasoline to wash your hands; there are excellent

Fig. 2 Don't work on a car for so long that you begin to lose your sense of reality

soaps available. Gasoline contains dangerous additives which can enter the body through a cut or through your pores. Gasoline also removes all the natural oils from the skin so that bone dry hands will suck up oil and grease.

• Don't service the air conditioning system unless you are equipped with the necessary tools and training. When liquid or compressed gas refrigerant is released to atmospheric pressure it will absorb heat from whatever it contacts. This will chill or freeze anything it touches. Although refrigerant is normally non-toxic, R-12 becomes a deadly poisonous gas in the presence of an open flame. One good whiff of the vapors from burning refrigerant can be fatal.

• Don't use screwdrivers for anything other than driving screws! A screwdriver used as an prying tool can snap when you least expect it, causing injuries. At the very least, you'll ruin a good screwdriver.

• Don't use a bumper or emergency jack (that little ratchet, scissors, or pantograph jack supplied with the vehicle) for anything other than changing a flat! These jacks are only intended for emergency use out on the road; they are NOT designed as a maintenance tool. If you are serious about maintaining your vehicle yourself, invest in a hydraulic floor jack of at least a 1½ ton capacity, and at least two sturdy jackstands.

FASTENERS, MEASUREMENTS AND CONVERSIONS

Bolts, Nuts and Other Threaded Retainers

Although there are a great variety of fasteners found in the modern car or truck, the most commonly used retainer is the threaded fastener (nuts, bolts, screws, studs, etc). Most threaded retainers may be reused, provided that they are not damaged in use or during the repair. Some retainers (such as stretch bolts or torque prevailing nuts) are designed to deform when tightened or in use and should not be reinstalled.

Whenever possible, we will note any special retainers which should be replaced during a procedure. But you should always inspect the condition of a retainer when it is removed and replace any that show signs of damage. Check all threads for rust or corrosion which can increase the torque necessary to achieve the desired clamp load for which that fastener was originally selected. Additionally, be sure that the driver surface of the fastener has not been compromised by rounding or other damage. In some cases a driver surface may become only partially rounded, allowing the driver to catch in only one direction. In many of these occurrences, a fastener may be installed and tightened, but the driver would not be able to grip and loosen the fastener again. (This could lead to frustration down the line should that component ever need to be disassembled again).

If you must replace a fastener, whether due to design or damage, you must ALWAYS be sure to use the proper replacement. In all cases, a retainer of the same design, material and strength should be used. Markings on the heads of most bolts will help determine the proper strength of the fastener. The same material, thread and pitch must be selected to assure proper installation and safe operation of the vehicle afterwards.

Thread gauges are available to help measure a bolt or stud's thread. Most automotive and hardware stores keep gauges available to help you select the proper size. In a pinch, you can use another nut or bolt for a thread gauge. If the bolt you are replacing is not too badly damaged, you can select a match by finding another bolt which will thread in its place. If you find a nut which

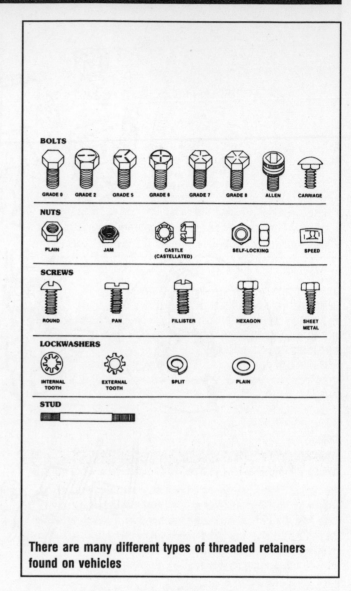

There are many different types of threaded retainers found on vehicles

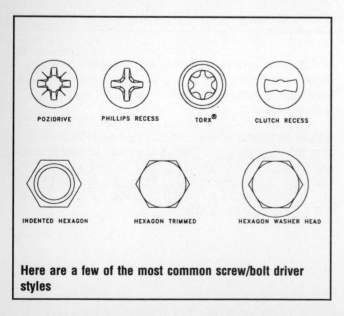

Here are a few of the most common screw/bolt driver styles

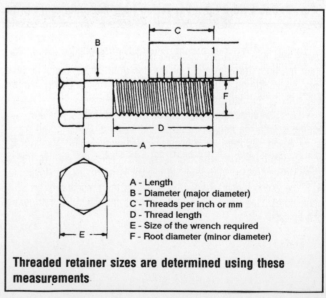

A - Length
B - Diameter (major diameter)
C - Threads per inch or mm
D - Thread length
E - Size of the wrench required
F - Root diameter (minor diameter)

Threaded retainer sizes are determined using these measurements

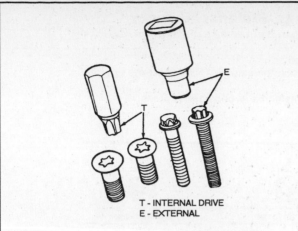

Special fasteners such as these Torx® head bolts are used by manufacturers to discourage people from working on vehicles without the proper tools

threads properly onto the damaged bolt, then use that nut to help select the replacement bolt. If however, the bolt you are replacing is so badly damaged (broken or drilled out) that its threads cannot be used as a gauge, you might start by looking for another bolt (from the same assembly or a similar location on your vehicle) which will thread into the damaged bolt's mounting. If so, the other bolt can be used to select a nut; the nut can then be used to select the replacement bolt.

In all cases, be absolutely sure you have selected the proper replacement. Don't be shy, you can always ask the store clerk for help.

✳✳ WARNING

Be aware that when you find a bolt with damaged threads, you may also find the nut or drilled hole it was threaded into has also been damaged. If this is the case, you may have to drill and tap the hole, replace the nut or otherwise repair the threads. NEVER try to force a replacement bolt to fit into the damaged threads.

Torque

Torque is defined as the measurement of resistance to turning or rotating. It tends to twist a body about an axis of rotation. A common example of this would be tightening a threaded retainer such as a nut, bolt or screw. Measuring torque is one of the most common ways to help assure that a threaded retainer has been properly fastened.

When tightening a threaded fastener, torque is applied in three distinct areas, the head, the bearing surface and the clamp load. About 50 percent of the measured torque is used in overcoming bearing friction. This is the friction between the bearing surface of the bolt head, screw head or nut face and the base material or washer (the surface on which the fastener is rotating). Approxi-

mately 40 percent of the applied torque is used in overcoming thread friction. This leaves only about 10 percent of the applied torque to develop a useful clamp load (the force which holds a joint together). This means that friction can account for as much as 90 percent of the applied torque on a fastener.

TORQUE WRENCHES

In most applications, a torque wrench can be used to assure proper installation of a fastener. Torque wrenches come in various designs and most automotive supply stores will carry a variety to suit your needs. A torque wrench should be used any time we supply a specific torque value for a fastener. A torque wrench can also be used if you are following the general guidelines in the accompanying charts. Keep in mind that because there is no worldwide standardization of fasteners, the charts are a general guideline and should be used with caution. Again, the general rule of "if you are using the right tool for the job, you should not have to strain to tighten a fastener" applies here.

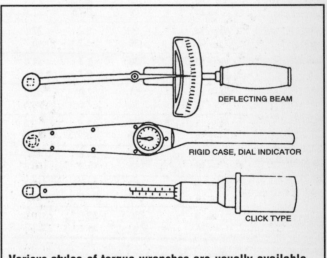

Various styles of torque wrenches are usually available at your local automotive supply store

Beam Type

The beam type torque wrench is one of the most popular types. It consists of a pointer attached to the head that runs the length of the flexible beam (shaft) to a scale located near the handle. As the wrench is pulled, the beam bends and the pointer indicates the torque using the scale.

Click (Breakaway) Type

Another popular design of torque wrench is the click type. To use the click type wrench you pre-adjust it to a torque setting. Once the torque is reached, the wrench has a reflex signalling feature that causes a momentary breakaway of the torque wrench body, sending an impulse to the operator's hand.

Standard Torque Specifications and Fastener Markings

In the absence of specific torques, the following chart can be used as a guide to the maximum safe torque of a particular size/grade of fastener.

- There is no torque difference for fine or coarse threads.
- Torque values are based on clean, dry threads. Reduce the value by 10% if threads are oiled prior to assembly.
- The torque required for aluminum components or fasteners is considerably less.

U.S. Bolts

SAE Grade Number	1 or 2			5			6 or 7		
Number of lines always 2 less than the grade number.									
Bolt Size (inches)—(Thread)	Ft./Lbs.	Kgm	Nm	Ft./Lbs.	Kgm	Nm	Ft./Lbs.	Kgm	Nm
¼ — 20	5	0.7	6.8	8	1.1	10.8	10	1.4	13.5
— 28	6	0.8	8.1	10	1.4	13.6			
5/16 — 18	11	1.5	14.9	17	2.3	23.0	19	2.6	25.8
— 24	13	1.8	17.6	19	2.6	25.7			
⅜ — 16	18	2.5	24.4	31	4.3	42.0	34	4.7	46.0
— 24	20	2.75	27.1	35	4.8	47.5			
7/16 — 14	28	3.8	37.0	49	6.8	66.4	55	7.6	74.5
— 20	30	4.2	40.7	55	7.6	74.5			
½ — 13	39	5.4	52.8	75	10.4	101.7	85	11.75	115.2
— 20	41	5.7	55.6	85	11.7	115.2			
9/16 — 12	51	7.0	69.2	110	15.2	149.1	120	16.6	162.7
— 18	55	7.6	74.5	120	16.6	162.7			
⅝ — 11	83	11.5	112.5	150	20.7	203.3	167	23.0	226.5
— 18	95	13.1	128.8	170	23.5	230.5			
¾ — 10	105	14.5	142.3	270	37.3	366.0	280	38.7	379.6
— 16	115	15.9	155.9	295	40.8	400.0			
⅞ — 9	160	22.1	216.9	395	54.6	535.5	440	60.9	596.5
— 14	175	24.2	237.2	435	60.1	589.7			
1 — 8	236	32.5	318.6	590	81.6	799.9	660	91.3	894.8
— 14	250	34.6	338.9	660	91.3	849.8			

Metric Bolts

Relative Strength Marking	4.6, 4.8			8.8		
Bolt Markings						
Bolt Size Thread Size x Pitch (mm)	Ft./Lbs.	Kgm	Nm	Ft./Lbs.	Kgm	Nm
6 x 1.0	2–3	.2–.4	3–4	3–6	4–.8	5–8
8 x 1.25	6–8	.8–1	8–12	9–14	1.2–1.9	13–19
10 x 1.25	12–17	1.5–2.3	16–23	20–29	2.7–4.0	27–39
12 x 1.25	21–32	2.9–4.4	29–43	35–53	4.8–7.3	47–72
14 x 1.5	35–52	4.8–7.1	48–70	57–85	7.8–11.7	77–110
16 x 1.5	51–77	7.0–10.6	67–100	90–120	12.4–16.5	130–160
18 x 1.5	74–110	10.2–15.1	100–150	130–170	17.9–23.4	180–230
20 x 1.5	110–140	15.1–19.3	150–190	190–240	26.2–46.9	160–320
22 x 1.5	150–190	22.0–26.2	200–260	250–320	34.5–44.1	340–430
24 x 1.5	190–240	26.2–46.9	260–320	310–410	42.7–56.5	420–550

Standard and metric bolt torque specifications based on bolt strengths—WARNING: use only as a guide

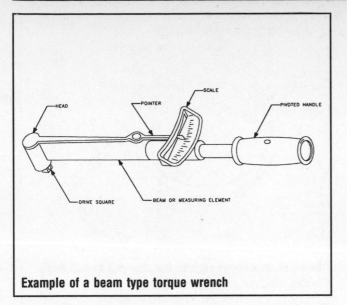

Example of a beam type torque wrench

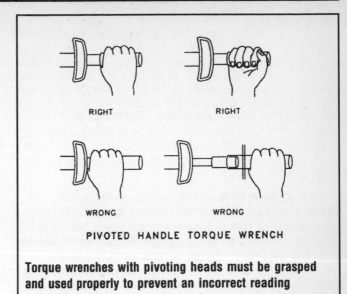

Torque wrenches with pivoting heads must be grasped and used properly to prevent an incorrect reading

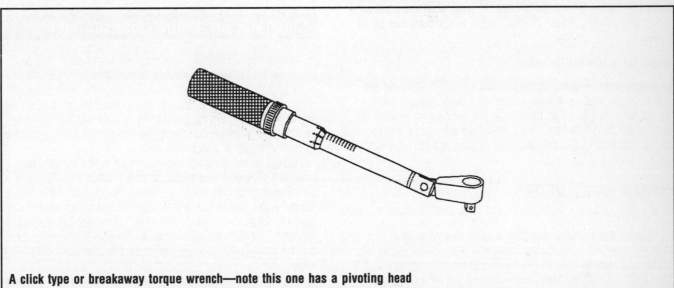

A click type or breakaway torque wrench—note this one has a pivoting head

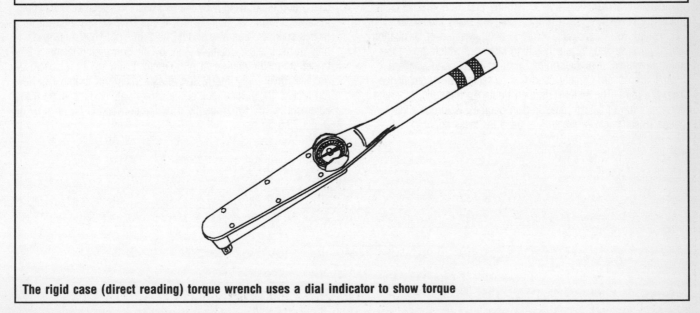

The rigid case (direct reading) torque wrench uses a dial indicator to show torque

Pivot Head Type

Some torque wrenches (usually of the click type) may be equipped with a pivot head which can allow it to be used in areas of limited access. BUT, it must be used properly. To hold a pivot head wrench, grasp the handle lightly, and as you pull on the handle, it should be floated on the pivot point. If the handle comes in contact with the yoke extension during the process of pulling, there is a very good chance the torque readings will be inaccurate because this could alter the wrench loading point. The design of the handle is usually such as to make it inconvenient to deliberately misuse the wrench.

➡ **It should be mentioned that the use of any U-joint, wobble or extension will have an effect on the torque readings, no matter what type of wrench you are using. For the most accurate readings, install the socket directly on the wrench driver. If necessary, straight extensions (which hold a socket directly under the wrench driver) will have the least effect on the torque reading. Avoid any extension that alters the length of the wrench from the handle to the head/driving point (such as a crow's foot). U-joint or Wobble extensions can greatly affect the readings; avoid their use at all times.**

Rigid Case (Direct Reading)

A rigid case or direct reading torque wrench is equipped with a dial indicator to show torque values. One advantage of these wrenches is that they can be held at any position on the wrench without affecting accuracy. These wrenches are often preferred because they tend to be compact, easy to read and have a great degree of accuracy.

TORQUE ANGLE METERS

Because the frictional characteristics of each fastener or threaded hole will vary, clamp loads which are based strictly on torque will vary as well. In most applications, this variance is not significant enough to cause worry. But, in certain applications, a manufacturer's engineers may determine that more precise clamp loads are necessary (such is the case with many aluminum cylinder heads). In these cases, a torque angle method of installation would be specified. When installing fasteners which are torque angle tightened, a predetermined seating torque and standard torque wrench are usually used first to remove any compliance from the joint. The fastener is then tightened the specified additional portion of a turn measured in degrees. A torque angle gauge (mechanical protractor) is used for these applications.

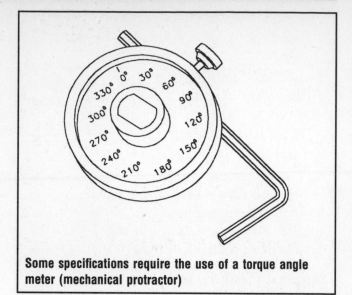

Some specifications require the use of a torque angle meter (mechanical protractor)

Standard and Metric Measurements

Throughout this manual, specifications are given to help you determine the condition of various components on your vehicle, or to assist you in their installation. Some of the most common measurements include length (in. or cm/mm), torque (ft. lbs., inch lbs. or Nm) and pressure (psi, in. Hg, kPa or mm Hg). In most cases, we strive to provide the proper measurement as determined by the manufacturer's engineers.

Though, in some cases, that value may not be conveniently measured with what is available in your toolbox. Luckily, many of the measuring devices which are available today will have two scales so the Standard or Metric measurements may easily be taken. If any of the various measuring tools which are available to you do not contain the same scale as listed in the specifications, use the accompanying conversion factors to determine the proper value.

The conversion factor chart is used by taking the given specification and multiplying it by the necessary conversion factor. For instance, looking at the first line, if you have a measurement in inches such as "free-play should be 2 in." but your ruler reads only in millimeters, multiply 2 in. by the conversion factor of 25.4 to get the metric equivalent of 50.8mm. Likewise, if the specification was given only in a Metric measurement, for example in Newton Meters (Nm), then look at the center column first. If the measurement is 100 Nm, multiply it by the conversion factor of 0.738 to get 73.8 ft. lbs.

CONVERSION FACTORS

LENGTH–DISTANCE

Inches (in.)	x 25.4	= Millimeters (mm)	x .0394 = Inches
Feet (ft.)	x .305	= Meters (m)	x 3.281 = Feet
Miles	x 1.609	= Kilometers (km)	x .0621 = Miles

VOLUME

Cubic Inches (in3)	x 16.387	= Cubic Centimeters	x .061 = in3
IMP Pints (IMP pt.)	x .568	= Liters (L)	x 1.76 = IMP pt.
IMP Quarts (IMP qt.)	x 1.137	= Liters (L)	x .88 = IMP qt.
IMP Gallons (IMP gal.)	x 4.546	= Liters (L)	x .22 = IMP gal.
IMP Quarts (IMP qt.)	x 1.201	= US Quarts (US qt.)	x .833 = IMP qt
IMP Gallons (IMP gal.)	x 1.201	= US Gallons (US gal.)	x .833 = IMP gal.
Fl. Ounces	x 29.573	= Milliliters	x .034 = Ounces
US Pints (US pt.)	x .473	= Liters (L)	x 2.113 = Pints
US Quarts (US qt.)	x .946	= Liters (L)	x 1.057 = Quarts
US Gallons (US gal.)	x 3.785	= Liters (L)	x .264 = Gallons

MASS–WEIGHT

Ounces (oz.)	x 28.35	= Grams (g)	x .035 = Ounces
Pounds (lb.)	x .454	= Kilograms (kg)	x 2.205 = Pounds

PRESSURE

Pounds Per Sq. In. (psi)	x 6.895	= Kilopascals (kPa)	x .145 = psi
Inches of Mercury (Hg)	x .4912	= psi	x 2.036 = Hg
Inches of Mercury (Hg)	x 3.377	= Kilopascals (kPa)	x .2961 = Hg
Inches of Water (H_2O)	x .07355	= Inches of Mercury	x 13.783 = H_2O
Inches of Water (H_2O)	x .03613	= psi	x 27.684 = H_2O
Inches of Water (H_2O)	x .248	= Kilopascals (kPa)	x 4.026 = H_2O

TORQUE

Pounds–Force Inches (in–lb)	x .113	= Newton Meters (N·m)	x 8.85 = in–lb
Pounds–Force Feet (ft–lb)	x 1.356	= Newton Meters (N·m)	x .738 = ft–lb

VELOCITY

Miles Per Hour (MPH)	x 1.609	= Kilometers Per Hour (KPH)	x .621 = MPH

POWER

Horsepower (Hp)	x .745	= Kilowatts	x 1.34 = Horsepower

FUEL CONSUMPTION*

Miles Per Gallon IMP (MPG)	x .354	= Kilometers Per Liter (Km/L)
Kilometers Per Liter (Km/L)	x 2.352	= IMP MPG
Miles Per Gallon US (MPG)	x .425	= Kilometers Per Liter (Km/L)
Kilometers Per Liter (Km/L)	x 2.352	= US MPG

*It is common to covert from miles per gallon (mpg) to liters/100 kilometers (1/100 km), where mpg (IMP) x 1/100 km = 282 and mpg (US) x 1/100 km = 235.

TEMPERATURE

Degree Fahrenheit (°F) = (°C x 1.8) + 32

Degree Celsius (°C) = (°F – 32) x .56

Standard and metric conversion factors chart

SERIAL NUMBER IDENTIFICATION

♦ See Figure 3

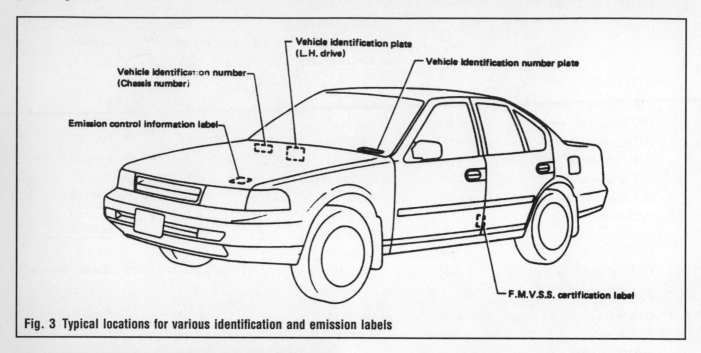

Fig. 3 Typical locations for various identification and emission labels

Vehicle

♦ **See Figures 4, 5, 6, 7 and 8**

The vehicle identification plate is located on the cowl at the rear of the engine compartment. The plate contains the model type, engine capacity, maximum horsepower, wheelbase and the engine and chassis serial numbers.

The vehicle or chassis serial number is broken down as shown in the illustration and described below. The Vehicle Identification Number (VIN) is also reproduced on a plate on the upper left surface of the instrument panel and can be seen from the outside through the windshield. **The VIN is broken down as follows:**

The Vehicle Identification Number (VIN) is stamped on a plate riveted to the firewall

- First three digits/letters: Manufacturer
- Fourth letter: Engine type
- Fifth letter: Vehicle line
- Sixth digit: Model change number (0–9)
- Seventh digit: Body type (sedan or wagon)
- Eighth letter: Restraint system. S means standard
- Ninth digit: Check digit 0–9 or X to verify that the serial number is being read off the car itself
- Tenth letter: Model year in a letter code
- Eleventh letter: Manufacturing plant code
- Last six digits: Vehicle serial (chassis) number

Fig. 4 A common Vehicle Identification Number (VIN) plate

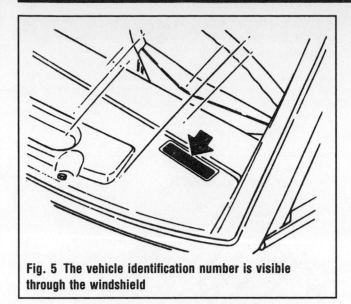

Fig. 5 The vehicle identification number is visible through the windshield

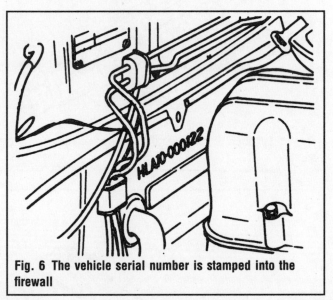

Fig. 6 The vehicle serial number is stamped into the firewall

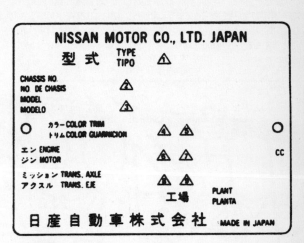

1   Type
2   Vehicle identification number (Chassis number)
3   Model
4   Body color code
5   Trim color code
6   Engine model
7   Engine displacement
8   Transmission model
9   Axle model

Vehicle identification plate

Fig. 7 Breakdown of a common vehicle identification plate

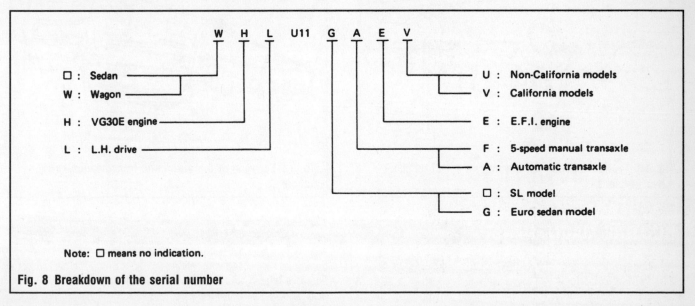

□ : Sedan
W : Wagon
H : VG30E engine
L : L.H. drive

U : Non-California models
V : California models
E : E.F.I. engine
F : 5-speed manual transaxle
A : Automatic transaxle
□ : SL model
G : Euro sedan model

Note: □ means no indication.

Fig. 8 Breakdown of the serial number

Engine

▶ **See Figures 9 and 10**

The engine serial number is stamped on the right side top edge of the cylinder block on all rear wheel drive models except the 1980 and later 200SX. 1980–81 200SX engine (Z20, Z22) numbers are stamped on the left side top edge of the cylinder block.

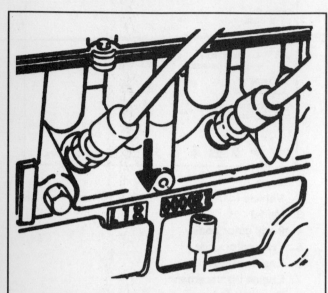

Fig. 9 Typical location for the engine serial number— gasoline engines

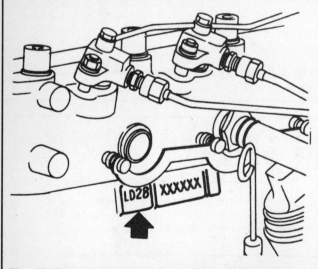

Fig. 10 Typical location for the engine serial number— diesel engines

Transmission

▶ **See Figures 11 and 12**

The transmission serial number is stamped on the front upper face of the transmission case on manual transmissions, or on the lower right side of the case on automatic transmissions.

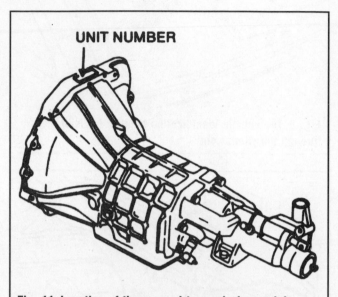

Fig. 11 Location of the manual transmission serial number

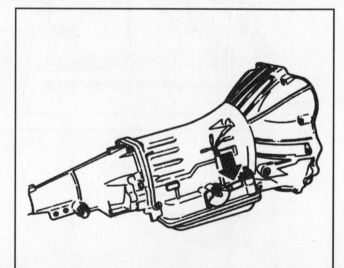

Fig. 12 Location of the automatic transmission serial number

ROUTINE MAINTENANCE

Routine maintenance is the self-explanatory term used to describe the sort of periodic work necessary to keep a car in safe and reliable working order. A regular program aimed at monitoring essential systems ensure that the car's components are functioning correctly (and will continue to do so until the next inspection, one hopes), and can prevent small problems from developing into major headaches. Routine maintenance also pays off big dividends in keeping major repair costs at a minimum, ex-

UNDERHOOD MAINTENANCE COMPONENT LOCATIONS (TYPICAL)

1. Automatic transmission dipstick
2. Brake master cylinder reservoir
3. Engine oil dipstick
4. Engine oil filler cap
5. Windshield washer fluid reservoir
6. Power steering fluid reservoir
7. Drive belts (below air cleaner duct)
8. Air cleaner housing
9. Battery terminals
10. Coolant overflow tank
11. Radiator cap
12. Air conditioning sight glass

tending the life of the car, and enhancing resale value, should you ever desire to part with your Datsun/Nissan.

A very definite maintenance schedule is provided by Nissan, and must be followed to keep the car working properly. The Maintenance Intervals chart in this chapter outlines the routine maintenance which must be performed according to intervals based on either accumulated mileage or time. Your car also came with a maintenance schedule provided by Nissan. Adherence to these schedules will result in a longer life for your car, and will, over the long run, save you money and time.

The checks and adjustments in the following sections generally require only a few minutes of attention every few weeks. The services to be performed can be easily accomplished in a morning. The most important part of any maintenance program is regularity. The few minutes or occasional morning spent on these seemingly trivial tasks will forestall or eliminate major problems later.

Air Cleaner

♦ **See Figure 13**

An air cleaner is used to keep airborne dirt and dust out of the air flowing through the engine. Proper maintenance is vital, as a clogged element will undesirably enrichen the fuel mixture, restrict air flow and power, and allow excessive contamination of the oil with abrasives.

Fig. 13 Air filter box—810 and Maxima style shown; 200SX and diesel engine vehicles similar

All models covered in this book are equipped with a disposable, paper cartridge air cleaner element. The filter should be checked at every tune-up (sooner if the car is operated in a dusty area). Loose dust can sometimes be removed by striking the filter against a hard surface several times or by blowing through it with compressed air. The filter should be replaced every 24,000 miles (30,000 miles, 1979 and later).

REMOVAL & INSTALLATION

♦ **See Figures 14 and 15**

1. Remove the wingnuts, if applicable, and/or lift off the thumb latches.

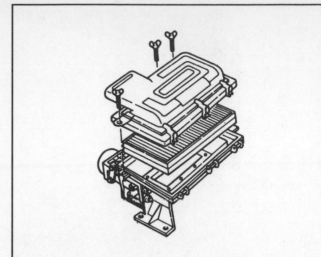

Fig. 14 Exploded view of a common air filter box—fuel injected engines

The air cleaner for this fuel injected car is in a plastic housing

2. Lift off the housing cover, then remove the filter element.
To install:
3. Wipe out the inside of the housing with a clean rag or paper towel.
4. Install the air cleaner element.
5. Seat the top cover and refasten it with the wingnuts and/or thumb latches.

➡**Fuel injected models (810, Maxima, and 1980–81 200SX) utilize a flat, cartridge type air cleaner element. Although removal and installation procedures for these models are the same as for those with round air cleaners, make sure that the word UP is facing up when you install the filter element.**

Unfasten the hold-down clips at the air filter housing

Lift off the housing lid to expose the air filter

Lift out the air filter element for inspection and/or replacement

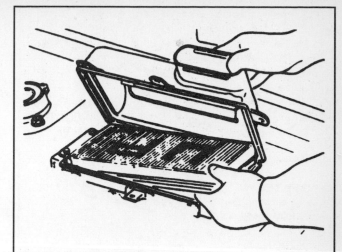

Fig. 15 On fuel injected models, install the air filter with the correct side (UP)

Air Induction Valve Filter

REMOVAL & INSTALLATION

◆ **See Figures 16 and 17**

Certain later models use an air induction valve filter. It is located in the side of the air cleaner housing and is easily replaced.

➡**Replacement intervals for this unit are every 30,000 miles.**

1. Unfasten the mounting screws and remove the valve filter case.
2. Pull the air induction valve out and remove the filter that lies underneath it.

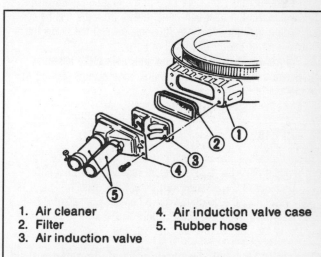

1. Air cleaner
2. Filter
3. Air induction valve
4. Air induction valve case
5. Rubber hose

Fig. 16 Exploded view of the air induction valve and filter assembly—carbureted engines

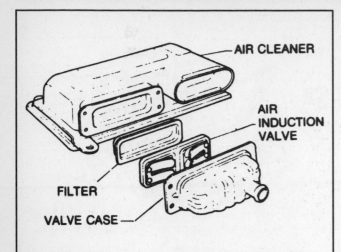

Fig. 17 Exploded view of the air induction valve and filter assembly—fuel injected engines

To install:

3. Install the new filter, then the valve. Pay particular attention to which way the valve is facing, so the exhaust gases will not flow backwards through the system.

4. Install the valve filter case.

Gasoline Fuel Filter

The fuel filter on all models is a disposable plastic unit. It's located on the right inner fender. The filter should be replaced at least every 24,000 miles. A dirty filter will starve the engine and cause poor running.

REMOVAL & INSTALLATION

510, 610, 710 and 1977–79 200SX

1. Locate fuel filter on right side of the engine compartment.
2. Disconnect the inlet and outlet hoses from the fuel filter. Make certain that the inlet hose (bottom) doesn't fall below the fuel tank level or the gasoline will drain out.
3. Pry the fuel filter from its clip and replace the assembly.
4. Replace the inlet, outlet lines and hose clamps. Secure the hose clamps to prevent leaks.
5. Start the engine and check for leaks.

1977–79 810

These models utilize an electric fuel pump. The pressure on these models must be released before removing the fuel filter.

1. Disconnect the negative cable from the battery.
2. Disconnect the cold start valve harness connector.
3. Use two jumper wires and connect one side of each to a terminal on the cold start valve connector.

➡**Be sure to keep both terminals separate in order to avoid short circuiting.**

4. Connect the two remaining terminals of the jumper wires to the negative and positive battery terminals in order to release the pressure in the fuel system.
5. Unfasten the clamps securing the fuel lines to the inlet and outlet sides of the fuel filter and then remove the fuel lines.
6. Remove the fuel filter.
7. Install new fuel filter with new hose clamps. Replace fuel lines if necessary.
8. Reconnect the cold start valve harness connector.
9. Connect the negative cable to the battery.
10. Start engine and check for leaks.

1980–84 810, Maxima, and 1977–81 200SX

◗ **See Figures 18, 19 and 20**

These models utilize an electric fuel pump. The pressure must be released on these models before removing the fuel filter. On later years, the fuel pump fuse should be removed, instead of the relay. Crank the engine a couple times to release pressure before removing the fuel filter. On some late models, the "Check Engine Light" will stay on after installation is completed. The memory

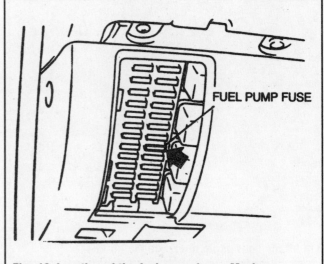

Fig. 18 Location of the fuel pump fuse—Maxima

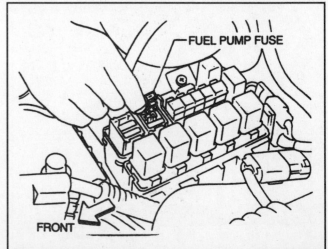

Fig. 19 On some models, it will be necessary to remove the fuel pump fuse

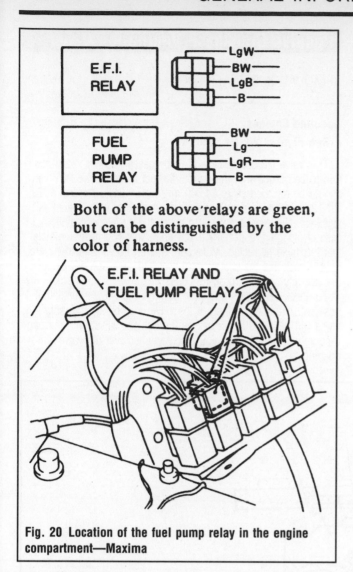

Both of the above relays are green, but can be distinguished by the color of harness.

Fig. 20 Location of the fuel pump relay in the engine compartment—Maxima

code in the control unit must be erased. To erase the code disconnect the battery cable for 10 seconds then reconnect after installation of fuel filter. Refer to Section 5 for more information.

1. Start the engine.
2. Disconnect the #2 fuel pump relay harness connector with the engine running.

➡**See Section 5 for illustrations.**

3. After the engine stalls, crank it two or three times.
4. Turn the ignition off and reconnect the #2 fuel pump relay harness connector.
5. Unfasten the clamps securing the fuel lines to the inlet and outlet side of the fuel filter and then disconnect the fuel lines.
6. Remove the fuel filter.
7. Install the fuel filter and new hose clamps. Replace fuel lines if necessary.
8. Start the engine and check for leaks.

Diesel Fuel Filter

The fuel filter on all diesel models is located on the right inner fender. The filter should be replaced at least every 30,000 miles. It should also be drained of water periodically.

REMOVAL & INSTALLATION

➤ **See Figure 21**

1. Locate the filter on the right side of the engine compartment.
2. Place a small pan or glass jar under the filter, unscrew the fuel filter sensor on the bottom and drain any fuel that is in the filter.
3. Using Datsun/Nissan special tool SP193200000 or a strap wrench, unscrew the filter from the mount.
4. Connect the fuel filter sensor to the new filter and then install the new filter.

➡**The new fuel filter should be screwed on hand-tight. DO NOT use the wrench to tighten the filter.**

5. Bleed the fuel system as detailed in Section 5.

Fig. 21 Remove the diesel fuel filter with a strap wrench (arrow)

DRAINING WATER FROM THE FUEL FILTER

➤ **See Figure 22**

1. Place a small pan or glass jar under the bottom of the fuel filter.
2. Unscrew the fuel filter sensor and let the filter drain.

➡**There is a round primer pump on top of the filter mount. Pumping it will quicken the draining process.**

3. The diesel fuel and the water will separate themselves in the container. The water is heavier and will therefore be on the bottom.
4. Allow the filter to drain until all the water has dripped out.
5. Replace the fuel sensor and then bleed the fuel system as detailed in Chapter 5.

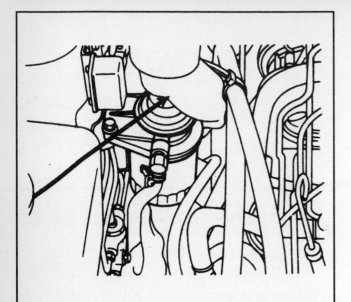

Fig. 22 Use the priming pump (underneath hand, at tip of arrow) to speed draining—diesel engines

Positive Crankcase Ventilation Valve

REMOVAL & INSTALLATION

Gasoline Engines
▶ See Figures 23, 24 and 25

This valve feeds crankcase blow-by gases into the intake manifold to be burned with the normal air/fuel mixture. The PCV valve should be replaced every 24,000 miles on models through 1979. On 1980 and later models, no strict interval for maintenance is specified. However, it is wise to check the system occasionally in case of clogging, especially if you know that you have a vehicle that has been neglected. Make sure that all PCV connections are tight. Check that the connecting hoses are clear and not clogged. Replace any brittle or broken hoses.

To check the valve's operation, remove the valve's ventilation hose with the engine idling. If the valve is working, a hissing noise will be heard as air passes through the valve, and a strong vacuum will be felt when you place a finger over the valve opening.

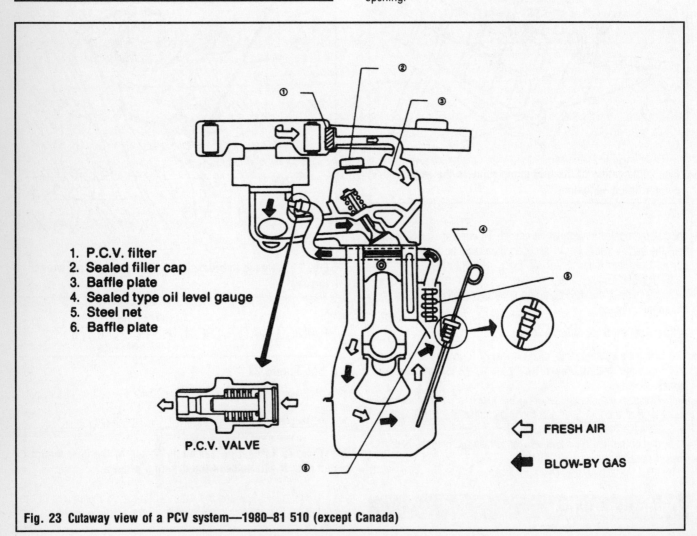

1. P.C.V. filter
2. Sealed filler cap
3. Baffle plate
4. Sealed type oil level gauge
5. Steel net
6. Baffle plate

P.C.V. VALVE

⇐ FRESH AIR

◀ BLOW-BY GAS

Fig. 23 Cutaway view of a PCV system—1980–81 510 (except Canada)

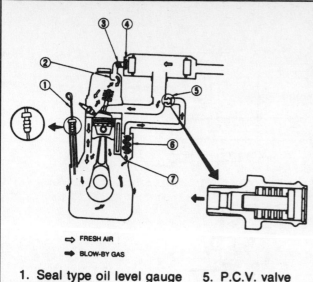

⇨ FRESH AIR

➡ BLOW-BY GAS

1. Seal type oil level gauge
2. Baffle plate
3. Flame arrester
4. Filter
5. P.C.V. valve
6. Steel net
7. Baffle plate

Fig. 24 Cutaway view of a PCV system—610 and 710, 1978–79 510 (all),1980 510 (Canada)

➡ **The PCV valve is located in the side or bottom of the intake manifold.**

1. Squeeze the hose clamp with pliers and remove the hose.
2. Using a wrench, unscrew the PCV valve and remove the valve.
3. Disconnect the ventilation hoses and flush with solvent.
4. Install the new PCV valve and replace the hoses and clamp.

Diesel Engines
▶ See Figure 26

These engines use a crankcase emission control valve in place of the PCV valve. Although different in configuration it is similar in function.

To replace the valve which is located inline between the cylinder head cover and the intake manifold:

1. Locate the valve. There should be three hoses attached to it.
2. Use a pair of pliers and squeeze the hose clamp on each hose so that you can remove the hose from the valve.
3. Install the new valve and reconnect all the hoses.

Evaporative Emission Control System

SERVICING

Gasoline Engines Only
▶ See Figures 27, 28, 29 and 30

Check the evaporation control system every 12,000 miles (15,000 miles, 1980 and later). Check the fuel and vapor lines for proper connections and correct routing as well as condition. Replace damaged or deteriorated parts as necessary. Remove and check the operation of the check valve on pre-1975 models in the following manner.

1. With all the hoses disconnected from the valve, apply air pressure to the fuel tank side of the valve. The air should flow through the valve and exit the crankcase side of the valve. If the valve does not behave in the above manner, replace.
2. Apply air pressure to the crankcase side valve. Air should not pass to either of the two outlets.
3. When air pressure is applied to the carburetor side of the

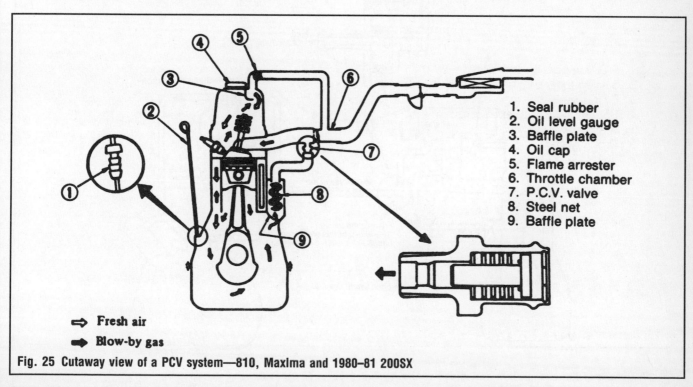

⇨ **Fresh air**

➡ **Blow-by gas**

1. Seal rubber
2. Oil level gauge
3. Baffle plate
4. Oil cap
5. Flame arrester
6. Throttle chamber
7. P.C.V. valve
8. Steel net
9. Baffle plate

Fig. 25 Cutaway view of a PCV system—810, Maxima and 1980–81 200SX

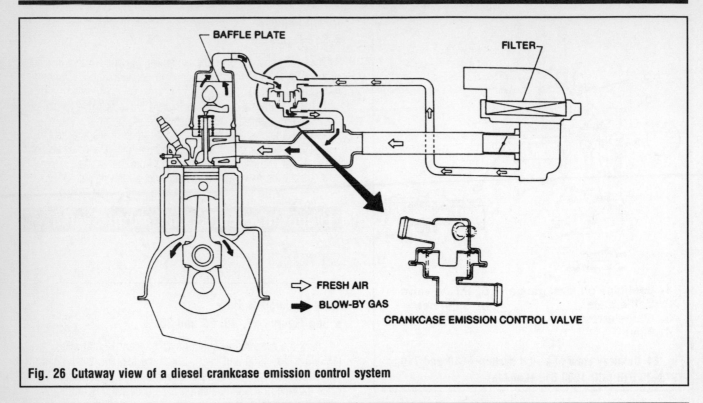

Fig. 26 Cutaway view of a diesel crankcase emission control system

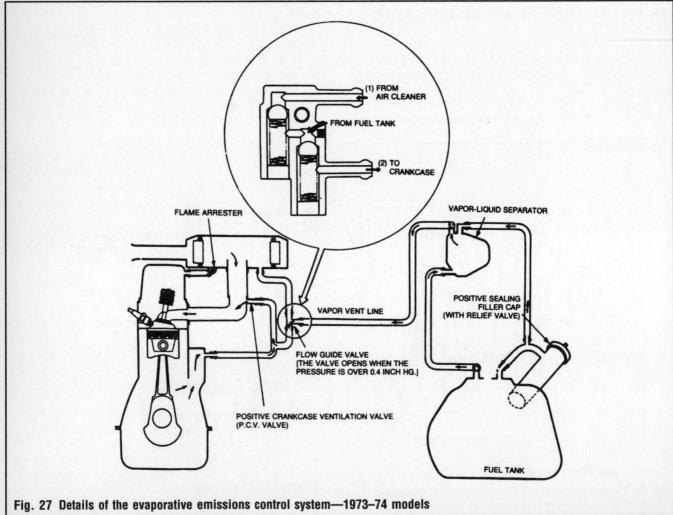

Fig. 27 Details of the evaporative emissions control system—1973–74 models

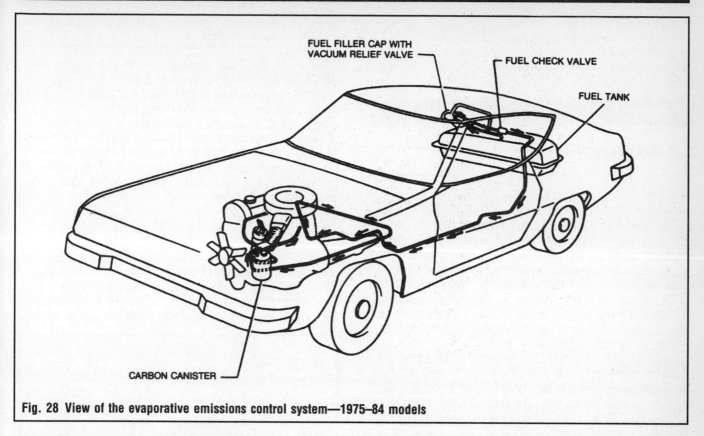

Fig. 28 View of the evaporative emissions control system—1975–84 models

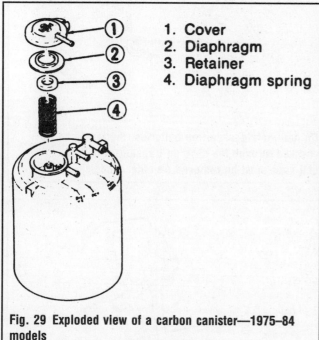

1. Cover
2. Diaphragm
3. Retainer
4. Diaphragm spring

Fig. 29 Exploded view of a carbon canister—1975–84 models

Fig. 30 Replace the carbon canister filter (at bottom of canister)

valve, the air should pass through to exit out the fuel tank and/or the crankcase side of the valve.

On 1975 and later models, the flow guide valve is replaced with a carbon filled storage canister which stores fuel vapors until the engine is started and the vapors are drawn into the combustion chambers and burned.

On those vehicles built through 1983, you should check the operation of the carbon canister purge valve. To do this, disconnect

the rubber hose between the canister control valve and the T-fitting, at the T-fitting. Apply vacuum to the hose leading to the control valve. The vacuum condition should be maintained indefinitely. If the control valve leaks, remove the top cover of the valve and check for a dislocated or cracked diaphragm. If the diaphragm is damaged, a repair kit containing a new diaphragm, retainer, and spring is available and should be installed.

The carbon canister has an air filter in the bottom of the canister. On models built in years up to and including 1982, the filter element should be checked every two years or 30,000 miles; more frequently if the car is operated in dusty areas. Replace the filter by pulling it out of the bottom of the canister and installing a new one.

Battery

GENERAL MAINTENANCE

All batteries, regardless of type, should be carefully secured by a battery hold-down device. If this is not done, the battery terminals or casing may crack from stress applied to the battery during vehicle operation. A battery which is not secured may allow acid to leak out, making it discharge faster; such leaking corrosive acid can also eat away components under the hood. A battery that is not sealed must be checked periodically for electrolyte level. You cannot add water to a sealed maintenance-free battery (though not all maintenance-free batteries are sealed), but a sealed battery must also be checked for proper electrolyte level as indicated by the color of the built-in hydrometer "eye."

Keep the top of the battery clean, as a film of dirt can help completely discharge a battery that is not used for long periods. A solution of baking soda and water may be used for cleaning, but be careful to flush this off with clear water. DO NOT let any of the solution into the filler holes. Baking soda neutralizes battery acid and will de-activate a battery cell.

❊❊ CAUTION

Always use caution when working on or near the battery. Never allow a tool to bridge the gap between the negative and positive battery terminals. Also, be careful not to allow a tool to provide a ground between the positive cable/terminal and any metal component on the vehicle. Either of these conditions will cause a short circuit leading to sparks and possible personal injury.

Batteries in vehicles which are not operated on a regular basis can fall victim to parasitic loads (small current drains which are constantly drawing current from the battery). Normal parasitic loads may drain a battery on a vehicle that is in storage and not used for 6–8 weeks. Vehicles that have additional accessories such as a cellular phone, an alarm system or other devices that increase parasitic load may discharge a battery sooner. If the vehicle is to be stored for 6–8 weeks in a secure area and the alarm system, if present, is not necessary, the negative battery cable should be disconnected at the onset of storage to protect the battery charge.

Remember that constantly discharging and recharging will shorten battery life. Take care not to allow a battery to be needlessly discharged.

BATTERY FLUID

❊❊ CAUTION

Battery electrolyte contains sulfuric acid. If you should splash any on your skin or in your eyes, flush the affected area with plenty of clear water. If it lands in your eyes, get medical help immediately.

The fluid (sulfuric acid solution) contained in the battery cells will tell you many things about the condition of the battery. Because the cell plates must be kept submerged below the fluid level in order to operate, maintaining the fluid level is extremely important. And, because the specific gravity of the acid is an indication of electrical charge, testing the fluid can be an aid in determining if the battery must be replaced. A battery in a vehicle with a properly operating charging system should require little maintenance, but careful, periodic inspection should reveal problems before they leave you stranded.

Fluid Level

Check the battery electrolyte level at least once a month, or more often in hot weather or during periods of extended vehicle operation. On non-sealed batteries, the level can be checked either through the case on translucent batteries or by removing the cell caps on opaque-cased types. The electrolyte level in each cell

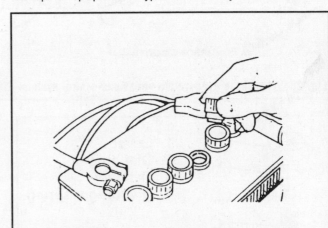

On non-maintenance free batteries, the level can be checked through the case on translucent batteries; the cell caps must be removed on other models

Check the specific gravity of the battery's electrolyte with a hydrometer

should be kept filled to the split ring inside each cell, or the line marked on the outside of the case.

If the level is low, add only distilled water through the opening until the level is correct. Each cell is separate from the others, so each must be checked and filled individually. Distilled water should be used, because the chemicals and minerals found in most drinking water are harmful to the battery and could significantly shorten its life.

If water is added in freezing weather, the vehicle should be driven several miles to allow the water to mix with the electrolyte. Otherwise, the battery could freeze.

Although some maintenance-free batteries have removable cell caps for access to the electrolyte, the electrolyte condition and level on all sealed maintenance-free batteries must be checked using the built-in hydrometer "eye." The exact type of eye varies between battery manufacturers, but most apply a sticker to the battery itself explaining the possible readings. When in doubt, refer to the battery manufacturer's instructions to interpret battery condition using the built-in hydrometer.

➡**Although the readings from built-in hydrometers found in sealed batteries may vary, a green eye usually indicates a properly charged battery with sufficient fluid level. A dark eye is normally an indicator of a battery with sufficient fluid, but one which may be low in charge. And a light or yellow eye is usually an indication that electrolyte supply has dropped below the necessary level for battery (and hydrometer) operation. In this last case, sealed batteries with an insufficient electrolyte level must usually be discarded.**

Specific Gravity

As stated earlier, the specific gravity of a battery's electrolyte level can be used as an indication of battery charge. At least once a year, check the specific gravity of the battery. It should be between 1.20 and 1.26 on the gravity scale. Most auto supply stores carry a variety of inexpensive battery testing hydrometers. These can be used on any non-sealed battery to test the specific gravity in each cell.

The battery testing hydrometer has a squeeze bulb at one end and a nozzle at the other. Battery electrolyte is sucked into the hydrometer until the float is lifted from its seat. The specific gravity

is then read by noting the position of the float. If gravity is low in one or more cells, the battery should be slowly charged and checked again to see if the gravity has come up. Generally, if after charging, the specific gravity between any two cells varies more than 50 points (0.50), the battery should be replaced as it can no longer produce sufficient voltage to guarantee proper operation.

On sealed batteries, the built-in hydrometer is the only way of checking specific gravity. Again, check with your battery's manufacturer for proper interpretation of its built-in hydrometer readings.

CABLES

Once a year (or as necessary), the battery terminals and the cable clamps should be cleaned. Loosen the clamps and remove the cables, negative cable first. On batteries with posts on top, the use of a puller specially made for this purpose is recommended. These are inexpensive and available in most auto parts stores. Side terminal battery cables are secured with a small bolt.

Clean the cable clamps and the battery terminal with a wire brush, until all corrosion, grease, etc., is removed and the metal is shiny. It is especially important to clean the inside of the clamp (an old knife is useful here) thoroughly, since a small deposit of foreign material or oxidation there will prevent a sound electrical connection and inhibit either starting or charging. Special tools are available for cleaning these parts, one type for conventional top post batteries and another type for side terminal batteries.

Before installing the cables, loosen the battery hold-down clamp or strap, remove the battery and check the battery tray. Clear it of any debris, and check it for soundness (the battery tray can be cleaned with a baking soda and water solution). Rust should be wire brushed away, and the metal given a couple coats of anti-rust paint. Install the battery and tighten the hold-down clamp or strap securely. Do not overtighten, as this can crack the battery case.

After the clamps and terminals are clean, reinstall the cables, negative cable last; DO NOT hammer the clamps onto post batteries. Tighten the clamps securely, but do not distort them. Give the clamps and terminals a thin external coating of grease after installation, to retard corrosion.

Check the cables at the same time that the terminals are

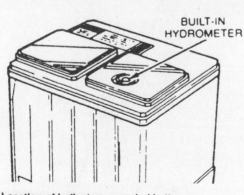

Location of indicator on sealed battery

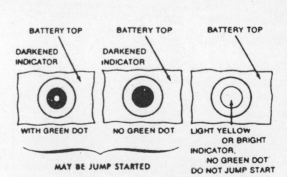

Check the appearance of the charge indicator on top of the battery before attempting a jump start; if it's not green or dark, do not jump start the car

A typical sealed (maintenance-free) battery with a built-in hydrometer—NOTE that the hydrometer eye may vary between battery manufacturers; always refer to the battery's label

Maintenance is performed with household items and with special tools like this post cleaner

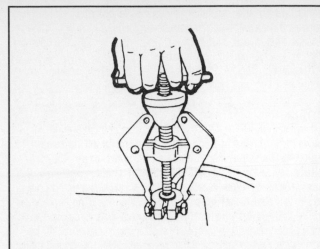

A special tool is available to pull the clamp from the post

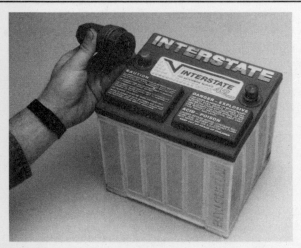

The underside of this special battery tool has a wire brush to clean post terminals

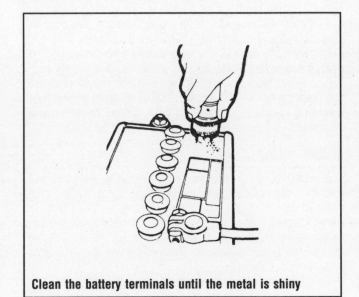

Clean the battery terminals until the metal is shiny

Place the tool over the terminals and twist to clean the post

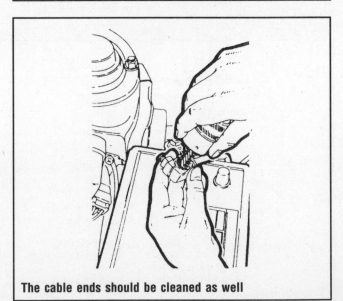

The cable ends should be cleaned as well

cleaned. If the cable insulation is cracked or broken, or if the ends are frayed, the cable should be replaced with a new cable of the same length and gauge.

CHARGING

> ### ✳✳ CAUTION
>
> **The chemical reaction which takes place in all batteries generates explosive hydrogen gas. A spark can cause the battery to explode and splash acid. To avoid serious personal injury, be sure there is proper ventilation and take appropriate fire safety precautions when connecting, disconnecting, or charging a battery and when using jumper cables.**

A battery should be charged at a slow rate to keep the plates inside from getting too hot. However, if some maintenance-free batteries are allowed to discharge until they are almost "dead," they may have to be charged at a high rate to bring them back to "life." Always follow the charger manufacturer's instructions on charging the battery.

REPLACEMENT

When it becomes necessary to replace the battery, select one with a rating equal to or greater than the battery originally installed. Deterioration and just plain aging of the battery cables, starter motor, and associated wires makes the battery's job harder in successive years. The slow increase in electrical resistance over time makes it prudent to install a new battery with a greater capacity than the old.

EFE System (Heat Riser)

SERVICING

Gasoline Engines Only
▶ See Figure 31

The heat riser, or Early Fuel Evaporative System, is a thermostatically operated valve in the exhaust manifold. It closes when the engine is warming up to direct hot exhaust gases to the intake manifold, in order to preheat the incoming air/fuel mixture. It is used on carbureted engines only. If it sticks shut, the result will be frequent stalling during warmup, especially in cold or damp weather. If it sticks open, the result will be a rough idle after the engine is warm.

The heat control valve should be checked for free operation every six months or 6,000 miles. Simply give the counterweight a twirl (engine cold) to make sure that no binding exists. If the valve sticks, apply a heat control solvent to the ends of the shaft. This type of solvent is available in auto parts stores. Sometimes lightly rapping the end of the shaft with a rubber hammer (engine hot) will break it loose. If this fails, the components will have to be removed from the car for repair.

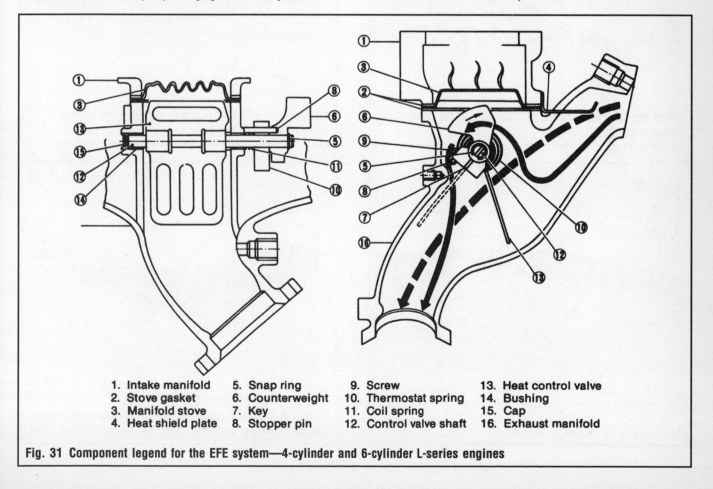

1. Intake manifold	5. Snap ring	9. Screw	13. Heat control valve
2. Stove gasket	6. Counterweight	10. Thermostat spring	14. Bushing
3. Manifold stove	7. Key	11. Coil spring	15. Cap
4. Heat shield plate	8. Stopper pin	12. Control valve shaft	16. Exhaust manifold

Fig. 31 Component legend for the EFE system—4-cylinder and 6-cylinder L-series engines

➡The 1980 and later carbureted engines do not use the heat control valve. Instead, these engines warm the fuel mixture by a coolant passage under the carburetor. No maintenance is required.

Belts

INSPECTION

Check the belts driving the fan, air pump, air conditioning compressor, and the alternator for cracks, fraying, wear, and tension every 12 months or 12,000 miles (15,000 miles, 1980 and later). Replace as necessary.

Belt deflection at the midpoint of the longest span between pulleys should not be more than ½″ with 22 lbs. of pressure applied to the belt.

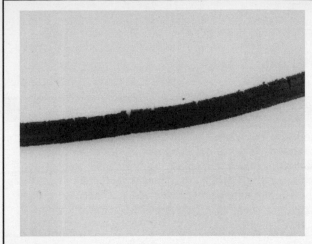

Deep cracks in this belt will cause flex, building up heat that will eventually lead to belt failure

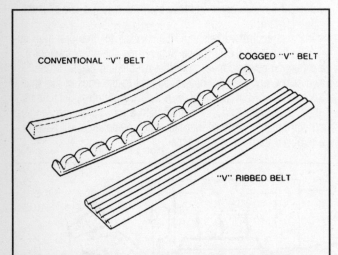

CONVENTIONAL "V" BELT   COGGED "V" BELT

"V" RIBBED BELT

There are typically 3 types of accessory drive belts found on vehicles today

The cover of this belt is worn, exposing the critical reinforcing cords to excessive wear

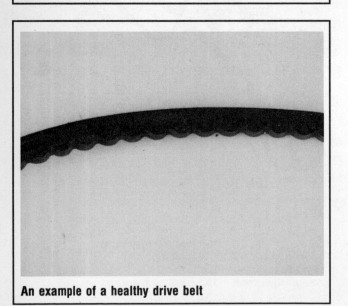

An example of a healthy drive belt

Installing too wide a belt can result in serious belt wear and/or breakage

ADJUSTING

▶ **See Figures 32 thru 39**

To adjust the tension on all components except the air conditioning compressor, power steering pump, and some late model air pumps, loosen the pivot and mounting bolts of the component which the belt is driving, then, using a wooden lever, pry the component toward or away from the engine until the proper tension is achieved. Tighten the component mounting bolts securely.

➡ **An overly tight belt will wear out the pulley bearings on the assorted components.**

Belt tension adjustments for the factory installed air conditioning compressor and power steering pump are made at the idler pulley. The idler pulley is the smallest of the three pulleys. At the top of the slotted bracket holding the idler pulley there is a bolt which is used to either raise or lower the pulley. To free the bolt for adjustment, it is necessary to loosen the locknut in the face of the idler pulley. After adjusting the belt tension, tighten the locknut in the face of the idler pulley.

➡ **1980 California Datsuns come equipped with special fan belts which, if loose, generate friction heat by slipping and shrink, taking up the slack. The air conditioning drive belt on those cars so equipped is adjusted in a similar fashion.**

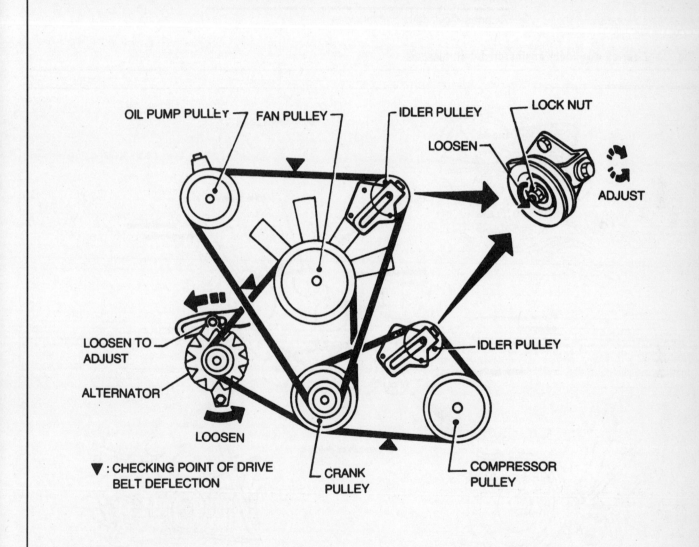

Fig. 32 Belt-to-pulley routing—Z series 4-cylinder engines

Drive Belt Deflection	Adjust Deflection of Used Belt	Set Deflection of New Belt
Cooling fan mm(in)	12–15 (0.47–0.59)	8–11 (0.31–0.43)
Air conditioner compressor mm(in)	10–13 (0.39–0.51)	7–10 (0.28–0.39)
Power steering oil pump mm(in)	15–18 (0.59–0.71)	12–15 (0.47–0.59)
Aplied pushing force N (kg, lb)	98 (10, 22)	

Z-series 4-cyl. drive belt tensions

Fig. 33 Z-series 4-cylinder engine drive belt tensions

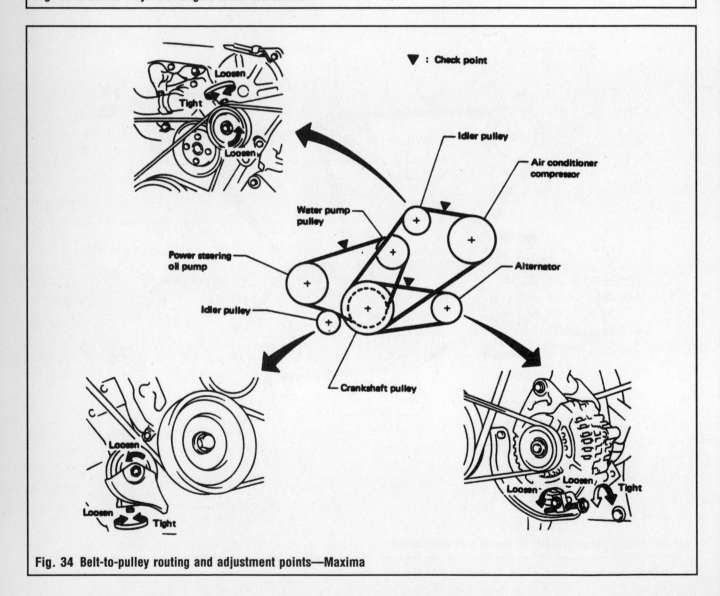

Fig. 34 Belt-to-pulley routing and adjustment points—Maxima

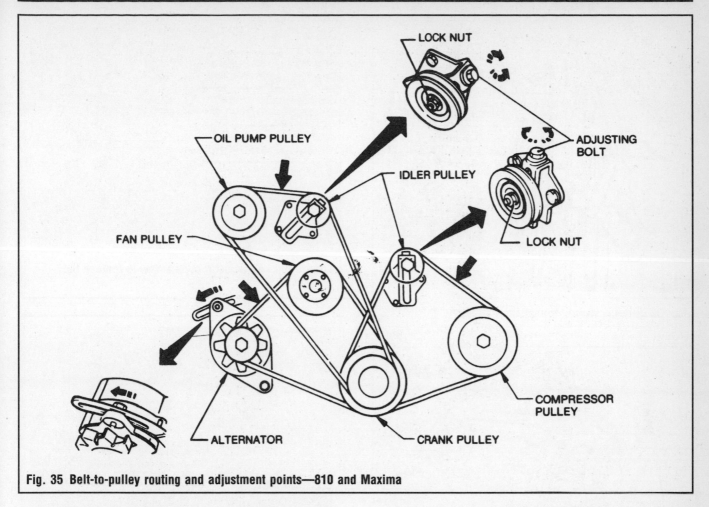

Fig. 35 Belt-to-pulley routing and adjustment points—810 and Maxima

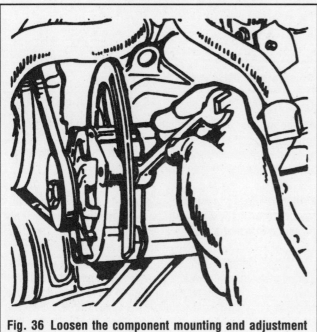

Fig. 36 Loosen the component mounting and adjustment bolts . . .

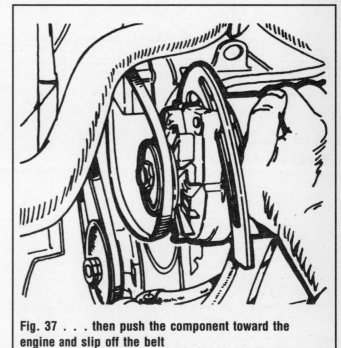

Fig. 37 . . . then push the component toward the engine and slip off the belt

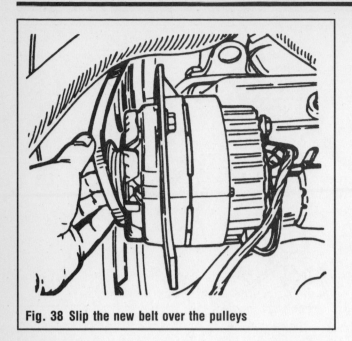

Fig. 38 Slip the new belt over the pulleys

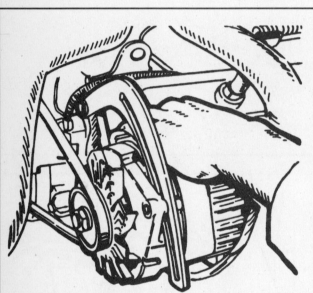

Fig. 39 Reverse the removal process to install the belt, then tighten to specification

REMOVAL & INSTALLATION

The replacement of the inner belt on multi-belted engines may require the removal of the outer belts. To replace a drive belt loosen the pivot and mounting bolts of the component which the belt is driving, then, using a wooden lever or equivalent pry the component inward to relieve the tension on the drive belt, always be careful where you locate the prybar not to damage the component. Slip the belt off the component pulley, match up the new

Loosen the belt adjuster mechanism to remove the belt(s)

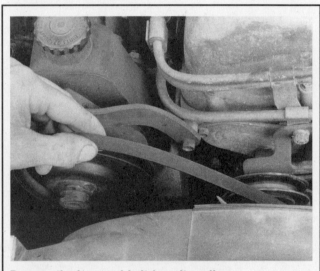

Remove the loosened belt from its pulleys

belt with the old belt for length and width, these measurement must be the same or problems will occur when you go to adjust the new belt. After new belt is installed correctly adjust the tension of the new belt.

➡**When replacing more than one belt it is a good idea, to make note or mark what belt goes around what pulley. This will make installation fast and easy.**

On air conditioning compressor and power steering pump belt replacements loosen the lockbolt for the adjusting bolt on idler pulley or power steering pump and then loosen the adjusting bolt. Pry pulley or pump inward to relieve the tension on the drive belt, always be careful where you locate the prybar not to damage the component or pulley.

Hoses

INSPECTION

Upper and lower radiator hoses along with the heater hoses should be checked for deterioration, leaks and loose hose clamps at least every 15,000 miles (24,000 km). It is also wise to check the hoses periodically in early spring and at the beginning of the fall or winter when you are performing other maintenance. A quick visual inspection could discover a weakened hose which might have left you stranded if it had remained unrepaired.

Whenever you are checking the hoses, make sure the engine and cooling system are cold. Visually inspect for cracking, rotting or collapsed hoses, and replace as necessary. Run your hand along the length of the hose. If a weak or swollen spot is noted when squeezing the hose wall, the hose should be replaced.

REMOVAL & INSTALLATION

1. Remove the radiator pressure cap.

✳✳ CAUTION

Never remove the pressure cap while the engine is running, or personal injury from scalding hot coolant or steam may result. If possible, wait until the engine has cooled to remove the pressure cap. If this is not possible, wrap a thick cloth around the pressure cap and turn it slowly to the stop. Step back while the pressure is released from the cooling system. When you are sure all the pressure has been released, use the cloth to turn and remove the cap.

2. Position a clean container under the radiator and/or engine draincock or plug, then open the drain and allow the cooling system to drain to an appropriate level. For some upper hoses, only a little coolant must be drained. To remove hoses positioned

A hose clamp that is too tight can cause older hoses to separate and tear on either side of the clamp

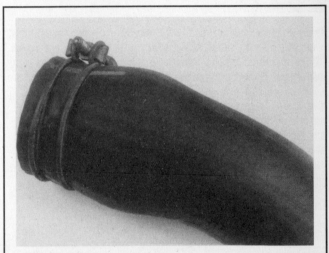

A soft spongy hose (identifiable by the swollen section) will eventually burst and should be replaced

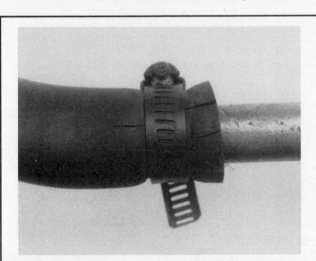

The cracks developing along this hose are a result of age-related hardening

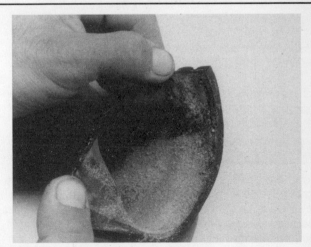

Hoses are likely to deteriorate from the inside if the cooling system is not periodically flushed

lower on the engine, such as a lower radiator hose, the entire cooling system must be emptied.

✳✳ CAUTION

When draining coolant, keep in mind that cats and dogs are attracted by ethylene glycol antifreeze, and are quite likely to drink any that is left in an uncovered container or in puddles on the ground. This will prove fatal in sufficient quantity. Always drain coolant into a sealable container. Coolant may be reused unless it is contaminated or several years old.

3. Loosen the hose clamps at each end of the hose requiring replacement. Clamps are usually either of the spring tension type (which require pliers to squeeze the tabs and loosen) or of the screw tension type (which require screw or hex drivers to loosen). Pull the clamps back on the hose away from the connection.

4. Twist, pull and slide the hose off the fitting, taking care not to damage the neck of the component from which the hose is being removed.

➡**If the hose is stuck at the connection, do not try to insert a screwdriver or other sharp tool under the hose end in an effort to free it, as the connection and/or hose may become damaged. Heater connections especially may be easily damaged by such a procedure. If the hose is to be replaced, use a single-edged razor blade to make a slice along the portion of the hose which is stuck on the connection, perpendicular to the end of the hose. Do not cut deep so as to prevent damaging the connection. The hose can then be peeled from the connection and discarded.**

5. Clean both hose mounting connections. Inspect the condition of the hose clamps and replace them, if necessary.

   To install:
6. Dip the ends of the new hose into clean engine coolant to ease installation.

7. Slide the clamps over the replacement hose, then slide the hose ends over the connections into position.

8. Position and secure the clamps at least ¼ in. (6.35mm) from the ends of the hose. Make sure they are located beyond the raised bead of the connector.

9. Close the radiator or engine drains and properly refill the cooling system with the clean drained engine coolant or a suitable mixture of ethylene glycol coolant and water.

10. If available, install a pressure tester and check for leaks. If a pressure tester is not available, run the engine until normal operating temperature is reached (allowing the system to naturally pressurize), then check for leaks.

✳✳ CAUTION

If you are checking for leaks with the system at normal operating temperature, BE EXTREMELY CAREFUL not to touch any moving or hot engine parts. Once temperature has been reached, shut the engine OFF, and check for leaks around the hose fittings and connections which were removed earlier.

Air Conditioning

➡**Be sure to consult the laws in your area before servicing the air conditioning system. In most areas, it is illegal to perform repairs involving refrigerant unless the work is done by a certified technician. Also, it is quite likely that you will not be able to purchase refrigerant without proof of certification.**

SAFETY PRECAUTIONS

There are two major hazards associated with air conditioning systems and they both relate to the refrigerant gas. First, the refrigerant gas (R-12) is an extremely cold substance. When exposed to air, it will instantly freeze any surface it comes in contact with, including your eyes. The other hazard relates to fire. Although normally non-toxic, the R-12 gas becomes highly poisonous in the presence of an open flame. One good whiff of the vapor formed by burning R-12 can be fatal. Keep all forms of fire (including cigarettes) well clear of the air conditioning system.

Because of the inherent dangers involved with working on air conditioning systems and R-12 refrigerant, these safety precautions must be strictly followed.

• Avoid contact with a charged refrigeration system, even when working on another part of the air conditioning system or vehicle. If a heavy tool comes into contact with a section of tubing or a heat exchanger, it can easily cause the relatively soft material to rupture.

• When it is necessary to apply force to a fitting which contains refrigerant, as when checking that all system couplings are securely tightened, use a wrench on both parts of the fitting involved, if possible. This will avoid putting torque on refrigerant tubing. (It is also advisable to use tube or line wrenches when tightening these flare nut fittings.)

➡**R-12 refrigerant is a chlorofluorocarbon which, when released into the atmosphere, can contribute to the depletion of the ozone layer in the upper atmosphere. Ozone filters out harmful radiation from the sun.**

• Do not attempt to discharge the system without the proper tools. Precise control is possible only when using the service gauges and a proper A/C refrigerant recovery station. Wear protective gloves when connecting or disconnecting service gauge hoses.

• Discharge the system only in a well ventilated area, as high concentrations of the gas which might accidentally escape can exclude oxygen and act as an anesthetic. When leak testing or soldering, this is particularly important, as toxic gas is formed when R-12 contacts any flame.

• Never start a system without first verifying that both service valves are properly installed, and that all fittings throughout the system are snugly connected.

• Avoid applying heat to any refrigerant line or storage vessel. Charging may be aided by using water heated to less than 125°F (50°C) to warm the refrigerant container. Never allow a refrigerant storage container to sit out in the sun, or near any other source of heat, such as a radiator or heater.

• Always wear goggles to protect your eyes when working on a system. If refrigerant contacts the eyes, it is advisable in all cases to consult a physician immediately.

• Frostbite from liquid refrigerant should be treated by first gradually warming the area with cool water, and then gently applying petroleum jelly. A physician should be consulted.

• Always keep refrigerant drum fittings capped when not in use. If the container is equipped with a safety cap to protect the valve, make sure the cap is in place when the can is not being used. Avoid sudden shock to the drum, which might occur from dropping it, or from banging a heavy tool against it. Never carry a drum in the passenger compartment of a vehicle.

• Always completely discharge the system into a suitable recovery unit before painting the vehicle (if the paint is to be baked on), or before welding anywhere near refrigerant lines.

• When servicing the system, minimize the time that any refrigerant line or fitting is open to the air in order to prevent moisture or dirt from entering the system. Contaminants such as moisture or dirt can damage internal system components. Always replace O-rings on lines or fittings which are disconnected. Prior to installation coat, but do not soak, replacement O-rings with suitable compressor oil.

GENERAL SERVICING PROCEDURES

➡**It is recommended, and possibly required by law, that a qualified technician perform the following services.**

The most important aspect of air conditioning service is the maintenance of a pure and adequate charge of refrigerant in the system. A refrigeration system cannot function properly if a significant percentage of the charge is lost. Leaks are common because the severe vibration encountered underhood in an automobile can easily cause a sufficient cracking or loosening of the air conditioning fittings; allowing, the extreme operating pressures of the system to force refrigerant out.

The problem can be understood by considering what happens to the system as it is operated with a continuous leak. Because the expansion valve regulates the flow of refrigerant to the evaporator, the level of refrigerant there is fairly constant. The receiver/drier stores any excess refrigerant, and so a loss will first appear there as a reduction in the level of liquid. As this level nears the bottom of the vessel, some refrigerant vapor bubbles will begin to appear in the stream of liquid supplied to the expansion valve. This vapor decreases the capacity of the expansion valve very little as the valve opens to compensate for its presence. As the quantity of liquid in the condenser decreases, the operating pressure will drop there and throughout the high side of the system. As the R-12 continues to be expelled, the pressure available to force the liquid through the expansion valve will continue to decrease, and, eventually, the valve's orifice will prove to be too much of a restriction for adequate flow even with the needle fully withdrawn.

At this point, low side pressure will start to drop, and a severe reduction in cooling capacity, marked by freeze-up of the evaporator coil, will result. Eventually, the operating pressure of the evaporator will be lower than the pressure of the atmosphere surrounding it, and air will be drawn into the system wherever there are leaks in the low side.

Because all atmospheric air contains at least some moisture, water will enter the system and mix with the R-12 and the oil. Trace amounts of moisture will cause sludging of the oil, and corrosion of the system. Saturation and clogging of the filter/drier, and freezing of the expansion valve orifice will eventually result. As air fills the system to a greater and greater extent, it will interfere more and more with the normal flows of refrigerant and heat.

From this description, it should be obvious that much of the repairman's focus in on detecting leaks, repairing them, and then restoring the purity and quantity of the refrigerant charge. A list of general rules should be followed in addition to all safety precautions:

• Keep all tools as clean and dry as possible.

• Thoroughly purge the service gauges/hoses of air and moisture before connecting them to the system. Keep them capped when not in use.

• Thoroughly clean any refrigerant fitting before disconnecting it, in order to minimize the entrance of dirt into the system.

• Plan any operation that requires opening the system beforehand, in order to minimize the length of time it will be exposed to open air. Cap or seal the open ends to minimize the entrance of foreign material.

• When adding oil, pour it through an extremely clean and dry tube or funnel. Keep the oil capped whenever possible. Do not use oil that has not been kept tightly sealed.

• Use only R-12 refrigerant. Purchase refrigerant intended for use only in automatic air conditioning systems.

• Completely evacuate any system that has been opened for service, or that has leaked sufficiently to draw in moisture and air. This requires evacuating air and moisture with a good vacuum pump for at least one hour. If a system has been open for a considerable length of time it may be advisable to evacuate the system for up to 12 hours (overnight).

• Use a wrench on both halves of a fitting that is to be disconnected, so as to avoid placing torque on any of the refrigerant lines.

• When overhauling a compressor, pour some of the oil into a clean glass and inspect it. If there is evidence of dirt, metal particles, or both, flush all refrigerant components with clean refrigerant before evacuating and recharging the system. In addition, if metal particles are present, the compressor should be replaced.

• Schrader valves may leak only when under full operating pressure. Therefore, if leakage is suspected but cannot be located, operate the system with a full charge of refrigerant and look for leaks from all Schrader valves. Replace any faulty valves.

Additional Preventive Maintenance

USING THE SYSTEM

The easiest and most important preventive maintenance for your A/C system is to be sure that it is used on a regular basis. Running the system for five minutes each month (no matter what the season) will help assure that the seals and all internal components remain lubricated.

ANTIFREEZE

In order to prevent heater core freeze-up during A/C operation, it is necessary to maintain a proper antifreeze protection. Use a hand-held antifreeze tester (hydrometer) to periodically check the condition of the antifreeze in your engine's cooling system.

➡ **Antifreeze should not be used longer than the manufacturer specifies.**

RADIATOR CAP

For efficient operation of an air conditioned vehicle's cooling system, the radiator cap should have a holding pressure which meets manufacturer's specifications. A cap which fails to hold these pressures should be replaced.

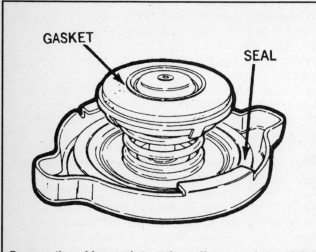

Be sure the rubber gasket on the radiator cap has a tight seal

CONDENSER

Any obstruction of or damage to the condenser configuration will restrict the air flow which is essential to its efficient operation. It is therefore a good rule to keep this unit clean and in proper physical shape.

➡ **Bug screens which are mounted in front of the condenser, (unless they are original equipment), are regarded as obstructions.**

CONDENSATION DRAIN TUBE

This single molded drain tube expels the condensation, which accumulates on the bottom of the evaporator housing, into the engine compartment. If this tube is obstructed, the air conditioning performance can be restricted and condensation buildup can spill over onto the vehicle's floor.

SYSTEM INSPECTION

➡ **R-12 refrigerant is a chlorofluorocarbon which, when released into the atmosphere, can contribute to the depletion of the ozone layer in the upper atmosphere. Ozone filters out harmful radiation from the sun.**

The easiest and often most important check for the air conditioning system consists of a visual inspection of the system components. Visually inspect the air conditioning system for refrigerant leaks, damaged compressor clutch, compressor drive belt tension and condition, plugged evaporator drain tube, blocked condenser fins, disconnected or broken wires, blown fuses, corroded connections and poor insulation.

A refrigerant leak will usually appear as an oily residue at the leakage point in the system. The oily residue soon picks up dust or dirt particles from the surrounding air and appears greasy.

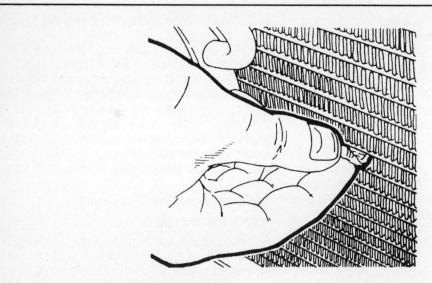

Periodically remove all debris from the radiator fins

An antifreeze tester can be used to determine the freezing and boiling levels of the coolant

Through time, this will build up and appear to be a heavy dirt impregnated grease. Most leaks are caused by damaged or missing O-ring seals at the component connections, damaged charging valve cores or missing service gauge port caps.

For a thorough visual and operational inspection, check the following:

1. Check the surface of the radiator and condenser for dirt, leaves or other material which might block air flow.

2. Check for kinks in hoses and lines. Check the system for leaks.

3. Make sure the drive belt is under the proper tension. When the air conditioning is operating, make sure the drive belt is free of noise or slippage.

4. Make sure the blower motor operates at all appropriate positions, then check for distribution of the air from all outlets with the blower on **HIGH**.

➡**Keep in mind that under conditions of high humidity, air discharged from the A/C vents may not feel as cold as expected, even if the system is working properly. This is because the vaporized moisture in humid air retains heat more effectively than does dry air, making the humid air more difficult to cool.**

Make sure the air passage selection lever is operating correctly. Start the engine and warm it to normal operating temperature, then make sure the hot/cold selection lever is operating correctly.

DISCHARGING, EVACUATING & CHARGING

Discharging, evacuating and charging the air conditioning system must be performed by a properly trained and certified mechanic in a facility equipped with refrigerant recovery/recycling equipment that meets SAE standards for the type of system to be serviced.

If you don't have access to the necessary equipment, we recommend that you take your vehicle to a reputable service station to have the work done. If you still wish to perform repairs on the vehicle, have them discharge the system, then take your vehicle home and perform the necessary work. When you are finished, return the vehicle to the station for evacuation and charging. Just be sure to cap ALL A/C system fittings immediately after opening them and keep them protected until the system is recharged.

Troubleshooting Basic Air Conditioning Problems

Problem	Cause	Solution
There's little or no air coming from the vents (and you're sure it's on)	• The A/C fuse is blown • Broken or loose wires or connections • The on/off switch is defective	• Check and/or replace fuse • Check and/or repair connections • Replace switch
The air coming from the vents is not cool enough	• Windows and air vent wings open • The compressor belt is slipping • Heater is on • Condenser is clogged with debris • Refrigerant has escaped through a leak in the system • Receiver/drier is plugged	• Close windows and vent wings • Tighten or replace compressor belt • Shut heater off • Clean the condenser • Check system • Service system
The air has an odor	• Vacuum system is disrupted • Odor producing substances on the evaporator case • Condensation has collected in the bottom of the evaporator housing	• Have the system checked/repaired • Clean the evaporator case • Clean the evaporator housing drains
System is noisy or vibrating	• Compressor belt or mountings loose • Air in the system	• Tighten or replace belt; tighten mounting bolts • Have the system serviced

Sight glass condition
  Constant bubbles, foam or oil streaks
  Clear sight glass, but no cold air
  Clear sight glass, but air is cold
  Clouded with milky fluid
	
	• Undercharged system
	
	• No refrigerant at all
	• System is OK
	• Receiver drier is leaking dessicant
		
		• Charge the system
		
		• Check and charge the system
		
		• Have system checked

Large difference in temperature of lines	• System undercharged	• Charge and leak test the system
Compressor noise	• Broken valves • Overcharged • Incorrect oil level • Piston slap • Broken rings • Drive belt pulley bolts are loose	• Replace the valve plate • Discharge, evacuate and install the correct charge • Isolate the compressor and check the oil level. Correct as necessary. • Replace the compressor • Replace the compressor • Tighten with the correct torque specification
Excessive vibration	• Incorrect belt tension • Clutch loose • Overcharged • Pulley is misaligned	• Adjust the belt tension • Tighten the clutch • Discharge, evacuate and install the correct charge • Align the pulley
Condensation dripping in the passenger compartment	• Drain hose plugged or improperly positioned • Insulation removed or improperly installed	• Clean the drain hose and check for proper installation • Replace the insulation on the expansion valve and hoses
Frozen evaporator coil	• Faulty thermostat • Thermostat capillary tube improperly installed • Thermostat not adjusted properly	• Replace the thermostat • Install the capillary tube correctly • Adjust the thermostat
Low side low—high side low	• System refrigerant is low • Expansion valve is restricted	• Evacuate, leak test and charge the system • Replace the expansion valve
Low side high—high side low	• Internal leak in the compressor—worn	• Remove the compressor cylinder head and inspect the compressor. Replace the valve plate assembly if necessary. If the compressor pistons, rings or

Troubleshooting Basic Air Conditioning Problems (cont.)

Problem	Cause	Solution
Low side high—high side low (cont.)		cylinders are excessively worn or scored replace the compressor
	• Cylinder head gasket is leaking	• Install a replacement cylinder head gasket
	• Expansion valve is defective	• Replace the expansion valve
	• Drive belt slipping	• Adjust the belt tension
Low side high—high side high	• Condenser fins obstructed	• Clean the condenser fins
	• Air in the system	• Evacuate, leak test and charge the system
	• Expansion valve is defective	• Replace the expansion valve
	• Loose or worn fan belts	• Adjust or replace the belts as necessary
Low side low—high side high	• Expansion valve is defective	• Replace the expansion valve
	• Restriction in the refrigerant hose	• Check the hose for kinks—replace if necessary
	• Restriction in the receiver/drier	• Replace the receiver/drier
	• Restriction in the condenser	• Replace the condenser
Low side and high side normal (inadequate cooling)	• Air in the system	• Evacuate, leak test and charge the system
	• Moisture in the system	• Evacuate, leak test and charge the system

Windshield Wipers

ELEMENT (REFILL) CARE & REPLACEMENT

For maximum effectiveness and longest element life, the windshield and wiper blades should be kept clean. Dirt, tree sap, road tar and so on will cause streaking, smearing and blade deterioration if left on the glass. It is advisable to wash the windshield carefully with a commercial glass cleaner at least once a month. Wipe off the rubber blades with the wet rag afterwards. Do not attempt to move wipers across the windshield by hand; damage to the motor and drive mechanism will result.

To inspect and/or replace the wiper blade elements, place the wiper switch in the **LOW** speed position and the ignition switch in the **ACC** position. When the wiper blades are approximately vertical on the windshield, turn the ignition switch to **OFF**.

Examine the wiper blade elements. If they are found to be cracked, broken or torn, they should be replaced immediately. Replacement intervals will vary with usage, although ozone deterioration usually limits element life to about one year. If the wiper pattern is smeared or streaked, or if the blade chatters across the glass, the elements should be replaced. It is easiest and most sensible to replace the elements in pairs.

If your vehicle is equipped with aftermarket blades, there are several different types of refills and your vehicle might have any kind. Aftermarket blades and arms rarely use the exact same type blade or refill as the original equipment. Here are some typical aftermarket blades; not all may be available for your vehicle:

The Anco® type uses a release button that is pushed down to allow the refill to slide out of the yoke jaws. The new refill slides back into the frame and locks in place.

Some Trico® refills are removed by locating where the metal backing strip or the refill is wider. Insert a small screwdriver blade between the frame and metal backing strip. Press down to release the refill from the retaining tab.

Other types of Trico® refills have two metal tabs which are unlocked by squeezing them together. The rubber filler can then be withdrawn from the frame jaws. A new refill is installed by inserting the refill into the front frame jaws and sliding it rearward

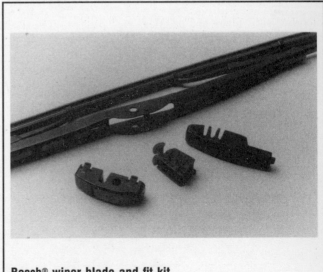

Bosch® wiper blade and fit kit

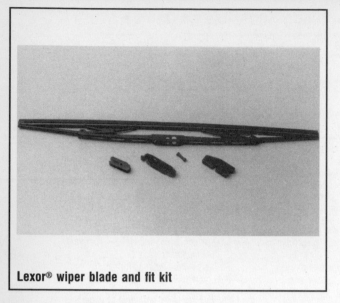

Lexor® wiper blade and fit kit

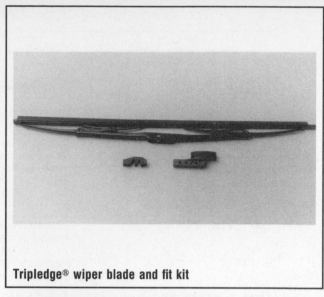

Tripledge® wiper blade and fit kit

Pylon® wiper blade and adaptor

To remove and install a Lexor® wiper blade refill, slip out the old insert and slide in a new one

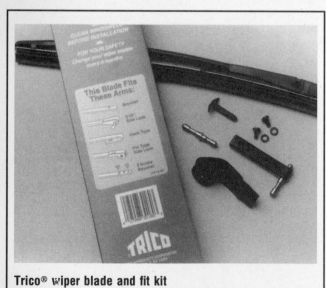

Trico® wiper blade and fit kit

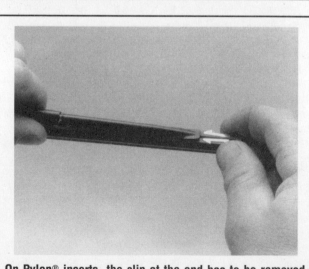

On Pylon® inserts, the clip at the end has to be removed prior to sliding the insert off

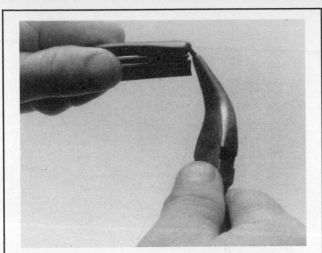

On Trico® wiper blades, the tab at the end of the blade must be turned up . . .

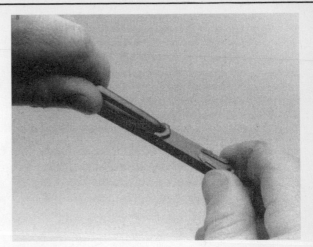

The Tripledge® wiper blade insert is removed and installed using a securing clip

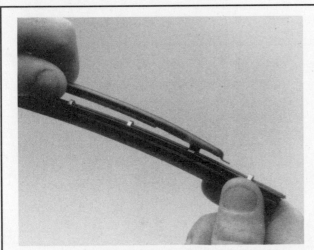

. . . then the insert can be removed. After installing the replacement insert, bend the tab back

these refills is molded into the end and they should be replaced with identical types.

Regardless of the type of refill used, be sure to follow the part manufacturer's instructions closely. Make sure that all of the frame jaws are engaged as the refill is pushed into place and locked. If the metal blade holder and frame are allowed to touch the glass during wiper operation, the glass will be scratched.

Tires and Wheels

Common sense and good driving habits will afford maximum tire life. Fast starts, sudden stops and hard cornering are hard on tires and will shorten their useful life span. Make sure that you don't overload the vehicle or run with incorrect pressure in the tires. Both of these practices will increase tread wear.

➡**For optimum tire life, keep the tires properly inflated, rotate them often and have the wheel alignment checked periodically.**

Inspect your tires frequently. Be especially careful to watch for bubbles in the tread or sidewall, deep cuts or underinflation. Replace any tires with bubbles in the sidewall. If cuts are so deep that they penetrate to the cords, discard the tire. Any cut in the sidewall of a radial tire renders it unsafe. Also look for uneven tread wear patterns that may indicate the front end is out of alignment or that the tires are out of balance.

TIRE ROTATION

Tires must be rotated periodically to equalize wear patterns that vary with a tire's position on the vehicle. Tires will also wear in an uneven way as the front steering/suspension system wears to the point where the alignment should be reset.

Rotating the tires will ensure maximum life for the tires as a set, so you will not have to discard a tire early due to wear on

to engage the remaining frame jaws. There are usually four jaws; be certain when installing that the refill is engaged in all of them. At the end of its travel, the tabs will lock into place on the front jaws of the wiper blade frame.

Another type of refill is made from polycarbonate. The refill has a simple locking device at one end which flexes downward out of the groove into which the jaws of the holder fit, allowing easy release. By sliding the new refill through all the jaws and pushing through the slight resistance when it reaches the end of its travel, the refill will lock into position.

To replace the Tridon® refill, it is necessary to remove the wiper blade. This refill has a plastic backing strip with a notch about 1 in. (25mm) from the end. Hold the blade (frame) on a hard surface so that the frame is tightly bowed. Grip the tip of the backing strip and pull up while twisting counterclockwise. The backing strip will snap out of the retaining tab. Do this for the remaining tabs until the refill is free of the blade. The length of

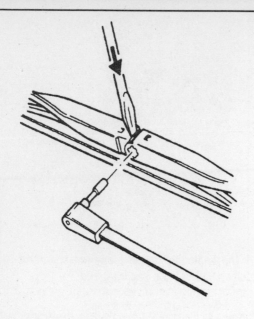

BLADE REPLACEMENT

1. CYCLE ARM AND BLADE ASSEMBLY TO UP POSITION-
   ON THE WINDSHIELD WHERE REMOVAL OF BLADE
   ASSEMBLY CAN BE PERFORMED WITHOUT
   DIFFICULTY. TURN IGNITION KEY OFF AT DESIRED
   POSITION.

2. TO REMOVE BLADE ASSEMBLY, INSERT
   SCREWDRIVER IN SLOT, PUSH DOWN ON SPRING
   LOCK AND PULL BLADE ASSEMBLY FROM PIN (VIEW
   A)

3. TO INSTALL, PUSH THE BLADE ASSEMBLY ON THE
   PIN SO THAT THE SPRING LOCK ENGAGES THE PIN
   (VIEW A). BE SURE THE BLADE ASSEMBLY IS
   SECURELY ATTACHED TO PIN

VIEW A

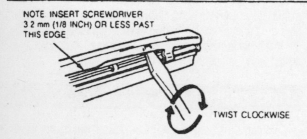

NOTE INSERT SCREWDRIVER
3 2 mm (1/8 INCH) OR LESS PAST
THIS EDGE

TWIST CLOCKWISE

ELEMENT REPLACEMENT

1 INSERT SCREWDRIVER BETWEEN THE EDGE OF THE
   SUPER STRUCTURE AND THE BLADE BACKING DRIP
   (VIEW B) TWIST SCREWDRIVER SLOWLY UNTIL
   ELEMENT CLEARS ONE SIDE OF THE SUPER STRUC-
   TURE CLAW

2 SLIDE THE ELEMENT INTO THE SUPER
   STRUCTURE CLAWS

VIEW B

4 INSERT ELEMENT INTO ONE SIDE OF THE END
   CLAWS (VIEW D) AND WITH A ROCKING MOTION
   PUSH ELEMENT UPWARD UNTIL IT SNAPS IN (VIEW
   E)

VIEW D

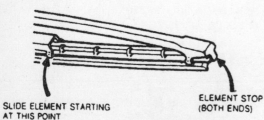

SLIDE ELEMENT STARTING
AT THIS POINT

ELEMENT STOP
(BOTH ENDS)

3. SLIDE THE ELEMENT INTO THE SUPER STRUCTURE
   CLAWS, STARTING WITH SECOND SET FROM EITHER
   END (VIEW C) AND CONTINUE TO SLIDE THE BLADE
   ELEMENT INTO ALL THE SUPER STRUCTURE CLAWS
   TO THE ELEMENT STOP (VIEW C)

VIEW C

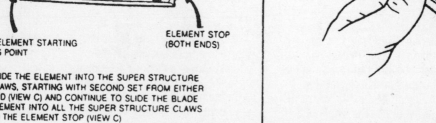

VIEW E

Trico® wiper blade insert (element) replacement

BLADE REPLACEMENT

1. Cycle arm and blade assembly to a position on the windshield where removal of blade assembly can be performed without difficulty. Turn ignition key off at desired position.
2. To remove blade assembly from wiper arm, pull up on spring lock and pull blade assembly from pin (View A). Be sure spring lock is not pulled excessively or it will become distorted.
3. To install, push the blade assembly onto the pin so that the spring lock engages the pin (View A). Be sure the blade assembly is securely attached to pin.

ELEMENT REPLACEMENT

1. In the plastic backing strip which is part of the rubber blade assembly, there is an 11.11mm (7/16 inch) long notch located approximately one inch from either end. Locate either notch.
2. Place the frame of the wiper blade assembly on a firm surface with either notched end of the backing strip visible.
3. Grasp the frame portion of the wiper blade assembly and push down until the blade assembly is tightly bowed.
4. With the blade assembly in the bowed position, grasp the tip of the backing strip firmly, pulling up and twisting C.C.W. at the same time. The backing strip will then snap out of the retaining tab on the end of the frame.
5. Lift the wiper blade assembly from the surface and slide the backing strip down the frame until the notch lines up with the next retaining tab, twist slightly, and the backing strip will snap out. Continue this operation with the remaining tabs until the blade element is completely detached from the frame.
6. To install blade element, reverse the above procedure, making sure all six (6) tabs are locked to the backing strip before installing blade to wiper arm.

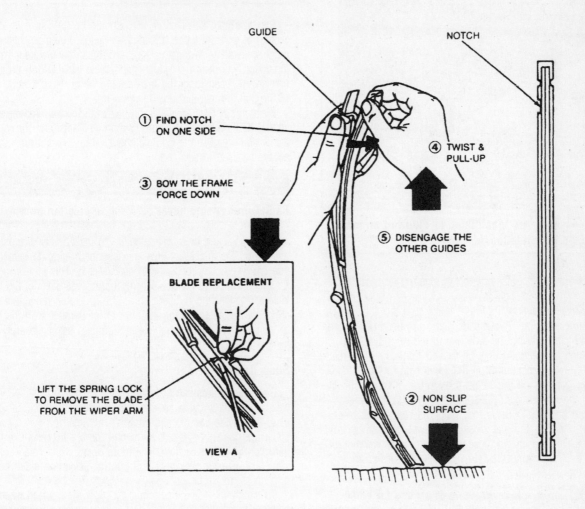

Tridon® wiper blade insert (element) replacement

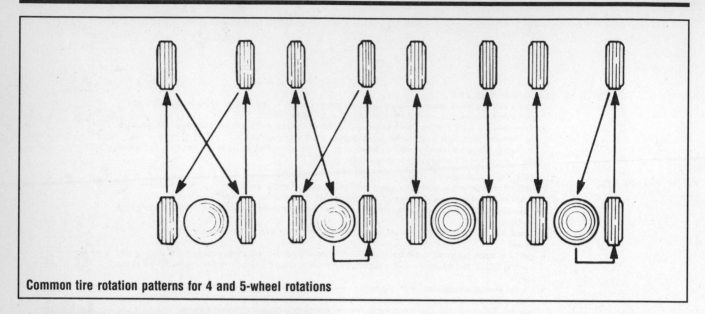

Common tire rotation patterns for 4 and 5-wheel rotations

Unidirectional tires are identifiable by sidewall arrows and/or the word ='rotation='

only part of the tread. Regular rotation is required to equalize wear.

When rotating "unidirectional tires," make sure that they always roll in the same direction. This means that a tire used on the left side of the vehicle must not be switched to the right side and vice-versa. Such tires should only be rotated front-to-rear or rear-to-front, while always remaining on the same side of the vehicle. These tires are marked on the sidewall as to the direction of rotation; observe the marks when reinstalling the tire(s).

Some styled or "mag" wheels may have different offsets front to rear. In these cases, the rear wheels must not be used up front and vice-versa. Furthermore, if these wheels are equipped with unidirectional tires, they cannot be rotated unless the tire is remounted for the proper direction of rotation.

➡**The compact or space-saver spare is strictly for emergency use. It must never be included in the tire rotation or placed on the vehicle for everyday use.**

TIRE DESIGN

For maximum satisfaction, tires should be used in sets of four. Mixing of different types (radial, bias-belted, fiberglass belted) must be avoided. In most cases, the vehicle manufacturer has designated a type of tire on which the vehicle will perform best. Your first choice when replacing tires should be to use the same type of tire that the manufacturer recommends.

When radial tires are used, tire sizes and wheel diameters should be selected to maintain ground clearance and tire load capacity equivalent to the original specified tire. Radial tires should always be used in sets of four.

✳✳ CAUTION

Radial tires should never be used on only the front axle.

When selecting tires, pay attention to the original size as marked on the tire. Most tires are described using an industry size code sometimes referred to as P-Metric. This allows the exact identification of the tire specifications, regardless of the manufacturer. If selecting a different tire size or brand, remember to check the installed tire for any sign of interference with the body or suspension while the vehicle is stopping, turning sharply or heavily loaded.

Snow Tires

Good radial tires can produce a big advantage in slippery weather, but in snow, a street radial tire does not have sufficient tread to provide traction and control. The small grooves of a street tire quickly pack with snow and the tire behaves like a billiard ball on a marble floor. The more open, chunky tread of a snow tire will self-clean as the tire turns, providing much better grip on snowy surfaces.

To satisfy municipalities requiring snow tires during weather emergencies, most snow tires carry either an M + S designation after the tire size stamped on the sidewall, or the designation "all-season." In general, no change in tire size is necessary when buying snow tires.

Most manufacturers strongly recommend the use of 4 snow tires on their vehicles for reasons of stability. If snow tires are fitted only to the drive wheels, the opposite end of the vehicle may become very unstable when braking or turning on slippery surfaces. This instability can lead to unpleasant endings if the driver can't counteract the slide in time.

Note that snow tires, whether 2 or 4, will affect vehicle handling in all non-snow situations. The stiffer, heavier snow tires will noticeably change the turning and braking characteristics of the vehicle. Once the snow tires are installed, you must re-learn the behavior of the vehicle and drive accordingly.

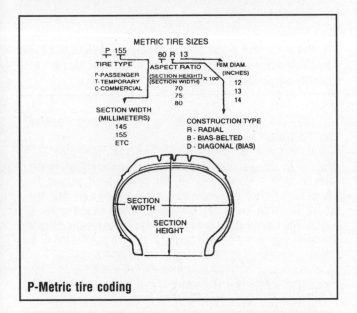

P-Metric tire coding

➡ **Consider buying extra wheels on which to mount the snow tires. Once done, the "snow wheels" can be installed and removed as needed. This eliminates the potential damage to tires or wheels from seasonal removal and installation. Even if your vehicle has styled wheels, see if inexpensive steel wheels are available. Although the look of the vehicle will change, the expensive wheels will be protected from salt, curb hits and pothole damage.**

TIRE STORAGE

If they are mounted on wheels, store the tires at proper inflation pressure. All tires should be kept in a cool, dry place. If they are stored in the garage or basement, do not let them stand on a concrete floor; set them on strips of wood, a mat or a large stack of newspaper. Keeping them away from direct moisture is of paramount importance. Tires should not be stored upright, but in a flat position.

INFLATION & INSPECTION

The importance of proper tire inflation cannot be overemphasized. A tire employs air as part of its structure. It is designed around the supporting strength of the air at a specified pressure.

For this reason, improper inflation drastically reduces the tires's ability to perform as intended. A tire will lose some air in day-to-day use; having to add a few pounds of air periodically is not necessarily a sign of a leaking tire.

Two items should be a permanent fixture in every glove compartment: an accurate tire pressure gauge and a tread depth gauge. Check the tire pressure (including the spare) regularly with a pocket type gauge. Too often, the gauge on the end of the air hose at your corner garage is not accurate because it suffers too much abuse. Always check tire pressure when the tires are cold, as pressure increases with temperature. If you must move the vehicle to check the tire inflation, do not drive more than a mile before checking. A cold tire is generally one that has not been driven for more than three hours.

A plate or sticker is normally provided somewhere in the vehicle (door post, hood, tailgate or trunk lid) which shows the proper pressure for the tires. Never counteract excessive pressure build-up by bleeding off air pressure (letting some air out). This will cause the tire to run hotter and wear quicker.

✳✳ CAUTION

Never exceed the maximum tire pressure embossed on the tire! This is the pressure to be used when the tire is at maximum loading, but it is rarely the correct pressure for everyday driving. Consult the owner's manual or the tire pressure sticker for the correct tire pressure.

Once you've maintained the correct tire pressures for several weeks, you'll be familiar with the vehicle's braking and handling personality. Slight adjustments in tire pressures can fine-tune these characteristics, but never change the cold pressure specification by more than 2 psi. A slightly softer tire pressure will give a softer ride but also yield lower fuel mileage. A slightly harder tire will give crisper dry road handling but can cause skidding on wet surfaces. Unless you're fully attuned to the vehicle, stick to the recommended inflation pressures.

All tires made since 1968 have built-in tread wear indicator bars that show up as ½ in. (13mm) wide smooth bands across the tire when 1/16 in. (1.5mm) of tread remains. The appearance of tread wear indicators means that the tires should be replaced. In

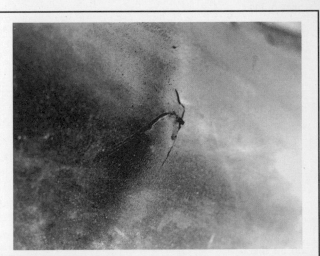

Tires should be checked frequently for any sign of puncture or damage

Tires with deep cuts, or cuts which show bulging should be replaced immediately

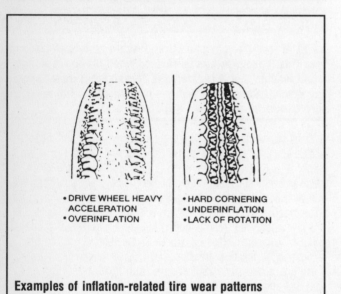

- DRIVE WHEEL HEAVY ACCELERATION
- OVERINFLATION

- HARD CORNERING
- UNDERINFLATION
- LACK OF ROTATION

Examples of inflation-related tire wear patterns

PROPERLY INFLATED   IMPROPERLY INFLATED
RADIAL TIRE

Radial tires have a characteristic sidewall bulge; don't try to measure pressure by looking at the tire. Use a quality air pressure gauge

fact, many states have laws prohibiting the use of tires with less than this amount of tread.

You can check your own tread depth with an inexpensive gauge or by using a Lincoln head penny. Slip the Lincoln penny (with Lincoln's head upside-down) into several tread grooves. If you can see the top of Lincoln's head in 2 adjacent grooves, the tire has less than 1/16 in. (1.5mm) tread left and should be replaced. You can measure snow tires in the same manner by using the "tails" side of the Lincoln penny. If you can see the top of the Lincoln memorial, it's time to replace the snow tire(s).

CARE OF SPECIAL WHEELS

If you have invested money in magnesium, aluminum alloy or sport wheels, special precautions should be taken to make sure your investment is not wasted and that your special wheels look good for the life of the vehicle.

Special wheels are easily damaged and/or scratched. Occasion-

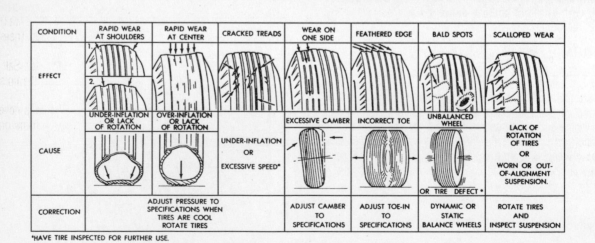

CONDITION	RAPID WEAR AT SHOULDERS	RAPID WEAR AT CENTER	CRACKED TREADS	WEAR ON ONE SIDE	FEATHERED EDGE	BALD SPOTS	SCALLOPED WEAR
EFFECT							
CAUSE	UNDER-INFLATION OR LACK OF ROTATION	OVER-INFLATION OR LACK OF ROTATION	UNDER-INFLATION OR EXCESSIVE SPEED*	EXCESSIVE CAMBER	INCORRECT TOE	UNBALANCED WHEEL OR TIRE DEFECT *	LACK OF ROTATION OF TIRES OR WORN OR OUT-OF-ALIGNMENT SUSPENSION.
CORRECTION	ADJUST PRESSURE TO SPECIFICATIONS WHEN TIRES ARE COOL ROTATE TIRES			ADJUST CAMBER TO SPECIFICATIONS	ADJUST TOE-IN TO SPECIFICATIONS	DYNAMIC OR STATIC BALANCE WHEELS	ROTATE TIRES AND INSPECT SUSPENSION

*HAVE TIRE INSPECTED FOR FURTHER USE.

Common tire wear patterns and causes

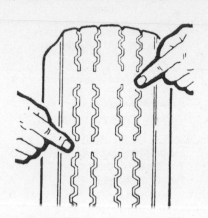

Tread wear indicators will appear when the tire is worn

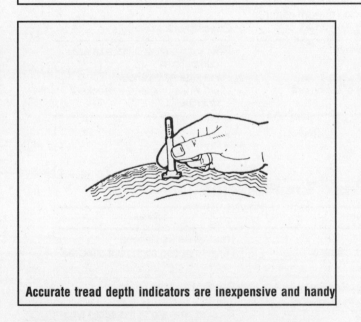

Accurate tread depth indicators are inexpensive and handy

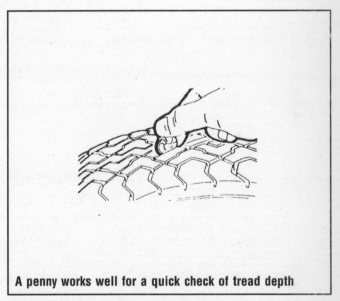

A penny works well for a quick check of tread depth

ally check the rims for cracking, impact damage or air leaks. If any of these are found, replace the wheel. But in order to prevent this type of damage and the costly replacement of a special wheel, observe the following precautions:

• Use extra care not to damage the wheels during removal, installation, balancing, etc. After removal of the wheels from the vehicle, place them on a mat or other protective surface. If they are to be stored for any length of time, support them on strips of wood. Never store tires and wheels upright; the tread may develop flat spots.

• When driving, watch for hazards; it doesn't take much to crack a wheel.

• When washing, use a mild soap or non-abrasive dish detergent (keeping in mind that detergent tends to remove wax). Avoid cleansers with abrasives or the use of hard brushes. There are many cleaners and polishes for special wheels.

• If possible, remove the wheels during the winter. Salt and sand used for snow removal can severely damage the finish of a wheel.

• Make certain the recommended lug nut torque is never exceeded or the wheel may crack. Never use snow chains on special wheels; severe scratching will occur.

Troubleshooting Basic Wheel Problems

Problem	Cause	Solution
The car's front end vibrates at high speed	• The wheels are out of balance • Wheels are out of alignment	• Have wheels balanced • Have wheel alignment checked/adjusted
Car pulls to either side	• Wheels are out of alignment • Unequal tire pressure • Different size tires or wheels	• Have wheel alignment checked/adjusted • Check/adjust tire pressure • Change tires or wheels to same size
The car's wheel(s) wobbles	• Loose wheel lug nuts • Wheels out of balance • Damaged wheel • Wheels are out of alignment • Worn or damaged ball joint • Excessive play in the steering linkage (usually due to worn parts) • Defective shock absorber	• Tighten wheel lug nuts • Have tires balanced • Raise car and spin the wheel. If the wheel is bent, it should be replaced • Have wheel alignment checked/adjusted • Check ball joints • Check steering linkage • Check shock absorbers
Tires wear unevenly or prematurely	• Incorrect wheel size • Wheels are out of balance • Wheels are out of alignment	• Check if wheel and tire size are compatible • Have wheels balanced • Have wheel alignment checked/adjusted

Troubleshooting Basic Tire Problems

Problem	Cause	Solution
The car's front end vibrates at high speeds and the steering wheel shakes	• Wheels out of balance • Front end needs aligning	• Have wheels balanced • Have front end alignment checked
The car pulls to one side while cruising	• Unequal tire pressure (car will usually pull to the low side) • Mismatched tires • Front end needs aligning	• Check/adjust tire pressure • Be sure tires are of the same type and size • Have front end alignment checked
Abnormal, excessive or uneven tire wear See "How to Read Tire Wear"	• Infrequent tire rotation • Improper tire pressure • Sudden stops/starts or high speed on curves	• Rotate tires more frequently to equalize wear • Check/adjust pressure • Correct driving habits
Tire squeals	• Improper tire pressure • Front end needs aligning	• Check/adjust tire pressure • Have front end alignment checked

Tire Size Comparison Chart

"Letter" sizes			Inch Sizes	Metric-inch Sizes		
"60 Series"	"70 Series"	"78 Series"	1965–77	"60 Series"	"70 Series"	"80 Series"
		Y78-12	5.50-12, 5.60-12 6.00-12	165/60-12	165/70-12	155-12
		W78-13	5.20-13	165/60-13	145/70-13	135-13
		Y78-13	5.60-13	175/60-13	155/70-13	145-13
			6.15-13	185/60-13	165/70-13	155-13, P155/80-13
A60-13	A70-13	A78-13	6.40-13	195/60-13	175/70-13	165-13
B60-13	B70-13	B78-13	6.70-13	205/60-13	185/70-13	175-13
			6.90-13			
C60-13	C70-13	C78-13	7.00-13	215/60-13	195/70-13	185-13
D60-13	D70-13	D78-13	7.25-13			
E60-13	E70-13	E78-13	7.75-13			195-13
			5.20-14	165/60-14	145/70-14	135-14
			5.60-14	175/60-14	155/70-14	145-14
			5.90-14			
A60-14	A70-14	A78-14	6.15-14	185/60-14	165/70-14	155-14
	B70-14	B78-14	6.45-14	195/60-14	175/70-14	165-14
	C70-14	C78-14	6.95-14	205/60-14	185/70-14	175-14
D60-14	D70-14	D78-14				
E60-14	E70-14	E78-14	7.35-14	215/60-14	195/70-14	185-14
F60-14	F70-14	F78-14, F83-14	7.75-14	225/60-14	200/70-14	195-14
G60-14	G70-14	G77-14, G78-14	8.25-14	235/60-14	205/70-14	205-14
H60-14	H70-14	H78-14	8.55-14	245/60-14	215/70-14	215-14
J60-14	J70-14	J78-14	8.85-14	255/60-14	225/70-14	225-14
L60-14	L70-14		9.15-14	265/60-14	235/70-14	
	A70-15	A78-15	5.60-15	185/60-15	165/70-15	155-15
B60-15	B70-15	B78-15	6.35-15	195/60-15	175/70-15	165-15
C60-15	C70-15	C78-15	6.85-15	205/60-15	185/70-15	175-15
	D70-15	D78-15				
E60-15	E70-15	E78-15	7.35-15	215/60-15	195/70-15	185-15
F60-15	F70-15	F78-15	7.75-15	225/60-15	205/70-15	195-15
G60-15	G70-15	G78-15	8.15-15/8.25-15	235/60-15	215/70-15	205-15
H60-15	H70-15	H78-15	8.45-15/8.55-15	245/60-15	225/70-15	215-15
J60-15	J70-15	J78-15	8.85-15/8.90-15	255/60-15	235/70-15	225-15
	K70-15		9.00-15	265/60-15	245/70-15	230-15
L60-15	L70-15	L78-15, L84-15	9.15-15			235-15
	M70-15	M78-15				255-15
		N78-15				

Note: Every size tire is not listed and many size comparisons are approximate, based on load ratings. Wider tires than those supplied new with the vehicle, should always be checked for clearance.

FLUIDS AND LUBRICANTS

▶ **See Figure 40**

Used fluids such as engine oil, transmission fluid, antifreeze and brake fluid are hazardous wastes and must be disposed of properly. Before draining any fluids, consult with the local authorities; in many areas, waste oil, etc. is being accepted as part of recycling programs. A number of service stations and auto parts stores are also accepting waste fluids for recycling. Be sure of the recycling center's policies before draining any fluids, as many will not accept different fluids that have been mixed together, such as oil and antifreeze.

Item	Lubricant
Engine Oil	API "SE" or "SF" API "SE/CC" or "SF/CC" (diesel)
Manual Transmission	SAE 80W GL-4 or SAE 80W/90 GL-4
Automatic Transmission	DEXRON® ATF
Rear Axle	SAE 80W GL-5 or SAE 80W/90 GL-5
Power Steering Reservoir	DEXRON® ATF
Brake and Clutch Fluid	DOT 3
Antifreeze	Ethylene Glycol
Chassis Lubrication	NLGI #2
Steering Gear	SAE 80W GL-4 or SAE 80W/90 GL-4

Fig. 40 Always replace fluids with the specified lubricant

Oil and Fuel Recommendations

OIL

▶ **See Figure 41**

The SAE (Society of Automotive Engineers) grade number indicates the viscosity of the engine oil and thus its ability to lubricate at a given temperature. The lower the SAE grade number, the lighter the oil. The lower the viscosity, and the easier it is to crank the engine in cold weather.

Oil viscosities should be chosen from those oils recommended for the lowest anticipated temperatures during the oil change interval.

Multi-viscosity oils (10W-30, 20W-50, etc.) offer the important advantage of being adaptable to temperature extremes. They allow easy starting at low temperatures, yet they give good protection at high speeds and engine temperatures. This is a decided advantage in changeable climates or in long distance touring.

Choose the viscosity range carefully, based upon the lowest expected temperature for the time of year. If the lowest expected temperature is 0°F (−18°C), you should use 10W-30. If it is 50°F (10°C), as in spring and fall, you can use 20W-40 and 20W-50 for their extra guarantee of sufficient viscosity at high temperatures.

The API (American Petroleum Institute) designation indicates the classification of engine oil used under certain given operating conditions. Only oils designated for use Service SE should be used. Oils of the SE type perform a variety of functions inside the engine in addition to the basic function as a lubricant. Through a balanced system of metallic detergents and polymeric dispersants, the oil prevents the formation of high and low temperature deposits and also keeps sludge and particles of dirt in suspension. Acids, particularly sulfuric acid, as well as other byproducts of combustion, are neutralized. Both the SAE grade number and the API designation can be found on top of the oil can.

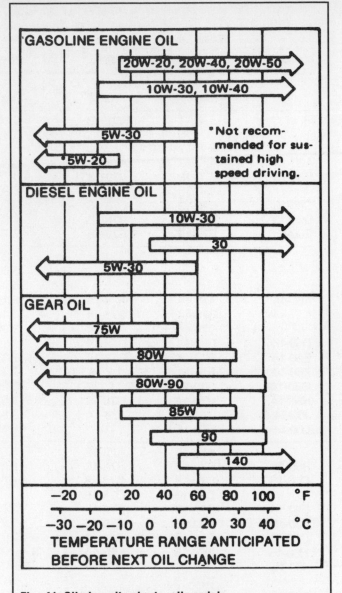

Fig. 41 Oil viscosity chart—all models

Look for the API oil identification label when choosing your engine oil

Diesel engines all require SE engine oil. In addition, the oil must qualify for ACC rating. The API has a number of different diesel engine ratings, including CB, CC and CD. Any of these other oils are fine as long as the designation CC appears on the can along with them. Do not use oil labeled only SE or only CC. Both designations must always appear together.

➡**As of late 1980, the API has come out with a new designation of motor oil, SF. Oils designated for use Service SF are equally acceptable in your Datsun/Nissan. Non-detergent or straight mineral oils should not be used in your car.**

SYNTHETIC OIL

There are excellent synthetic and fuel efficient oils available that, under the right circumstances, can help provide better fuel mileage and better engine protection. However, these advantages come at a price, which can be three or four times the price per quart of conventional motor oils.

Before pouring any synthetic oils into your car's engine, you should consider the condition of the engine and the type of driving you do. Also, check the car's warranty conditions regarding the use of synthetics.

Generally, it is best to avoid the use of synthetic oil in both brand new and older, high mileage engines. New engines require a proper break-in, and the synthetics are so slippery that they can prevent this. Most manufacturers recommend that you wait at least 5,000 miles before switching to a synthetic oil. Conversely, older engines are looser and tend to use more oil. Synthetics will slip past worn parts more readily than regular oil, and will be used up faster. If your car already leaks and/or uses oil (due to worn parts and bad seals or gaskets), it will leak and use more with a slippery synthetic oil inside.

Consider your type of driving. If most of your accumulated mileage is on the highway at higher, steadier speeds, a synthetic oil will reduce friction and probably help deliver better fuel mileage. Under such ideal highway conditions, the oil change interval can be extended, as long as the oil filter will operate effectively for the extended life of the oil. If the filter can't do its job for this extended period, dirt and sludge will build up in your engine's crankcase, sump, oil pump and lines, no matter what type of oil is used. If using synthetic oil in this manner, you should continue to change the oil filter at the recommended intervals.

Cars used under harder, stop-and-go, short hop circumstances should always be serviced more frequently, and for these cars synthetic oil may not be a wise investment. Because of the necessary shorter change interval needed for this type of driving, you cannot take advantage of the long recommended change interval of most synthetic oils.

Finally, most synthetic oils are not compatible with conventional oils and cannot be added to them. This means you should always carry a couple of quarts of synthetic oil with you while on a long trip, as not all service stations carry this oil.

FUEL

All Datsun gasoline engined models covered in this book have been designed to run on regular low-lead or unleaded fuel, 1973–79, with the exception of those models built for use in California (1975 and later) which require the use of unleaded fuel. All 1980 and later models must also use only unleaded fuel. 1975 and later California cars and all 1980 and later models utilize a catalytic converter. The use of leaded fuel will plug the catalyst, rendering it inoperative, and will increase the exhaust back pressure to the point where engine output will be severely reduced. The minimum octane requirement for all engines using unleaded fuel is 91 RON (87 CLC). All unleaded fuels sold in the U.S. are required to meet this minimum octane rating.

The use of a fuel too low in octane (a measurement of anti-knock quality) will result in spark knock. Since many factors such as altitude, terrain, air temperature and humidity affect operating efficiency, knocking may result even though the recommended fuel is being used. If persistent knocking occurs, it may be necessary to switch to a higher grade of fuel. Continuous or heavy knocking may result in engine damage.

➡**Your engine's fuel requirement can change with time, mainly due to carbon buildup, which will in turn increase the temperatures in the combustion chamber and change the compression ratio. If your engine pings, knocks, or runs on, switch to a higher grade of fuel. Sometimes just changing brands will cure the problem. If it becomes necessary to retard the timing from specifications, don't change it more than about two degrees. Retarded timing will reduce power output and fuel mileage, in addition to increasing the engine temperature.**

Datsun diesels require the exclusive use of diesel fuel. At NO time should gasoline be substituted or mixed with diesel fuel. Two grades of diesel fuel are manufactured, #1 and #2, although #2 is generally more available. Better fuel economy results from the use of #2 grade fuel. In some northern parts of the U.S. and in most parts of Canada, #1 grade fuel is available in the winter or, if not, a winterized blend of #2 grade is supplied. When the temperature falls below 20°F (−7°C), #1 grade or winterized #2 grade fuel are the only fuels that can be used. Temperatures below 20°F. cause unwinterized #2 to thicken (it actually gels), blocking the fuel lines and preventing the engine from running.

Diesel Cautions:

• Do not use heating oil in your car. While in some cases, home heating refinement levels equal those of diesel fuel, at times they are far below diesel engine requirements. The result of using dirty home heating oil will be a clogged fuel system, in which case the entire system may have to be dismantled and cleaned. There may also be engine running problems such as ignition lag (see below).

• Do not use ether or starting assist fluids in your car.

• Do not use any fuel additives recommended for use in gasoline engines.

It is normal that the engine noise level is louder during the warm-up period in winter. This occurs due to a normal diesel phenomenon known as ignition lag. It relates to the lower temperatures reached through compression if the combustion chambers are cold, and normally does not indicate any engine abnormality. It is also normal that whitish-blue smoke may be emitted from the exhaust shortly after starting and during warm-up. The amount of smoke depends upon the outside temperature.

If the increases in noise and smoke levels at cold temperatures seem extreme, you may wish to check on the fuel's cetane rating (you may have to ask your fuel dealer what the rating is). This is a measurement of the fuel's ability to ignite at low temperatures. The rating should be at least 42 (higher cetane numbers are more desirable).

Engine

OIL LEVEL CHECK

The best time to check the engine oil is before operating the engine or after it has been sitting for at least 10 minutes in order to gain an accurate reading. This will allow the oil to drain back in the crankcase. To check the engine oil level, make sure that the vehicle is resting on a level surface, remove the oil dipstick, wipe it clean and reinsert the stick firmly for an accurate reading. The oil dipstick has two marks to indicate high and low oil level. If the oil is at or below the "low level" mark on the dipstick, oil should be added as necessary. The oil level should be maintained in the safety margin, neither going above the "high level" mark or below the "low level" mark.

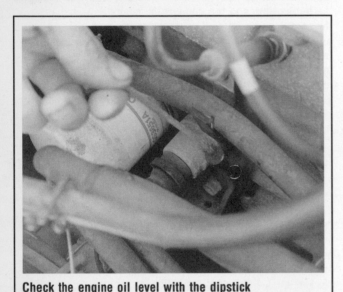

Check the engine oil level with the dipstick

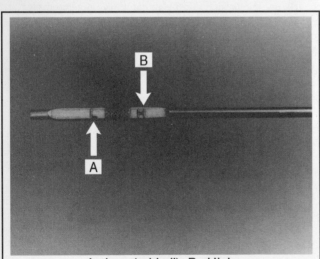

A. Low (add oil) B. High
Check the engine oil dipstick to determine oil level

OIL & FILTER CHANGE

▶ **See Figure 42**

The Datsun/Nissan factory maintenance intervals (every 7,500 miles or 6 months) specify changing the oil filter at every second oil change after the initial service. We recommend replacing the oil filter with every oil change. For the small price of an oil filter, it's cheap insurance to replace the filter at every oil change. One of the larger filter manufacturers points out in its advertisements that not changing the filter leaves 1 quart of dirty oil in the engine. This claim is true and should be kept in mind when changing your oil.

➡**On turbocharged engines factory maintenance intervals are every 5,000 miles/6 months and diesel maintenance intervals are 7,500 miles/6 months.**

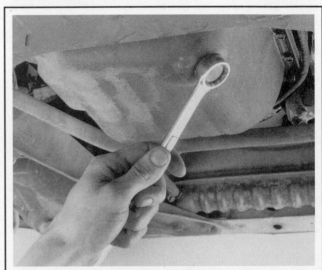

Use a wrench to loosen the oil drain plug, then . . .

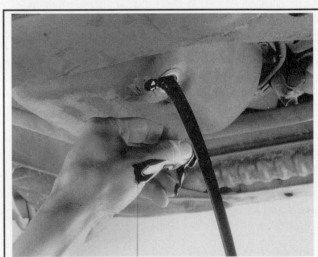

. . . . keeping inward pressure, unscrew and remove the plug by hand

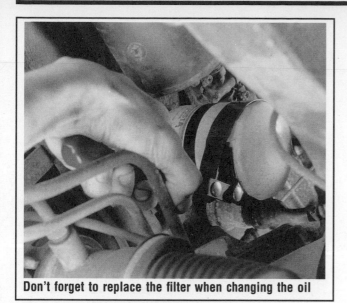

Don't forget to replace the filter when changing the oil

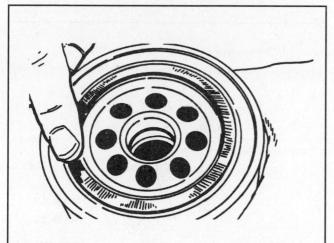

Fig. 42 Coat the new oil filter gasket with clean engine oil

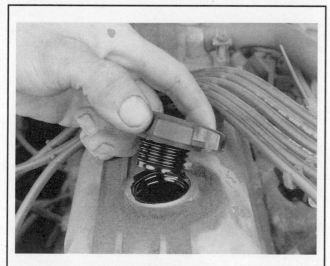

Remove the filler cap to add the oil

Use a funnel to avoid spillage

1. Run the engine until it reaches normal operating temperature.

2. Jack up the front of the car and support it on jackstands if necessary to gain access to the filter.

3. Slide a drain pan of at least 6 quarts capacity under the oil pan.

✳✳ CAUTION

The EPA warns that prolonged contact with used engine oil may cause a number of skin disorders, including cancer! You should make every effort to minimize your exposure to used engine oil. Protective gloves should be worn when changing the oil. Wash your hands and any other exposed skin areas as soon as possible after exposure to used engine oil. Soap and water, or waterless hand cleaner should be used.

4. Loosen the drain plug. Turn the plug out by hand. By keeping an inward pressure on the plug as you unscrew it, oil won't escape past the threads and you can remove it without being burned by hot oil.

5. Allow the oil to drain completely and then install the drain plug. Don't overtighten the plug or you'll be buying a new pan or a trick replacement plug for damaged threads.

6. Using a strap wrench, remove the oil filter. Keep in mind that it's holding about one quart of dirty, hot oil.

7. Empty the old filter into the drain pan and dispose of the filter and old oil.

➡**One ecologically desirable solution to the used oil disposal problem is to find a cooperative gas station owner who will allow you to dump your used oil into his tank or take the oil to a reclamation center (often at garages and gas stations).**

8. Using a clean rag, wipe off the filter adapter on the engine block. Be sure that the rag doesn't leave any lint which could clog an oil passage.

9. Coat the rubber gasket on the filter with fresh oil. Spin it onto the engine *by hand;* when the gasket touches the adapter sur-

Before installing a new oil filter, lightly coat the rubber gasket with clean oil

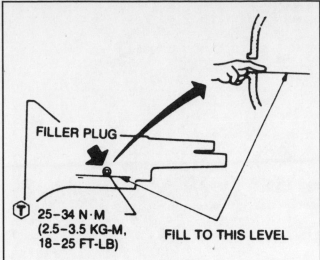

FILLER PLUG

25–34 N·M
(2.5–3.5 KG-M,
18–25 FT-LB)

FILL TO THIS LEVEL

Fig. 43 Transmission oil should be level with the bottom of the filler opening on manual transmissions

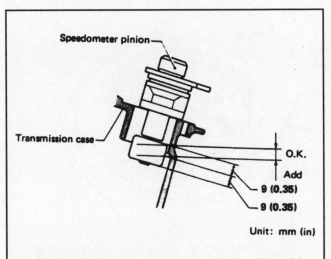

Speedometer pinion

Transmission case

O.K.
Add
9 (0.35)
9 (0.35)

Unit: mm (in)

Fig. 44 Check that the manual transmission oil level is within specifications

face give it another ½–¾ turn. No more or you'll squash the gasket and it will leak.

10. Refill the engine with the correct amount of fresh oil. See the Capacities chart.

11. Crank the engine over several times and then start it. If the oil pressure indicator light doesn't go out or the pressure gauge shows zero, shut the engine down and find out what's wrong.

12. If the oil pressure is OK and there are no leaks, shut the engine off and lower the car.

Manual Transmission

FLUID RECOMMENDATION

For manual transmission be sure to use fluid with an API GL-4 rating.

LEVEL CHECK

◆ **See Figures 43 and 44**

You should inspect the manual transmission gear oil at 7,500 miles or 6 months (12 months or 15,000 miles 1980 and later), at this point you should correct the level or replace the oil as necessary. The lubricant level should be even with the bottom of the filler hole. Hold in on the filler plug when unscrewing it. When you are sure that all of the threads of the plug are free of the transaxle case, move the plug away from the case slightly. If lubricant begins to flow out of the transmission, then you know it is full. If not, add the correct gear oil as necessary.

DRAIN & REFILL

◆ **See Figures 43 and 44**

➡**It is recommended that the manual transmission/ transaxle fluid be changed every 30,000 miles if the vehicle is used in severe service. You may also want to change it if**

you have bought your car used or if it has been driven in water deep enough to reach the transaxle case.

1. Run the engine until it reaches normal operating temperature then turn key to the **OFF** position.

2. Jack up the front of the car and support it on safety stands level, if necessary to gain access.

3. Remove the filler plug from the left-side of the transmission or remove the speedometer cable from the transaxle, to provide a vent.

4. The drain plug is located on the bottom of the transmission/ transaxle case. Place a pan under the drain plug and remove it.

✳✳ CAUTION

The oil will be HOT. Push up against the threads as you unscrew the plug to prevent leakage.

5. Allow the oil to drain completely. Clean off the plug and replace it. DO NOT OVERTIGHTEN PLUG.

6. Fill the transmission/transaxle with gear oil through the filler plug hole. Use API service GL-4 gear oil of the proper viscosity. This oil usually comes in a squeeze bottle with a long nozzle. If yours isn't, use a plastic squeeze bottle (the type used in the kitchen). Refer to the "Capacities" chart for the amount of oil needed.

7. The oil level should come up to the edge of the filler hole. You can stick your finger in to verify this. Watch out for sharp threads.

8. Replace the filler plug or speedometer cable. Lower the vehicle, dispose of the old oil in the same manner as old engine oil.

9. Test drive the vehicle, stop and check for leaks.

Automatic Transmission

FLUID RECOMMENDATIONS

All automatic transmissions use Dexron®II ATF (automatic transmission fluid).

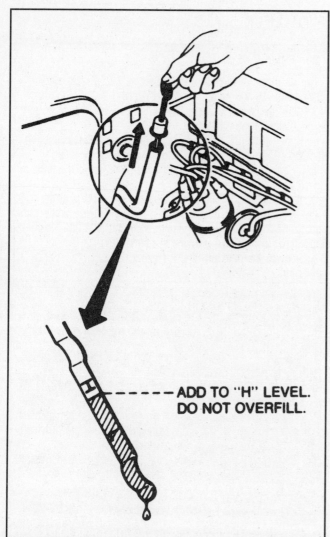

ADD TO "H" LEVEL.
DO NOT OVERFILL.

Fig. 45 Check the automatic transmission dipstick with the vehicle level, while the engine is warm and idling in Park

LEVEL CHECK

▶ **See Figures 45 and 46**

The fluid level in the automatic transmission (or transaxle on late model Maximas) should be checked every 6 months or 7,500 miles (12 months or 15,000 miles, 1980 and later), whichever comes first. The transmission has a dipstick for fluid level checks.

1. Drive the car until it is at normal operating temperature. The level should not be checked immediately after the car has been driven for a long time at high speed, or in city traffic in hot weather. In those cases, the transmission should be given a half hour to cool down.

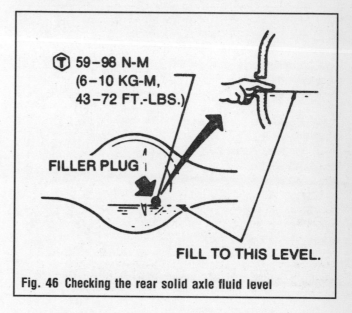

59–98 N-M
(6–10 KG-M,
43–72 FT.-LBS.)

FILLER PLUG

FILL TO THIS LEVEL.

Fig. 46 Checking the rear solid axle fluid level

2. Stop the car, apply the parking brake, then shift slowly through all gear positions, ending in Park. Let the engine idle for about five minutes with the transmission or transaxle in Park. The car should be on a level surface.

3. With the engine still running, remove the dipstick, wipe it clean, then reinsert it, pushing it fully home.

4. Pull the dipstick again and, holding it horizontally, read the fluid level.

5. Cautiously feel the end of the dipstick to determine the temperature. Note that on Datsuns/Nissans there is a scale on each side, HOT on one, COLD on the other. If the fluid level is not in the correct area, more will have to be added.

6. Fluid is added through the dipstick tube. You will probably need the aid of a spout or a long necked funnel. Be sure that whatever you pour through is perfectly clean and dry. Use an automatic transmission fluid marked DEXRON®II. Add fluid slowly, and in small amounts, checking the level frequently between additions. Do not overfill, which will cause foaming, fluid loss, slippage, and possible transmission damage. It takes only one pint to raise the level from L to H when the transaxle is hot.

DRAIN & REFILL

➡It is recommended that the automatic transmission fluid be changed every 30,000 miles if the vehicle is used in severe service. You may also want to change it if you have bought your car used or if it has been driven in water deep enough to reach the transmission case.

Transmission

◆ **See Figure 45**

1. There is no drain plug. The fluid pan must be removed. Partially remove the pan screws until the pan can be pulled down at one corner. Place a container under the transmission, lower a rear corner of the pan, and allow the fluid to drain.

2. After draining, remove the pan screws completely, and remove the pan and gasket.

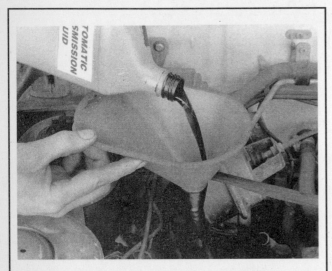

Using a funnel, add ATF through the dipstick tube

3. Clean the pan thoroughly and allow it to air dry. If you wipe it out with a rag you risk leaving bits of lint in the pan which will clog the tiny hydraulic passages in the transmission.

➡**It is very important to clean the old gasket from the oil pan, to prevent leaks upon installation, a razor blade does a excellent job at this.**

4. Install the pan using a new gasket. If you decide to use sealer on the gasket apply it only in a very thin bead running to the outside of the pan screw holes. Tighten the pan screws evenly in rotation from the center outwards, to 36–60 inch lbs.

5. It is a good idea to measure the amount of fluid drained to determine how much fresh fluid to add. This is because some part of the transmission, such as the torque converter, will not drain completely, and using the dry refill amount specified in the Capacities chart may lead to overfilling. Fluid is added through the dipstick tube. Make sure that the funnel, hose, or whatever you are using is completely clean and dry before pouring transmission fluid through it. Use DEXRON®II automatic transmission fluid.

6. Replace the dipstick after filling. Start the engine and allow it to idle. Do NOT race the engine. Check the installation of the new pan gasket for leaks.

7. After the engine has idled for a few minutes, shift the transmission slowly through the gears, then return the lever to Park. With the engine idling, check the fluid level on the dipstick. It

should be between the H and L marks. If below L, add sufficient fluid to raise the level to between the marks.

8. Drive the car until it is at operating temperature. The fluid should be at the H mark. If not, add sufficient fluid until this is the case. Be careful not to overfill. Overfilling causes slippage, overheating, and seal damage.

➡**If the drained fluid is discolored (brown or black), thick, or smells burnt, serious transmission problems due to overheating should be suspected. Your car's transmission should be inspected by a transmission specialist to determine the cause.**

Rear Drive Axle

FLUID RECOMMENDATIONS

Use only standard GL-5 hypoid type gear oil: SAE 80W or SAE 80W/90.

LEVEL CHECK

◆ **See Figures 46 and 47**

The oil in the differential should be checked at least every 7,500 miles (15,000 miles, 1980 and later).

1. With the car on a level surface, remove the filler plug from the back side of the differential.

2. If the oil begins to trickle out of the hole, there is enough. Otherwise, carefully insert your finger (watch out for sharp threads) into the hole and check that the oil is up to the bottom edge of the filler hole.

3. If not, add oil through the hole until the level is at the edge of the hole. Most gear oils come in a plastic squeeze bottle with a nozzle; making additions is simple. You can also use a common kitchen baster. Use only the specified fluid.

4. Replace the plug and check for leaks.

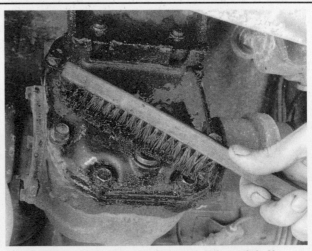

Use a stiff brush to de-gunk the rear differential, if necessary

A half inch breaker bar or ratchet works well to loosen the differential filler plug

Remove the plug once you have loosened it with the breaker bar or ratchet

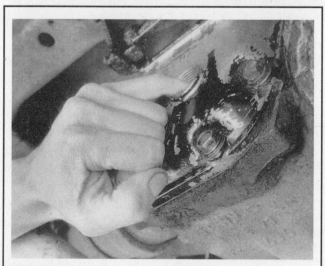

Check the hypold gear oil level with your finger

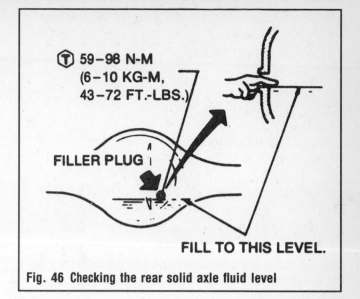

59–98 N-M
(6–10 KG-M,
43–72 FT.-LBS.)

FILLER PLUG

FILL TO THIS LEVEL.

Fig. 46 Checking the rear solid axle fluid level

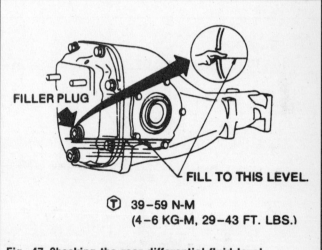

FILLER PLUG

FILL TO THIS LEVEL.

39–59 N-M
(4–6 KG-M, 29–43 FT. LBS.)

Fig. 47 Checking the rear differential fluid level—models with an independent rear suspension

DRAIN & REFILL

▶ **See Figures 48 and 49**

The axle lubricant should be changed according to the schedule in the Maintenance Intervals chart. You may also want to change it if you have bought your car used, or if it has been driven in water deep enough to reach the axle.

1. Park the car on a level surface. Place a pan of at least two quarts capacity underneath the drain plug. The drain plug is located on the center rear of the differential carrier, just below the filler plug on some models, on others it can be found at the bottom of the carrier. Remove the drain plug.

2. Allow the lubricant to drain completely.

3. Install the drain plug. Tighten it so that it will not leak, but do not overtighten. If you have a torque wrench, recommended torque is 29–43 ft. lbs.

4. Refill the differential housing with API GL-5 gear oil of

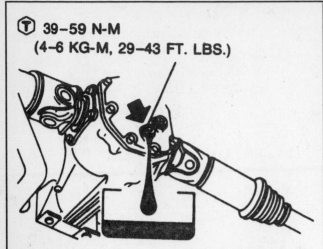

Fig. 48 Drain the differential fluid and retighten the plug to specifications (shown)—models with an independent rear suspension

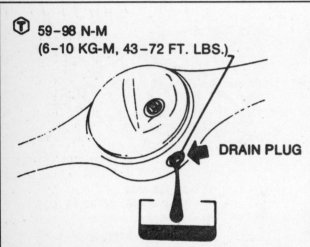

Fig. 49 Drain the solid rear axle as shown, then tighten the drain plug to specifications

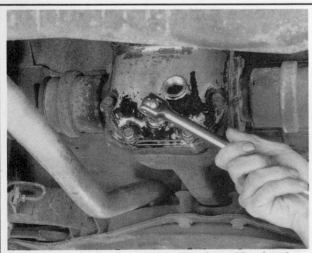

To drain the differential, loosen the plug with a breaker bar or ratchet . . .

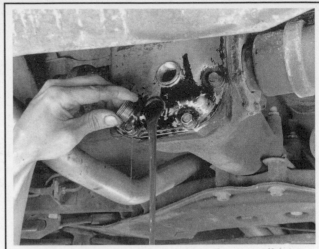

. . . then remove the plug and drain the gear oil into a suitable receptacle

the proper viscosity. The correct level is to the edge of the filler hole.

5. Install the filler plug. Tighten to 29–43 ft. lbs.

Cooling System

FLUID RECOMMENDATION

The cooling fluid or antifreeze, should be changed every 30,000 miles or 24 months. When replacing the fluid, use a mixture of 50% water and 50% ethylene glycol antifreeze.

Check the freezing protection rating at least once a year, preferably just before the winter sets in. This can be done with an antifreeze tester (most service stations will have one on hand and will probably check it for you, if not, they are available at an auto parts store). Maintain a protection rating of at least −20°F (−29°C) to prevent engine damage as a result of freezing and to assure the proper engine operating temperature.

It is also a good idea to have the cooling system checked for leaks. A pressure test gauge is available to perform such a task. Checking and repairing a coolant leak in the early stages will save time and money.

LEVEL CHECK

Check the coolant level every 3,000 miles or once a month. In hot weather operation, it may be a good idea to check the level once a week. Check for loose connections and signs of deterioration of the coolant hoses. Maintain the coolant level ¾–1¼″ below the level of the filler neck when the engine is cold. If the engine is equipped with a coolant recovery bottle check the coolant level in the bottle when the engine is cold, the level should be up to the MAX mark. If the bottle is empty, check the level in the radiator and refill as necessary, then fill the bottle up to the MAX level.

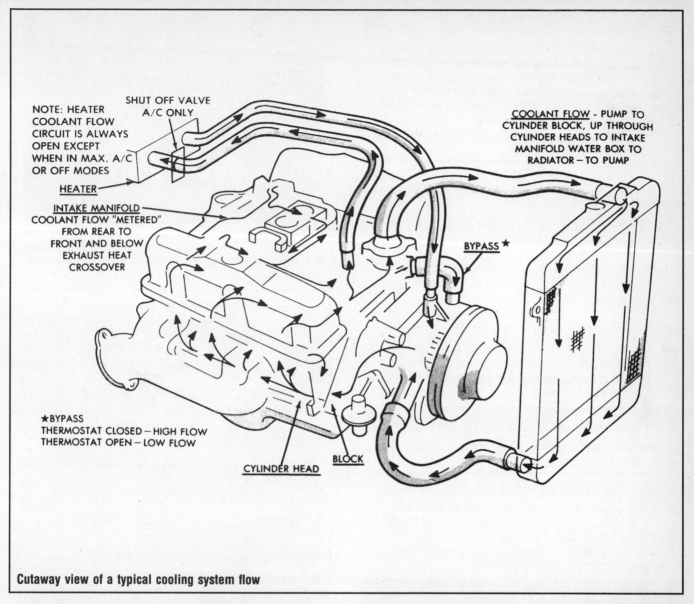

NOTE: HEATER COOLANT FLOW CIRCUIT IS ALWAYS OPEN EXCEPT WHEN IN MAX. A/C OR OFF MODES

SHUT OFF VALVE A/C ONLY

HEATER

INTAKE MANIFOLD COOLANT FLOW "METERED" FROM REAR TO FRONT AND BELOW EXHAUST HEAT CROSSOVER

COOLANT FLOW – PUMP TO CYLINDER BLOCK, UP THROUGH CYLINDER HEADS TO INTAKE MANIFOLD WATER BOX TO RADIATOR – TO PUMP

BYPASS ★

★BYPASS
THERMOSTAT CLOSED – HIGH FLOW
THERMOSTAT OPEN – LOW FLOW

CYLINDER HEAD

BLOCK

Cutaway view of a typical cooling system flow

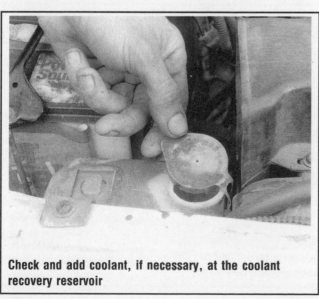

Check and add coolant, if necessary, at the coolant recovery reservoir

Use a funnel when adding coolant to avoid spillage

✳✳ CAUTION

Never remove the radiator cap when the vehicle is hot or overheated. Wait until it has cooled. Place a thick cloth over the radiator cap to shield yourself from the heat and turn the radiator cap, SLIGHTLY, until the sound of escaping pressure can be heard. DO NOT turn any more; allow the pressure to release gradually. When no more pressure can be heard escaping, remove the cap with the heavy cloth, CAUTIOUSLY.

➡**Never add cold water to an overheated engine while the engine is not running.**

After filling the radiator, run the engine until it reaches normal operating temperature, to make sure that the thermostat has opened and all the air is bled from the system.

DRAIN & REFILL

To drain the cooling system, allow the engine to cool down **BEFORE ATTEMPTING TO REMOVE THE RADIATOR CAP.** Then turn the cap until it hisses. Wait until all pressure is off the cap before removing it completely.

✳✳ CAUTION

To avoid burns and scalding, always handle a warm radiator cap with a heavy rag.

1. At the dash, set the heater TEMP control lever to the fully HOT position. If the vehicle is equipped with automatic air conditioning turn ignition switch ON and set temperature at MAXIMUM. Then turn the ignition switch OFF.
2. With the radiator cap removed, drain the radiator by loosening the petcock at the bottom of the radiator.

✳✳ CAUTION

When draining the coolant, keep in mind that cats and dogs are attracted by ethylene glycol antifreeze, and are quite likely to drink any that is left in an uncovered container or in puddles on the ground. This will prove fatal in sufficient quantity. Always drain the coolant into a sealable container. Coolant should be reused unless it is contaminated or several years old.

3. Close the petcock. Be careful not to damage the petcock when closing.
4. Refill the system with a 50/50 mix of ethylene glycol or other suitable antifreeze; fill the system to ¾–1¼" from the bottom of the filler neck. Reinstall the radiator cap.

➡**If equipped with a fluid reservoir tank, fill the reservoir tank up to the MAX level.**

5. Operate the engine at 2,000 rpm for a few minutes and check the system for signs of leaks and for the correct level.

If there is no petcock, loosen the lowest radiator hose to drain the fluid

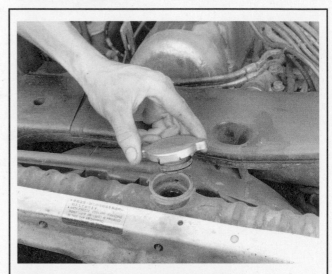

Remove the radiator cap to fill the system

Using a funnel, fill the system with the correct mixture and quantity of coolant

FLUSHING & CLEANING THE SYSTEM

To flush the system you must first, drain the cooling system but do not close the petcock valve on the bottom of the radiator. You can insert a garden hose, in the filler neck, turn the water pressure on moderately then start the engine. After about 10 minutes or less the water coming out of the bottom of the radiator should be clear. Shut off the engine and water supply, allow the radiator to drain, then refill and bleed the system as necessary.

➡**DO NOT allow the engine to overheat. The supply of water going in the top must be equal in amount to the water draining from the bottom, this way the radiator will always be full when the engine is running.**

Usually flushing the radiator using water is all that is necessary to maintain the proper condition in the cooling system.

Radiator flush is the only cleaning agent that can be used to clean the internal portion of the radiator. Radiator flush can be purchased at any auto supply store. Follow the directions on the label.

Brake and Clutch Master Cylinders

FLUID RECOMMENDATION

When adding or changing the fluid in the systems, use a quality brake fluid of the DOT 3 specifications.

➡**Never reuse old brake fluid.**

LEVEL CHECK

The brake and clutch master cylinders are located under the hood, in the left rear section of the engine compartment. They are made of translucent plastic so that the levels may be checked without removing the tops. The fluid level in both reservoirs should

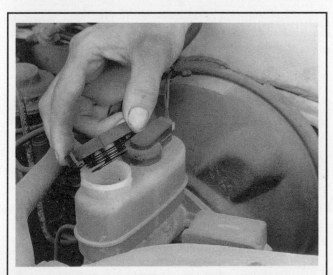

Remove the master cylinder cap to add brake fluid

Pour fresh brake fluid into the reservoir using a funnel—note that brake fluid is highly corrosive

be checked at least every 7,500 miles (15,000 miles, 1980 and later). The fluid level should be maintained at the upper most mark on the side of the reservoir. Any sudden decrease in the level indicates a possible leak in the system and should be checked out immediately.

➡**Some models may have two reservoirs for the brake master cylinder, while other models (those with an automatic transmission/transaxle) will not have a clutch master cylinder at all.**

When making additions of brake fluid, use only fresh, uncontaminated brake fluid meeting or exceeding DOT 3 standards. Be careful not to spill any brake fluid on painted surfaces, as it eats the paint. Do not allow the brake fluid container or the master cylinder reservoir to remain open any longer than necessary. Brake fluid absorbs moisture from the air, reducing its effectiveness and causing corrosion in the lines.

Power Steering Pump

FLUID RECOMMENDATION

When adding or changing the power steering fluid, use Dexron®II ATF (Automatic Transmission Fluid).

LEVEL CHECK

The power steering hydraulic fluid level is checked with a dipstick inserted into the pump reservoir cap. The level can be checked with the fluid either warm or cold. The car should be parked on a level surface. Check the fluid level every 6 months or 7,500 miles (12 months or 15,000 miles, 1980 and later), whichever comes first.

1. With the engine off, unscrew the dipstick and check the level. If the engine is warm, the level should be within the proper range on the HOT scale. If the engine is cold, the level should be within the proper range on the COLD scale (see illustrations).

Remove the power steering pump reservoir cap to check and/or add fluid

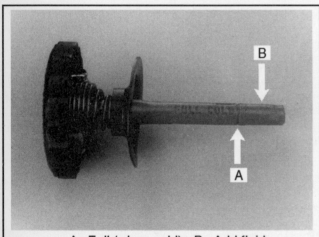

A. Full (when cold)   B. Add fluid

Check the power steering fluid dipstick, which is found under the cap on most models

2. If the level is low, add DEXRON®II ATF until correct. Be careful not to overfill, which will cause fluid loss and seal damage.

Steering Gear

FLUID RECOMMENDATIONS

When fill the steering gear box use only standard GL-4 hypoid type gear oil, SAE 80W or SAE 80W/90.

LEVEL CHECK

▶ **See Figure 50**

Check the level of the lubricant in the steering gear every 12,000 miles (15,000 miles, 1979 and later). If the level is low, check for leakage. Any oily film is not considered a leak; solid

⬤ : CHECK FLUID LEAKS.

🝰 : ADD FLUID.

Fig. 50 Check and add fluid for the manual steering gearbox through the filler hole

grease must be present. The lubricant is added and checked through the filler plug hole in the top of the steering gearbox.

Chassis Greasing

The manufacturer doesn't install lubrication fittings in lube points on the steering linkage or suspension. You can buy metric threaded fittings to grease these points or use a pointed, rubber tip end on your grease gun. Lubricate all joints equipped with a plug, every 15,000 miles or once a year with NLGI No. 2 (Lithium base) grease. Replace the plugs after lubrication.

Body Lubrication and Maintenance

Lubricate all locks and hinges with multipurpose grease every 6,000 miles (7,500 miles, 1980 and later).

Wheel Bearings

Clean and repack wheel bearings every 30,000 miles on rear wheel drive vehicles. In order to clean and repack the front wheel bearings on the rear wheel drive vehicle the wheel bearings must be removed from the wheel hub. You should also check that the wheel bearings operate smoothly and there is no excess amount of play (looseness) in the bearing assembly before removing the wheel bearing. To remove the wheel bearing refer to Chapter 8.

On front wheel drive vehicles, the front wheel bearings are different than on rear wheel drive vehicles. The front hub must be removed. The rear wheel bearings on front wheel drive vehicles are similar to the front bearings on rear wheel drive vehicles. Refer to Section 8 for both of the above procedures.

TRAILER TOWING

General Recommendations

Your vehicle was primarily designed to carry passengers and cargo. It is important to remember that towing a trailer will place additional loads on your vehicles engine, drivetrain, steering, braking and other systems. However, if you decide to tow a trailer, using the prior equipment is a must.

Local laws may require specific equipment such as trailer brakes or fender mounted mirrors. Check your local laws.

Trailer Weight

The weight of the trailer is the most important factor. A good weight-to-horsepower ratio is about 35:1, 35 lbs. of Gross Combined Weight (GCW) for every horsepower your engine develops. Multiply the engine's rated horsepower by 35 and subtract the weight of the vehicle passengers and luggage. The number remaining is the approximate ideal maximum weight you should tow, although a numerically higher axle ratio can help compensate for heavier weight.

Hitch (Tongue) Weight

Calculate the hitch weight in order to select a proper hitch. The weight of the hitch is usually 9–11% of the trailer gross weight and should be measured with the trailer loaded. Hitches fall into various categories: those that mount on the frame and rear bumper, the bolt-on type, or the weld-on distribution type used for larger trailers. Axle mounted or clamp-on bumper hitches should never be used.

Check the gross weight rating of your trailer. Tongue weight is usually figured as 10% of gross trailer weight. Therefore, a trailer with a maximum gross weight of 2000 lbs. will have a maximum tongue weight of 200 lbs. Class I trailers fall into this category. Class II trailers are those with a gross weight rating of 2000–

3000 lbs., while Class III trailers fall into the 3500–6000 lbs. category. Class IV trailers are those over 6000 lbs. and are for use with fifth wheel trucks, only.

When you've determined the hitch that you'll need, follow the manufacturer's installation instructions, exactly, especially when it comes to fastener torques. The hitch will subjected to a lot of stress and good hitches come with hardened bolts. Never substitute an inferior bolt for a hardened bolt.

Cooling

ENGINE

Overflow Tank

One of the most common, if not THE most common, problems associated with trailer towing is engine overheating. If you have a cooling system without an expansion tank, you'll definitely need to get an aftermarket expansion tank kit, preferably one with at least a 2 quart capacity. These kits are easily installed on the radiator's overflow hose, and come with a pressure cap designed for expansion tanks.

Flex Fan

Another helpful accessory for vehicles using a belt-driven radiator fan is a flex fan. These fans are large diameter units designed to provide more airflow at low speeds, by using fan blades that have deeply cupped surfaces. The blades then flex, or flatten out, at high speed, when less cooling air is needed. These fans are far lighter in weight than stock fans, requiring less horsepower to drive them. Also, they are far quieter than stock fans. If you do decide to replace your stock fan with a flex fan, note that if your vehicle has a fan clutch, a spacer will be needed between the flex fan and water pump hub.

Oil Cooler

Aftermarket engine oil coolers are helpful for prolonging engine oil life and reducing overall engine temperatures. Both of these factors increase engine life. While not absolutely necessary in towing Class I and some Class II trailers, they are recommended for heavier Class II and all Class III towing. Engine oil cooler systems usually consist of an adapter, screwed on in place of the oil filter, a remote filter mounting and a multi-tube, finned heat exchanger, which is mounted in front of the radiator or air conditioning condenser.

TRANSMISSION

An automatic transmission is usually recommended for trailer towing. Modern automatics have proven reliable and, of course, easy to operate, in trailer towing. The increased load of a trailer, however, causes an increase in the temperature of the automatic transmission fluid. Heat is the worst enemy of an automatic trans-

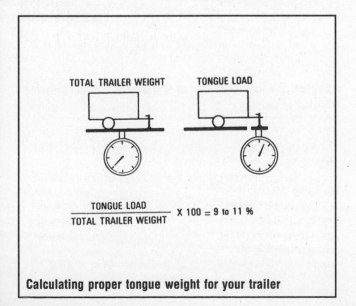

Calculating proper tongue weight for your trailer

mission. As the temperature of the fluid increases, the life of the fluid decreases.

It is essential, therefore, that you install an automatic transmission cooler. The cooler, which consists of a multi-tube, finned heat exchanger, is usually installed in front of the radiator or air conditioning compressor, and hooked in-line with the transmission cooler tank inlet line. Follow the cooler manufacturer's installation instructions.

Select a cooler of at least adequate capacity, based upon the combined gross weights of the vehicle and trailer.

Cooler manufacturers recommend that you use an aftermarket cooler in addition to, and not instead of, the present cooling tank in your radiator. If you do want to use it in place of the radiator cooling tank, get a cooler at least two sizes larger than normally necessary.

➡A transmission cooler can, sometimes, cause slow or harsh shifting in the transmission during cold weather, until the fluid has a chance to come up to normal operating temperature. Some coolers can be purchased with or retrofitted with a temperature bypass valve which will allow fluid flow through the cooler only when the fluid has reached above a certain operating temperature.

Handling A Trailer

Towing a trailer with ease and safety requires a certain amount of experience. It's a good idea to learn the feel of a trailer by practicing turning, stopping and backing in an open area such as an empty parking lot.

TOWING THE VEHICLE

On rear wheel drive vehicles, the car can be flat-towed safely (with the transmission in Neutral) from the front at speeds of 20 mph or less. The car must either be towed with the rear wheels off the ground or the driveshaft disconnected if: towing speeds are to be over 20 mph, or towing distance is over 50 miles, or transmission or rear axle problems exist.

When towing the car on its front wheels, the steering wheel must be secured in a straight-ahead position and the steering column unlocked. Tire-to-ground clearance should not exceed 6″ during towing.

On all models there are towing hooks under the vehicle to attach tow hooks. If any question concerning towing are in doubt, check with the "Towing Procedure Manual" at your local Datsun/Nissan dealer.

JUMP STARTING A DEAD BATTERY

Whenever a vehicle is jump started, precautions must be followed in order to prevent the possibility of personal injury. Remember that batteries contain a small amount of explosive hydrogen gas which is a by-product of battery charging. Sparks should always be avoided when working around batteries, especially when attaching jumper cables. To minimize the possibility of accidental sparks, follow the procedure carefully.

❊❊ CAUTION

NEVER hook the batteries up in a series circuit or the entire electrical system will go up in smoke, including the starter!

Vehicles equipped with a diesel engine may utilize two 12 volt batteries. If so, the batteries are connected in a parallel circuit (positive terminal to positive terminal, negative terminal to negative terminal). Hooking the batteries up in parallel circuit increases battery cranking power without increasing total battery voltage output. Output remains at 12 volts. On the other hand, hooking two 12 volt batteries up in a series circuit (positive terminal to negative terminal, positive terminal to negative terminal) increases total battery output to 24 volts (12 volts plus 12 volts).

Jump Starting Precautions

• Be sure that both batteries are of the same voltage. Vehicles covered by this manual and most vehicles on the road today utilize a 12 volt charging system.
• Be sure that both batteries are of the same polarity (have the same terminal, in most cases NEGATIVE grounded).

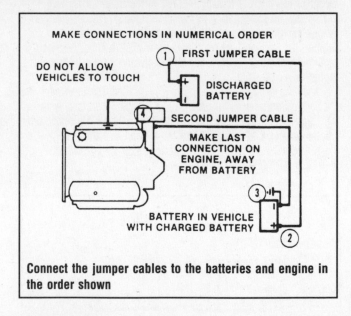

Connect the jumper cables to the batteries and engine in the order shown

• Be sure that the vehicles are not touching or a short could occur.
• On serviceable batteries, be sure the vent cap holes are not obstructed.
• Do not smoke or allow sparks anywhere near the batteries.
• In cold weather, make sure the battery electrolyte is not frozen. This can occur more readily in a battery that has been in a state of discharge.
• Do not allow electrolyte to contact your skin or clothing.

Jump Starting Procedure

1. Make sure that the voltages of the 2 batteries are the same. Most batteries and charging systems are of the 12 volt variety.

2. Pull the jumping vehicle (with the good battery) into a position so the jumper cables can reach the dead battery and that vehicle's engine. Make sure that the vehicles do NOT touch.

3. Place the transmissions/transaxles of both vehicles in **Neutral** (MT) or **P** (AT), as applicable, then firmly set their parking brakes.

➡️ **If necessary for safety reasons, the hazard lights on both vehicles may be operated throughout the entire procedure without significantly increasing the difficulty of jumping the dead battery.**

4. Turn all lights and accessories OFF on both vehicles. Make sure the ignition switches on both vehicles are turned to the **OFF** position.

5. Cover the battery cell caps with a rag, but do not cover the terminals.

6. Make sure the terminals on both batteries are clean and free of corrosion or proper electrical connection will be impeded. If necessary, clean the battery terminals before proceeding.

7. Identify the positive (+) and negative (−) terminals on both batteries.

8. Connect the first jumper cable to the positive (+) terminal of the dead battery, then connect the other end of that cable to the positive (+) terminal of the booster (good) battery.

9. Connect one end of the other jumper cable to the negative (−) terminal on the booster battery and the final cable clamp to an engine bolt head, alternator bracket or other solid, metallic point on the engine with the dead battery. Try to pick a ground on the engine that is positioned away from the battery in order to

minimize the possibility of the 2 clamps touching should one loosen during the procedure. DO NOT connect this clamp to the negative (−) terminal of the bad battery.

10. Check to make sure that the cables are routed away from any moving parts, then start the donor vehicle's engine. Run the engine at moderate speed for several minutes to allow the dead battery a chance to receive some initial charge.

11. With the donor vehicle's engine still running slightly above idle, try to start the vehicle with the dead battery. Crank the engine for no more than 10 seconds at a time and let the starter cool for at least 20 seconds between tries. If the vehicle does not start in 3 tries, it is likely that something else is also wrong or that the battery needs additional time to charge.

12. Once the vehicle is started, allow it to run at idle for a few seconds to make sure that it is operating properly.

13. Turn ON the headlights, heater blower and, if equipped, the rear defroster of both vehicles in order to reduce the severity of voltage spikes and subsequent risk of damage to the vehicles' electrical systems when the cables are disconnected. This step is especially important to any vehicle equipped with computer control modules.

14. Carefully disconnect the cables in the reverse order of connection. Start with the negative cable that is attached to the engine ground, then the negative cable on the donor battery. Disconnect the positive cable from the donor battery and finally, disconnect the positive cable from the formerly dead battery. Be careful when disconnecting the cables from the positive terminals not to allow the alligator clips to touch any metal on either vehicle or a short and sparks will occur.

JACKING

▶ **See Figure 51**

Your vehicle was supplied with a jack for emergency road repairs. This jack is fine for changing a flat tire or other short term procedures not requiring you to go beneath the vehicle. If it is used in an emergency situation, carefully follow the instructions provided either with the jack or in your owner's manual. Do not attempt to use the jack on any portions of the vehicle other than specified by the vehicle manufacturer. Always block the diagonally opposite wheel when using a jack.

A more convenient way of jacking is the use of a garage or floor jack.

Never place the jack under the radiator, engine or transmission components. Severe and expensive damage will result when the jack is raised. Additionally, never jack under the floorpan or bodywork; the metal will deform.

Whenever you plan to work under the vehicle, you must support it on jackstands or ramps. Never use cinder blocks or stacks of wood to support the vehicle, even if you're only going to be under it for a few minutes. Never crawl under the vehicle when it is supported only by the tire-changing jack or other floor jack.

➡️ **Always position a block of wood or small rubber pad on top of the jack or jackstand to protect the lifting point's finish when lifting or supporting the vehicle.**

Small hydraulic, screw, or scissors jacks are satisfactory for raising the vehicle. Drive-on trestles or ramps are also a handy and safe way to both raise and support the vehicle. Be careful though, some ramps may be too steep to drive your vehicle onto without scraping the front bottom panels. Never support the vehicle on any suspension member (unless specifically instructed to do so by a repair manual) or by an underbody panel.

Jacking Precautions

The following safety points cannot be overemphasized:
• Always block the opposite wheel or wheels to keep the vehicle from rolling off the jack.

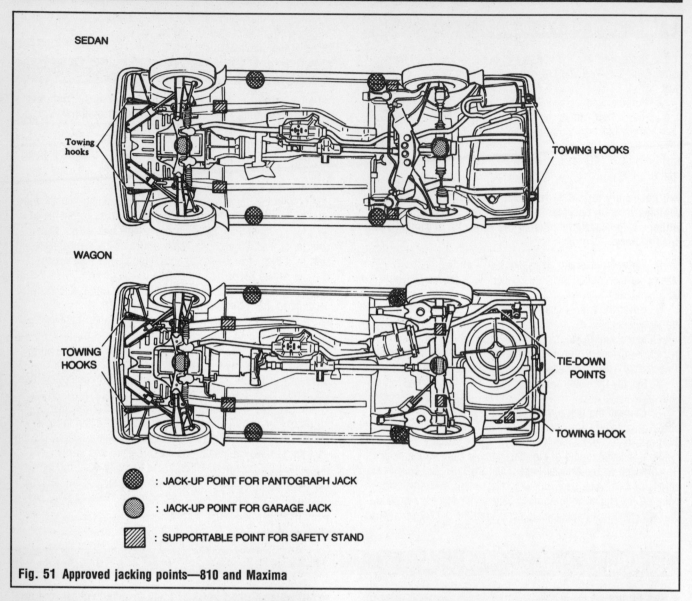

SEDAN

Towing hooks

TOWING HOOKS

WAGON

TOWING HOOKS

TIE-DOWN POINTS

TOWING HOOK

⬤ : JACK-UP POINT FOR PANTOGRAPH JACK

◉ : JACK-UP POINT FOR GARAGE JACK

▨ : SUPPORTABLE POINT FOR SAFETY STAND

Fig. 51 Approved jacking points—810 and Maxima

Use a reliable floor jack—never work under the car unless it is properly supported

Wood blocks atop the jackstands are gentler on unibody seams and will better distribute the weight

Only jack the vehicle at approved jacking points—front end shown

With the jackstand positioned, carefully lower the vehicle. Make sure it is well supported

• When raising the front of the vehicle, firmly apply the parking brake.

• When the drive wheels are to remain on the ground, leave the vehicle in gear to help prevent it from rolling.

HOW TO BUY A USED VEHICLE

Many people believe that a two or three year old used car or truck is a better buy than a new vehicle. This may be true as most new vehicles suffer the heaviest depreciation in the first two years and, at three years old, a vehicle is usually not old enough to present a lot of costly repair problems. But keep in mind, when buying a non-warranted automobile, there are no guarantees. Whatever the age of the used vehicle you might want to purchase, this section and a little patience should increase your chances of selecting one that is safe and dependable.

Tips

1. First decide what model you want, and how much you want to spend.

2. Check the used car lots and your local newspaper ads. Privately owned vehicles are usually less expensive, however, you may not get a warranty that, in many cases, comes with a used vehicle purchased from a lot. Of course, some aftermarket warranties may not be worth the extra money, so this is a point you will have to debate and consider based on your priorities.

3. Never shop at night. The glare of the lights make it easy to miss faults on the body caused by accident or rust repair.

4. Try to get the name and phone number of the previous owner. Contact him/her and ask about the vehicle. If the owner of a lot refuses this information, look for a vehicle somewhere else.

A private seller can tell you about the vehicle and maintenance. But remember, there's no law requiring honesty from private citizens selling used vehicles. There is a law that forbids tampering with or turning back the odometer mileage. This includes both the private citizen and the lot owner. The law also requires that the seller or anyone transferring ownership of the vehicle must pro-

vide the buyer with a signed statement indicating the mileage on the odometer at the time of transfer.

5. You may wish to contact the National Highway Traffic Safety Administration (NHTSA) to find out if the vehicle has ever been included in a manufacturer's recall. Write down the year, model and serial number before you buy the vehicle, then contact NHTSA (there should be a 1-800 number that your phone company's information line can supply). If the vehicle was listed for a recall, make sure the needed repairs were made.

6. Refer to the Used Vehicle Checklist in this section and check all the items on the vehicle you are considering. Some items are more important than others. Only you know how much money you can afford for repairs, and depending on the price of the vehicle, may consider performing any needed work yourself. Beware, however, of trouble in areas that will affect operation, safety or emission. Problems in the Used Vehicle Checklist break down as follows:

• Numbers 1–8: Two or more problems in these areas indicate a lack of maintenance. You should beware.

• Numbers 9–13: Problems here tend to indicate a lack of proper care, however, these can usually be corrected with a tune-up or relatively simple parts replacement.

• Numbers 14–17: Problems in the engine or transmission can be very expensive. Unless you are looking for a project, walk away from any vehicle with problems in 2 or more of these areas.

7. If you are satisfied with the apparent condition of the vehicle, take it to an independent diagnostic center or mechanic for a complete check. If you have a state inspection program, have it inspected immediately before purchase, or specify on the bill of sale that the sale is conditional on passing state inspection.

8. Road test the vehicle—refer to the Road Test Checklist in this section. If your original evaluation and the road test agree—the rest is up to you.

• Always use jackstands to support the vehicle when you are working underneath. Place the stands beneath the vehicle's jacking brackets. Before climbing underneath, rock the vehicle a bit to make sure it is firmly supported.

USED VEHICLE CHECKLIST

➡**The numbers on the illustrations refer to the numbers on this checklist.**

1. Mileage: Average mileage is about 12,000–15,000 miles per year. More than average mileage may indicate hard usage or could indicate many highway miles (which could be less detrimental than half as many tough around town miles).

2. Paint: Check around the tailpipe, molding and windows for overspray indicating that the vehicle has been repainted.

3. Rust: Check fenders, doors, rocker panels, window moldings, wheelwells, floorboards, under floormats, and in the trunk for signs of rust. Any rust at all will be a problem. There is no way to permanently stop the spread of rust, except to replace the part or panel.

➡**If rust repair is suspected, try using a magnet to check for body filler. A magnet should stick to the sheet metal parts of the body, but will not adhere to areas with large amounts of filler.**

4. Body appearance: Check the moldings, bumpers, grille, vinyl roof, glass, doors, trunk lid and body panels for general overall condition. Check for misalignment, loose hold-down clips, ripples, scratches in glass, welding in the trunk, severe misalignment of body panels or ripples, any of which may indicate crash work.

5. Leaks: Get down and look under the vehicle. There are no normal leaks, other than water from the air conditioner evaporator.

6. Tires: Check the tire air pressure. One old trick is to pump the tire pressure up to make the vehicle roll easier. Check the tread wear, then open the trunk and check the spare too. Uneven wear is a clue that the front end may need an alignment.

7. Shock absorbers: Check the shock absorbers by forcing downward sharply on each corner of the vehicle. Good shocks will not allow the vehicle to bounce more than once after you let go.

8. Interior: Check the entire interior. You're looking for an interior condition that agrees with the overall condition of the vehicle. Reasonable wear is expected, but be suspicious of new seat covers on sagging seats, new pedal pads, and worn armrests. These indicate an attempt to cover up hard use. Pull back the carpets and look for evidence of water leaks or flooding. Look for missing hardware, door handles, control knobs, etc. Check lights and signal operations. Make sure all accessories (air conditioner, heater, radio, etc.) work. Check windshield wiper operation.

9. Belts and Hoses: Open the hood, then check all belts and hoses for wear, cracks or weak spots.

10. Battery: Low electrolyte level, corroded terminals and/or cracked case indicate a lack of maintenance.

11. Radiator: Look for corrosion or rust in the coolant indicating a lack of maintenance.

12. Air filter: A severely dirty air filter would indicate a lack of maintenance.

13. Ignition wires: Check the ignition wires for cracks, burned spots, or wear. Worn wires will have to be replaced.

14. Oil level: If the oil level is low, chances are the engine uses oil or leaks. Beware of water in the oil (there is probably a cracked block or bad head gasket), excessively thick oil (which is often used to quiet a noisy engine), or thin, dirty oil with a distinct gasoline smell (this may indicate internal engine problems).

15. Automatic Transmission: Pull the transmission dipstick out when the engine is running. The level should read FULL, and the fluid should be clear or bright red. Dark brown or black fluid that has distinct burnt odor, indicates a transmission in need of repair or overhaul.

16. Exhaust: Check the color of the exhaust smoke. Blue smoke indicates, among other problems, worn rings. Black smoke can indicate burnt valves or carburetor problems. Check the exhaust system for leaks; it can be expensive to replace.

17. Spark Plugs: Remove one or all of the spark plugs (the most accessible will do, though all are preferable). An engine in good condition will show plugs with a light tan or gray deposit on the firing tip.

ROAD TEST CHECKLIST

1. Engine Performance: The vehicle should be peppy whether cold or warm, with adequate power and good pickup. It should respond smoothly through the gears.

2. Brakes: They should provide quick, firm stops with no noise, pulling or brake fade.

3. Steering: Sure control with no binding harshness, or looseness and no shimmy in the wheel should be expected. Noise or vibration from the steering wheel when turning the vehicle means trouble.

4. Clutch (Manual Transmission/Transaxle): Clutch action should give quick, smooth response with easy shifting. The clutch pedal should have free-play before it disengages the clutch. Start the engine, set the parking brake, put the transmission in first gear and slowly release the clutch pedal. The engine should begin to stall when the pedal is ½–¾ of the way up.

5. Automatic Transmission/Transaxle: The transmission should shift rapidly and smoothly, with no noise, hesitation, or slipping.

6. Differential: No noise or thumps should be present. Differentials have no normal leaks.

7. Driveshaft/Universal Joints: Vibration and noise could mean driveshaft problems. Clicking at low speed or coast conditions means worn U-joints.

8. Suspension: Try hitting bumps at different speeds. A vehicle that bounces excessively has weak shock absorbers or struts. Clunks mean worn bushings or ball joints.

9. Frame/Body: Wet the tires and drive in a straight line. Tracks should show two straight lines, not four. Four tire tracks indicate a frame/body bent by collision damage. If the tires can't be wet for this purpose, have a friend drive along behind you and see if the vehicle appears to be traveling in a straight line.

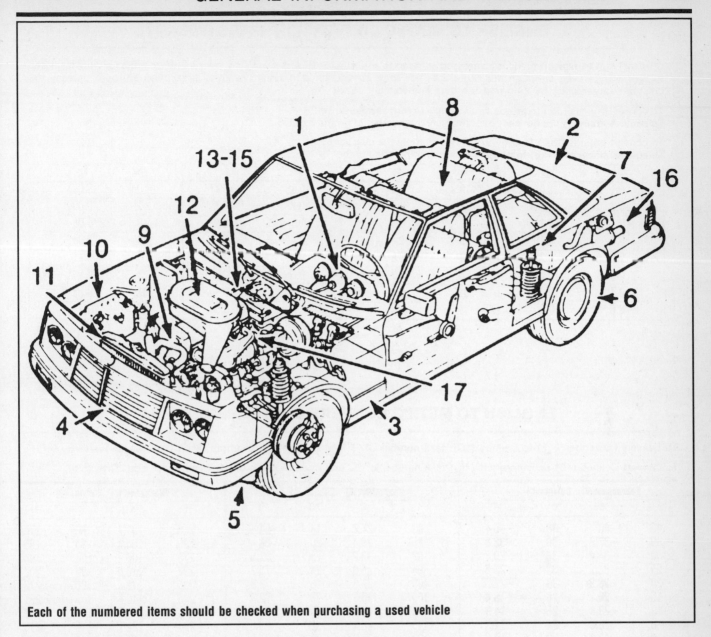

Each of the numbered items should be checked when purchasing a used vehicle

ENGLISH TO METRIC CONVERSION: MASS (WEIGHT)

Current **mass** measurement is expressed in pounds and ounces (lbs. & ozs.). The metric unit of mass (or weight) is the kilogram (kg). Even although this table does not show conversion of masses (weights) larger than 15 lbs, it is easy to calculate larger units by following the data immediately below.

To convert ounces (oz.) to grams (g): multiply th number of ozs. by 28
To convert grams (g) to ounces (oz.): multiply the number of grams by .035

To convert pounds (lbs.) to kilograms (kg): multiply the number of lbs. by .45
To convert kilograms (kg) to pounds (lbs.): multiply the number of kilograms by 2.2

lbs	kg	lbs	kg	oz	kg	oz	kg
0.1	0.04	0.9	0.41	0.1	0.003	0.9	0.024
0.2	0.09	1	0.4	0.2	0.005	1	0.03
0.3	0.14	2	0.9	0.3	0.008	2	0.06
0.4	0.18	3	1.4	0.4	0.011	3	0.08
0.5	0.23	4	1.8	0.5	0.014	4	0.11
0.6	0.27	5	2.3	0.6	0.017	5	0.14
0.7	0.32	10	4.5	0.7	0.020	10	0.28
0.8	0.36	15	6.8	0.8	0.023	15	0.42

ENGLISH TO METRIC CONVERSION: TEMPERATURE

To convert Fahrenheit (°F) to Celsius (°C): take number of °F and subtract 32; multiply result by 5; divide result by 9

To convert Celsius (°C) to Fahrenheit (°F): take number of °C and multiply by 9; divide result by 5; add 32 to total

Fahrenheit (F)		Celsius (C)		Fahrenheit (F)		Celsius (C)		Fahrenheit (F)		Celsius (C)	
°F	°C	°C	°F	°F	°C	°C	°F	°F	°C	°C	°F
−40	−40	−38	−36.4	80	26.7	18	64.4	215	101.7	80	176
−35	−37.2	−36	−32.8	85	29.4	20	68	220	104.4	85	185
−30	−34.4	−34	−29.2	90	32.2	22	71.6	225	107.2	90	194
−25	−31.7	−32	−25.6	95	35.0	24	75.2	230	110.0	95	202
−20	−28.9	−30	−22	100	37.8	26	78.8	235	112.8	100	212
−15	−26.1	−28	−18.4	105	40.6	28	82.4	240	115.6	105	221
−10	−23.3	−26	−14.8	110	43.3	30	86	245	118.3	110	230
−5	−20.6	−24	−11.2	115	46.1	32	89.6	250	121.1	115	239
0	−17.8	−22	−7.6	120	48.9	34	93.2	255	123.9	120	248
1	−17.2	−20	−4	125	51.7	36	96.8	260	126.6	125	257
2	−16.7	−18	−0.4	130	54.4	38	100.4	265	129.4	130	266
3	−16.1	−16	3.2	135	57.2	40	104	270	132.2	135	275
4	−15.6	−14	6.8	140	60.0	42	107.6	275	135.0	140	284
5	−15.0	−12	10.4	145	62.8	44	112.2	280	137.8	145	293
10	−12.2	−10	14	150	65.6	46	114.8	285	140.6	150	302
15	−9.4	−8	17.6	155	68.3	48	118.4	290	143.3	155	311
20	−6.7	−6	21.2	160	71.1	50	122	295	146.1	160	320
25	−3.9	−4	24.8	165	73.9	52	125.6	300	148.9	165	329
30	−1.1	−2	28.4	170	76.7	54	129.2	305	151.7	170	338
35	1.7	0	32	175	79.4	56	132.8	310	154.4	175	347
40	4.4	2	35.6	180	82.2	58	136.4	315	157.2	180	356
45	7.2	4	39.2	185	85.0	60	140	320	160.0	185	365
50	10.0	6	42.8	190	87.8	62	143.6	325	162.8	190	374
55	12.8	8	46.4	195	90.6	64	147.2	330	165.6	195	383
60	15.6	10	50	200	93.3	66	150.8	335	168.3	200	392
65	18.3	12	53.6	205	96.1	68	154.4	340	171.1	205	401
70	21.1	14	57.2	210	98.9	70	158	345	173.9	210	410
75	23.9	16	60.8	212	100.0	75	167	350	176.7	215	414

ENGLISH TO METRIC CONVERSION: LENGTH

To convert inches (ins.) to millimeters (mm): multiply number of inches by 25.4

To convert millimeters (mm) to inches (ins.): multiply number of millimeters by .04

Inches	Decimals	Milli-meters	Inches to millimeters (inches)	(mm)	Inches	Decimals	Milli-meters	Inches to millimeters (inches)	(mm)
1/64	0.051625	0.3969	0.0001	0.00254	33/64	0.515625	13.0969	0.6	15.24
1/32	0.03125	0.7937	0.0002	0.00508	17/32	0.53125	13.4937	0.7	17.78
3/64	0.046875	1.1906	0.0003	0.00762	35/64	0.546875	13.8906	0.8	20.32
1/16	0.0625	1.5875	0.0004	0.01016	9/16	0.5625	14.2875	0.9	22.86
5/64	0.078125	1.9844	0.0005	0.01270	37/64	0.578125	14.6844	1	25.4
3/32	0.09375	2.3812	0.0006	0.01524	19/32	0.59375	15.0812	2	50.8
7/64	0.109375	2.7781	0.0007	0.01778	39/64	0.609375	15.4781	3	76.2
1/8	0.125	3.1750	0.0008	0.02032	5/8	0.625	15.8750	4	101.6
9/64	0.140625	3.5719	0.0009	0.02286	41/64	0.640625	16.2719	5	127.0
5/32	0.15625	3.9687	0.001	0.0254	21/32	0.65625	16.6687	6	152.4
11/64	0.171875	4.3656	0.002	0.0508	43/64	0.671875	17.0656	7	177.8
3/16	0.1875	4.7625	0.003	0.0762	11/16	0.6875	17.4625	8	203.2
13/64	0.203125	5.1594	0.004	0.1016	45/64	0.703125	17.8594	9	228.6
7/32	0.21875	5.5562	0.005	0.1270	23/32	0.71875	18.2562	10	254.0
15/64	0.234375	5.9531	0.006	0.1524	47/64	0.734375	18.6531	11	279.4
1/4	0.25	6.3500	0.007	0.1778	3/4	0.75	19.0500	12	304.8
17/64	0.265625	6.7469	0.008	0.2032	49/64	0.765625	19.4469	13	330.2
9/32	0.28125	7.1437	0.009	0.2286	25/32	0.78125	19.8437	14	355.6
19/64	0.296875	7.5406	0.01	0.254	51/64	0.796875	20.2406	15	381.0
5/16	0.3125	7.9375	0.02	0.508	13/16	0.8125	20.6375	16	406.4
21/64	0.328125	8.3344	0.03	0.762	53/64	0.828125	21.0344	17	431.8
11/32	0.34375	8.7312	0.04	1.016	27/32	0.84375	21.4312	18	457.2
23/64	0.359375	9.1281	0.05	1.270	55/64	0.859375	21.8281	19	482.6
3/8	0.375	9.5250	0.06	1.524	7/8	0.875	22.2250	20	508.0
25/64	0.390625	9.9219	0.07	1.778	57/64	0.890625	22.6219	21	533.4
13/32	0.40625	10.3187	0.08	2.032	29/32	0.90625	23.0187	22	558.8
27/64	0.421875	10.7156	0.09	2.286	59/64	0.921875	23.4156	23	584.2
7/16	0.4375	11.1125	0.1	2.54	15/16	0.9375	23.8125	24	609.6
29/64	0.453125	11.5094	0.2	5.08	61/64	0.953125	24.2094	25	635.0
15/32	0.46875	11.9062	0.3	7.62	31/32	0.96875	24.6062	26	660.4
31/64	0.484375	12.3031	0.4	10.16	63/64	0.984375	25.0031	27	690.6
1/2	0.5	12.7000	0.5	12.70					

ENGLISH TO METRIC CONVERSION: TORQUE

To convert foot-pounds (ft. lbs.) to Newton-meters: multiply the number of ft. lbs. by 1.3

To convert inch-pounds (in. lbs.) to Newton-meters: multiply the number of in. lbs. by .11

in lbs	N-m	in lbs	N-m	in lbs	N-m	in lbs	N-m	in lbs	N-m
0.1	0.01	1	0.11	10	1.13	19	2.15	28	3.16
0.2	0.02	2	0.23	11	1.24	20	2.26	29	3.28
0.3	0.03	3	0.34	12	1.36	21	2.37	30	3.39
0.4	0.04	4	0.45	13	1.47	22	2.49	31	3.50
0.5	0.06	5	0.56	14	1.58	23	2.60	32	3.62
0.6	0.07	6	0.68	15	1.70	24	2.71	33	3.73
0.7	0.08	7	0.78	16	1.81	25	2.82	34	3.84
0.8	0.09	8	0.90	17	1.92	26	2.94	35	3.95
0.9	0.10	9	1.02	18	2.03	27	3.05	36	4.0

ENGLISH TO METRIC CONVERSION: TORQUE

Torque is now expressed as either foot-pounds (ft./lbs.) or inch-pounds (in./lbs.). The metric measurement unit for torque is the Newton-meter (Nm). This unit—the Nm—will be used for all SI metric torque references, both the present ft./lbs. and in./lbs.

ft lbs	N-m	ft lbs	N-m	ft lbs	N-m	ft lbs	N-m
0.1	0.1	33	44.7	74	100.3	115	155.9
0.2	0.3	34	46.1	75	101.7	116	157.3
0.3	0.4	35	47.4	76	103.0	117	158.6
0.4	0.5	36	48.8	77	104.4	118	160.0
0.5	0.7	37	50.7	78	105.8	119	161.3
0.6	0.8	38	51.5	79	107.1	120	162.7
0.7	1.0	39	52.9	80	108.5	121	164.0
0.8	1.1	40	54.2	81	109.8	122	165.4
0.9	1.2	41	55.6	82	111.2	123	166.8
1	1.3	42	56.9	83	112.5	124	168.1
2	2.7	43	58.3	84	113.9	125	169.5
3	4.1	44	59.7	85	115.2	126	170.8
4	5.4	45	61.0	86	116.6	127	172.2
5	6.8	46	62.4	87	118.0	128	173.5
6	8.1	47	63.7	88	119.3	129	174.9
7	9.5	48	65.1	89	120.7	130	176.2
8	10.8	49	66.4	90	122.0	131	177.6
9	12.2	50	67.8	91	123.4	132	179.0
10	13.6	51	69.2	92	124.7	133	180.3
11	14.9	52	70.5	93	126.1	134	181.7
12	16.3	53	71.9	94	127.4	135	183.0
13	17.6	54	73.2	95	128.8	136	184.4
14	18.9	55	74.6	96	130.2	137	185.7
15	20.3	56	75.9	97	131.5	138	187.1
16	21.7	57	77.3	98	132.9	139	188.5
17	23.0	58	78.6	99	134.2	140	189.8
18	24.4	59	80.0	100	135.6	141	191.2
19	25.8	60	81.4	101	136.9	142	192.5
20	27.1	61	82.7	102	138.3	143	193.9
21	28.5	62	84.1	103	139.6	144	195.2
22	29.8	63	85.4	104	141.0	145	196.6
23	31.2	64	86.8	105	142.4	146	198.0
24	32.5	65	88.1	106	143.7	147	199.3
25	33.9	66	89.5	107	145.1	148	200.7
26	35.2	67	90.8	108	146.4	149	202.0
27	36.6	68	92.2	109	147.8	150	203.4
28	38.0	69	93.6	110	149.1	151	204.7
29	39.3	70	94.9	111	150.5	152	206.1
30	40.7	71	96.3	112	151.8	153	207.4
31	42.0	72	97.6	113	153.2	154	208.8
32	43.4	73	99.0	114	154.6	155	210.2

ENGLISH TO METRIC CONVERSION: FORCE

Force is presently measured in pounds (lbs.). This type of measurement is used to measure spring pressure, specifically how many pounds it takes to compress a spring. Our present force unit (the pound) will be replaced in SI metric measurements by the Newton (N). This term will eventually see use in specifications for electric motor brush spring pressures, valve spring pressures, etc.

To convert pounds (lbs.) to Newton (N): multiply the number of lbs. by 4.45

lbs	N	lbs	N	lbs	N	oz	N
0.01	0.04	21	93.4	59	262.4	1	0.3
0.02	0.09	22	97.9	60	266.9	2	0.6
0.03	0.13	23	102.3	61	271.3	3	0.8
0.04	0.18	24	106.8	62	275.8	4	1.1
0.05	0.22	25	111.2	63	280.2	5	1.4
0.06	0.27	26	115.6	64	284.6	6	1.7
0.07	0.31	27	120.1	65	289.1	7	2.0
0.08	0.36	28	124.6	66	293.6	8	2.2
0.09	0.40	29	129.0	67	298.0	9	2.5
0.1	0.4	30	133.4	68	302.5	10	2.8
0.2	0.9	31	137.9	69	306.9	11	3.1
0.3	1.3	32	142.3	70	311.4	12	3.3
0.4	1.8	33	146.8	71	315.8	13	3.6
0.5	2.2	34	151.2	72	320.3	14	3.9
0.6	2.7	35	155.7	73	324.7	15	4.2
0.7	3.1	36	160.1	74	329.2	16	4.4
0.8	3.6	37	164.6	75	333.6	17	4.7
0.9	4.0	38	169.0	76	338.1	18	5.0
1	4.4	39	173.5	77	342.5	19	5.3
2	8.9	40	177.9	78	347.0	20	5.6
3	13.4	41	182.4	79	351.4	21	5.8
4	17.8	42	186.8	80	355.9	22	6.1
5	22.2	43	191.3	81	360.3	23	6.4
6	26.7	44	195.7	82	364.8	24	6.7
7	31.1	45	200.2	83	369.2	25	7.0
8	35.6	46	204.6	84	373.6	26	7.2
9	40.0	47	209.1	85	378.1	27	7.5
10	44.5	48	213.5	86	382.6	28	7.8
11	48.9	49	218.0	87	387.0	29	8.1
12	53.4	50	224.4	88	391.4	30	8.3
13	57.8	51	226.9	89	395.9	31	8.6
14	62.3	52	231.3	90	400.3	32	8.9
15	66.7	53	235.8	91	404.8	33	9.2
16	71.2	54	240.2	92	409.2	34	9.4
17	75.6	55	244.6	93	413.7	35	9.7
18	80.1	56	249.1	94	418.1	36	10.0
19	84.5	57	253.6	95	422.6	37	10.3
20	89.0	58	258.0	96	427.0	38	10.6

ENGLISH TO METRIC CONVERSION: LIQUID CAPACITY

Liquid or fluid capacity is presently expressed as pints, quarts or gallons, or a combination of all of these. In the metric system the liter (l) will become the basic unit. Fractions of a liter would be expressed as deciliters, centiliters, or most frequently (and commonly) as milliliters.

To convert pints (pts.) to liters (l): multiply the number of pints by .47
To convert liters (l) to pints (pts.): multiply the number of liters by 2.1
To convert quarts (qts.) to liters (l): multiply the number of quarts by .95

To convert liters (l) to quarts (qts.): multiply the number of liters by 1.06
To convert gallons (gals.) to liters (l): multiply the number of gallons by 3.8
To convert liters (l) to gallons (gals.): multiply the number of liters by .26

gals	liters	qts	liters	pts	liters
0.1	0.38	0.1	0.10	0.1	0.05
0.2	0.76	0.2	0.19	0.2	0.10
0.3	1.1	0.3	0.28	0.3	0.14
0.4	1.5	0.4	0.38	0.4	0.19
0.5	1.9	0.5	0.47	0.5	0.24
0.6	2.3	0.6	0.57	0.6	0.28
0.7	2.6	0.7	0.66	0.7	0.33
0.8	3.0	0.8	0.76	0.8	0.38
0.9	3.4	0.9	0.85	0.9	0.43
1	3.8	1	1.0	1	0.5
2	7.6	2	1.9	2	1.0
3	11.4	3	2.8	3	1.4
4	15.1	4	3.8	4	1.9
5	18.9	5	4.7	5	2.4
6	22.7	6	5.7	6	2.8
7	26.5	7	6.6	7	3.3
8	30.3	8	7.6	8	3.8
9	34.1	9	8.5	9	4.3
10	37.8	10	9.5	10	4.7
11	41.6	11	10.4	11	5.2
12	45.4	12	11.4	12	5.7
13	49.2	13	12.3	13	6.2
14	53.0	14	13.2	14	6.6
15	56.8	15	14.2	15	7.1
16	60.6	16	15.1	16	7.6
17	64.3	17	16.1	17	8.0
18	68.1	18	17.0	18	8.5
19	71.9	19	18.0	19	9.0
20	75.7	20	18.9	20	9.5
21	79.5	21	19.9	21	9.9
22	83.2	22	20.8	22	10.4
23	87.0	23	21.8	23	10.9
24	90.8	24	22.7	24	11.4
25	94.6	25	23.6	25	11.8
26	98.4	26	24.6	26	12.3
27	102.2	27	25.5	27	12.8
28	106.0	28	26.5	28	13.2
29	110.0	29	27.4	29	13.7
30	113.5	30	28.4	30	14.2

2

ENGINE PERFORMANCE AND TUNE-UP

Tune-Up Specifications

When analyzing compression test results, look for uniformity among cylinders, rather than specific pressures.

Year	Model	Spark Plug Type	Spark Plug Gap (in.)	Distributor Point Dwell (deg)	Distributor Point Gap (in.)	Ignition Timing (deg) ● MT	Ignition Timing (deg) ● AT	Fuel Pump Pressure (psi)	Idle Speed (rpm) MT	Idle Speed (rpm) AT ▲	Valve Clearance (in.) In	Valve Clearance (in.) Ex	Percentage of CO at idle
1973	610	BP-6ES	0.028–0.031	49–55	0.018–0.022	5B	5B	2.6–3.4	800	650	0.008 COLD 0.010 HOT	0.010 COLD 0.012 HOT	1.5
1974	610	B6ES	0.028–0.031	49–55	0.018–0.022	12B	12B	3.0–3.8	750	650	0.008 COLD 0.010 HOT	0.010 COLD 0.012 HOT	3.0
	710	B6ES	0.028–0.031	49–55	0.018–0.022	12B	12B	2.6–3.4	800	650	0.008 COLD 0.010 HOT	0.010 COLD 0.012 HOT	1.5
1975	610	BP-6ES	0.031–0.035	49–55①	0.018–② 0.022	12B	12B	3.8	750	650	0.010 HOT	0.012 HOT	2.0
	710	BP-6ES	0.031–0.035	49–55①	0.018–② 0.022	12B	12B	3.8	750	650	0.010 HOT	0.012 HOT	2.0
1976	610	BP-6ES	0.031–③ 0.035	49–55①	0.018–② 0.022	12B	12B	3.8	750	650	0.008 COLD 0.010 HOT	0.010 COLD 0.012 HOT	2.0
	710	BP-6ES	0.031–③ 0.035	49–55①	0.018–② 0.022	12B	12B	3.8	750	650	0.008 COLD 0.010 HOT	0.010 COLD 0.012 HOT	2.0
1977	710	BP-6ES	0.039–④ 0.043	49–55①	0.018–② 0.022	12B	12B	3.8	600⑤	600⑥	0.008 COLD 0.010 HOT	0.010 COLD 0.012 HOT	1.0⑦
	810	BP-6ES	0.039–0.043	ELECTRONIC	②	10B	10B	35 EFI	700	650	0.008 COLD 0.010 HOT	0.010 COLD 0.012 HOT	1.0⑧
	200SX	BP-6ES	0.039–④ 0.043	49–55①	0.018–② 0.022	9B⑨	12B	3.8	600⑤	600⑥	0.008 COLD 0.010 HOT	0.010 COLD 0.012 HOT	1.0⑦
1978	510	BP-6ES	0.039–0.043	ELECTRONIC	②	12B	12B	3.8	600	600	0.010 HOT	0.012 HOT	1.0
	810	B6ES	0.039–0.043	ELECTRONIC	②	8B⑩	8B⑩	36 EFI	700	650	0.010 HOT	0.012 HOT	1.0⑧
	200SX	BP-6ES	0.039–0.043	ELECTRONIC	②	12B	12B	3.8	600	600	0.010 HOT	0.012 HOT	1.0
1979	510	BP-6ES	0.039–④ 0.043	ELECTRONIC	②	11B⑨	12B	3.8	600	600	0.010 HOT	0.012 HOT	1.0
	810	B6ES	0.039–0.043	ELECTRONIC	②	10B	10B	37⑰ EFI	700	650	0.010 HOT	0.012 HOT	2.0⑧
	200SX	BP-6ES	0.039–④ 0.043	ELECTRONIC	②	9B⑨	12B	3.8	600	600	0.010 HOT	0.012 HOT	1.0
1980	510 (L20B)	BPR6ES	0.031–0.035	ELECTRONIC	②	12B	12B	3.8	600	600	0.010 HOT	0.012 HOT	1.0
	510 (Z20S)	BP-6ES	0.031–0.035	ELECTRONIC	②	8B⑪	8B⑪	3.8	600	600	0.012 HOT	0.012 HOT	1.5⑫
	810	BP6ES-11	0.039–0.043	ELECTRONIC	②	10B	10B	37⑰ EFI	700	650	0.010 HOT	0.012 HOT	1.0⑫
	200SX	BP-6ES	0.031–0.035	ELECTRONIC	②	8B⑪	8B⑪	37⑰ EFI	700	700	0.012 HOT	0.012 HOT	1.3⑫
1981	510	BP-6ES⑬	0.031–0.035	ELECTRONIC	②	6B	6B	3.8	600	600	0.012 HOT	0.012 HOT	⑭
	810	BP6ES-11	0.039–0.043	ELECTRONIC	②	10B	10B	37⑰ EFI	700	650	0.010 HOT	0.012 HOT	⑭
	200SX	BP-6ES⑬	0.031–0.035	ELECTRONIC	②	6B⑮	6B⑮	37⑰ EFI	750	700	0.012 HOT	0.012 HOT	⑯
1982–84	810 Maxima	BPR-6ES-11	0.039–0.043	ELECTRONIC	②	8B	8B	37⑰ EFI	700	650	0.010 HOT	0.012 HOT	⑭

● At idle
▲ In drive
N.A. Nonadjustable
① California cars are equipped with electronic ignition—dwell is pre-set and non-adjustable
② Electronic ignition—Air gap: 0.008–0.016 in. (1975–78)
   0.012–0.020 in. (1979 and later)
③ All models with electronic ignition—0.039–0.043 in.
④ 0.031–0.035 in.—Canada
⑤ 750—Canada
⑥ 650—Canada
⑦ 2%—Canada
⑧ 0.5%—California
⑨ 12B—California and Canada
⑩ 10B—California
⑪ 6B—California
⑫ Idle mixture screw is pre-set and nonadjustable on California cars
⑬ BPR6ES—Canada
⑭ Idle mixture screw is pre-set and nonadjustable
⑮ 8B—Canada
⑯ U.S.A.—idle mixture screw is pre-set and nonadjustable. Canada—1.3%
⑰ Note that fuel pressure is 37 p.s.i. *above* intake manifold pressure. Pressure must be measured in conjunction with a vacuum gauge.

Diesel Tune-Up Specifications

Year Model	Engine Displacement cu. in. (cc)	Warm Valve Clearance (in.)		Intake Valve Opens (deg)	Injection Pump Setting (deg)	Injection Nozzle Pressure (psi)		Idle Speed (rpm)	Compression Pressure (psi)
		In	Ex			New	Used		
1981–83	170 (2,793)	0.010	0.012	NA	align marks	1,920– 2,033	1,778– 1,920	650	455 @ 200 rpm

SPARK PLUGS AND WIRES

In order to extract the full measure of performance and economy from your engine it is essential that it is properly tuned at regular intervals. A regular tune-up will keep your Datsun's engine running smoothly and will prevent the annoying breakdowns and poor performance often associated with an unmaintained engine.

➡**All 1973–77 models use the conventional breaker point ignition system except for 1975–77 California cars and 1977 810's which use an electronic system. All models made in 1978 and later (except diesels) utilize this system also.**

On 1979 and earlier cars, a complete tune-up should be performed at least every 15,000 miles (24,000 km) or twelve months, whichever comes first.

On 1980 and later models the interval is 30,000 miles (48,000 km).

This interval should be halved if the car is operated under severe conditions such as trailer towing, prolonged idling, start-and-stop driving, or if starting or running problems are noticed. It is assumed that the routine maintenance described in Chapter 1 has been kept up, as this will have a decided effect on the results of a tune-up. All of the applicable steps of a tune-up should be followed in order, as the result is a cumulative one.

If the specifications on the underhood tune-up sticker in the engine compartment of your car disagree with the Tune-Up Specifications chart in this chapter, the figures on the sticker must be used. The sticker often reflects changes made during the production run.

Other than the periodic changing of oil, air and fuel filters as outlined in Section 1, diesel engines do not require a tune-up, as there is no ignition system.

Spark Plugs

A typical spark plug consists of a metal shell surrounding a ceramic insulator. A metal electrode extends downward through the center of the insulator and protrudes a small distance. Located at the end of the plug and attached to the side of the outer metal shell is the side electrode. This side electrode bends in a 90° so its tip is even with, parallel to, the tip of the center electrode. This distance between these two electrodes is called spark plug gap. The spark plug in no way produces a spark but merely provides a gap across which the current can arc. The coil produces 20,000–25,000 V (transistorized ignition produces considerably more voltage than the standard type, approximately 50,000 volts), which travels to the distributor where it is distributed through the spark plug wires to the plugs. The current passes along the center electrode and jumps the gap to the side electrode and, in so doing, ignites the air/fuel mixture in the combustion chamber. All plugs used in Datsun/Nissan have a resistor built into the center electrode to reduce interference to any nearby radio and television receivers. The resistor also cuts down on erosion of plug electrodes caused by excessively long sparking. Resistor spark plug wiring is original equipment on all Datsun/Nissan vehicles.

Spark plug life and efficiency depend upon the condition of the engine and the temperatures to which the plug is exposed. Combustion chamber temperatures are affected by many factors such as compression ratio of the engine, fuel/air mixtures, exhaust emission equipment, and the type of driving you do. Spark plugs are designed and classified by number according to the heat range at which they will operate most efficiently. The amount of heat that the plug absorbs is determined by the length of the lower insulator. The longer the insulator (it extends farther into the engine), the hotter the plug will operate. A plug that has a short path for heat transfer and remains too cool will quickly accumulate deposits of oil and carbon since it is not hot enough to burn them off. This leads to plug fouling and consequently to misfiring. A plug that has a long path for heat transfer will have no deposits but, due to the excessive heat, the electrodes will burn away quickly and, in some instances, pre-ignition may result.

Preignition takes place when plug tips get so hot that they glow sufficiently to ignite the fuel/air mixture before the spark does. This early ignition will usually cause a pinging during low speeds and heavy loads. In sever cases, the heat may become enough to start the fuel/air mixture burning throughout the combustion chamber rather than just to the front of the plug as in normal operation. At this time, the piston is rising in the cylinder making its compression stroke. The burning mass is compressed and an explosion results producing tremendous pressure. Something has to give, and it does. Pistons are often damaged. Obviously, this detonation (explosion) is a destructive condition that can be avoided by installed a spark plug designed and specified for your particular engine.

A set of spark plugs usually requires replacement after 12,000 miles (19,000 km) depending on the type of driving for 1979 and earlier models, or 30,000 miles (48,000 km) for all 1980 and later models. The electrode on a new spark plug has a sharp edge but, with use, this edge becomes rounded by erosion causing the plug gap to increase. In normal operation, plug gap increases about 0.001″ in every 1,000–2,000 miles (1,600–3,200 km). As the gap increases, the plug's voltage requirement also increases. It requires a greater voltage to jump the wider gap and about two to three times as much voltage to fire a plug at high speeds and acceleration than at idle.

The higher voltage produced by the ignition coil is one of the primary reasons for the prolonged replacement interval for spark plugs in later cars. A consistently hotter spark prevents the fouling of plugs for much longer than could normally be expected. This spark is also able to jump across a larger gap more efficiently than a spark from a conventional system.

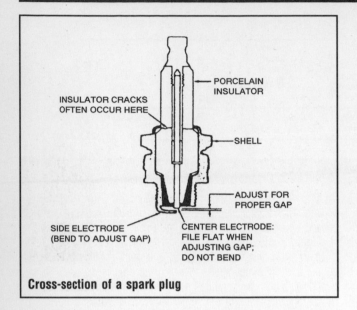

Cross-section of a spark plug

Worn plugs become obvious during acceleration. Voltage requirement is greatest during acceleration and a plug with an enlarged gap may require more voltage than the coil is able to produce. As a result, the engine misses and sputters until acceleration is reduced. Reducing acceleration reduces the plug's voltage requirement and the engine runs smoother. Slow, city driving is hard on plugs. The long periods of idle experienced in traffic creates an overly rich gas mixture. The engine isn't running fast enough to completely burn the gas and, consequently, the plugs are fouled with gas deposits and engine idle becomes rough. In many cases driving under right conditions can effectively clean these fouled plugs.

➡**There are several reasons why a spark plug will foul and you can usually learn which is at fault by just looking at the plug. A few of the most common reasons for plug fouling, and a description of the fouled plug's appearance can be found in the photographs of failed or damaged spark plugs later in this section.**

Accelerate your car to the speed where the engine begins to miss and then slow down to the point where the engine smooths out. Run at this speed for a few minutes and then accelerate again to the point of engine miss. With each repetition this engine miss should occur at increasingly higher speeds and then disappear altogether. Do not attempt to shortcut this procedure by hard acceleration. This approach will compound problems by fusing deposits into a hard permanent glaze. Dirty, fouled plugs may be cleaned by sandblasting. Many shops have a spark plug sandblaster. After sandblasting, the electrode should be filed to a sharp, square shape and then gapped to specifications. Gapping a plug too close will produce rough idle, while gapping it too wide will increase its voltage requirement and cause missing at high speeds and during acceleration.

SPARK PLUG HEAT RANGE

Spark plug heat range is the ability of the plug to dissipate heat. The longer the insulator (or the farther it extends into the engine), the hotter the plug will operate; the shorter the insulator (the closer the electrode is to the block's cooling passages) the

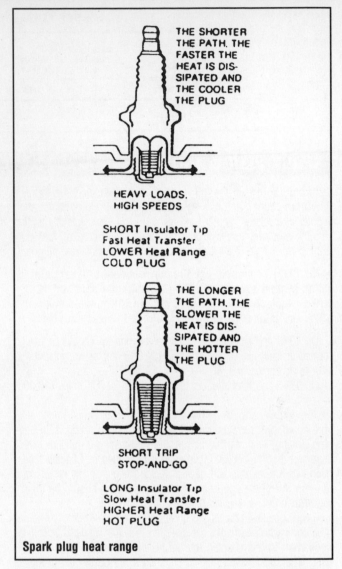

Spark plug heat range

cooler it will operate. A plug that absorbs little heat and remains too cool will quickly accumulate deposits of oil and carbon since it is not hot enough to burn them off. This leads to plug fouling and consequently to misfiring. A plug that absorbs too much heat will have no deposits but, due to the excessive heat, the electrodes will burn away quickly and might possibly lead to preignition or other ignition problems. Preignition takes place when plug tips get so hot that they glow sufficiently to ignite the air/fuel mixture before the actual spark occurs. This early ignition will usually cause a pinging during low speeds and heavy loads.

The general rule of thumb for choosing the correct heat range when picking a spark plug is: if most of your driving is long distance, high speed travel, use a colder plug; if most of your driving is stop and go, use a hotter plug. Original equipment plugs are generally a good compromise between the 2 styles and most people never have the need to change their plugs from the factory-recommended heat range.

The type of driving you do may require a change in spark plug heat range. If the majority of your driving is done in the city and rarely at high speeds, plug fouling may necessitate changing to a plug with a heat range number one lower than that specified by the car manufacturer. For example, a 1980 810 requires a BP6ES-11 plug. Frequent city driving may foul these plugs making engine operation rough. A BP5ES-11 is the next hottest plug and its insulator is longer than the BP6ES-11 so that it can absorb and retain more heat than the shorter BP6ES-11. This hotter BPES-11 burns off deposits even at low city speeds but would be too hot for prolonged turnpike driving. Using this plug at high speeds would create dangerous pre-ignition. On the other hand, if the aforementioned 810 were used almost exclusively for long distance high speed driving, the specified BP6ES-11 might be too hot, resulting in rapid electrode wear and dangerous pre-ignition. In this case, it might be wise to change to a colder BP7ES-11. If the car is used for abnormal driving (as in the examples above), or the engine has been modified for higher performance, then a change to a plug of a different heat range may be necessary. For a modified car, it is always wise to go to a colder plug as a protection against pre-ignition. It will require more frequent plug cleaning, but destructive detonation during acceleration will be avoided.

Pull the plug wire by the connector boot, not the wire

Use a spark plug socket to remove the plug from the cylinder head

Remove the plug for inspection or replacement

REMOVAL

➡**Some 1980 Calif. and all 1981 510 and 200SX models equipped with the Z20 engine have two plugs for each cylinder. All eight plugs should be replaced at every tune-up for maximum fuel efficiency and power.**

When you're removing spark plugs, you should work on one at a time. Don't start by removing the plug wires all at once because unless you number them, they're going to get mixed up. On some models though, it will be more convenient for you to remove all the wires before you start to work on the plugs. If this is necessary, take a minute before you begin and number the wires with tape before you take them off. The time you spend here will pay off later on.

1. Twist the spark plug boot and remove the boot from the plug. You may also use a plug wire removal tool designed especially for this purpose. Do not pull on the wire itself. When the wire has been removed, take a wire brush and clean around the plug. Make sure that all the grime is removed so that none will enter the cylinder after the plug has been removed.

2. Remove the plug using the proper size socket, extensions, and universals as necessary. The Datsun/Nissan cylinder head is aluminum, which is easily stripped. Remove plugs ONLY when the engine is cold.

3. If removing the plug is difficult, drip some penetrating oil on the plug threads, allow it to work, then remove the plug. Also, be sure that the socket is straight on the plug, especially on those hard to reach plugs.

INSPECTION & GAPPING

Check the plugs for deposits and wear. If they are not going to be replaced, clean the plugs thoroughly. Remember that any kind of deposit will decrease the efficiency of the plug. Plugs can be cleaned on a spark plug cleaning machine, which can sometimes be found in service stations, or you can do an acceptable job of cleaning with a stiff brush. If the plugs are cleaned, the electrodes must be filed flat. Use an ignition points file, not an emery board or the like, which will leave deposits. The electrodes must be filed perfectly flat with sharp edges; rounded edges reduce the spark plug voltage by as much as 50%.

Check spark plug gap before installation. The ground electrode (the L-shaped one connected to the body of the plug) must be parallel to the center electrode and the specified size wire gauge (please refer to the Tune-Up Specifications chart for details) must pass between the electrodes with a slight drag.

➡**NEVER adjust the gap on a used platinum type spark plug.**

Always check the gap on new plugs as they are not always set correctly at the factory. Do not use a flat feeler gauge when measuring the gap on a used plug, because the reading may be inaccurate. A round-wire type gapping tool is the best way to check the gap. The correct gauge should pass through the electrode gap with a slight drag. If you're in doubt, try one size smaller and one larger. The smaller gauge should go through easily, while the larger one shouldn't go through at all. Wire gapping tools usually have a bending tool attached. Use that to adjust the side electrode until the proper distance is obtained. Absolutely never attempt to bend the center electrode. Also, be careful not to bend the side electrode too far or too often as it may weaken and break off

A carbon fouled plug, identified by soft, sooty, black deposits, may indicate an improperly tuned vehicle. Check the air cleaner, ignition components and engine control system

A normally worn spark plug should have light tan or gray deposits on the firing tip

A variety of tools and gauges are needed for spark plug service

A physically damaged spark plug may be evidence of severe detonation in that cylinder. Watch that cylinder carefully between services, as a continued detonation will not only damage the plug, but could also damage the engine

An oil fouled spark plug indicates an engine with worn piston rings and/or bad valve seals allowing excessive oil to enter the chamber

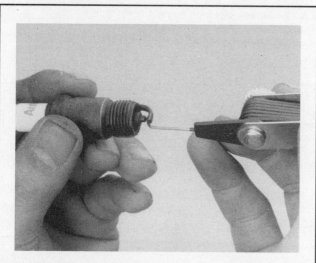

Checking the spark plug gap with a feeler gauge

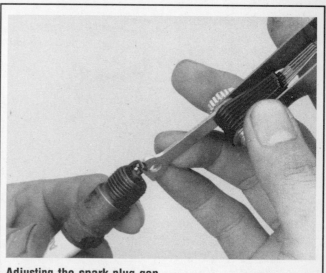

Adjusting the spark plug gap

This spark plug has been left in the engine too long, as evidenced by the extreme gap—Plugs with such an extreme gap can cause misfiring and stumbling accompanied by a noticeable lack of power

A bridged or almost bridged spark plug, identified by a build-up between the electrodes caused by excessive carbon or oil build-up on the plug

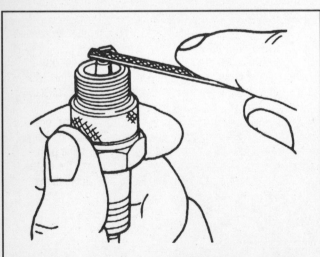

If the standard plug is in good condition, the electrode may be filed flat—CAUTION: do not file platinum plugs

within the engine, requiring removal of the cylinder head to retrieve it.

INSTALLATION

1. Lubricate the threads of the spark plugs with drop of oil. Install the plugs and tighten them hand-tight. Take care not to crossthread them.

2. Tighten the spark plugs with the socket. Do not apply the same amount of force you would use for a bolt; just snug them in. If a torque wrench is available, tighten to 11–15 ft. lbs.

3. Install the wires on their respective plugs. Make sure the wires are firmly connected. You will be able to feel them click into place.

Spark Plug Wires

REPLACING & TESTING

Every 15,000 miles (24,000 km), inspect the spark plug wires for burns, cuts, or breaks in the insulation. Check the boots and the nipples on the distributor cap. Replace any damaged wiring.

Every 45,000 miles (72,000 km) or so, the resistance of the wires should be checked with an ohmmeter. Wires with excessive resistance will cause misfiring, and may make the engine difficult to start in damp weather. Generally, the useful life of the cables is 45,000–60,000 miles (72,000–96,000 km).

To check resistance, remove the distributor cap, leaving the wires in place. Connect one lead of an ohmmeter to an electrode within the cap. Connect the other lead to the corresponding spark plug terminal (remove it from the spark plug for this test). Replace any wire which shows a resistance over 30,000Ω. Resis-

Disconnect both ends of the wire, then remove it from the vehicle

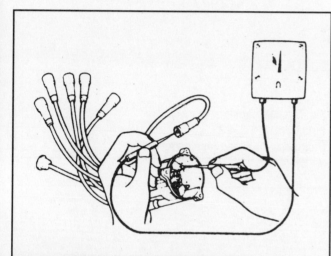

Checking plug wire resistance through the distributor cap with an ohmmeter

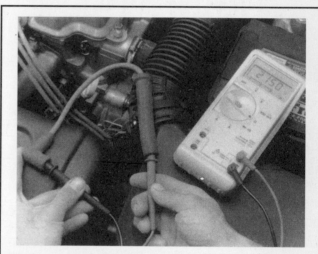

Checking individual plug wire resistance with a digital ohmmeter

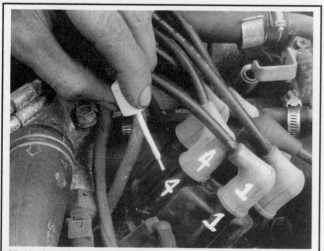

Mark the wires and distributor cap to take the guesswork out of reinstallation

tance should not be over 25,000Ω, and 30,000Ω must be considered the outer limit of acceptability.

It should be remembered that resistance is also a function of length; the longer the wire, the greater the resistance. Thus, if the wires on your car are longer than the factory originals, resistance will be higher, quite possibly outside these limits.

When installing new wires, replace them one at a time to avoid mixups. Start by replacing the longest one first. Install the boot firmly over the spark plug. Route the wire over the same path as the original. Insert the nipple firmly onto the tower on the distributor cap, then install the cap cover and latches to secure the wires.

FIRING ORDERS

◆ **See Figures 1 thru 6**

➡️**To avoid confusion, remove and tag the spark plug wires one at a time, for replacement.**

If a distributor is not keyed for installation with only one orientation, it could have been removed previously and rewired. The resultant wiring would hold the correct firing order, but could change the relative placement of the plug towers in relation to the engine. For this reason it is imperative that you label all wires before disconnecting any of them. Also, before removal, compare the current wiring with the accompanying illustrations. If the current wiring does not match, make notes in your book to reflect how your engine is wired.

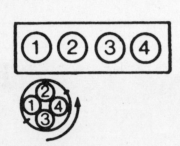

Fig. 1 1973 L18 engine
Firing order: 1-3-4-2
Distributor rotation: counterclockwise

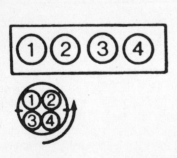

Fig. 2 1974 L18 engine
Firing order: 1-3-4-2
Distributor rotation: counterclockwise

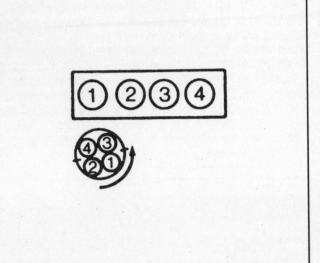

Fig. 3 L20B engine
Firing order: 1-3-4-2
Distributor rotation: counterclockwise

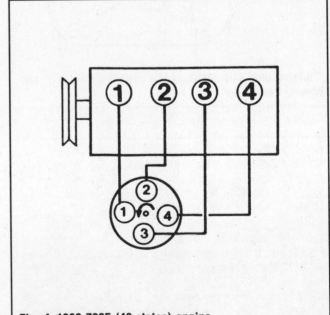

Fig. 4 1980 Z20E (49 states) engine
Firing order: 1-3-4-2
Distributor rotation: counterclockwise

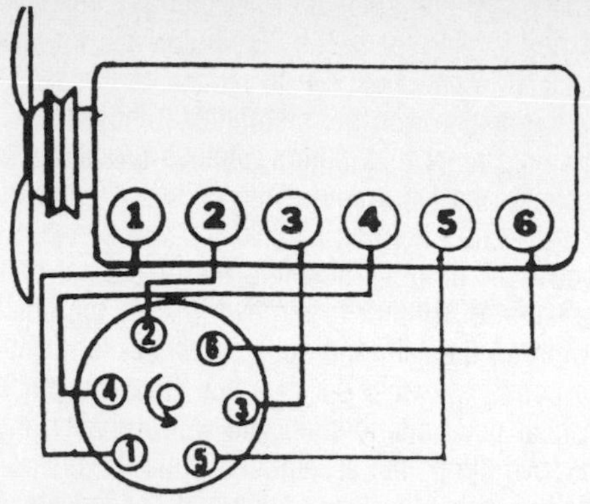

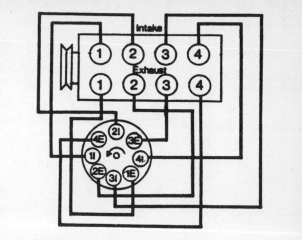

L24, L28 engines
Firing order: 1–5–3–6–2–4
Distributor rotation: counterclockwise

Fig. 5 L24 engines
Firing order: 1-5-3-6-2-4
Distributor rotation: counterclockwise

Fig. 6 Z20 engines, except 1980 49 state version
Firing order: 1-3-4-2
Distributor rotation: counterclockwise

POINT TYPE IGNITION

Breaker Points and Condenser

➡**Certain 1975–77 and virtually all 1978 and later Datsuns are equipped with electronic, breakerless ignition systems. See the following section for maintenance procedures.**

The points function as a circuit breaker for the primary circuit of the ignition system. The ignition coil must boost the 12 volts of electrical pressure supplied by the battery to as much as 25,000 volts in order to fire the plugs. To do this, the coil depends on the points and the condenser to make a clean break in the primary circuit.

The coil has both primary and secondary circuits. When the ignition is turned on, the battery supplies voltage through the coil and onto the points. The points are connected to ground, completing the primary circuit. As the current passes through the coil, a magnetic field is created in the iron center core of the coil. When the cam in the distributor turns, the points open, breaking the primary circuit. The magnetic field in the primary circuit of the coil then collapses and cuts through the secondary circuit windings around the iron core. Because of the physical principle called electromagnetic induction, the battery voltage is increased to a level sufficient to fire the spark plugs.

When the points open, the electrical charge in the primary circuit tries to jump the gap created between the two open contacts of the points. If this electrical charge were not transferred elsewhere, the metal contacts of the points would start to change rapidly.

The function of the condenser is to absorb excessive voltage from the points when they open and thus prevent the points from becoming pitted or burned.

If you have ever wondered why it is necessary to tune-up your engine occasionally, consider the fact that the ignition system must complete the above cycle each time a spark plug fires. On a 4-cylinder, 4-cycle engine, two of the four plugs must fire once for every engine revolution. If the idle speed of your engine is 800 revolutions per minutes (800 rpm), the breaker points open and close two times for each revolution. For every minute your engine idles, your points open and close 1,600 times $(2 \times 800 = 1,600)$. And that is just at idle. What about at 60 mph?

There are two ways to check breaker point gap: with a feeler gauge or with a dwell meter. Either way you set the points, you are adjusting the amount of time (in degrees of distributor rotation) that the points will remain open. If you adjust the points with a feeler gauge, you are setting the maximum amount the points will open when the rubbing block on the points is on a high point of the distributor cam. When you adjust the points with a dwell meter, you are measuring the number of degrees (of distributor cam rotation) that the points will remain closed before they start to open as a high point of the distributor cam approaches the rubbing block of the points.

If you still do not understand how the points function, take a friend, go outside, and remove the distributor cap from your engine. Have your friend operate the starter (make sure that the transmission is not in gear) as you look at the exposed parts of the distributor.

There are two rules that should always be followed when adjusting or replacing points. The points and condenser are a matched set. Never replace one without replacing the other. If you change the point gap or dwell of the engine, you also change the ignition timing. Therefore, if you adjust the points, you must also adjust the timing.

INSPECTION

♦ **See Figure 7**

A dual breaker point distributor was used on the 610 in 1973 as part of the emissions control system. The point sets are wired parallel in the primary ignition circuit. The two sets have a phase difference of 7°, making one a retard set and the other an advance. Ignition timing is advanced or retarded depending on which set is switching. Which set the engine operates on is con-

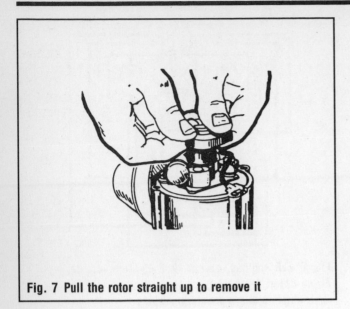

Fig. 7 Pull the rotor straight up to remove it

trolled by a relay which in turn is connected to throttle position, temperature, and transmission switches. The dual points are adjusted with a feeler gauge in the same manner as the single point distributor.

1. Mark and disconnect the high tension wire from the top of the distributor and the coil.

2. Remove the distributor cap by prying off the spring clips on the sides of the cap.

3. Remove the rotor from the distributor shaft by pulling it straight up. Examine the condition of the rotor. If it is cracked or the metal tip is excessively worn or burned, it should be replaced. Clean the tip with fine emery paper, or equivalent.

➡️ **It is a good idea at this time, to check the distributor cap for small cracks as this will affect the performance of the engine.**

4. Pry open the contacts of the points with a screwdriver and check the condition of the contacts. If they are excessively worn, burned or pitted, they should be replaced.

5. If the points are in good condition, adjust them and replace the rotor and the distributor cap. If the points need to be replaced, follow the replacement procedure given below.

REMOVAL & INSTALLATION

1. Mark or tag then remove the coil high tension wire from the top of the distributor cap. Remove the distributor cap and place it out of the way. Remove the rotor from the distributor shaft by pulling up.

2. On single point distributors, remove the condenser from the distributor body. On early dual point distributors, you will find that one condenser is virtually impossible to reach without removing the distributor from the engine. To do this, first note and mark the position of the distributor on the small timing scale on the front of the distributor. Then mark the position of the rotor in relation to the distributor body. Do this by simply replacing the rotor on the distributor shaft and marking the spot on the distributor body where the rotor is pointing. Be careful not to turn the engine over while performing this operation.

3. Remove the distributor on dual point models by removing the small bolt at the rear of the distributor. Lift the distributor out of the block. It is now possible to remove the rear condenser. Do not crank the engine with the distributor removed.

4. On single point distributors, remove the points assembly attaching screws and then remove the points. A magnetic screwdriver or one with a holding mechanism will come in handy here, so that you don't drop a screw into the distributor and have to remove the entire distributor to retrieve it. After the points are removed, wipe off the cam and apply new cam lubricant. If you don't, the points will wear out in a few thousand miles.

5. On dual point distributors, you will probably find it easier to simply remove the points assemblies while the distributor is out of the engine. Install the new points and condensers. You can either set the point gap now or later after you have reinstalled the distributor.

To install:

6. On dual point models, install the distributor, making sure the marks made earlier are lined up. Note that the slot for the oil pump drive is tapered and will only fit one way.

7. On single point distributors, slip the new set of points onto the locating dowel and install the screws that hold the assembly onto the plate. Don't tighten them all the way yet, since you'll only have to loosen them to set the point gap.

8. Install the new condenser on single point models and attach the condenser lead to the points.

9. Set the point gap and dwell (see the following sections).

ADJUSTMENT WITH A FEELER GAUGE

Single Point Distributor
▶ **See Figures 8, 9, 10 and 11**

1. If the contact points of the assembly are not parallel, bend the stationary contact so that they make contact across the entire surface of the contacts. Bend only the stationary bracket part of the point assembly; not the movable contact.

2. Turn the engine until the rubbing block of the points is on one of the high points of the distributor cam. You can do this by either turning the ignition switch to the start position and releas-

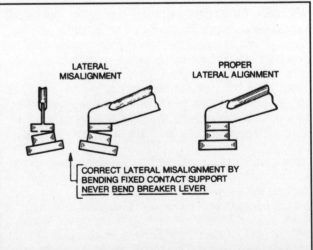

Fig. 8 Check the points alignment along the parameters shown

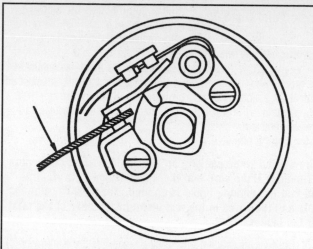

Fig. 9 Use a feeler gauge (arrow) to determine point gap

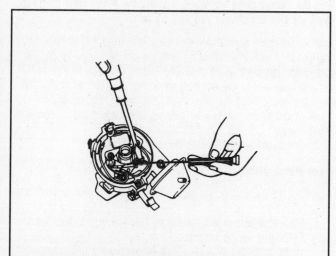

Fig. 10 Turn the eccentric screw to adjust the point gap—single point distributor

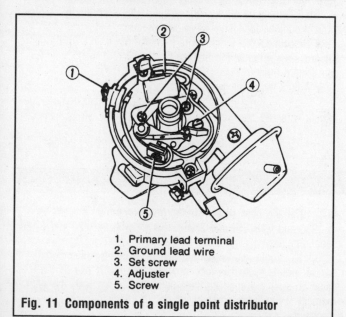

1. Primary lead terminal
2. Ground lead wire
3. Set screw
4. Adjuster
5. Screw

Fig. 11 Components of a single point distributor

ing it quickly (bumping the engine) or by using a wrench on the bolt which holds the crankshaft pulley to the crankshaft.

3. Place the correct size feeler gauge between the contacts (see the Tune-Up chart). Make sure that it is parallel with the contact surfaces.

4. With your free hand, insert a screwdriver into the eccentric adjusting screw, then twist the screwdriver to either increase or decrease the gap to the proper setting.

5. Tighten the adjustment lockscrew and recheck the contact gap to make sure that didn't change when the lockscrew was tightened.

6. Replace the rotor and distributor cap, and the high tension wire which connects the top of the distributor and the oil. Make sure that the rotor is firmly seated all the way onto the distributor shaft and that the tab of the rotor is aligned with notch in the shaft. Align the tab in the base of the distributor cap with the notch in the distributor body. Make sure that the cap is firmly seated on the distributor and that the retainer clips are in place. Make sure that the end of the high tension wire is firmly placed in the top of the distributor and the coil.

Dual Point Distributor
▶ See Figures 12 and 13

The two sets of breaker points are adjusted with a feeler gauge in the same manner as those in a single point distributor, except that you do the actual adjusting by twisting a screwdriver in the point set notch. Check the Tune-up Specifications chart for the correct setting. Both are set to the same opening.

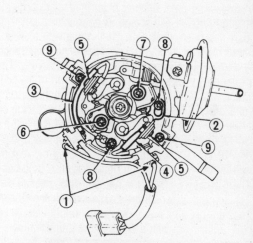

1. Lead wire terminal set screws
2. Adjuster plate
3. Primary lead wire—advanced points
4. Primary lead wire—retarded points
5. Primary lead wire set screw
6. Set screw—advanced points
7. Set screw—retarded points
8. Adjuster plate set screws
9. Breaker plate set screws

Fig. 12 Components of the dual point distributor— NEVER disturb the adjuster plate setscrews (No. 8) when adjusting or replacing points

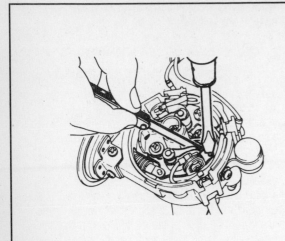

Fig. 13 Turn a screwdriver in the notch to adjust the point gap—dual point distributor

DWELL ADJUSTMENT

The dwell angle or cam angle is the number of degrees that the distributor cam rotates while the points are closed. There is an inverse relationship between dwell angle and point gap. Increasing the point gap will decrease the dwell angle and vice versa. Checking the dwell angle with a meter is a far more accurate method of measuring point opening than the feeler gauge method.

After setting the point gap to specification with a feeler gauge as previously described, check the dwell angle with a meter. Attach the dwell meter according to the manufacturer's instruction sheet. The negative lead is grounded and the positive lead is connected to the primary wire terminal which runs from the coil to the distributor. Start the engine, let it idle and reach operating temperature, and observe the dwell on the meter. The reading should fall within the allowable range. If it does not, the gap will have to be reset or the breaker points will have to be replaced.

Dwell can be checked with the engine running or cranking. Decrease dwell by increasing the point gap; increase by decreasing the gap. Dwell angle is simply the number of degrees of distributor shaft rotation during which the points stay closed. Theoretically, if the point gap is correct, the dwell should also be correct or nearly so. Adjustment with a dwell meter produces more exact, consistent results since it is a dynamic adjustment. If dwell varies more than 3° from idle speed to 1,750 engine rpm, the distributor is worn.

Single Point Distributor

1. Adjust the points with a feeler gauge as previously described.
2. Connect the dwell meter to the ignition circuit as according to the manufacturer's instructions. One lead of the meter is connected to a ground and the other lead is connected to the distributor post on the coil. An adapter is usually provided for this purpose.
3. If the dwell meter has a set line on it, adjust the meter to zero the indicator.
4. Start the engine.

➡ **Be careful when working on any vehicle while the engine is running. Make sure that the transmission is in Neutral and that the parking brake is applied. Keep hands, clothing, tools and the wires of the test instruments clear of the rotating fan blades.**

5. Observe the reading on the dwell meter. If the reading is within the specified range, turn off the engine and remove the dwell meter.

➡ **If the meter does not have a scale for 4-cylinder engines, multiply the 8-cylinder reading by two.**

6. If the reading is above the specified range, the breaker point gap is too small. If the reading is below the specified range, the gap is too large. In either case, the engine must be stopped and the gap adjusted in the manner previously covered. After making the adjustment, start the engine and check the reading on the dwell meter. When the correct reading is obtained, disconnect the dwell meter.
7. Check the adjustment of the ignition timing.

Dual Point Distributor

Adjust the point gap of a dual point distributor with a dwell meter as follows:

1. Mark and disconnect the wiring harness of the distributor from the engine wiring harness.
2. Using a jumper wire, connect the black wire of the engine side of the harness to the black wire of the distributor side of the harness (advance points).
3. Start the engine and observe the reading on the dwell meter. Shut the engine off and adjust the points accordingly as previously outlined for single point distributors.
4. Disconnect the jumper wire from the black wire of the distributor side of the wiring harness and connect it to the yellow wire (retard points).
5. Adjust the point gap as necessary.
6. After the dwell of both sets of points is correct, remove the jumper wire and connect the engine-to-distributor wiring harness securely.

ELECTRONIC IGNITION

Description and Operation

In 1975, in order to comply with California's tougher emission laws, Datsun/Nissan introduced electronic ignition systems for all models sold in that state. Since that time, the Datsun electronic ignition system has undergone a metamorphosis from a standard transistorized circuit (1975–78) to an Integrated Circuit system (IC), 1979 and later, to the special dual spark plug system used in 1980 and later 510 and 200SX models with the Z20 and CA20 series engine.

The electronic ignition system differs from the conventional breaker points system in form only. Its function is exactly the same: to supply a spark to the spark plugs at precisely the right moment to ignite the compressed gas in the cylinders and create mechanical movement.

➡ On Maxima models, a crank angle sensor mounted in the distributor is the basic component of the entire E.C.C.S. (Electronic Concentrated Control System). There are no adjustments necessary.

Located in the distributor, in addition to the normal rotor cap, is a spoked rotor (reluctor) which fits on the distributor shaft where the breaker points cam is found on nonelectronic ignitions. The rotor (reluctor) revolves with the top rotor cap and, as it passes a pickup coil inside the distributor body, breaks a high flux phase which occurs while the space between the reluctor spokes passes the pickup coil. This allows current to flow to the pickup coil. Primary ignition current is then cut off by the electronic ignition unit, allowing the magnetic field in the ignition coil to collapse, creating the spark which the distributor passes on to the spark plug.

The 1979 and later IC ignition system uses a ring type pickup coil which surrounds the reluctor instead of the single post type pickup coil on earlier models.

The dual spark plug ignition system used on some 1980 and later uses two ignition coils and each cylinder has two spark plugs which fire simultaneously. In this manner the engine is able to consume large quantities of recirculated exhaust gas which would cause a single spark plug cylinder to misfire and idle roughly.

Because no points or condenser are used, and because dwell is determined by the electronic unit, no adjustments are necessary. Ignition timing is checked in the usual way, but unless the distributor is disturbed it is not likely to ever change very much.

Adjustments

◆ **See Figures 14, 15 and 16**

The adjustment service consists of inspection of the distributor cap, rotor, and ignition wires, replacing when necessary. These parts can be expected to last for at least 40,000 miles (64,000 km). In addition, the reluctor air gap should be checked periodically.

1. The distributor cap is held on by two clips. Release them with a screwdriver and lift the cap straight up and off, with the

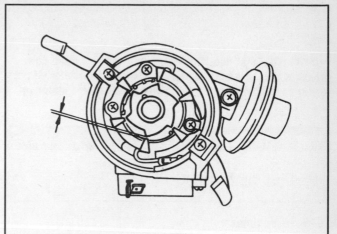

Fig. 15 Adjust the air gap so that the dimension between the arrows is 0.30–0.50mm—1979–84 models, except Z20 engines

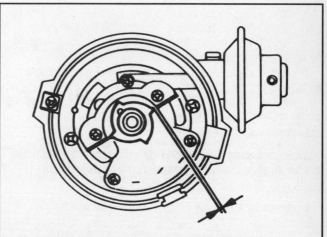

Fig. 16 Adjust the air gap so that the dimension between the arrows is 0.30–0.50mm—1980–81 Z20 engines

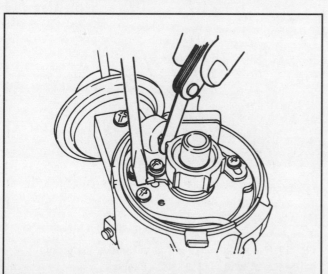

Fig. 14 Check the air gap as shown—1975–78 models

wires attached. Inspect the cap for cracks, carbon tracks, or a worn center contact. Replace it if necessary, transferring the wires one at a time from the old cap to the new.

2. Pull the ignition rotor (not the spoked reluctor) straight up to remove. Replace it if its contacts are worn, burned, or pitted. Do not file the contacts. To replace, press it firmly onto the shaft. It only goes on one way, so be sure it is fully seated.

3. Before replacing the ignition rotor, check the reluctor air gap. Use a non-magnetic feeler gauge. Rotate the engine until a reluctor spoke is aligned with the pick-up coil (either bump the engine around with the starter, or turn it with a wrench on the crankshaft pulley bolt). The gap should measure 0.20–0.40mm through 1978, or 0.30–0.50mm for 1979 and later. Adjustment, if necessary, is made by loosening the pickup coil mounting screws and shifting the coil either closer to, or farther from the reluctor. On 1979 and later models, center the pickup coil (ring) around the reluctor. Tighten the screws and recheck the gap.

4. Inspect the wires for cracks or brittleness. Replace them one at a time to prevent crosswiring, carefully pressing the replace-

ment wires into place. The cores of electronic wires are more susceptible to breakage than those of standard wires, so treat them gently.

➡ **On models that use IC ignition unit and no pickup coil measure the air gap between the reluctor and stator. If not within specifications (0.30–0.50mm), loosen the stator retaining screws and adjust.**

Parts Replacement

PICK-UP COIL & RELUCTOR

1975–78 Vehicles

◆ **See Figures 17 and 18**

The reluctor cannot be removed on some early models. It is an integral part of the distributor shaft. Non-removable reluctors can be distinguished by the absence of a roll pin (retaining pin) which locks the reluctor in place on the shaft.

To replace the pick-up coil:

1. Remove the distributor cap by releasing the two spring clips. Remove the ignition rotor by pulling it straight up and off the shaft.

2. Disconnect the distributor wiring harness at the terminal block.

3. Remove the two pick-up coil mounting screws. Remove the screws retaining the wiring harness to the distributor.

4. Remove the pick-up coil.

➡ **When replacing the the pick-up coil, leave the mounting screws slightly loose to facilitate air gap adjustment.**

To install:

1. Remove the distributor cap, ignition rotor and the pick-up coil.

2. Use two prybars to pry the reluctor from the distributor shaft. Be extremely careful not to damage the reluctor teeth. Remove the roll pin.

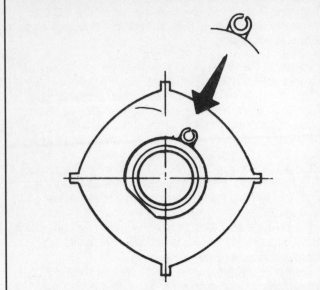

Fig. 18 Install the roll pin where indicated—1975–78 4-cylinder models

3. To replace, press the reluctor firmly onto the shaft. Install a new roll pin with the slit facing away from the distributor shaft. Do not reuse the old roll pin.

1979–84 Vehicles

◆ **See Figures 19, 20 and 21**

➡ **The 1980 200SX and 510 models (Calif. only) and 1981 200SX and 510 models (ex. Canada) use the Z20 engine. This engine is equipped with a slightly different ignition system and does not utilize a pick-up coil.**

1. Remove the distributor cap. Remove the ignition rotor by pulling the rotor straight up and off the shaft.

2. On all models, use a pair of needle nose pliers to discon-

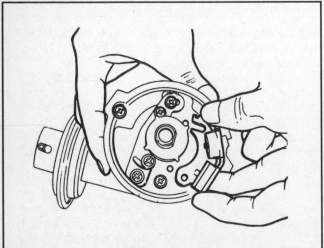

Fig. 17 Remove the pickup coil as shown—1975–78 models

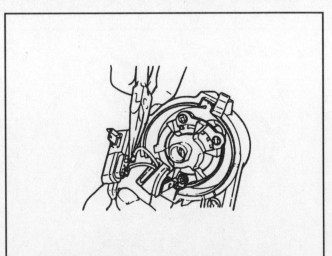

Fig. 19 Use needlenose pliers to remove the pickup coil—except twin plug Z-series engines

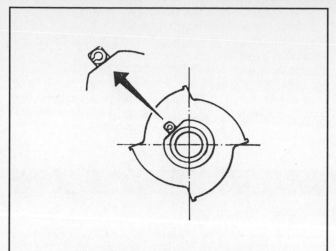

Fig. 20 Install the roll pin where shown—1979–84 models, except 810 and Maxima

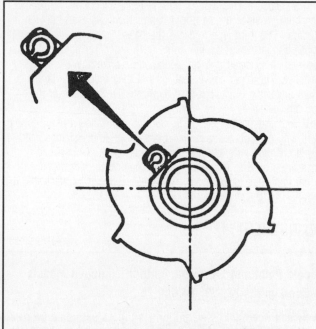

Fig. 21 Install the roll pin where shown—1979–84 810 and Maxima

nect the pick-up coil spade connectors from the ignition unit. Do not pull on the pick-up coil wires themselves.

3. Remove the toothed stator and the ring magnet underneath it by removing the three mounting screws.

4. Remove the reluctor by prying it from the distributor shaft with two small prybars or a small puller. Be careful not to damage any of the reluctor teeth. Remove the roll pin.

5. Remove the screw retaining the pick-up coil wiring harness to the distributor. Remove the pick-up coil.

To install:

6. Install the pick-up coil into place in the distributor body. Replace the wiring harness retainer.

7. Press the reluctor firmly into place on the shaft. Install a new roll pin with the slit in the pin parallel to the flat on the shaft.

8. Install the magnet and stator, and center the stator around the reluctor. Air gap is 0.30–0.50mm.

9. Press the pick-up coil spade connectors onto the ignition unit terminals with your fingers. The proper connections can be determined from the color code marked on the grommet. Replace the ignition rotor and the distributor cap.

RELUCTOR AND IC IGNITION UNIT

1. Remove the distributor cap and rotor. The rotor is held to the distributor shaft by a retaining screw, which must be removed.

2. Remove the wiring harness and the vacuum controller from the housing.

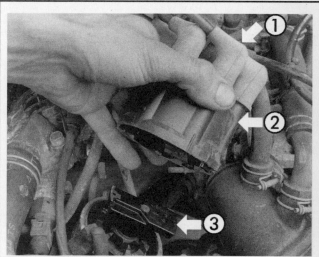

1. Spark plug wires (still attached)
2. Distributor cap
3. Rotor (transmits spark sequentially to cap and wires)

Disconnect the clips, then lift off the cap with wires still connected

Pull the rotor straight off the shaft

3. Using 2 flat bladed prytools place one on each side of the reluctor, and pry it from the distributor shaft.

➡**When removing the reluctor, be careful not to damage or distort the teeth.**

4. Remove the roll pin from the reluctor.

➡**To remove the IC unit, mark and remove the breaker plate assembly and separate the IC unit from it. Be careful not to loose the spacers when you remove the IC unit.**

5. Install the IC unit to the breaker plate assembly.

6. Install the wiring harness and the vacuum controller to the distributor housing. When you install the roll pin into the reluctor position the cutout direction of the roll pin in parallel with the notch in the reluctor. Make sure that the harness to the IC ignition unit is tightly secured, then adjust the air gap between the reluctor and the stator to 0.30–0.50mm. Refer to the exploded views of the distributor in this book.

IGNITION TIMING

Gasoline Engines

Ignition timing is the measurement in degrees of crankshaft rotation, of the point at which the spark plugs fire in each of the cylinders. It is measured in degrees before or after Top Dead Center (TDC) of the compression stroke.

Because it takes a fraction of a second for the spark plug to ignite the mixture in the cylinder, the spark plug must fire a little before the piston reaches TDC. Otherwise, the mixture will not be completely ignited as the piston passes TDC and the full power of the explosion will not be used by the engine.

The timing measurement is given in degrees of crankshaft rotation before the piston reaches TDC (BTDC). If the setting for the ignition timing is 5° BTDC, the spark plug must fire 5° before each piston reaches TDC. This only holds true, however, when the engine is at idle speed.

As the engine speed increases, the pistons go faster. The spark plugs have to ignite the fuel even sooner if it is to be completely ignited when the piston reaches TDC. To do this, the distributor has two means to advance the timing of the spark as the engine speed increases: a set of centrifugal weights within the distributor, and a vacuum diaphragm, mounted on the side of the distributor.

➡**On Maxima models a crank angle sensor in the distributor is used. This sensor controls ignition timing and has other engine control functions. There is no vacuum or centrifugal advance all timing settings are controlled by the Electronic Control Unit (ECU).**

If the ignition is set too far advanced (BTDC), the ignition and expansion of the fuel in the cylinder will occur too soon and tend to force the piston down while it is still traveling up. This causes engine ping. If the ignition spark is set too far retarded, after TDC (ATDC), the piston will have already passed TDC and started on its way down when the fuel is ignited. This will cause the piston to be forced down for only a portion of its travel. This will result in poor engine performance and lack of power.

Timing marks consist of a notch on the rim of the crankshaft pulley and a scale of degrees attached to the front of the engine. The notch corresponds to the position of the piston in the number 1 cylinder. A stroboscopic (dynamic) timing light is used, which is hooked into the circuit of the No. 1 cylinder spark plug. Every time the spark plug fires, the timing light flashes. By aiming the timing light at the timing marks, the exact position of the piston within the cylinder can be read, since the stroboscopic flash makes the mark on the pulley appear to be standing still. Proper timing is indicated when the notch is aligned with the correct number on the scale.

There are three basic types of timing lights available. The first is a simple neon bulb with two wire connections (one for the spark plug and one for the plug wire, connecting the light in series). This type of light is quite dim, and must be held closely to the marks to be seen, but it is inexpensive. The second type of light operates from the car battery. Two alligator clips connect to the battery terminals, while a third wire connects to the spark plug with an adapter. This type of light is more expensive, but the xenon bulb provides a nice bright flash which can even be seen in sunlight. The third type replaces the battery source with 110 volt house current. Some timing lights have other functions built into them, such as dwell meters, tachometers, or remote starting switches. These are convenient, in that they reduce the tangle of wires under the hood, but may duplicate the functions of tools you already have.

If your Datsun has electronic ignition, you should use a timing light with an inductive pickup. This pickup simply clamps onto the No. 1 plug wire, eliminating the adapter. It is not prone to crossfiring or false triggering, which may occur with a conventional light, due to the greater voltages produced by electronic ignition.

ADJUSTMENT

Single Point and Electronic Ignition Equipped Models
◆ **See Figures 22, 23, 24 and 25**

➡**Nissan does not give ignition timing adjustments for 1980 California models or for any 1981 200SXs and for 1981–84 810s and Maxima models. If timing requires adjustment, please refer to the underhood specifications sticker for applicable procedures.**

1. Set the dwell of the breaker points to the proper specification.

2. Locate the timing marks on the crankshaft pulley and the front of the engine.

3. Clean off the timing marks, so that you can see them.

4. Use chalk or white paint to color the mark on the crankshaft pulley and the mark on the scale which will indicate the correct timing when aligned with the notch on the crankshaft pulley.

5. Attach a tachometer to the engine.

6. Attach a timing light to the engine, according to the manufacturer's instructions. If the timing light has three wires, one, usually green or blue, is attached to the No. 1 spark plug with an adapter. The other wires are connected to the battery. The red wire

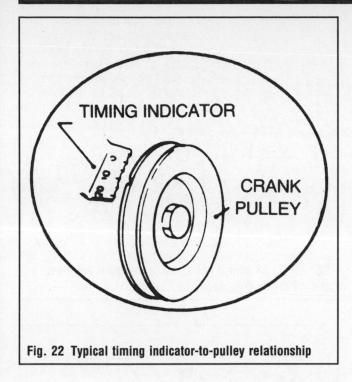

Fig. 22 Typical timing indicator-to-pulley relationship

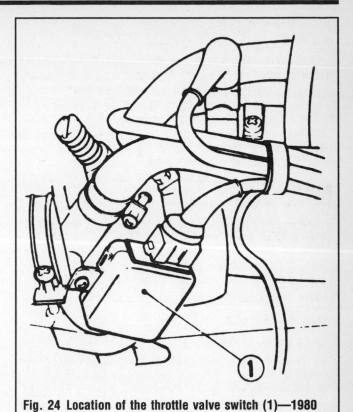

Fig. 24 Location of the throttle valve switch (1)—1980 models

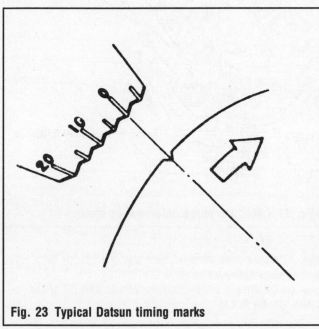

Fig. 23 Typical Datsun timing marks

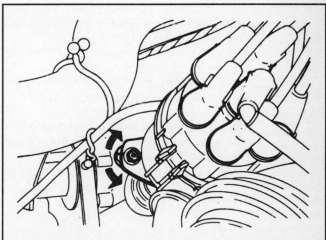

Fig. 25 Loosen the lockbolt, then turn the distributor to advance (upper arrow), or retard the timing (lower arrow)

goes to the positive side of the battery and the black wire is connected to the negative terminal of the battery.

7. Leave the vacuum hose connected to the distributor advance vacuum diaphragm on all models through 1979.

On 1980 models: disconnect the throttle valve switch harness connector (810 only). Disconnect and plug the canister purge hose from the intake manifold (810 only). Plug the opening in the intake manifold. On 1980 49 State models, also disconnect the hoe from the air induction pipe and cap the pipe, and disconnect and plug the vacuum advance hose at the distributor. Note that the disconnect and plug instructions for the air induction pipe and the distributor vacuum advance do not apply to 1980 models sold in Canada.

8. Check that all of the wires clear the fan, pulleys, and belts, and then start the engine. Allow the engine to reach normal operating temperature.

✳✳ CAUTION

Block the front wheels and set the parking brake. Shift the manual transmission to Neutral or the automatic transmission to Drive. Do not stand in front of the car when making adjustments!

9. Adjust the idle to the correct setting. See the Idle Speed and Mixture section later in this section.

10. Aim the timing light at the timing marks. If the marks which you put on the pulley and the engine are aligned when the light flashes, the timing is correct. Turn off the engine and remove the tachometer and the timing light. If the marks are not in alignment, proceed with the following steps.

11. Turn off the engine.

12. Loosen the distributor lockbolt just enough so that the distributor can be turned with a little effort.

13. Start the engine. Keep the wires of the timing light clear of the fan.

14. With the timing light aimed at the pulley and the marks on the engine, turn the distributor in the direction of rotor rotation to retard the spark, and in the opposite direction of rotor rotation to advance the spark. Align the marks on the pulley and the engine with the flashes of the timing light.

15. Tighten the distributor lockbolt and recheck the timing.

Models With Dual Points

PHASE DIFFERENCE

▶ **See Figures 26 and 27**

1. Disconnect the wiring harness of the distributor from the engine harness.

2. Connect the black wire of the engine harness to the black wire of the distributor harness with a jumper wire. This connects the advanced set of points.

3. With the engine idling, adjust the ignition timing by rotating the distributor.

4. Disconnect the jumper wire from the black wire of the distributor harness and connect it to the yellow wire of the distributor harness. The retarded set of points is now activated.

5. With the engine idling, check the ignition timing. The timing should be retarded from the advanced setting 7°.

6. To adjust the out of phase angle of the ignition timing, loosen the adjuster plate set screws on the same side as the retarded set of points.

7. Place the blade of a screwdriver in the adjusting notch of the adjuster plate and turn the adjuster plate as required to obtain the correct retarded ignition timing specification. The ignition timing is retarded when the adjuster plate is turned counterclockwise. There are graduations on the adjuster plate to make the adjustment easier. One graduation is equal to 4° of crankcase rotation.

8. Replace the distributor cap, start the engine and check the ignition timing with the retarded set of points activated (yellow

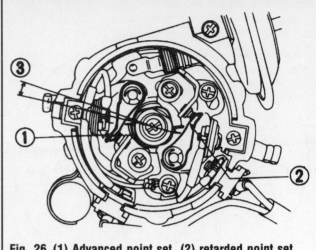

Fig. 26 (1) Advanced point set, (2) retarded point set, and (3) phase difference

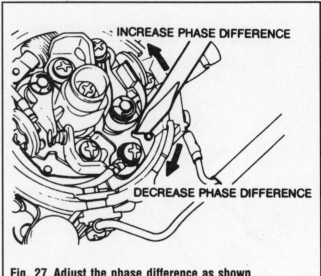

Fig. 27 Adjust the phase difference as shown

wire of the distributor wiring harness connected to the black wire of the engine wiring harness).

9. Repeat the steps above as necessary to gain the proper retarded ignition timing.

VALVE LASH

Description

Valve adjustment determines how far the valves enter the cylinder and how long they stay open and closed.

If the valve clearance is too large, part of the lift of the camshaft will be used in removing the excessive clearance. Consequently, the valve will not be opening for as long as it should. This condition has two effects: the valve train components will emit a tapping sound as they take up the excessive clearance and the engine will perform poorly because the valves don't open fully

and allow the proper amount of gases to flow into and out of the engine.

If the valve clearance is too small, the intake valves and the exhaust valves will open too far and they will not fully seat on the cylinder head when they close. When a valve seats itself on the cylinder head, it does two things: it seals the combustion chamber so that one of the gases in the cylinder escape and it cools itself by transferring some of the heat it absorbs from the combustion in the cylinder to the cylinder head and to the engine's cooling system. If the valve clearance is too small, the engine will run poorly because of the gases escaping from the combustion chamber. The valves will also become overheated and will warp, since they cannot transfer heat unless they are touching the valve seat in the cylinder head.

➡**While all valve adjustments must be made as accurately as possible, it is better to have the valve adjustment slightly loose than slightly tight, as a burned valve may result from overly tight adjustments.**

ADJUSTMENT

610, 710 and 1977–80 510, 200SX (Single Plug Engine)
◆ **See Figures 28, 29 and 30**

1. The valves are adjusted with the engine at normal operating temperature. Oil temperature, and the resultant parts expansion, is much more important than water temperature. Run the engine for at least fifteen minutes to ensure that all the parts have reached their full expansion. After the engine is warmed up, shut it off.

2. Purchase either a new gasket or some silicone gasket seal before removing the camshaft cover. Note the location of any wires and hoses which may interfere with cam cover removal, disconnect them and move them aside. Then remove the bolts which hold the cam cover in place and remove the cam cover.

3. Place a wrench on the crankshaft pulley bolt and turn the engine over until the valves for No. 1 cylinder are closed. When both cam lobes are pointing up, the valves are closed. If you have not done this before, it is a good idea to turn the engine over slowly several times and watch the valve action until you have a clear idea of just when the valve is closed.

4. Check the clearance of the intake and exhaust valves. You

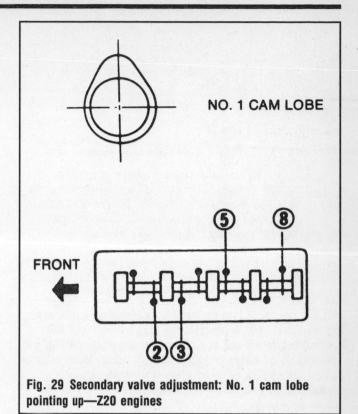

Fig. 29 Secondary valve adjustment: No. 1 cam lobe pointing up—Z20 engines

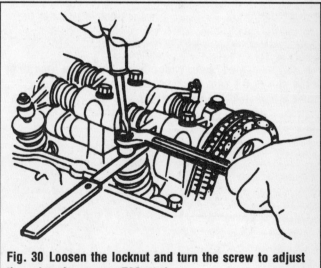

Fig. 30 Loosen the locknut and turn the screw to adjust the valve clearance—Z20 engines

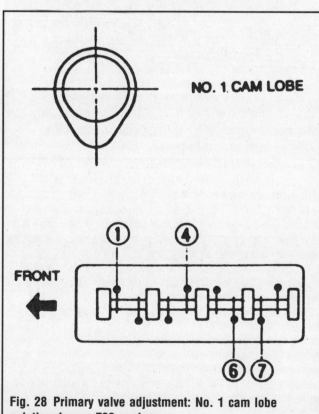

Fig. 28 Primary valve adjustment: No. 1 cam lobe pointing down—Z20 engines

can differentiate between them by lining them up with the tubes of the intake and exhaust manifolds. The correct size feeler gauge should pass between the base circle of the cam and the rocker arm with just a slight drag. Be sure the feeler gauge is inserted straight and not on an angle.

5. If the valves need adjustment, loosen the locking nut and then adjust the clearance with the adjusting screw. You will probably find it necessary to hold the locking nut while you turn the adjuster. After you have the correct clearance, tighten the locking nut and recheck the clearance. Remember, it's better to have them too loose than too tight, especially exhaust valves.

6. Repeat this procedure (Steps 3–5) until you have checked

and/or adjusted all the valves. (Be sure to adjust in the firing order.) Keep in mind that all that is necessary is to have the valves closed and the camshaft lobes pointing up.

7. Install the cam cover gasket, the cam cover, and any wires and hoses which were removed.

810 and Maxima
▶ See Figures 31 and 32

➡The 810 and Maxima engine valves are adjusted hot.

1. Note the locations of all hoses or wires that would interfere with valve cover removal, disconnect them and move them aside. Then, remove the six bolts which hold the valve cover in place.

2. Bump one end of the cover sharply to loosen the gasket and then pull the valve cover off the engine vertically.

3. Place a wrench on the crankshaft pulley bolt and turn the engine over until the first cam lobe is pointing straight up. The timing marks on the crankshaft pulley should be lined up approximately where they would be when the No. 1 spark plug fires.

➡If you decide to turn the engine by bumping it with the starter, be sure to disconnect the high tension wire from the coil to prevent the engine from accidentally starting and spewing oil all over the engine compartment. Never attempt to turn the engine by using a wrench on the camshaft sprocket bolt. This would put a tremendous strain on the timing chain.

4. See the illustration for primary adjustment and check the clearance for valves (1), (3), (7), (8), (9) and (11) using a flat bladed feeler gauge. The feeler gauge should pass between the cam and the cam follower with a very slight drag. Insert the feeler gauge straight, not at an angle.

➡A narrow angled feeler gauge blade should be used to fit in the slot of the cam follower. Do not angle the feeler gauge when checking the clearance.

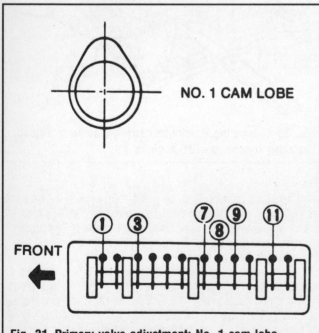

Fig. 31 Primary valve adjustment: No. 1 cam lobe pointing up—810 and Maxima

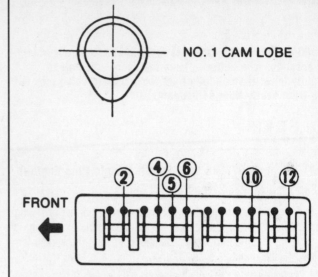

Fig. 32 Secondary valve adjustment: No. 1 cam lobe pointing down—810 and Maxima

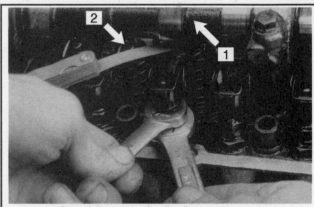

1. Cam lobe must be "up"
2. Check clearance with the feeler gauge before and after adjusting the locking nuts

Use two wrenches and a feeler gauge to adjust the valves—Maxima engine shown

5. If the clearance is not within the specified limits, loosen the pivot locking nut and then insert the feeler gauge between the cam and the cam follower. Adjust the pivot screw until there is a very slight drag on the gauge, tighten the locking nut, recheck the adjustment and correct as necessary.

6. Turn the engine over so that the first cam lobe is pointing straight down. See the illustration for secondary adjustment and then check the clearance on valves (2), (4), (5), (6), (10) and (12). If clearance is not within specifications, adjust as detailed in Step 5.

7. Clean all traces of old gasket material from the valve cover and the head. Install the new gasket in the valve cover with sealer and install the valve cover. Tighten the valve cover bolts evenly in several stages going around the cover to ensure a good seal. Reconnect all hoses and wires securely and operate the engine to check for leaks.

8. Road test the vehicle for proper operation.

1980–83 510 and 1981 200SX (Twin Plug Engines)

1. The valves must be adjusted with the engine warm, so start the car and run the engine until the needle on the temperature gauge reaches the middle of the gauge. After the engine is warm, shut it off.

2. Purchase either a new gasket or some silicone gasket sealer before removing the camshaft cover. Counting on the old gasket to be in good shape is a losing proposition. Always use new gaskets. Note the location of any wires and hoses which may interfere with cam cover removal, disconnect them and move them to one side. Remove the bolts holding the cover in place and remove the cover. Remember, the engine will be hot, so be careful.

3. Place a wrench on the crankshaft pulley bolt and turn the engine over until the first cam lobe behind the camshaft timing chain sprocket is pointing straight down.

➡ **If you decide to turn the engine by bumping it with the starter, be sure to disconnect the high tension wire from the coil(s) to prevent the engine from accidentally starting and spewing oil all over the engine compartment. Never at-** tempt to turn the engine by using a wrench on the camshaft sprocket bolt. There is a one to two turning ratio between the camshaft and the crankshaft which will put a tremendous strain on the timing chain.

4. See the illustration for primary adjustment and check the clearance of valves (1), (4), (6), and (7) using a flat bladed feeler gauge. The feeler gauge should pass between the valve stem end and the rocker arm screw with a very slight drag. Insert the feeler gauge straight, not at an angle.

5. If the clearance is not within specified value, loosen the rocker arm locknut and turn the rocker arm screw to obtain the proper clearance. After correct clearance is obtained, tighten the locknut.

6. Turn the engine over so that the first cam lobe behind the camshaft timing chain sprocket is pointing straight up and check the clearance of the valves marked (2), (3), (5), and (8) in the secondary adjustment illustration. They, too, should be adjusted to specifications as in Step 5.

7. Install the cam cover gasket, the cam cover and any wires and hoses which were removed.

IDLE SPEED AND MIXTURE

This section contains only tune-up adjustment procedures for carburetors. Descriptions, adjustments, and overhaul procedures for fuel systems can be found in Section 5.

Carbureted Engines

When the engine is running, the air/fuel mixture from the carburetor is being drawn into the engine by a partial vacuum which is created by the movement of the pistons downward on the intake stroke. The amount of air/fuel mixture that enters into the engine is controlled by the throttle plate(s) in the bottom of the carburetor. When the engine is not running the throttle plate(s) is closed, completely blocking off the bottom of the carburetor from the inside of the engine. The throttle plates are connected by the throttle linkage to the accelerator pedal in the passenger compartment of the vehicle. When you depress the pedal, you open the throttle plates in the carburetor to admit more air/fuel mixture to the engine.

When the engine is not running, the throttle plates are closed. When the engine is idling, it is necessary to have the throttle plates open slightly. To prevent having to hold your foot on the pedal when the engine is idling, an idle speed adjusting screw was added to the carburetor linkage.

The idle adjusting screw contacts a lever (throttle lever) on the outside of the carburetor. When the screw is turned, it either opens or closes the throttle plates of the carburetor, raising or lowering the idle speed of the engine. This screw is called the curb idle adjusting screw.

ADJUSTMENT

◆ **See Figure 33**

➡ The 1980 model Datsun/Nissan require a CO meter to adjust their mixture ratios, therefore, no procedures concerning this adjustment are given. Also, many California model

Datsun/Nissan have a plug over their mixture control screw. It is suggested that in both of these cases, mixture adjustment be left to a qualified technician.

1. Start the engine and allow it to run until it reaches normal operating temperature.

2. Allow the engine idle speed to stabilize by running the engine at idle for at least two minutes.

3. If you have not done so already, check and adjust the ignition timing to the proper setting.

4. Shut off the engine and connect a tachometer as per the manufacturer's instructions.

5. Disconnect and plug the air hose between the three-way connector and the check valve, if equipped. On 1980 models with

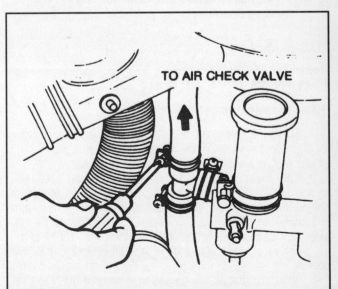

TO AIR CHECK VALVE

Fig. 33 Disconnect the air hose between the three-way connector and the check valve—510 shown

the Z20S engine, disconnect the air induction hose and plug the pipe, also disconnect and plug the vacuum hose at the distributor. With the transmission in Neutral, check the idle speed on the tachometer. If the reading is correct, continue on to Step 6 for 1973–79 models. For 1980 and later, and certain California models, proceed to Step 10 below if the idle is correct. If the idle is not correct, for all models, turn the idle speed adjusting screw clockwise with a screwdriver to increase idle speed or counterclockwise to decrease it.

6. With the automatic transmission in Drive (wheels blocked and parking brake on) or the manual transmission in Neutral, turn the mixture screw out until the engine rpm starts to drop due to an overly rich mixture.

7. Turn the screw until just before the rpm starts to drop due to an overly lean mixture. Turn the mixture screw in until the idle speed drops 60–70 rpm with manual transmission, or 15–25 rpm with automatic transmission (in Drive) for 1975–76 610 and 710 models; 45–55 rpm for all 1977 710's, and 1978–79 510's and 200SX's. If the mixture limited cap will not allow this adjustment, remove it, make the adjustment, and install it. Go on to Step 10 for all 1975–79 models.

8. On 1973–74 models, turn the mixture screw back out to the point midway between the two extreme positions where the engine began losing rpm to achieve the fastest and smoothest idle.

9. Adjust the curb idle speed to the proper specification, on 1973–74 models, with the idle speed adjusting screw.

10. Install the air hose (if so equipped). If the engine speed increases, reduce it with the idle speed screw.

Electronic Fuel Injected Engines

These cars use a rather complex electronic fuel injection system which is controlled by a series of temperature, altitude (for California) and air flow sensors which feed information into a central control unit. The control unit then relays an electronic signal to the injector nozzle at each cylinder, which allows a predetermined amount of fuel into the combustion chamber. To adjust the mixture controls on these units requires a CO meter and several special Datsun/Nissan tools. Therefore, we will confine ourselves to idle speed adjustment.

ADJUSTMENT

◆ **See Figures 34, 35, 36, 37 and 38**

➡**This procedure covers idle speed only.**

1. Start the engine and run it until the water temperature indicator points to the middle of the temperature gauge. It might be quicker to take a short spin down the road and back.

2. Open the engine hood. Run the engine at about 2,000 rpm for a few minutes with the transmission in Neutral and all accessories off. If you have not already done so, check the ignition timing and make sure it is correct. Hook up a tachometer as per the manufacturer's instructions. For automatic transmission, set the parking brake, block the wheels and set the shift selector in the Drive position.

3. Run the engine at idle speed and disconnect the hose from

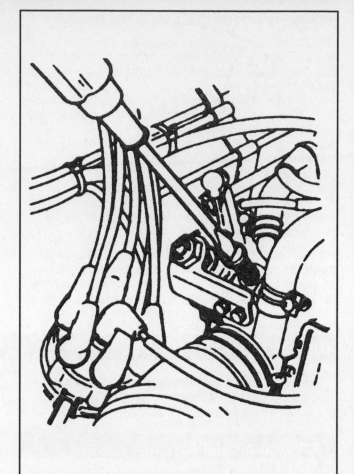

Fig. 34 To set the idle speed, turn the adjustment screw

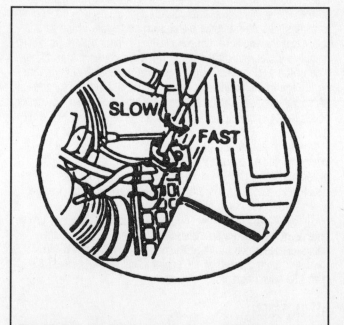

Fig. 35 Turn the idle speed screw for adjustment— 200SX shown

Fig. 36 Turn the idle speed screw for adjustment— 1977–80 810 shown

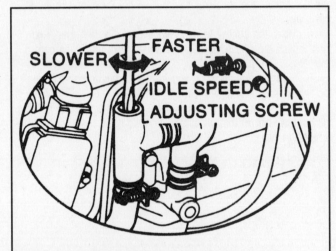

Fig. 37 Turn the idle speed screw for adjustment— 1981–84 810 and Maxima shown

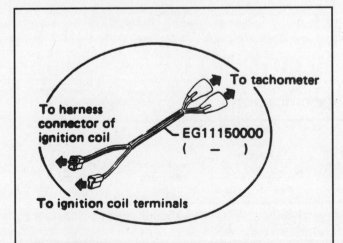

Fig. 38 Use this special tool adapter, or equivalent, for tachometer installation

the air induction pipe, then plug the pipe. Allow the engine to run for about a minute at idle speed.

4. Check the idle against the specifications given earlier in this chapter. Adjust the idle speed by turning the idle speed adjusting screw, located near the air cleaner on the 200SX and the throttle chamber on the 810. Turn the screw clockwise for slower idle speed and counterclockwise for faster idle speed.

5. Connect the hose and disconnect the tachometer. If idle speed increases, adjust it with the idle speed adjusting screw.

Diesel Engines

ADJUSTMENT

▶ **See Figures 39, 40, 41 and 42**

➡**This procedure covers idle speed only.**

1. Make sure all electrical accessories are turned off.
2. Start the engine and run it until it reaches the normal operating temperature.

➡**A special diesel tachometer will be required for this procedure. A normal tachometer will not work.**

3. The automatic transmission (if so equipped) should be in D with the parking brake on and the wheels blocked.
4. Attach the diesel tachometer's pick-up to the No. 1 injection tube.

➡**In order to obtain a more accurate reading of the idle speed, you may wish to remove all the clamps on the No. 1 injection tube.**

5. Run the engine at about 2,000 rpm for two minutes under no-load conditions.
6. Slow the engine down to idle speed for about 1 min. and then check the idle.
7. If the engine is not idling at the proper speed, turn it off

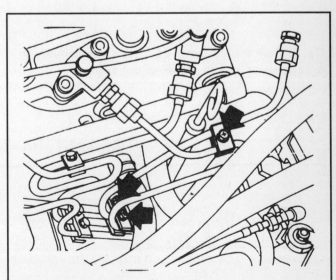

Fig. 39 You may wish to remove all the clamps on the No. 1 injection tube to obtain a more accurate reading— diesel engines

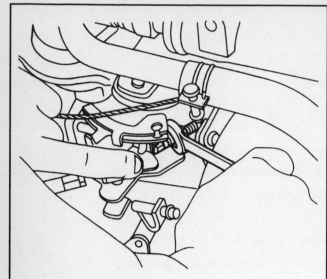

Fig. 40 Loosen the idle screw locknut while holding the control lever—diesel engines

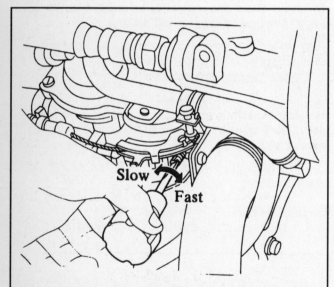

Fig. 41 Turn the idle speed adjusting screw as shown to raise or lower the idle speed—diesel engines

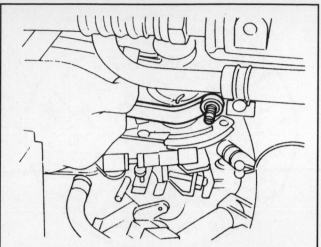

Fig. 42 Tighten the idle speed adjusting screw locknut when the adjustment is completed—diesel engines

and disconnect the accelerator wire from the injection pump control lever.

8. Move the control lever to the full acceleration side, and then loosen the idle screw locknut while still holding the control lever.

9. Start the engine again and turn the adjusting screw until the proper idle is obtained. Stop the engine.

10. Tighten the idle adjusting screw locknut while still holding the control level to the full acceleration side and then connect the accelerator wire.

Diesel Tune-Up Specifications

Year Model	Engine Displacement cu. in. (cc)	Warm Valve Clearance (in.)		Intake Valve Opens (deg)	Injection Pump Setting (deg)	Injection Nozzle Pressure (psi)		Idle Speed (rpm)	Compression Pressure (psi)
		In	Ex			New	Used		
1981–83	170 (2,793)	0.010	0.012	NA	align marks	1,920– 2,033	1,778– 1,920	650	455 @ 200 rpm

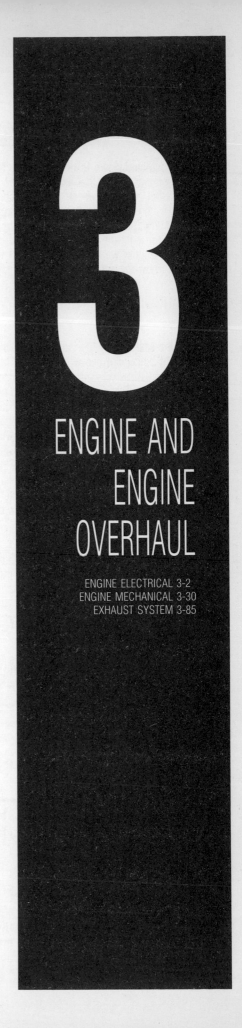

3

ENGINE AND ENGINE OVERHAUL

ENGINE ELECTRICAL

Understanding Electricity

For any electrical system to operate, there must be a complete circuit. This simply means that the power flow from the battery must make a full circle. When an electrical component is operating, power flows from the battery to the components, passes through the component (load) causing it to function, and returns to the battery through the ground path of the circuit. This ground may be either another wire or a metal part of the vehicle (depending upon how the component is designed).

BASIC CIRCUITS

Perhaps the easiest way to visualize a circuit is to think of connecting a light bulb (with two wires attached to it) to the battery. If one of the two wires was attached to the negative post (−) of the battery and the other wire to the positive post (+), the circuit would be complete and the light bulb would illuminate. Electricity could follow a path from the battery to the bulb and back to the battery. It's not hard to see that with longer wires on our light bulb, it could be mounted anywhere on the vehicle. Further, one wire could be fitted with a switch so that the light could be turned on and off. Various other items could be added to our primitive circuit to make the light flash, become brighter or dimmer under certain conditions, or advise the user that it's burned out.

Ground

Some automotive components are grounded through their mounting points. The electrical current runs through the chassis of the vehicle and returns to the battery through the ground (−) cable; if you look, you'll see that the battery ground cable connects between the battery and the body of the vehicle.

Load

Every complete circuit must include a "load" (something to use the electricity coming from the source). If you were to connect a wire between the two terminals of the battery (DON'T do this, but take our word for it) without the light bulb, the battery would attempt to deliver its entire power supply from one pole to another almost instantly. This is a short circuit. The electricity is taking a short cut to get to ground and is not being used by any load in the circuit. This sudden and uncontrolled electrical flow can cause great damage to other components in the circuit and can develop a tremendous amount of heat. A short in an automotive wiring harness can develop sufficient heat to melt the insulation on all the surrounding wires and reduce a multiple wire cable to one sad lump of plastic and copper. Two common causes of shorts are broken insulation (thereby exposing the wire to contact with surrounding metal surfaces or other wires) or a failed switch (the pins inside the switch come out of place and touch each other).

Switches and Relays

Some electrical components which require a large amount of current to operate also have a relay in their circuit. Since these circuits carry a large amount of current (amperage or amps), the thickness of the wire in the circuit (wire gauge) is also greater. If this large wire were connected from the load to the control switch on the dash, the switch would have to carry the high amperage load and the dash would be twice as large to accommodate wiring harnesses as thick as your wrist. To prevent these problems, a relay is used. The large wires in the circuit are connected from the battery to one side of the relay and from the opposite side of the relay to the load. The relay is normally open, preventing current from passing through the circuit. An additional, smaller wire is connected from the relay to the control switch for the circuit. When the control switch is turned on, it grounds the smaller wire to the relay and completes its circuit. The main switch inside the relay closes, sending power to the component without routing the main power through the inside of the vehicle. Some common circuits which may use relays are the horn, headlights, starter and rear window defogger systems.

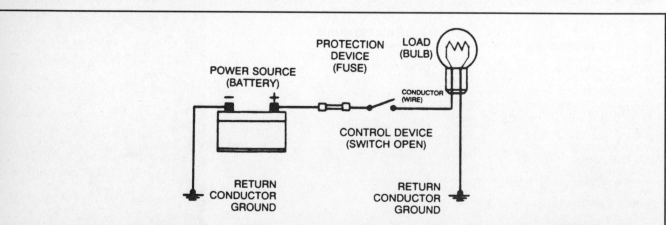

Here is an example of a simple automotive circuit. When the switch is closed, power from the positive battery terminal flows through the fuse, the switch and then the load (light bulb). The light illuminates and the circuit is completed through the return conductor and the vehicle ground. If the light did not work, the tests could be made with a voltmeter or test light at the battery, fuse, switch or bulb socket

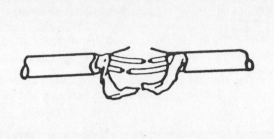

Damaged insulation can allow wires to break (causing an open circuit) or touch (causing a short circuit)

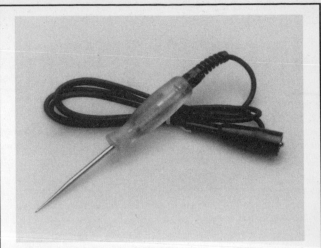

A 12 volt test light is useful when checking parts of a circuit for power

Protective Devices

It is possible for larger surges of current to pass through the electrical system of your vehicle. If this surge of current were to reach the load in the circuit, it could burn it out or severely damage it. To prevent this, fuses, circuit breakers and/or fusible links are connected into the supply wires of the electrical system. These items are nothing more than a built-in weak spot in the system. It's much easier to go to a known location (the fusebox) to see why a circuit is inoperative than to dissect 15 feet of wiring under the dashboard, looking for what happened.

When an electrical current of excessive power passes through the fuse, the fuse blows (the conductor melts) and breaks the circuit, preventing the passage of current and protecting the components.

A circuit breaker is basically a self repairing fuse. It will open the circuit in the same fashion as a fuse, but when either the short is removed or the surge subsides, the circuit breaker resets itself and does not need replacement.

A fuse link (fusible link or main link) is a wire that acts as a fuse. One of these is normally connected between the starter relay and the main wiring harness under the hood. Since the starter is usually the highest electrical draw on the vehicle, an internal short during starting could direct about 130 amps into the wrong places. Consider the damage potential of introducing this current into a system whose wiring is rated at 15 amps and you'll understand the need for protection. Since this link is very early in the electrical path, it's the first place to look if nothing on the vehicle works, but the battery seems to be charged and is properly connected.

TROUBLESHOOTING

Electrical problems generally fall into one of three areas:
• The component that is not functioning is not receiving current.
• The component is receiving power but is not using it or is using it incorrectly (component failure).
• The component is improperly grounded.
The circuit can be can be checked with a test light and a

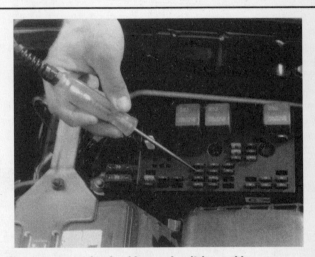

Here, someone is checking a circuit by making sure there is power to the component's fuse

jumper wire. The test light is a device that looks like a pointed screwdriver with a wire on one end and a bulb in its handle. A jumper wire is simply a piece of wire with alligator clips or special terminals on each end. If a component is not working, you must follow a systematic plan to determine which of the three causes is the villain.

1. Turn ON the switch that controls the item not working.

➡**Some items only work when the ignition switch is turned ON.**

2. Disconnect the power supply wire from the component.
3. Attach the ground wire of a test light or a voltmeter to a good metal ground.
4. Touch the end probe of the test light (or the positive lead of the voltmeter) to the power wire; if there is current in the wire, the light in the test light will come on (or the voltmeter will indicate the amount of voltage). You have now established that current is getting to the component.
5. Turn the ignition or dash switch **OFF** and reconnect the wire to the component.

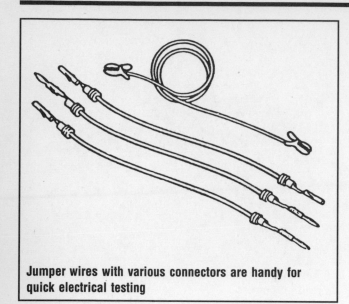

Jumper wires with various connectors are handy for quick electrical testing

If there was no power, then the problem is between the battery and the component. This includes all the switches, fuses, relays and the battery itself. The next place to look is the fusebox; check carefully either by eye or by using the test light across the fuse clips. The easiest way to check is to simply replace the fuse. If the fuse is blown, and upon replacement, immediately blows again, there is a short between the fuse and the component. This is generally (not always) a sign of an internal short in the component. Disconnect the power wire at the component again and replace the fuse; if the fuse holds, the component is the problem.

⁂ WARNING

DO NOT test a component by running a jumper wire from the battery UNLESS you are certain that it operates on 12 volts. Many electronic components are designed to operate with less voltage and connecting them to 12 volts could destroy them. Jumper wires are best used to bypass a portion of the circuit (such as a stretch of wire or a switch) that DOES NOT contain a resistor and is suspected to be bad.

If all the fuses are good and the component is not receiving power, find the switch for the circuit. Bypass the switch with the jumper wire. This is done by connecting one end of the jumper to the power wire coming into the switch and the other end to the wire leaving the switch. If the component comes to life, the switch has failed.

⁂ WARNING

Never substitute the jumper for the component. The circuit needs the electrical load of the component. If you bypass it, you will cause a short circuit.

Checking the ground for any circuit can mean tracing wires to the body, cleaning connections or tightening mounting bolts for the component itself. If the jumper wire can be connected to the case of the component or the ground connector, you can ground the other end to a piece of clean, solid metal on the vehicle. Again, if the component starts working, you've found the problem. A systematic search through the fuse, connectors, switches and

the component itself will almost always yield an answer. Loose and/or corroded connectors, particularly in ground circuits, are becoming a larger problem in modern vehicles. The computers and on-board electronic (solid state) systems are highly sensitive to improper grounds and will change their function drastically if one occurs.

Remember that for any electrical circuit to work, ALL the connections must be clean and tight.

➡**For more information on Understanding and Troubleshooting Electrical Systems, please refer to Section 6 of this manual.**

Battery, Starting and Charging Systems

BASIC OPERATING PRINCIPLES

Battery

The battery is the first link in the chain of mechanisms which work together to provide cranking of the automobile engine. In most modern vehicles, the battery is a lead/acid electrochemical device consisting of six 2v subsections (cells) connected in series so the unit is capable of producing approximately 12v of electrical pressure. Each subsection consists of a series of positive and negative plates held a short distance apart in a solution of sulfuric acid and water.

The two types of plates are of dissimilar metals. This sets-up a chemical reaction, and it is this reaction which produces current flow from the battery when its positive and negative terminals are connected to an electrical accessory such as a lamp or motor. The continued transfer of electrons would eventually convert the sulfuric acid to water, and make the two plates identical in chemical composition. As electrical energy is removed from the battery, its voltage output tends to drop. Thus, measuring battery voltage and battery electrolyte composition are two ways of checking the ability of the unit to supply power. During engine cranking, electrical energy is removed from the battery. However, if the charging circuit is in good condition and the operating conditions are normal, the power removed from the battery will be replaced by the alternator which will force electrons back through the battery, reversing the normal flow, and restoring the battery to its original chemical state.

Starting System

The battery and starting motor are linked by very heavy electrical cables designed to minimize resistance to the flow of current. Generally, the major power supply cable that leaves the battery goes directly to the starter, while other electrical system needs are supplied by a smaller cable. During starter operation, power flows from the battery to the starter and is grounded through the vehicle's frame/body or engine and the battery's negative ground strap.

The starter is a specially designed, direct current electric motor capable of producing a great amount of power for its size. One thing that allows the motor to produce a great deal of power is its tremendous rotating speed. It drives the engine through a tiny pinion gear (attached to the starter's armature), which drives the very large flywheel ring gear at a greatly reduced speed. Another factor allowing it to produce so much power is that only intermittent operation is required of it. Thus, little allowance for air circulation is necessary, and the windings can be built into a very small space.

The starter solenoid is a magnetic device which employs the small current supplied by the start circuit of the ignition switch. This magnetic action moves a plunger which mechanically engages the starter and closes the heavy switch connecting it to the battery. The starting switch circuit usually consists of the starting switch contained within the ignition switch, a neutral safety switch or clutch pedal switch, and the wiring necessary to connect these in series with the starter solenoid or relay.

The pinion, a small gear, is mounted to a one way drive clutch. This clutch is splined to the starter armature shaft. When the ignition switch is moved to the **START** position, the solenoid plunger slides the pinion toward the flywheel ring gear via a collar and spring. If the teeth on the pinion and flywheel match properly, the pinion will engage the flywheel immediately. If the gear teeth butt one another, the spring will be compressed and will force the gears to mesh as soon as the starter turns far enough to allow them to do so. As the solenoid plunger reaches the end of its travel, it closes the contacts that connect the battery and starter, then the engine is cranked.

As soon as the engine starts, the flywheel ring gear begins turning fast enough to drive the pinion at an extremely high rate of speed. At this point, the one-way clutch begins allowing the pinion to spin faster than the starter shaft so that the starter will not operate at excessive speed. When the ignition switch is released from the starter position, the solenoid is de-energized, and a spring pulls the gear out of mesh interrupting the current flow to the starter.

Some starters employ a separate relay, mounted away from the starter, to switch the motor and solenoid current on and off. The relay replaces the solenoid electrical switch, but does not eliminate the need for a solenoid mounted on the starter used to mechanically engage the starter drive gears. The relay is used to reduce the amount of current the starting switch must carry.

Charging System

The automobile charging system provides electrical power for operation of the vehicle's ignition system, starting system and all electrical accessories. The battery serves as an electrical surge or storage tank, storing (in chemical form) the energy originally produced by the engine driven generator. The system also provides a means of regulating output to protect the battery from being overcharged and to avoid excessive voltage to the accessories.

The storage battery is a chemical device incorporating parallel lead plates in a tank containing a sulfuric acid/water solution. Adjacent plates are slightly dissimilar, and the chemical reaction of the two dissimilar plates produces electrical energy when the battery is connected to a load such as the starter motor. The chemical reaction is reversible, so that when the generator is producing a voltage (electrical pressure) greater than that produced by the battery, electricity is forced into the battery, and the battery is returned to its fully charged state.

Newer automobiles use alternating current generators or alternators, because they are more efficient, can be rotated at higher speeds, and have fewer brush problems. In an alternator, the field usually rotates while all the current produced passes only through the stator winding. The brushes bear against continuous slip rings. This causes the current produced to periodically reverse the direction of its flow. Diodes (electrical one way valves) block the flow of current from traveling in the wrong direction. A series of diodes is wired together to permit the alternating flow of the stator to be rectified back to 12 volts DC for use by the vehicle's electrical system.

The voltage regulating function is performed by a regulator. The regulator is often built in to the alternator; this system is termed an integrated or internal regulator.

SAFETY PRECAUTIONS

Observing these precautions will ensure safe handling of the electrical system components, and will avoid damage to the vehicle's electrical system:

• Be absolutely sure of the polarity of a booster battery before making connections. Connect the cables positive to positive, and negative to negative. Connect positive cables first and then make the last connection to a ground on the body of the booster vehicle so that arcing cannot ignite hydrogen gas that may have accumulated near the battery. Even momentary connection of a booster battery with the polarity reversed will damage alternator diodes.

• Disconnect both vehicle battery cables before attempting to charge a battery.

• Never ground the alternator or generator output or battery terminal. Be cautious when using metal tools around a battery to avoid creating a short circuit between the terminals.

• Never ground the field circuit between the alternator and regulator.

• Never run an alternator or generator without load unless the field circuit is disconnected.

• Never attempt to polarize an alternator.

• Keep the regulator cover in place when taking voltage and current limiter readings.

• Use insulated tools when adjusting the regulator.

• Whenever DC generator-to-regulator wires have been disconnected, the generator must be repolarized. To do this with an externally grounded, light duty generator, momentarily place a jumper wire between the battery terminal and the generator terminal of the regulator. With an internally grounded heavy duty unit, disconnect the wire to the regulator field terminal and touch the regulator battery terminal with it.

For safety, whenever working on the vehicle, disconnect the negative battery cable

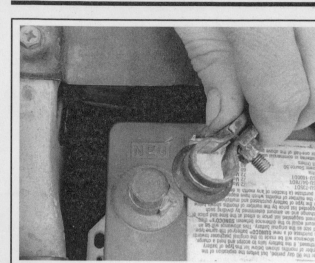

Make sure polarity is correct before making the connection

Electronic Ignition System Coil/Module

TESTING

1975–78 Models

♦ See Figures 1 and 2

The main differences between the 1975–77 and 1978 systems are: (1) the 1975–77 system uses an external ballast resistor located next to the ignition coil, and (2) the earlier system uses a wiring harness with individual eyelet connectors to the electronic unit, while the later system uses a multiple plug connector. You will need an accurate voltmeter and ohmmeter for these tests, which must be performed in the order given.

1. Check all connections for corrosion, looseness, breaks, etc., and correct if necessary. Clean and gap the spark plugs.

2a. Disconnect the harness (connector of plug) from the electronic unit. Turn the ignition switch On. Set the voltmeter to the DC 50v range. Connect the positive (+) voltmeter lead to the black/white wire terminal, and the negative (−) lead to the black wire terminal. Battery, voltage should be obtained. If not, check the black/white and black wires for continuity; check the battery terminals for corrosion; check the battery state of charge.

2b. Next, connect the voltmeter (+) lead to the blue wire and the (−) lead to the black wire. Battery voltage should be obtained. If not check the blue wire for continuity; check the ignition coil terminals for corrosion or looseness; check the coil for continuity. On 1975–77 models, also check the external ballast resistor.

3. Disconnect the distributor harness wires from the ignition coil ballast resistor on 1975–77 models, leaving the ballast resistor-to-coil wires attached. On 1978 models, disconnect the ignition coil wires. Connect the leads of an ohmmeter to the ballast resistor outside terminals (at each end) for 1975–77, and to the two coil terminals for 1978. With the ohmmeter set in the X1 range, the following model years should show a reading of 1.6–2.0Ω: 1976 710, 610; 1977 810, 710 models.

The following models should show a reading of approximately 0Ω: 1975 710; 1978 810, 200SX. The maximum allowable limit for the 1.6–2.0Ω range models is 2.0Ω. The limit for the 0Ω models is 1.8Ω. If a reading higher than the limit is received, replace the ignition coil assembly.

4. Disconnect the harness from the electronic control unit. Connect an ohmmeter to the red and the green wire terminals. Resistance should be 720Ω. If far more or far less, replace the distributor pick-up coil.

5. Disconnect the anti-dieseling solenoid connector. Connect a voltmeter to the red and green terminals of the electronic control harness. When the starter is cranked, the needle should deflect slightly. If not, replace the distributor pick-up coil.

6. Reconnect the ignition coil and the electronic control unit. Leave the anti-dieseling solenoid wire disconnected. Unplug the high tension lead (coil to distributor) from the distributor and hole it ⅛–¼″ from the cylinder head with a pair of insulated pliers and a heavy glove. When the engine is cranked, a spark should be observed. If not, check the lead, and replace if necessary. If still no spark, replace the electronic control unit.

7. Reconnect all wires.

1976–77: connect the voltmeter (+) lead to the blue electronic control harness connector and the (−) lead to the black wire. The harness should be attached to the control unit.

1978: Connect the voltmeter (+) lead to the (−) terminal of the ignition coil and the (−) lead to ground.

As soon as the ignition switch is turned ON, the meter should indicate battery voltage. If not, replace the electronic control unit.

1979–84 Models

510, 810 AND MAXIMA AND 1979–81 200SX (SINGLE PLUG ENGINE) MODELS

♦ See Figures 3, 4, 5 and 6

1. Make a check of the power supply circuit. Turn the ignition OFF, Disconnect the connector from the top of the IC unit. Turn the ignition ON. Measure the voltage at each terminal of the connector in turn by touch the probe of the positive lead of the voltmeter to one of the terminals, and touching the probe of the negative lead of the voltmeter to a ground, such as the engine. In each case, battery voltage should be indicated. If not, check all wiring, the ignition switch, and all connectors for breaks, corrosion, discontinuity, etc., and repair as necessary.

2. Check the primary windings of the ignition coil. Turn the ignition OFF. Disconnect the harness connector from the negative coil terminal. Use an ohmmeter to measure the resistance between the positive and negative coil terminals. If resistance is 0.84–1.02Ω the coil is OK. Replace if far from this range. If the power supply, circuits, wiring, and coil are in good shape, check the IC unit and pick-up coil, as follows:

3. Turn the ignition OFF. Remove the distributor cap and ignition rotor. Use an ohmmeter to measure the resistance between the two terminals of the pick-up coil, where they attach to the IC unit. Measure the resistance by reversing the polarity of the probes. If approximately 400Ω are indicated, the pick-up coil is OK, but the IC unit is bad and must be replaced. If other than 400Ω are measured, go to the next step.

4. Be certain the two pin connector to the IC unit is secure. Turn the ignition ON. Measure the voltage at the ignition coil negative terminal. Turn the ignition OFF.

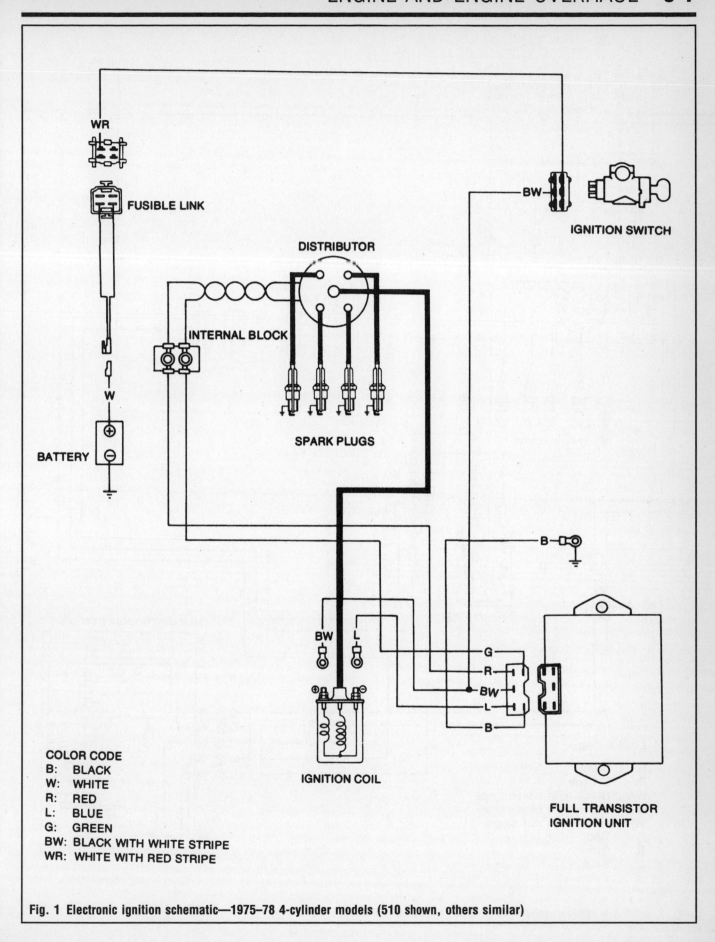

Fig. 1 Electronic ignition schematic—1975–78 4-cylinder models (510 shown, others similar)

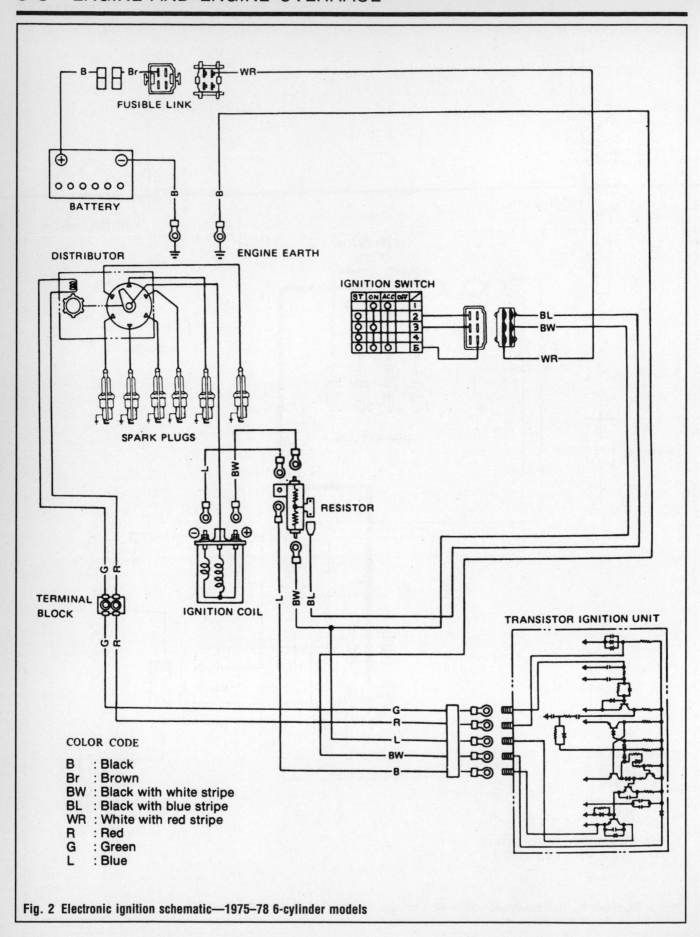

Fig. 2 Electronic ignition schematic—1975–78 6-cylinder models

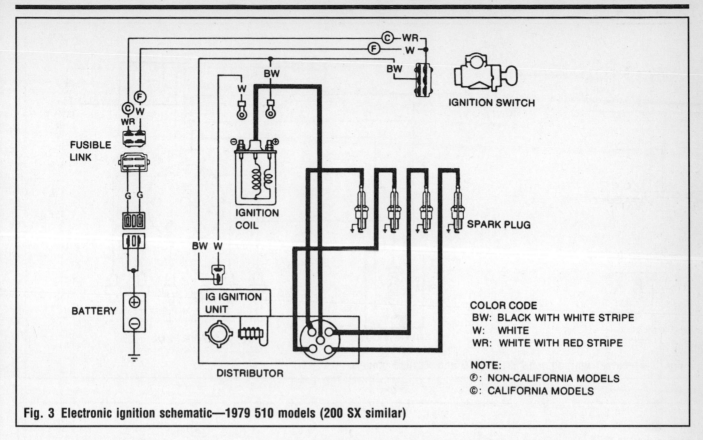

Fig. 3 Electronic ignition schematic—1979 510 models (200 SX similar)

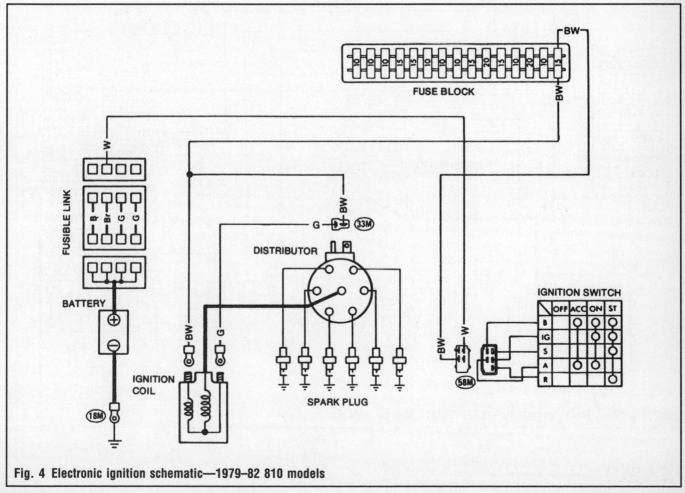

Fig. 4 Electronic ignition schematic—1979-82 810 models

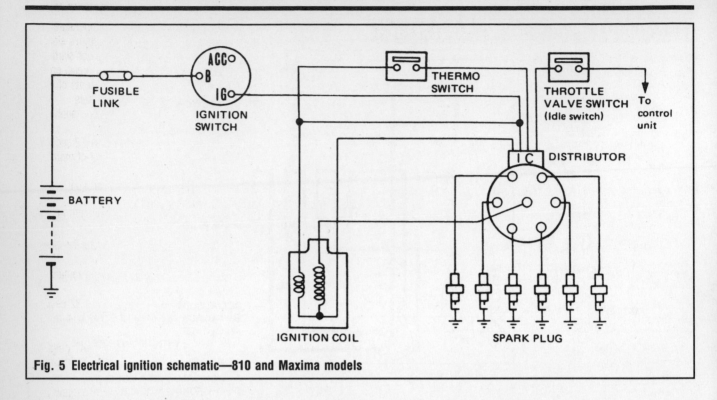

Fig. 5 Electrical ignition schematic—810 and Maxima models

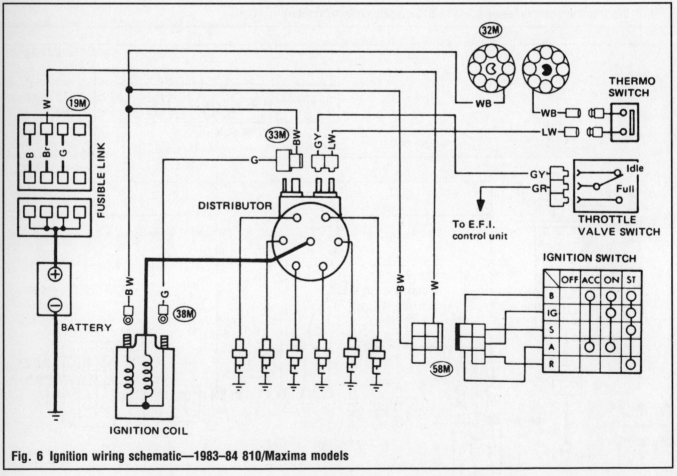

Fig. 6 Ignition wiring schematic—1983–84 810/Maxima models

❄❄ CAUTION

Remove the tester probe from the coil negative terminal before switching the ignition OFF, to prevent burning out the tester.

If zero voltage is indicated, the IC unit is bad and must be replaced. If battery voltage is indicated, proceed.

5. Remove the IC unit from the distributor:

a. Disconnect the battery ground (negative) cable.

b. Remove the distributor cap and ignition rotor.

c. Disconnect the harness connector at the top of the IC unit.

d. Remove the two screws securing the IC unit to the distributor.

e. Disconnect the two pick-up coil wires from the IC unit.

❄❄ CAUTION

Pull the connectors free with a pair of needlenosed pliers. Do not pull on the wires to detach the connectors.

f. Remove the IC unit.

6. Measure the resistance between the terminals of the pick-up coil. It should be approximately 400Ω. If so, the pick-up coil is OK, and the IC unit is bad. If not approximately 400Ω, the pick-up coil is bad and must be replaced.

7. With a new pick-up coil installed, install the IC unit. Check for a spark at one of the spark plugs. If a good spark is obtained, the IC unit is OK. If not, replace the IC unit.

1980–83 510 and 1980–81 200SX (Twin Plug Engine) Models

◆ **See Figure 7**

Complete Step 1–2 of the previous procedure; the resistance should be between 1.04–1.27Ω. If not, replace ignition coil(s).

➥ **The manufacturer does not give a complete system of tests for the 1980 200SX/510 California ignition system. Therefore, before attempting anything else, try this spark performance test:**

1. Turn the ignition switch to the OFF position.

2. On the 510 cut off the fuel supply to the engine. On the 200SX, disconnect the electronic fuel injection (EFI) fusible link.

3. Disconnect the high tension cable from the distributor. Hold the cable with insulated pliers to avoid getting shocked. Position the wire about a ¼" from the engine block and have an assistant turn over the engine using the starter. A spark should jump from the cable to the engine block. If not, there is probably something wrong with the ignition system. Further testing should be left to an authorized service technician with the proper test equipment.

Diesel Engine Auto-Glow System

◆ **See Figure 8**

The glow plug circuit is used on diesel engines to initially start the engine from cold. The glow plugs heat up the combustion chambers prior to cranking the engine. This heat, combined with the first squirt of fuel from the injectors and the extremely high cylinder pressures, fires the engine during cold starts. After normal operating temperature is reached, the water temperature sensor wired in the glow plug system changes the system's electrical resistance and cancels glow plug operation during hot starting.

The fast glow control units on 810 and Maxima diesel engines have multiple functions, controlling various components of the glow plug system. The unit has a total of ten terminals:

• No.1 Terminal: A terminal at which voltage being applied to the glow plug is measured. It serves two functions:

a. Determines the pre-glow time (approx. 4 to 12 seconds)

b. Stops after-glow operations when a voltage of more than 7 volts is detected after pre-glow operation

• No.2 Terminal: Control unit's power source terminal

• No.3 Terminal: Control unit's ground terminal

• No.4 Terminal: A terminal that controls the ON/OFF operation of glow plug relay 1.

• No.5 Terminal: A terminal connected to the water temperature sensor to serve three functions:

a. Determines the period that the warning lamp remains illuminated (approx. 1 to 9 seconds)

b. Determines the after-glow time (approx. 5 to 32 seconds)

c. Stops pre-glow operation when coolant temperature is higher than 50°C (122°F)

• No.6 Terminal: A terminal connected to the START position of the ignition switch (When the ignition key is returned from START to ON, after-glow operation begins.)

• No.7 Terminal: Controls the ON/OFF operation of glow plug relay 2.

• No.8 Terminal: A grounding terminal for the water temperature sensor.

• No.9 Terminal: A terminal for the flow/fuel filter warning lamp

• No.10 Terminal: A terminal used to determine whether the engine has started or not (Glow plug relay is turned OFF by means of terminal (4) immediately after the engine has started.)

GLOW PLUG REMOVAL & INSTALLATION

LD28 Diesel Engine

◆ **See Figure 9**

1. Disconnect the glow plug electrical leads. Remove the glow plug connecting plate.

2. Remove the glow plugs by unscrewing them from the cylinder head.

3. Inspect the tips of the plugs for any evidence of melting. If even one glow plug tip looks bad, all the glow plugs must be replaced. This is a general rule-of-thumb which applies to all diesel engines.

To install:

To install the glow plugs, screw the glow plugs into the cylinder head just like spark plugs. Install the glow plug connecting plate. Tighten the glow plugs to 14–18 ft. lbs., and the glow plug connecting plate bolts to 12 inch lbs.

TESTING

Glow Plugs

Glow plugs are tested by checking their resistance with an ohmmeter. The plugs can be tested either while removed from the cyl-

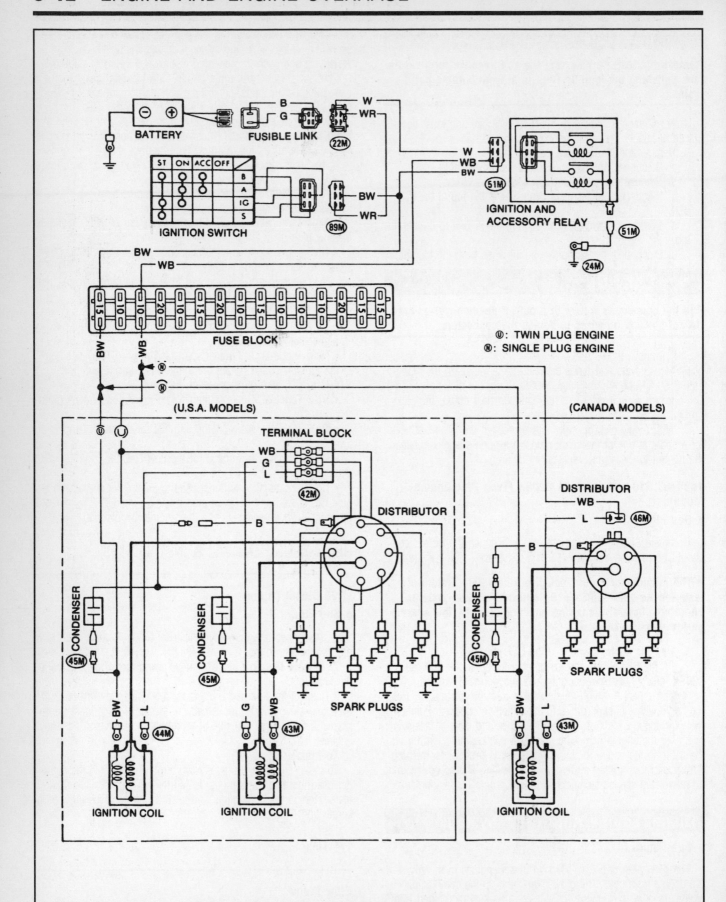

Fig. 7 Electronic ignition schematic—1980–82 510 and 200SX models

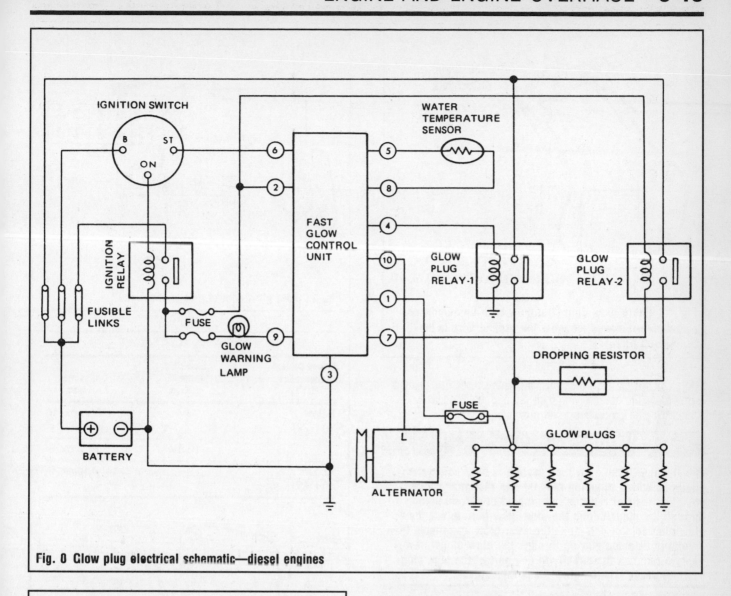

Fig. 0 Glow plug electrical schematic—diesel engines

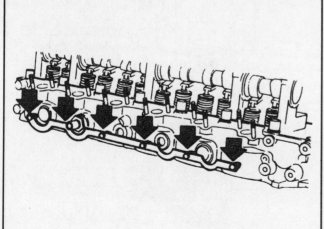

Fig. 9 Remove the fasteners (arrows) to remove the glow plug connector plate

inder head or while still in position. To test them while removed, connect the ground side of the ohmmeter to the threaded section of the plug, and the other side to the plug's tip as shown in the illustration. If a minimum of continuity is shown on the meter, the plug is OK. If no continuity whatsoever is shown the plug must be replaced. To check the glow plugs without removing them from the cylinder head, connect the ground side of the ohmmeter to the engine block (or any other convenient ground) and the other end to the glow plug tip. Likewise, a minimum of continuity shown signifies that the plug is OK; a lack of continuity and the plug must be replaced.

GLOW PLUG CONNECTIONS

▸ **See Figure 10**

A diesel engine's reluctance to start can often be traced to the glow plug busbar (the wire connections to the plugs.) Because diesel engines have a certain degree of vibration when running, they

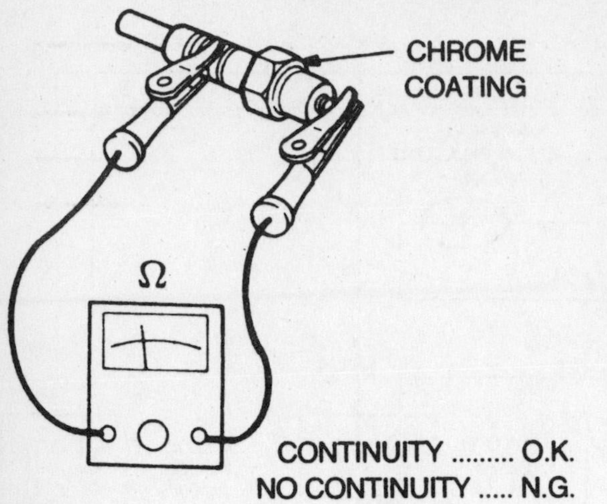

Fig. 10 Check glow plug continuity with an ohmmeter (glow plug removed; connect the ground wire to the threaded portion)

tend to loosen the glow plug busbars. This causes hard starting, as the plugs are not receiving their full current. Periodically tighten the wire connection to all glow plugs.

✲✲ CAUTION

The Datsun/Nissan glow plug system is a 12 volt system equipped with a dropping resistor and fast glow control unit. The resistor reduces the amount of current flowing through the plugs during the after-glow period, and the glow plug control unit stops the after-glow when more than 7 volts is detected flowing through the glow plugs. Never apply a full 12 volts directly to any part of the glow plug system, especially the glow plugs themselves.

Pre-Glow System

See Figures 11 and 12

1. Connect a test light to the blue/yellow wire leading to the glow control unit. Measure the length of time that the test light is lighted.

2. Standard operation (except restart operation within 60 seconds):

Restart operation (within 80 seconds): The length of time the light is ON should be less than 6.5 seconds. For example, when restarting the engine 5 seconds after the ignition switch is turned off, the lamp should be ON for 1.5 seconds (with engine coolant temperature below 122°F and glow plug voltage 10.5 volts).

After-Glow Operation

See Figures 13 and 14

1. Connect a test light to the blue/red wire leading to the glow control unit. Measure the length of time that the light is lighted. In the normal condition, when the ignition switch is turned ON from ST or OFF, and the ignition switch in ST, the test light is on continuously. Refer to the accompanying illustration.

2. After the pre-glow system turns off, check the operation of

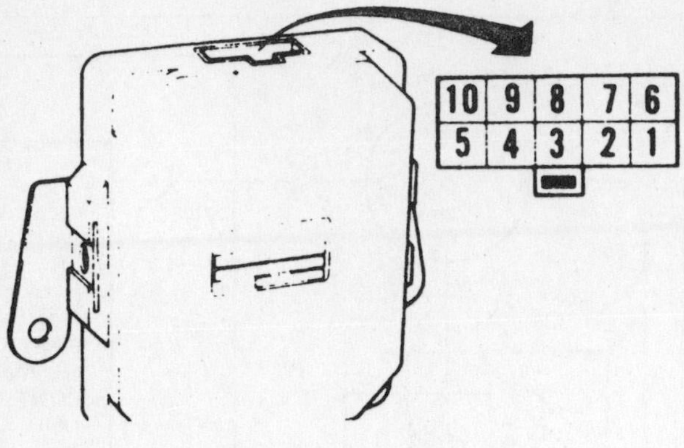

Fig. 11 Fast glow control unit connections

Engine Coolant Temperature °C (°F)	Glow Plug Terminal Voltage	Time (sec.)
Below 50 (122)	8V	Approx. 13
	10.5V	Approx. 6
Above 50 (122)	—	Approx. 0

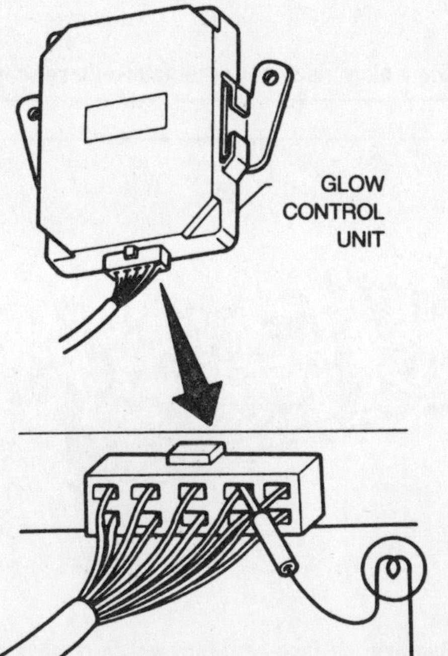

Fig. 12 To check the pre-glow system, connect a test light to the blue/yellow wire leading into the fast glow control unit

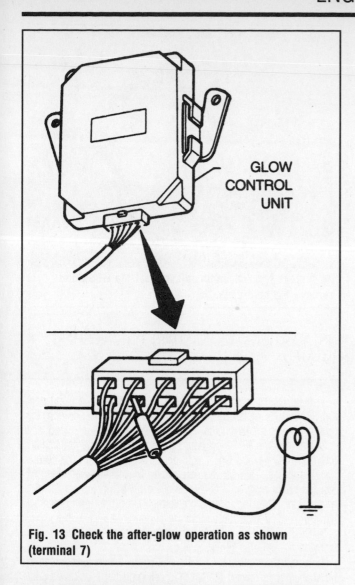

Fig. 13 Check the after-glow operation as shown (terminal 7)

Glow Plug Terminal Voltage	Test Lamp ②
Above 7V	OFF
Below 7V	ON

Fig. 14 Test the on/off operation of the glow plug relays 1 and 2 as shown

the test light (2) in the accompanying illustration; (test light no. (1) in the illustration is OFF).

Water Temperature Sensor

The water temperature sensor is connected to the fast glow control unit. Sensor resistance varies with changes in the temperature of the engine coolant.

◆ See Figure 15

The sensor is tested by measuring resistance while removed from the engine and inserted in a vessel of water as shown in the illustration. Replace the sensor if resistance figures vary greatly from those shown.

Distributor

REMOVAL & INSTALLATION

◆ See Figures 16, 17, 18, 19 and 20

1. Unfasten the retaining clips and lift the distributor cap straight up. It will be easier to install the distributor if the spark plug wires are not disconnected from the cap. If the wires must

be removed from the cap remove the wires one at a time, mark or tag their positions to aid in installation.

2. Disconnect the distributor wiring harness and or the electrical connection if so equipped.

➡**On late model Datsun/Nissan a crank angle sensor is the basic component of the distributor. No vacuum lines are used, just one electrical connection.**

3. Disconnect the vacuum lines if so equipped.
4. Note the position of the rotor in relation to the base. Scribe a mark on the base of the distributor and on the engine block to facilitate reinstallation. Align the marks with the direction the metal tip of the rotor is pointing.
5. Remove the bolt(s) which holds the distributor to the engine.
6. Carefully lift the distributor assembly from the engine.
   To install:

➡**If the crankshaft or camshaft was rotated, refer to the special installation procedure in this section.**

7. Insert the distributor shaft and assembly into the engine. Line up the mark on the distributor and the one on the engine

TEMPERATURE °C ((°F)	RESISTANCE kΩ
10(50)	3.25 – 4.15
20(68)	2.25 – 2.75
50(122)	0.74 – 0.94
80(176)	0.29 – 0.36

Fig. 15 Test the water temperature sensor with an ohmmeter

To remove the distributor, disconnect the wires and remove the hold-down bolt

with the metal tip of the rotor. Make sure that the vacuum advance diaphragm if so equipped is pointed in the same direction as it was pointed originally. This will be done automatically if the marks on the engine and the distributor are lined up with the rotor.

8. Install the distributor hold-down bolt and clamp. Leave the screw loose enough so that you can move the distributor with heavy hand pressure.

9. Connect the primary wire to the coil and or the electrical connection. Install the distributor cap on the distributor housing. Secure the distributor cap with the spring clips.

10. Install the spark plug wires if removed. Make sure that the wires are pressed all the way into the top of the distributor cap and firmly onto the spark plug. Make sure the correct firing order is maintained.

11. Adjust the point dwell if so equipped and set the ignition timing.

➡ If the crankshaft has been turned or the engine disturbed in any manner (i.e., disassembled and rebuilt) while the distributor was removed, or if the marks were not drawn, it will be necessary to initially time the engine. Follow the procedure given below.

INSTALLATION—CRANKSHAFT OR CAMSHAFT ROTATED

1. It is necessary to place the No. 1 cylinder in the firing position to correctly install the distributor. To locate this position, the ignition timing marks on the crankshaft front pulley are used.

2. Remove the No. 1 cylinder spark plug. Turn the crankshaft until the piston in the No. 1 cylinder is moving up on the compression stroke. This can be determined by placing your thumb over the spark plug hole and feeling the air being forced out of the cylinder. Stop turning the crankshaft when the timing marks that are used to time the engine are aligned.

3. Oil the distributor housing lightly where the distributor bears on the cylinder block.

4. Install the distributor so that the rotor, which is mounted on the shaft, points toward the No. 1 spark plug terminal tower position when the cap is installed. Of course you won't be able to see the direction in which the rotor is pointing if the cap is on the distributor. Lay the cap on the top of the distributor and make a mark on the side of the distributor housing just below the No. 1 spark plug terminal. Make sure that the rotor points toward that mark when you install the distributor.

5. When the distributor shaft has reached the bottom of the hole, move the rotor back and forth slightly until the driving lug on the end of the shaft enters the slots cut in the end of the oil pump shaft and the distributor assembly slides down into place.

6. When the distributor is correctly installed, the breaker points should be in such a position that they are just ready to break contact with each other; or, on engines with electronic ignition, the reluctor teeth should be aligned with the pick-up coil. This can be accomplished by rotating the distributor body after it has been installed in the engine. Once again, line up the marks that you made before the distributor was removed.

7. Install the distributor hold-down bolt.

8. Install the spark plug into the No. 1 spark plug hole and continue from Step 3 of the preceding distributor installation procedure.

If your engine has a distributor with a crankangle sensor set up read the above section and then you will be able to remove and install the distributor.

Basically, you have to remove the distributor cap, mark or tag all the spark plug wires and the electrical connections then remove them. Next, mark the postion of the base of the distributor with relation to the engine mounting location and the rotor position as opposed to the the base of the distributor.

When installing the distributor, line up your marks and gently install the distributor and reconnect all spark wires and electrical connections. If you disturb the engine while the distributor is removed you will have to set initial timing.

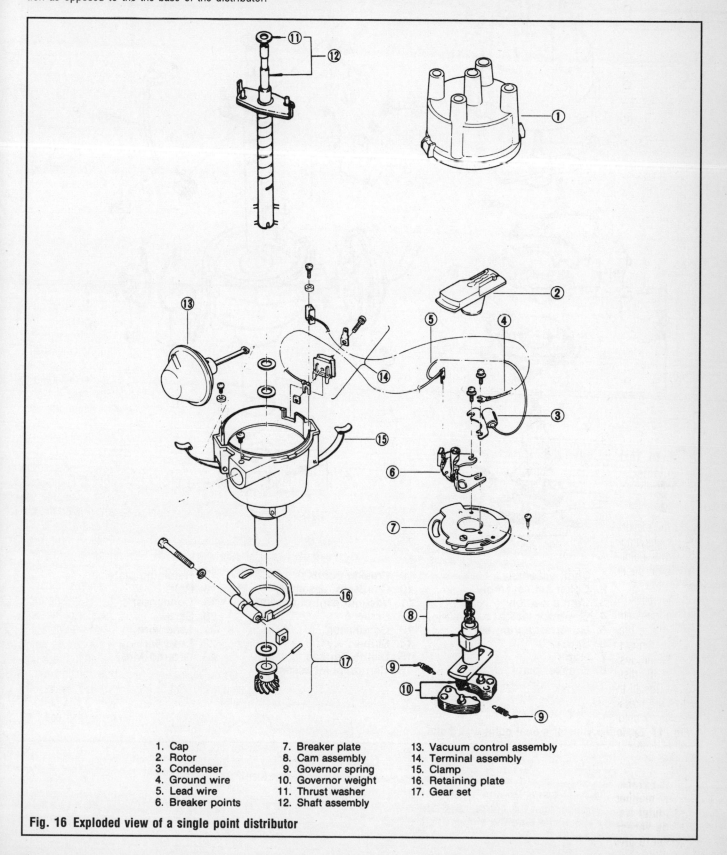

1. Cap
2. Rotor
3. Condenser
4. Ground wire
5. Lead wire
6. Breaker points
7. Breaker plate
8. Cam assembly
9. Governor spring
10. Governor weight
11. Thrust washer
12. Shaft assembly
13. Vacuum control assembly
14. Terminal assembly
15. Clamp
16. Retaining plate
17. Gear set

Fig. 16 Exploded view of a single point distributor

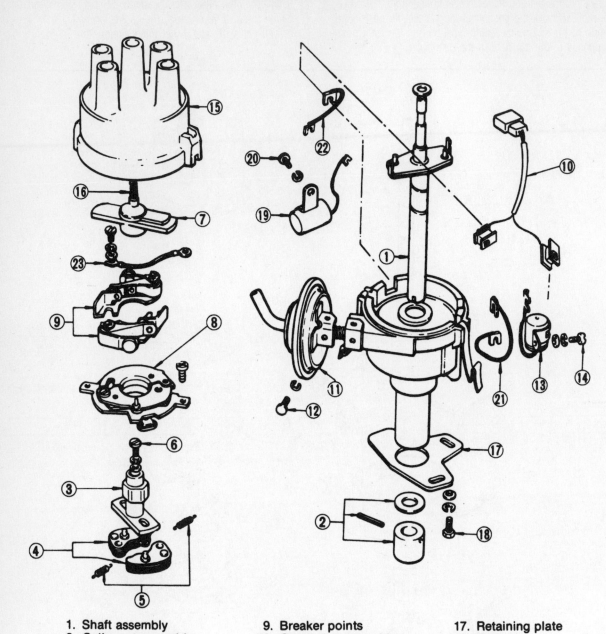

1. Shaft assembly
2. Collar set assembly
3. Cam assembly
4. Governor weight assembly
5. Governor spring set
6. Screw
7. Rotor
8. Breaker plate
9. Breaker points
10. Connector assembly
11. Vacuum control assembly
12. Screw
13. Condenser
14. Screw
15. Distributor cap
16. Carbon point assembly
17. Retaining plate
18. Bolt
19. Condenser
20. Screw
21. Lead wire
22. Lead wire
23. Ground wire

Fig. 17 Exploded view of a dual point distributor

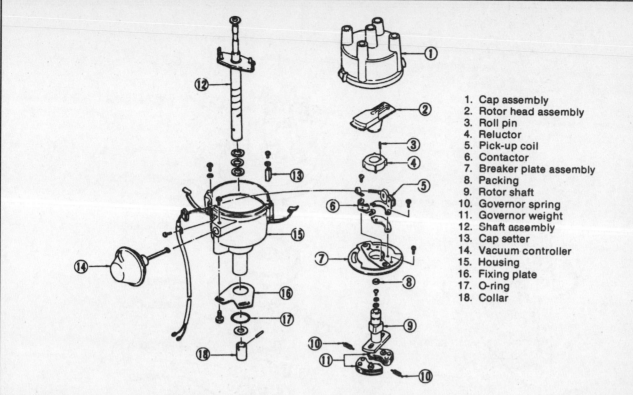

1. Cap assembly
2. Rotor head assembly
3. Roll pin
4. Reluctor
5. Pick-up coil
6. Contactor
7. Breaker plate assembly
8. Packing
9. Rotor shaft
10. Governor spring
11. Governor weight
12. Shaft assembly
13. Cap setter
14. Vacuum controller
15. Housing
16. Fixing plate
17. O-ring
18. Collar

Fig. 18 Exploded view of the distributor—1975–77 610, 710 and 200SX California models and 1977–78 510, 200SX and 810 models

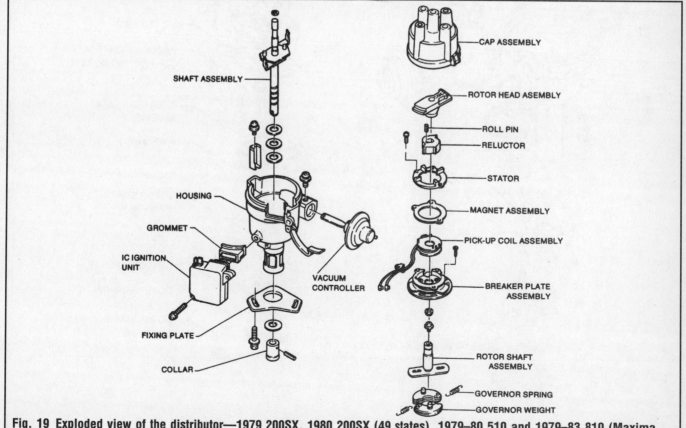

Fig. 19 Exploded view of the distributor—1979 200SX, 1980 200SX (49 states), 1979–80 510 and 1979–83 810 (Maxima similar)

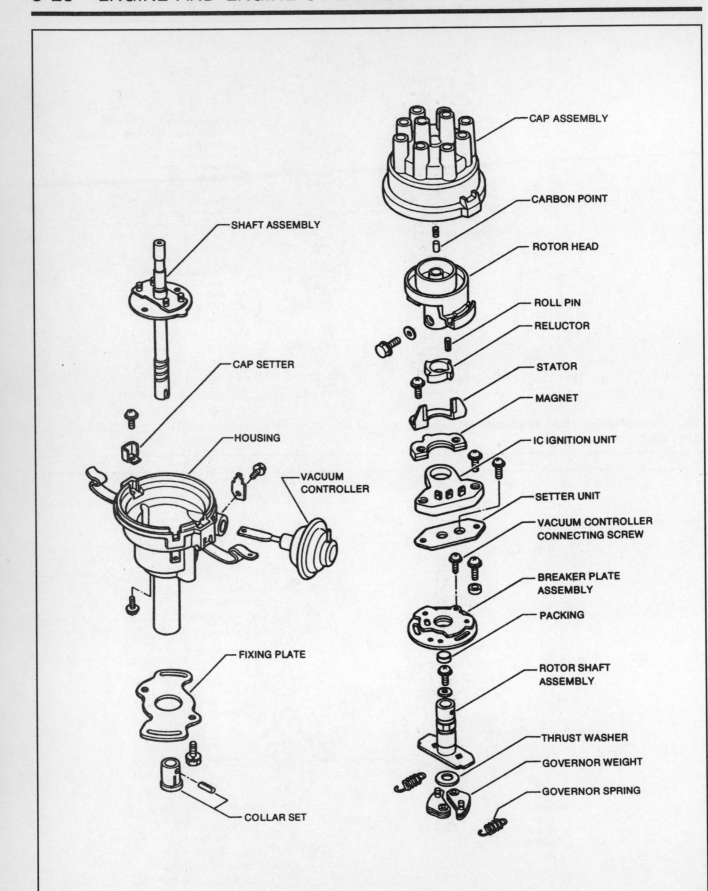

Fig. 20 Exploded view of the twin plug distributor—1980–82 510 and 200SX models

Alternator

♦ **See Figures 21, 22 and 23**

PRECAUTIONS

To prevent damage to the alternator and regulator, the following precautionary measures must be taken when working with the electrical system.

1. Never reverse battery connections.
2. Booster batteries for starting must be connected properly. Make sure that the positive cable of the booster battery is connected to the positive terminal of the battery that is getting the boost. This applies to both negative and ground cables.
3. Disconnect the battery cables before using a fast charger; the charger has a tendency to force current through the diodes in the opposite direction for which they are designed. This burns out the diodes.
4. Never use a fast charger as a booster for starting the vehicle.
5. Never disconnect the voltage regulator while the engine is running.
6. Do not ground the alternator output terminal.
7. Do not operate the alternator on an open circuit with the field energized.
8. Do not attempt to polarize an alternator.

REMOVAL & INSTALLATION

1. Disconnect the negative battery terminal.
2. Disconnect the two lead wires and connector from the alternator.

➡**Depending on the year and model vehicle you are working on, it may be easier to access the lead wires, etc. from either above or below the vehicle.**

3. Loosen the drive belt adjusting bolt and remove the belt.
4. Unscrew the alternator attaching bolts and remove the alternator from the vehicle.
To install:
5. Mount the alternator to the engine and partially tighten the attaching bolts.
6. Reconnect the lead wires and connector to the alternator.
7. Install the alternator drive belt.

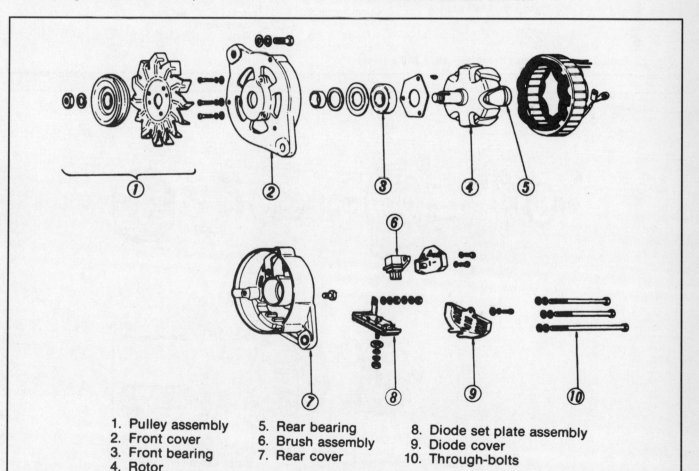

1. Pulley assembly
2. Front cover
3. Front bearing
4. Rotor
5. Rear bearing
6. Brush assembly
7. Rear cover
8. Diode set plate assembly
9. Diode cover
10. Through-bolts

Fig. 21 Exploded view of the alternator—1973–78 models

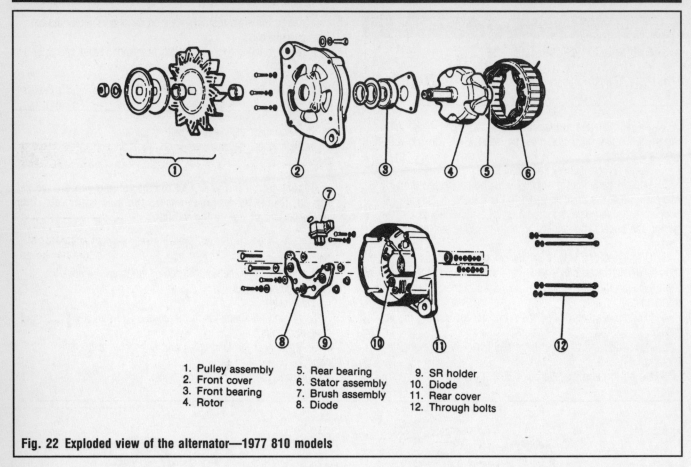

1. Pulley assembly
2. Front cover
3. Front bearing
4. Rotor
5. Rear bearing
6. Stator assembly
7. Brush assembly
8. Diode
9. SR holder
10. Diode
11. Rear cover
12. Through bolts

Fig. 22 Exploded view of the alternator—1977 810 models

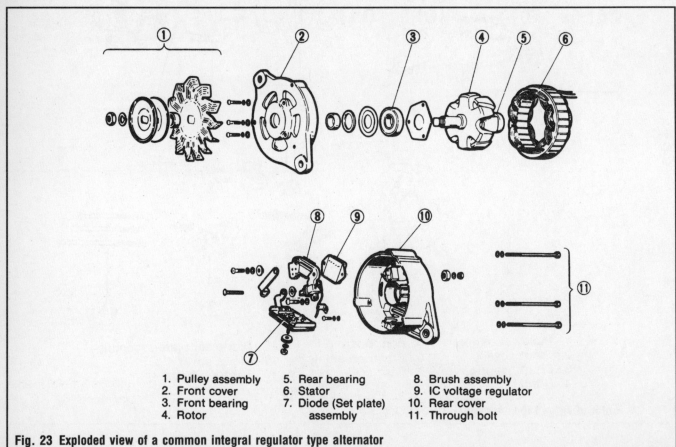

1. Pulley assembly
2. Front cover
3. Front bearing
4. Rotor
5. Rear bearing
6. Stator
7. Diode (Set plate) assembly
8. Brush assembly
9. IC voltage regulator
10. Rear cover
11. Through bolt

Fig. 23 Exploded view of a common integral regulator type alternator

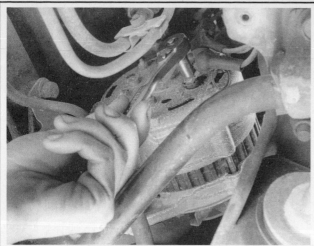

To remove the alternator, remove the nut retaining the main power cable

Disengage the two lead wires from the back of the alternator

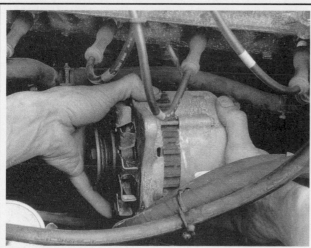

After removing the belts and the alternator attaching bolts, lift the unit from the engine

8. Adjust the alternator belt correctly and completely tighten the mounting bolts.

9. Connect the battery cable. Start the engine and check for proper operation.

➡**The alternator belt tension is quite critical. A belt that is too tight may cause alternator bearing failure; one that is too loose will cause a gradual battery discharge.**

Regulator

REMOVAL & INSTALLATION

➡**1978–84 models are equipped with integral regulator alternators. Since the regulator is part of the alternator no adjustments are possible or necessary.**

1. Disconnect the negative battery terminal.
2. Disconnect the electrical lead connector of the regulator.
3. Remove the two mounting screws and remove the regulator from the vehicle.
4. Install the regulator in the reverse order of removal.

ADJUSTMENT

◆ **See Figures 24, 25 and 26**

1. Adjust the voltage regulator core gap on regulators that are adjustable by loosening the screw which is used to secure the contact set on the yoke, and move the contact up or down as necessary. Retighten the screw. The gap should be 0.60–1.00mm.

2. Adjust the point gap of the voltage regulator coil by loosening the screw used to secure the upper contact and move the upper contact up or down. The gap for 1973–75 models is 0.30–0.40mm. The point gap for all other models is 0.35–0.45mm.

3. The core gap and point gap on the charge relay coil is or are adjusted in the same manner as previously outlined for the voltage regulator coil. The core gap is to be set at 0.80–1.00mm and the point gap adjusted to 0.40–0.60mm.

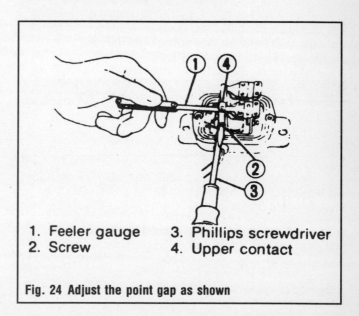

1. Feeler gauge
2. Screw
3. Phillips screwdriver
4. Upper contact

Fig. 24 Adjust the point gap as shown

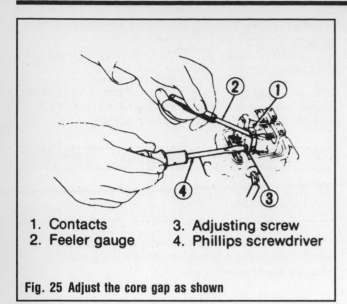

1. Contacts
2. Feeler gauge
3. Adjusting screw
4. Phillips screwdriver

Fig. 25 Adjust the core gap as shown

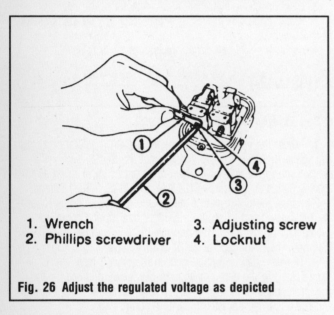

1. Wrench
2. Phillips screwdriver
3. Adjusting screw
4. Locknut

Fig. 26 Adjust the regulated voltage as depicted

4. The regulated voltage is adjusted by loosening the locknut and turning the adjusting screw clockwise to increase, or counterclockwise to decrease the regulated voltage. The voltage should be between 14.3–15.3 volts at 68°F.

Battery

REMOVAL & INSTALLATION

1. Disconnect the negative (ground) cable from the terminal, and then the positive cable. Special pullers are available to remove the cable clamps.

➡**To avoid sparks, always disconnect the ground cable first, and connect it last.**

2. Remove the battery hold-down clamp.
3. Remove the battery, being careful not to spill the acid.

➡**Spilled acid can be neutralized with a baking soda/water solution. If you somehow get acid into your eyes, flush it out with lots of water and get to a doctor.**

4. Clean the battery posts thoroughly before reinstalling, or when installing a new battery.
5. Clean the cable clamps, using a wire brush, both inside and out.
6. Install the battery and the hold-down clamp or strap. Connect the positive, and then the negative cable. Do not hammer them in place. The terminals should be coated lightly (externally) with grease to prevent corrosion. There are also felt washers impregnated with an anti-corrosion substance which are slipped over the battery posts before installing the cables; these are available in auto parts stores.

➡**Make absolutely sure that the battery is connected properly before you turn on the ignition switch. Reversed polarity can burn out your alternator and regulator within a matter of seconds.**

Starter

Datsun/Nissan began using a reduction gear starter in 1978 on the 810 and in the Canadian versions of the 510 and 200SX. They were also available as an option on the U.S. 510 and 200SX. The differences between the gear reduction and conventional starters are: the gear reduction starter has a set of ratio reduction gears while the conventional starter does not; the brushes on the gear reduction starter are located on a plate behind the starter drive housing, while the conventional starter's brushes are located in its rear cover. The extra gears on the gear reduction starter make the starter pinion gear turn at about half the speed of the starter, giving the starter twice the turning power of a conventional starter.

REMOVAL & INSTALLATION

1. Disconnect the negative battery cable from the battery.
2. Disconnect the starter wiring at the starter, taking note of the positions for correct installation.
3. Remove the bolts attaching the starter to the engine and remove the starter from the vehicle.
4. Install the starter to the engine.
5. Tighten the attaching bolts. Be careful not overtighten the mounting bolts as this will crack the nose of the starter case.
6. Install the starter wiring in the correct location.
7. Connect the negative battery cable.
8. Start the engine a few times to make sure of proper operation.

SOLENOID REPLACEMENT

➡**The starter solenoid is also know as the magnetic switch assembly.**

1. Remove the starter from the engine as outlined above.
2. Place the starter in a vise or equivalent to hold the starter in

Alternator and Regulator Specifications

Year	Model	Alternator Identification Number	Rated Output @ 5000 RPM	Output @ 2500 RPM (not less than)	Brush Length (in.)	Brush Spring Tension (oz)	Regulated Voltage
1973	610	LT150-05B	50	37.5	0.571	8.8–12.32	14.3–15.3
1974	610	LT150-05B	50	37.5	0.571	8.8–12.32	14.3–15.3
	710	LT150-13	50	37.5	0.571	8.80	14.3–15.3
1975	610	LT150-13	50	37.5	0.310	9.0–12.2	14.3–15.3
	710	LT150-13	50	37.5	0.571	8.80	14.3–15.3
1976	610	LT150-13	50	37.5	0.310	9.0–12.2	14.3–15.3
	710	LT150-13	50	37.5	0.295	9.0–12.2	14.3–15.3
1977	710	LT150-25	50	37.5	0.295	9.0–12.2	14.3–15.3
	810	LT160-39	60	40	0.310	9.0–12.2	14.3–15.3
	200SX	LT150-35 ①	50	40	0.295	8.99–12.17	14.4–15.0
1978	810	LR160-42 ①	60	40	0.280	8.99–12.17	14.4–15.0
	510	LR150-35 ①	50	40	0.295	8.99–12.17	14.4–15.0
		LR160-47 ①②	60	41	0.295	8.99–12.17	14.4–15.0
	200SX	LR150-35 ①	50	40	0.295	8.99–12.17	14.4–15.0
1979	810	LR160-42 ①	60	40	0.280	8.99–12.17	14.4–15.0
	510	LR150-35 ①	50	40	0.295	8.99–12.17	14.4–15.0
		LR160-47 ①②	60	41	0.295	8.99–12.17	14.4–15.0
	200SX	LR150-35 ①	50	40	0.295	8.99–12.17	14.4–15.0
1980	810	LR160-42B ①	60	50	0.295	8.99–12.17	14.4–15.0
	510	LR150-52 ①	50	40	0.295	8.99–12.17	14.4–15.0
	200SX	LR160-47 ①	60	45	0.295	8.99–12.17	14.4–15.0
1981	810 (L24)	LR160-82 ①	60	50	0.280	8.99–12.17	14.4–15.0
	810 (LD28)	LR160-97 ①	60	52	0.240	10.79–14.60	14.4–15.0
	510	LR150-98 ①	50	40	0.295	8.99–12.17	14.4–15.0
		LR160-78 ①②	60	50	0.276	8.99–12.17	14.4–15.0
	200SX	LR160-78 ①	60	50	0.280	8.99–12.17	14.4–15.0
1982	810 (L24)	LR160-82B ①	60	50	0.280	8.99–12.17	14.4–15.0
	810 (LD28)	LR160-97B ①	60	52	0.240	10.79–14.60	14.4–15.0
1983–84	Maxima (L24E)	LR160-82B ①	60	50	0.280	8.99–12.17	14.4–15.0
	Maxima (LD28)	LR160-97C ①	60	50	0.280	8.99–12.17	14.4–15.0

① Uses integral voltage regulator
② Optional in US, standard in Canada

place while you are working on the solenoid. DO NOT tighten the vise to tight around the case of the starter. The case will crack if you tighten the vise to much.

3. Loosen the locknut and remove the connection from the starter motor going to the **M** terminal of the solenoid or bottom terminal of the solenoid.

4. Remove the securing screws and remove the solenoid.

5. Install the solenoid to the starter and tighten the securing screws.

6. Install the connection and locknut at bottom terminal of the starter.

OVERHAUL

Brush Replacement

NON-REDUCTION GEAR TYPE

▶ See Figure 27

1. With the starter out of the vehicle, remove the bolts holding the solenoid to the top of the starter and remove the solenoid.

2. To remove the brushes, remove the 2 through-bolts, the 2 rear cover attaching screws (some models) and the rear cover.

To remove the starter, disconnect the lead wires, then unbolt the unit from the engine

Pull the starter away from the engine, wiggling it slightly if necessary, to disengage the gears

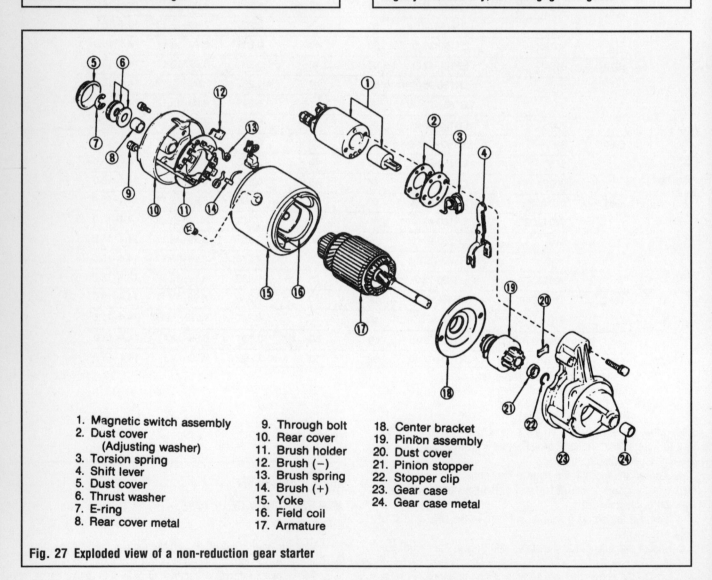

1. Magnetic switch assembly
2. Dust cover
   (Adjusting washer)
3. Torsion spring
4. Shift lever
5. Dust cover
6. Thrust washer
7. E-ring
8. Rear cover metal
9. Through bolt
10. Rear cover
11. Brush holder
12. Brush (−)
13. Brush spring
14. Brush (+)
15. Yoke
16. Field coil
17. Armature
18. Center bracket
19. Pinion assembly
20. Dust cover
21. Pinion stopper
22. Stopper clip
23. Gear case
24. Gear case metal

Fig. 27 Exploded view of a non-reduction gear starter

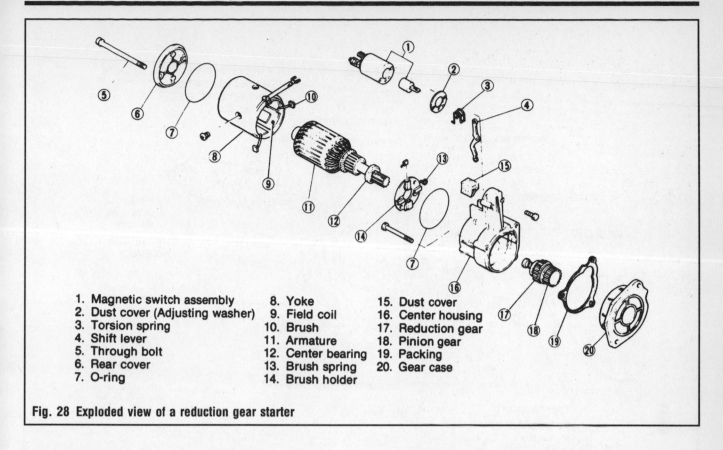

1. Magnetic switch assembly
2. Dust cover (Adjusting washer)
3. Torsion spring
4. Shift lever
5. Through bolt
6. Rear cover
7. O-ring
8. Yoke
9. Field coil
10. Brush
11. Armature
12. Center bearing
13. Brush spring
14. Brush holder
15. Dust cover
16. Center housing
17. Reduction gear
18. Pinion gear
19. Packing
20. Gear case

Fig. 28 Exploded view of a reduction gear starter

➡ **Remove the dust cover, E-ring and thrust washers from the armature shaft before the rear cover.**

3. Using a wire hook, lift the brush springs to separate the brushes from the commutator.

4. Install the brushes in the reverse order of removal and reassemble the rear cover to the starter.

REDUCTION GEAR TYPE

▶ **See Figures 28 and 29**

1. Remove the starter, then the solenoid or magnetic switch.
2. Remove the dust cover, E-ring and thrust washers.
3. Remove the starter through-bolts and brush holder setscrews.
4. Remove the rear cover. The rear cover can be pried off with a screwdriver, be careful not to damage the O-ring or gasket if equipped.
5. Remove the starter housing, armature and brush holder from the center housing. They can be removed as an assembly.
6. Using a wire hook on the spring, lift the spring then remove the positive side brush from its holder. The positive brush is insulated from the brush holder and its lead wire is connected to the field coil.
7. Using a wire hook on the spring, lift the spring and remove the negative brush from the holder.
8. Replace all the brushes in the starter assembly.
9. Insert the new brushes in the brush holder.

10. Install the starter housing, armature and brush holder to the center housing.
11. Install the brush holder setscrews, rear cover and starter through-bolts.
12. Install the thrust washers, E-ring and dust cover.
13. Install the solenoid or magnetic switch.

Starter Drive Replacement

NON-REDUCTION GEAR TYPE

▶ **See Figure 30**

1. With the starter motor removed from the vehicle, remove the solenoid from the starter.
2. Remove the 2 through-bolts at the rear cover but do not disassemble the entire starter. Mark the front gear cover with relationship to the yoke housing.
3. Separate the front gear case from the yoke housing, then the shift lever from the armature, without removing the armature from starter assembly.
4. Push the pinion stopper toward the rear cover, then remove the pinion stopper clip and the pinion stopper.
5. Slide the starter drive from the armature shaft.
6. Install the starter drive on the armature shaft.
7. Install pinion stopper and stopper clip.
8. Reassemble the front gear case to the yoke and the shift lever to the armature.
9. Install the rear cover through-bolts.
10. Install the solenoid or the magnetic switch.

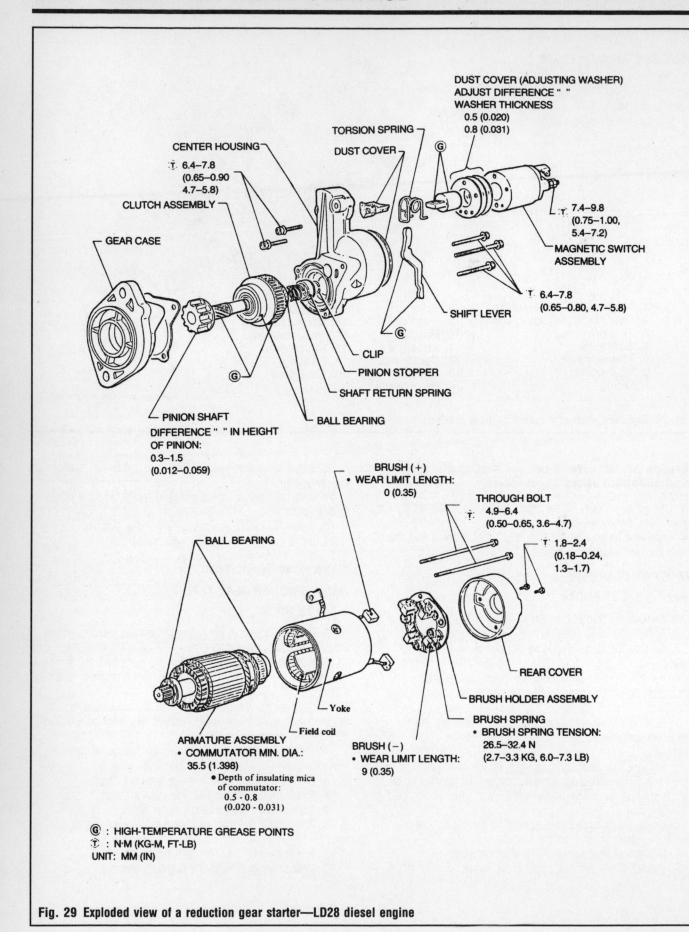

Fig. 29 Exploded view of a reduction gear starter—LD28 diesel engine

REDUCTION GEAR TYPE

1. Remove the starter.
2. Remove the solenoid and the torsion spring. Mark the front housing with relationship to the center housing.
3. Remove the center housing-to-front housing bolts, then separate the front housing from the center housing. Do not disassemble the entire starter.
4. Remove the pinion/reduction gear assembly from the armature shaft.

➡It may be necessary to remove the shift lever pivot pin, to disconnect the pinion/reduction gear assembly from the armature shaft.

5. Installation is the reverse of the removal procedures. The best idea is to try not to disassemble the entire starter when removing the pinion/reduction gear. Do not disturb the brush assembly in the rear cover.

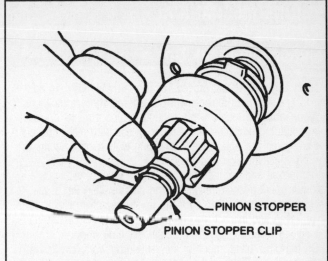

Fig. 30 Remove the pinion stopper as shown

Battery and Starter Specifications

All cars use 12 volt, negative ground electrical systems

| Year | Model | Battery Amp Hour Capacity | Starter | | | | | | | Brush Spring Tension (oz) | Min Brush Length (in.) |
| | | | Lock Test | | | No Load Test | | | | |
			Amps	Volts	Torque (ft. lbs.)	Amps	Volts	RPM		
1973–77	610, 710	50, 60	430 MT	6.0	6.3	60	12	7,000	49–64	0.47
			540 AT	5.0	6.0	60	12	6,000	49–64	0.47
1977–78	200SX, 510	60	—	—	—	60 MT	12	7,000	49–64	0.47
						60 AT	12	6,000	49–64	0.47
						100 RG	12	4,300	56–70	0.43
1979–82	200SX, 510	60 ①	—	—	—	60 MT	11.5	7,000	49–64	0.47
						60 AT	11.5	6,000	49–64	0.47
						100 RG	11.0	3,900	56–70	0.43
1977–79	810	60 ②	—	—	—	100 RG	12	4,300	56–70	0.43
1980–82	810 (L24)	60 ②	—	—	—	100 RG	11	3,900	56–70	0.43
	810 (LD28)	80	—	—	—	100 RG	11	3,900	96–116.8	0.35
1983–84	Maxima (L24E)	60 ②	—	—	—	100 RG	11	3,900	56–70	0.43
	Maxima (LD28)	80	—	—	—	140 RG	11	3,900	96–116.8	0.35

MT: Manual Transmission
AT: Automatic Transmission
RG: Reduction Gear Starter
—: Not Recommended
① Canada—65
② Canada, optional U.S.—70

ENGINE MECHANICAL

Engine Overhaul Tips

Most engine overhaul procedures are fairly standard. In addition to specific parts replacement procedures and specifications for your individual engine, this section is also a guide to acceptable rebuilding procedures. Examples of standard rebuilding practice are given and should be used along with specific details concerning your particular engine.

Competent and accurate machine shop services will ensure maximum performance, reliability and engine life. In most instances it is more profitable for the do-it-yourself mechanic to remove, clean and inspect the component, buy the necessary parts and deliver these to a shop for actual machine work.

On the other hand, much of the rebuilding work (crankshaft, block, bearings, piston rods, and other components) is well within the scope of the do-it-yourself mechanic's tools and abilities. You will have to decide for yourself the depth of involvement you desire in an engine repair or rebuild.

TOOLS

The tools required for an engine overhaul or parts replacement will depend on the depth of your involvement. With a few exceptions, they will be the tools found in a mechanic's tool kit (see Section 1 of this manual). More in-depth work will require some or all of the following:
- A dial indicator (reading in thousandths) mounted on a universal base
- Micrometers and telescope gauges
- Jaw and screw-type pullers
- Scraper
- Valve spring compressor
- Ring groove cleaner
- Piston ring expander and compressor
- Ridge reamer
- Cylinder hone or glaze breaker
- Plastigage®
- Engine stand

The use of most of these tools is illustrated in this chapter. Many can be rented for a one-time use from a local parts jobber or tool supply house specializing in automotive work.

Occasionally, the use of special tools is called for. See the information on Special Tools and the Safety Notice in the front of this book before substituting another tool.

INSPECTION TECHNIQUES

Procedures and specifications are given in this chapter for inspecting, cleaning and assessing the wear limits of most major components. Other procedures such as Magnaflux® and Zyglo® can be used to locate material flaws and stress cracks. Magnaflux® is a magnetic process applicable only to ferrous materials. The Zyglo® process coats the material with a fluorescent dye penetrant and can be used on any material.

Checking for suspected surface cracks can be more readily made using spot check dye. The dye is sprayed onto the suspected area, wiped off and the area sprayed with a developer. Cracks will show up brightly.

OVERHAUL TIPS

Aluminum has become extremely popular for use in engines, due to its low weight. Observe the following precautions when handling aluminum parts:
- Never hot tank aluminum parts (the caustic hot tank solution will eat the aluminum.
- Remove all aluminum parts (identification tag, etc.) from engine parts prior to the tanking.
- Always coat threads lightly with engine oil or anti-seize compounds before installation, to prevent seizure.
- Never overtorque bolts or spark plugs especially in aluminum threads.

Stripped threads in any component can be repaired using any of several commercial repair kits (Heli-Coil®, Microdot®, Keenserts®, etc.).

When assembling the engine, any parts that will be exposed to frictional contact must be prelubed to provide lubrication at initial start-up. Any product specifically formulated for this purpose can be used, but engine oil is not recommended as a prelube in most cases.

When semi-permanent (locked, but removable) installation of bolts or nuts is desired, threads should be cleaned and coated with Loctite® or another similar, commercial non-hardening sealant.

REPAIRING DAMAGED THREADS

Several methods of repairing damaged threads are available. Heli-Coil® (shown here), Keenserts® and Microdot® are among the most widely used. All involve basically the same principle—drilling out stripped threads, tapping the hole and installing a prewound insert—making welding, plugging and oversize fasteners unnecessary.

Two types of thread repair inserts are usually supplied: a standard type for most inch coarse, inch fine, metric course and metric fine thread sizes and a spark lug type to fit most spark plug port sizes. Consult the individual tool manufacturer's catalog to determine exact applications. Typical thread repair kits will contain a selection of prewound threaded inserts, a tap (corresponding to the outside diameter threads of the insert) and an installation tool. Spark plug inserts usually differ because they require a tap equipped with pilot threads and a combined reamer/tap section. Most manufacturers also supply blister-packed thread repair inserts separately in addition to a master kit containing a variety of taps and inserts plus installation tools.

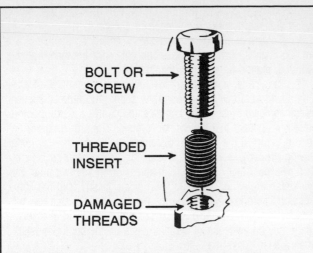

Damaged bolt hole threads can be replaced with thread repair inserts

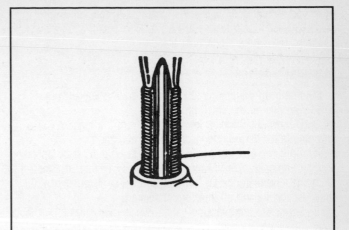

Using the kit, tap the hole in order to receive the thread insert. Keep the tap well oiled and back it out frequently to avoid clogging the threads

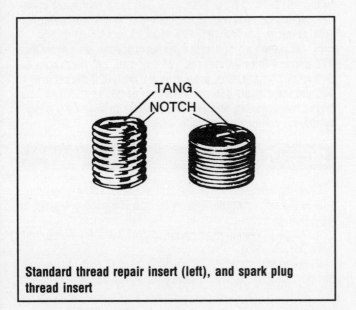

Standard thread repair insert (left), and spark plug thread insert

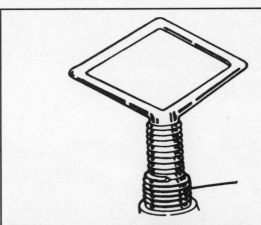

Screw the insert onto the installer tool until the tang engages the slot. Thread the insert into the hole until it is 1/4–1/2 turn below the top surface, then remove the tool and break off the tang using a punch

Before attempting to repair a threaded hole, remove any snapped, broken or damaged bolts or studs. Penetrating oil can be used to free frozen threads. The offending item can usually be removed with locking pliers or using a screw/stud extractor. After the hole is clear, the thread can be repaired, as shown in the series of accompanying illustrations and in the kit manufacturer's instructions.

Checking Engine Compression

A noticeable lack of engine power, excessive oil consumption and/or poor fuel mileage measured over an extended period are all indicators of internal engine war. Worn piston rings, scored or worn cylinder bores, blown head gaskets, sticking or burnt valves and worn valve seats are all possible culprits here. A check of each cylinder's compression will help you locate the problems.

As mentioned in the Tools and Equipment section of Chapter 1, a screw-in type compression gauge is more accurate that the

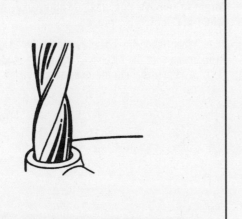

Drill out the damaged threads with the specified size bit. Be sure to drill completely through the hole or to the bottom of a blind hole

type you simply hold against the spark plug hole, although it takes slightly longer to use. It's worth it to obtain a more accurate reading. Follow the procedures below.

Gasoline Engines

1. Warm up the engine to normal operating temperature.
2. Remove all the spark plugs.
3. Disconnect the high tension lead from the ignition coil or the distributor harness connection if so equipped.
4. On carbureted cars fully open the throttle either by operating the carburetor throttle linkage by hand or by having an assistant floor the accelerator pedal. On fuel injected cars, disconnect the cold start valve and all injector connections.
5. Screw the compression gauge into the No.1 spark plug hole until the fitting is snug.

➡️**Be careful not to crossthread the plug hole. On aluminum cylinder heads use extra care, as the threads in these heads are easily ruined.**

6. Ask an assistant to depress the accelerator pedal fully on both carbureted and fuel injected vehicles. Then, while you read the compression gauge, ask the assistant to crank the engine four times in short bursts using the ignition switch.
7. Read the compression gauge at the end of each series of cranks, and record the highest of these readings. Repeat this procedure for each of the engine's cylinders. Compare the highest

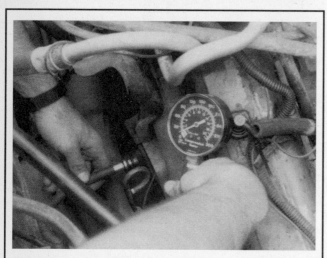

A screw-in type compression gauge is more accurate and easier to use without an assistant

reading of each cylinder to the compression pressure specification in the Tune-Up Specifications chart in Section 2.

A cylinder's compression pressure is usually acceptable if it is not less than 80% of maximum. The difference between any two cylinders should be no more than 12–14 psi.

8. If a cylinder is unusually low, pour a tablespoon of clean engine oil into the cylinder through the spark plug hole and repeat the compression test. If the compression comes up after adding the oil, it appears that the cylinder's piston rings or bore are damaged or worn. If the pressure remains low, the valves may not be seating properly (a valve job is needed), or the head gasket may be blown near that cylinder. If compression in any two adjacent cylinders is low, and if the addition of oil doesn't help the compression, there is leakage past the head gasket. Oil and coolant water in the combustion chamber can result from this problem. There may be evidence of water droplets on the engine dipstick when a head gasket has blown.

➡️**Maximum cylinder compression for all Datsun/Nissan gasoline engines covered in this guide (except the L24 engine in the 1977–78 810) is 171 psi at 350 rpm. Minimum cylinder compression is 128 psi at 350 rpm. Maximum compression pressure for the 1977–78 810 L24 is 185 psi at 350 rpm. Maximum compression pressure for the V6 engine is 173 psi and the minimum is 128 psi; both are measured at 300 rpm. Compression pressures for the LD28 diesel are 455 psi maximum, 356 psi minimum at 200 rpm. When analyzing compression test results, look for uniformity among cylinders, rather than specific pressures.**

Diesel Engines

Checking compression on the Datsun/Nissan LD28 diesel engine is the same procedure as on the gasoline engines, except for the following:

1. A special compression gauge adaptor suitable for diesel engines must be used.
2. Begin the procedure by removing the spill tube assembly, the injection tubes on the nozzle side, and nozzle assemblies.

➡️**Remove the nozzle washer with a pair of tweezers. Don't forget to remove this washer; otherwise, it may get lost when the engine is cranked.**

3. When fitting the compression gauge adaptor to the cylinder head, make sure the bleeder of the gauge is closed.
4. When reinstalling the injector assemblies, install new nozzle washers.

General Engine Specifications

Year	Car Model	Engine Model	Engine Displacement Cu. in. (cc)	Carburetor Type	Horsepower (@ rmp)	Torque (@ rpm (ft. lbs.)	Bore x Stroke (in.)	Compression Ratio	Oil Pressure @ rpm (psi)
1973	610	L18	108.0 (1770)	2 BBL	105 @ 6000	108 @ 3600	3.35 x 3.307	8.5:1	50–57
1974	610	L20B	119.1 (1952)	2 BBL	110 @ 3500	112 @ 3600	3.35 x 3.39	8.5:1	50–57
	710	L18	108.0 (1770)	2 BBL	105 @ 6000	108 @ 3600	3.35 x 3.307	8.5:1	50–57
1975	610	L20B	119.1 (1952)	2 BBL	110 @ 5600	112 @ 3600	3.35 x 3.39	8.5:1	50–57
	710	L20B	119.1 (1952)	2 BBL	100 @ 5600	100 @ 3600	3.35 x 3.39	8.5:1	50–57
1976	610	L20B	119.1 (1952)	2 BBL	112 @ 5600	108 @ 3600	3.35 x 3.39	8.5:1	50–57
	710	L20B	119.1 (1952)	2 BBL	110 @ 5600	112 @ 5600	3.35 x 3.39	8.5:1	50–57
1977	200SX	L20B	119.1 (1952)	2 BBL	97 @ 5600	102 @ 3200	3.35 x 3.39	8.5:1	50–57
	710	L20B	119.1 (1952)	2 BBL	110 @ 5600	112 @ 5600	3.35 x 3.39	8.5:1	50–57
	810	L24	146.0 (2393)	EFI	154 @ 5600	155 @ 4400	3.27 x 2.90	8.6:1	50–57
1978	200SX	L20B	119.1 (1952)	2 BBL	97 @ 5600	102 @ 3200	3.35 x 3.39	8.5:1	50–57
	510	L20B	119.1 (1952)	2 BBL	97 @ 5600	102 @ 3200	3.35 x 3.39	8.5:1	50–57
	810	L24	146.0 (2393)	EFI	154 @ 5600	155 @ 4400	3.27 x 2.90	8.6:1	50–57
1979	200SX	L20B	119.1 (1952)	2 BBL	92 @ 5600	107 @ 3200	3.35 x 3.39	8.5:1	50–57
	510	L20B	119.1 (1952)	2 BBL	92 @ 5600	107 @ 3200	3.35 x 3.39	8.5:1	50–57
	810	L24	146.0 (2393)	EFI	120 @ 5200	125 @ 4400	3.27 x 2.90	8.9:1	50–60
1980	200SX	Z20E	119.1 (1952)	EFI	100 @ 5200	112 @ 3200	3.35 x 3.39	8.5:1	50–60
	510	L20B ② Z20E ③	119.1 (1952)	2 BBL	92 @ 5200	112 @ 2800	3.35 x 3.39	8.5:1	50–60
	810	L24	119.1 (1952)	EFI	120 @ 5200	125 @ 4400	3.27 x 2.90	8.9:1 ①	50–60
1981	200SX	Z20E	119.1 (1952)	EFI	100 @ 5200	112 @ 3200	3.35 x 3.39	8.5:1	50–60
	510	Z20S	119.1 (1952)	2 BBL	92 @ 5200	112 @ 2800	3.35 x 3.39	8.5:1	50–60
	810	L24E	146.0 (2393)	EFI	120 @ 5200	134 @ 2800	3.27 x 2.90	8.9:1	50–60
	810 Diesel	LD28	170.0 (2793)	DFI	80 @ 4600	120 @ 2400	3.33 x 3.27	22.7:1	NA
1982–83	810 Maxima	L24E	146.0 (2393)	EFI	120 @ 5200	134 @ 2800	3.27 x 2.90	8.9:1	50–60
	810 Diesel	LD28	170.0 (2793)	DFI	80 @ 4600	120 @ 2400	3.33 x 3.27	22.7:1	NA
1984	Maxima	L24E	146.0 (2393)	EFI	120 @ 5200	134 @ 2800	3.27 x 2.90	8.9:1	50–60

NA: Not Available
DFI: Diesel Fuel Injection
① 8.6 in California
② Canadian models
③ U.S. models

Valve Specifications

Engine	Seat Angle (deg)	Face Angle (deg)	Spring Test Pressure (lbs. @ in.)		Spring Installed Height (in.)		Stem to Guide Clearance (in.)		Stem Diameter (in.)	
			Outer	Inner	Outer	Inner	Intake	Exhaust	Intake	Exhaust
L18, L20B	45	45	108 @ 1.161	56.2 @ 0.965	1.575	1.378	0.0008–0.0021	0.0016–0.0029	0.3136–0.3142	0.3128–0.3134
Z20E, Z20S	45	45	115.3 @ 1.18	57 @ 0.98	1.575	1.378	0.0008–0.0021	0.0016–0.0029	0.3136–0.3142	0.3128–0.3434
L24	45	45	108 @ 1.161 ①	56.2 @ 0.965 ①	1.575	1.378	0.0008–0.0021	0.0016–0.0029	0.3136–0.3142	0.3128–0.3134
LD28	45	45	115.3 @ 1.181	—	1.575	—	0.0008–0.0021	0.0016–0.0029	0.3136–0.3142	0.3128–0.3134

① Figure is for Exhaust; for Intake: Outer 105.2 @ 1.181
Inner 54.9 @ 0.984

Camshaft Specifications
(All measurements in inches)

Engine	Journal Diameter					Bearing Clearance	Lobe Lift		Camshaft End-Play
	1	2	3	4	5		Intake	Exhaust	
L18, L20B	1.8878–1.8883	1.8878–1.8883	1.8878–1.8883	1.8878–1.8883	—	0.0015–0.0026	0.276	0.276	0.0031–0.0150
Z20E, Z20S, Z22E	1.2967–1.2974	1.2967–1.2974	1.2967–1.2974	1.2967–1.2974	—	0.0018–0.0035	NA	NA	0.008
L24, LD28	1.8878–1.8883	1.8878–1.8883	1.8878–1.8883	1.8878–1.8883	1.8878–1.8883	0.0015–0.0026	0.262	0.276	0.0031–0.0150

Crankshaft and Connecting Rod Specifications
All measurements given in inches

Engine Model	Crankshaft				Connecting Rod Bearings		
	Main Brg Journal Dia	Main Brg Oil Clearance	Shaft End-Play	Thrust on No.	Journal Dia	Oil Clearance	Side Clearance
L18	2.1631–2.1636	0.001–0.002	0.002–0.007	3	1.9670–1.9675	0.001–0.002	0.008–0.012
L18 (710)	2.3599–2.360	0.0008–0.002	0.002–0.007	3	1.967–1.9675	0.001–0.002	0.008–0.012
L20B	2.3599–2.360	0.0008–0.0024	0.002–0.007	3	1.9660–1.9670	0.001–0.002	0.008–0.012
Z20S, Z20E	2.1631–2.1636	0.0008–0.0024	0.002–0.0071	3	1.967–1.9675	0.001–0.0022	0.008–0.012
L24	2.1631–2.1636	0.0008–0.0026	0.002–0.0071	Center	1.9670–1.9675	0.001–0.003	0.008–0.012
L24E	2.1631–2.1636	0.0008–0.0026	0.0020–0.0071	Center	1.7701–1.7706	0.0009–0.0024	0.008–0.012
LD28	2.1631–2.1636	0.0008–0.0024	0.0020–0.0071	Center	1.9670–1.9675	0.0008–0.0024	0.008–0.012

Piston and Ring Specifications

All measurements in inches

Engine Model	Piston Clearance	Ring Gap			Ring Side Clearance		
		Top Compression	Bottom Compression	Oil Control	Top Compression	Bottom Compression	Oil Control
L18	0.001–0.002	0.014–0.022	0.012–0.020	0.012–0.035	0.002–0.003	0.002–0.003	—
L20B	0.001–0.002	0.010–0.016	0.012–0.020	0.012–0.035	0.002–0.003	0.001–0.003	—
Z20E, Z20S	0.001–0.002	0.0098–0.016	0.006–0.012	0.012–0.035	0.002–0.003	0.001–0.0025	—
L24	0.001–0.002	0.010–0.016	0.006–0.012	0.012–0.035	0.002–0.003	0.001–0.003	①
LD28	0.0020–0.0028	②	0.0079–0.0138	0.0118–0.0177	0.0024–0.0039	0.0016–0.0031	0.0012–0.0028

—Not applicable
① 1977–80—combined
   1981—0.009–0.0028
   1982—0.010
② Without mark—0.0079–0.0114
   With mark—0.0055–0.0087

Torque Specifications

All readings in ft. lbs.

Engine Model	Cylinder Head Bolts	Main Bearing Bolts	Rod Bearing Bolts	Crankshaft Pulley Bolts	Flywheel to Crankshaft Bolts	Manifold	
						Intake	Exhaust
L18	47–62	33–40	33–40	87–116	101–116	9–12	9–12
L20B	51–61	33–40	33–40	87–116	101–116	9–12	9–12
Z20E, Z20S	51–58	33–40	33–40	87–116	101–116	12–15	12–15
L24	51–61	33–40	33–40	101–116	94–108	①	
LD28	87–94	51–61	33–40	101–116	101–116	②	

① M10 bolt: 25–35 ft. lbs.
  M8 bolt: 11–18 ft. lbs.
  M8 nut: 9–12 ft. lbs.
② Upper bolt (M10): 24–27 ft. lbs.
  Lower nut and bolt (M8): 12–18 ft. lbs.

Engine

REMOVAL & INSTALLATION

▶ **See Figure 31**

Rear Wheel Drive Models
▶ **See Figure 32**

The engine and transmission are removed together and then separated when out of the car. Always observe the following cautions:

• Make sure the vehicle is on a flat and leevel surface and that wheels are tightly chocked. Use the chocks on both sides of the rear wheels on front wheel drive cars.

• Allow the exhaust system to cool completely before starting work to prevent burns and possible fire as fuel lines are disconnected.

• Release fuel pressure from the fuel system before attempting to disconnect any fuel lines.

• When lifting the engine out, guide it carefully to avoid hitting parts such as the master cylinder.

• Mount the engine securely and then release the tension of lifting chains to avoid injury as you work on the engine.

1. Mark the location of the hinges on the hood. Unbolt and remove the hood.

2. Disconnect the battery cables. Remove the battery from the models with the L16 engine and Z20E models with air conditioning.

3. Drain the coolant and automatic transmission fluid.

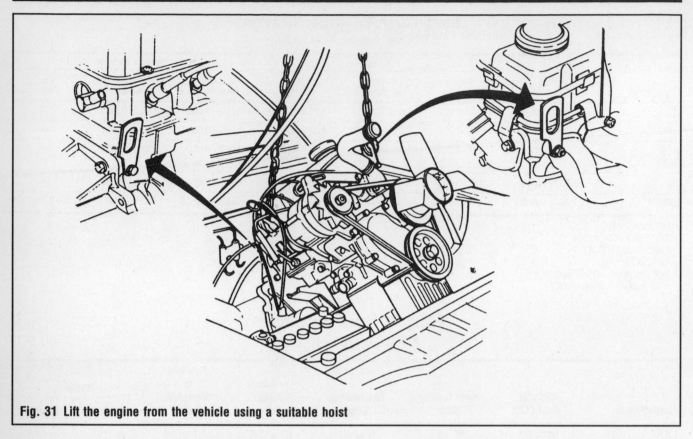

Fig. 31 Lift the engine from the vehicle using a suitable hoist

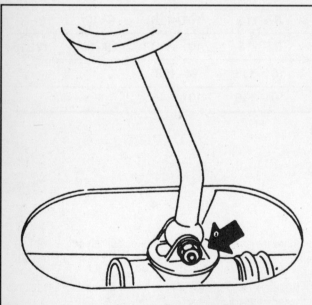

Fig. 32 Remove the gearshift lever, if necessary, to remove the engine/transmission assembly

➡When draining the coolant, keep in mind that cats and dogs are attracted by ethylene glycol antifreeze, and are quite likely to drink any that is left in an uncovered container or in puddles on the ground. This will prove fatal in sufficient quantity. Always drain the coolant into a sealable container. Coolant should be reused unless it is contaminated or several years old.

4. Remove the grille on the 510, 610, and 710 models. Remove the radiator and radiator shroud after disconnecting the automatic transmission coolant tubes.
5. Remove the air cleaner.
6. Remove the fan and pulley.
7. Disconnect:
   a. water temperature gauge wire;
   b. oil pressure sending unit wire;
   c. ignition distributor primary wire;
   d. starter motor connections;
   e. fuel hose;

✳✳ CAUTION

On all fuel injected models, the fuel pressure must be released before the fuel lines can be disconnected. See the pressure releasing procedure under Gasoline Engine Fuel Filter in Section 1.

   f. alternator leads;
   g. heater hoses;
   h. throttle and choke connections;
   i. engine ground cable;
   j. thermal transmitter wire;
   k. wire to fuel cut-off solenoid;
   l. vacuum cut solenoid wire.

➡A good rule of thumb when disconnecting the rather complex engine wiring of today's cars is to put a piece of masking tape on the wire and on the connection you removed the wire from, then mark both pieces of tape 1, 2, 3, etc. When replacing wiring, simply match the pieces of tape.

8. Disconnect the power brake booster hose from the engine.

9. Remove the clutch operating cylinder and return spring.

10. Disconnect the speedometer cable from the transmission. Disconnect the backup light switch and any other wiring or attachments to the transmission. On cars with the L18 models, remove the boot, withdraw the lock pin, and remove the lever from inside the car.

11. Detach the exhaust pipe from the exhaust manifold. Remove the front section of the exhaust system. Be careful not to break the retaining bolts to manifold. If the bolts or studs break in the manifold remove the manifold and drill and tap the hole.

12. Mark the relationship of the driveshaft flanges and remove the driveshaft.

13. Place a jack under the transmission. Remove the rear crossmember.

14. Attach a hoist to the lifting hooks on the engine (at either end of the cylinder head). Support the engine.

15. Unbolt the front engine mounts. Tilt the engine by lowering the jack under the transmission and raising the hoist.

16. With the engine/transmission assembly mounted safely on the engine hoist slowly lower the engine/transmission assembly into place.

17. Support the transmission with a jack or equivalent until the crossmember is installed.

18. Tighten the front engine mounts. It may be necessary to lower or raise the engine hoist to correctly position the engine assembly to line up with the mount holes. Remove the engine hoist.

19. Install the crossmember then remove the jack or equivalent supporting the transmission.

20. Install the driveshaft in the correct marked position.

21. Reconnect the front exhaust system to the exhaust manifold. Be careful not to tighten retaining bolts to manifold to tight. If the bolts or studs break in the manifold remove the manifold and drill and tap the hole.

22. Reconnect all wiring at the transmission and the speedometer cable.

23. On cars with the L18 engine, install the lever, lock pin and shift boot.

24. Install the clutch cylinder and return spring. Reconnect the power brake hose to the engine if so equipped.

25. Install all wiring, brackets, vacuum hoses and water hoses to the engine. Make sure all connections are tight and in the correct location. It is always a good idea to replace all the old water hoses when installing the engine.

26. Install the fan and fan pulley.

27. Install the radiator shroud than the radiator reconnect the transmission lines if so equipped. Install the front grille if it was removed.

28. Refill the radiator and all other fluid levels.

29. Install the air cleaner, battery and reconnect the battery cables.

30. Install the hood in the same location as you removed it from.

31. Check all fluids, start the engine, let it warm up and check for leaks.

32. Road test vehicle after you are sure there are no leaks.

Front Wheel Drive Models

On these models no standard engine removal and installation procedures are given by the manufacturer. However it is recommended the engine and transaxle be removed as a single unit. Always release the fuel pressure in the system before disconnecting the fuel lines. Situate the vehicle on as flat and solid a surface as possible. Place chocks or equivalent at front and rear of rear wheels to stop vehicle from rolling while working on the vehicle. To remove the engine and transaxle assembly the front halfshafts will have to be removed from the transaxle refer to Section 7 in this book.

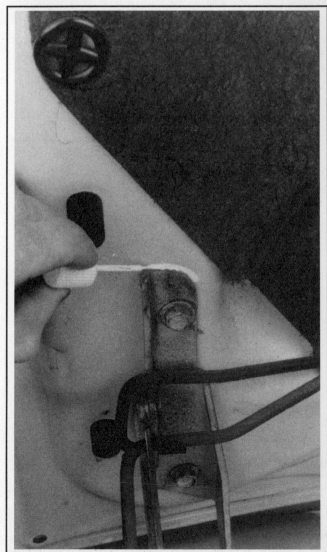

Prior to removing the engine, trace a line around the hood hinge to gain room to work

Rocker Cover/Shaft

REMOVAL & INSTALLATION

Rocker Cover/Shaft removal and installation procedures are included in the Camshaft Removal and Installation procedure in this section.

Thermostat

REMOVAL & INSTALLATION

▶ **See Figures 33, 34, 35 and 36**

1. Drain the engine coolant into a clean container so that the level is below the thermostat housing.

✳✳ CAUTION

When draining the coolant, keep in mind that cats and dogs are attracted by ethylene glycol antifreeze, and are quite likely to drink any that is left in an uncovered container or in puddles on the ground. This will prove fatal in sufficient quantity. Always drain the coolant into a sealable container. Coolant should be reused unless it is contaminated or several years old.

2. Disconnect the upper radiator hose at the water outlet.
3. Loosen the two securing nuts and remove the water otlet, gasket, and the thermostat from the thermostat housing.
4. Install the thermostat to the engine, using a new gasket with sealer and with the thermostat spring toward the inside of the engine.
5. Reconnect the upper radiator hose.
6. Refill the cooling system. Refer to Section 1 for Drain And Refill procedures if necessary. Make sure to let the engine reach normal operating temperature then check coolant for the correct level.

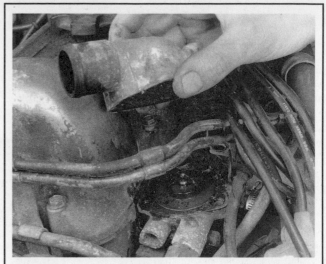

Lift off the thermostat housing to expose the thermostat

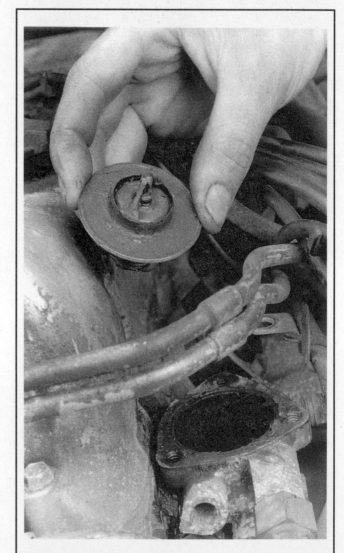

Remove the thermostat, then scrape the gasket material from the housing mating surfaces

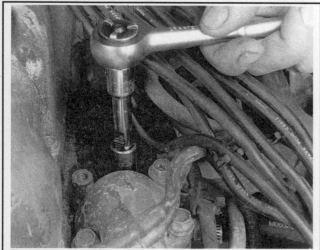

To remove the thermostat, remove the attaching bolts, then the housing

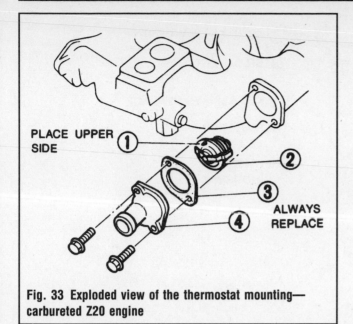

PLACE UPPER SIDE

① ② ③ ④

ALWAYS REPLACE

Fig. 33 Exploded view of the thermostat mounting—carbureted Z20 engine

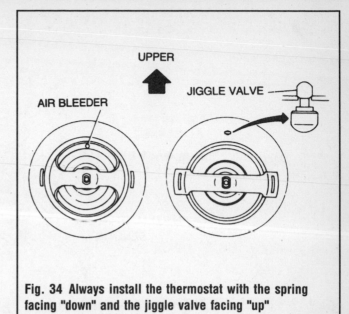

UPPER

AIR BLEEDER

JIGGLE VALVE

Fig. 34 Always install the thermostat with the spring facing "down" and the jiggle valve facing "up"

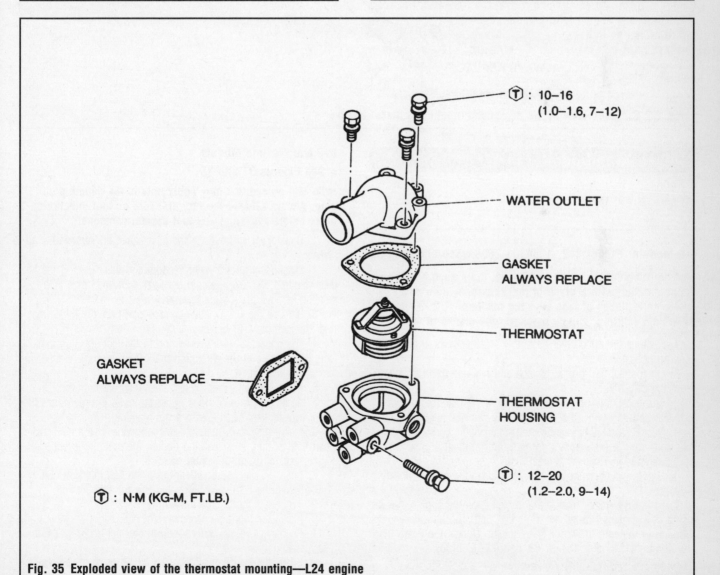

Ⓣ : 10–16
(1.0–1.6, 7–12)

WATER OUTLET

GASKET
ALWAYS REPLACE

THERMOSTAT

GASKET
ALWAYS REPLACE

THERMOSTAT
HOUSING

Ⓣ : 12–20
(1.2–2.0, 9–14)

Ⓣ : N·M (KG-M, FT.LB.)

Fig. 35 Exploded view of the thermostat mounting—L24 engine

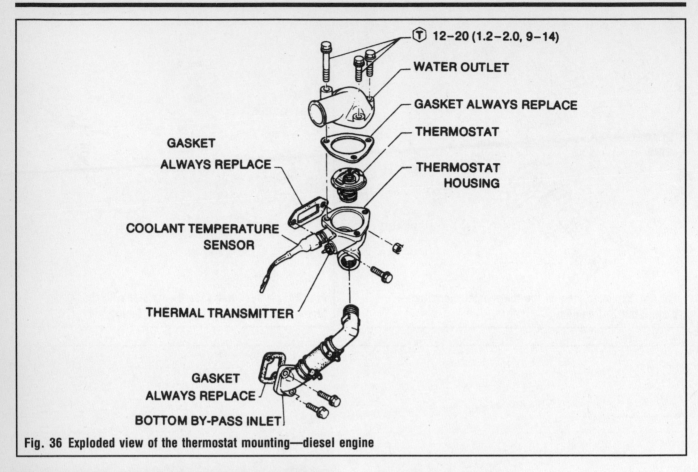

Ⓣ 12–20 (1.2–2.0, 9–14)

WATER OUTLET

GASKET ALWAYS REPLACE

THERMOSTAT

THERMOSTAT HOUSING

GASKET ALWAYS REPLACE

COOLANT TEMPERATURE SENSOR

THERMAL TRANSMITTER

GASKET ALWAYS REPLACE

BOTTOM BY-PASS INLET

Fig. 36 Exploded view of the thermostat mounting—diesel engine

Intake Manifold

REMOVAL & INSTALLATION

All Models, Except 810, 1980–81 200SX/510 and Maxima

➡When unplugging wires and hoses, mark each hose and its connection with a piece of masking tape, then match code the 2 pieces of tape with the numbers 1, 2, 3, etc. When assembling, simply match up the pieces of tape.

1. Remove the air cleaner assembly together with all of the attending hoses.

2. Disconnect the throttle linkage and fuel and vacuum lines from the carburetor.

3. The carburetor can be removed from the manifold at this point or can be removed as an assembly with the intake manifold.

4. Loosen the intake manifold attaching nuts, working from the two ends toward the center, and then remove them.

5. Remove the intake manifold from the engine.

6. Using a putty knife or equivalent, clean the gasket mounting surfaces.

7. Install the intake manifold and gasket on the engine. Always use a new gasket. Tighten the mounting bolts from the center working to the end, in two or three stages. Tighten the intake manifold bolts to 14–19 ft. lbs. or the nuts 12–15 ft. lbs.

8. Install throttle linkage, fuel and vacuum lines and the air cleaner assembly.

9. Start engine and check for leaks.

810 and Maxima Models

▸ **See Figures 37 and 38**

➡Certain procedures may apply only to the gasoline engine. Always release the fuel pressure on fuel injected engines before removing any fuel system component.

1. Disconnect all hoses to the air cleaner and remove the air cleaner.

2. Disconnect all air, water vacuum and fuel hoses to the intake manifold. Remove the cold start valve and fuel pipe as an assembly. Remove the throttle linkage.

3. Remove the B.P.T. valve control tube from the intake manifold. Remove the EGR hoses.

4. Disconnect all electrical wiring to the fuel injection unit. Note the location of the wires and mark them in some manner to facilitate reinstallation.

5. Make sure all wires, hoses, lines, etc. are removed. Unscrew the intake manifold bolts. Keep the bolts in order since they are of two different sizes. Remove the manifold.

6. Install the intake manifold to the engine. Use a new gasket, clean both sealing surfaces, and tighten the bolts in several stages, working from the center outward.

7. Reconnect all electrical wiring to the fuel injection unit.

8. Install the EGR valve hose and B.P.T. valve control.

9. Reconnect the throttle linkage.

10. Install the fuel pipe assembly and the cold start valve.

11. Reconnect all air, water vacuum and fuel hoses to the intake manifold.

12. Install the air cleaner reconnect all hoses to the correct location.

13. Start engine and check for leaks.

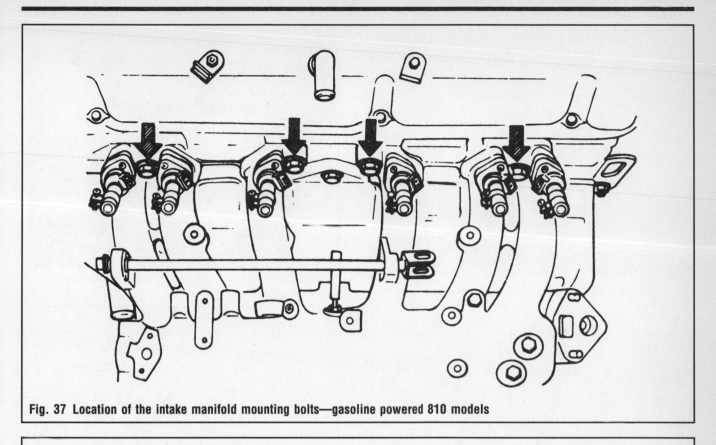

Fig. 37 Location of the intake manifold mounting bolts—gasoline powered 810 models

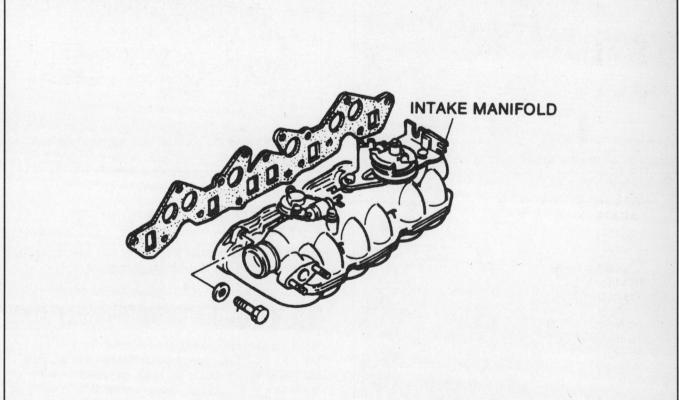

INTAKE MANIFOLD

Fig. 38 Exploded view of the intake manifold-to-gasket relationship—diesel powered 810 models

To remove the intake manifold, unbolt the upper bolts

Before re-installation, the gasket surfaces must be scraped clean thoroughly

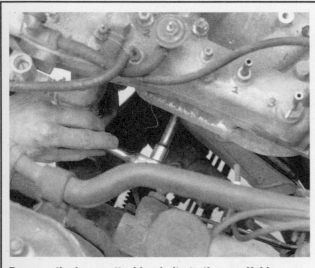

Remove the lower attaching bolts to the manifold

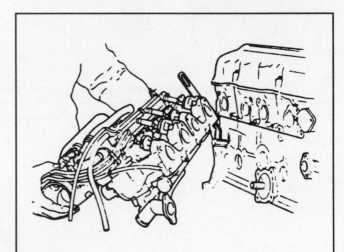

Fig. 39 Remove the manifold with injectors, etc. still attached

Lift the manifold away from the cylinder head

1980–81 200SX/510 Models

♦ See Figure 39

➡Always release the fuel pressure on fuel injected engines before removing any fuel system component.

1. Drain the coolant and disconnect the battery cable.

✳✳ CAUTION

When draining the coolant, keep in mind that cats and dogs are attracted by ethylene glycol antifreeze, and are quite likely to drink any that is left in an uncovered container or in puddles on the ground. This will prove fatal in sufficient quantity. Always drain the coolant into a sealable container. Coolant should be reused unless it is contaminated or several years old.

2. On the fuel injected engine, remove the air cleaner hoses. On the carbureted engine, remove the air cleaner.

3. Remove the radiator hoses from the manifold.

4. For the carbureted engine, remove the fuel, air and vacuum hoses from the carburetor. Remove the throttle linkage and remove the carburetor.

5. Remove the throttle cable and disconnect the fuel pipe and the return fuel line on fuel injection engines. Plug the fuel pipe to prevent spilling fuel.

➡When unplugging wires and hoses, mark each hose and its connection with a piece of masking tape, then match code the two pieces of tape with the numbers 1, 2, 3, etc. When assembling, simply match the pieces of tape.

6. Remove all remaining wires, tubes, the air cleaner bracket (carbureted engines) and the E.G.R. and P.C.V. tubes from the rear of the intake manifold. Remove the air induction pipe from the front of the carbureted engine. Remove the manifold supports on the fuel injected engine.

7. Unbolt and remove the intake manifold. On fuel injected engines, remove the manifold with injectors, E.G.R. valve, fuel tubes, etc., still attached.

8. Clean the gasket mounting surfaces then install the intake manifold on the engine. Always use a new intake manifold gasket.

9. Connect all electrical connections, tubes, the air cleaner bracket (carbureted engines) and the E.G.R. and P.C.V. tubes to the rear of the intake manifold. Install the air induction pipe to the front of the carbureted engine. Install the manifold supports on the fuel injected engine.

10. Install the throttle cable and reconnect the fuel pipe and the return fuel line on fuel injection engines.

11. Install the carburetor and throttle linkage. Reconnect the fuel, air and vacuum hoses to the carburetor on these models.

12. Install the radiator hoses to the intake manifold.

13. On the fuel injected engine, install the air cleaner hoses. On the carbureted engine, install the air cleaner.

14. Refill the coolant level and connect the battery cable. Start the engine and check for leaks.

Exhaust Manifold

REMOVAL & INSTALLATION

All Models
◆ See Figure 40

➡You may find that removing the intake manifold will provide better access to the exhaust manifold on some early models.

1. Remove the air cleaner assembly, if necessary for access. Remove the heat shield.

2. Disconnect and tag the high tension wires from the spark plugs on the exhaust side of the engine.

3. Disconnect the exhaust pipe from the exhaust manifold.

➡Soak the exhaust pipe retaining bolts with penetrating oil if necessary to loosen them.

4. On the carbureted models, remove the air induction and/or the EGR tubes from the exhaust manifold. On the fuel injected

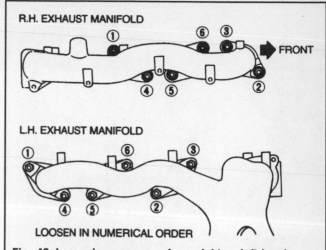

Fig. 40 Loosening sequence for a right or left-hand exhaust manifold fasteners

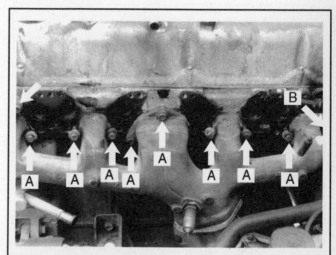

When removing the exhaust manifold, be prepared to remove bolts (A) and nuts (B)

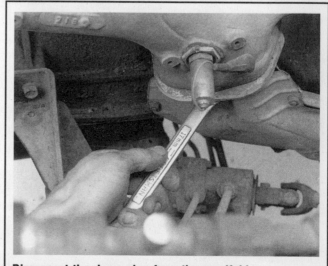

Disconnect the down pipe from the manifold

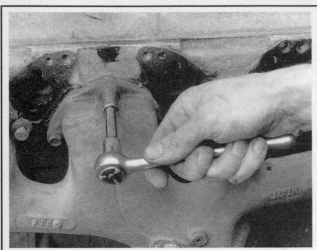

Remove the manifold bolts—intake manifold was removed for ease of access

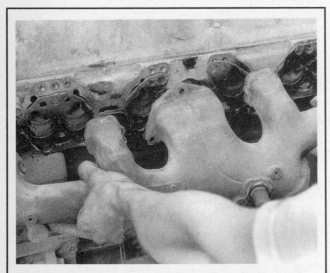

Lift away the exhaust manifold from the cylinder head

Remove the gasket, then scrape the surfaces clean—use a new gasket upon installation

models, disconnect the exhaust gas sensor electrical connector.

5. Remove the exhaust manifold mounting fasteners and the manifold from the cylinder head.

6. Using a putty knife, clean the gasket mounting surfaces.

7. Install the manifold onto the engine, use new gaskets and from the center working to the end. Tighten the exhaust manifold nuts/bolts to 14–22 ft. lbs.

8. Install the air induction and/or the EGR tubes to the exhaust manifold or the exhaust gas sensor electrical connector.

9. Reconnect exhaust pipe.

10. Connect plug wires and air cleaner and any related hoses.

11. Start the engine and check for exhaust leaks.

Radiator

REMOVAL & INSTALLATION

▶ See Figures 41, 42, 43 and 44

➡**On some models, it may be necessary to remove the front grille to remove the radiator. The cooling system can be drained from opening the drain cock at the bottom of the radiator or by removing the bottom hose at the radiator. Be careful not to damage the fins or core tubes when removing and installing the radiator to the vehicle. NEVER OPEN THE RADIATOR CAP WHEN HOT!**

1. Drain the engine coolant into a clean container. On fuel injected models, remove the air cleaner inlet pipe.

✳✳ CAUTION

When draining the coolant, keep in mind that cats and dogs are attracted by ethylene glycol antifreeze, and are quite likely to drink any that is left in an uncovered container or in puddles on the ground. This will prove fatal in sufficient quantity. Always drain the coolant into a sealable container. Coolant should be reused unless it is contaminated or several years old.

To remove the radiator, disconnect all hoses to and from the unit

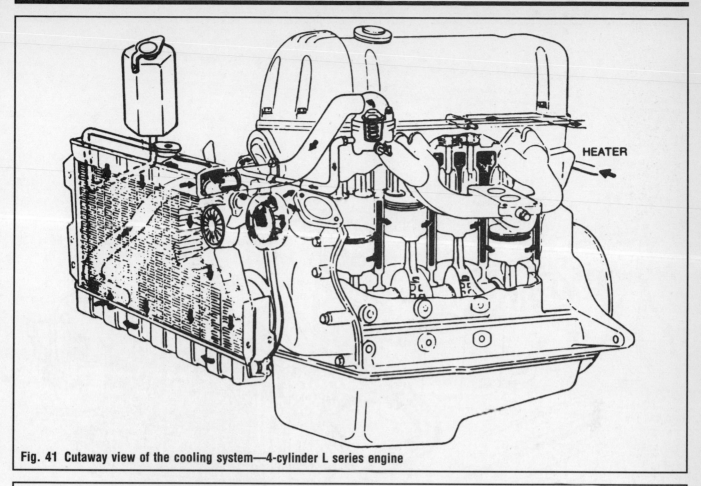

Fig. 41 Cutaway view of the cooling system—4-cylinder L series engine

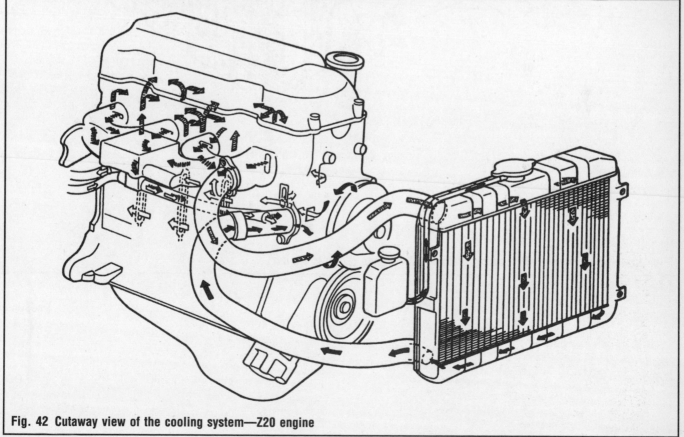

Fig. 42 Cutaway view of the cooling system—Z20 engine

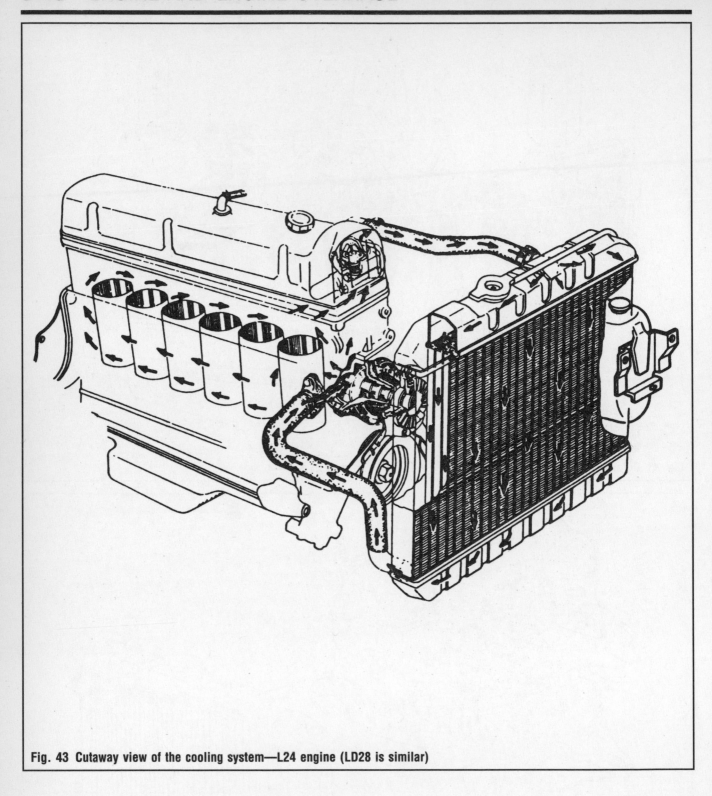

Fig. 43 Cutaway view of the cooling system—L24 engine (LD28 is similar)

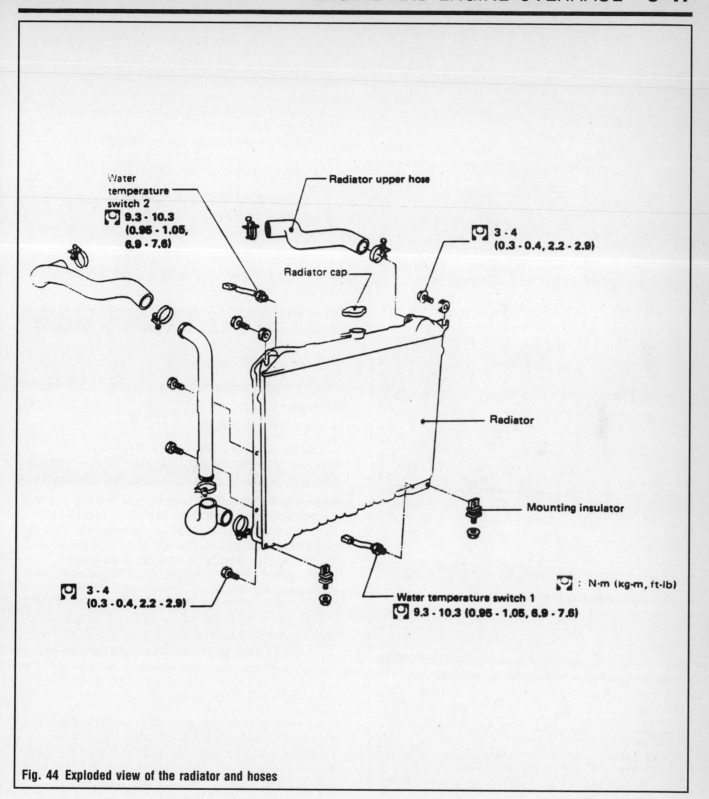

Water temperature switch 2
⬚ 9.3 - 10.3
(0.95 - 1.05, 6.9 - 7.6)

Radiator upper hose

Radiator cap

⬚ 3 - 4
(0.3 - 0.4, 2.2 - 2.9)

Radiator

Mounting insulator

⬚ : N·m (kg-m, ft-lb)

⬚ 3 - 4
(0.3 - 0.4, 2.2 - 2.9)

Water temperature switch 1
⬚ 9.3 - 10.3 (0.95 - 1.05, 6.9 - 7.6)

Fig. 44 Exploded view of the radiator and hoses

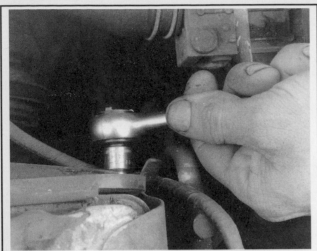

Disconnect the radiator by removing all retaining fasteners

If necessary, disconnect and remove the fan shroud

When detached, lift out the radiator from the vehicle

2. Disconnect the upper and lower radiator hoses and the coolant reserve tank hose.

3. Disconnect the automatic transmission oil cooler lines if so equipped. Cap the lines to keep dirt out of them.

4. If the fan has a shroud, unbolt the shroud and move it back, hanging it over the fan.

5. Remove the radiator mounting bolts and the radiator.

6. Install the radiator in the vehicle and tighten the mounting bolts evenly.

7. If equipped with an automatic transmission, connect the cooling lines at the radiator.

8. Connect the upper and lower hoses and the coolant reserve tank hose.

9. Refill the cooling system (refer to Section 1) and automatic transmission if necessary, operate the engine until warm and then check the coolant level and for leaks.

Water Pump

REMOVAL & INSTALLATION

All Models
▶ See Figures 45 and 46

1. Drain the engine coolant into a clean container.

✳✳ CAUTION

When draining the coolant, keep in mind that cats and dogs are attracted by ethylene glycol antifreeze, and are quite likely to drink any that is left in an uncovered container or in puddles on the ground. This will prove fatal in sufficient quantity. Always drain the coolant into a sealable container. Coolant should be reused unless it is contaminated or several years old.

2. Loosen the four bolts retaining the fan shroud to the radiator and remove the shroud.

3. Loosen the belt, then remove the fan and pulley from the water pump hub.

4. Remove the bolts retaining the pump and remove the pump together with the gasket from the front cover.

5. Remove all traces of gasket material and install the water pump to the engine with a new gasket and sealer. Tighten the bolts uniformly and to specifications.

6. Install the fan and pulley to the water pump hub.

7. Install and adjust the drive belt.

8. Install the radiator fan shroud.

9. Refill the cooling system and start the engine and check for leaks. Refer to Section 1 for necessary procedure.

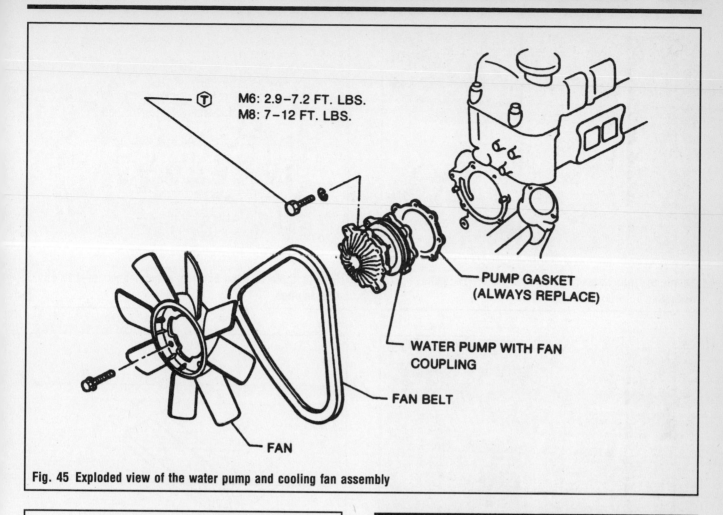

M6: 2.9–7.2 FT. LBS.
M8: 7–12 FT. LBS.

PUMP GASKET
(ALWAYS REPLACE)

WATER PUMP WITH FAN
COUPLING

FAN BELT

FAN

Fig. 45 Exploded view of the water pump and cooling fan assembly

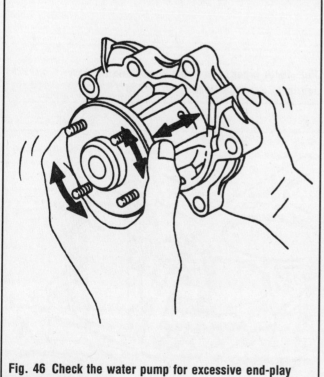

Fig. 46 Check the water pump for excessive end-play and rough operation

Cylinder Head

REMOVAL & INSTALLATION

▶ See Figures 47, 48, 49 and 50

➡ To prevent distortion or warping of the cylinder head, allow the engine to cool completely before removing the head bolts.

L18 and L20B Engines

1. Crank the engine until the No. 1 piston is TDC of the compression stroke and disconnect the negative battery cable, drain the cooling system and remove the air cleaner and attending hoses.

✳ CAUTION

When draining the coolant, keep in mind that cats and dogs are attracted by ethylene glycol antifreeze, and are quite likely to drink any that is left in an uncovered container or in puddles on the ground. This will prove fatal in sufficient quantity. Always drain the coolant into a sealable container. Coolant should be reused unless it is contaminated or several years old.

To remove the water pump, remove all belts, pulleys and other interfering components

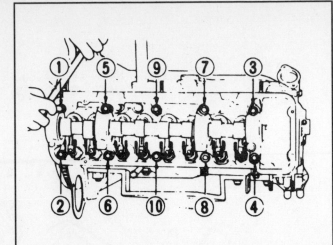

Fig. 47 Cylinder head bolt loosening sequence—L18 and L20 engines

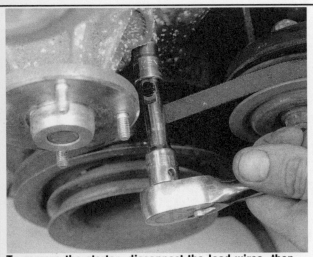

To remove the starter, disconnect the lead wires, then unbolt the unit from the engine

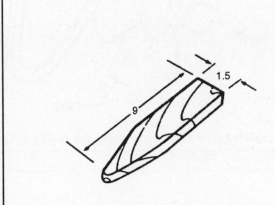

Fig. 48 In order to hold the cam chain in place, fabricate a wooden wedge as shown

Lift off the water pump, then carefully and completely clean the mating surfaces

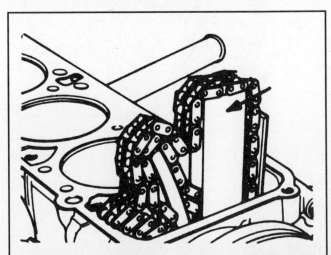

Fig. 49 Use a wooden block as shown to keep the chain from falling into the engine—overhead camshaft engines

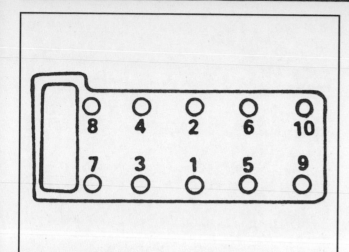

Fig. 50 Cylinder head torque sequence—L-series 4-cylinder engine

2. Remove the alternator.

3. Disconnect the carburetor throttle linkage, the fuel line and any other vacuum lines or electrical leads, and remove the carburetor.

4. Disconnect the exhaust pipe from the exhaust manifold.

5. Remove the fan and fan pulley.

6. Remove the spark plugs to protect them from damage. Lay the spark plugs aside and out of the way.

7. Remove the rocker cover.

8. Remove the water pump.

9. Remove the fuel pump.

10. Remove the fuel pump drive cam.

11. Mark the relationship of the camshaft sprocket to the timing chain with paint or chalk. If this is done, it will not be necessary to locate the factory timing marks. Before removing the camshaft sprocket, it will be necessary to wedge the chain in place so that it will not fall down into the front cover. The factory procedure is to wedge the timing chain in place with the wooden wedge shown here. The problem with this procedure is that it may allow the chain tensioner to move out far enough to cock itself against the chain. If this happens, you'll find that the chain won't go back over the sprocket after you've put the sprocket back on. In this case, you'll have to remove the front cover and push the tensioner back. After you've wedged the chain, unbolt the camshaft sprocket and remove it.

12. Loosen and remove the cylinder head bolts. You will need a 10mm Allen wrench to remove the head bolts. Keep the bolts in order since they are different sizes. Lift the cylinder head assembly from the engine. Remove the intake and exhaust manifolds as necessary.

To install:

13. Thoroughly clean the cylinder block and head mating surfaces and install a new cylinder head gasket. Check for head and block warpage; see Cleaning and Inspection and Resurfacing below. Do not use sealer on the cylinder head gasket.

14. With the crankshaft turned so that the No. 1 piston is at TDC of the compression stroke (if not already done so as mentioned in Step 1), make sure that the camshaft sprocket timing mark and the oblong groove in the plate are aligned.

15. Place the cylinder head in position on the cylinder block, being careful not to allow any of the valves to come in contact with any of the pistons. Do not rotate the crankshaft or camshaft separately because of possible damage which might occur to the valves.

16. Temporarily tighten the two center right and left cylinder head bolts to 14.5 ft. lbs.

17. Install the camshaft sprocket together with the timing chain to the camshaft. Make sure the marks you made earlier line up with each other. If you get into trouble, see Timing Chain Removal and Installation for timing procedures.

18. Install the cylinder head bolts. Note that there are two sizes of bolts used; the longer bolts are installed on the driver's side of the engine with a smaller bolt in the center position. The remaining small bolts are installed on the opposite side of the cylinder head.

19. Tighten the cylinder head bolts in three stages: first to 29 ft. lbs., second to 43 ft. lbs., and lastly to 62 ft. lbs. Tighten the cylinder head bolts on all models in the proper sequence.

20. Install the fuel pump assembly, water pump and rocker cover.

21. Clean and regap the spark plugs then install plugs into the cylinder head. DO NOT OVER TORQUE THE SPARK PLUGS.

22. Install the fan pulley and cooling fan. Connect the exhaust pipe to the exhaust manifold.

23. Install the carburetor and connect the carburetor throttle linkage, the fuel line and any other vacuum lines or electrical leads.

24. Install the alternator, electrical connections to the alternator and drive belt.

25. Adjust the valves. Fill the cooling system start the engine and run it until normal operating temperature is reached. Retighten the cylinder head bolts to specifications, the readjust the valves. Retighten the head bolts again after 600 miles, and readjust the valves at that time.

L24 and LD28 Engines

◗ See Figures 51 and 52

1. Crank the engine until the No. 1 piston is at TDC of the compression stroke, disconnect the battery, and drain the cooling system.

➡**To set the No. 1 piston at TDC of the compression stroke on the LD28 engine, remove the blind plug from the rear plate. Rotate the crankshaft until the marks on the flywheel and rear plate are in alignment. The No. 1 piston should now be at TDC.**

2. Remove the radiator hoses and the heater hoses. Unbolt the alternator mounting bracket and move the alternator to one side, if necessary.

✳✳ CAUTION

When draining the coolant, keep in mind that cats and dogs are attracted by ethylene glycol antifreeze, and are quite likely to drink any that is left in an uncovered container or in puddles on the ground. This will prove fatal in sufficient quantity. Always drain the coolant into a sealable container. Coolant should be reused unless it is contaminated or several years old.

To remove the camshaft cover, disconnect all hoses, wires, or other interfering components

Using a long-handled breaker bar and the correct socket, remove the cylinder head bolts

Remove the attaching bolts to the camshaft cover

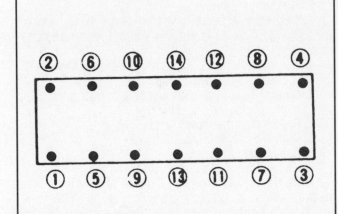

Fig. 51 Cylinder head bolt loosening sequence—L24 and LD28 engines

Lift off the camshaft cover to expose the cylinder head bolts

Lift the cylinder head from the block

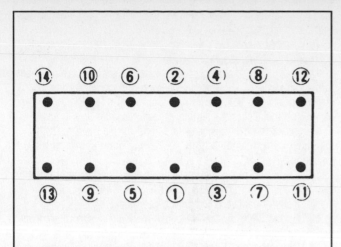

Fig. 52 Cylinder head bolt tightening sequence—L24 and LD28 engines

3. If the car is equipped with air conditioning, unbolt the compressor and place it to one side. Do not disconnect the compressor lines. Severe injury could result.

4. Remove the power steering pump.

5. Remove the spark plug leads and spark plugs (gasoline engine only).

6. Remove the cold start valve and the fuel pipe as an assembly. Remove the throttle linkage.

7. Remove all lines and hoses from the intake manifold. Mark them first so you will know where they go.

8. Unbolt the exhaust manifold from the exhaust pipe. The cylinder head can be removed with both the intake and exhaust manifolds in place.

9. Remove the camshaft cover.

10. Mark the relationship of the camshaft sprocket to the timing chain with paint. There are timing marks on the chain and the sprocket which should be visible when the No. 1 piston is at TDC, but the marks are quite small and not particularly useful.

11. Before removing the camshaft sprocket, it will be necessary to wedge the chain in place so that it will not fall down into the front cover. The factory procedure is to wedge the timing chain in place with the wooden wedge as detailed in the previous procedure. The problem with this procedure is that it may allow the chain tensioner to move out far enough to cock itself against the chain. If this happens, you'll find that the chain won't go back over the sprocket after you've put the sprocket back on. In this case, you'll have to remove the front cover and push the tensioner back. After you've wedged the chain, unbolt the camshaft sprocket and remove it.

12. Remove the cylinder head bolts. They require an Allen wrench type socket adapter. Keep the bolts in order as two different sizes are used.

13. Lift off the cylinder head. You may have to tap it lightly with a rubber hammer.

To install:

14. Install a new head gasket and place the head in position on the block.

15. Install the head bolts in their original locations.

16. Tighten the head bolts in three stages: first to 29 ft. lbs., then to 43 ft. lbs., then to 61 ft. lbs.

17. Reinstall the camshaft sprocket in its original location. The chain is installed at the same time as the sprocket. Make sure the marks you made earlier line up. If the chain has slipped, or the engine has been disturbed, correct the timing as described under Timing Chain Removal and Installation.

18. Install the camshaft cover and exhaust pipe to the exhaust manifold.

19. Reconnect all lines and hoses to the intake manifold.

20. Install the throttle linkage, cold start valve and fuel pipe assembly.

21. Clean and regap the spark plugs if so equipped. Install the spark plugs in the cylinder head. DO NOT OVER TORQUE THE SPARK PLUGS.

22. Install the power steering pump and correctly adjust the drive belt.

23. Install the air conditioning compressor and correctly adjust the drive belt.

24. Install the alternator mounting bracket, alternator, electrical connections to the alternator and adjust the drive belt.

25. Reconnect the heater and radiator hoses.

26. Refill the cooling system. Adjust the valves.

27. Start engine, run engine to normal operating temperature, check for the correct coolant level.

28. Check for leaks and roadtest vehicle for proper operation.

➡**After 600 miles of driving, retighten the head bolts and readjust the valves.**

Z20E and Z20S Engines

▶ **See Figures 53 and 54**

1. Complete Steps 1–5 under L24. Observe the following note for Step 5.

➡**The spark plug leads should be marked; however, it would be wise to mark them yourself, especially on the dual spark plug models.**

2. Disconnect the throttle linkage, the air cleaner or its intake hose assembly (fuel injection). Disconnect the fuel line, the return fuel line and any other vacuum lines or electrical leads. On the Z20S, remove the carburetor to avoid damaging it while removing the head.

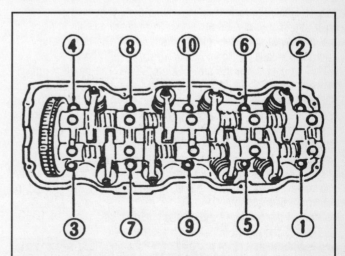

Fig. 53 Cylinder head bolt loosening sequence—Z-series engines

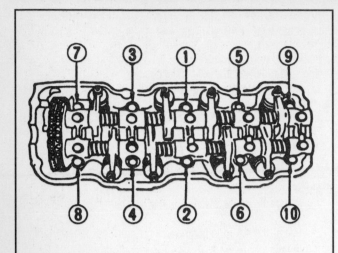

Fig. 54 Cylinder head bolt tightening sequence—Z-series engines

➡**A good rule of thumb when disconnecting the rather complex engine wiring of today's automobiles is to put a piece of masking tape on the wire or hose and one the connection you removed the wire or hose from, then mark both pieces of tape 1, 2, 3, etc. When replacing wiring, simply match the pieces of tape.**

3. Remove the E.G.R. tube from around the rear of the engine.

4. Remove the exhaust air induction tubes from around the front of the engine on Z20S engines and from the exhaust manifold on Z20E engines.

5. Unbolt the exhaust manifold from the exhaust pipe. On the Z20S, remove the fuel pump.

6. On the Z20E, remove the intake manifold supports from under the manifold. Remove the P.C.V. valve from around the rear of the engine if necessary.

7. Remove the spark plugs to protect them from damage. Remove the valve cover.

8. Mark the relationship of the camshaft sprocket to the timing chain with paint or chalk. If this is done, it will not be necessary to locate the factory timing marks. Before removing the camshaft sprocket, it will be necessary to wedge the chain in place so that it will not fall down into the front cover. The factory procedure is to wedge the timing chain in place with the wooden wedge as detailed in the previous procedure. The problem with this procedure is that it may allow the chain tensioner to move out far enough to cock itself against the chain. If this happens, you'll find that the chain won't go back over the sprocket after you've put the sprocket back on. In this case, you'll have to remove the front cover and push the tensioner back. After you've wedged the chain, unbolt the camshaft sprocket and remove it.

9. Working from both ends in, loosen the cylinder head bolts and remove them. Remove the bolts securing the cylinder head to the front cover assembly.

10. Lift the cylinder head off the engine block. It may be necessary to tap the head lightly with a rubber mallet to loosen it.

11. Thoroughly clean the cylinder block and head surfaces and check both for warpage.

12. Fit the new head gasket. Don't use sealant. Make sure that no open valves are in the way of raised pistons, and do not rotate the crankshaft or camshaft separately because of possible damage which might occur to the valves.

13. Temporarily tighten the two center right and left cylinder head bolts to 14 ft. lbs.

14. Install the camshaft sprocket together with the timing chain to the camshaft. Make sure the marks you made earlier line up with each other. If you get into trouble, see Timing Chain Removal and Installation for timing procedures.

15. Install the cylinder head bolts and torque them to 20 ft. lbs., then 40 ft. lbs., then 58 ft. lbs. in the order shown in the illustration.

16. Clean and regap the spark plugs then install them in the cylinder head. DO NOT OVER TORQUE THE SPARK PLUGS.

17. Install the valve cover with a new gasket.

18. On the Z20E, install the intake manifold supports from under the manifold. Install the P.C.V. valve if it was removed.

19. Connect the exhaust pipe to exhaust manifold. On the Z20S, install the fuel pump.

20. Install the exhaust air induction tubes to the front of the engine on Z20S engines and to the exhaust manifold on Z20E engines.

21. Install the E.G.R. tube from around the rear of the engine.

22. On the Z20S, install the carburetor. Connect the throttle linkage, the air cleaner or its intake hose assembly (fuel injection). Reconnect the fuel line, the return fuel line and any other vacuum lines or electrical leads.

23. Install the power steering pump if so equipped and correctly adjust the drive belt.

24. Install the air conditioning compressor and correctly adjust the drive belt.

25. Install the alternator mounting bracket, alternator, electrical connections to the alternator and adjust the drive belt.

26. Reconnect the heater and radiator hoses.

27. Refill the cooling system. Adjust the valves.

28. Start engine, run engine to normal operating temperature, check for the correct coolant level.

29. Check for leaks and roadtest vehicle for proper operation.

➡**It is always wise to drain the crankcase oil after the cylinder head has been installed to avoid coolant contamination.**

CLEANING & INSPECTION

All Cylinder Heads

1. With the valves installed to protect the valve seats, remove deposits from the combustion chambers and valve heads with a scraper and a wire brush. Be careful not to damage the cylinder head gasket surface. After the valves are removed, clean the valve guide bores with a valve guide cleaning tool. Using cleaning solvent to remove dirt, grease and other deposits, clean all bolt holes; be sure the oil passages are clean.

2. Remove all deposits from the valves with a fine wire brush or buffing wheel.

3. Inspect the cylinder head for cracks or excessively burned areas in the exhaust outlet ports.

4. Check the cylinder head for cracks and inspect the gasket surface for burrs and nicks. Replace the head if it is cracked.

5. On cylinder heads that incorporate valve seat inserts, check the inserts for excessive wear, cracks or looseness.

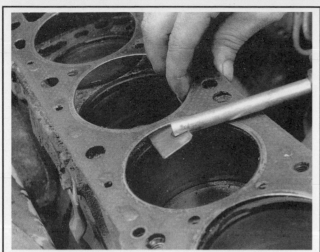

Remove the gasket—take care not to damage the aluminum surfaces

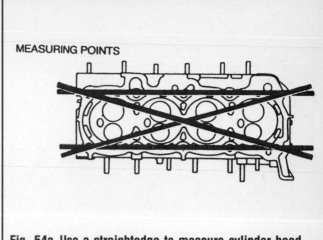

MEASURING POINTS

Fig. 54a Use a straightedge to measure cylinder head flatness along these lines

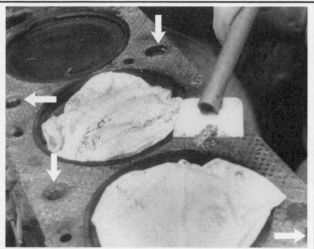

Fig. 35 Exploded view of the thermostat mounting—L24 engine

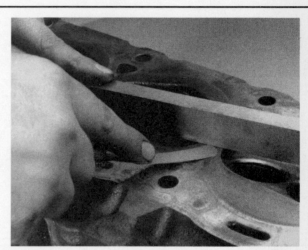

Check the cylinder head for flatness across the head surface

RESURFACING

Cylinder Head Flatness

▶ See Figure 54a

When a cylinder head is removed, check the flatness of the cylinder head gasket surface.

1. Place a straight edge across the gasket surface of the cylinder head. Using feeler gauges, determine the clearance at the center of the straightedge.

2. If warpage exceeds 0.10mm over the total length, the cylinder head must be resurfaced. Cylinder head height after resurfacing must not exceed specifications.

3. If necessary to refinish the cylinder head gasket surface, do not plane or grind off more than 0.2mm from the original gasket surface.

➡Cylinder head resurfacing should be done only by a competent machine shop.

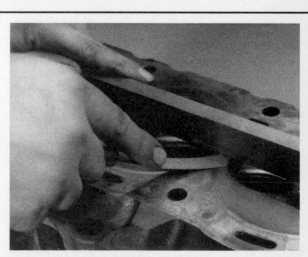

Checks should be made both straight across the cylinder head and at both diagonals

Valves

REMOVAL & INSTALLATION

All Engines

▶ **See Figures 55 and 56**

The cylinder head must be removed on all engines before the valves can be removed.

A valve spring compressor is needed to remove the valves and springs; these are available at most auto parts and auto tool shops. A small magnet is very helpful for removing the keepers and spring seats.

Set the head on its side on the bench. Install the spring compressor so that the fixed side of the tool is flat against the valve head in the combustion chamber, and the screw side is against the retainer. Slowly turn the screw in towards the head, compressing the spring. As the spring compresses, the keepers will be revealed; pick them off of the valve stem with the magnet as they are easily fumbled and lost. When the keepers are removed, slowly back the screw out and remove the retainers and springs. Remove the compressor and pull the valves out of the head from the other side. Remove the valve seals by hand and remove the spring seats with the magnet.

Since it is very important that each valve and its spring, retainer, spring seat and keepers is reassembled in its original location, you must keep these parts in order. The best way to do this is to cut either eight (four cylinder) or twelve (six cylinder) holes in a piece of heavy cardboard or wood. Label each hole with the cylinder number and either IN or EX, corresponding to the location of each valve in the head. As you remove each valve, insert it into the holder, and assemble the seats, springs, keepers and retainers to the stem on the labeled side of the holder. This way each valve and its attending parts are kept together, and can be put back into the head in their proper locations.

Oil each valve stem, and install each valve into the cylinder head in the reverse order of removal, so that all parts except the keepers are assembled on the stem. Always use new valve stem

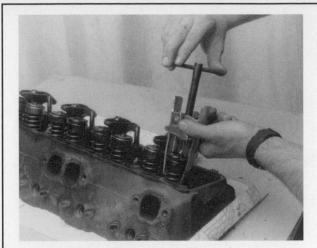

Use a valve spring compressor tool to relieve spring tension from the valve caps

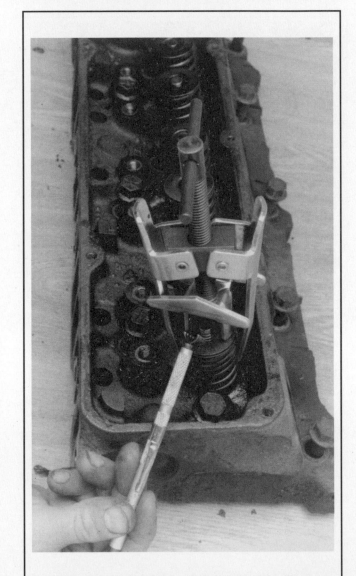

A magnet may be helpful in removing the valve keepers

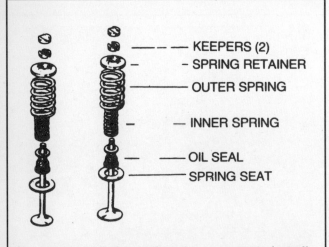

KEEPERS (2)
SPRING RETAINER
OUTER SPRING
INNER SPRING
OIL SEAL
SPRING SEAT

Fig. 55 Exploded view of the valve components (not all engines have double valve springs)

Remove the spring from the valve stem in order to access the seal

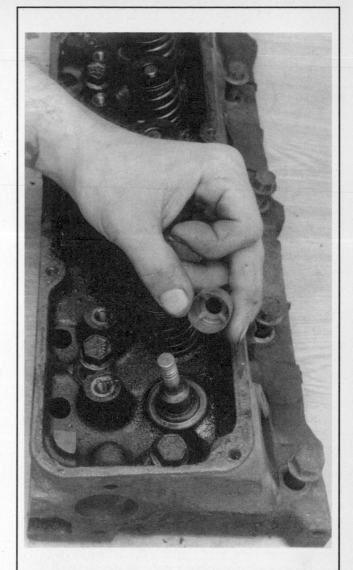

Remove the valve stem seal from the cylinder head

Once the spring has been removed, the O-ring may be removed from the valve stem

Invert the cylinder head and withdraw the valve from the cylinder head bore

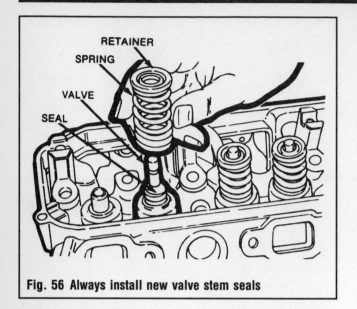

RETAINER

SPRING

VALVE

SEAL

Fig. 56 Always install new valve stem seals

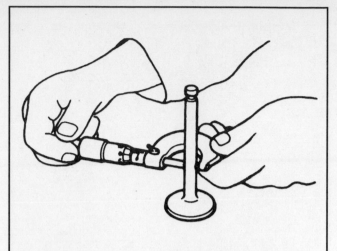

Fig. 57 Measure the valve stem diameter on the center of the stem

seals. Install the spring compressor, and compress the retainer and spring until the keeper groove on the valve stem is fully revealed. Coat the groove with a wipe of grease (to hold the keepers until the retainer is released) and install both keepers, wide end up. Slowly back the screw of the compressor out until the spring retainer covers the keepers. Remove the tool. Lightly tap the end of each valve stem with a rubber hammer to ensure proper fit of the retainers and keepers. Adjust the valves.

INSPECTION

◆ **See Figures 57, 58 and 59**

Before the valves can be properly inspected, the stem, lower end of the stem and the entire valve face and head must be cleaned. An old valve works well for clipping carbon from the valve head, and a wire brush, gasket scraper or putty knife can be used for cleaning the valve face and the area between the face and lower stem. Do not scratch the valve face during cleaning. Clean the entire stem with a rag soaked in thinners to remove all varnish and gum.

Thorough inspection of the valves requires the use of a micrometer, and a dial indicator is needed to measure the inside diameter of the valve guides. If these instruments are not available to you, the valves and head can be taken to a reputable machine shop for inspection. Refer to the Valve Specifications chart for valve stem and stem-to-guide specifications.

If the above instruments are at your disposal, measure the diameter of each valve stem at the locations illustrated. Jot these measurements down. Using the dial indicator, measure the inside diameter of the valve guides at their bottom, top and midpoint 90° apart. Jot these measurements down also. Subtract the valve stem measurement from the valve guide inside measurement; if the clearance exceeds that listed in the specifications chart under Stem-to-Guide Clearance, replace the valve(s). Stem-to-guide clearance can also be checked at a machine shop, where a dial indicator would be used.

Check the top of each valve stem for pitting and unusual wear due to improper rocker adjustment, etc. The stem tip can be ground flat if it is worn, but no more than 0.5mm can be removed; if this limit must be exceeded to make the tip flat and

Fig. 58 Use an inside dial indicator to measure the valve guide inside diameter (ID)

square, then the valve must be replaced. If the valve stem tips are ground, make sure you fix the valve securely into a jig designed for this purpose, so the tip contacts the grinding wheel squarely at exactly 90°. Most machine shops that handle automotive work are equipped for this job.

STEM-TO-GUIDE CLEARANCE

Valve stem-to-guide clearance should be checked upon assembling the cylinder head, and is especially necessary if the valve guides have been reamed or knurled, or if oversize valves have been installed. Excessive oil consumption often is a result of too much clearance between the valve guide and valve stem.

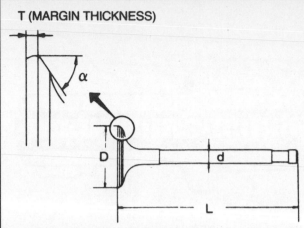

Fig. 59 Critical valve dimensions. When the head has been worn to 0.020 in. margin thickness, replace the valve

A wire wheel may be used to clean the combustion chambers of carbon deposits

A dial gauge may be used to check valve stem-to-guide clearance

1. Clean the valve stem with lacquer thinner or a similar solvent to remove all gum and varnish. Clean the valve guides using solvent and an expanding wire-type valve guide cleaner (a rifle cleaning brush works well here).

2. Mount a dial indicator so that the stem is at 90° to the valve stem and as close to the valve guide as possible.

3. Move the valve off its seat, and measure the valve guide-to-stem clearance by rocking the stem back and forth to actuate the dial indicator. Measure the valve stems using a micrometer and compare to specifications, to determine whether stem or guide wear is responsible for excessive clearance.

Valve Guide

INSPECTION

Valve guides should be cleaned as outlined earlier, and checked when valve stem diameter and stem-to-guide clearance is checked. Generally, if the engine is using oil through the guides (assuming the valve seals are OK) and the valve stem diameter is within specification, it is the guides that are worn and need replacing.

REMOVAL & INSTALLATION

♦ See Figure 60

The valve guides in all engines covered in this guide may be replaced. To remove the guide(s), heat the cylinder head to 302–320°F (150–160°C). Drive out the guides using a 2 ton press (many machine shops have this equipment) or a hammer and brass drift which has been modified with washers as in the accompanying illustration.

➡**Some valve guides are retained by snaprings, which must be removed prior to guide removal.**

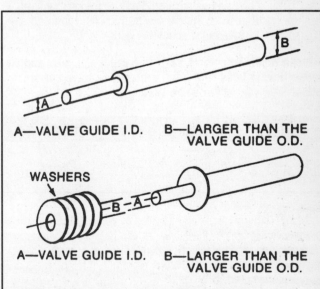

A—VALVE GUIDE I.D. B—LARGER THAN THE VALVE GUIDE O.D.

WASHERS

A—VALVE GUIDE I.D. B—LARGER THAN THE VALVE GUIDE O.D.

Fig. 60 A brass drift can be modified for valve guide removal

With the guide(s) removed, the cylinder head valve guide holes should be reamed to accept the new guides. The head should then be heated again and the new guides pressed or driven into place. On engines which utilize valve guide snaprings, install the snapring to the guide first, then install the guide into the head. Ream the new valve guide bores to 8.00–8.01mm.

KNURLING

▶ **See Figure 61**

Valve guides which are not excessively worn or distorted may, in some cases, be knurled rather than reamed. Knurling is a process in which metal inside the valve guide bore is displaced and raised (forming a very fine cross-hatch pattern), thereby reducing clearance. Knurling also provides for excellent oil control. The possibility of knurling rather than reaming the guides should be discussed with a machinist.

REFACING

Valve refacing should only be handled by a reputable machine shop, as the experience and equipment needed to do the job are beyond that of the average owner/mechanic. During the course of a normal valve job, refacing is necessary when simply lapping the valves into their seats will not correct the seat and face wear. When the valves are reground (resurfaced), the valve seats must also be recut, again requiring special equipment and experience.

Valve Seats

REPLACEMENT

Check the valve seat inserts for any evidence of pitting or excessive wear at the valve contact surface. The valve seats in all engines covered here can be replaced. Because the cylinder head must be machined to accept the new seat inserts, consult an engine specialist or machinist about this work.

➡**When repairing a valve seat, first check the valve and guide; if wear is evident here, replace the valve and/or guide, then correct the valve seat.**

Valve Springs

REMOVAL & INSTALLATION

Z20 Engines

The valve springs in these engines can be removed without removing the camshaft, while the cylinder head is in place. Follow the Valves Removal and Installation procedure if the head has already been removed.

1. Remove the rocker cover. Set the cylinder on which you will be working to TDC on the compression stroke.
2. Remove the rocker shaft assembly.

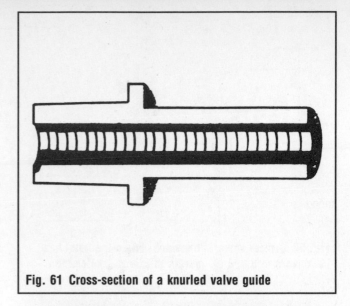

Fig. 61 Cross-section of a knurled valve guide

With the valve spring out of the way, the valve stem seals may now be replaced

3. Remove one spark plug on whichever cylinder you are working.
4. Install an air hose adaptor into the spark plug hole and apply about 71 psi of pressure into the cylinder. This will hole the valves in place, preventing them from dropping into the cylinder when the springs are removed.
5. Install a valve spring compressing tool similar to the one illustrated and remove the valve spring and valve steam seal. Use care not to lose the keepers.

➡**Always install new oil seals during reassembly.**

6. Reassemble the valve and components. Making sure the air pressure in the cylinder is at 71 psi while the springs are being installed.
7. Remove air adaptor and install the spark plug.
8. Install the rocker shaft and rocker cover with a new gasket.

L18, L20, L24, LD28 Engines

The camshafts in these engines must be removed in order to remove the valve springs. Follow the Camshaft Removal and Installation procedure, then follow the valve spring removal procedure listed above for the Z-series engines. If you are removing the valve springs with the cylinder head already removed from the engine, follow the procedure under Valves Removal and Installation.

HEIGHT & PRESSURE CHECK

1. Place the valve spring on a flat, clean surface next to a square.

2. Measure the height of the spring, and rotate it against the edge of the square to measure distortion (out-of-roundness). If spring height varies between springs by more than 1.5mm or if the distortion exceeds 1.5mm, replace the spring(s) in question. Outer valve spring squareness should not exceed 2.2mm; inner spring squareness should not exceed 1.9mm.

A valve spring tester is needed to test spring test pressure, so the valve springs usually must be taken to a machinist or engine specialist for this test. Compare the tested pressure with the pressures listed in the Valve Specifications chart in this section.

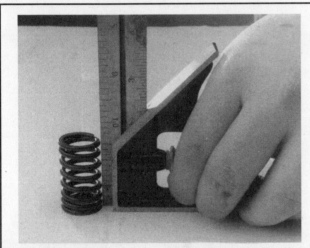

Check the valve spring for squareness on a flat service; a carpenter's square can be used

Oil Pan

REMOVAL & INSTALLATION

All Engines
♦ See Figures 62 and 63

To remove the oil pan it will be necessary to unbolt the motor mounts and jack up the engine to gain clearance. Drain the oil, remove the attaching screws, and remove the oil pan and gasket.

✳✳ CAUTION

The EPA warns that prolonged contact with used engine oil may cause a number of skin disorders, including cancer! You should make every effort to minimize your exposure to used engine oil. Protective gloves should be worn when changing the oil. Wash your hands and any other exposed skin areas as soon as possible after exposure to used engine oil. Soap and water, or waterless hand cleaner should be used.

Do not insert a prytool into the oil pan to remove it, because this may bend or deform the oil pan flange. Install the oil pan with a new gasket and sealant at the points indicated, tightening the screws to 48–84 in. lbs. Wait at least 30 minutes before refilling engine oil. Overtightening will distort the pan lip, causing leakage. Do not use a liquid gasket for the oil pan if original equipment was a rubber gasket.

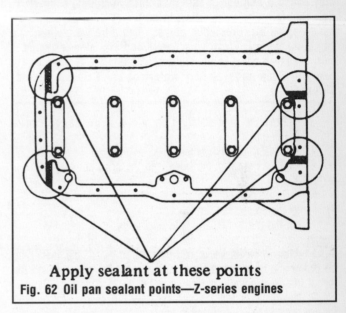

Apply sealant at these points
Fig. 62 Oil pan sealant points—Z-series engines

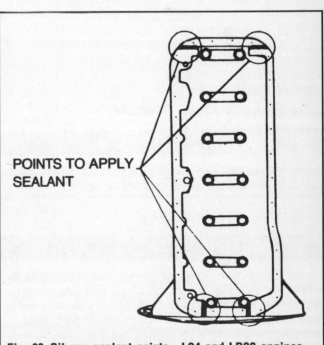

POINTS TO APPLY SEALANT

Fig. 63 Oil pan sealant points—L24 and LD28 engines

Oil Pump

REMOVAL & INSTALLATION

1973–79

1. Remove the distributor on the L18, L20B and L24 engines.
2. Drain the engine oil.

✳✳ CAUTION

The EPA warns that prolonged contact with used engine oil may cause a number of skin disorders, including cancer! You should make every effort to minimize your exposure to used engine oil. Protective gloves should be worn when changing the oil. Wash your hands and any other exposed skin areas as soon as possible after exposure to used engine oil. Soap and water, or waterless hand cleaner should be used.

3. Remove the front stabilizer bar if it is in the way of removing the oil pump.
4. Remove the splash shield.
5. Remove the oil pump body with the drive spindle assembly.
6. Turn the crankshaft so that the No. 1 piston is at TDC of the compression stroke.
7. Fill the pump housing with engine oil, then align the punch mark on the spindle with the hole in the oil pump.
8. With a new gasket placed over the drive spindle, install the oil pump and drive spindle assembly so that the projection on the top of the drive spindle is located in the 11:25 o'clock position.
9. Install the distributor with the metal tip of the rotor pointing toward the No. 1 spark plug tower of the distributor cap.
10. Install the splash shield and front stabilizer bar if it was removed.
11. Refill the engine oil. Start the engine, check ignition timing and check for oil leaks.

1980–84 Models
♦ See Figures 64, 65, 66, 67 and 68

✳✳ CAUTION

Before attempting to remove the oil pump on 1980 models, you must perform the following procedures:

a. Drain the oil from the oil pan.

✳✳ CAUTION

The EPA warns that prolonged contact with used engine oil may cause a number of skin disorders, including cancer! You should make every effort to minimize your exposure to used engine oil. Protective gloves should be worn when changing the oil. Wash your hands and any other exposed skin areas as soon as possible after exposure to used engine oil. Soap and water, or waterless hand cleaner should be used.

Fig. 64 Remove the oil pump—Z-series and L-series engines

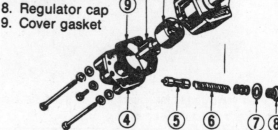

1. Oil pump body
2. Inner rotor and shaft
3. Outer rotor
4. Oil pump cover
5. Regulator valve
6. Regulator spring
7. Washer
8. Regulator cap
9. Cover gasket

Fig. 65 Exploded view of the oil pump—Z-series and L-series engines

b. Turn the crankshaft so that No. 1 piston is at TDC on its compression stroke.

c. Remove the distributor cap and mark the position of the distributor rotor in relation to the distributor base with a piece of chalk (gasoline engine only).

1. Remove the front stabilizer bar, if so equipped.
2. Remove the splash shield.
3. Remove the oil pump body with the drive spindle assembly.
4. To install, fill the pump housing with engine oil, align the punch mark on the spindle with the hole in the pump. No. 1 piston should be at TDC on its compression stroke.
5. With a new gasket placed over the drive spindle, install the oil pump and drive spindle assembly. On gasoline engines make sure the tip of the drive spindle fits into the distributor shaft

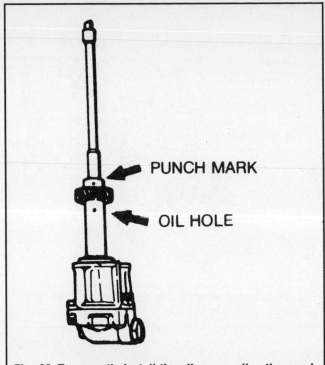

Fig. 66 To correctly install the oil pump, align the punch marks—Z-series and L-series engines

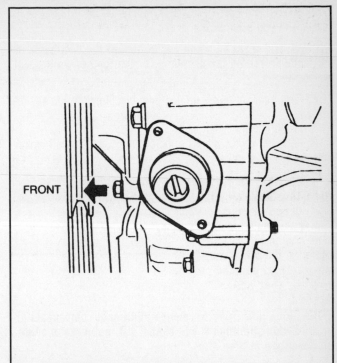

Fig. 67 Position the distributor drive spindle as shown—L-series engines

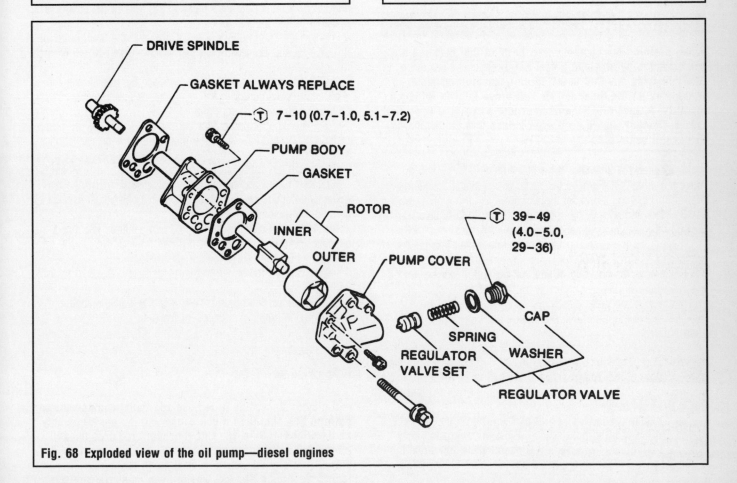

Fig. 68 Exploded view of the oil pump—diesel engines

notch securely. The distributor rotor should be pointing to the matchmark you made earlier.

➡️**Great care must be taken not to disturb the distributor rotor while installing the oil pump, or the ignition timing will be wrong.**

6. Install the splash shield and front stabilizer bar if it was removed.

7. Install the distributor cap.

8. Refill the engine oil. Start the engine, check ignition timing and check for oil leaks.

Timing Chain Cover

REMOVAL & INSTALLATION

All Gasoline Engines

◆ **See Figure 69**

➡️**It may be necessary to remove additional components to perform this operation if you cannot cut the gasket cleanly as described in Step 10.**

1. Disconnect the negative battery cable from the battery, drain the cooling system, and remove the radiator together with the upper and lower radiator hoses.

✳️✳️ CAUTION

When draining the coolant, keep in mind that cats and dogs are attracted by ethylene glycol antifreeze, and are quite likely to drink any that is left in an uncovered container or in puddles on the ground. This will prove fatal in sufficient quantity. Always drain the coolant into a sealable container. Coolant should be reused unless it is contaminated or several years old.

2. Loosen the alternator drive belt adjusting screw and remove the drive belt. Remove the bolts, which attach the alternator bracket to the engine and set the alternator aside out of the way.

3. Mark and remove the distributor. Refer to Distributor Removal and Installation, if necessary.

4. Remove the oil pump attaching screws, then take out the pump and its drive spindle.

5. Remove the cooling fan and the fan pulley together with the drive belt.

6. Remove the water pump.

7. Remove the crankshaft pulley bolt and remove the crankshaft pulley.

8. Remove the bolts holding the front cover to the front of the cylinder block, the four bolts which retain the front of the oil pan to the bottom of the front cover, and the two bolts which are screwed down through the front of the cylinder head and into the top of the front cover.

9. Carefully pry the front cover off the front of the engine.

10. Cut the exposed front section of the oil pan gasket away from the oil pan. Do the same to the gasket at the top of the front cover. Remove the two side gaskets and clean all of the mating surfaces.

11. Cut the portions needed from a new oil pan gasket and top front cover gasket.

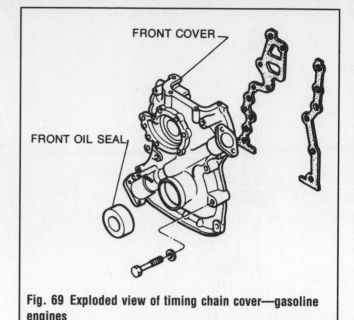

Fig. 69 Exploded view of timing chain cover—gasoline engines

12. Apply sealer to all of the gaskets and position them on the engine in their proper places.

13. Apply a light coating of grease to the crankshaft oil seal and carefully mount the front cover to the front of the engine and install all of the mounting bolts.

Tighten the 8mm bolts to 7–12 ft. lbs. and the 6mm bolts to 36–72 inch lbs. Tighten the oil pan attaching bolts to 48–84 inch lbs.

14. Before installing the oil pump, place the gasket over the shaft and make sure that the mark on the drive spindle faces (aligned) with the oil pump hole.

15. Install the oil pump after priming it with oil. For oil pump installation procedures, see Oil Pump Removal and Installation in this section.

16. Install the crankshaft pulley and bolt.

17. Install the water pump with a new gasket. Install the fan pulley and cooling fan. Install the drive belt and adjust the belt to the correct tension.

18. Install the distributor in the correct position. Reconnect the alternator bracket and alternator if it was removed. Install the drive belt and adjust the belt to the correct tension.

19. Reconnect the upper and lower radiator hoses and refill the cooling system.

20. Reconnect the negative battery cable. Start the engine, check ignition timing and check for leaks.

Diesel Engine

◆ **See Figures 70 and 71**

➡️**It may be necessary to remove additional components to perform this operation if you cannot cut the gasket cleanly as described in Step 18. This procedure requires the removal and subsequent installation of the fuel injection pump. It is a good idea to read through the Diesel Fuel Injection section in Section 4 before you continue with this procedure. You may decide that the job is better left to a qualified service technician.**

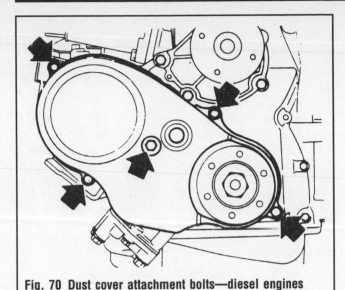

Fig. 70 Dust cover attachment bolts—diesel engines

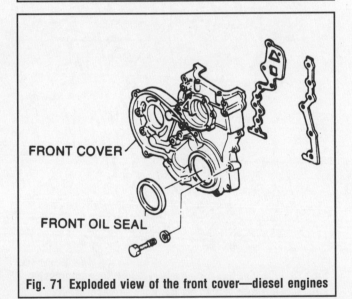

FRONT COVER

FRONT OIL SEAL

Fig. 71 Exploded view of the front cover—diesel engines

1. Disconnect the negative battery cable. Drain the cooling system and then remove the radiator together with the upper and lower radiator hoses.

✳✳ CAUTION

When draining the coolant, keep in mind that cats and dogs are attracted by ethylene glycol antifreeze, and are quite likely to drink any that is left in an uncovered container or in puddles on the ground. This will prove fatal in sufficient quantity. Always drain the coolant into a sealable container. Coolant should be reused unless it is contaminated or several years old.

2. Remove the fan, fan coupling and fan pulley.
3. Unscrew the retaining bolts on the crankshaft damper pulley. Use a plastic mallet and lightly tap around the outer edges of the pulley; this should loosen it enough so that you can pull it off. If not, use a two armed gear puller.
4. Remove the power steering pump, bracket and idler pulley (if so equipped).

5. Unscrew the five mounting bolts and remove the front dust cover.
6. Remove the thermostat housing and the bottom bypass inlet with the hose.
7. Remove the engine slinger.
8. Tag and disconnect all hoses and lines running from the injection pump. Make sure to plug any hoses or lines to prevent dust or dirt from entering.
9. Drain the engine oil.

✳✳ CAUTION

The EPA warns that prolonged contact with used engine oil may cause a number of skin disorders, including cancer! You should make every effort to minimize your exposure to used engine oil. Protective gloves should be worn when changing the oil. Wash your hands and any other exposed skin areas as soon as possible after exposure to used engine oil. Soap and water, or waterless hand cleaner should be used.

10. Remove the oil cooler and coolant hose together with the oil filter.
11. Remove the water inlet, the oil dipstick and the right side engine mounting bracket.
12. Remove the oil pump.
13. Remove the injection pump as detailed in Section 4.
14. Remove the water pump.
15. Loosen the mounting bolt and remove the injection pump drive crank pulley. You will need a two armed gear puller.
16. Remove the bolts holding the front cover to the front of the cylinder block, the four bolts which retain the front of the oil pan to the bottom of the front cover, and the two bolts which are screwed down through the front of the cylinder head and into the top of the front cover.
17. Carefully pry the front cover off the front of the engine.
18. Cut the exposed front section of the oil pan gasket away from the oil pan. Do the same to the gasket at the top of the front cover. Remove the two side gaskets and clean all of the mating surfaces.
19. Cut the portions needed from a new oil pan gasket and top front cover gasket.
20. Apply sealer to all of the gaskets and position them on the engine in their proper places.
21. Apply a light coating of grease to the crankshaft oil seal and carefully mount the front cover to the front of the engine and install all of the mounting bolts.
22. Tighten the 8mm bolts to 7–12 ft. lbs. and the 6mm bolts to 36–72 inch lbs. Tighten the oil pan attaching bolts to 48–84 inch lbs.
23. Before installing the oil pump, place the gasket over the shaft and make sure that the mark on the drive spindle faces (aligned) with the oil pump hole.
24. Install the oil pump after priming it with oil. For oil pump installation procedures, see Oil Pump Removal and Installation in this section.
25. Install the injection drive crank pulley and mounting bolt.
26. Install the water pump with a new gasket.
27. Install the injection pump. Refer to Injection Pump Removal and Installation.
28. Reconnect the right side engine bracket, oil dipstick and the water outlet. Install the oil cooler, filter and necessary hoses.

29. Reconnect all lines and hoses to the injection pump. Install the engine slinger.

30. Install the thermostat housing and bypass inlet with the hose.

31. Install the front dust cover and install the idler pulley, power steering bracket and power steering pump.

32. Install the crankshaft damper pulley, cooling fan pulley, fan coupling and cooling fan.

33. Install all the drive belts that were removed and adjust the belts to the proper tension.

34. Connect the upper and lower radiator hoses and refill the cooling system. Reconnect the negative battery cable.

35. Check the injection pump timing and check for leaks.

Timing Chain, Gears and Tensioner

REMOVAL & INSTALLATION

All Gasoline Engines

♦ **See Figures 72, 73 and 74**

1. Before beginning any disassembly procedures, position the No. 1 piston at TDC on the compression stroke.

2. Remove the front cover as previously outlined. Remove the camshaft cover and remove the fuel pump if it runs off a cam lobe in front of the camshaft sprocket.

3. With the No. 1 piston at TDC, the timing marks in the camshaft sprocket and the timing chain should be visible. Mark both of them with paint. Also mark the relationship of the camshaft sprocket to the camshaft. At this point you will notice that there are three sets of timing marks and locating holes in the sprocket. They are for making adjustments to compensate for timing chain stretch. See the Timing Chain Adjustment for more details.

4. With the timing marks on the cam sprocket clearly marked, locate and mark the timing marks on the crankshaft sprocket. Also mark the chain timing mark. Of course, if the chain is not to be re-used, marking it is useless.

5. Unbolt the camshaft sprocket and remove the sprocket along with the chain. As you remove the chain, hold it where the chain

tensioner contacts it. When the chain is removed, the tensioner is going to come apart. Hold on to it and you won't lose any of the parts. There is no need to remove the chain guide unless it is being replaced.

6. Using a suitable gear puller, remove the crankshaft sprocket assembly.

To install:

7. Install the timing chain and the camshaft sprocket together after first positioning the chain over the crankshaft sprocket. Position the sprocket so that the marks made earlier line up. This is assuming that the engine has not been disturbed. The camshaft and crankshaft keys should both be pointed upward. If a new chain and/or gear is being installed, position the sprocket so that the timing marks on the chain align with the marks on the crankshaft sprocket and the camshaft sprocket (with both keys pointing

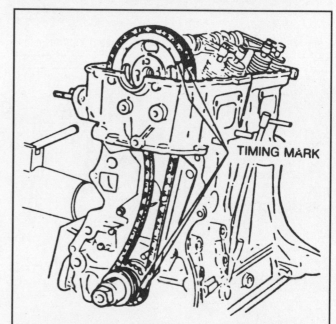

Fig. 73 With the No. 1 piston at TDC of the compression stroke, the timing marks on the chain and sprockets respectively should align as shown—Z20 engines

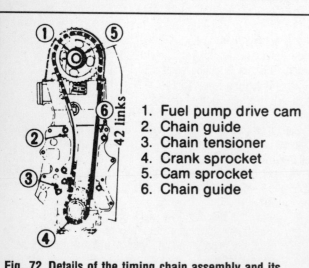

1. Fuel pump drive cam
2. Chain guide
3. Chain tensioner
4. Crank sprocket
5. Cam sprocket
6. Chain guide

Fig. 72 Details of the timing chain assembly and its alignment—L-series engines

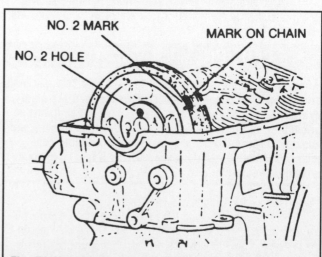

Fig. 74 Use the No. 2 mark and hole to align the camshaft—Z20 engines

To remove the timing chain, position the No. 1 cylinder at TDC of the compression stroke

If you are re-using the timing chain, mark it with paint to ensure accurate installation

Mark the camshaft sprocket and chain for reference—note (UP) indicator for TDC (arrow)

up). The marks are on the right-hand side of the sprockets as you face the engine. The L18 has 42 pins between the mating marks of the chain and sprockets when the chain is installed correctly. The L20B has 44 pins. The 1977–78 L24 engine used in the 810 has 42 pins between timing marks. The L24 (1979–84), Z20E and Z20S engines do not use the pin counting method for finding correct valve timing. Instead, position the key in the crankshaft sprocket so that it is pointing upward and install the camshaft sprocket on the camshaft with its dowel pin at the top using the No. 2 (No. 1 on the L24) mounting hole and timing mark. The painted links of the chain should be on the right-hand side of the sprockets as you face the engine. See the illustration.

➡The factory manual refers to the pins you are to count in the L-series engines as links, but in the U.S., this is not correct. Count the pins. There are two pins per link. This is an important step. If you do not get the exact number of pins between the timing marks, valve timing will be incorrect and the engine will either not run at all, in which case

Remove the camshaft sprocket bolt

Lift out the timing chain and camshaft sprocket as an assembly

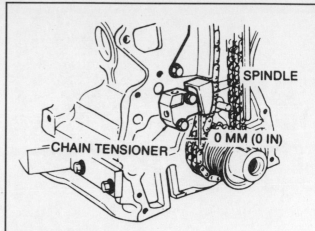

Fig. 75 If the chain tensioner was removed, install it as shown—1979–84 810/Maxima gasoline and diesel engines

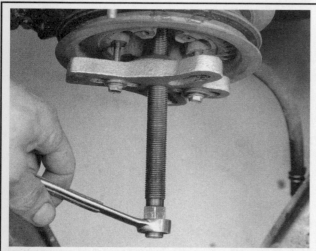

Using a suitable gear puller, remove the crankshaft sprocket

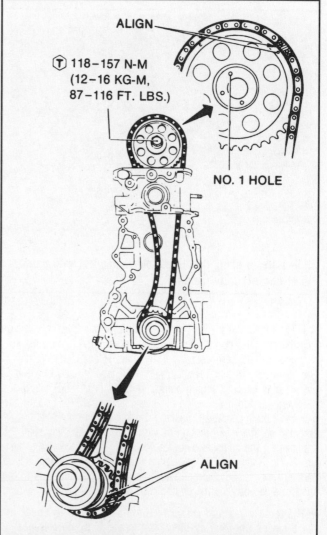

Fig. 76 Align the timing chain and sprockets as shown—1979–84 810/Maxima gasoline and diesel engines

you may stand the chance of bending the valves, or the engine will run very poorly.

8. Install the chain tensioner and the front cover assembly.

If timing chain assembly uses chain guides these guides do not have to be removed to replace the timing chain. Check the timing chain for cracks and excessive wear.

Diesel Engine

▶ **See Figures 75 and 76**

1. Follow Steps 1–6 of the preceding Gasoline Engine procedure. You need not remove the fuel pump as detailed in Step 2.

2. Install the crankshaft sprocket. Make sure that the mating marks on the sprocket face the front of the car.

3. Install the timing chain and the camshaft sprocket together after first positioning the chain over the crankshaft sprocket. Position the cam sprocket so that the marks made earlier line up. This

is assuming that the engine has not been disturbed. The camshaft and crankshaft keys should be pointing upward. If a new chain and/or gear is being installed, position the sprocket so that the timing marks on the chain align with the marks on the crankshaft and camshaft sprockets (with both keys pointing up). The marks are on the right-hand side of the sprockets as you face the engine. Insert the camshaft dowel pin into the No. 1 hole in the camshaft sprocket. Install and tighten the camshaft sprocket bolt.

4. Install the chain guide (if removed) and the chain tensioner. Tighten the slack side (left side when facing the engine) chain guide mounting bolt so that the protrusion of the chain tensioner spindle is 0.

5. Install the front cover assembly.

TIMING CHAIN ADJUSTMENT

▶ See Figure 77

When the timing chain stretches excessively, the valve timing will be adversely affected. There are three sets of holes and timing marks on the camshaft sprocket.

If the stretch of the chain roller links is excessive, adjust camshaft sprocket location by transferring the set position of the camshaft sprocket from the factory position of No. 1 or No. 2 to one of the other positions as follows:

1. Turn the crankshaft until the No. 1 piston is at TDC on the compression stroke. Examine whether the camshaft sprocket location notch is to the left of the oblong groove on the camshaft retaining plate. If the notch in the sprocket is to the left of the groove in the retaining plate, then the chain is stretched and needs adjusting.

2. Remove the camshaft sprocket together with the chain and reinstall the sprocket and chain with the locating dowel on the camshaft inserted into either the No. 2 or 3 hole of the sprocket. The timing mark on the timing chain must be aligned with the

mark on the sprocket. The amount of modification is 4° of crankshaft rotation for each mark.

3. Recheck the valve timing as outlined in Step 1. The notch in the sprocket should be to the right of the groove in the camshaft retaining plate.

4. If and when the notch cannot be brought to the right of the groove, the timing chain is worn beyond repair and must be replaced.

Timing Belt

REMOVAL & INSTALLATION

▶ See Figures 78, 79, 80, 81 and 82

1. Remove the battery ground cable.
2. Remove the cooling fan.
3. Remove the power steering, alternator, and air conditioner compressor belts if so equipped.
4. Set the No. 1 cylinder at TDC on the compression stroke. The accompanying illustration shows the timing mark alignment for TDC.
5. Remove the front upper and lower timing belt covers.
6. Loosen the timing belt tensioner and return spring, then remove the timing belt.
7. Carefully inspect the condition of the timing belt. There should be no breaks or cracks anywhere on the belt. Especially check around the bottoms of the teeth, where they intersect the belt; cracks often show up here. Evidence of any wear or damage on the belt means the belt should be replaced.
8. To install the belt, first make sure that No. 1 cylinder is set at TDC on compression. Install the belt tensioner and return spring.

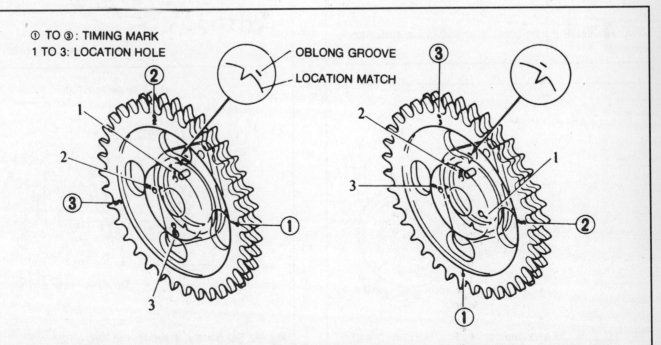

Fig. 77 Use this illustration to make sure you have the timing chain sprockets correctly aligned before and after chain adjustment

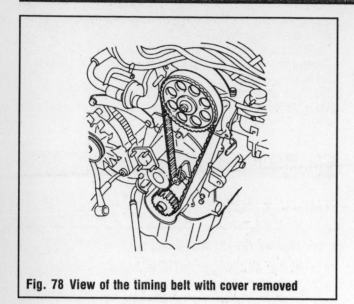

Fig. 78 View of the timing belt with cover removed

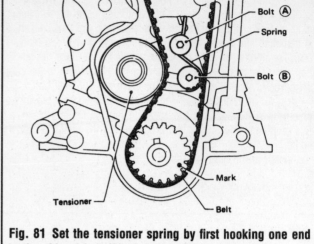

Fig. 81 Set the tensioner spring by first hooking one end to the side of bolt (B), then the other on the pawl bracket

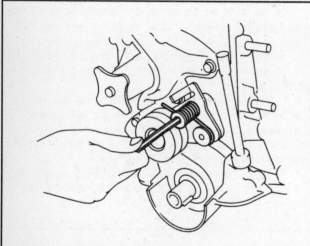

Fig. 79 Install the belt tensioner and return spring as shown

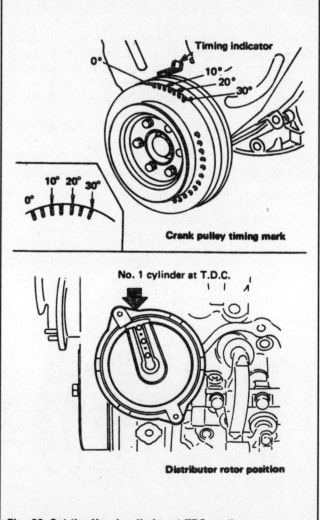

Fig. 82 Set the No. 1 cylinder at TDC on the compression stroke

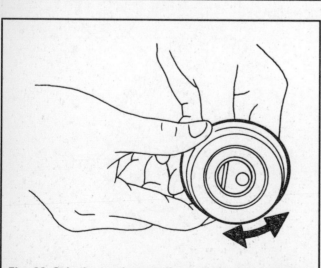

Fig. 80 Spin the tensioner pulley to make sure it works smoothly

➡If the coarse stud has been removed, apply Loctite® or another locking thread sealer to the stud threads before installing.

9. Make sure the tensioner bolts are not securely tightened before the drive belt is installed. Make sure the tensioner pulley can be rotated smoothly.

10. Make sure the timing belt is in good condition and clean. Do not bend it. Place the belt in position, aligning the white lines on the timing belt with the punch mark on the camshaft pulleys and the crankshaft pulley. Make sure the arrow on the belt is pointing toward the front belt covers.

11. Tighten the belt tensioner and assemble the spring. To set the spring, first hook one end on bolt B side, then hook the other end on the tensioner bracket pawl. Rotate the crankshaft two turns clockwise, then tighten bolt B then bolt A. At this point, belt tension will automatically be at the specified value.

12. Install the upper and lower timing belt covers.

13. Install and adjust all the drive belts.

14. Connect the battery cable, start engine and check the ignition timing.

Camshaft Sprocket

REMOVAL & INSTALLATION

1. Refer to the "Timing Belt/Chain, Removal and Installation" procedures, in this section and remove the timing chain/belt.

2. Remove the sprocket retaining bolt and remove the sprocket from the camshaft. On engines with a timing chain the chain and sprocket are removed at the same time.

3. To install reverse the removal procedures.

➡On the belt driven engines make sure to install the crank pulley plate in the correct position. On chain driven engines make sure oil thrower, oil pump drive gear are installed in the correct position.

Camshaft

REMOVAL & INSTALLATION

L18, L20B, and L24 Engines
◆ **See Figures 83, 84 and 85**

➡Removal of the cylinder head from the engine is optional. The camshaft cover and rocker cover are one and the same. Mark and keep all parts in order for correct installation.

1. Remove the camshaft sprocket from the camshaft together with the timing chain. Refer to the Timing Chain procedures, if necessary.

2. Loosen the valve rocker pivot locknut and remove the rocker arm by pressing down on the valve spring.

3. Remove the two retaining nuts on the camshaft retainer plate at the front of the cylinder head and carefully slide the camshaft out (towards the front of the vehicle) of the camshaft carrier.

4. Check camshaft runout, end-play, wear and journal clearance as described in this chapter.

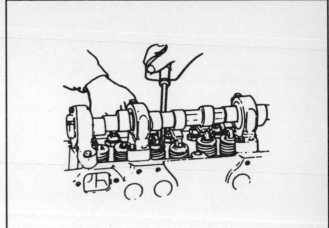
Fig. 83 Remove the rocker arm by pressing down on the valve spring

Fig. 84 Carefully slide the camshaft out of the carrier

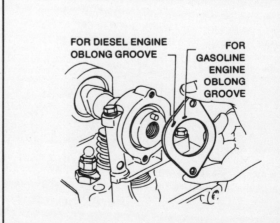
Fig. 85 When installing the retaining plate, make sure the oblong groove is facing the front of the engine

5. Lightly coat the camshaft bearings with clean motor oil and carefully slide the camshaft into place in the camshaft carrier.

6. Install the camshaft retainer plate with the oblong groove in the face of the plate facing toward the front of the engine.

7. Check the valve timing as outlined under Timing Chain Removal and Installation and install the timing sprocket on the camshaft, tightening the bolt together with the fuel pump cam (gasoline engines only) to 86–116 ft. lbs.

8. Install the rocker arms by pressing down the valve springs with a screwdriver and install the valve rocker springs.

9. Install the cylinder head, if it was removed, and assemble the rest of the engine.

10. Start and run engine to normal operating temperature. Remove rocker cover, check and adjust valves if necessary. Install rocker cover with new gasket and check for oil leaks.

Z20E and Z20S Engines

◆ **See Figures 86, 87, 88 and 89**

➡**Removal of the cylinder head from the engine is optional. Mark and keep all parts in order for correct installation.**

1. Remove the camshaft sprocket from the camshaft together with the timing chain, after setting the No. 1 piston at TDC on its compression stroke. Refer to the Timing Chain Removal and Installation procedures.

2. Loosen the bolts holding the rocker shaft assembly in place and remove the six center bolts. Do not pull the four end bolts out of the rocker assembly because they hold the unit together.

➡**When loosening the bolts, work from the ends in and loosen all of the bolts a little at a time so that you do not strain the camshaft or the rocker assembly. Remember, the camshaft is under pressure from the valve springs.**

3. After removing the rocker assembly, remove the camshaft. Slide the camshaft carefully out of the front of the vehicle.

➡**Mark and keep the disassembled parts in order.**

If you disassembled the rocker unit, assemble as follows.

4. Install the mounting brackets, valve rockers and springs observing the following considerations:

a. The two rocker shafts are different. Both have punch marks in the ends that face the front of the engine. The rocker shaft that goes on the side of the intake manifold has two slits in its end just below the punch mark. The exhaust side rocker shaft does not have slits.

b. The rocker arms for the intake and exhaust valves are interchangeable between cylinders one and three and are identified by the mark 1. Similarly, the rockers for cylinders two and four are interchangeable and are identified by the mark 2.

c. The rocker shaft mounting brackets are also coded for correct placement with either an A or a Z plus a number code. See the illustration for proper placement.

5. Check camshaft runout, end-play wear and journal clearance as described in this chapter.

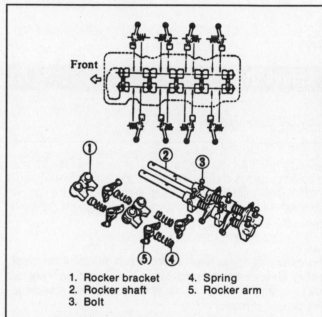

1. Rocker bracket
2. Rocker shaft
3. Bolt
4. Spring
5. Rocker arm

Fig. 87 Exploded view of the rocker shaft assembly and mounting position—Z20 engines

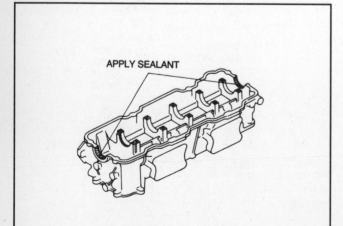

APPLY SEALANT

Fig. 86 Apply sealant at the points indicated just before camshaft installation—Z-series engines

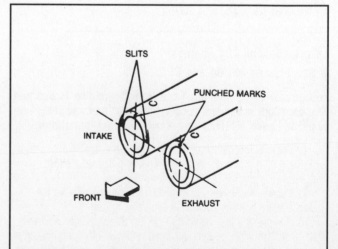

SLITS

PUNCHED MARKS

INTAKE

FRONT

EXHAUST

Fig. 88 Note the difference in rocker shafts—Z20 engines

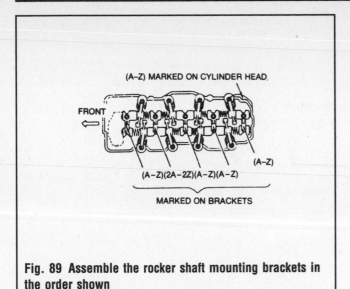

Fig. 89 Assemble the rocker shaft mounting brackets in the order shown

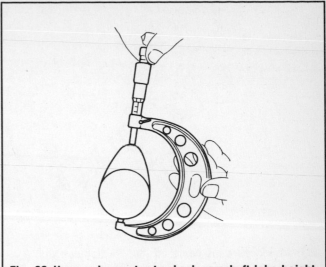

Fig. 90 Use a micrometer to check camshaft lobe height

6. Apply sealant to the end camshaft saddles as shown in the accompanying illustration. Place the camshaft on the head with its dowel pin pointing up.

7. Fit the rocker assembly on the head, making sure you mount it on its knock pin.

8. Tighten the bolts to 11–18 ft. lbs., in several stages working from the middle bolts and moving outwards on both sides.

➡**Make sure the engine is on TDC of the compression stroke for No. 1 piston or you may damage some valves.**

9. Adjust the valves. Refer to the Valve Adjustment procedure.

CHECKING CAMSHAFT RUN-OUT

Camshaft runout should be checked when the camshaft has been removed from the cylinder head. An accurate dial indicator is needed for this procedure; engine specialists and most machine shops have this equipment. If you have access to a dial indicator, or can take your cam to someone who does, measure cam bearing journal runout. The maximum (limit) runout on the L18, L20, L24 and LD28 camshafts is 0.02mm. The runout limit on the Z20 and Z22 series camshafts is 0.20mm. If the runout exceeds the limit replace the camshaft.

CHECKING CAMSHAFT LOBE HEIGHT

◗ **See Figure 90**

Use a micrometer to check cam (lobe) height, making sure the anvil and the spindle of the micrometer are positioned directly on the heel and tip of the cam lobe as shown in the accompanying illustration. Use the specifications in the following chart to determine the lobe wear.

CAMSHAFT LOBE SPECIFICATIONS

Engine	Lobe	Lobe Height (in.)	Wear Limit (in.)
L18	Int. and Exh.	1.5728 to 1.3748	0.0098
L20	Int. and Exh.	1.5866 to 1.5886	0.0098
L24, LD28	Intake	1.5728 to 1.5748	0.0059
	Exhaust	1.5866 to 1.5886	0.0059
Z20	Int. and Exh.	1.5148 to 1.5168	0.0098

CHECKING CAMSHAFT JOURNALS & CAMSHAFT BEARING SADDLES

◗ **See Figure 91 and 92**

While the camshaft is still removed from the cylinder head, the camshaft bearing journals should be measured with a micrometer. Compare the measurements with those listed in the Camshaft Specifications chart in this section. If the measurements are less than the limits listed in the chart, the camshaft will have to be replaced, since the camshafts in all of the engines covered in this guide run directly on the cylinder head surface; no actual bearings or bushings are used, so no oversize bearings or bushings are available.

Using an inside dial gauge or inside micrometer, measure the inside diameter of the camshaft saddles (the camshaft mounts that are either integrally cast as part of the cylinder head, or are a bolted on, one piece unit. The Z-series engines use a saddle-and-cap arrangement. The inside diameter of the saddles on all engines is 48.00–48.01mm. The inside diameter on the KA24E with the camshaft bracket and rocker shaft torque to specifications is 31.5–33.00mm. The camshaft journal oil clearances are listed in the Camshaft Specifications chart in this section. If the saddle in-

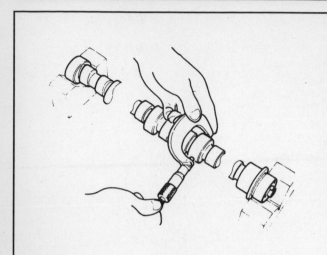

Fig. 91 Measure the camshaft journal diameter with a micrometer

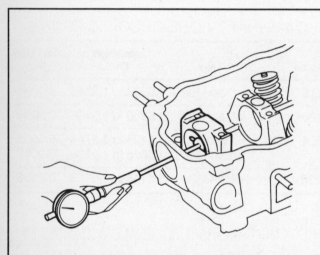

Fig. 92 Use an inside micrometer or dial gauge to measure camshaft bearing saddle diameters

side diameters exceed those listed above, the cylinder head must be replaced (again, because oversize bearings or bushings are not available).

CHECKING CAMSHAFT END-PLAY

After the camshaft has been installed, end-play should be checked. The camshaft sprocket should not be installed on the cam. Use a dial gauge to check the end-play, by moving the camshaft forward and backward in the cylinder head. End-play specifications for the Z20/22 series engines should not exceed 0.20mm. L18, L20, L24 and LD28 camshaft end-play should not exceed 0.38mm.

Pistons and Connecting Rods

REMOVAL

All Engines
◗ **See Figures 93 and 94**

 1. Remove the cylinder head.
 2. Remove the oil pan.
 3. Remove any carbon buildup from the cylinder wall at the top end of the piston travel with a ridge reamer tool.

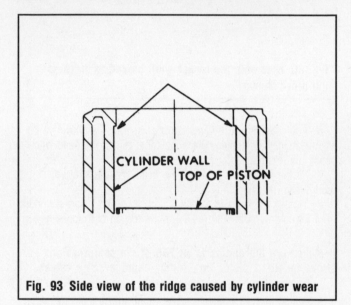

Fig. 93 Side view of the ridge caused by cylinder wear

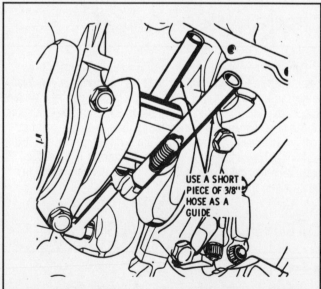

Fig. 94 Install lengths of rubber tubing on the rod bolts to protect the cylinder walls from scoring

4. Position the piston to be removed at the bottom of its stroke so that the connecting rod bearing cap can be reached easily from under the engine.

5. Unscrew the connecting rod bearing cap nuts and remove the cap and lower half of the bearing. Cover the rod bolts with lengths of rubber tubing or hose to protect the cylinder walls when the rod and piston assembly is driven out.

6. Push the piston and connecting rod up and out of the cylinder block with a length of wood. Use care not to scratch the cylinder wall with the connecting rod or the wooden tool.

INSTALLATION

Except LD28 Diesel/Engine

1. Keep all of the components from each cylinder together and install them in the cylinder from which they were removed.

2. Coat the bearing face of the connecting rod and the outer face of the pistons with engine oil.

3. See the illustrations, the correct placement of the piston rings for your model and engine size.

4. Turn the crankshaft until the rod journal of the particular cylinder you are working on is brought to the TDC position.

5. With the piston and rings clamped in a ring compressor, the notched mark on the head of the piston toward the front of the engine, and the oil hole side of the connecting rod toward the fuel pump side of the engine, push the piston and connecting rod assembly into the cylinder bore until the big bearing end of the connecting rod contacts and is seated on the rod journal of the crankshaft. Use care not to scratch the cylinder wall with the connecting rod.

➡ **See LD28 Diesel below for piston installation details on that engine.**

6. Push down farther on the piston and turn the crankshaft while the connecting rod rides around on the crankshaft rod journal. Turn the crankshaft until the crankshaft rod journal is at BDC (bottom dead center).

7. Align the mark on the connecting rod bearing cap with that on the connecting rod and tighten the bearing cap bolts to the specified torque.

8. Install all of the piston/connecting rod assemblies in the manner outlined above.

9. Install the oil strainer, pickup tube and oil pan.

10. Install the cylinder head.

11. Install engine assembly in vehicle.

12. Check all fluid levels and road test.

LD28 Diesel

▶ **See Figures 95 thru 101**

When replacing pistons in the LD28 diesel engine, the amount of projection of each piston crown above the deck of the block must be measured.

1. Clean the deck of the cylinder block completely.

2. Set a dial gauge, as shown on the cylinder block surface in the illustration, to zero.

3. For every cylinder, measure the piston projection and record the length.

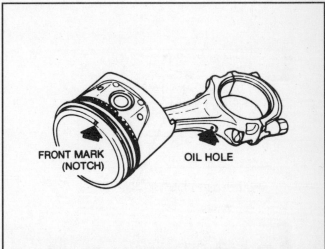

Fig. 95 View of the correct piston-to-rod relationship—except LD28 engine

Installing the piston into the block using a ring compressor and the handle of a hammer

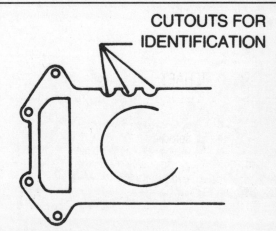

Fig. 96 View of the head gasket cutouts for identification, determining piston projection and gasket thickness—LD28 engine

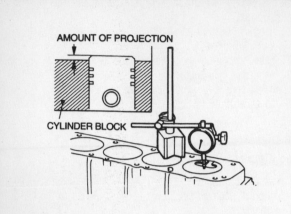

Fig. 97 Set the dial gauge at zero, then measure and record the length of each piston projection—LD28 engine

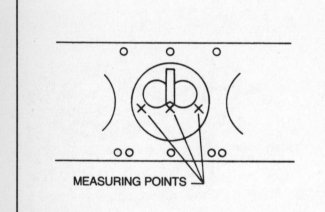

Fig. 98 Piston projection measuring points—LD28 engine

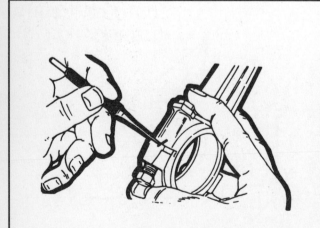

Fig. 99 Matchmark each rod cap to its connecting rod

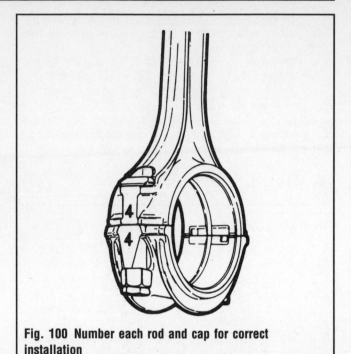

Fig. 100 Number each rod and cap for correct installation

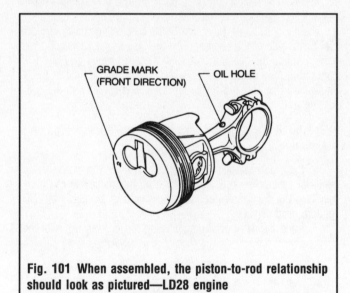

Fig. 101 When assembled, the piston-to-rod relationship should look as pictured—LD28 engine

➡ Be sure to measure the length of piston projection at at least three points for every cylinder.

4. Determine the maximum length of piston projection and select the suitable head gasket according to the chart below.

➡ The head gaskets have cutout(s) in them for identification purposes. When a head gasket needs to be replaced, always install a gasket of the same thickness.

CLEANING & INSPECTION

Clean the piston after removing the rings (See Piston Ring and Wrist Pin Removal and Installation), by first scraping any carbon from the piston top. Do not scratch the piston in any way during

Diesel Engine Head Gasket Selection Chart

Piston Projection mm (in)	Cylinder Head Gasket Thickness mm (in)	No. of Cutouts in Cylinder Head Gasket
Below 0.487 (0.0192)	1.12 (0.0441)	1
0.487–0.573 (0.0192–0.0226)	1.2 (0.047)	2
Above 0.573 (0.0226)	1.28 (0.0504)	3

cleaning. Use a broken piston ring or ring cleaning tool to clean out the ring grooves. Clean the entire piston with solvent and a brush (NOT a wire brush).

Once the piston is thoroughly cleaned, insert the side of a good piston ring (both No. 1 and No. 2 compression on each piston) into its respective groove. Using a feeler gauge, measure the clearance between the ring and its groove. (See Piston Ring Side Clearance Check for more details). If clearance is greater than the maximum listed under Ring Side Clearance in the Piston and Ring chart, replace the ring(s) and if necessary, the piston.

To check ring end-gap, insert a compression ring into the cylinder. Lightly oil the cylinder bore and push the ring down into the cylinder with a piston, to the bottom of its travel. Measure the ring end-gap with a feeler gauge. If the gap is not within specification, replace the ring; DO NOT file the ring ends.

CYLINDER BORE INSPECTION

Place a rag over the crankshaft journals. Wipe out each cylinder with a clean, solvent soaked rag. Visually inspect the cylinder bores for roughness, scoring or scuffing; also check the bores by feel. Measure the cylinder bore diameter with an inside micrometer, or a telescope gauge and micrometer. Measure the bore at

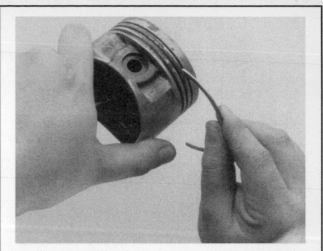

You can use a piece of an old ring to clean the piston grooves, BUT be careful, the ring is sharp

Checking the ring-to-ring groove clearance

Clean the piston grooves using a ring groove cleaner

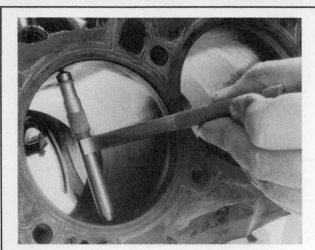

A telescoping gauge may be used to measure the cylinder bore diameter

Measure the piston's outer diameter using a micrometer

Using a ball type cylinder hone is an easy way to hone the cylinder bore

A solid hone can also be used to cross-hatch the cylinder bore

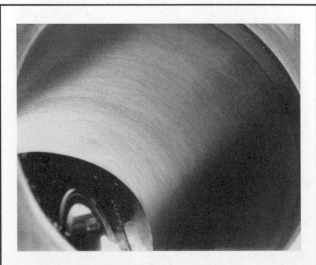

A properly cross-hatched cylinder bore

points parallel and perpendicular to the engine centerline at the top (below the ridge) and bottom of the bore. Subtract the bottom measurements from the top to determine cylinder taper.

Measure the piston diameter with a micrometer; since this micrometer may not be part of your tool kit as it is necessarily large, you may have to have the pistons measured at a machine shop. Take the measurements at right angles to the wrist pin center line, about an inch down the piston skirt from the top.

Compare this measurement to the bore diameter of each cylinder. The difference is the piston clearance. If the clearance is greater than that specified in the Piston and Ring Specifications chart, have the cylinders honed or rebored and replace the pistons with an oversize set. Piston clearance can also be checked by inverting a piston into an oiled cylinder, and sliding in a feeler gauge between the two.

➡**When any one cylinder needs boring, all cylinders must be bored.**

IDENTIFICATION & POSITIONING

The pistons are marked with a number or **F** in the piston head. When installed in the engine the number or **F** markings are to be facing toward the front of the engine.

The connecting rods are installed in the engine with the oil hole facing toward the fuel pump side (right) of the engine.

➡**It is advisable to number the pistons, connecting rods, and bearing caps in some manner so that they can be reinstalled in the same cylinder, facing in the same direction from which they are removed.**

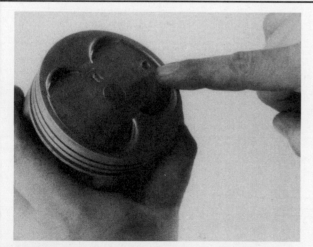

Most pistons are marked to indicate positioning in the engine (usually a mark means the side facing front)

PISTON RING & WRIST PIN REMOVAL

A piston ring expander is necessary for removing piston rings without damaging them; any other method (prytool blades, pliers, etc.) usually results in the rings being bent, scratched or distorted, or the piston itself being damaged. When the rings are removed, clean the ring grooves using an appropriate ring groove

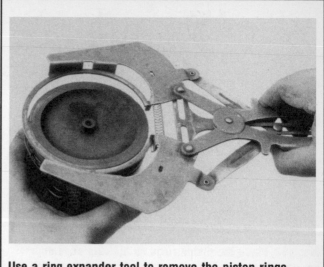

Use a ring expander tool to remove the piston rings

cleaning tool, using care not to cut too deeply. Thoroughly clean all carbon and varnish from the piston with solvent.

All the Datsun/Nissan pistons covered in this guide have a pressed in wrist pin, requiring a special press for removal. Take the piston and connecting rod assemblies to an engine specialist or machinist for wrist pin removal. The pins must also be pressed in during assembly.

PISTON RING END-GAP

Piston ring end-gap should be checked while the rings are removed from the pistons. Incorrect end-gap indicates that the wrong size rings are being used; ring breakage could occur.

Compress the piston rings to be used in a cylinder, one at a time, into that cylinder. Squirt clean oil into the cylinder, so that the rings and the top 50mm of cylinder wall are coated. Using an inverted piston, press the rings approximately 25mm below the deck of the block. Measure the ring end-gap with a feeler gauge, and compare to the Ring Gap chart in this section. Replace the ring if necessary.

PISTON RING SIDE CLEARANCE CHECK & INSTALLATION

◆ **See Figures 102, 103, 104, 105 and 106**

Check the pistons to see that the ring grooves and oil return holes have been properly cleaned. Slide a piston ring into its groove, and check the side clearance with a feeler gauge. On gasoline engines, make sure you insert the gauge between the ring and its lower land (lower edge of the groove), because any wear that occurs forms a step at the inner portion of the lower land. If the piston grooves have worn to the extent that relatively high steps exist on the lower land, the piston should be replaced, because these will interfere with the operation of the new rings and ring clearances will be excessive. Piston rings are not furnished in oversize widths to compensate for ring groove wear.

Install the rings on the piston, lowest ring first, using a piston ring expander. There is a high risk of breaking or distorting the

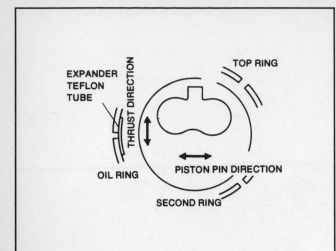

Fig. 102 Place the piston rings so the ring edge gaps are 120 degrees apart from each other—LD28 engine

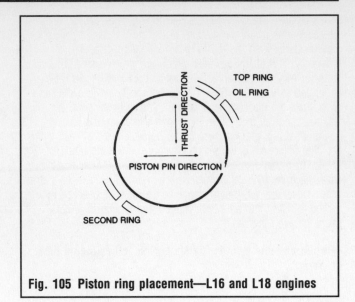

Fig. 105 Piston ring placement—L16 and L18 engines

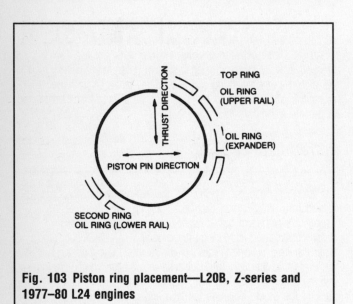

Fig. 103 Piston ring placement—L20B, Z-series and 1977–80 L24 engines

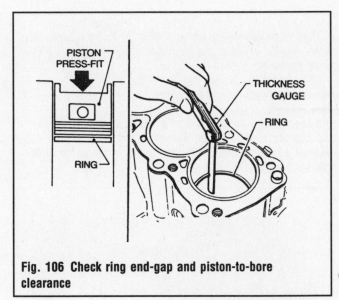

Fig. 106 Check ring end-gap and piston-to-bore clearance

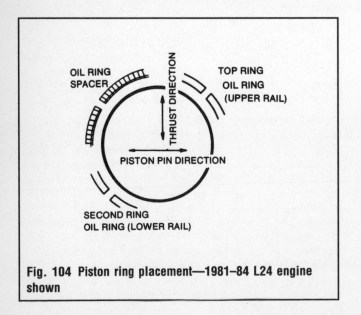

Fig. 104 Piston ring placement—1981–84 L24 engine shown

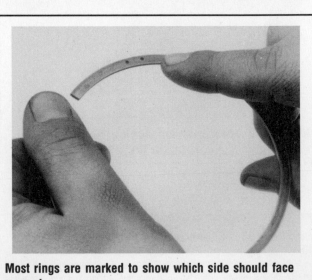

Most rings are marked to show which side should face upward

rings, or scratching the piston, if the rings are installed by hand or other means.

Position the rings on the piston as illustrated; spacing of the various piston ring gaps is crucial to proper oil retention and even cylinder wear. When installing new rings, refer to the installation diagram furnished with the new parts.

CONNECTION ROD INSPECTION & BEARING REPLACEMENT

♦ See Figure 107

Connecting rod side clearance and big end bearing inspection and replacement should be performed while the rods are still installed in the engine. Determine the clearance between the connecting rod sides and the crankshaft using a feeler gauge. If clearance is below the minimum tolerance, check with a machinist about machining the rod to provide adequate clearance. If clearance is excessive, substitute an unworn rod and recheck; if clearance is still outside specifications, the crankshaft must be welded and reground, or replaced.

1. To check connecting rod big end bearing clearances, remove the rod bearing caps one at a time. Using a clean, dry shop rag, thoroughly clean all oil from the crank journal and bearing insert in the cap.

➡ **The Plastigage® gauging material you will be using to check clearances with is soluble in oil; therefore any oil on the journal or bearing could result in an incorrect reading.**

2. Lay a strip of Plastigage® along the full length of the bearing insert (along the crank journal if the engine is out of the car and inverted). Reinstall the cap and torque to specifications listed in the Torque Specifications chart.

3. Remove the rod cap and determine bearing clearance by comparing the width of the now flattened Plastigage® to the scale on the Plastigage® envelope. Journal taper is determined by comparing the width of the Plastigage® strip near its ends. Rotate the crankshaft 90° and retest, to determine journal eccentricity.

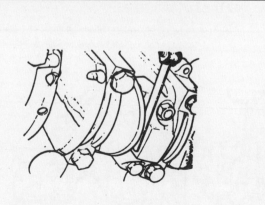

Fig. 107 To check connecting rod side clearance, make sure the feeler gauge is between the shoulder of the crank journal and the side of the rod

➡**Do not rotate the crankshaft with the Plastigage® installed.**

4. If the bearing insert and crank journal appear intact and are within tolerances, no further service is required and the bearing caps can be reinstalled (remove Plastigage® before installation). If clearances are not within tolerances, the bearing inserts in both the connecting rod and rod cap must be replaced with undersize inserts, and/or the crankshaft must be reground. To install the bearing insert halves, press them into the bearing caps and connecting rods. Make sure the tab in each insert fits into the notch in each rod and cap. Lube the face of each insert with engine oil prior to installing each rod into the engine.

5. The connecting rods can be further inspected when they are removed from the engine and separated from their pistons. Rod alignment (straightness and squareness) must be checked by a machinist, as the rod must be set in a special fixture. Many machine shops also perform a Magnafluxing service, which is a process that shows up any tiny cracks that you may be unable to see with the naked eye.

Rear Main Seal

REMOVAL & INSTALLATION

All Engines

In order to replace the rear main oil seal, the rear main bearing cap must be removed. Removal of the rear main bearing cap requires the use of a special rear main bearing cap puller. Also, the oil seal is installed with a special crankshaft rear oil seal drift. Unless these or similar tools are available to you, it is recommended that the oil seal be replaced by a Nissan/Datsun service center or an independent shop that has the proper equipment.

1. Remove the engine and transmission assembly from the vehicle.

2. Remove the transmission from the engine. Remove the oil pan.

3. Remove the clutch from the flywheel.

4. Remove the flywheel from the crankshaft.

5. Remove the rear main bearing cap together with the bearing cap side seals.

6. Remove the rear main oil seal from around the crankshaft.

7. Apply lithium grease around the sealing lip of the oil seal and install the seal around the crankshaft using a suitable tool.

8. Apply sealer to the rear main bearing cap as indicated, install the rear main bearing cap, and tighten the cap bolts to 33–40 ft. lbs.

9. Apply sealant to the rear main bearing cap side seals and install the side seals, driving the seals into place with a suitable drift.

10. Install the oil pan with a new gasket.

11. Install the flywheel and clutch assembly.

12. Install the transmission to the engine and install the engine/transmission assembly in the vehicle. Refer to the Engine Removal and Installation procedure.

13. Check all fluid levels, start the engine and check for any leaks. Roadtest the vehicle for proper operation.

Crankshaft and Main Bearings

REMOVAL & INSTALLATION

♦ **See Figures 108, 109, 110 and 111**

➡**Before removing the crankshaft, check main bearing clearances as described under Main Bearing Clearance Check.**

1. Remove the piston and connecting rod assemblies following the procedure in this section.
2. Check crankshaft thrust clearance (end-play) before removing the crank from the block. Using a prybar, pry the crankshaft the extent of its travel forward, and measure thrust clearance at the center main bearing (No. 4 bearing on 6-cylinder engines, No. 3 on 4-cylinder engines) with a feeler gauge. Pry the crankshaft the extent of its rearward travel, and measure the other side of the bearing. If clearance is greater than specified, the thrust washers must be replaced (see Main Bearing Replacement):
3. Using a punch, mark the corresponding main bearing caps and saddles according to position. One punch on the front main cap and saddle, two on the second, three on the third, etc. This ensures correct reassembly.
4. Remove the main bearing caps after they have been marked.
5. Remove the crankshaft from the block.
6. Follow the crankshaft inspection, main bearing clearance checking and replacement procedures below before reinstalling the crankshaft.

INSPECTION

Crankshaft inspection and servicing should be handled exclusively by a reputable machinist, as most of the necessary procedures require a dial indicator and fixing jig, a large micrometer, and machine tools such as a crankshaft grinder. While at the machine shop, the crankshaft should be thoroughly cleaned (especially the oil passages),; magnafluxed (to check for minute cracks) and the following checks made: Main journal diameter, crank pin (connecting rod journal) diameter, taper and out-of-round, and run-out. Wear, beyond specification limits, in any of these areas means the crankshaft must be reground or replaced.

CLEARANCE CHECK

Checking main bearing clearances is done in the same manner as checking connecting rod big end clearances.

1. With the crankshaft installed, remove the main bearing cap. Clean all oil from the bearing insert in the cap and from the crankshaft journal, as the Plastigage® material is oil soluble.
2. Lay a strip of Plastigage® along the full width of the bearing cap (or along the width of the crank journal if the engine is out of the car and inverted).
3. Install the bearing cap and torque to specification. Tighten bearing caps gradually in two or three stages.

➡**Do not rotate the crankshaft with the Plastigage® installed.**

4. Remove the bearing cap and determine bearing clearance by comparing the width of the now flattened Plastigage® with the scale on the Plastigage® envelope. Journal taper is determined by comparing the width of the Plastigage® strip near its ends. Rotate the crankshaft 90° and retest, to determine journal eccentricity.
5. Repeat the above for the remaining bearings. If the bearing journal and insert appear in good shape (with no unusual wear visible) and are within tolerances, no further main bearing service is required. If unusual wear is evident and/or the clearances are outside specifications, the bearings must be replaced and the cause of their wear found.

REPLACEMENT

Main bearings can be replaced with the crankshaft both in the engine (with the engine still in the car) and out of the engine (with the engine on a workstand or bench). Both procedures are covered here. The main bearings must be replaced if the crankshaft has been reground; the replacement bearings being available in various undersize increments from most auto parts jobbers or your local Datsun/Nissan dealer.

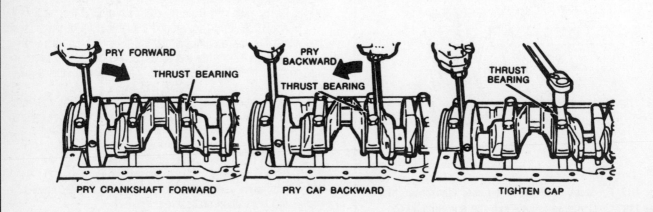

Fig. 108 Check the crankshaft thrust as shown

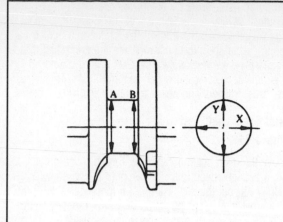

Fig. 109 Check the crankshaft journal eccentricity and taper at these points

Carefully pry the shaft back and forth while reading the dial gauge for play

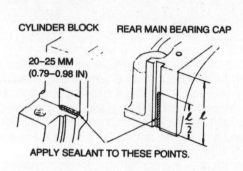

Fig. 110 Apply sealant to the engine main bearing caps where shown—L-series 4-cylinder and 6-cylinder engines

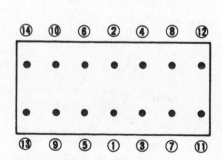

Fig. 111 Tighten the bearing caps in the sequence shown gradually in two or three stages—L24 and LD28 engines

Mounting a dial gauge to read crankshaft run-out

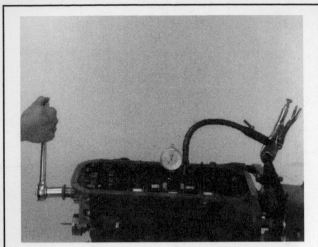

Turn the crankshaft slowly by hand while checking the gauge

The notch on the the side of the bearing cap matches the groove on the bearing insert

Engine Out of Car

1. Remove the crankshaft from the engine block.

2. Remove the main bearing inserts from the bearing caps and from the main bearing saddles. Remove the thrust washers from the No. 3 (4-cylinder) or No. 4 (6-cylinder) crank journal.

3. Thoroughly clean the saddles, bearing caps, and crankshaft.

4. Make sure the crankshaft has been fully checked and is ready for reassembly. Place the upper main bearings in the block saddles so that the oil grooves and/or oil holes are correctly aligned with their corresponding grooves or holes in the saddles.

5. Install the thrust washers on the center main bearing, with the oil grooves facing out.

6. Lubricate the faces of all bearings with clean engine oil, and place the crankshaft in the block.

7. Install the main bearing caps in numbered order with the arrows or any other orientation marks facing forward. Torque all bolts except the center cap bolts in sequence in two or three passes to the specified torque. Rotate the crankshaft after each pass to ensure even tightness.

8. Align the thrust bearing by prying the crankshaft the extent of its axial travel several times with a prybar. On last movement hold the crankshaft toward the front of the engine and tighten the thrust bearing cap to specifications. Measure the crankshaft thrust clearance (end-play) as previously described in this chapter. If clearance is outside specifications (too sloppy), install a new set of oversize thrust washers and check clearance again.

Engine and Crankshaft Installed

▶ **See Figure 112**

1. Remove the main bearing caps and keep them in order.

2. Make a bearing rollout pin from a cotter pin as shown.

3. Carefully roll out the old inserts from the upper side of the crankshaft journal, noting the positions of the oil grooves and/or oil holes so the new inserts can be correctly installed.

4. Roll each new insert into its saddle after lightly oiling the crankshaft side face of each. Make sure the notches and/or oil holes are correctly positioned.

5. Replace the bearing inserts in the caps with new inserts. Oil the face of each, and install the caps in numbered order with the arrows or other orientation marks facing forward. Tighten the bolts to the specified torque in two or three passes in the sequence shown.

Cylinder Block

Most inspection and service work on the cylinder block should be handled by a machinist or professional engine rebuilding shop. Included in this work are bearing alignment checks, line boring, deck resurfacing, hot-tanking and cylinder honing or boring. A block that has been checked and properly serviced will last much longer than one which has not had the proper attention when the opportunity was there for it.

Cylinder deglazing (honing) can, however, be performed by the owner/mechanic who is careful and takes his or her time. The cylinder bores become glazed during normal operation as the rings continually ride up and down against them. This shiny glaze must be removed in order for a new set of piston rings to be able to properly seat themselves.

Cylinder hones are available at most auto tool stores and parts jobbers. With the piston and rod assemblies removed from the

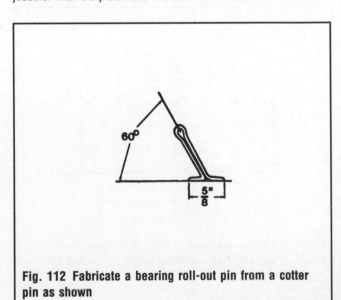

Fig. 112 Fabricate a bearing roll-out pin from a cotter pin as shown

block, cover the crankshaft completely with a rag or cover to keep grit from the hone and cylinder material off of it. Chuck a hone into a variable speed power drill (preferable here to a constant speed drill), and insert it into the cylinder.

➡**Make sure the drill and hone are kept square to the cylinder bore throughout the entire honing operation.**

Start the hone and move it up and down in the cylinder at a rate which will produce approximately a 60° crosshatch pattern. DO NOT extend the hone below the cylinder bore! After developing the pattern, remove the hone and recheck piston fit. Wash the cylinders with a detergent and water solution to remove the hone and cylinder grit. Wipe the bores out several times with a clean rag soaked in clean engine oil. Remove the cover from the crankshaft, and check closely to see that no grit has found its way onto the crankshaft.

Flywheel and Ring Gear

REMOVAL & INSTALLATION

➡**The clutch cover and the pressure plate are balanced as an assembly; if replacement of either part becomes neces-**sary, replace both parts as an assembly. If vehicle is equipped with a automatic transmission use this procedure as a guide. See exploded view of engine assembly for flywheel/drive plate installation and quick torque reference.

1. Refer to the Clutch Removal and Installation procedures in Section 7 and remove the clutch assembly.
2. Remove the flywheel-to-crankshaft bolts and the flywheel.

➡**If necessary the clutch disc should be inspected and/or replaced at this time; the clutch lining wear limit is 0.30mm above the rivet heads.**

3. To install, reverse the removal procedures. Tighten the flywheel-to-crankshaft bolts to specifications, the clutch cover-to-flywheel bolts and the bearing housing-to-clutch housing bolts to specifications. Refer to the Torque Specification Chart or Section 7.

EXHAUST SYSTEM

◆ **See Figure 113**

Safety Precautions

For a number of reasons, exhaust system work can be dangerous. Always observe the following precautions:
1. Support the vehicle securely by using jackstands or equivalent under the frame of the vehicle.
2. Wear safety goggles to protect your eyes from metal chips that may fly free while working on the exhaust system.
3. If you are using a torch be careful not to come close to any fuel lines.
4. Always use the proper tool for the job.

Special Tools

A number of special exhaust tools can be rented or bought from a local auto parts store. It may also be quite helpful to use solvents designed to loosen rusted nuts or bolts. Remember that these products are often flammable, apply only to parts after they are cool.

Front Pipe

REMOVAL & INSTALLATION

1. Support the vehicle securely by using jackstands or equivalent under the frame of the vehicle.
2. Remove the exhaust pipe clamps and any front exhaust pipe shield.

3. Soak the exhaust manifold front pipe mounting studs with penetrating oil. Remove attaching nuts and gasket from the manifold.

➡**If these studs snap off, while removing the front pipe the manifold will have to be removed and the stud will have to be drill out and the hole tapped.**

4. Remove any exhaust pipe mounting hanger or bracket.
5. Remove front pipe from the catalytic converter.
6. Install the front pipe on the manifold with seal if so equipped.
7. Install the pipe on the catalytic converter. Assemble all parts loosely and position pipe to insure proper clearance from body of vehicle.
8. Tighten mounting studs, bracket bolts on exhaust clamps.
9. Install exhaust pipe shield.
10. Start engine and check for exhaust leaks.

Catalytic Converter

REMOVAL & INSTALLATION

1. Remove the converter lower shield.
2. Disconnect converter from front pipe.
3. Disconnect converter from center pipe.

➡**Assemble all parts loosely and position converter before tightening the exhaust clamps.**

4. Remove catalytic converter.

5. To install reverse the removal procedures. Always use new clamps and exhaust seals, start engine and check for leaks.

Tailpipe and Muffler

REMOVAL & INSTALLATION

1. Remove tailpipe connection at center pipe.
2. Remove all brackets and exhaust clamps.

3. Remove tailpipe from muffler. On some models the tailpipe and muffler are one piece.

4. To install reverse the removal procedures. Always use new clamps and exhaust seals, start engine and check for leaks.

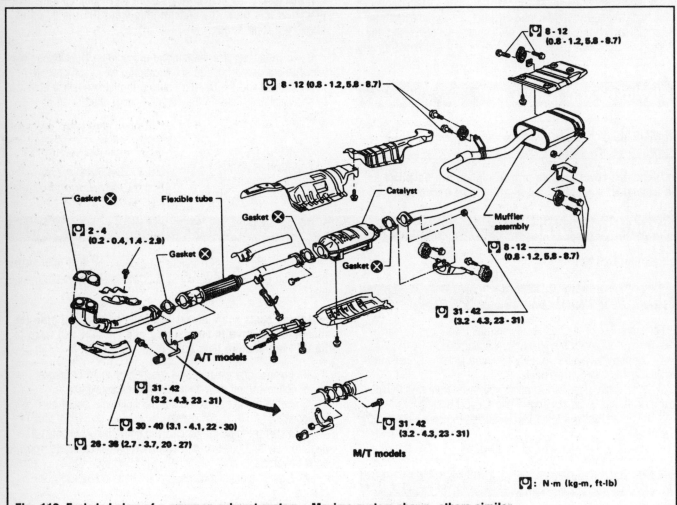

Fig. 113 Exploded view of a common exhaust system—Maxima system shown, others similar

USING A VACUUM GAUGE

White needle = steady needle   *Dark needle = drifting needle*

The vacuum gauge is one of the most useful and easy-to-use diagnostic tools. It is inexpensive, easy to hook up, and provides valuable information about the condition of your engine.

Indication: Normal engine in good condition

Gauge reading: Steady, from 17–22 in./Hg.

Indication: Sticking valve or ignition miss

Gauge reading: Needle fluctuates from 15–20 in./Hg. at idle

Indication: Late ignition or valve timing, low compression, stuck throttle valve, leaking carburetor or manifold gasket.

Gauge reading: Low (15–20 in./Hg.) but steady

Indication: Improper carburetor adjustment, or minor intake leak at carburetor or manifold

NOTE: Bad fuel injector O-rings may also cause this reading.

Gauge reading: Drifting needle

Indication: Weak valve springs, worn valve stem guides, or leaky cylinder head gasket (vibrating excessively at all speeds).

NOTE: A plugged catalytic converter may also cause this reading.

Gauge reading: Needle fluctuates as engine speed increases

Indication: Burnt valve or improper valve clearance. The needle will drop when the defective valve operates.

Gauge reading: Steady needle, but drops regularly

Indication: Choked muffler or obstruction in system. Speed up the engine. Choked muffler will exhibit a slow drop of vacuum to zero.

Gauge reading: Gradual drop in reading at idle

Indication: Worn valve guides

Gauge reading: Needle vibrates excessively at idle, but steadies as engine speed increases

Troubleshooting Engine Mechanical Problems

Problem	Cause	Solution
External oil leaks	• Cylinder head cover RTV sealant broken or improperly seated	• Replace sealant; inspect cylinder head cover sealant flange and cylinder head sealant surface for distortion and cracks
	• Oil filler cap leaking or missing	• Replace cap
	• Oil filter gasket broken or improperly seated	• Replace oil filter
	• Oil pan side gasket broken, improperly seated or opening in RTV sealant	• Replace gasket or repair opening in sealant; inspect oil pan gasket flange for distortion
	• Oil pan front oil seal broken or improperly seated	• Replace seal; inspect timing case cover and oil pan seal flange for distortion
	• Oil pan rear oil seal broken or improperly seated	• Replace seal; inspect oil pan rear oil seal flange; inspect rear main bearing cap for cracks, plugged oil return channels, or distortion in seal groove
	• Timing case cover oil seal broken or improperly seated	• Replace seal
	• Excess oil pressure because of restricted PCV valve	• Replace PCV valve
	• Oil pan drain plug loose or has stripped threads	• Repair as necessary and tighten
	• Rear oil gallery plug loose	• Use appropriate sealant on gallery plug and tighten
	• Rear camshaft plug loose or improperly seated	• Seat camshaft plug or replace and seal, as necessary
Excessive oil consumption	• Oil level too high	• Drain oil to specified level
	• Oil with wrong viscosity being used	• Replace with specified oil
	• PCV valve stuck closed	• Replace PCV valve
	• Valve stem oil deflectors (or seals) are damaged, missing, or incorrect type	• Replace valve stem oil deflectors
	• Valve stems or valve guides worn	• Measure stem-to-guide clearance and repair as necessary
	• Poorly fitted or missing valve cover baffles	• Replace valve cover
	• Piston rings broken or missing	• Replace broken or missing rings
	• Scuffed piston	• Replace piston
	• Incorrect piston ring gap	• Measure ring gap, repair as necessary
	• Piston rings sticking or excessively loose in grooves	• Measure ring side clearance, repair as necessary
	• Compression rings installed upside down	• Repair as necessary
	• Cylinder walls worn, scored, or glazed	• Repair as necessary

Troubleshooting Engine Mechanical Problems

Problem	Cause	Solution
Excessive oil consumption (cont.)	• Piston ring gaps not properly staggered	• Repair as necessary
	• Excessive main or connecting rod bearing clearance	• Measure bearing clearance, repair as necessary
No oil pressure	• Low oil level	• Add oil to correct level
	• Oil pressure gauge, warning lamp or sending unit inaccurate	• Replace oil pressure gauge or warning lamp
	• Oil pump malfunction	• Replace oil pump
	• Oil pressure relief valve sticking	• Remove and inspect oil pressure relief valve assembly
	• Oil passages on pressure side of pump obstructed	• Inspect oil passages for obstruction
	• Oil pickup screen or tube obstructed	• Inspect oil pickup for obstruction
	• Loose oil inlet tube	• Tighten or seal inlet tube
Low oil pressure	• Low oil level	• Add oil to correct level
	• Inaccurate gauge, warning lamp or sending unit	• Replace oil pressure gauge or warning lamp
	• Oil excessively thin because of dilution, poor quality, or improper grade	• Drain and refill crankcase with recommended oil
	• Excessive oil temperature	• Correct cause of overheating engine
	• Oil pressure relief spring weak or sticking	• Remove and inspect oil pressure relief valve assembly
	• Oil inlet tube and screen assembly has restriction or air leak	• Remove and inspect oil inlet tube and screen assembly. (Fill inlet tube with lacquer thinner to locate leaks.)
	• Excessive oil pump clearance	• Measure clearances
	• Excessive main, rod, or camshaft bearing clearance	• Measure bearing clearances, repair as necessary
High oil pressure	• Improper oil viscosity	• Drain and refill crankcase with correct viscosity oil
	• Oil pressure gauge or sending unit inaccurate	• Replace oil pressure gauge
	• Oil pressure relief valve sticking closed	• Remove and inspect oil pressure relief valve assembly
Main bearing noise	• Insufficient oil supply	• Inspect for low oil level and low oil pressure
	• Main bearing clearance excessive	• Measure main bearing clearance, repair as necessary
	• Bearing insert missing	• Replace missing insert
	• Crankshaft end-play excessive	• Measure end-play, repair as necessary
	• Improperly tightened main bearing cap bolts	• Tighten bolts with specified torque
	• Loose flywheel or drive plate	• Tighten flywheel or drive plate attaching bolts
	• Loose or damaged vibration damper	• Repair as necessary

Troubleshooting Engine Mechanical Problems

Problem	Cause	Solution
Connecting rod bearing noise	• Insufficient oil supply	• Inspect for low oil level and low oil pressure
	• Carbon build-up on piston	• Remove carbon from piston crown
	• Bearing clearance excessive or bearing missing	• Measure clearance, repair as necessary
	• Crankshaft connecting rod journal out-of-round	• Measure journal dimensions, repair or replace as necessary
	• Misaligned connecting rod or cap	• Repair as necessary
	• Connecting rod bolts tightened improperly	• Tighten bolts with specified torque
Piston noise	• Piston-to-cylinder wall clearance excessive (scuffed piston)	• Measure clearance and examine piston
	• Cylinder walls excessively tapered or out-of-round	• Measure cylinder wall dimensions, rebore cylinder
	• Piston ring broken	• Replace all rings on piston
	• Loose or seized piston pin	• Measure piston-to-pin clearance, repair as necessary
	• Connecting rods misaligned	• Measure rod alignment, straighten or replace
	• Piston ring side clearance excessively loose or tight	• Measure ring side clearance, repair as necessary
	• Carbon build-up on piston is excessive	• Remove carbon from piston
Valve actuating component noise	• Insufficient oil supply	• Check for: (a) Low oil level (b) Low oil pressure (c) Wrong hydraulic tappets (d) Restricted oil gallery (e) Excessive tappet to bore clearance
	• Rocker arms or pivots worn	• Replace worn rocker arms or pivots
	• Foreign objects or chips in hydraulic tappets	• Clean tappets
	• Excessive tappet leak-down	• Replace valve tappet
	• Tappet face worn	• Replace tappet; inspect corresponding cam lobe for wear
	• Broken or cocked valve springs	• Properly seat cocked springs; replace broken springs
	• Stem-to-guide clearance excessive	• Measure stem-to-guide clearance, repair as required
	• Valve bent	• Replace valve
	• Loose rocker arms	• Check and repair as necessary
	• Valve seat runout excessive	• Regrind valve seat/valves
	• Missing valve lock	• Install valve lock
	• Excessive engine oil	• Correct oil level

Troubleshooting Engine Performance

Problem	Cause	Solution
Hard starting (engine cranks normally)	• Faulty engine control system component • Faulty fuel pump • Faulty fuel system component • Faulty ignition coil • Improper spark plug gap • Incorrect ignition timing • Incorrect valve timing	• Repair or replace as necessary • Replace fuel pump • Repair or replace as necessary • Test and replace as necessary • Adjust gap • Adjust timing • Check valve timing; repair as necessary
Rough idle or stalling	• Incorrect curb or fast idle speed • Incorrect ignition timing • Improper feedback system operation • Faulty EGR valve operation • Faulty PCV valve air flow • Faulty TAC vacuum motor or valve • Air leak into manifold vacuum • Faulty distributor rotor or cap • Improperly seated valves • Incorrect ignition wiring • Faulty ignition coil • Restricted air vent or idle passages • Restricted air cleaner	• Adjust curb or fast idle speed (If possible) • Adjust timing to specification • Refer to Chapter 4 • Test EGR system and replace as necessary • Test PCV valve and replace as necessary • Repair as necessary • Inspect manifold vacuum connections and repair as necessary • Replace rotor or cap (Distributor systems only) • Test cylinder compression, repair as necessary • Inspect wiring and correct as necessary • Test coil and replace as necessary • Clean passages • Clean or replace air cleaner filter element
Faulty low-speed operation	• Restricted idle air vents and passages • Restricted air cleaner • Faulty spark plugs • Dirty, corroded, or loose ignition secondary circuit wire connections • Improper feedback system operation • Faulty ignition coil high voltage wire • Faulty distributor cap	• Clean air vents and passages • Clean or replace air cleaner filter element • Clean or replace spark plugs • Clean or tighten secondary circuit wire connections • Refer to Chapter 4 • Replace ignition coil high voltage wire (Distributor systems only) • Replace cap (Distributor systems only)
Faulty acceleration	• Incorrect ignition timing • Faulty fuel system component • Faulty spark plug(s) • Improperly seated valves • Faulty ignition coil	• Adjust timing • Repair or replace as necessary • Clean or replace spark plug(s) • Test cylinder compression, repair as necessary • Test coil and replace as necessary

Troubleshooting Engine Performance

Problem	Cause	Solution
Faulty acceleration (cont.)	• Improper feedback system operation	• Refer to Chapter 4
Faulty high speed operation	• Incorrect ignition timing	• Adjust timing (if possible)
	• Faulty advance mechanism	• Check advance mechanism and repair as necessary (Distributor systems only)
	• Low fuel pump volume	• Replace fuel pump
	• Wrong spark plug air gap or wrong plug	• Adjust air gap or install correct plug
	• Partially restricted exhaust manifold, exhaust pipe, catalytic converter, muffler, or tailpipe	• Eliminate restriction
	• Restricted vacuum passages	• Clean passages
	• Restricted air cleaner	• Cleaner or replace filter element as necessary
	• Faulty distributor rotor or cap	• Replace rotor or cap (Distributor systems only)
	• Faulty ignition coil	• Test coil and replace as necessary
	• Improperly seated valve(s)	• Test cylinder compression, repair as necessary
	• Faulty valve spring(s)	• Inspect and test valve spring tension, replace as necessary
	• Incorrect valve timing	• Check valve timing and repair as necessary
	• Intake manifold restricted	• Remove restriction or replace manifold
	• Worn distributor shaft	• Replace shaft (Distributor systems only)
	• Improper feedback system operation	• Refer to Chapter 4
Misfire at all speeds	• Faulty spark plug(s)	• Clean or relace spark plug(s)
	• Faulty spark plug wire(s)	• Replace as necessary
	• Faulty distributor cap or rotor	• Replace cap or rotor (Distributor systems only)
	• Faulty ignition coil	• Test coil and replace as necessary
	• Primary ignition circuit shorted or open intermittently	• Troubleshoot primary circuit and repair as necessary
	• Improperly seated valve(s)	• Test cylinder compression, repair as necessary
	• Faulty hydraulic tappet(s)	• Clean or replace tappet(s)
	• Improper feedback system operation	• Refer to Chapter 4
	• Faulty valve spring(s)	• Inspect and test valve spring tension, repair as necessary
	• Worn camshaft lobes	• Replace camshaft
	• Air leak into manifold	• Check manifold vacuum and repair as necessary
	• Fuel pump volume or pressure low	• Replace fuel pump
	• Blown cylinder head gasket	• Replace gasket
	• Intake or exhaust manifold passage(s) restricted	• Pass chain through passage(s) and repair as necessary
Power not up to normal	• Incorrect ignition timing	• Adjust timing
	• Faulty distributor rotor	• Replace rotor (Distributor systems only)

Troubleshooting Engine Performance

Problem	Cause	Solution
Power not up to normal (cont.)	• Incorrect spark plug gap • Faulty fuel pump • Faulty fuel pump • Incorrect valve timing • Faulty ignition coil • Faulty ignition wires • Improperly seated valves • Blown cylinder head gasket • Leaking piston rings • Improper feedback system operation	• Adjust gap • Replace fuel pump • Replace fuel pump • Check valve timing and repair as necessary • Test coil and replace as necessary • Test wires and replace as necessary • Test cylinder compression and repair as necessary • Replace gasket • Test compression and repair as necessary • Refer to Chapter 4
Intake backfire	• Improper ignition timing • Defective EGR component • Defective TAC vacuum motor or valve	• Adjust timing • Repair as necessary • Repair as necessary
Exhaust backfire	• Air leak into manifold vacuum • Faulty air injection diverter valve • Exhaust leak	• Check manifold vacuum and repair as necessary • Test diverter valve and replace as necessary • Locate and eliminate leak
Ping or spark knock	• Incorrect ignition timing • Distributor advance malfunction • Excessive combustion chamber deposits • Air leak into manifold vacuum • Excessively high compression • Fuel octane rating excessively low • Sharp edges in combustion chamber • EGR valve not functioning properly	• Adjust timing • Inspect advance mechanism and repair as necessary (Distributor systems only) • Remove with combustion chamber cleaner • Check manifold vacuum and repair as necessary • Test compression and repair as necessary • Try alternate fuel source • Grind smooth • Test EGR system and replace as necessary
Surging (at cruising to top speeds)	• Low fuel pump pressure or volume • Improper PCV valve air flow • Air leak into manifold vacuum • Incorrect spark advance • Restricted fuel filter • Restricted air cleaner • EGR valve not functioning properly • Improper feedback system operation	• Replace fuel pump • Test PCV valve and replace as necessary • Check manifold vacuum and repair as necessary • Test and replace as necessary • Replace fuel filter • Clean or replace air cleaner filter element • Test EGR system and replace as necessary • Refer to Chapter 4

Troubleshooting the Serpentine Drive Belt

Problem	Cause	Solution
Tension sheeting fabric failure (woven fabric on outside circumference of belt has cracked or separated from body of belt)	• Grooved or backside idler pulley diameters are less than minimum recommended • Tension sheeting contacting (rubbing) stationary object • Excessive heat causing woven fabric to age • Tension sheeting splice has fractured	• Replace pulley(s) not conforming to specification • Correct rubbing condition • Replace belt • Replace belt
Noise (objectional squeal, squeak, or rumble is heard or felt while drive belt is in operation)	• Belt slippage • Bearing noise • Belt misalignment • Belt-to-pulley mismatch • Driven component inducing vibration • System resonant frequency inducing vibration	• Adjust belt • Locate and repair • Align belt/pulley(s) • Install correct belt • Locate defective driven component and repair • Vary belt tension within specifications. Replace belt.
Rib chunking (one or more ribs has separated from belt body)	• Foreign objects imbedded in pulley grooves • Installation damage • Drive loads in excess of design specifications • Insufficient internal belt adhesion	• Remove foreign objects from pulley grooves • Replace belt • Adjust belt tension • Replace belt
Rib or belt wear (belt ribs contact bottom of pulley grooves)	• Pulley(s) misaligned • Mismatch of belt and pulley groove widths • Abrasive environment • Rusted pulley(s) • Sharp or jagged pulley groove tips • Rubber deteriorated	• Align pulley(s) • Replace belt • Replace belt • Clean rust from pulley(s) • Replace pulley • Replace belt
Longitudinal belt cracking (cracks between two ribs)	• Belt has mistracked from pulley groove • Pulley groove tip has worn away rubber-to-tensile member	• Replace belt • Replace belt
Belt slips	• Belt slipping because of insufficient tension • Belt or pulley subjected to substance (belt dressing, oil, ethylene glycol) that has reduced friction • Driven component bearing failure • Belt glazed and hardened from heat and excessive slippage	• Adjust tension • Replace belt and clean pulleys • Replace faulty component bearing • Replace belt
"Groove jumping" (belt does not maintain correct position on pulley, or turns over and/or runs off pulleys)	• Insufficient belt tension • Pulley(s) not within design tolerance • Foreign object(s) in grooves	• Adjust belt tension • Replace pulley(s) • Remove foreign objects from grooves

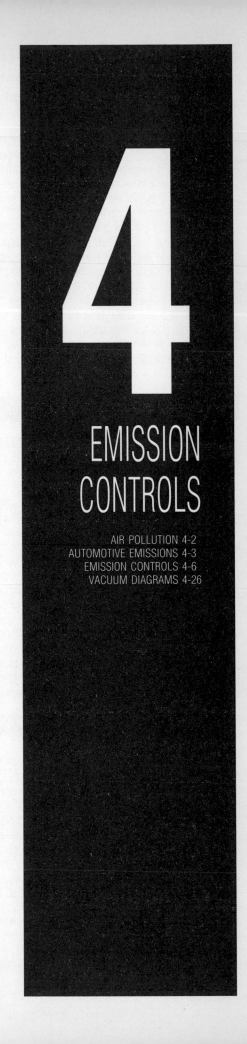

4

EMISSION CONTROLS

AIR POLLUTION

The earth's atmosphere, at or near sea level, consists approximately of 78 percent nitrogen, 21 percent oxygen and 1 percent other gases. If it were possible to remain in this state, 100 percent clean air would result. However, many varied sources allow other gases and particulates to mix with the clean air, causing our atmosphere to become unclean or polluted.

Some of these pollutants are visible while others are invisible, with each having the capability of causing distress to the eyes, ears, throat, skin and respiratory system. Should these pollutants become concentrated in a specific area and under certain conditions, death could result due to the displacement or chemical change of the oxygen content in the air. These pollutants can also cause great damage to the environment and to the many man made objects that are exposed to the elements.

To better understand the causes of air pollution, the pollutants can be categorized into 3 separate types, natural, industrial and automotive.

Natural Pollutants

Natural pollution has been present on earth since before man appeared and continues to be a factor when discussing air pollution, although it causes only a small percentage of the overall pollution problem. It is the direct result of decaying organic matter, wind born smoke and particulates from such natural events as plain and forest fires (ignited by heat or lightning), volcanic ash, sand and dust which can spread over a large area of the countryside.

Such a phenomenon of natural pollution has been seen in the form of volcanic eruptions, with the resulting plume of smoke, steam and volcanic ash blotting out the sun's rays as it spreads and rises higher into the atmosphere. As it travels into the atmosphere the upper air currents catch and carry the smoke and ash, while condensing the steam back into water vapor. As the water vapor, smoke and ash travel on their journey, the smoke dissipates into the atmosphere while the ash and moisture settle back to earth in a trail hundreds of miles long. In some cases, lives are lost and millions of dollars of property damage result.

Industrial Pollutants

Industrial pollution is caused primarily by industrial processes, the burning of coal, oil and natural gas, which in turn produce smoke and fumes. Because the burning fuels contain large amounts of sulfur, the principal ingredients of smoke and fumes are sulfur dioxide and particulate matter. This type of pollutant occurs most severely during still, damp and cool weather, such as at night. Even in its less severe form, this pollutant is not confined to just cities. Because of air movements, the pollutants move for miles over the surrounding countryside, leaving in its path a barren and unhealthy environment for all living things.

Working with Federal, State and Local mandated regulations and by carefully monitoring emissions, big business has greatly reduced the amount of pollutant introduced from its industrial sources, striving to obtain an acceptable level. Because of the mandated industrial emission clean up, many land areas and streams in and around the cities that were formerly barren of vegetation and life, have now begun to move back in the direction of nature's intended balance.

Automotive Pollutants

The third major source of air pollution is automotive emissions. The emissions from the internal combustion engines were not an appreciable problem years ago because of the small number of registered vehicles and the nation's small highway system. However, during the early 1950's, the trend of the American people was to move from the cities to the surrounding suburbs. This caused an immediate problem in transportation because the majority of suburbs were not afforded mass transit conveniences. This lack of transportation created an attractive market for the automobile manufacturers, which resulted in a dramatic increase in the number of vehicles produced and sold, along with a marked increase in highway construction between cities and the suburbs. Multi-vehicle families emerged with a growing emphasis placed on an individual vehicle per family member. As the increase in vehicle ownership and usage occurred, so did pollutant levels in and around the cities, as suburbanites drove daily to their businesses and employment, returning at the end of the day to their homes in the suburbs.

It was noted that a smoke and fog type haze was being formed and at times, remained in suspension over the cities, taking time to dissipate. At first this "smog," derived from the words "smoke" and "fog," was thought to result from industrial pollution but it was determined that automobile emissions shared the blame. It was discovered that when normal automobile emissions were exposed to sunlight for a period of time, complex chemical reactions would take place.

It is now known that smog is a photo chemical layer which develops when certain oxides of nitrogen (NOx) and unburned hydrocarbons (HC) from automobile emissions are exposed to sunlight. Pollution was more severe when smog would become stagnant over an area in which a warm layer of air settled over the top of the cooler air mass, trapping and holding the cooler mass at ground level. The trapped cooler air would keep the emissions from being dispersed and diluted through normal air flows. This type of air stagnation was given the name "Temperature Inversion."

TEMPERATURE INVERSION

In normal weather situations, surface air is warmed by heat radiating from the earth's surface and the sun's rays. This causes it to rise upward, into the atmosphere. Upon rising it will cool through a convection type heat exchange with the cooler upper air. As warm air rises, the surface pollutants are carried upward and dissipated into the atmosphere.

When a temperature inversion occurs, we find the higher air is no longer cooler, but is warmer than the surface air, causing the cooler surface air to become trapped. This warm air blanket can extend from above ground level to a few hundred or even a few thousand feet into the air. As the surface air is trapped, so are the pollutants, causing a severe smog condition. Should this stagnant air mass extend to a few thousand feet high, enough air movement with the inversion takes place to allow the smog layer to rise above ground level but the pollutants still cannot dissipate. This inversion can remain for days over an area, with the smog level only rising or lowering from ground level to a few hundred feet high. Meanwhile, the pollutant levels increase, causing eye irritation, respiratory problems, reduced visibility, plant damage and in some cases, even disease.

This inversion phenomenon was first noted in the Los Angeles, California area. The city lies in terrain resembling a basin and with certain weather conditions, a cold air mass is held in the basin while a warmer air mass covers it like a lid.

Because this type of condition was first documented as prevalent in the Los Angeles area, this type of trapped pollution was named Los Angeles Smog, although it occurs in other areas where a large concentration of automobiles are used and the air remains stagnant for any length of time.

HEAT TRANSFER

Consider the internal combustion engine as a machine in which raw materials must be placed so a finished product comes out. As in any machine operation, a certain amount of wasted material is formed. When we relate this to the internal combustion engine, we find that through the input of air and fuel, we obtain power during the combustion process to drive the vehicle. The by-product or waste of this power is, in part, heat and exhaust gases with which we must dispose.

The heat from the combustion process can rise to over 4000°F (2204°C). The dissipation of this heat is controlled by a ram air effect, the use of cooling fans to cause air flow and a liquid coolant solution surrounding the combustion area to transfer the heat of combustion through the cylinder walls and into the coolant. The coolant is then directed to a thin-finned, multi-tubed radiator, from which the excess heat is transferred to the atmosphere by 1 of the 3 heat transfer methods, conduction, convection or radiation.

The cooling of the combustion area is an important part in the control of exhaust emissions. To understand the behavior of the combustion and transfer of its heat, consider the air/fuel charge. It is ignited and the flame front burns progressively across the combustion chamber until the burning charge reaches the cylinder walls. Some of the fuel in contact with the walls is not hot enough to burn, thereby snuffing out or quenching the combustion process. This leaves unburned fuel in the combustion chamber. This unburned fuel is then forced out of the cylinder and into the exhaust system, along with the exhaust gases.

Many attempts have been made to minimize the amount of unburned fuel in the combustion chambers due to quenching, by increasing the coolant temperature and lessening the contact area of the coolant around the combustion area. However, design limitations within the combustion chambers prevent the complete burning of the air/fuel charge, so a certain amount of the unburned fuel is still expelled into the exhaust system, regardless of modifications to the engine.

AUTOMOTIVE EMISSIONS

Before emission controls were mandated on internal combustion engines, other sources of engine pollutants were discovered along with the exhaust emissions. It was determined that engine combustion exhaust produced approximately 60 percent of the total emission pollutants, fuel evaporation from the fuel tank and carburetor vents produced 20 percent, with the final 20 percent being produced through the crankcase as a by-product of the combustion process.

Exhaust Gases

The exhaust gases emitted into the atmosphere are a combination of burned and unburned fuel. To understand the exhaust emission and its composition, we must review some basic chemistry.

When the air/fuel mixture is introduced into the engine, we are mixing air, composed of nitrogen (78 percent), oxygen (21 percent) and other gases (1 percent) with the fuel, which is 100 percent hydrocarbons (HC), in a semi-controlled ratio. As the combustion process is accomplished, power is produced to move the vehicle while the heat of combustion is transferred to the cooling system. The exhaust gases are then composed of nitrogen, a diatomic gas (N_2), the same as was introduced in the engine, carbon dioxide (CO_2), the same gas that is used in beverage carbonation, and water vapor (H_2O). The nitrogen (N_2), for the most part, passes through the engine unchanged, while the oxygen (O_2) re-acts (burns) with the hydrocarbons (HC) and produces the carbon dioxide (CO_2) and the water vapors (H_2O). If this chemical process would be the only process to take place, the exhaust emissions would be harmless. However, during the combustion process, other compounds are formed which are considered dangerous. These pollutants are hydrocarbons (HC), carbon monoxide (CO), oxides of nitrogen (NOx) oxides of sulfur (SOx) and engine particulates.

HYDROCARBONS

Hydrocarbons (HC) are essentially fuel which was not burned during the combustion process or which has escaped into the atmosphere through fuel evaporation. The main sources of incomplete combustion are rich air/fuel mixtures, low engine temperatures and improper spark timing. The main sources of hydrocarbon emission through fuel evaporation on most vehicles used to be the vehicle's fuel tank and carburetor float bowl.

To reduce combustion hydrocarbon emission, engine modifications were made to minimize dead space and surface area in the combustion chamber. In addition, the air/fuel mixture was made more lean through the improved control which feedback carburetion and fuel injection offers and by the addition of external controls to aid in further combustion of the hydrocarbons outside the engine. Two such methods were the addition of air injection systems, to inject fresh air into the exhaust manifolds and the installation of catalytic converters, units that are able to burn traces of hydrocarbons without affecting the internal combustion process or fuel economy.

To control hydrocarbon emissions through fuel evaporation, modifications were made to the fuel tank to allow storage of the fuel vapors during periods of engine shut-down. Modifications were also made to the air intake system so that at specific times during engine operation, these vapors may be purged and burned by blending them with the air/fuel mixture.

CARBON MONOXIDE

Carbon monoxide is formed when not enough oxygen is present during the combustion process to convert carbon (C) to carbon dioxide (CO_2). An increase in the carbon monoxide (CO) emission is normally accompanied by an increase in the hydrocarbon (HC) emission because of the lack of oxygen to completely burn all of the fuel mixture.

Carbon monoxide (CO) also increases the rate at which the photo chemical smog is formed by speeding up the conversion of nitric oxide (NO) to nitrogen dioxide (NO_2). To accomplish this, carbon monoxide (CO) combines with oxygen (O_2) and nitric oxide (NO) to produce carbon dioxide (CO_2) and nitrogen dioxide (NO_2). ($CO + O_2 + NO \rightarrow CO_2 + NO_2$).

The dangers of carbon monoxide, which is an odorless and colorless toxic gas are many. When carbon monoxide is inhaled into the lungs and passed into the blood stream, oxygen is replaced by the carbon monoxide in the red blood cells, causing a reduction in the amount of oxygen supplied to the many parts of the body. This lack of oxygen causes headaches, lack of coordination, reduced mental alertness and, should the carbon monoxide concentration be high enough, death could result.

NITROGEN

Normally, nitrogen is an inert gas. When heated to approximately 2500°F (1371°C) through the combustion process, this gas becomes active and causes an increase in the nitric oxide (NO) emission.

Oxides of nitrogen (NOx) are composed of approximately 97–98 percent nitric oxide (NO). Nitric oxide is a colorless gas but when it is passed into the atmosphere, it combines with oxygen and forms nitrogen dioxide (NO_2). The nitrogen dioxide then combines with chemically active hydrocarbons (HC) and when in the presence of sunlight, causes the formation of photo-chemical smog.

Ozone

To further complicate matters, some of the nitrogen dioxide (NO_2) is broken apart by the sunlight to form nitric oxide and oxygen. ($NO_2 + sunlight \rightarrow NO + O$). This single atom of oxygen then combines with diatomic (meaning 2 atoms) oxygen (O_2) to form ozone (O_3). Ozone is one of the smells associated with smog. It

has a pungent and offensive odor, irritates the eyes and lung tissues, affects the growth of plant life and causes rapid deterioration of rubber products. Ozone can be formed by sunlight as well as electrical discharge into the air.

The most common discharge area on the automobile engine is the secondary ignition electrical system, especially when inferior quality spark plug cables are used. As the surge of high voltage is routed through the secondary cable, the circuit builds up an electrical field around the wire, which acts upon the oxygen in the surrounding air to form the ozone. The faint glow along the cable with the engine running that may be visible on a dark night, is called the "corona discharge." It is the result of the electrical field passing from a high along the cable, to a low in the surrounding air, which forms the ozone gas. The combination of corona and ozone has been a major cause of cable deterioration. Recently, different and better quality insulating materials have lengthened the life of the electrical cables.

Although ozone at ground level can be harmful, ozone is beneficial to the earth's inhabitants. By having a concentrated ozone layer called the "ozonosphere," between 10 and 20 miles (16–32 km) up in the atmosphere, much of the ultra violet radiation from the sun's rays are absorbed and screened. If this ozone layer were not present, much of the earth's surface would be burned, dried and unfit for human life.

OXIDES OF SULFUR

Oxides of sulfur (SOx) were initially ignored in the exhaust system emissions, since the sulfur content of gasoline as a fuel is less than $1/10$ of 1 percent. Because of this small amount, it was felt that it contributed very little to the overall pollution problem. However, because of the difficulty in solving the sulfur emissions in industrial pollutions and the introduction of catalytic converter to the automobile exhaust systems, a change was mandated. The automobile exhaust system, when equipped with a catalytic converter, changes the sulfur dioxide (SO_2) into sulfur trioxide (SO_3).

When this combines with water vapors (H_2O), a sulfuric acid mist (H_2SO_4) is formed and is a very difficult pollutant to handle since it is extremely corrosive. This sulfuric acid mist that is formed, is the same mist that rises from the vents of an automobile battery when an active chemical reaction takes place within the battery cells.

When a large concentration of vehicles equipped with catalytic converters are operating in an area, this acid mist may rise and be distributed over a large ground area causing land, plant, crop, paint and building damage.

PARTICULATE MATTER

A certain amount of particulate matter is present in the burning of any fuel, with carbon constituting the largest percentage of the particulates. In gasoline, the remaining particulates are the burned remains of the various other compounds used in its manufacture. When a gasoline engine is in good internal condition, the particulate emissions are low but as the engine wears internally, the particulate emissions increase. By visually inspecting the tail pipe emissions, a determination can be made as to where an engine defect may exist. An engine with light gray or blue smoke emitting from the tail pipe normally indicates an increase in the oil consumption through burning due to internal engine wear. Black smoke would indicate a defective fuel delivery system, causing the engine to operate in a rich mode. Regardless of the color of the smoke, the internal part of the engine or the fuel delivery system should be repaired to prevent excess particulate emissions.

Diesel and turbine engines emit a darkened plume of smoke from the exhaust system because of the type of fuel used. Emission control regulations are mandated for this type of emission and more stringent measures are being used to prevent excess emission of the particulate matter. Electronic components are being introduced to control the injection of the fuel at precisely the proper time of piston travel, to achieve the optimum in fuel ignition and fuel usage. Other particulate after-burning components are being tested to achieve a cleaner emission.

Good grades of engine lubricating oils should be used, which meet the manufacturers specification. Cut-rate oils can contribute to the particulate emission problem because of their low flash or ignition temperature point. Such oils burn prematurely during the combustion process causing emission of particulate matter.

The cooling system is an important factor in the reduction of particulate matter. The optimum combustion will occur, with the cooling system operating at a temperature specified by the manufacturer. The cooling system must be maintained in the same manner as the engine oiling system, as each system is required to perform properly in order for the engine to operate efficiently for a long time.

Crankcase Emissions

Crankcase emissions are made up of water, acids, unburned fuel, oil fumes and particulates. These emissions are classified as hydrocarbons (HC) and are formed by the small amount of unburned, compressed air/fuel mixture entering the crankcase from the combustion area (between the cylinder walls and piston rings) during the compression and power strokes. The head of the compression and combustion help to form the remaining crankcase emissions.

Since the first engines, crankcase emissions were allowed into the atmosphere through a road draft tube, mounted on the lower side of the engine block. Fresh air came in through an open oil filler cap or breather. The air passed through the crankcase mixing with blow-by gases. The motion of the vehicle and the air blowing past the open end of the road draft tube caused a low pressure area (vacuum) at the end of the tube. Crankcase emissions were simply drawn out of the road draft tube into the air.

To control the crankcase emission, the road draft tube was deleted. A hose and/or tubing was routed from the crankcase to the intake manifold so the blow-by emission could be burned with the air/fuel mixture. However, it was found that intake manifold vac-

uum, used to draw the crankcase emissions into the manifold, would vary in strength at the wrong time and not allow the proper emission flow. A regulating valve was needed to control the flow of air through the crankcase.

Testing, showed the removal of the blow-by gases from the crankcase as quickly as possible, was most important to the longevity of the engine. Should large accumulations of blow-by gases remain and condense, dilution of the engine oil would occur to form water, soots, resins, acids and lead salts, resulting in the formation of sludge and varnishes. This condensation of the blow-by gases occurs more frequently on vehicles used in numerous starting and stopping conditions, excessive idling and when the engine is not allowed to attain normal operating temperature through short runs.

Evaporative Emissions

Gasoline fuel is a major source of pollution, before and after it is burned in the automobile engine. From the time the fuel is refined, stored, pumped and transported, again stored until it is pumped into the fuel tank of the vehicle, the gasoline gives off unburned hydrocarbons (HC) into the atmosphere. Through the redesign of storage areas and venting systems, the pollution factor was diminished, but not eliminated, from the refinery standpoint. However, the automobile still remained the primary source of vaporized, unburned hydrocarbon (HC) emissions.

Fuel pumped from an underground storage tank is cool but when exposed to a warmer ambient temperature, will expand. Before controls were mandated, an owner might fill the fuel tank with fuel from an underground storage tank and park the vehicle for some time in warm area, such as a parking lot. As the fuel would warm, it would expand and should no provisions or area be provided for the expansion, the fuel would spill out of the filler neck and onto the ground, causing hydrocarbon (HC) pollution and creating a severe fire hazard. To correct this condition, the vehicle manufacturers added overflow plumbing and/or gasoline tanks with built in expansion areas or domes.

However, this did not control the fuel vapor emission from the fuel tank. It was determined that most of the fuel evaporation occurred when the vehicle was stationary and the engine not operating. Most vehicles carry 5–25 gallons (19–95 liters) of gasoline. Should a large concentration of vehicles be parked in one area, such as a large parking lot, excessive fuel vapor emissions would take place, increasing as the temperature increases.

To prevent the vapor emission from escaping into the atmosphere, the fuel systems were designed to trap the vapors while the vehicle is stationary, by sealing the system from the atmosphere. A storage system is used to collect and hold the fuel vapors from the carburetor (if equipped) and the fuel tank when the engine is not operating. When the engine is started, the storage system is then purged of the fuel vapors, which are drawn into the engine and burned with the air/fuel mixture.

EMISSION CONTROLS

There are three sources of automotive pollutants: Crankcase fumes, exhaust gases and gasoline evaporation. The pollutants formed from these substances fall into three categories: unburnt hydrocarbons (HC), carbon monoxide (CO) and oxides of nitrogen (NOx). The equipment that is used to limit these pollutants is commonly called emission control equipment.

Crankcase Ventilation System

GENERAL INFORMATION

▶ **See Figures 1, 2, 3, 4 and 5**

The crankcase emission control equipment consists of a positive crankcase ventilation valve (PCV), a closed or open oil filler cap and hoses to connect this equipment.

➡**The crankcase emission control system on the diesel engine is basically the same as that which is on the gasoline engine. Its major difference is the crankcase emission control valve. Although its function is the same as the gasoline engine's PCV valve, it's shape and location are different.**

When the engine is running, a small portion of the gases which are formed in the combustion chamber during combustion leak by the piston rings and enter the crankcase. Since these gases are under pressure they tend to escape from the crankcase and enter into the atmosphere. If these gases were allowed to re-main in the crankcase for any length of time, they would contaminate the engine oil and cause sludge to build up. If the gases are allowed to escape into the atmosphere, they would pollute the air, as they contain unburned hydrocarbons. The crankcase emission control equipment recycles these gases back into the engine combustion chamber where they are burned.

Crankcase gases are recycled in the following manner: while the engine is running, clean filtered air is drawn into the crankcase through the air filter and then through a hose leading to the rocker cover. As the air passes through the crankcase it picks up the combustion gases and carries them out of the crankcase, up through the PCV valve and into the intake manifold. After they enter the intake manifold they are drawn into the combustion chamber and burned.

The most critical component in the system is the PCV valve. This vacuum controlled valve regulates the amount of gases which are recycled into the combustion changer. At low engine speeds the valve is partially closed, limiting the flow of gases into the intake manifold. As engine speed increases, the valve opens to admit greater quantities of the gases into the intake manifold. If the valve should become blocked or plugged, the gases will be prevented from escaping from the crankcase by the normal route. Since these gases are under pressure, they will find their own way out of the crankcase. This alternate route is usually a weak oil seal or gasket in the engine. As the gas escapes by the gasket it also creates an oil leak. Besides causing oil leaks, a clogged PCV valve also allows these gases to remain in the crankcase for an extended period of time, promoting the formation of sludge in the engine.

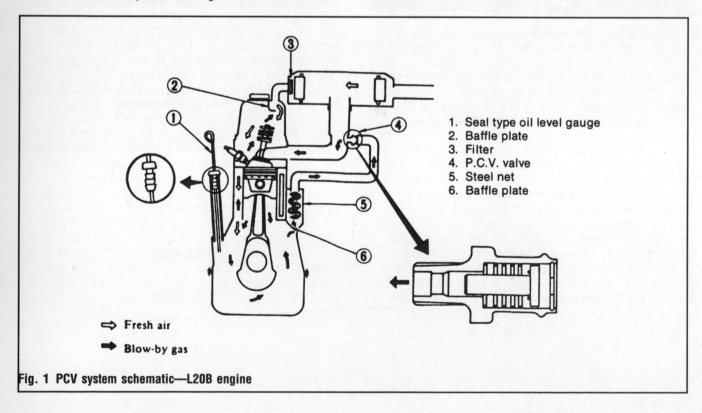

1. Seal type oil level gauge
2. Baffle plate
3. Filter
4. P.C.V. valve
5. Steel net
6. Baffle plate

⇨ Fresh air

➡ Blow-by gas

Fig. 1 PCV system schematic—L20B engine

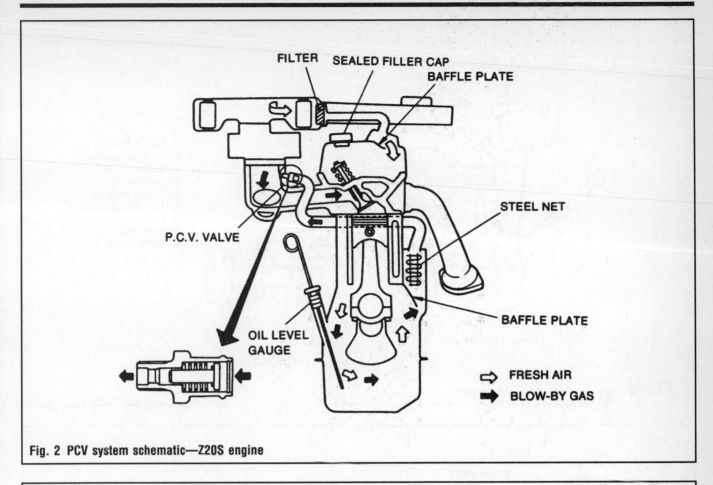

Fig. 2 PCV system schematic—Z20S engine

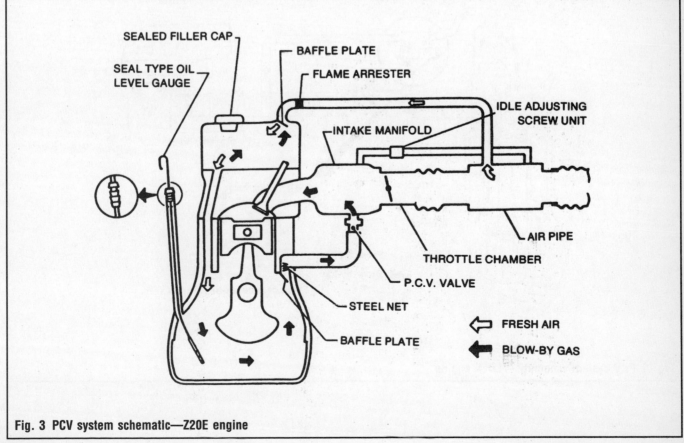

Fig. 3 PCV system schematic—Z20E engine

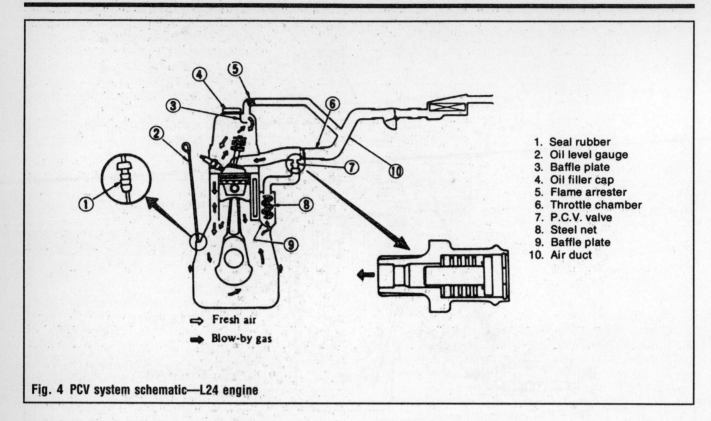

1. Seal rubber
2. Oil level gauge
3. Baffle plate
4. Oil filler cap
5. Flame arrester
6. Throttle chamber
7. P.C.V. valve
8. Steel net
9. Baffle plate
10. Air duct

⇨ Fresh air

➡ Blow-by gas

Fig. 4 PCV system schematic—L24 engine

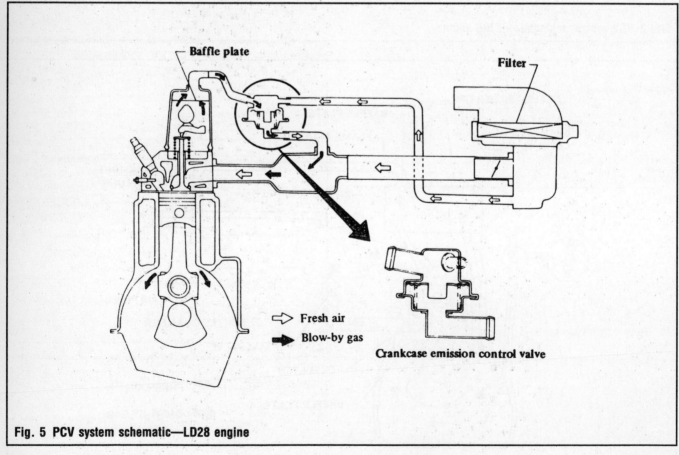

Baffle plate

Filter

⇨ Fresh air

➡ Blow-by gas

Crankcase emission control valve

Fig. 5 PCV system schematic—LD28 engine

TESTING

Check the PCV system hoses and connections, to see that there are no leaks. Then replace or tighten, as necessary.

Gasoline Engines

To check the valve, remove it and blow through both of its ends. When blowing from the side which goes toward the intake manifold, very little air should pass through it. When blowing from the crankcase (valve cover) side, air should pass through freely.

Replace the valve with a new one, if the valve fails to function as outlined.

➡**Do not attempt to clean or adjust the valve. Replace it with a new one.**

Diesel Engines

Remove the crankcase emission control valve and suck on the pipe that leads to the intake manifold. Air should flow freely. You should be able to hear the diaphragm in the valve click open while you are sucking. If the valve fails to function as detailed, replace it with a new one.

REMOVAL & INSTALLATION

To remove the PCV valve, simply loosen the hose clamp and remove the valve from the manifold-to-crankcase hose and intake manifold. Install the PCV valve in the reverse order of removal.

Removal and installation procedures for the diesel crankcase emission control valve are detailed in Section 1.

Evaporative Emission Control System

DESCRIPTION

◆ **See Figure 6**

When raw fuel evaporates, the vapors contain hydrocarbons. To prevent these fumes from escaping into the atmosphere, the fuel evaporative emission control system was developed.

There are two different evaporative emission control systems used on Datsun/Nissan. The system used through 1974 consists of a sealed fuel tank, a vapor/liquid separator, a flow guide (check) valve, and all of the hoses connecting these components, in the above order, leading from the fuel tank to the PCV hose, which connects the crankcase to the PCV valve.

In operation, the vapor formed in the fuel tank passes through the vapor separator, onto the flow guide valve and the crankcase. When the engine is not running, if the fuel vapor pressure in the vapor separator goes about 0.4 in. Hg, the flow guide valve opens and allows the vapor to enter the engine crankcase. Otherwise the flow guide valve is closed to the vapor separator while the engine is not running. When the engine is running, and a vacuum is developed in the fuel tank or in the engine crankcase and the difference of pressure between the relief side and the fuel tank or crankcase becomes 2 in. Hg, the relief valve opens and allows ambient air from the air cleaner into the fuel tank or the engine crankcase.

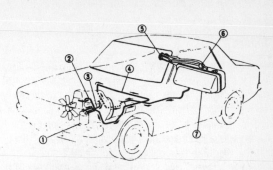

1. Carbon canister
2. Vacuum signal line
3. Canister vent line
4. Vapor vent line
5. Fuel filler cap with vacuum relief valve
6. Fuel check valve
7. Fuel tank

Fig. 6 Components of the evaporative emission control system

This ambient air replaces the vapor within the fuel tank or crankcase, bring the fuel tank or crankcase back into a neutral or positive pressure range.

The system used on 1975 and later models consists of a sealed fuel tank, a vapor/liquid separator (certain models only), a vapor vent line, a carbon canister, a vacuum signal line and a canister purge line.

In operation, fuel vapors and/or liquid are routed to the liquid/vapor separator or check valve where liquid fuel is directed back into the fuel tank as fuel vapors flow into the charcoal filled canister. The charcoal absorbs and stores the fuel vapors when the engine is not running or is at idle. When the throttle valves in the carburetor (or air intakes for fuel injection) are opened, vacuum from above the throttle valves is routed through a vacuum signal line to the purge control valve on the canister. The control valve opens and allows the fuel vapors to be drawn from the canister through a purge line and into the intake manifold and the combustion chambers.

INSPECTION AND SERVICE

Check the hoses for proper connections and damage. Replace as necessary. Check the vapor separator tank for fuel leaks, distortion and dents, and replace as necessary.

Flow Guide Valve
1973–74 MODELS ONLY

Remove the flow guide valve and inspect it for leakage by blowing air into the ports in the valve. When air is applied from the fuel tank side, the flow guide valve is normal if the air passes into the check side (crankcase side), but not into the relief side (air cleaner side). When air is applied from the check side, the valve is normal if the passage of air is restricted: When air is applied from the relief side (air cleaner side), the valve is normal if air passes into the fuel tank side or into the check side.

Carbon Canister and Purge Control Valve

1975–84 MODELS

▶ See Figure 7

To check the operation of the carbon canister purge control valve, disconnect the rubber hose between the canister control valve and the T-fitting, at the T-fitting. Apply vacuum to the hose leading to the control valve. The vacuum condition should be maintained indefinitely. If the control valve leaks, remove the top cover of the valve and check for a dislocated or cracked diaphragm. If the diaphragm is damaged, a repair kit containing a new diaphragm, retainer, and spring is available and should be installed.

The carbon canister has an air filter in the bottom of the canister. The filter element should be checked once a year or every 12,000 miles; more frequently if the car is operated in dusty areas. Replace the filter by pulling it out of the bottom of the canister and installing a new one.

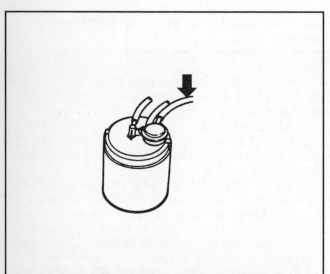

Fig. 7 Apply vacuum to check the purge control valve

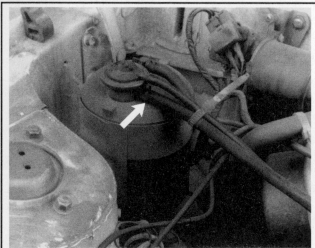

Check the hose (arrow) leading to the canister purge control valve every year or 12,000 miles

REMOVAL & INSTALLATION

Removal and installation of the various evaporative emission control system components consists of disconnecting the hoses, loosening retaining screws, and remove the part which is to be replaced or checked. Install in the reverse order. When replacing hose, make sure that it is fuel and vapor resistant.

Spark Timing Control System

DESCRIPTION

Except 1973 610 Models

The spark timing control system has been used in different forms on NissanDatsuns since 1972. The first system, Transmission Controlled Spark System (TCS) was used on most Nissan/Datsuns through 1979. This system consists of a thermal vacuum valve, a vacuum switching valve, a high gear detecting switch, and a number of vacuum hoses. Basically, the system is designed to retard full spark advance except when the car is in high gear and the engine is at normal operating temperature. At all other times, the spark advance is retarded to one degree or another.

The 1980 and later Spark Timing Control System replaces the TCS system. The major difference is that it works solely from engine water temperature changes rather than a transmission mounted switch. The system includes a thermal vacuum valve, a vacuum delay valve, and attendant hoses. It performs the same function as the earlier TCS system. To retard full spark advance at times when high levels of pollutants would otherwise be given off.

1973 610 With Dual Point Distributor

▶ See Figure 8

The dual point distributor has two sets of breaker points which operate independently of each other and are positioned with a relative phase angle of 7° apart. This makes one set the advanced points and the other set the retarded points.

The two sets of points, which mechanically operate continuously, are connected in parallel to the primary side of the ignition circuit. One set of points controls the firing of the spark plugs and hence, the ignition timing, depending on whether or not the retarded set of points is energized.

When both sets of points are electrically energized, the first set to open (the advanced set, 7° sooner) has no control over breaking the ignition coil primary circuit because the retarded set is still closed and maintaining a complete circuit to ground. When the retarded set of points opens, the advanced set is still open, and the primary circuit is broken causing the electromagnetic field in the coil to collapse and the ignition spark is produced.

When the retarded set of points is removed from the primary ignition circuit through the operation of a distributor relay inserted into the retarded points circuit, the advanced set of points controls the primary circuit. The retarded set of points is activated as follows:

The retarded set of points is activated only while the throttle is partially open, the temperature is above 50°F (10°C) and the transmission is any gear but fourth gear.

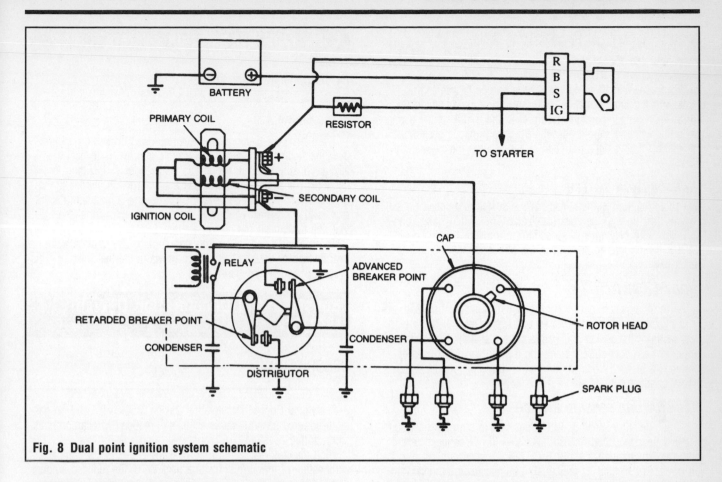

Fig. 8 Dual point ignition system schematic

➡**When the ambient temperature is below 30°F (−1°C), the retarded set of points is removed from the ignition circuit no matter what switch is ON.**

In the case of an automatic transmission, the retarded set of points is activated at all times except under heavy acceleration and high speed cruising (wide open throttle) with the ambient temperature about 50°F (10°C).

There are three switches which control the operation of the distributor relay. All of the switches must be ON in order to energize the distributor relay, thus energizing the retarded set of points.

The switches and their operation are as follows:

A transmission switch located in the transmission closes an electrical circuit when the transmission is all gears except Fourth gear.

A throttle switch located on the throttle linkage at the carburetor is ON when the throttle valve is removed within a 45° angle.

The temperature sensing switch is located near the hood release level inside the passenger compartment. The temperature sensing switch comes on between 41°F (5°C) and 55°F (13°C) and rising and goes OFF above 34°F (1°C) when the temperature falls.

The distributor vacuum advance mechanism produced a spark advance based on the amount of vacuum in the intake manifold. With a high vacuum, less air/fuel mixture enters the engine cylinders and the mixture is therefore less highly compressed. Consequently, this mixture burns more slowly and the advance mechanism gives it more time to burn. This longer burning time results in higher combustion temperatures at peak pressure and hence, more time for nitrogen to react with oxygen and form nitrogen oxides (NOx). At the same time, this advanced timing results in less

complete combustion due to the greater area of cylinder wall (quench area) exposed at the instant of ignition. This cooled fuel will not burn as readily and hence, results in higher unburned hydrocarbons (HC). The production of NOx and HC resulting from the vacuum advance is highest during the moderate acceleration in lower gears.

Retardation of the ignition timing is necessary to reduce NOx and HC emissions. Various ways of retarding the ignition spark have been used in automobiles, all of which remove vacuum to the distributor vacuum advance mechanism at different times under certain conditions. Another way of accomplishing the same goal is the dual point distributor system.

INSPECTION & ADJUSTMENTS

Except 1973 610 Models

Normally the TCS and Spark Timing Control systems should be trouble-free. However, if you suspect a problem in the system, first check to make sure all wiring (if so equipped) and hoses are connected and free from dirt. Also check to make sure the distributor vacuum advance is working properly. If everything appears all right, connect a timing light to the engine and make sure the initial timing is correct. On vehicles with the TCS system, run the engine until it reaches normal operating temperature, and then have an assistant sit in the car and shift the transmission through all the gears slowly. If the system is functioning properly, the timing will be 10–15° advanced in high gear (compared to the other gear positions). If the system is still not operating correctly, you will have to check for continuity at all the connections with a test light.

To test the Spark Timing Control System, connect a timing light and check the ignition timing while the temperature gauge is in the cold position. Write down the reading. Allow the engine to run with the timing light attached until the temperature needle reaches the center of the gauge. As the engine is warming up, check with the timing light to make sure the ignition timing retards. When the temperature needle is in the middle of the gauge, the ignition timing should advance from its previous position. If the ignition timing does not change, replace the thermal vacuum valve.

TRANSMISSION SWITCH

Disconnect the electrical leads at the switch and connect a self powered test light to the electrical leads. The switch should conduct electricity only when the gearshift is moved to fourth gear.

If the switch fails to perform in the above manner, replace it with a new one.

THROTTLE SWITCH

The throttle switch located on the throttle linkage at the carburetor is checked with a self powered test light. Disconnect the electrical leads of the switch and connect the test light. The switch should not conduct current when the throttle valve is closed or opened, up to 45°. When the throttle is fully opened, the switch should conduct current.

TEMPERATURE SENSING SWITCH

The temperature sensing switch mounted in the passenger compartment near the hood release lever should not conduct current when the temperature is above 55°F (13°C) when connected to a self powered test light as previously outlined for the throttle switch.

Dual Spark Plug Ignition System

DESCRIPTION

Z20E and Z20S Engines

The 1980 California model and all 1981–83 Z-series engines have two spark plugs per cylinder. This arrangement allows the engine to burn large amounts of recirculated exhaust gases without affecting performance. In fact, the system works so well it improves gas mileage under most circumstances.

Both spark plugs fire simultaneously, which substantially shortens the time required to burn the air/fuel mixture when exhaust gases (EGR) are not being recirculated. When gases are being recirculated, the dual spark plug system brings the ignition level up to that of a single plug system which is not recirculating exhaust gases.

ADJUSTMENT

The only adjustments necessary are the tune-up and maintenance procedures outlined in Sections 1 and 2.

Early Fuel Evaporation System

DESCRIPTION

▶ **See Figure 9**

The Early Fuel Evaporation System is used on some gasoline-powered L-series engines. The system's purpose is to heat the air/fuel mixture when the engine is below normal operating temperature. The L-series engines use a system much similar to the old style exhaust manifold heat riser. The only adjustment necessary is to occasionally lubricate the counterweight. Other than that, the system should be trouble-free.

The 1980–81 and later carbureted engines use coolant water heat instead of exhaust gas heat to prewarm the fuel mixture. This system should be trouble-free.

Boost Control Deceleration Device (BCDD)

DESCRIPTION

The Boost Control Deceleration Device (BCDD) is used on gasoline-powered (only) L-series engines to reduce hydrocarbon emissions during coasting conditions.

High manifold vacuum during coasting prevents the complete combustion of the air/fuel mixture because of the reduced amount of air. This condition will result in a large amount of HC emission. Enriching the air/fuel mixture for a short time (during the high vacuum condition) will reduce the emission of the HC.

However, enriching the air/fuel mixture with only the mixture adjusting screw will cause poor engine idle or invite an increase in the carbon monoxide (CO) content of the exhaust gases. The BCDD consists of an independent system that kicks in when the engine is coasting and enriches the air/fuel mixture, which reduces the hydrocarbon content of the exhaust gases. This is accomplished without adversely affecting engine idle and the carbon monoxide content of the exhaust gases.

ADJUSTMENT

▶ **See Figure 10**

Normally, the BCDD does not need adjustment. However, if the need should arise because of suspected malfunction of the system, proceed as follows:

1. Connect the tachometer to the engine.
2. Connect a quick response vacuum gauge to the intake manifold.
3. Disconnect the solenoid valve electrical leads.
4. Start and warm up the engine until it reaches normal operating temperature.
5. Adjust the idle speed to the proper specification.
6. Raise the engine speed to 3,000–3,500 rpm under no-load

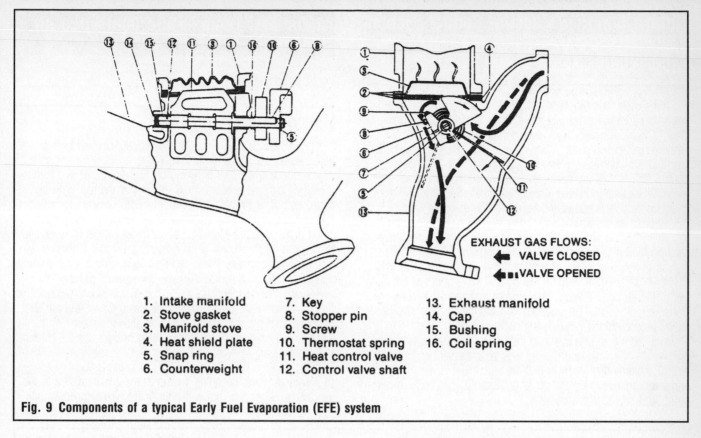

1. Intake manifold
2. Stove gasket
3. Manifold stove
4. Heat shield plate
5. Snap ring
6. Counterweight
7. Key
8. Stopper pin
9. Screw
10. Thermostat spring
11. Heat control valve
12. Control valve shaft
13. Exhaust manifold
14. Cap
15. Bushing
16. Coil spring

EXHAUST GAS FLOWS:
◄ **VALVE CLOSED**
◄▪ı **VALVE OPENED**

Fig. 9 Components of a typical Early Fuel Evaporation (EFE) system

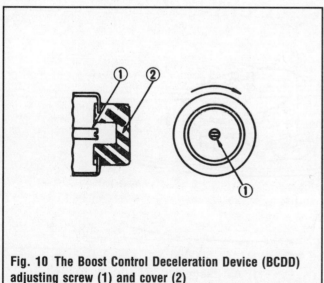

Fig. 10 The Boost Control Deceleration Device (BCDD) adjusting screw (1) and cover (2)

(transmission in Neutral or Park), then allow the throttle to close quickly. Take notice as to whether or not the engine rpm returns to idle speed and if it does, how long the fall in rpm is interrupted before it reaches idle speed.

At the moment the throttle is snapped closed at high engine rpm and the vacuum in the intake manifold reaches between 23 in. Hg and 27.7 in. Hg and then gradually falls to about 15.6 in. Hg at idle speed. The process of the fall of the intake manifold vacuum and the engine rpm will take one of the following three forms:

a. When the operating pressure of the BCDD is too high, the system remains inoperative, and the vacuum in the intake manifold decreases without interruption just like that of an engine without a BCDD.

b. When the operating pressure is lower than that of the case given above, but still higher than the proper set pressure, the fall of vacuum in the intake manifold is interrupted and kept constant at a certain level (operating pressure) for about one second and then gradually falls down to the normal vacuum at idle speed.

c. When the set of operating pressure of the BCDD is lower than the intake manifold vacuum when the throttle is suddenly released, the engine speed will not lower to idle speed.

To adjust the set operating pressure of the BCDD, remove the adjusting screw cover from the BCDD mechanism mounted on the side of the carburetor. On 810 models, the BCDD system is installed under the throttle chamber.

The adjusting screw is a left-hand threaded screw. Late models may have an adjusting nut instead of a screw. Turning the screw ⅛ of a turn in either direction will change the operation pressure about 0.8 in. Hg. Turning the screw counterclockwise will increase the amount of vacuum needed to operate the mechanism. Turning the screw clockwise will decrease the amount of vacuum needed to operate the mechanism.

The operating pressure for the BCDD on most models should be between 19.9 to 22.05 in. Hg. The decrease in intake manifold vacuum should be interrupted at these levels for about one second when the BCDD is operating correctly.

Don't forget to install the adjusting screw cover after the system is adjusted.

Intake Manifold Vacuum Control System

DESCRIPTION

This system, used in 1980–81 510s, is designed to reduce the engine's oil consumption when the intake manifold vacuum increases to an extremely high level during deceleration. The system consists of two units. A boost control unit as the vacuum sensor, and a by-pass air control unit as an actuator. The boost control unit senses the manifold vacuum. When the level of the manifold vacuum increases above the predetermined value, the boost control valve opens and transmits the manifold vacuum to the by-pass air air control unit. The manifold vacuum then pulls the diaphragm in and opens the by-pass air control valve, thereby causing the air to be bypassed to the intake manifold. After completion of the air by-pass, the manifold vacuum is lowered. This results in the closing of the boost control valve and then the closing of the air control valve. This system operates in a tightly controlled circuit so that the manifold vacuum can be kept very close to the predetermined value during deceleration.

Aside from a routine check of the hoses and their connections, no service or adjustments should ever be necessary on this system. If at some time you feel that an adjustment is required, it is suggested that you take the car to a Nissan/Datsun dealer or an authorized service representative.

Automatic Temperature Controlled Air Cleaner

DESCRIPTION

▶ **See Figure 11**

This system is used on all Datsun models covered in this guide except the 810 and the 200SX.

The rate at which fuel is drawn into the air-stream in a carburetor varies with the temperature of the air that the fuel is being mixed with. The air/fuel ratio cannot be held constant for efficient fuel combustion with a wide range of air temperatures. Cold air being drawn into the engine causes a richer air/fuel mixture, and thus, more hydrocarbons in the exhaust gas. Hot air being drawn into the engine causes a leaner air/fuel mixture and more efficient combustion for less hydrocarbons in the exhaust gases.

The automatic temperature controlled air cleaner is designed so that the temperature of the ambient air being drawn into the engine is automatically controlled, to hold the temperature of the air and, consequently, the fuel/air ratio at a constant rate for efficient fuel combustion.

A temperature sensing vacuum switch controls vacuum applied to a vacuum motor operating a valve in the intake snorkle of the air cleaner. When the engine is cold or the air being drawn into

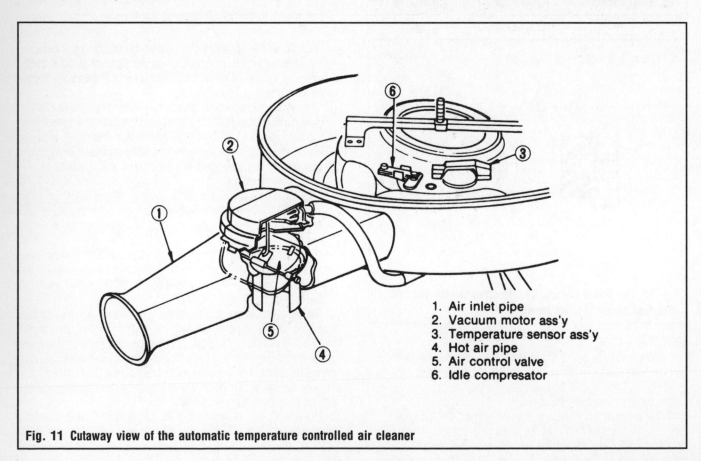

1. Air inlet pipe
2. Vacuum motor ass'y
3. Temperature sensor ass'y
4. Hot air pipe
5. Air control valve
6. Idle compresator

Fig. 11 Cutaway view of the automatic temperature controlled air cleaner

the engine is cold, the vacuum motor opens the valve, allowing air heated by the exhaust manifold to be drawn into the engine. As the engine warms up, the temperature sensing unit shuts off the vacuum applied to the vacuum motor which allows the valve to close, shutting off the heated air and allowing cooler, outside (under hood) air to be drawn into the engine.

TESTING

When the air around the temperature sensor of the unit mounted inside the air cleaner housing reaches 100°F (38°C), the sensor should allow vacuum to pass onto the air valve vacuum motor thus blocking off the air cleaner snorkle to under hood (unheated) air.

When the temperature around the sensor is above 188°F (87°C), the air control valve should be completely open to under hood air.

If the air cleaner fails to operate correctly, check for loose or broken vacuum hoses. If the hoses are not the cause, replace the vacuum motor in the air cleaner.

Exhaust Gas Recirculation (EGR)

DESCRIPTION

Gasoline Engines
▶ **See Figures 12 and 13**

This system is used on all 1974–84 and later models. Exhaust gas recirculation is used to reduce combustion temperatures in the engine, thereby reducing the oxides of nitrogen emissions.

An EGR valve is mounted on the center of the intake manifold. The recycled exhaust gas is drawn into the bottom of the intake manifold riser portion through the exhaust manifold heat stove and EGR valve. A vacuum diaphragm is connected to a timed signal port at the carburetor flange.

As the throttle valve is opened, vacuum is applied to the EGR valve vacuum diaphragm. When the vacuum reaches about 2 in. Hg, the diaphragm moves against string pressure and is in a fully up position at 8 in. Hg of vacuum. As the diaphragm moves up, it opens the exhaust gas metering valve which allows exhaust gas to be pulled into the engine intake manifold. The system does not operate when the engine is idling because the exhaust gas recirculation would cause a rough idle.

On 1975–84 and later models, a thermal vacuum valve inserted in the engine thermostat housing controls the application of the vacuum to the EGR valve. When the engine coolant reaches a predetermined temperature, the thermal vacuum valve opens and allows vacuum to be routed to the EGR valve. Below the predetermined temperature, the thermal vacuum valve closes and blocks vacuum to the EGR valve.

All 1978–79 models, the 1980 810 and the 1980–81 510 (Canadian), 200SX (Canadian) have a B.P.T. valve installed between the EGR valve and the thermal vacuum valve. The B.P.T. valve has a diaphragm which is raised or lowered by exhaust back pressure. The diaphragm opens or closes an air bleed, which is connected into the EGR vacuum line. High pressure results in higher levels of EGR, because the diaphragm is raised, closing off the air bleed, which allows more vacuum to reach and open the EGR

valve. Thus the amount of recirculated exhaust gas varies with exhaust pressure.

All 1980 200SX (USA) models and all 1980–81 510 (USA) models use a V.V.T. valve (venturi vacuum transducer valve) instead of the B.P.T. valve. The V.V.T. valve monitors exhaust pressure and carburetor vacuum in order to activate the diaphragm which controls the throttle vacuum applied to the EGR control valve. This system expands the operating range of the EGR flow rate as compared to the B.P.T. unit.

➡ **1981 510s built for California are equipped with two EGR valves. The second one is directly below the normal one.**

Many 1975 and later Datsuns are equipped with an EGR warning system which signals via a light in the dashboard that the EGR system may need service. The EGR warning light should come on every time the starter is engaged as a test to make sure the bulb is not blown. The system uses a counter which works in conjunction with the odometer, and lights the warning signal after the vehicle has traveled a predetermined number of miles.

To reset the counter, which is mounted in the engine compartment, remove the grommet installed in the side of the counter and insert the tip of a small screwdriver into the hole. Press down on the knob inside the hole. Reinstall the grommet.

Diesel Engines

This system is designed to control the formation of NOx emissions by recirculating the exhaust gas into the intake manifold passage through the control valve.

The EGR flow rate is controlled in three stages in accordance with the engine speed and load. The first stage, High EGR, is obtained through the combination of a closed throttle valve and an open EGR valve. The second stage, Low EGR, is obtained through the opening of the throttle valve. The third stage, Zero EGR, is obtained closing the EGR valve.

The engine load signal is picked up by the potentiometer installed on the injection pump control lever. The engine speed sig-

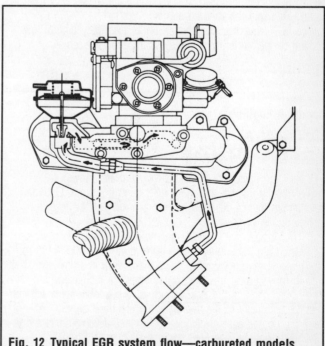

Fig. 12 Typical EGR system flow—carbureted models

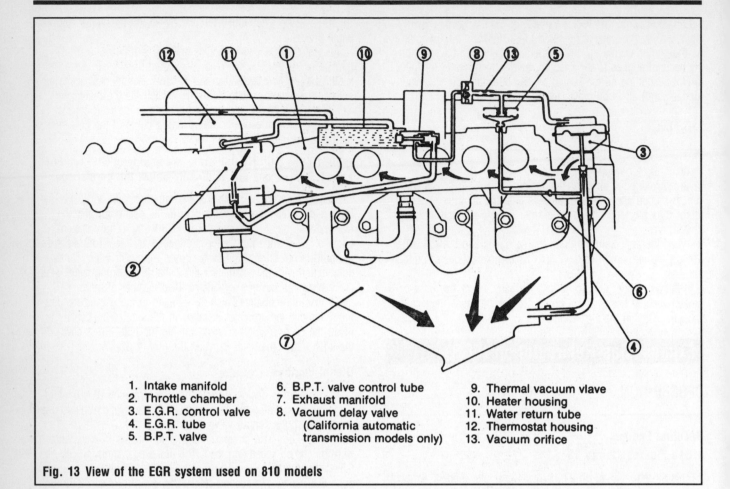

1. Intake manifold
2. Throttle chamber
3. E.G.R. control valve
4. E.G.R. tube
5. B.P.T. valve
6. B.P.T. valve control tube
7. Exhaust manifold
8. Vacuum delay valve
   (California automatic
   transmission models only)
9. Thermal vacuum vlave
10. Heater housing
11. Water return tube
12. Thermostat housing
13. Vacuum orifice

Fig. 13 View of the EGR system used on 810 models

nal is transmitted by an electromagnetic revolution sensor attached to the front cover. The throttle diaphragm and the EGR valve are both actuated by vacuum generated at the vacuum pump. Solenoids are used to convert the electrical signal from the control unit into the vacuum signal.

The EGR system is deactivated under extremely high or low coolant temperatures in order to assure good driveability.

TESTING

Gasoline Engines

1974 MODELS

▶ **See Figures 14 and 15**

Check the operation of the EGR system as follows:

1. Visually inspect the entire EGR control system. Clean the mechanism free of oil and dirt. Replace any rubber hoses found to be cracked or broken.
2. Make sure that the EGR solenoid valve is properly wired.
3. Increase the engine speed from idling to 2,000–3,500 rpm. The plate of the EGR control valve diaphragm and the valve shaft should move upward as the engine speed is increased.
4. Disconnect the EGR solenoid valve electrical leads and connect them directly to the vehicle's 12v electrical supply (battery). Race the engine again with the EGR solenoid valve connected to a 12v power source. The EGR control valve should remain stationary.

5. With the engine running at idle, push up on the EGR control valve diaphragm with your finger. When this is done, the engine idle should become rough and uneven.

Inspect the two components of the EGR system as necessary in the following manner:

 a. Remove the EGR control valve from the intake manifold.
 b. Apply 4.7–5.1 in. Hg of vacuum to the EGR control valve

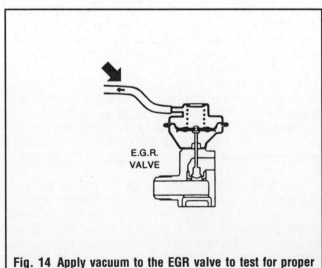

E.G.R. VALVE

Fig. 14 Apply vacuum to the EGR valve to test for proper operation

Fig. 15 Clean the seat of the EGR valve with a stiff brush

by sucking on a tube attached to the outlet on top of the valve. The valve should move to the full up position. The valve should remain open for more than 30 seconds after the application of vacuum is discontinued and the vacuum hose is blocked.

c. Inspect the EGR valve for any signs of warpage or damage.

d. Clean the EGR valve seat with a brush and compressed air to prevent clogging.

e. Connect the EGR solenoid valve to a 12v DC power source and notice if the valve clicks when intermittently electrified. If the valve clicks, it is considered to be working properly.

f. Check the EGR temperature sensing switch by removing it from the engine and placing it in a container of water together with a thermometer. Connect a self powered test light to the two electrical leads of the switch.

g. Heat the container of water.

h. The switch should conduct current when the water temperature is below 77°F (25°C) and stop conducting current when the water reaches a temperature somewhere between 88–106°F (31–41°C). Replace the switch if it functions otherwise.

1975–84 MODELS

1. Remove the EGR valve and apply enough vacuum to the diaphragm to open the valve.

2. The valve should remain open for over 30 seconds after the vacuum is removed.

3. Check the valve for damage, such as warpage, cracks, and excessive wear around the valve and seat.

4. Clean the seat with a brush and compressed air and remove any deposits from around the valve and port (seat).

5. To check the operation of the thermal vacuum valve, remove the valve from the engine and apply vacuum to the ports of the valve. The valve should not allow vacuum to pass.

6. Place the valve in a container of water with a thermometer and heat the water. When the temperature of the water reaches 134–145°F (57–63°C), remove the valve and apply vacuum to the ports. The valve should allow vacuum to pass through it.

7. To test the B.P.T. valve installed on 1978 and later models, disconnect the two vacuum hoses from the valve. Plug one of the ports. While applying pressure to the bottom of the valve, apply

vacuum to the unplugged port and check for leakage. If any exists, replace the valve.

8. To test the check valve installed in some 1978 and later models, remove the valve and blow into the side which connects the EGR valve. Air should flow. When air is supplied to the other side, air flow resistance should be greater. If not, replace the valve.

9. To check the V.V.T. valve which replaces the B.P.T. valve on some 1980 and later models, disconnect the top and bottom center hoses and apply a vacuum to the top hose. Check for leaks. If a leak is present, replace the valve.

Diesel Engines
▶ **See Figures 16 and 17**

1. Visually check the entire EGR system as detailed in the previous Gasoline Engine section.

2. With the engine off, check the EGR control valve and throttle body for an indication of binding or sticking by moving the diaphragm/rod upward with your finger.

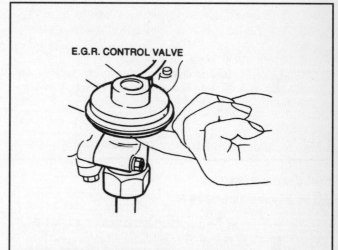

E.G.R. CONTROL VALVE

Fig. 16 To check the EGR valve for binding or sticking, push your finger up on the diaphragm—diesel engine

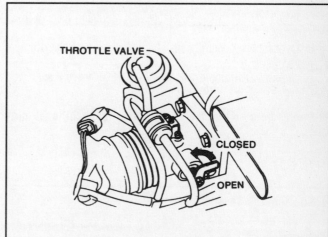

THROTTLE VALVE

CLOSED

OPEN

Fig. 17 The position of this lever will tell you whether the throttle valve is open or closed

3. Start the engine and place your finger on the underside of the EGR valve. You should feel the diaphragm.

✳✳ CAUTION

Be careful that your finger doesn't get caught between the diaphragm and the body of the valve.

4. When the temperature of the engine is at or below 86°F (30°C), make sure that the EGR valve does not operate and the throttle valve is open when the engine is revved.

5. If the EGR valve operates or the throttle valve is closed, check the water temperature sensor. If the sensor appears normal, replace the EGR control unit.

6. When the temperature of the engine is high, above 86°F (30°C), make sure that the EGR valve operates and the throttle valve is closed when the engine is idling.

7. Increase the engine speed gradually and make sure that the throttle valve opens and the EGR valve closes in this order.

8. If the EGR valve and/or the throttle valve do not operate properly in this step, check them as follows:

a. Run the engine at idle and disconnect the harness connector at the solenoid valve. Apply battery voltage to the connector and check that the EGR valve and the throttle valve operate normally.

b. If they do not, check the EGR valve and the throttle diaphragm independently. If they operate normally, check the rev sensor, the potentiometer and all electrical circuits. If they appear normal, replace the EGR control unit.

REMOVAL & INSTALLATION

EGR Control Valve
◆ **See Figures 18 and 19**

1. Remove the nuts which attach the EGR tube and/or the BP tube to the EGR valve (if so equipped).

2. Unscrew the mounting bolts and remove the heat shield plate from the EGR control valve (if so equipped).

3. Tag and disconnect the EGR vacuum hose(s).

4. Unscrew the mounting bolts and remove the EGR control valve.

5. Install the EGR valve assembly with mounting bolts to intake manifold location.

6. Connect all vacuum hoses and install the heat shield if so equipped.

7. Connect EGR tube or BP tube to the EGR valve if so equipped.

➡**Always be sure that the new valve is identical to the old one.**

TESTING

◆ **See Figures 18 and 19**

1. Visually check the entire EGR system as detailed in the previous Gasoline Engine section.

2. With the engine off, check the EGR control valve and throttle body for an indication of binding or sticking by moving the diaphragm/rod upward with your finger.

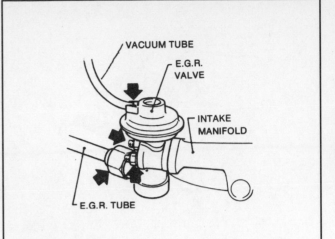

Fig. 18 Disconnect the following to remove the EGR valve where shown

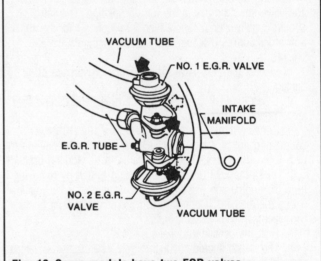

Fig. 19 Some models have two EGR valves

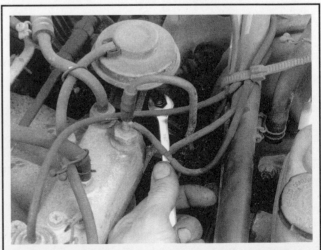

To remove the EGR valve, unbolt it from the exhaust manifold flange

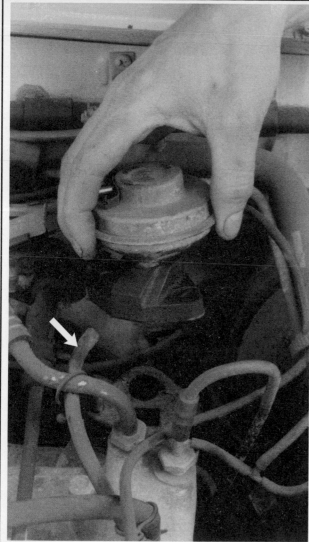

Lift off the EGR valve from its flange—you may want to label the vacuum hose (arrow)

3. Start the engine and place your finger on the underside of the EGR valve. You should feel the diaphragm.

❋❋ CAUTION

Be careful that your finger doesn't get caught between the diaphragm and the body of the valve.

4. When the temperature of the engine is at or below 86°F (30°C), make sure that the EGR valve does not operate and the throttle valve is open when the engine is revved.

5. If the EGR valve operates or the throttle valve is closed, check the water temperature sensor. If the sensor appears normal, replace the EGR control unit.

6. When the temperature of the engine is high, above 86°F (30°C), make sure that the EGR valve operates and the throttle valve is closed when the engine is idling.

7. Increase the engine speed gradually and make sure that the throttle valve opens and the EGR valve closes in this order.

8. If the EGR valve and/or the throttle valve do not operate properly in this step, check them as follows:

a. Run the engine at idle and disconnect the harness connector at the solenoid valve. Apply battery voltage to the connector and check that the EGR valve and the throttle valve operate normally.

b. If they do not, check the EGR valve and the throttle diaphragm independently. If they operate normally, check the rev sensor, the potentiometer and all electrical circuits. If they appear normal, replace the EGR control unit.

Air Injection Reactor System

DESCRIPTION

▶ **See Figure 20**

This system is used on 1974–79 gasoline engines (only). In gasoline engines, it is difficult to completely burn the air/fuel mixture through normal combustion in the combustion chambers. Under certain operating conditions, unburned fuel is exhausted into the atmosphere.

The air injection reactor system is designed so that ambient air, pressurized by the air pump, is injected through the injection nozzles into the exhaust ports near each exhaust valve. The exhaust gases are at high temperatures and ignite when brought into contact with the oxygen. Unburned fuel is then burned in the exhaust ports and manifold.

In 1976 California models utilized a secondary system consisting of an air control valve which limits injection of secondary air and an emergency relief valve which controls the supply of secondary air. This system protects the catalytic converter from overheating. In 1977 the function of these two valves was taken by a single combined air control (C.A.C.) valve.

All engines with the air pump system have a series of minor alterations to accommodate the system. These are:

1. Special close tolerance carburetor. Most engines, except the L16, require a slightly rich idle mixture adjustment.

2. Distributor with special advance curve. Ignition timing is retarded about 10° at idle in most cases.

3. Cooling system changes such as larger fan, higher fan speed, and thermostatic fan clutch. This is required to offset the increase in temperature caused by retarded timing at idle.

4. Faster idle speed.

5. Heated air intake on some engines.

The only periodic maintenance required on the air pump system is replacement of the drive belt.

TESTING

Air Pump

If the air pump makes an abnormal noise and cannot be corrected without removing the pump from the vehicle, check the following in sequence:

1. Turn the pulley ¾ of a turn in the clockwise direction and ¼ of a turn in the counterclockwise direction. If the pulley is binding and if rotation is not smooth, a defective bearing is indicated.

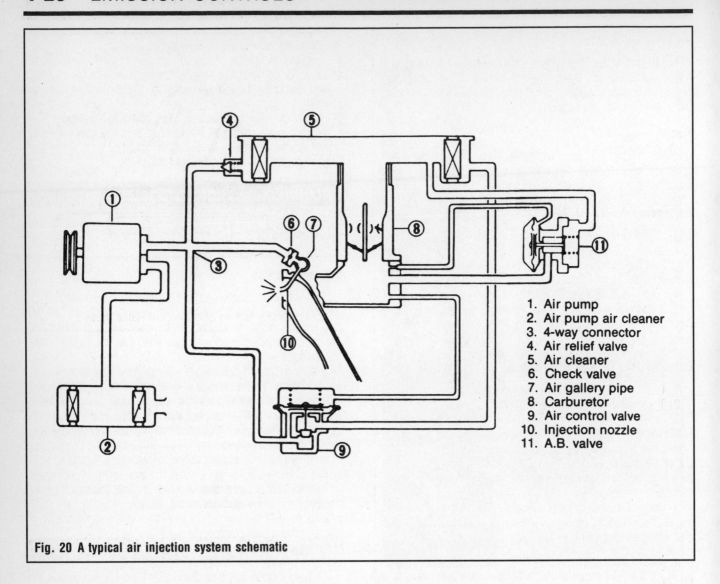

Fig. 20 A typical air injection system schematic

1. Air pump
2. Air pump air cleaner
3. 4-way connector
4. Air relief valve
5. Air cleaner
6. Check valve
7. Air gallery pipe
8. Carburetor
9. Air control valve
10. Injection nozzle
11. A.B. valve

2. Check the inner wall of the pump body, vanes and rotor for wear. If the rotor has abnormal wear, replace the air pump.

3. Check the needle roller bearing for wear and damage. If the bearings are defective, the air pump should be replaced.

4. Check and replace the rear side seal if abnormal wear or damage is noticed.

5. Check and replace the carbon shoes holding the vanes if they are found to be worn or damaged.

6. A deposit of carbon particles on the inner wall of the pump body and vanes is normal, but should be removed with compressed air before reassembling the air pump.

Check Valve

Remove the check valve from the air pump discharge line. Test it for leakage by blowing air into the valve from the air pump side and from the air manifold side. Air should only pass through the valve from the air pump side if the valve is functioning normally. A small amount of air leakage from the manifold side can be overlooked. Replace the check valve if it is found to be defective.

Anti-Backfire Valve

Disconnect the rubber hose connecting the mixture control valve with the intake manifold and plug the hose. If the mixture control valve is operating correctly, air will continue to blow out the mixture control valve for a few seconds after the accelerator pedal is fully depressed (engine running) and released quickly. If air continues to blow out for more than five seconds, replace the mixture control valve.

Air Pump Relief Valve

Disconnect the air pump discharge hose leading to the exhaust manifold. With the engine running, restrict the air flow coming from the pump. The air pump relief valve should vent the pressurized air to the atmosphere if it is working properly.

➡ **When performing this test do not completely block the discharge line of the air pump as damage may result if the relief valve fails to function properly.**

Air Injection Nozzles

Check around the air manifold for air leakage with the engine running at 2,000 rpm. If air is leaking from the eye joint bolt, retighten or replace the gasket. Check the air nozzles for restrictions by blowing air into the nozzles.

Hoses

Check and replace hoses if they are found to be weakened or cracked. Check all hose connections and clips. Be sure that the hoses are not in contact with other parts of the engine.

Emergency Air Relief Valve

1. Warm up the engine.
2. Check all hoses for leaks, kinks, improper connections, etc.
3. Run the engine up to 2,000 rpm under no load. No air should be discharged from the valve.
4. Disconnect the vacuum hose from the valve. This is the hose which runs to the intake manifold. Run the engine up to 2,000 rpm. Air should be discharged from the valve. If not, replace it.

Combined Air Control (CAC) Valve

1. Check all hoses for leaks, kinks, and improper connections.
2. Thoroughly warm up the engine.
3. With the engine idling, check for air discharge from the relief opening in the air cleaner case.
4. Disconnect and plug the vacuum hose from the valve. Air should be discharged from the valve with the engine idling. If the disconnect vacuum hose is not plugged, the engine will stumble.
5. Connect a hand operated vacuum pump to the vacuum fitting on the valve and apply 7.8–9.8 in. Hg of vacuum. Run the engine speed up to 3,000 rpm. No air should be discharged from the valve.
6. Disconnect and plug the air hose at the check valve, with the conditions as in the preceding step. This should cause the valve to discharge air. If not, or if any of the conditions in this procedure are not met, replace the valve.

Air Induction System

DESCRIPTION

▶ **See Figure 21**

➡ **This system is applicable to gasoline engines only.**

Models using this system include the 1980–81 510, the 1980 200SX and the 49 state version of the 1980 810. The air induction system is used to send fresh, secondary air to the exhaust manifold by utilizing vacuum created by the exhaust pulsation in the manifold.

The exhaust pressure usually pulsates in response to the opening and closing of the exhaust valve and it periodically decreases

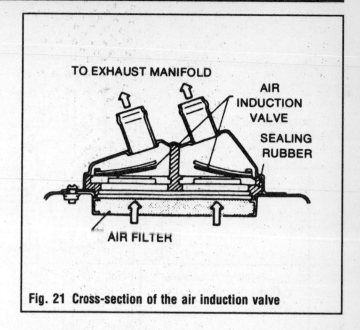

TO EXHAUST MANIFOLD

AIR INDUCTION VALVE

SEALING RUBBER

AIR FILTER

Fig. 21 Cross-section of the air induction valve

below atmospheric pressure. If a secondary air intake pipe is opened to the atmosphere under a vacuum condition, secondary air can then be drawn into the exhaust manifold in proportion of the vacuum. Because of this, the air induction system is able to reduce the CO and HC content in the exhaust gases. The system consists of two air induction valves, a filter, hoses and E.A.I. tubes.

The only periodic maintenance required is replacement of the air induction filter as detailed in Section 1.

Fuel Shut-Off System

DESCRIPTION

▶ **See Figure 22**

This system, used only in the 1980–81 510, is designed to reduce HC emissions and also to improve fuel economy during deceleration.

The system is operated by an anti-dieseling solenoid valve in the carburetor which is controlled by a vacuum switch. When the intake manifold vacuum increases to an extremely high level (which it does during deceleration), the fuel flow of the slow system is shut off by the anti-dieseling solenoid valve. When the intake manifold vacuum drops to a low level again, the fuel flow the slow system is resupplied.

The fuel shut-off system is further controlled by the clutch switch and gear position switches such as the neutral switch (manual transmission) and the inhibitor switch (automatic transmission) to ensure that fuel cannot be shut off even if the manifold vacuum is high enough to trigger the normal fuel shut-off operation.

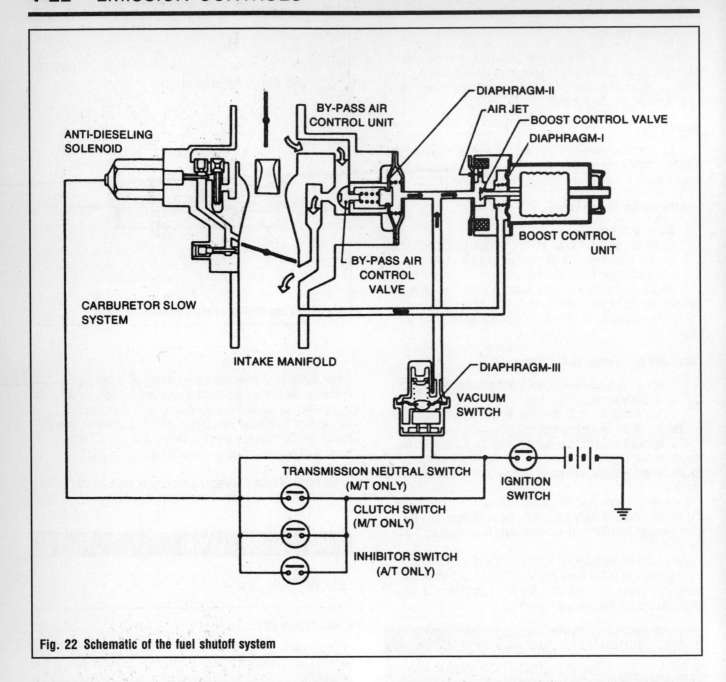

Fig. 22 Schematic of the fuel shutoff system

Injection Timing Advance System

DESCRIPTION

➡ **This system applies to diesel engines only.**

This system is designed to control the formation of HC emissions. It controls the amount of recirculating fuel in the fuel injection pump in order to control the injection timing.

The injection timing advance system is composed of an injection timing control solenoid valve, a potentiometer, and EGR control unit and a revolution sensor. This system is also called a Partial Load Advancer (PLA). The system operates along much the same lines as the EGR system and shares many of the same components.

High Altitude Emission Control System

DESCRIPTION

◆ **See Figure 23**

➡ **This system applies to diesel engines only.**

The high altitude emission control system is designed to control the formation of HC and CO emissions and to improve the driveability of the car in high altitude areas. In order to ensure decreased exhaust emissions, the injection timing and EGR tube have to be changed/replaced.

There is an altitude compensator located on top of the injection pump. The altitude shaft is in contact with a pin which is connected to the control lever which is in contact with the governor

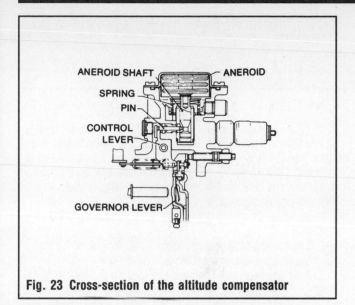

Fig. 23 Cross-section of the altitude compensator

lever. The higher the altitude, the lower the atmospheric pressure. Due to this fact, the pressure inside the aneroid is higher than that of the atmosphere at high altitudes, which causes the aneroid to expand like a balloon. When this happens, the aneroid shaft is pushed down, changing the contact surface with the pin, thus decreasing the fuel. Hence, the system controls the amount of fuel supplied in direct proportion to the altitude.

Electric Choke

DESCRIPTION

The purpose of the electric choke, used on all models, except the 810, and Z20E (200XS) covered in this guide, is to shorten the time the choke is in operation after the engine is started, thus shortening the time of high HC output.

An electric heater warms the bimetal spring which controls the opening and closing of the choke valve. The heater starts to heat as soon as the engine starts.

Catalytic Converter

DESCRIPTION

➡ **The catalytic converter is utilized in gasoline engines only.**

The catalytic converter is a muffler-like container built into the exhaust system to aid in the reduction of exhaust emissions. The catalyst element consists of individual pellets or a honeycomb monolithic substrate coated with a noble metal such as platinum, palladium, rhodium or a combination. When the exhaust gases come into contact with the catalyst, a chemical reaction occurs which will reduce the pollutants into harmless substances like water and carbon dioxide.

There are essentially two types of catalytic converters: an oxidizing type is used on all 1975–79 models built for California, all 1980 200SX models, the 49 state version of the 1980 810, and 1980–81 510s. It requires the addition of oxygen to spur the catalyst into reducing the engine's HC and CO emissions into H_2O and CO_2. Because of this need for oxygen, the Air Injection system is used with all these models.

The oxidizing catalytic converter, while effectively reducing HC and CO emissions, does little, if anything in the way of reducing NOx emissions. Thus, the three way catalytic converter.

The three way converter, unlike the oxidizing type, is capable of reducing HC, CO and NOx emissions; all at the same time. In theory, it seems impossible to reduce all three pollutants in one system since the reduction of HC and CO requires the addition of oxygen, while the reduction of NOx calls for the removal of oxygen. In actuality, the three way system really can reduce all three pollutants, but only if the amount of oxygen in the exhaust system is precisely controlled. Due to this precise oxygen control requirement, the three way converter system is used only in cars equipped with an oxygen sensor system: the 1980 810 (Calif.), the 1981–82 810 (all) and the 1981 200SX.

1975–78 models (all California models) have a floor temperature warning system, consisting of a temperature sensor installed onto the floor of the car above the converter, a relay, located under the passenger seat, and a light, installed on the instrument panel. The lamp illuminates when floor temperatures become abnormally high, due to converter or engine malfunction. The light also comes on when the ignition switch is turned to Start, to check its operation. 1979 and later models do not have the warning system.

All models with the three-way converter have an oxygen sensor warning light on the dashboard, which illuminates at the first 30,000 mile interval, signaling the need for oxygen sensor replacement. The oxygen sensor is part of the Mixture Ratio Feedback System, described in this section. The Feedback System uses the three way converter as one of its major components.

No regular maintenance is required for the catalytic converter system, except for periodic replacement of the Air Induction System filter (if so equipped). The Air Induction System is described earlier in this chapter. Filter replacement procedures are in Chapter 1. The Air Induction System is used to supply the catalytic converter with fresh air. Oxygen present in the air is used in the oxidation process.

PRECAUTIONS

1. Use only unleaded fuel.
2. Avoid prolonged idling. The engine should run on longer than 20 minutes at curb idle and no longer than 10 minutes at fast idle.
3. Do not disconnect any of the spark plug leads while the engine is running.
4. Make engine compression checks as quickly as possible.

TESTING

As long as you avoid severe overheating and the use of leaded fuels it is reasonably safe to assume that the converter is working properly. If you are in doubt, take the car to a diagnostic center that has a tester.

➡ **If the catalytic converter becomes blocked the engine will not run.**

Mixture Ratio Feedback System

DESCRIPTION

➡**The mixture ratio feedback system is utilized in gasoline engines only.**

The need for better fuel economy coupled to increasingly strict emission control regulations dictates a more exact control of the engine air/fuel mixture. Datsun/Nissan has developed a Mixture Ratio Feedback System in response to these needs. The system is installed on all 1980 810s sold in California, all 1981 200SX, 1981–83 810 and Maxima models.

The principle of the system is to control the air/fuel mixture exactly, so that more complete combustion can occur in the engine, and more thorough oxidation and reduction of the exhaust gases can occur in the catalytic converter. The object is to maintain a stoichiometric air/fuel mixture, which is chemically correct for theoretically complete combustion. The stoichiometric ratio is 14.7:1 (air to fuel). At that point, the converter's efficiency is greatest in oxidizing and reducing HC, CO, and NOx into CO_2, H_2O, O_2, and N_2.

Components used in the system include an oxygen sensor, installed in the exhaust manifold upstream of the converter, a three-way oxidation reduction catalytic converter, an electronic control unit, and the fuel injection system itself.

The oxygen sensor reads the oxygen content of the exhaust gases. It generates an electric signal which is sent to the control unit. The control unit then decides how to adjust the mixture to keep it at the correct air/fuel ratio. For example, if the mixture is too lean, the control unit increases the fuel metering to the injectors. The monitoring process is a continual one, so that fine mixture adjustments are going on at all times.

The system has two modes of operation: open loop and closed loop. Open loop operation takes place when the engine is still cold. In this mode, the control unit ignores signals from the oxygen sensor and provides a fixed signal to the fuel injection unit. Closed loop operation takes place when the engine and catalytic converter have warmed to normal operating temperature. In closed loop operation, the control unit uses the oxygen sensor signals to adjust the mixture. The burned mixture's oxygen content is read by the oxygen sensor, which continues to signal the control unit, and so on. Thus, the closed loop mode is an interdependent system of information feedback.

Mixture is, of course, not readily adjustable in this system. All system adjustments require the use of a CO meter. Thus, they should be entrusted to a qualified dealer with access to the equipment and special training in the system's repair. The only regularly scheduled maintenance is replacement of the oxygen sensor at 30,000 mile intervals. This procedure is covered in the following section.

It should be noted that proper operation of the system is entirely dependent on the oxygen sensor. Thus, if the sensor is not replaced at the correct interval, or if the sensor fails during normal operation, the engine fuel mixture will be incorrect, resulting in poor fuel economy, starting problems, or stumbling and stalling of the engine when warm.

Oxygen Sensor

INSPECTION

▶ **See Figure 24**

An exhaust gas sensor warning light will illuminate on the instrument panel when the car has reached 30,000 miles This is a signal that the oxygen sensor must be replaced. It is important to replace the oxygen sensor every 30,000 miles, to ensure proper monitoring and control of the engine air/fuel mixture. Refer to "Maintenance Reminder Lights" section.

1. Start the engine and allow it to reach normal operating temperature.
2. Run the engine at approximately 2,000 rpm under no load. Block the front wheels and set the parking brake.
3. An inspection lamp has been provided on the bottom of the control unit, which is located in the passenger compartment on the driver's side kick panel, next to the clutch or brake pedal. If the oxygen sensor is operating correctly, the inspection lamp will go on and off more than 5 times in 10 seconds. The inspection lamp can be more easily seen with the aid of a mirror.
4. If the lamp does not go on and off as specified, the system

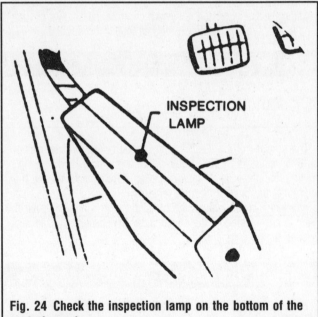

Fig. 24 Check the inspection lamp on the bottom of the control panel

is not operating correctly. Check the battery, ignition system, engine oil and coolant levels, all fuses, the fuel injection wiring harness connectors, all vacuum hoses, the oil filler cap and dipstick for proper seating, and the valve clearance and engine compression. If all of these parts are in good order, and the inspection lamp still does not go on and off at least 5 times in 10 seconds, the oxygen sensor is probably faulty. However, the possibility exists that the malfunction could be in the fuel injection control unit. The system should be tested by a qualified dealer with specific training in the Mixture Ratio Feedback System.

REMOVAL & INSTALLATION

▶ **See Figures 25 and 26**

1. Disconnect the negative battery cable and the sensor electrical lead. Unscrew the sensor from the exhaust manifold.

2. Coat the threads of the replacement sensor with a nickel base anti-seize compound. Do not use other types of compounds, since they may electrically insulate the sensor. Do not get compound on sensor housing. Install the sensor into the manifold. Installation torque for the sensor is about 18–25 ft. lbs. Connect the electrical lead. Be careful handling the electrical lead. It is easily damaged.

3. Reconnect the battery cable.

➡The oxygen sensor is installed in the exhaust manifold and is removed in the same manner as a spark plug. Exercise care when handling the sensor do not drop or handle the sensor roughly. Care should be used not to get compound on the sensor itself.

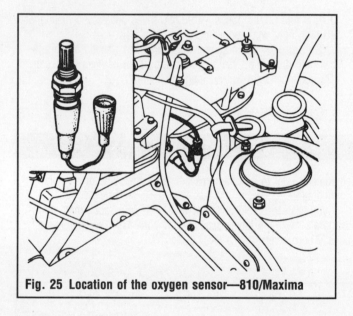

Fig. 25 Location of the oxygen sensor—810/Maxima

Maintenance Reminder Lights

WARNING LIGHT CONNECTOR LOCATIONS

▶ **See Figures 27 and 28**

After 30,000 miles on Datsun/Nissan 1981 200SX Models, disconnect a green/green and white stripe wire under the right side of the instrument panel. On 810/Maxima models 1982–84 disconnect warning lamp harness connector at the left of the brake pedal.

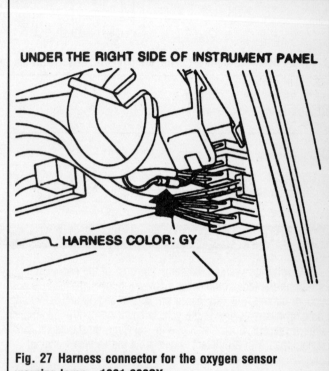

UNDER THE RIGHT SIDE OF INSTRUMENT PANEL

HARNESS COLOR: GY

Fig. 27 Harness connector for the oxygen sensor warning lamp—1981 200SX

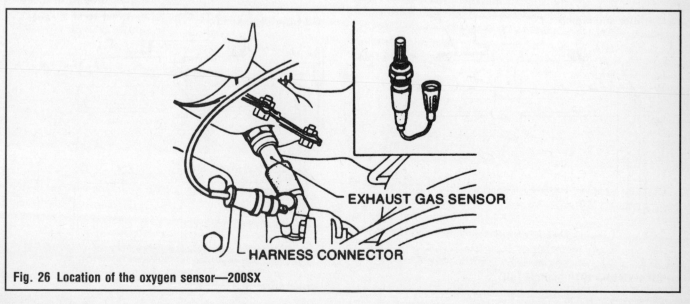

EXHAUST GAS SENSOR

HARNESS CONNECTOR

Fig. 26 Location of the oxygen sensor—200SX

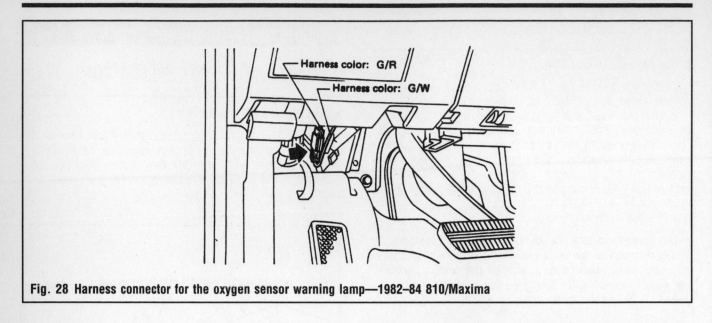

Fig. 28 Harness connector for the oxygen sensor warning lamp—1982–84 810/Maxima

RESETTING

U.S. Models

On models with a sensor relay, reset the relay by pushing or inserting a small screwdriver into the reset hole. Reset relay at 30,000 and 60,000 miles. At 90,000 miles, locate and disconnect warning light wire connector.

On models without sensor light relay and Canada models locate and disconnect the single warning light harness connector. The reminder light will no longer function.

VACUUM DIAGRAMS

Following are vacuum diagrams for most of the engine and emissions package combinations covered by this manual. Because vacuum circuits will vary based on various engine and vehicle options, always refer first to the vehicle emission control information label, if present. Should the label be missing, or should vehicle be equipped with a different engine from the vehicle's original equipment, refer to the diagrams below for the same or similar configuration.

If you wish to obtain a replacement emissions label, most manufacturers make the labels available for purchase. The labels can usually be ordered from a local dealer.

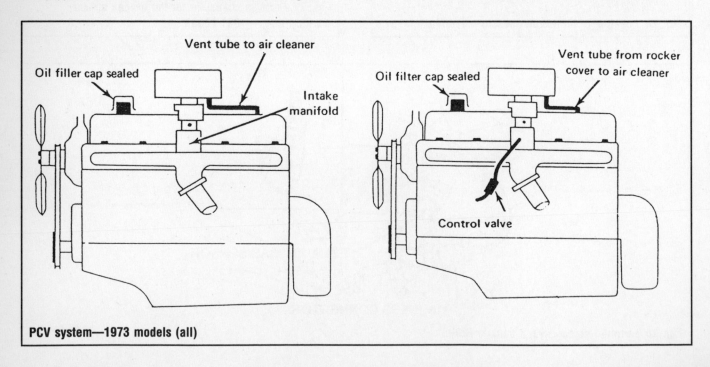

PCV system—1973 models (all)

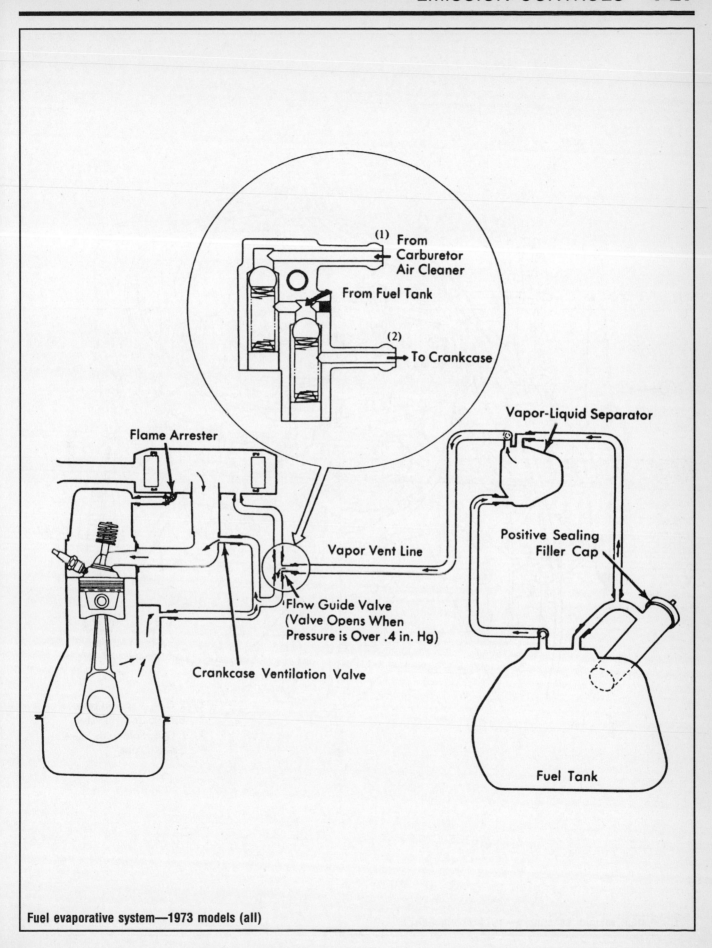

(1) From
Carburetor
Air Cleaner

From Fuel Tank

(2) To Crankcase

Flame Arrester

Vapor-Liquid Separator

Vapor Vent Line

Positive Sealing
Filler Cap

Flow Guide Valve
(Valve Opens When
Pressure is Over .4 in. Hg)

Crankcase Ventilation Valve

Fuel Tank

Fuel evaporative system—1973 models (all)

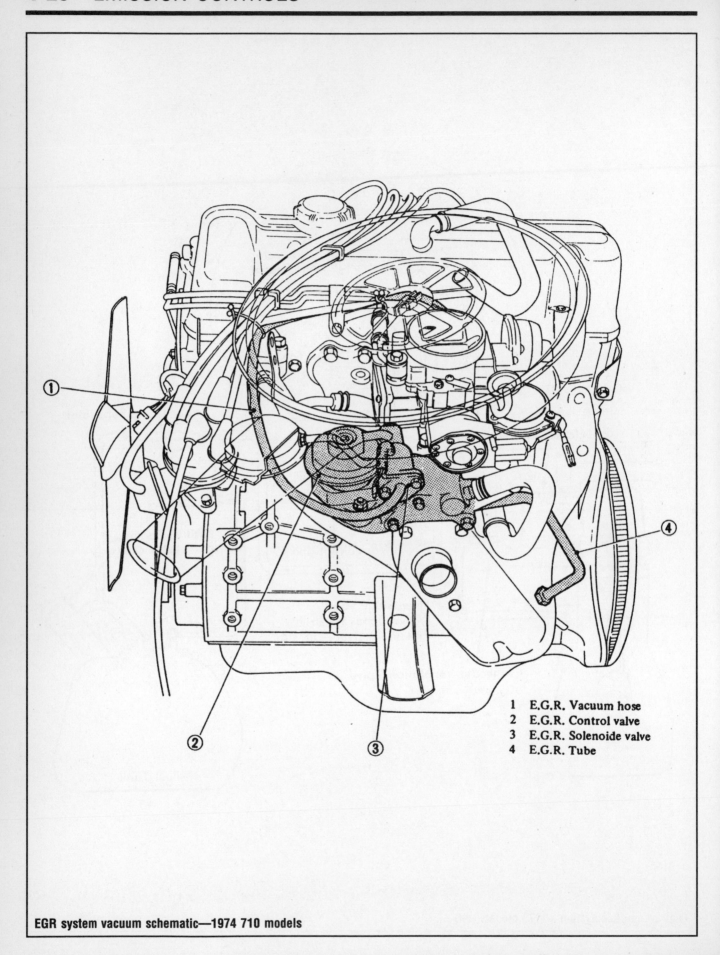

1 E.G.R. Vacuum hose
2 E.G.R. Control valve
3 E.G.R. Solenoide valve
4 E.G.R. Tube

EGR system vacuum schematic—1974 710 models

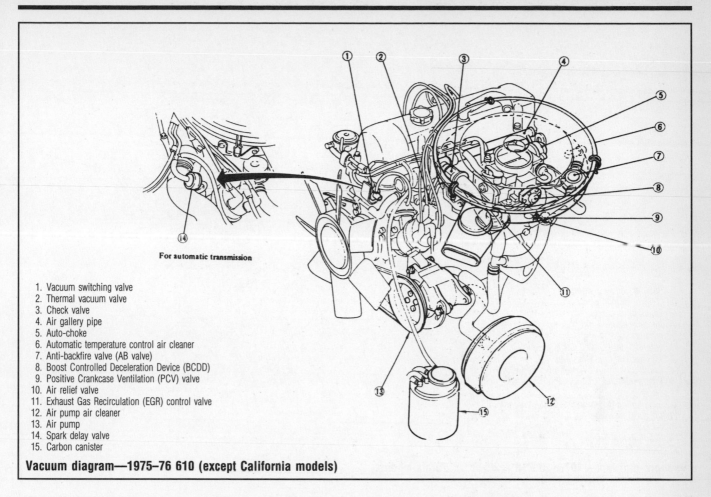

For automatic transmission

1. Vacuum switching valve
2. Thermal vacuum valve
3. Check valve
4. Air gallery pipe
5. Auto-choke
6. Automatic temperature control air cleaner
7. Anti-backfire valve (AB valve)
8. Boost Controlled Deceleration Device (BCDD)
9. Positive Crankcase Ventilation (PCV) valve
10. Air relief valve
11. Exhaust Gas Recirculation (EGR) control valve
12. Air pump air cleaner
13. Air pump
14. Spark delay valve
15. Carbon canister

Vacuum diagram—1975–76 610 (except California models)

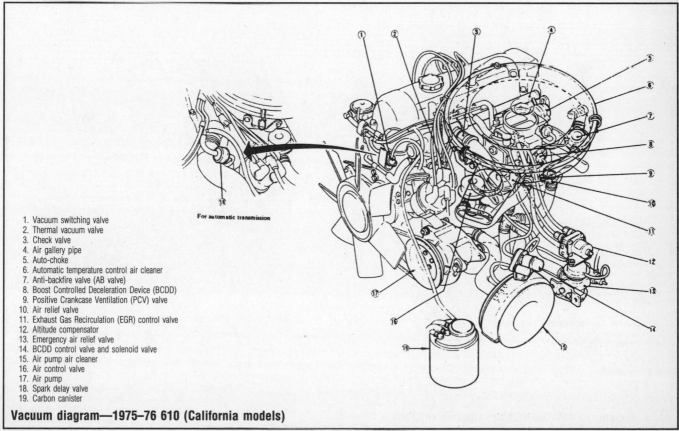

For automatic transmission

1. Vacuum switching valve
2. Thermal vacuum valve
3. Check valve
4. Air gallery pipe
5. Auto-choke
6. Automatic temperature control air cleaner
7. Anti-backfire valve (AB valve)
8. Boost Controlled Deceleration Device (BCDD)
9. Positive Crankcase Ventilation (PCV) valve
10. Air relief valve
11. Exhaust Gas Recirculation (EGR) control valve
12. Altitude compensator
13. Emergency air relief valve
14. BCDD control valve and solenoid valve
15. Air pump air cleaner
16. Air control valve
17. Air pump
18. Spark delay valve
19. Carbon canister

Vacuum diagram—1975–76 610 (California models)

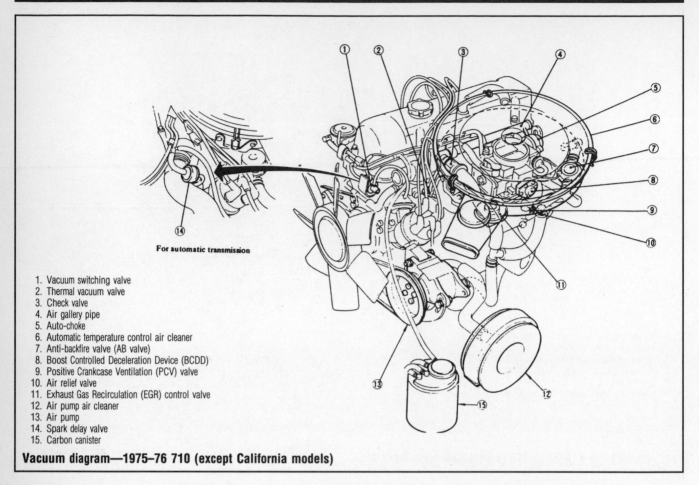

For automatic transmission

1. Vacuum switching valve
2. Thermal vacuum valve
3. Check valve
4. Air gallery pipe
5. Auto-choke
6. Automatic temperature control air cleaner
7. Anti-backfire valve (AB valve)
8. Boost Controlled Deceleration Device (BCDD)
9. Positive Crankcase Ventilation (PCV) valve
10. Air relief valve
11. Exhaust Gas Recirculation (EGR) control valve
12. Air pump air cleaner
13. Air pump
14. Spark delay valve
15. Carbon canister

Vacuum diagram—1975–76 710 (except California models)

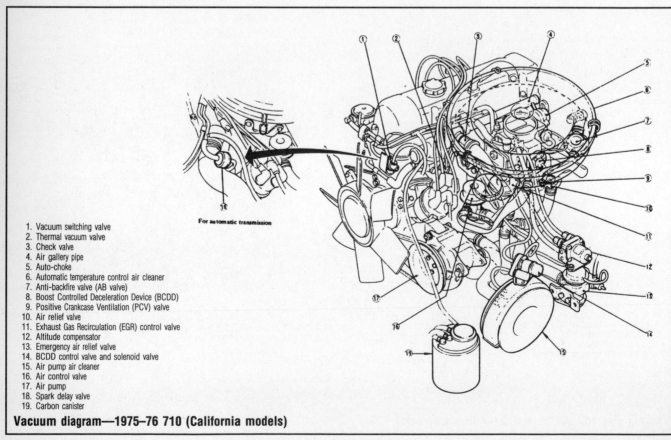

For automatic transmission

1. Vacuum switching valve
2. Thermal vacuum valve
3. Check valve
4. Air gallery pipe
5. Auto-choke
6. Automatic temperature control air cleaner
7. Anti-backfire valve (AB valve)
8. Boost Controlled Deceleration Device (BCDD)
9. Positive Crankcase Ventilation (PCV) valve
10. Air relief valve
11. Exhaust Gas Recirculation (EGR) control valve
12. Altitude compensator
13. Emergency air relief valve
14. BCDD control valve and solenoid valve
15. Air pump air cleaner
16. Air control valve
17. Air pump
18. Spark delay valve
19. Carbon canister

Vacuum diagram—1975–76 710 (California models)

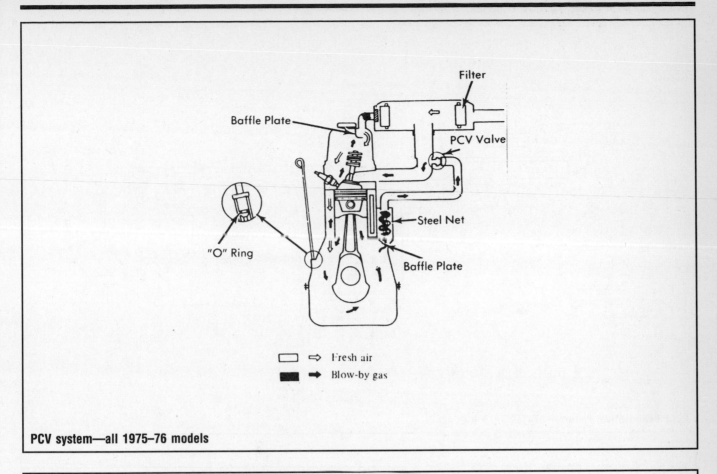

PCV system—all 1975–76 models

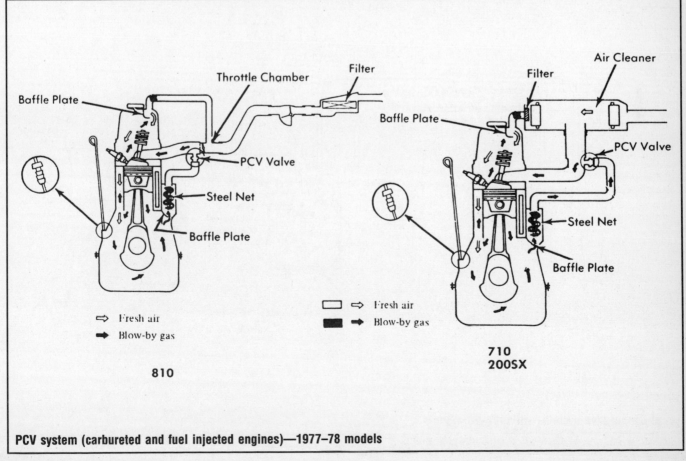

PCV system (carbureted and fuel injected engines)—1977–78 models

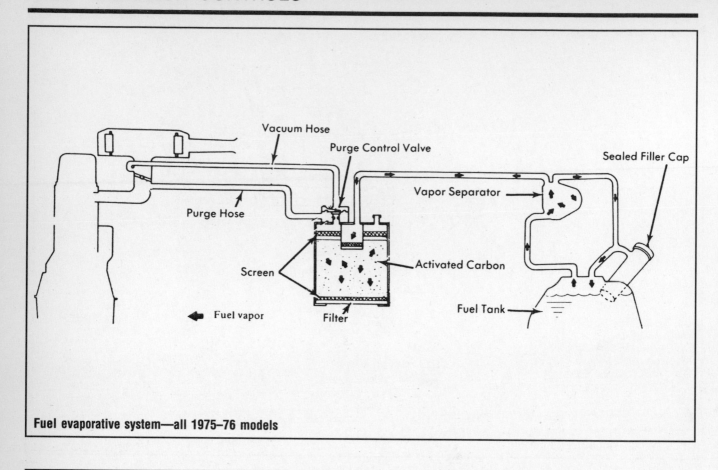

Fuel evaporative system—all 1975–76 models

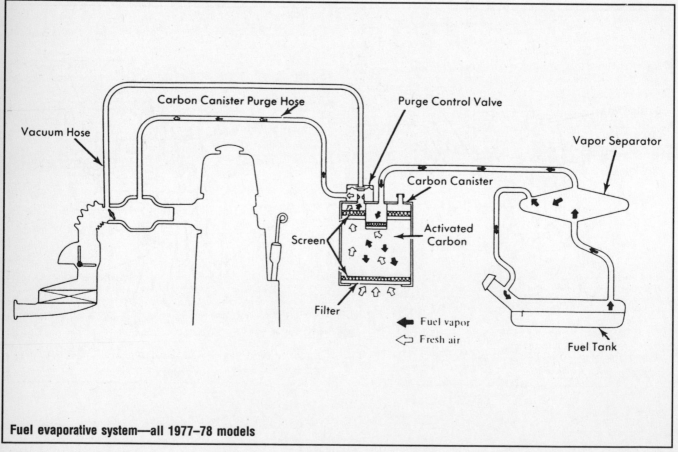

Fuel evaporative system—all 1977–78 models

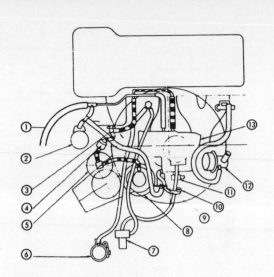
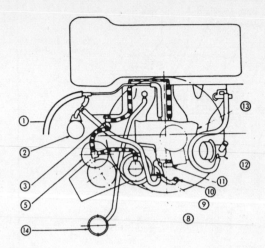

1 — To Canister Purge Cont. Valve
2 — Distributor
3 — Thermal Vacuum Valve
4 — Vac. Delay Valve (Cal. Only)
5 — Backpressure Transducer Valve

6 — C.A.C. Valve (Cal. Only)
7 — Boost-Controlled Decel. Device Vac. Control Valve
8 — EGR Valve
9 — Vac. Switching Valve (M/T Only)

10 — To Air Cleaner (M/T Only)
11 — Int. Man. Vacuum Port
12 — Anti-Backfire Valve
13 — Carburetor
14 — Air Control Valve (Fed. Only)

Vacuum diagram—1978 200 SX (left) and 510 (right) models

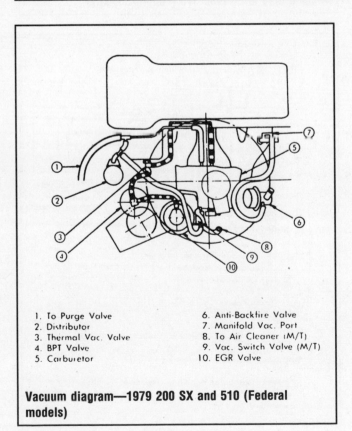

1. To Purge Valve
2. Distributor
3. Thermal Vac. Valve
4. BPT Valve
5. Carburetor

6. Anti-Backfire Valve
7. Manifold Vac. Port
8. To Air Cleaner (M/T)
9. Vac. Switch Valve (M/T)
10. EGR Valve

Vacuum diagram—1979 200 SX and 510 (Federal models)

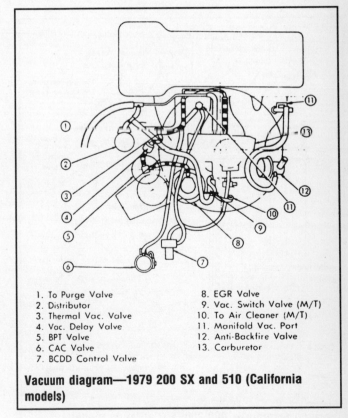

1. To Purge Valve
2. Distributor
3. Thermal Vac. Valve
4. Vac. Delay Valve
5. BPT Valve
6. CAC Valve
7. BCDD Control Valve

8. EGR Valve
9. Vac. Switch Valve (M/T)
10. To Air Cleaner (M/T)
11. Manifold Vac. Port
12. Anti-Backfire Valve
13. Carburetor

Vacuum diagram—1979 200 SX and 510 (California models)

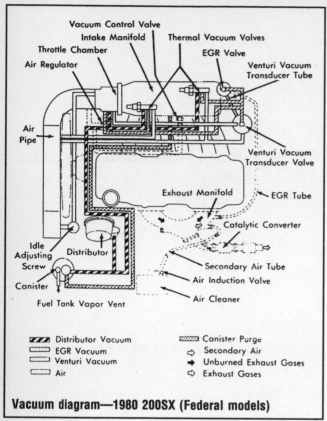

Vacuum diagram—1980 200SX (Federal models)

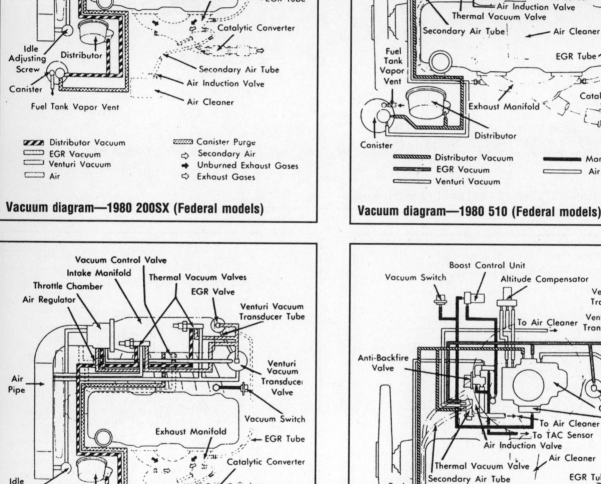

Vacuum diagram—1980 510 (Federal models)

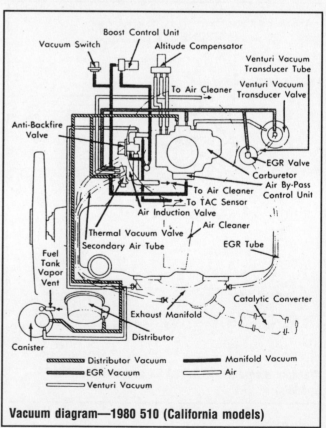

Vacuum diagram—1980 200SX (California models)

Vacuum diagram—1980 510 (California models)

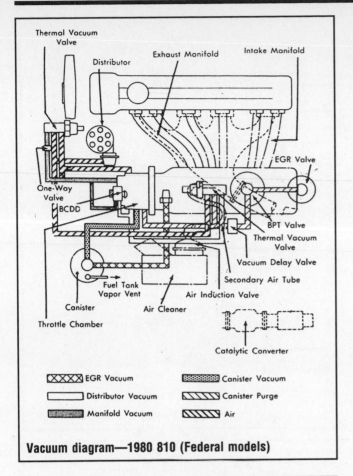

Vacuum diagram—1980 810 (Federal models)

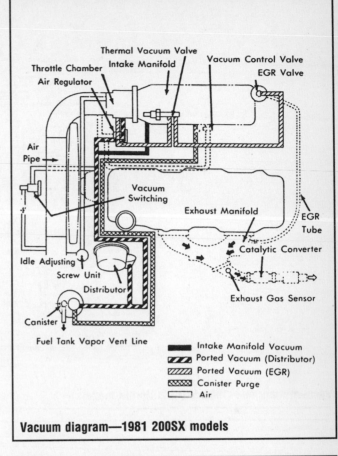

Vacuum diagram—1981 200SX models

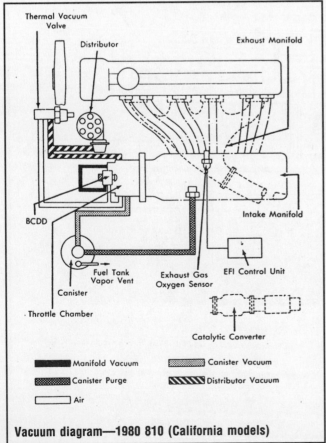

Vacuum diagram—1980 810 (California models)

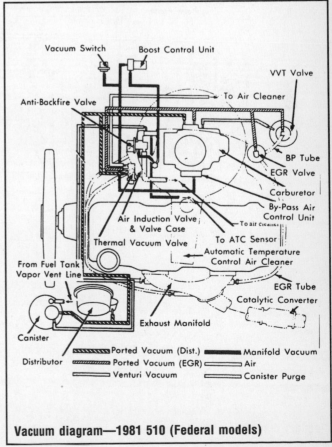

Vacuum diagram—1981 510 (Federal models)

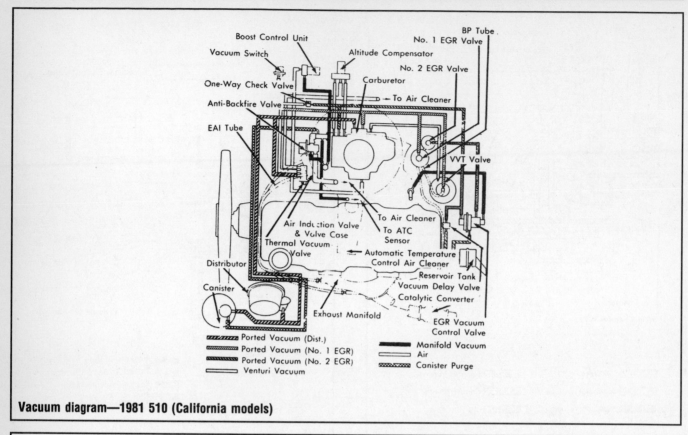

Vacuum diagram—1981 510 (California models)

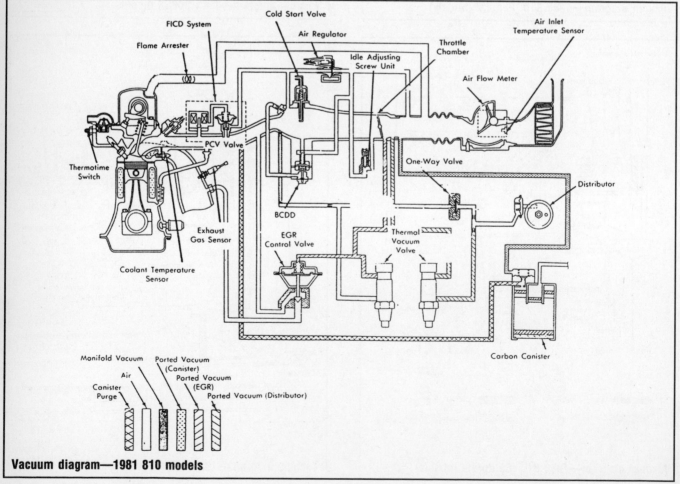

Vacuum diagram—1981 810 models

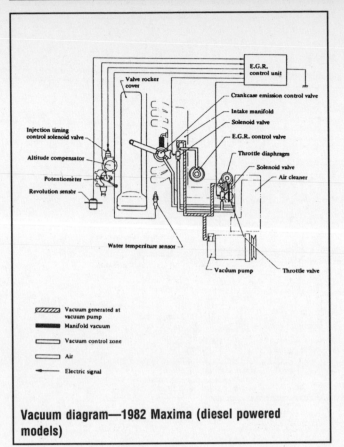

Vacuum diagram—1982 Maxima (diesel powered models)

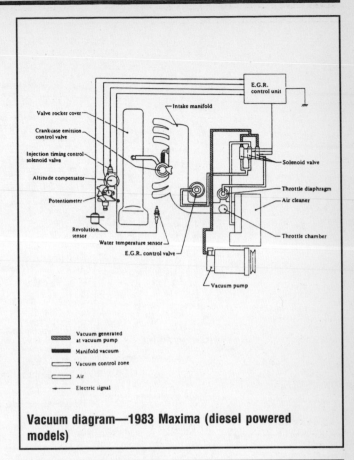

Vacuum diagram—1983 Maxima (diesel powered models)

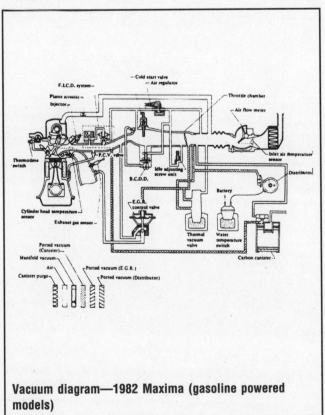

Vacuum diagram—1982 Maxima (gasoline powered models)

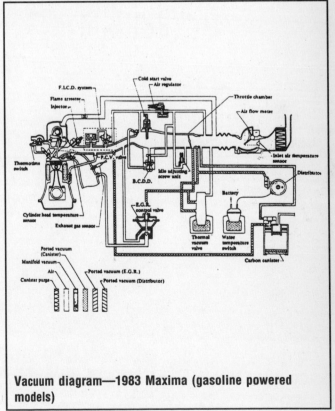

Vacuum diagram—1983 Maxima (gasoline powered models)

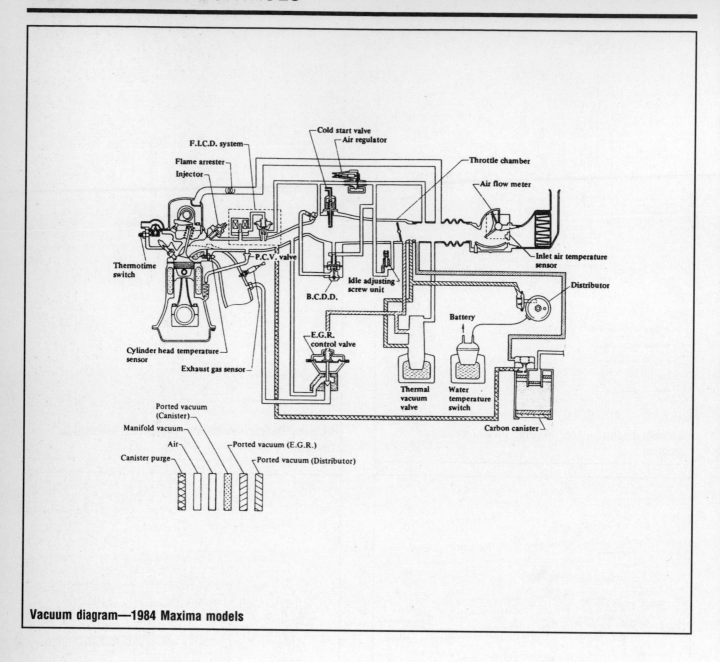

Vacuum diagram—1984 Maxima models

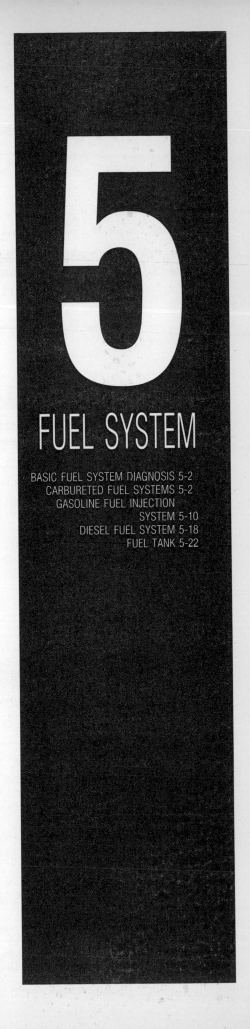

5

FUEL SYSTEM

BASIC FUEL SYSTEM DIAGNOSIS

When there is a problem starting or driving a vehicle, two of the most important checks involve the ignition and the fuel systems. The questions most mechanics attempt to answer first, "is there spark?" and "is there fuel?" will often lead to solving most basic problems. For ignition system diagnosis and testing, please refer to the information on engine electrical components and ignition systems found earlier in this manual. If the ignition system checks out (there is spark), then you must determine if the fuel system is operating properly (is there fuel?).

CARBURETED FUEL SYSTEMS

Mechanical Fuel Pump

REMOVAL & INSTALLATION

▶ **See Figures 1 and 2**

✳✳ CAUTION

Never smoke when working around gasoline! Avoid all sources of sparks or ignition. Gasoline vapors are EXTREMELY volatile!

1. Disconnect the two fuel lines from the fuel pump. Be sure to keep the line leading from the fuel tank up high to prevent the excess loss of fuel.
2. Remove the two fuel pump mounting nuts and remove the fuel pump assembly from the side of the engine.
3. Install the fuel pump in the reverse order of removal, using a new gasket and sealer on the mating surface.

TESTING

✳✳ CAUTION

Never smoke when working around gasoline! Avoid all sources of sparks or ignition. Gasoline vapors are EXTREMELY volatile!

The fuel pump is a mechanically operated, diaphragm type, driven by the fuel pump eccentric on the camshaft. Design of the fuel pump permits disassembly, cleaning, and repair or replacement of defective parts. The fuel pump is mounted on the right side of the cylinder block, near the front.

1. Disconnect the line between the carburetor and the pump at the carburetor.
2. Connect a fuel pump pressure gauge on the line.
3. Start the engine. The pressure should be between 3.0 and 3.9 psi. There is usually enough gas in the float bowl to perform this test.
4. If the pressure is ok, perform a capacity test. Remove the gauge from the line. Use a graduated container to catch the gas from the fuel line. Fill the carburetor float bowl with gas. Run the engine for one minute at about 1,000 rpm. The pump should deliver 1,000cc in a minute or less.

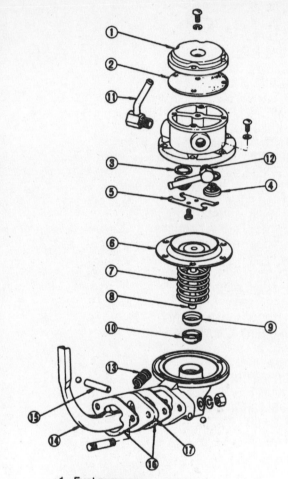

1. Fuel pump cap
2. Cap gasket
3. Valve packing assembly
4. Fuel pump valve assembly
5. Valve retainer
6. Diaphragm assembly
7. Diaphragm spring
8. Pull rod
9. Lower body seal washer
10. Lower body seal
11. Inlet connector
12. Outlet connector
13. Rocker arm spring
14. Rocker arm
15. Rocker arm side pin
16. Fuel pump packing
17. Spacer-fuel pump to cylinder block

Fig. 1 Exploded view of the fuel pump—L-series engines

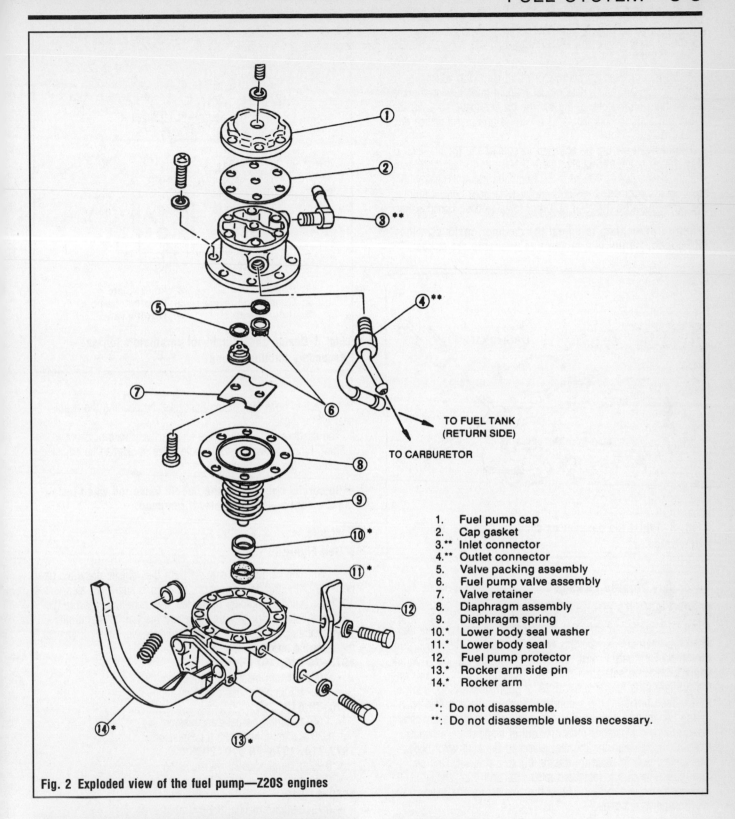

1. Fuel pump cap
2. Cap gasket
3.** Inlet connector
4.** Outlet connector
5. Valve packing assembly
6. Fuel pump valve assembly
7. Valve retainer
8. Diaphragm assembly
9. Diaphragm spring
10.* Lower body seal washer
11.* Lower body seal
12. Fuel pump protector
13.* Rocker arm side pin
14.* Rocker arm

*: Do not disassemble.
**: Do not disassemble unless necessary.

TO FUEL TANK
(RETURN SIDE)

TO CARBURETOR

Fig. 2 Exploded view of the fuel pump—Z20S engines

Carburetor

The carburetor used is a 2-barrel downdraft type with a low speed (primary) side and a high speed (secondary) side.

All models have an electrically operated anti-dieseling solenoid. As the ignition switch is turned off, the valve is energized and shuts off the supply of fuel to the idle circuit of the carburetor.

ADJUSTMENTS

Throttle Linkage

On all models, make sure the throttle is wide open when the accelerator pedal is floored. Some models have an adjustable accelerator pedal stop to prevent strain on the linkage.

Dashpot
♦ See Figure 3

A dashpot is used on carburetor of all cars with automatic transmissions and many late model manual transmission models. The dashpot slowly closes the throttle on automatic transmissions to prevent stalling and serves as an emission control device on all late model vehicles.

The dashpot should be adjusted to contact the throttle lever on deceleration at approximately 1,900–2,100 rpm for automatic transmissions or 1,600–1,800 rpm for automatic transmissions with the L-series engines. The Z20S engine's dashpot contact point should be between 1,400–1,600 rpm for automatic transmissions.

➡**Before attempting to adjust the dashpot, make sure the idle speed, timing and mixture adjustments are correct.**

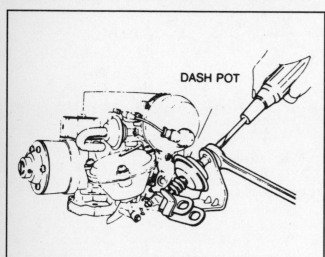

Fig. 3 Adjust the dashpot as shown—L-series unit illustrated

Secondary Throttle Linkage
♦ See Figure 4

All Datsun/Nissan carburetors discussed in this book are two stage type carburetors. On this type of carburetor, the engine runs on the primary barrel most of the time, with the secondary barrel being used for acceleration purposes. When the throttle valve on the primary side opens to an angle of approximately 50° from its fully closed position, the secondary throttle valve is pulled open by the connecting linkage. The 50° angle of throttle valve opening works out to a clearance measurement of somewhere between 6.5–8.0mm between the throttle valve and the carburetor body. The easiest way to measure this is to use a drill bit. Drill bits from size H to size P (standard letter size drill bits) should fit. If an adjustment is necessary, bend the connecting link between the two linkage assemblies.

Float Level
♦ See Figure 5

The fuel level is normal if it is within the lines on the window glass of the float chamber (or the sight glass) when the vehicle is resting on level ground and the engine is off.

If the fuel level is outside the lines, remove the float housing cover. Have an absorbent cloth under the cover to catch the fuel

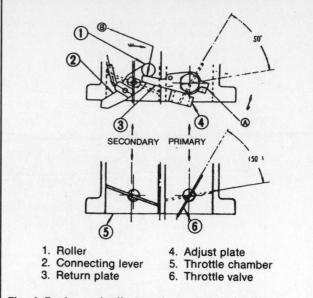

1. Roller
2. Connecting lever
3. Return plate
4. Adjust plate
5. Throttle chamber
6. Throttle valve

Fig. 4 Design and adjustment parameters for the secondary throttle linkage

from the fuel bowl. Adjust the float level by bending the needle seat on the float.

The needle valve should have an effective stroke of about 1.5mm. When necessary, the needle valve stroke can be adjusted by bending the float stopper.

➡**Be careful not to bend the needle valve rod when installing the float and baffle plate, if removed.**

Fast Idle
♦ See Figure 6

1. With the carburetor removed from the vehicle, place the upper side of the fast idle screw on the second step (first step for 1977–81 L and Z engines) of the fast idle cam and measure the clearance between the throttle valve and the wall of the throttle valve chamber at the center of the throttle valve. Check it against the following specifications:

1973–74 610, 1974 710:
• 0.90–1.00mm manual transmission
• 1.10–1.20mm automatic transmission

1975–76 610, 710:
• 1.00–1.20mm manual transmission
• 1.25–1.33mm automatic transmission

1977 710, 1978–79 510, 200SX:
• 0.95–1.15mm manual transmission
• 1.15–1.40mm automatic transmission

1980–81 510:
• 0.75–0.90mm manual transmission
• 0.95–1.10mm automatic transmission

➡**The first step of the fast idle adjustment procedure is not absolutely necessary.**

2. Install the carburetor on the engine.
3. Start the engine and measure the fast idle rpm with the engine at operating temperature. The cam should be at the 2nd step.
1974–76 710, 610:

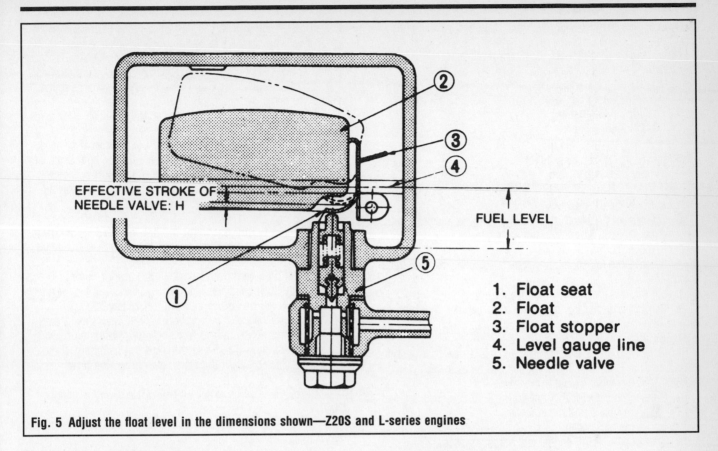

EFFECTIVE STROKE OF NEEDLE VALVE: H

FUEL LEVEL

1. Float seat
2. Float
3. Float stopper
4. Level gauge line
5. Needle valve

Fig. 5 Adjust the float level in the dimensions shown—Z20S and L-series engines

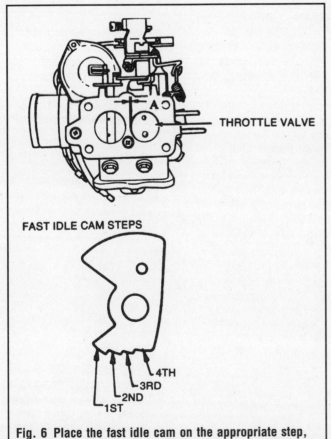

THROTTLE VALVE

FAST IDLE CAM STEPS

4TH
3RD
2ND
1ST

Fig. 6 Place the fast idle cam on the appropriate step, then adjust until the proper clearance at (A) is obtained

- MT 1,900–2,100 rpm
- AT 2,300–2,500 rpm

1977 710, 1978–79 510, 200SX:
- manual transmission 1,900–2,800 rpm
- automatic transmission 2,200–3,200 rpm

4. To adjust the fast idle speed, turn the fast idle adjusting screw counterclockwise to increase the fast idle speed and clockwise to decrease the fast idle speed.

Automatic Choke

1. With the engine cold, make sure the choke is fully closed (press the gas pedal all the way to the floor and release).

2. Check the choke linkage for binding. The choke plate should be easily opened and closed with your finger. If the choke sticks or binds, it can usually be freed with a liberal application of a carburetor cleaner made for the purpose. If not, the carburetor will have to be disassembled for repairs.

3. The choke is correctly adjusted when the index mark on the choke housing (notch) aligns with the center mark on the carburetor body. If the setting is incorrect, loosen the three screws clamping the choke body in place and rotate the choke cover left or right until the marks align. Tighten the screws carefully to avoid cracking the housing.

Choke Unloader

1. Close the choke valve completely.
2. Hold the choke valve closed by stretching a rubber band between the choke piston lever and a stationary part of the carburetor.
3. Open the throttle lever fully.

4. Adjust the gap between the choke plate and the carburetor body to:

L-series engines, 1980–81 Z20S engine:
- 1973–74: 4.4mm
- 1975–77:
     Exc. 710: 2.4mm
         710: 2.05–2.85mm
- 1978–80: 2.05–2.85mm

REMOVAL & INSTALLATION

1. Remove the air cleaner.
2. Disconnect the electrical connector(s) if so equipped, the fuel and the vacuum hoses from the carburetor.
3. Remove the throttle lever.
4. Remove the four nuts and washers retaining the carburetor to the manifold.
5. Lift the carburetor from the manifold.
6. Remove and discard the gasket used between the carburetor and the manifold.

To install:
7. Install carburetor on the manifold, use a new base gasket and tighten the carburetor mounting nuts to 9–13 ft. lbs.
8. Install the throttle lever.
9. Connect the electrical connector(s) if so equipped, the fuel and the vacuum hoses to the carburetor.
10. Install the air cleaner.
11. Start engine, warm engine and adjust as necessary.

OVERHAUL

◆ **See Figures 7 and 8**

❊❊ CAUTION

Never smoke when working around gasoline! Avoid all sources of sparks or ignition. Gasoline vapors are EXTREMELY volatile!

Efficient carburetion depends greatly on careful cleaning and inspection during overhaul, since dirt, gum, water, or varnish in or on the carburetor parts are often responsible for poor performance.

Overhaul your carburetor in a clean, dust-free area. Carefully disassemble the carburetor, referring often to the exploded views. Keep all similar and look-alike parts segregated during disassembly and cleaning to avoid accidental interchange during assembly. Make a note of all jet sizes.

When the carburetor is disassembled, wash all parts (except diaphragms, electric choke units, pump plunger, and any other plastic, leather, fiber, or rubber parts) in clean carburetor solvent. Do not leave parts in the solvent any longer than is necessary to sufficiently loosen the deposits. Excessive cleaning may remove the special finish from the float bowl and choke valve bodies, leaving these parts unfit for service. Rinse all parts in clean solvent and blow them dry with compressed air to allow them to air dry. Wipe clean all cork, plastic, leather, and fiber parts with a clean, lint-free cloth.

Blow out all passages and jets with compressed air and be sure that there are no restrictions or blockages. Never use wire or similar tools to clean jets, fuel passages, or air bleeds. Clean all jets and valves separately to avoid accidental interchange.

Check all parts for wear or damage. If wear or damage is found, replace the defective parts. Especially check the following:
1. Check the float needle and seat for wear. If wear is found, replace the complete assembly.
2. Check the float hinge pin for wear and the float(s) for dents or distortion. Replace the float if fuel has leaked into it.
3. Check the throttle and choke shaft bores for wear or an out-of-round condition. Damage or wear to the throttle arm, shaft, or shaft bore will often require replacement of the throttle body. These parts require a close tolerance of fit. Wear may allow air leakage, which could affect starting and idling.

➡**Throttle shafts and bushings are not included in overhaul kits. They can be purchased separately.**

4. Inspect the idle mixture adjusting needles for burrs or grooves. Any such condition requires replacement of the needle, since you will not be able to obtain a satisfactory idle.
5. Test the accelerator pump check valves. They should pass air one way but not the other. Test for proper seating by blowing and sucking on the valve. Replace the valve if necessary. If the valve is satisfactory, wash the valve again to remove breath moisture.
6. Check the bowl cover for warped surfaces with a straightedge.
7. Closely inspect the valves and seats for wear and damage, replacing as necessary.
8. After the carburetor is assembled, check the choke valve for freedom of operation.

Carburetor overhaul kits are recommended for each overhaul. These kits contain all gaskets and new parts to replace those that deteriorate most rapidly. Failure to replace all parts supplied with the kit (especially gaskets) can result in poor performance later.

Some carburetor manufacturers supply overhaul kits of three basic types: minor repair, major repair, and gasket kits. Basically, they contain the following:

Minor Repair Kits:
- All gaskets
- Float needle valve
- Volume control screw
- All diaphragms
- Spring for the pump diaphragm

Major Repair Kits:
- All jets and gaskets
- All diaphragms
- Float needle valve
- Volume control screw
- Pump ball valve
- Main jet carrier
- Float

Gasket Kits:
- All gaskets

After cleaning and checking all components, reassemble the carburetor, using new parts and referring to the exploded view. When reassembling, make sure that all screws and jets are tight in their seats, but do not overtighten as the tips will be distorted. Tighten all screws gradually in rotation. Do not tighten needle valves into their seats; uneven jetting will result. Always use new gaskets. Be sure to adjust the float level when reassembling.

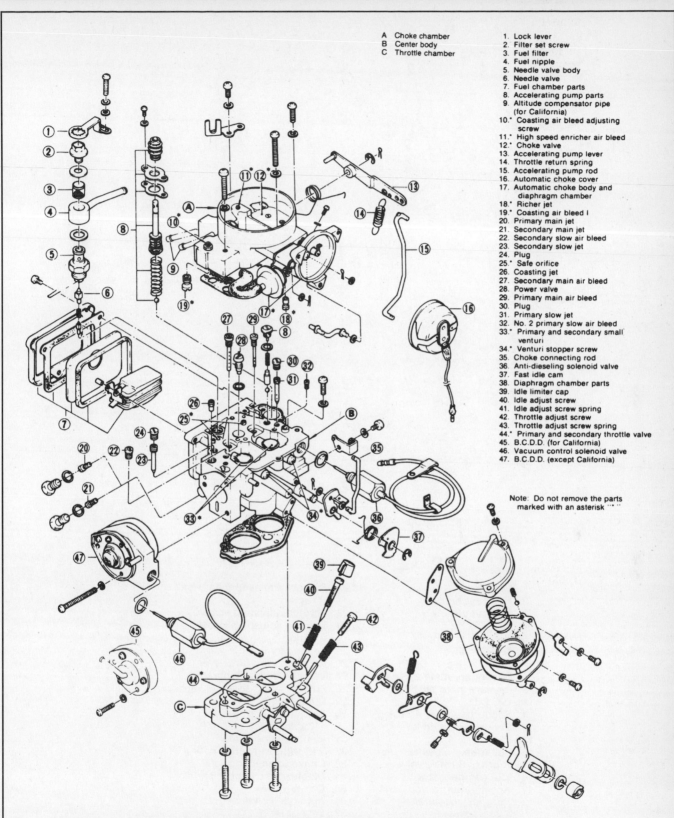

A Choke chamber
B Center body
C Throttle chamber

1. Lock lever
2. Filter set screw
3. Fuel filter
4. Fuel nipple
5. Needle valve body
6. Needle valve
7. Fuel chamber parts
8. Accelerating pump parts
9. Altitude compensator pipe
   (for California)
10.* Coasting air bleed adjusting
    screw
11.* High speed enricher air bleed
12.* Choke valve
13. Accelerating pump lever
14. Throttle return spring
15. Accelerating pump rod
16. Automatic choke cover
17. Automatic choke body and
    diaphragm chamber
18.* Richer jet
19.* Coasting air bleed I
20. Primary main jet
21. Secondary main jet
22. Secondary slow air bleed
23. Secondary slow jet
24. Plug
25.* Safe orifice
26. Coasting jet
27. Secondary main air bleed
28. Power valve
29. Primary main air bleed
30. Plug
31. Primary slow jet
32. No. 2 primary slow air bleed
33.* Primary and secondary small
    venturi
34.* Venturi stopper screw
35. Choke connecting rod
36. Anti-dieseling solenoid valve
37. Fast idle cam
38. Diaphragm chamber parts
39. Idle limiter cap
40. Idle adjust screw
41. Idle adjust screw spring
42. Throttle adjust screw
43. Throttle adjust screw spring
44.* Primary and secondary throttle valve
45. B.C.D.D. (for California)
46. Vacuum control solenoid valve
47. B.C.D.D. (except California)

Note: Do not remove the parts
marked with an asterisk "*"

Fig. 7 Exploded view of the carburetor—1975 710 unit shown, other L-series carburetors similar

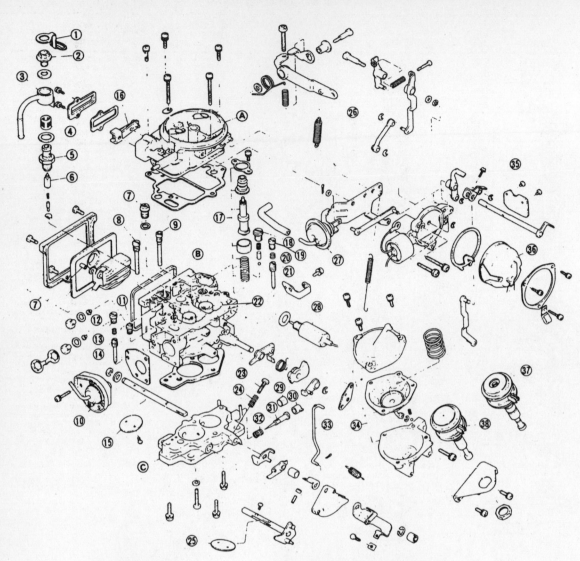

1. Lock lever
2. Filter set screw
3. Fuel nipple
4. Fuel filter
5. Needle valve body
6. Needle valve
7. Power valve
8. Secondary main air bleed
9. Primary main air bleed
10. B.C.D.D.
11. Secondary slow air bleed
12. Secondary main jet
13. Plug
14. Secondary slow jet
15. Primary throttle valve
16. Idle compensator
17. Accelerating pump parts
18. Plug for accelerating mechanism
19. Plug
20. Spring
21. Primary slow jet
22. Primary and secondary small venturi
23. Throttle adjusting screw
24. Throttle adjusting screw spring
25. Secondary throttle valve
26. Accelerating pump lever
27. Vacuum break diaphragm
28. Anti-dieseling solenoid valve
29. Blind plug (California)
30. Idle limiter cap (Except California)
31. Idle adjusting screw
32. Idle adjusting screw spring
33. Choke connecting rod
34. Diaphragm chamber parts
35. Choke valve
36. Automatic choke cover
37. F.I. pot (A/T)
38. F.I.C.D. actuator (M/T air conditioner equipped models only)

Fig. 8 Exploded view of the carburetor—1980 510 (Z20S engine) unit shown

Carburetor Specifications

Year	Engine	Vehicle Model	Carb Model	Main Jet #		Main Air Bleed #		Slow Jet #		Float Level (in.)	Power Jet #
				Primary	Secondary	Primary	Secondary	Primary	Secondary		
1973	L18	610	DCH340-2 ① DCH340-1 ②	97.5	170	65	60	48 ③	90 ③	0.906	53
1974	L18	710	DCH340-10 ① DCH340-11 ②	100	170	60	60	45 ③	90 ③	0.906	41
	L20B	610	DCH340-15 ① DCH340-14 ②	102	170	60	60	46 ③	160 ③	0.906	50
1975	L20B (California)	710	DCH340-41 ① DCH340-42 ②	99	160	70	60	48	80	0.906	43
	L20B (Federal)	710	DCH340-43 ① DCH340-44 ②	97	160	70	60	48	100	0.906	48
1976	L20B (California)	710, 610	DCH340-41A ① DCH340-42B ②	101	160	70	60	48	80	0.906	40
	L20B (Federal)	710, 610	DCH340-43A ① DCH340-44A ②	99	160	70	60	48	100	0.906	43
1977	L20B (California)	710	DCH340-41B ① DCH340-42C ②	101	160	70	60	48	80	0.91	40
	L20B (Federal)	710	DCH340-51A ① DCH340-52A ②	105	165	60	60	48	100	0.91	43
	L20B (California)	200SX	DCH340-49A ① DCH340-50A ②	101	160	70	60	48	80	0.91	43
	L20B (Federal)	200SX	DCH340-53B ① DCH340-54B ②	105	165	60	60	48	100	0.91	43
1978	L20B (California)	200SX	DCH340-91A ① DCH340-92A ②	102	158	70	60	48	70	0.91	40
	L20B (Federal)	200SX	DCH340-93A ① DCH340-94A ②	104	160	60	60	48	70	0.91	43
	L20B (California)	510	DCH340-99 ① DCH340-92A ②	103 102	158	70	60	48	70	0.91	35 40
	L20B (Federal)	510	DCH340-93A ① DCH340-94A ②	104	160	60	60	48	70	0.91	43
1979	L20B (California)	200SX	DCH340-91C ① DCH340-92C ②	102	158	70	60	48	70	0.91	40
	L20B (Federal)	200SX	DCH340-69 ① DCH340-94B ②	104	160	60	60	48	70	0.91	35 43
	L20B (California)	510	DCH340-99C ① DCH340-92C ②	103 102	158	70	60	48	70	0.91	35 40
	L20B (Fedral)	510	DCH340-69 ① DCH340-94B ②	104	160	60	60	48	70	0.91	35 43
1980	Z20S (California)	510	All	107	170	110	60	47	100	0.91	35
	Z20S (Federal)	510	All	99	166	90	60	47	100	0.91	40
1981	Z20S (California)	510	All	112	155	90	60	47	100	0.91	35 ④
	Z20S (Federal)	510	All	112	155	90	60	47	100	0.91	35

① Manual Transmission
② Automatic Transmission
③ Slow jet air bleed: Primary #145, Secondary #100
④ Models with A/T: #45

GASOLINE FUEL INJECTION SYSTEM

Description

♦ **See Figures 9 and 10**

The Electronic Fuel Injection (EFI) system uses various types of sensors to convert engine operating conditions into electronic signals. This generated information is fed to a control unit, where it is analyzed, then calculated electrical signals are sent to various equipment, to control idle speed, timing and amount of fuel being injected into the engine.

For the most part, diagnosing and testing the system is a very difficult job requiring specialized training and equipment. It should be left to a highly qualified professional.

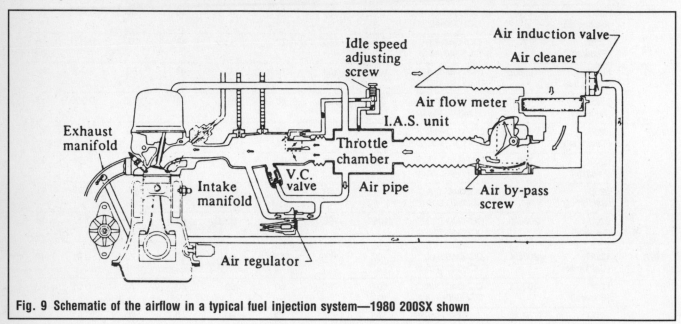

Fig. 9 Schematic of the airflow in a typical fuel injection system—1980 200SX shown

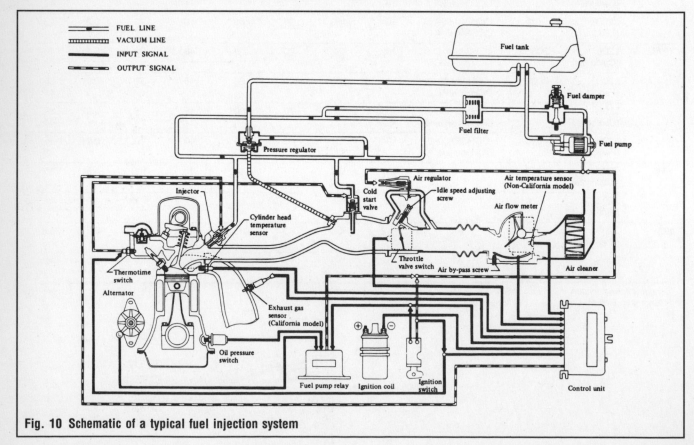

Fig. 10 Schematic of a typical fuel injection system

1. Fuel pressure regulator
2. Fuel injector harness connector (1 of 4)
3. Fuel injector (1 of 4)
4. Fuel inlet pipe
5. Fuel outlet pipe

Common fuel system components

Relieving Fuel System Pressure

✳✳ CAUTION

Never smoke when working around gasoline! Avoid all sources of sparks or ignition. Gasoline vapors are EXTREMELY volatile!

Any time the fuel system is being worked on always keep a dry chemical (Class B) fire extinguisher near the work area.

1. Remove the fuel pump fuse from the fuse block, fuel pump relay or disconnect the harness connector at the tank while engine is running.

2. It should run and then stall when the fuel in the lines is exhausted. When the engine stops, crank the starter for about 5 seconds to make sure all pressure in the fuel lines is released.

3. Install the fuel pump fuse, relay or harness connector after repair is made.

On 1977–79 810, disconnect the ground cable from the battery. Disconnect the cold start valve wiring harness at the connector. Connect two jumper wires to the terminals of the cold start valve. Touch the other ends of the jumpers to the positive and negative terminals of the battery for a few seconds to release the pressure.

For 1980–84 810, Maxima and 1980–81 200SX, start the engine, disconnect the harness connector of fuel pump relay 2 while the engine is running. After the engine stalls, crank it over two or three times to make sure all of the fuel pressure is released.

Electric Fuel Pump

REMOVAL & INSTALLATION

External Mount Electric Pump
▶ **See Figures 11 and 12**

1. Before disconnecting the fuel lines or any of the fuel system components, refer to Fuel Pressure Release procedures and release the fuel pressure.

2. Disconnect the electrical harness connector at the pump. The 810/Maxima (rear wheel drive) pump is located near the fuel tank. The 200SX pump is located near the center of the car.

3. Clamp the hose between the fuel tank and the pump to prevent gas from spewing out from the tank.

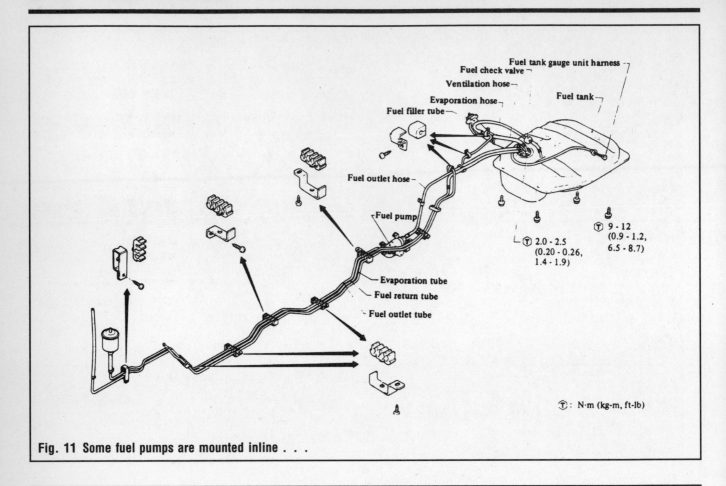

Fuel tank gauge unit harness
Fuel check valve
Ventilation hose
Evaporation hose
Fuel filler tube
Fuel tank

Fuel outlet hose

Fuel pump

Ⓣ 2.0 - 2.5
(0.20 - 0.26,
1.4 - 1.9)

Ⓣ 9 - 12
(0.9 - 1.2,
6.5 - 8.7)

Evaporation tube
Fuel return tube
Fuel outlet tube

Ⓣ : N·m (kg-m, ft-lb)

Fig. 11 Some fuel pumps are mounted inline . . .

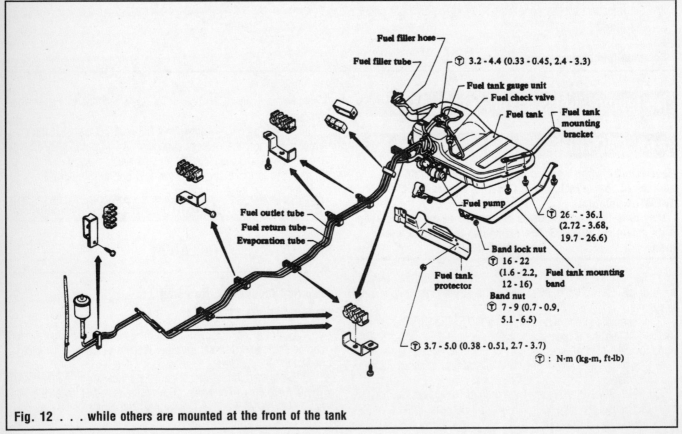

Fuel filler hose
Fuel filler tube
Ⓣ 3.2 - 4.4 (0.33 - 0.45, 2.4 - 3.3)

Fuel tank gauge unit
Fuel check valve
Fuel tank
Fuel tank mounting bracket

Fuel outlet tube
Fuel return tube
Evaporation tube

Fuel pump

Ⓣ 26.7 - 36.1
(2.72 - 3.68,
19.7 - 26.6)

Fuel tank protector

Band lock nut
Ⓣ 16 - 22
(1.6 - 2.2,
12 - 16)

Fuel tank mounting band

Band nut
Ⓣ 7 - 9 (0.7 - 0.9,
5.1 - 6.5)

Ⓣ 3.7 - 5.0 (0.38 - 0.51, 2.7 - 3.7)

Ⓣ : N·m (kg-m, ft-lb)

Fig. 12 . . . while others are mounted at the front of the tank

4. Remove the inlet and outlet hoses at the pump. Unclamp the inlet hose and allow the fuel lines to drain into a suitable container.

5. Unbolt and remove the pump. The 200SX pump and fuel damper can be removed at the same time.

To install:

6. Install the fuel pump in the correct position. Reconnect all hoses. Use new clamps and be sure all hoses are properly seated on the fuel pump body.

7. Reconnect the electrical harness connector at the pump. Start engine and check for fuel leaks.

TESTING

♦ **See Figure 13**

1. Release the fuel pressure. Connect a fuel pressure gauge between the fuel filter outlet and fuel feed pipe.

2. Start the engine and read the pressure. All models should have 30 psi at idle, and 37 psi at the moment the accelerator pedal is fully depressed.

➡**Make sure that the fuel filter is not blocked before replacing any fuel system components.**

3. If pressure is not as specified, replace the pressure regulator and repeat the test. If the pressure is still incorrect, check for clogged or deformed fuel lines, then replace the fuel pump.

Throttle Body/Chamber

REMOVAL & INSTALLATION

✳✳ CAUTION

Never smoke when working around gasoline! Avoid all sources of sparks or ignition. Gasoline vapors are EXTREMELY volatile!

1. Disconnect the negative battery cable and remove the intake duct from the throttle chamber.

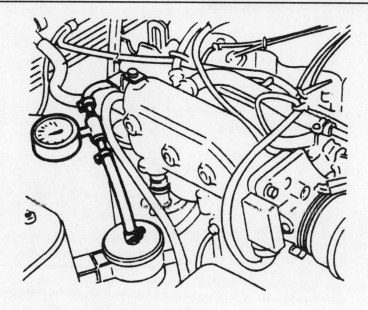

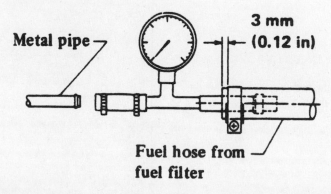

Fig. 13 Install a pressure gauge as shown

2. Disconnect the vacuum hoses and the electrical harness connector from the throttle chamber. Disconnect the accelerator cable from the throttle chamber.

3. Remove the mounting bolts and the throttle chamber from the intake manifold.

To install:

4. Use a new gasket and reverse the removal procedures. Tighten the throttle chamber bolts to 13–16 ft. lbs. Adjust the throttle cable if necessary.

Check the throttle for smooth operation and make sure the by-pass port is free from obstacles and is clean. Check to make sure the idle speed adjusting screw moves smoothly.

Do not touch the EGR vacuum port screw or, on some later models, the throttle valve stopper screw, as they are factory adjusted.

Because of the sensitivity of the air flow meter, there cannot be any air leaks in the fuel system. Even the smallest leak could unbalance the system and affect the performance of the automobile.

During every check pay attention to hose connections, dipstick and oil filler cap for evidence of air leaks. Should you encounter any, take steps to correct the problem.

Fuel Injectors

REMOVAL & INSTALLATION

▶ **See Figures 14 and 15**

Z-Series 4-Cylinder Engines

➡**Review the entire procedure before starting this repair.**

1. Release fuel pressure by following the correct procedure. Refer to Fuel Pressure Release Procedure.

2. Disconnect the negative battery cable and the accelerator cable.

3. Disconnect the injector harness connector.

4. Tag and disconnect the vacuum hose at the fuel pipe connection end. Disconnect the air regulator and its harness connector, and tag and disconnect any other hoses that may hinder removal of the injection assembly.

5. Disconnect the fuel feed hose and fuel return hose from the fuel pipe.

➡**Place a rag under the fuel pipe to prevent splashing of the fuel.**

6. Remove the vacuum hose connecting the pressure regulator to the intake manifold.

7. Remove the bolts securing the fuel pipe and pressure regulator.

8. Remove the screws securing the fuel injectors. Remove the fuel pipe assembly, by pulling out the fuel pipe, injectors and pressure regulator as an assembly.

9. Unfasten the hose clamp on the injectors and remove the injectors from the fuel pipe.

To install:

10. Install the fuel injectors in the fuel pipe with new hose clamps.

11. Install the fuel pipe assembly, injectors with new O-rings and pressure regulator as an assembly.

12. Connect the fuel feed hose and fuel return hose to the fuel pipe. Use new hose clamps on all connections. Reconnect all vacuum hoses and electrical connections.

13. Reconnect the accelerator cable and battery cable. Note the following:

a. When installing the injectors, check that there are no scratches or abrasion at the lower rubber insulator, and securely install it, making sure it is air-tight.

b. When installing the fuel hose, make sure the hose end is inserted onto the metal pipe until the end contacts the unit, as far as it will go. Push the end of the injector rubber hose onto the fuel pipe until it is 25mm from the end of the pipe.

c. Never reuse hose clamps on the injection system. Always renew the clamps. When tightening clamps, make sure the screw does not come in contact with adjacent parts.

14. Start the engine and check for fuel leaks.

L-Series 6-Cylinder Engines

1. Release fuel pressure by following the correct procedure. Refer to Fuel Pressure Release Procedure. Disconnect the negative battery cable.

When removing fuel injectors, tag all hoses and wires to ensure correct reinstallation

Unplug the hose connecting the pressure regulator and the intake manifold

You'll want a supply of wire ties on hand for reinstallation after you snip off the various old ones

When fully detached, carefully lift away the fuel rail from the intake manifold

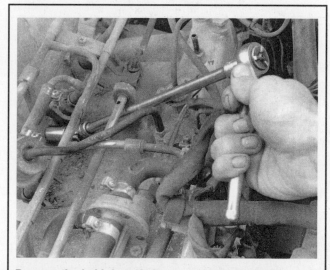

Remove the hold-down bolts securing the fuel pipe

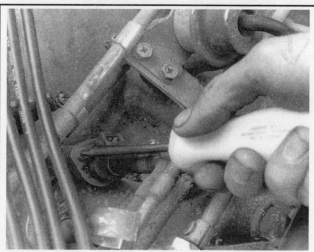

Remove the screws attaching the injectors to the manifold

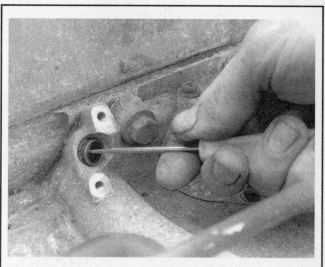

Remove and replace the old injector O-rings

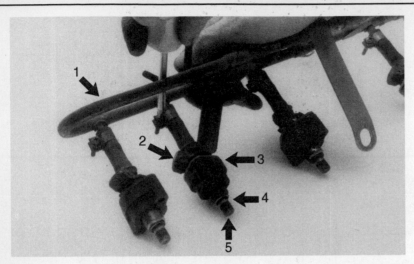

1. Fuel rail
2. Electrical connector
3. Injector
4. O-ring (replace)
5. Injector pintle

To remove the individual injectors from the rail, unscrew the hose clamp . . .

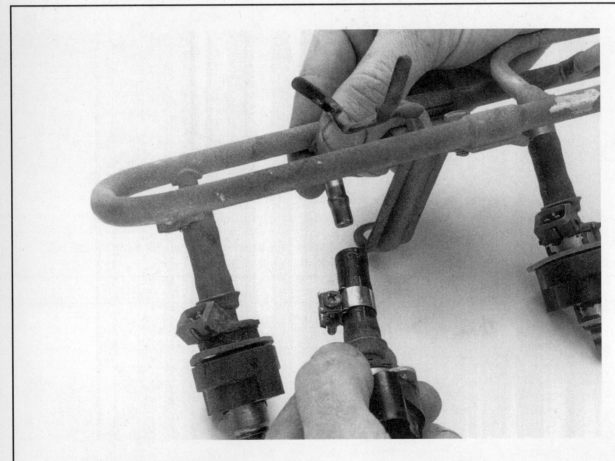

. . . then pull the injector from the rail

2. Disconnect the electric connector from the injector and cold start valve.

3. Disengage the harness from the fuel pipe wire clamp.

4. Disconnect the blow-by hose at the side of the rocker cover.

5. Disconnect the vacuum tube, which connects the pressure regulator to the intake manifold, from the pressure regulator.

6. Remove the air regulator pipe.

7. Disconnect the fuel feed hose and fuel return hose from the fuel pipe.

➡**Place a rag underneath the fuel pipe to catch fuel spillage.**

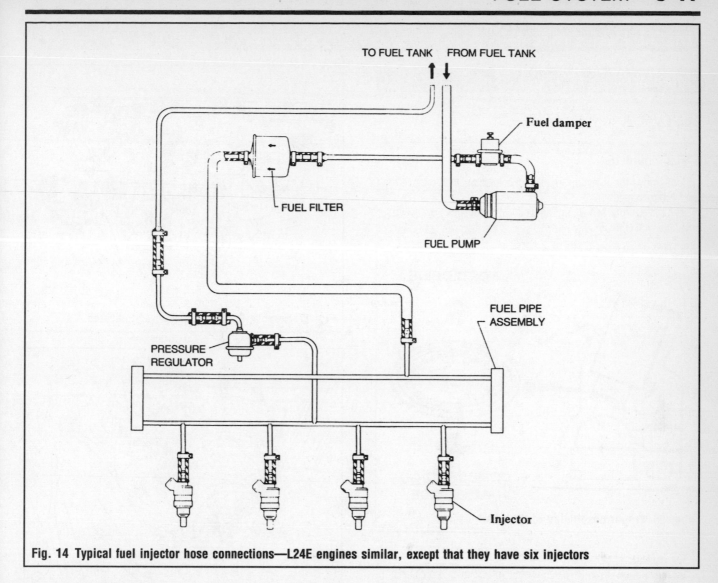

TO FUEL TANK   FROM FUEL TANK

Fuel damper

FUEL FILTER

FUEL PUMP

FUEL PIPE
ASSEMBLY

PRESSURE
REGULATOR

Injector

Fig. 14 Typical fuel injector hose connections—L24E engines similar, except that they have six injectors

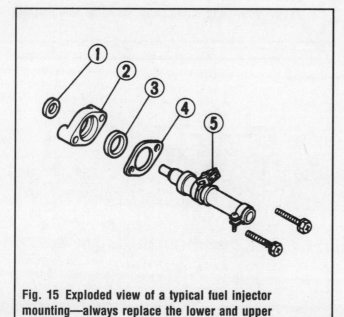

Fig. 15 Exploded view of a typical fuel injector mounting—always replace the lower and upper insulators (part No. 1 and 3)

8. Remove the bolts securing the fuel pipe and cold start valve. Remove the screws securing the fuel injectors.

9. Remove the fuel pipe assembly by pulling out the fuel pipe, injectors, pressure regulator and cold start valve as an assembly.

10. Unfasten the hose clamp on the injectors and remove the injectors from the fuel pipe.

To install:

11. Install the fuel injectors in the fuel pipe with a new hose clamps.

12. Install the fuel pipe assembly, injectors with new O-rings, pressure regulator and cold start valve as an assembly.

13. Connect the fuel feed hose and fuel return hose to the fuel pipe. Always use new hose clamps.

14. Install the air regulator pipe.

15. Reconnect the vacuum tube to the pressure regulator. The vacuum tube connects the pressure regulator to the intake manifold.

16. Connect the blow-by hose to the side of the rocker cover. Reconnect all vacuum hoses if removed and all electrical connections.

17. Reconnect the negative battery cable. Start the engine and check for fuel leaks.

DIESEL FUEL SYSTEM

Injectors

REMOVAL & INSTALLATION

▶ **See Figure 16**

1. Remove the injection tubes at the injector, then remove the spill tube assembly.
2. Unscrew the two mounting bolts and pull out the injectors and their washers.

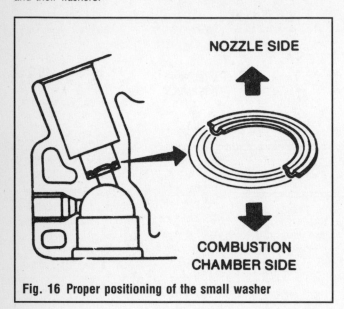

Fig. 16 Proper positioning of the small washer

To install:

3. Installation is in the reverse order of removal. Tighten the injector mounting nuts to 12–15 ft. lbs. (16–21 Nm). Tighten the injection tube-to-injector nut to 16–18 ft. lbs. (22–25 Nm). Always use a new injector small washer.

Injection Pump

➡ The diesel injection pump is located at the right front side of the engine. In case of pump failure or damage, the pump must be replaced as an assembly, except for certain simple parts on the outside of the pump.

REMOVAL & INSTALLATION

▶ **See Figures 17, 18, 19 and 20**

1. Disconnect the negative battery cable.
2. Remove the air cleaner duct. Remove the engine under cover.
3. Drain the engine coolant and then remove the radiator and its shroud.
4. Loosen the fan pulley nuts, then remove the drive belts (air conditioning, alternator and power steering pump).

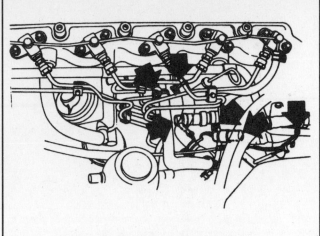

Fig. 17 Remove the hoses and wires indicated

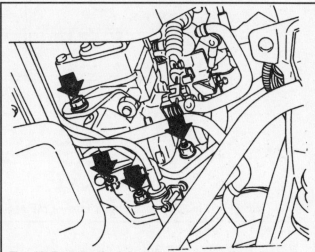

Fig. 18 Remove the injection pump mounting nuts and bolts

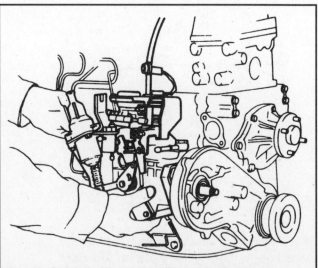

Fig. 19 Carefully lift out the diesel injection pump

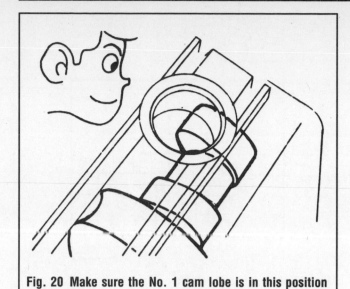

Fig. 20 Make sure the No. 1 cam lobe is in this position

5. Disconnect the power steering oil pump and position it out of the way.

6. Tag and disconnect the accelerator wire, the overflow hose (on the spill tube side), the fuel cut solenoid connector and the fuel return hose.

7. Tag and disconnect the potentiometer, the injection timing control solenoid valve wire, the cold start device water hoses (at the 4-way connector side) and the vacuum hoses for the vacuum modulator (automatic transmission models only).

8. Remove the crank damper pulley. Use a plastic mallet and tap lightly around the sides. If this does not loosen the pulley you will need a two armed gear puller.

9. Remove the pulley bracket and the idler pulley (if so equipped) and then remove the front dust cover.

10. Loosen the spring set pin, set the tensioner pulley to the free tension position and then tighten them.

11. Slide the injection pump drive belt off its pulleys.

12. Loosen the retaining nut and remove the injection pump drive gear. You may need a two armed gear puller.

13. Disconnect the injection tubes at the injection nozzle side.

14. Unscrew the injection pump fixing nuts and the bracket bolt.

15. Remove the injection pump assembly with the injection tubes attached.

➡**If you plan to measure plunger lift, remove the injection tubes before removing the pump.**

To install:

16. Install the injection pump assembly and bracket in the correct position. Observe the following:

    a. Set the No. 1 cylinder at TDC of the compression stroke. Make sure that the grooves in the rear plate and the flywheel align and that the No. 1 cam lobe on the camshaft is in the position shown.

    b. Install the injection pump and temporarily tighten the mounting bolts.

    c. Use the alignment marks as shown in the illustration and install the injection pump drive gear. Tighten the nut to 43–51 ft. lbs. (59–69 Nm).

➡**The injection pump drive shaft is tapered.**

If the drive gear is difficult to install, use a plastic mallet and drive it into place.

17. Make sure that the tensioner pulley is still in the free position and slide the injection drive belt over the pulleys.

18. The drive belt should have two timing marks on it. Align one with the mark on the crank pulley and the other with the mark on the drive gear. If the timing marks on the drive belt are not clear enough to read, set the marks on the drive gear and the crank pulley so that there are 20 cogs of the drive belt between them when it is installed.

19. Loosen the spring set pin and the tensioner so that the belt is automatically set to the tension position.

20. Adjust the injection timing as detailed in this chapter.

21. Tighten the injection pump nuts to 12–15 ft. lbs. (16–21 Nm) and the bracket bolt to 22–26 ft. lbs. (30–35 Nm).

22. Reconnect the injection tubes. Connect them to the cylinders in this order: 4, 2, 6, 1, 5, 3.

23. Bleed the air from the fuel system as detailed in this chapter.

24. Install the idler pulley and bracket if so equipped. Install the crank damper pulley.

25. Reconnect the potentiometer, the injection timing control solenoid valve wire, the cold start device water hoses (at the 4-way connector side) and the vacuum hoses to the vacuum modulator (automatic transmission models only).

26. Connect the accelerator wire, the overflow hose (on the spill tube side), the fuel cut solenoid connector and the fuel return hose.

27. Install the power steering oil pump and all drive belts. Adjust all drive belts to the correct tension.

28. Install the radiator and shroud, refill the cooling system.

29. Install the air cleaner duct and engine undercover. Reconnect the negative battery cable.

30. Check all fluid levels, start the engine and inspect for any leaks. Road test the vehicle for proper operation.

INJECTION PUMP TIMING

◆ **See Figures 21, 22, 23, 24 and 25**

1. Remove the under cover and drain the coolant.

2. Remove the coolant hoses that are connected to the cold start device.

3. Remove the power steering pump.

4. Set the No. 1 cylinder at TDC of its compression stroke. Make sure that the grooves in the rear plate and the drive plate are aligned with each other. Make sure that the No. 1 camshaft lobe is in the position shown in the illustration.

5. Using two wrenches, remove the fuel injection tubes.

6. Loosen the fork retaining screw on the cold start device. Turn the fork 90° and then set the cold start device in the free position.

➡**Never remove the screw on the cold start device wire. If it should be removed accidentally, the pump assembly should be readjusted at a service shop specified by the manufacturer.**

7. Remove the plug bolt from the rear side of the injection pump and, in its place, attach a dial indicator.

8. Loosen the injection pump mounting nuts and bracket bolt.

9. Turn the crankshaft counterclockwise 15–20° from the No. 1 cylinder TDC position.

10. Find the dial indicator needle rest point and set the gauge to zero.

11. Turn the crankshaft clockwise two complete revolutions in order to remove the play in the camshaft mechanism. Loosen the tensioner and then retighten it.

12. Turn the crankshaft clockwise until the No. 1 cylinder is again at TDC and then read the dial indicator.

13. If the dial indicator is not within the above range, turn the injection pump counterclockwise to increase the reading and clockwise to decrease it.

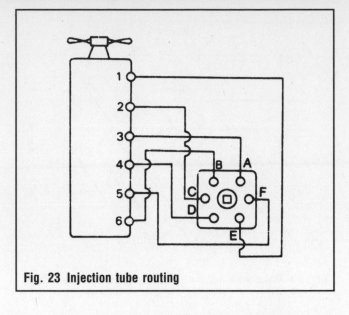

Fig. 23 Injection tube routing

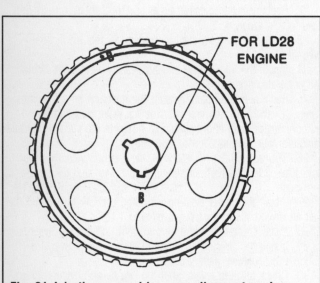

Fig. 21 Injection pump drive gear alignment marks

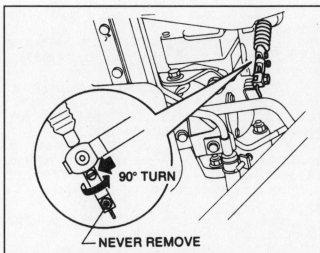

Fig. 24 Loosen the fork retaining screw on the cold start device

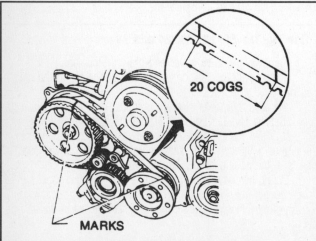

Fig. 22 Align the timing marks as shown on the injection pump drive belt

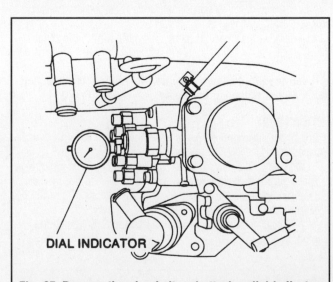

Fig. 25 Remove the plug bolt and attach a dial indicator

	Plunger Lift mm (in) For Low Altitudes
M/T	0.85 ± 0.03 (0.0335 ± 0.0012)
A/T	0.81 − 0.03 (0.0319 ± 0.0012)

	For High Altitudes (Non-California Model Only)
M/T	0.90 ± 0.03 (0.0354 ± 0.0012)
A/T	0.85 ± 0.03 (0.0335 ± 0.0012)

14. Tighten the injection pump mounting nuts and bracket bolt (torque figures are given in the preceding section).

15. Remove the dial indicator and reinstall the plug bolt with a new washer. Tighten the plug bolt to 10–14 ft. lbs. (14–20 Nm).

16. Set the fork at the cold start device in its original position by pulling on the cold start device wire and then tighten the fork screw.

17. Connect the injection tubes.

18. Install the power steering pump, connect the cold start device water hoses, refill with coolant and install the under cover.

BLEEDING THE FUEL SYSTEM

♦ **See Figures 26 and 27**

➡ **Air should be bled from the fuel system whenever the injection pump is removed or the fuel system is repaired.**

1. Loosen the priming pump vent screw and pump a few times. Make sure that the fuel overflows at the vent screw.

2. Tighten the vent screw.

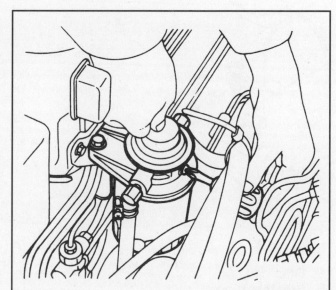

Fig. 26 Loosen the priming pump vent screw on the fuel filter

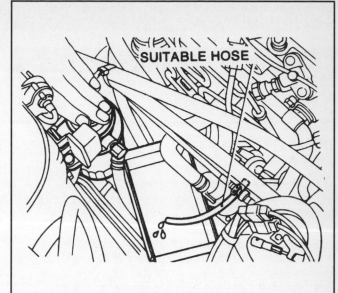

Fig. 27 Install a suitable hose over the overflow connector

3. Disconnect the fuel return hose and install a suitable hose over the overflow connector. Place a small pan under the overflow hose.

4. Prime the priming pump to make sure that the fuel overflows at the open end of the hose.

5. Remove the pan and the overflow hose and then install the return hose.

Glow Plugs

REMOVAL & INSTALLATION

1. Disconnect the glow plug electrical leads. Remove the glow plug connecting plate.

2. Remove the glow plug by unscrewing them from the cylinder head.

3. Inspect the tips of the plugs for any evidence of melting. If even one glow plug tip looks bad, all the glow plugs must be replaced. This a general rule-of-thumb which applies to all diesel engines.

To install:

4. Install the glow plugs in the cylinder head. Tighten the glow plugs to 14–18 ft. lbs.

5. Install the glow plug connecting plates.

6. Reconnect the glow plug electrical leads.

FUEL TANK

Tank Assembly

REMOVAL & INSTALLATION

610 and 710 Station Wagon
♦ **See Figure 28**

1. Disconnect the battery ground cable.
2. Remove the inspection plate from the rear floor. Disconnect the gauge wiring.
3. Remove the spare tire.
4. Place a pan under the drain plug and remove the plug.
5. Disconnect the filler hose, ventilation lines, and the fuel line from the tank.
6. Remove the retaining bolts and remove the tank.
To install:
7. Install the tank with retaining bolts to vehicle.
8. Reconnect all fuel lines, filler hose, ventilation hoses and the electrical connection.
9. Install the spare tire and inspection plate. Connect the battery ground cable.

1977–79 200SX
♦ **See Figure 29**

1. Disconnect the battery ground cable.
2. Remove the rubber plug located on the floor panel above the left side rear axle.
3. Remove the drain plug and drain the tank.
4. Detach the rear set cushion, seat back, and rear seat backboard.
5. Disconnect the fuel hose.
6. Remove the two bolts which secure the fuel tank in the front.
7. Open the trunk, remove the trim in front of the tank if necessary, and remove all the hoses and lines.
8. Remove the two bolts which hold the fuel tank in the back and remove the tank.
To install:
9. Install the fuel tank with retaining bolts to vehicle.
10. Reconnect all fuel hoses and lines and install trim if removed.
11. Reconnect the rear seat assembly. Install the drain plug and rubber access plug.
12. Connect the battery ground cable.

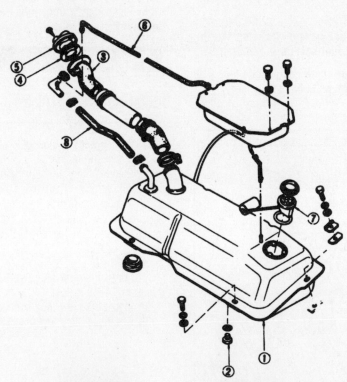

1.	Fuel tank	5.	Filler cap
2.	Drain plug	6.	Breather tube
3.	Filler hose	7.	Fuel gauge unit
4.	Filler neck	8.	Ventilation hose

Fig. 28 Fuel tank design and components—710

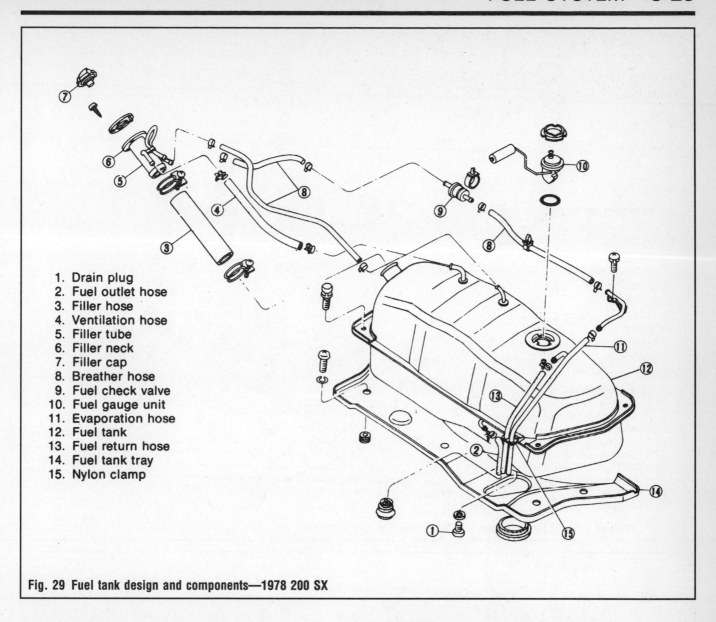

1. Drain plug
2. Fuel outlet hose
3. Filler hose
4. Ventilation hose
5. Filler tube
6. Filler neck
7. Filler cap
8. Breather hose
9. Fuel check valve
10. Fuel gauge unit
11. Evaporation hose
12. Fuel tank
13. Fuel return hose
14. Fuel tank tray
15. Nylon clamp

Fig. 29 Fuel tank design and components—1978 200 SX

810 and Maxima (Rear Wheel Drive) Sedan
▶ See Figure 30

1. Disconnect the battery ground cable.
2. Remove the mat and the spare tire from the trunk.
3. Place a suitable container under the fuel tank and drain the tank. There is a drain plug in the bottom of the tank.
4. Disconnect the filler hose, the vent tube, and the outlet hose.
5. Disconnect the wires from the sending unit.
6. Remove the four bolts securing the fuel tank and remove the tank.
   To install:
7. Install the fuel tank with retaining bolts to vehicle.
8. Reconnect all fuel lines, filler hose, outlet hose, vent tube and the electrical connection.
9. Install the spare tire and mat. Connect the battery ground cable.

810 and Maxima (Rear Wheel Drive) Station Wagon
▶ See Figure 31

1. Disconnect the battery ground cable.
2. Loosen the tire hanger and take out the spare tire.
3. Loosen the drain plug and drain the tank.
4. Disconnect the filler hose, ventilation hose, evaporation hose, and outlet hose.
5. Remove the tire stopper. Disconnect the wiring from the gauge.
6. Remove the four bolts securing the fuel tank and remove the tank.
   To install:
7. Install the fuel tank with retaining bolts to vehicle.
8. Install the tire stopper.
9. Connect the filler hose, ventilation hose, evaporation hose, and outlet hose.
10. Install the spare tire in the correct manner. Connect the battery ground cable.

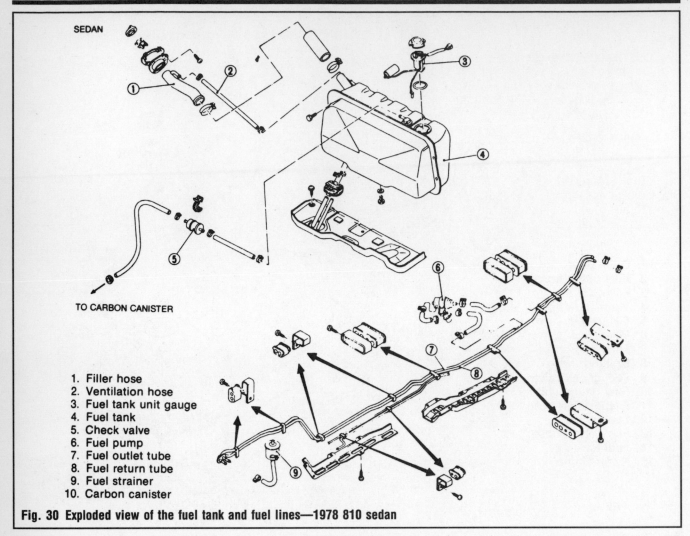

SEDAN

TO CARBON CANISTER

1. Filler hose
2. Ventilation hose
3. Fuel tank unit gauge
4. Fuel tank
5. Check valve
6. Fuel pump
7. Fuel outlet tube
8. Fuel return tube
9. Fuel strainer
10. Carbon canister

Fig. 30 Exploded view of the fuel tank and fuel lines—1978 810 sedan

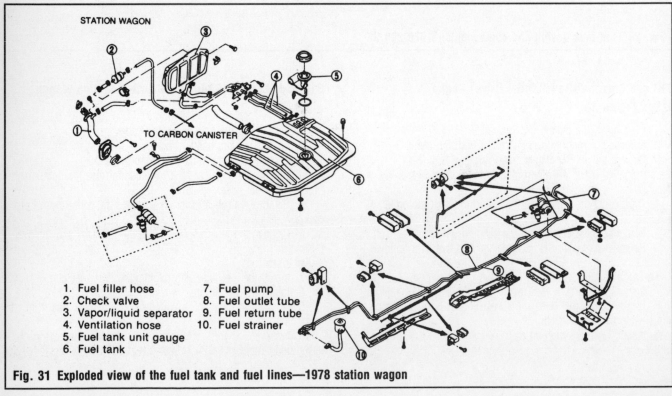

STATION WAGON

TO CARBON CANISTER

1. Fuel filler hose
2. Check valve
3. Vapor/liquid separator
4. Ventilation hose
5. Fuel tank unit gauge
6. Fuel tank
7. Fuel pump
8. Fuel outlet tube
9. Fuel return tube
10. Fuel strainer

Fig. 31 Exploded view of the fuel tank and fuel lines—1978 station wagon

1978–81 510 Sedan

1. Disconnect the battery ground cable.
2. Remove the back seat trim in the luggage compartment.
3. Drain the fuel in the fuel tank.
4. Remove the bolts securing the tank and remove the tank.
5. Installation is in the reverse order of removal.

1978–81 510 Hatchback

▶ **See Figure 32**

1. Disconnect the battery ground cable. Drain the fuel from the tank, then disconnect the fuel hose.

2. Remove the luggage carpet, luggage board, and fuel filler hose protector.
3. Disconnect all the hoses and wires to the tank and unbolt the fuel tank and remove it.
4. Installation is in the reverse order of removal.

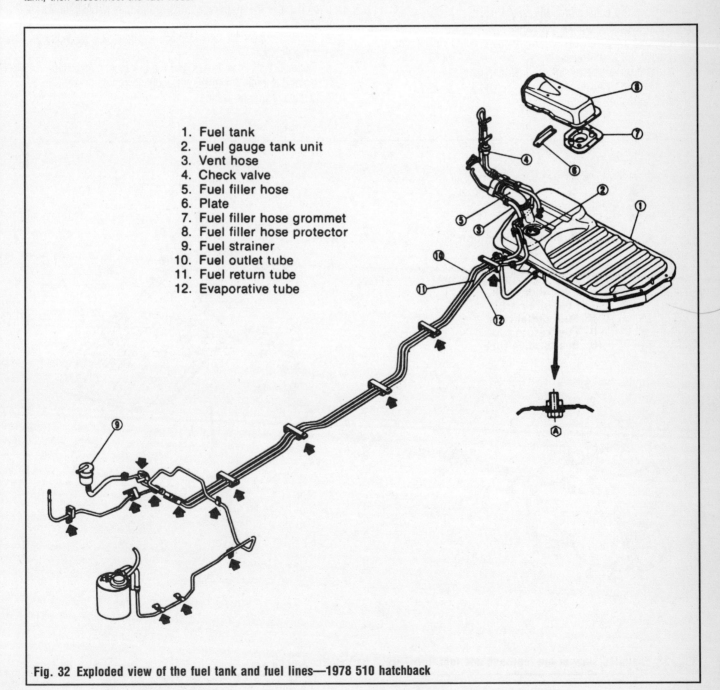

1. Fuel tank
2. Fuel gauge tank unit
3. Vent hose
4. Check valve
5. Fuel filler hose
6. Plate
7. Fuel filler hose grommet
8. Fuel filler hose protector
9. Fuel strainer
10. Fuel outlet tube
11. Fuel return tube
12. Evaporative tube

Fig. 32 Exploded view of the fuel tank and fuel lines—1978 510 hatchback

1978–81 510 Station Wagon

◆ **See Figure 33**

1. Disconnect the battery ground cable.
2. Drain the fuel from the tank. Disconnect all the hoses and lines.
3. Remove the spare tire and fuel tank support.
4. Unbolt and remove the tank.
5. Installation is in the reverse order of removal.

1980–81 200SX

◆ **See Figure 34**

1. Remove the battery ground cable.
2. Drain the fuel from the fuel tank.
3. Remove the protector from the luggage compartment, and then remove the following parts:
   a. Harness connector for the fuel tank gauge unit.
   b. Ventilation hose.
   c. Evaporation hoses

   d. Fuel filler hose (Hatchback)
4. Remove the following parts from beneath the floor:
   a. Fuel outlet hose
   b. Fuel return hose
   c. Evaporation hose
   d. Fuel filler hose (Hardtop)
5. Remove the bolts which secure the fuel tank and remove the tank.
6. To remove the Reservoir tank from the Hatchback:
   a. Remove the battery cable.
   b. Remove the protector from the luggage compartment. Also remove the right-hand speaker and side lower finisher.
   c. Remove the evaporation hoses and then remove the reservoir tank.
7. Install the reservoir tank in place and fuel tank assembly in the correct position.
8. Reconnect all lines, hoses and the electrical connection.
9. Install the protector in the the luggage compartment. Connect the battery ground cable.

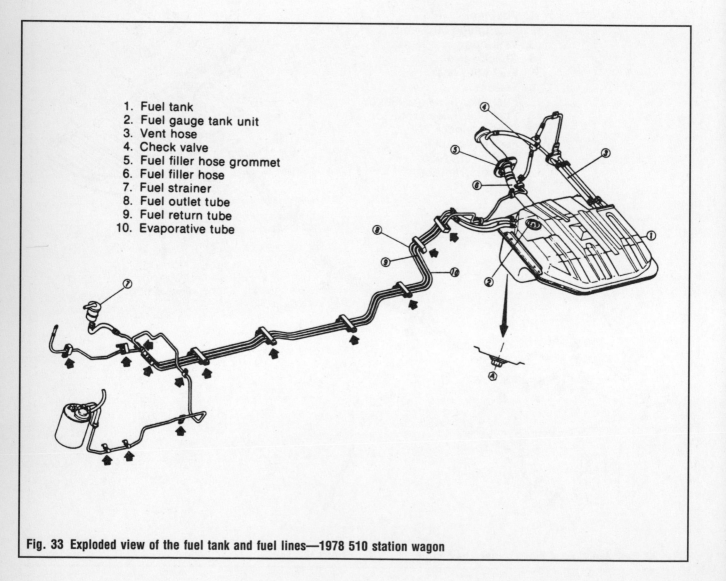

1. Fuel tank
2. Fuel gauge tank unit
3. Vent hose
4. Check valve
5. Fuel filler hose grommet
6. Fuel filler hose
7. Fuel strainer
8. Fuel outlet tube
9. Fuel return tube
10. Evaporative tube

Fig. 33 Exploded view of the fuel tank and fuel lines—1978 510 station wagon

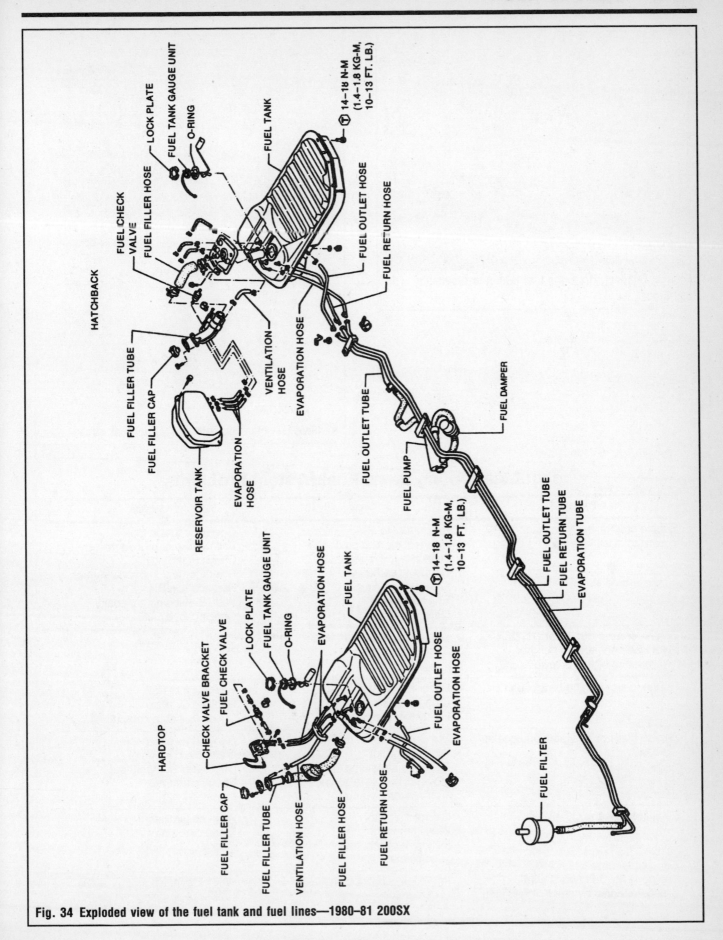

Fig. 34 Exploded view of the fuel tank and fuel lines—1980–81 200SX

Prior to removal, drain the fuel tank into a suitable container

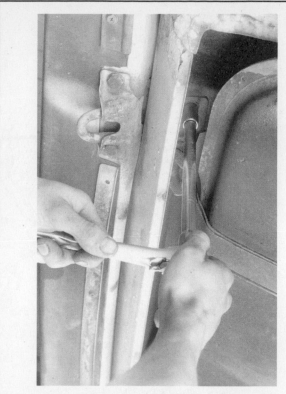

Remove the attaching bolts to the fuel tank straps

Troubleshooting Basic Fuel System Problems

Problem	Cause	Solution
Engine cranks, but won't start (or is hard to start) when cold	• Empty fuel tank • Incorrect starting procedure • Defective fuel pump • No fuel in carburetor • Clogged fuel filter • Engine flooded • Defective choke	• Check for fuel in tank • Follow correct procedure • Check pump output • Check for fuel in the carburetor • Replace fuel filter • Wait 15 minutes; try again • Check choke plate
Engine cranks, but is hard to start (or does not start) when hot—(presence of fuel is assumed)	• Defective choke	• Check choke plate
Rough idle or engine runs rough	• Dirt or moisture in fuel • Clogged air filter • Faulty fuel pump	• Replace fuel filter • Replace air filter • Check fuel pump output
Engine stalls or hesitates on acceleration	• Dirt or moisture in the fuel • Dirty carburetor • Defective fuel pump • Incorrect float level, defective accelerator pump	• Replace fuel filter • Clean the carburetor • Check fuel pump output • Check carburetor
Poor gas mileage	• Clogged air filter • Dirty carburetor • Defective choke, faulty carburetor adjustment	• Replace air filter • Clean carburetor • Check carburetor
Engine is flooded (won't start accompanied by smell of raw fuel)	• Improperly adjusted choke or carburetor	• Wait 15 minutes and try again, without pumping gas pedal • If it won't start, check carburetor

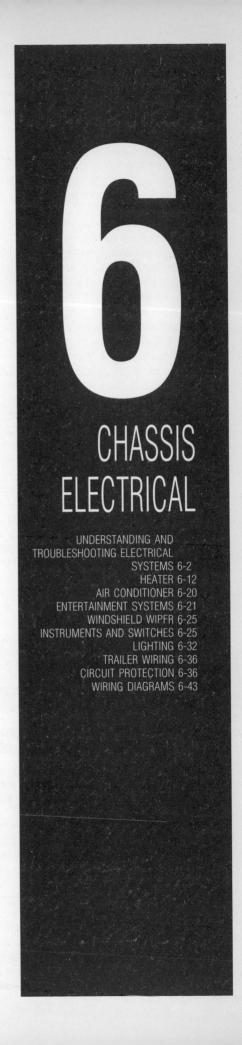

6

CHASSIS
ELECTRICAL

UNDERSTANDING AND TROUBLESHOOTING ELECTRICAL SYSTEMS

Over the years import and domestic manufacturers have incorporated electronic control systems into their production lines. In fact, electronic control systems are so prevalent that all new cars and trucks built today are equipped with at least one on-board computer. These electronic components (with no moving parts) should theoretically last the life of the vehicle, provided that nothing external happens to damage the circuits or memory chips.

While it is true that electronic components should never wear out, in the real world malfunctions do occur. It is also true that any computer-based system is extremely sensitive to electrical voltages and cannot tolerate careless or haphazard testing/service procedures. An inexperienced individual can literally cause major damage looking for a minor problem by using the wrong kind of test equipment or connecting test leads/connectors with the ignition switch **ON**. When selecting test equipment, make sure the manufacturer's instructions state that the tester is compatible with whatever type of system is being serviced. Read all instructions carefully and double check all test points before installing probes or making any test connections.

The following section outlines basic diagnosis techniques for dealing with automotive electrical systems. Along with a general explanation of the various types of test equipment available to aid in servicing modern automotive systems, basic repair techniques for wiring harnesses and connectors are also given. Read the basic information before attempting any repairs or testing. This will provide the background of information necessary to avoid the most common and obvious mistakes that can cost both time and money. Although the replacement and testing procedures are simple in themselves, the systems are not, and unless one has a thorough understanding of all components and their function within a particular system, the logical test sequence these systems demand cannot be followed. Minor malfunctions can make a big difference, so it is important to know how each component affects the operation of the overall system in order to find the ultimate cause of a problem without replacing good components unnecessarily. It is not enough to use the correct test equipment; the test equipment must be used correctly.

Safety Precautions

✳✳ CAUTION

Whenever working on or around any electrical or electronic systems, always observe these general precautions to prevent the possibility of personal injury or damage to electronic components.

• Never install or remove battery cables with the key **ON** or the engine running. Jumper cables should be connected with the key **OFF** to avoid power surges that can damage electronic control units. Engines equipped with computer controlled systems should avoid both giving and getting jump starts due to the possibility of serious damage to components from arcing in the engine compartment if connections are made with the ignition **ON**.

• Always remove the battery cables before charging the battery. Never use a high output charger on an installed battery or attempt to use any type of "hot shot" (24 volt) starting aid.

• Exercise care when inserting test probes into connectors to insure good contact without damaging the connector or spreading the pins. Always probe connectors from the rear (wire) side, NOT the pin side, to avoid accidental shorting of terminals during test procedures.

• Never remove or attach wiring harness connectors with the ignition switch **ON**, especially to an electronic control unit.

• Do not drop any components during service procedures and never apply 12 volts directly to any component (like a solenoid or relay) unless instructed specifically to do so. Some component electrical windings are designed to safely handle only 4 or 5 volts and can be destroyed in seconds if 12 volts are applied directly to the connector.

• Remove the electronic control unit if the vehicle is to be placed in an environment where temperatures exceed approximately 176°F (80°C), such as a paint spray booth or when arc/gas welding near the control unit location.

Understanding Basic Electricity

Understanding the basic theory of electricity makes electrical troubleshooting much easier. Several gauges are used in electrical troubleshooting to see inside the circuit being tested. Without a basic understanding, it will be difficult to understand testing procedures.

THE WATER ANALOGY

Electricity is the flow of electrons—hypothetical particles thought to constitute the basic stuff of electricity. Many people have been taught electrical theory using an analogy with water. In a comparison with water flowing in a pipe, the electrons would be the water. As the flow of water can be measured, the flow of electricity can be measured. The unit of measurement is amperes, frequently abbreviated amps. An ammeter will measure the actual amount of current flowing in the circuit.

Just as the water pressure is measured in units such as pounds per square inch, electrical pressure is measured in volts. When a voltmeter's two probes are placed on two live portions of an electrical circuit with different electrical pressures, current will flow through the voltmeter and produce a reading which indicates the difference in electrical pressure between the two parts of the circuit.

While increasing the voltage in a circuit will increase the flow of current, the actual flow depends not only on voltage, but on the resistance of the circuit. The standard unit for measuring circuit resistance is an ohm, measured by an ohmmeter. The ohmmeter is somewhat similar to an ammeter, but incorporates its own source of power so that a standard voltage is always present.

CIRCUITS

An actual electric circuit consists of four basic parts. These are: the power source, such as a generator or battery; a hot wire, which conducts the electricity under a relatively high voltage to the component supplied by the circuit; the load, such as a lamp, motor, resistor or relay coil; and the ground wire, which carries the current back to the source under very low voltage. In such a circuit the bulk of the resistance exists between the point where the hot wire is connected to the load, and the point where the load is grounded. In an automobile, the vehicle's frame or body, which is made of steel, is used as a part of the ground circuit for many of the electrical devices.

Remember that, in electrical testing, the voltmeter is connected in parallel with the circuit being tested (without disconnecting any wires) and measures the difference in voltage between the locations of the two probes; that the ammeter is connected in series with the load (the circuit is separated at one point and the ammeter inserted so it becomes a part of the circuit); and the ohmmeter is self-powered, so that all the power in the circuit should be off and the portion of the circuit to be measured contacted at either end by one of the probes of the meter.

For any electrical system to operate, it must make a complete circuit. This simply means that the power flow from the battery must make a complete circle. When an electrical component is operating, power flows from the battery to the component, passes through the component causing it to perform it to function (such as lighting a light bulb) and then returns to the battery through the ground of the circuit. This ground is usually (but not always) the metal part of the vehicle on which the electrical component is mounted.

Perhaps the easiest way to visualize this is to think of connecting a light bulb with two wires attached to it to your vehicle's battery. The battery in your vehicle has two posts (negative and positive). If one of the two wires attached to the light bulb was attached to the negative post of the battery and the other wire was attached to the positive post of the battery, you would have a complete circuit. Current from the battery would flow out one post, through the wire attached to it and then to the light bulb, where it would pass through causing it to light. It would then leave the light bulb, travel through the other wire, and return to the other post of the battery.

AUTOMOTIVE CIRCUITS

The normal automotive circuit differs from this simple example in two ways. First, instead of having a return wire from the bulb to the battery, the light bulb return the current to the battery through the chassis of the vehicle. Since the negative battery cable is attached to the chassis and the chassis is made of electrically conductive metal, the chassis of the vehicle can serve as a ground wire to complete the circuit. Secondly, most automotive circuits contain switches to turn components on and off.

Some electrical components which require a large amount of current to operate also have a relay in their circuit. Since these circuits carry a large amount of current, the thickness of the wire in the circuit (gauge size) is also greater. If this large wire were connected from the component to the control switch on the instrument panel, and then back to the component, a voltage drop would occur in the circuit. To prevent this potential drop in voltage, an electromagnetic switch (relay) is used. The large wires in the circuit are connected from the vehicle battery to one side of the relay, and from the opposite side of the relay to the component. The relay is normally open, preventing current from passing through the circuit. An additional, smaller wire is connected from the relay to the control switch for the circuit. When the control switch is turned on, it grounds the smaller wire from the relay and completes the circuit.

SHORT CIRCUITS

If you were to disconnect the light bulb (from the previous example of a light-bulb being connected to the battery by two wires) from the wires and touch the two wires together (please take our word for this; don't try it), the result will be a shower of sparks. A similar thing happens (on a smaller scale) when the power supply wire to a component or the electrical component itself becomes grounded before the normal ground connection for the circuit. To prevent damage to the system, the fuse for the circuit blows to interrupt the circuit—protecting the components from damage. Because grounding a wire from a power source makes a complete circuit—less the required component to use the power—the phenomenon is called a short circuit. The most common causes of short circuits are: the rubber insulation on a wire breaking or rubbing through to expose the current carrying core of the wire to a metal part of the car, or a shorted switch.

Some electrical systems on the vehicle are protected by a circuit breaker which is, basically, a self-repairing fuse. When either of the described events takes place in a system which is protected by a circuit breaker, the circuit breaker opens the circuit the same way a fuse does. However, when either the short is removed from the circuit or the surge subsides, the circuit breaker resets itself and does not have to be replaced as a fuse does.

Troubleshooting

When diagnosing a specific problem, organized troubleshooting is a must. The complexity of a modern automobile demands that you approach any problem in a logical, organized manner. There are certain troubleshooting techniques that are standard:

1. Establish when the problem occurs. Does the problem appear only under certain conditions? Were there any noises, odors, or other unusual symptoms?

2. Isolate the problem area. To do this, make some simple tests and observations; then eliminate the systems that are working properly. Check for obvious problems such as broken wires, dirty connections or split/disconnected vacuum hoses. Always check the obvious before assuming something complicated is the cause.

3. Test for problems systematically to determine the cause once the problem area is isolated. Are all the components functioning properly? Is there power going to electrical switches and motors? Is there vacuum at vacuum switches and/or actuators? Is there a mechanical problem such as bent linkage or loose mounting screws? Performing careful, systematic checks will often turn up most causes on the first inspection without wasting time checking components that have little or no relationship to the problem.

4. Test all repairs after the work is done to make sure that the problem is fixed. Some causes can be traced to more than one component, so a careful verification of repair work is important in order to pick up additional malfunctions that may cause a problem to reappear or a different problem to arise. A blown fuse, for example, is a simple problem that may require more than another fuse to repair. If you don't look for a problem that caused a fuse to blow, a shorted wire (for example) may go undetected.

Experience has shown that most problems tend to be the result of a fairly simple and obvious cause, such as loose or corroded connectors or air leaks in the intake system. This makes careful inspection of components during testing essential to quick and accurate troubleshooting.

BASIC TROUBLESHOOTING THEORY

Electrical problems generally fall into one of three areas:
- The component that is not functioning is not receiving current.
- The component itself is not functioning.
- The component is not properly grounded.

Problems that fall into the first category are by far the most complicated. It is the current supply system to the component which contains all the switches, relay, fuses, etc.

The electrical system can be checked with a test light and a jumper wire. A test light is a device that looks like a pointed screwdriver with a wire attached to it. It has a light bulb in its handle. A jumper wire is a piece of insulated wire with an alligator clip attached to each end.

If a light bulb is not working, you must follow a systematic plan to determine which of the three causes is the villain.

1. Turn on the switch that controls the inoperable bulb.
2. Disconnect the power supply wire from the bulb.
3. Attach the ground wire to the test light to a good metal ground.
4. Touch the probe end of the test light to the end of the power supply wire that was disconnected from the bulb. If the bulb is receiving current, the test light will go on.

➡️**If the bulb is one which works only when the ignition key is turned on (turn signal), make sure the key is turned on.**

If the test light does not go on, then the problem is in the circuit between the battery and the bulb. As mentioned before, this includes all the switches, fuses, and relays in the system. Turn to a wiring diagram and find the bulb on the diagram. Follow the wire that runs back to the battery. The problem is an open circuit between the battery and the bulb. If the fuse is blown and, when replaced, immediately blows again, there is a short circuit in the system which must be located and repaired. If there is a switch in the system, bypass it with a jumper wire. This is done by connecting one end of the jumper wire to the power supply wire into the switch and the other end of the jumper wire to the wire coming out of the switch. If the test light illuminates with the jumper wire installed, the switch or whatever was bypassed is defective.

➡️**Never substitute the jumper wire for the bulb, as the bulb is the component required to use the power from the power source.**

5. If the bulb in the test light goes on, then the current is getting to the bulb that is not working in the car. This eliminates the first of the three possible causes. Connect the power supply wire and connect a jumper wire from the bulb to a good metal ground. Do this with the switch which controls the bulb works with jumper wire installed, then it has a bad ground. This is usually caused by the metal area on which the bulb mounts to the vehicle being coated with some type of foreign matter.

6. If neither test located the source of the trouble, then the light bulb itself is defective.

The above test procedure can be applied to any of the components of the chassis electrical system by substituting the component that is not working for the light bulb. Remember that for any electrical system to work, all connections must be clean and tight.

TEST EQUIPMENT

➡️**Pinpointing the exact cause of trouble in an electrical system can sometimes only be accomplished by the use of special test equipment. The following describes different types of commonly used test equipment and explains how to use them in diagnosis. In addition to the information covered below, the tool manufacturer's instructions booklet (provided with the tester) should be read and clearly understood before attempting any test procedures.**

Jumper Wires

Jumper wires are simple, yet extremely valuable, pieces of test equipment. They are basically test wires which are used to bypass sections of a circuit. The simplest type of jumper wire is a length of multi-strand wire with an alligator clip at each end. Jumper wires are usually fabricated from lengths of standard automotive wire and whatever type of connector (alligator clip, spade connector or pin connector) that is required for the particular vehicle being tested. The well equipped tool box will have several different styles of jumper wires in several different lengths. Some jumper wires are made with three or more terminals coming from a common splice for special purpose testing. In cramped, hard-to-reach areas it is advisable to have insulated boots over the jumper wire terminals in order to prevent accidental grounding, sparks, and possible fire, especially when testing fuel system components.

Jumper wires are used primarily to locate open electrical circuits, on either the ground (−) side of the circuit or on the hot (+) side. If an electrical component fails to operate, connect the jumper wire between the component and a good ground. If the component operates only with the jumper installed, the ground circuit is open. If the ground circuit is good, but the component does not operate, the circuit between the power feed and component may be open. By moving the jumper wire successively back from the lamp toward the power source, you can isolate the area of the circuit where the open is located. When the component stops functioning, or the power is cut off, the open is in the segment of wire between the jumper and the point previously tested.

You can sometimes connect the jumper wire directly from the

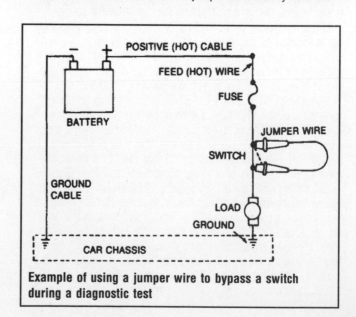

Example of using a jumper wire to bypass a switch during a diagnostic test

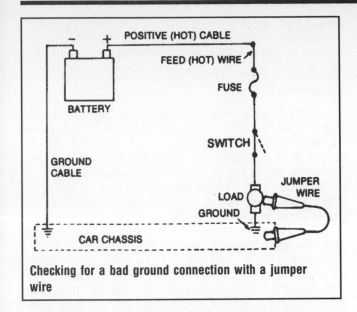

Checking for a bad ground connection with a jumper wire

battery to the hot terminal of the component, but first make sure the component uses 12 volts in operation. Some electrical components, such as fuel injectors, are designed to operate on about 4 volts and running 12 volts directly to the injector terminals can cause damage.

By inserting an in-line fuse holder between a set of test leads, a fused jumper wire can be used for bypassing open circuits. Use a 5 amp fuse to provide protection against voltage spikes. When in doubt, use a voltmeter to check the voltage input to the component and measure how much voltage is normally being applied.

✳✳ CAUTION

Never use jumpers made from wire that is of lighter gauge than that which is used in the circuit under test. If the jumper wire is of too small a gauge, it may overheat and possibly melt. Never use jumpers to bypass high resistance loads in a circuit. Bypassing resistances, in effect, creates a short circuit. This may, in turn, cause damage and fire. Jumper wires should only be used to bypass lengths of wire.

Unpowered Test Lights

The 12 volt test light is used to check circuits and components while electrical current is flowing through them. It is used for voltage and ground tests. Twelve volt test lights come in different styles but all have three main parts; a ground clip, a probe, and a light. The most commonly used 12 volt test lights have pick-type probes. To use a 12 volt test light, connect the ground clip to a good ground and probe wherever necessary with the pick. The pick should be sharp so that it can be probed into tight spaces.

✳✳ CAUTION

Do not use a test light to probe electronic ignition spark plug or coil wires. Never use a pick-type test light to probe wiring on computer controlled systems unless specifically instructed to do so. Any wire insulation that is pierced by the test light probe should be taped and sealed with silicone after testing.

Like the jumper wire, the 12 volt test light is used to isolate opens in circuits. But, whereas the jumper wire is used to bypass the open to operate the load, the 12 volt test light is used to locate the presence of voltage in a circuit. If the test light glows, you know that there is power up to that point; if the 12 volt test light does not glow when its probe is inserted into the wire or connector, you know that there is an open circuit (no power). Move the test light in successive steps back toward the power source until the light in the handle does glow. When it glows, the open is between the probe and point which was probed previously.

➡ **The test light does not detect that 12 volts (or any particular amount of voltage) is present; it only detects that some voltage is present. It is advisable before using the test light to touch its terminals across the battery posts to make sure the light is operating properly.**

Self-Powered Test Lights

The self-powered test light usually contains a 1.5 volt penlight battery. One type of self-powered test light is similar in design to the 12 volt unit. This type has both the battery and the light in the handle, along with a pick-type probe tip. The second type has the light toward the open tip, so that the light illuminates the contact point. The self-powered test light is a dual purpose piece of test equipment. It can be used to test for either open or short circuits when power is isolated from the circuit (continuity test). A powered test light should not be used on any computer controlled system or component unless specifically instructed to do so. Many engine sensors can be destroyed by even this small amount of voltage applied directly to the terminals.

Voltmeters

A voltmeter is used to measure voltage at any point in a circuit, or to measure the voltage drop across any part of a circuit. It can also be used to check continuity in a wire or circuit by indicating current flow from one end to the other. Analog voltmeters usually have various scales on the meter dial and a selector switch to allow the selection of different voltages. The voltmeter has a positive and a negative lead. To avoid damage to the meter, always connect the negative lead to the negative (−) side of the circuit (to ground or nearest the ground side of the circuit) and connect the positive lead to the positive (+) side of the circuit (to the power source or the nearest power source). Note that the negative voltmeter lead will always be black and that the positive voltmeter will always be some color other than black (usually red).

Depending on how the voltmeter is connected into the circuit, it has several uses. A voltmeter can be connected either in parallel or in series with a circuit and it has a very high resistance to current flow. When connected in parallel, only a small amount of current will flow through the voltmeter current path; the rest will flow through the normal circuit current path and the circuit will work normally. When the voltmeter is connected in series with a circuit, only a small amount of current can flow through the circuit. The circuit will not work properly, but the voltmeter reading will show if the circuit is complete or not.

Ohmmeters

The ohmmeter is designed to read resistance (which is measured in ohms or Ω) in a circuit or component. Although there are several different styles of ohmmeters, all analog meters will usually have a selector switch which permits the measurement of different ranges of resistance (usually the selector switch allows the multiplication of the meter reading by 10, 100, 1000, and 10,000). A calibration knob allows the meter to be set at zero for accurate measurement. Since all ohmmeters are powered by an internal battery, the ohmmeter can be used as a self-powered test light. When the ohmmeter is connected, current from the ohmmeter flows through the circuit or component being tested. Since the ohmmeter's internal resistance and voltage are known values, the amount of current flow through the meter depends on the resistance of the circuit or component being tested.

The ohmmeter can be used to perform a continuity test for opens or shorts (either by observation of the meter needle or as a self-powered test light), and to read actual resistance in a circuit. It should be noted that the ohmmeter is used to check the resistance of a component or wire while there is no voltage applied to the circuit. Current flow from an outside voltage source (such as the vehicle battery) can damage the ohmmeter, so the circuit or component should be isolated from the vehicle electrical system before any testing is done. Since the ohmmeter uses its own voltage source, either lead can be connected to any test point.

➡️**When checking diodes or other solid state components, the ohmmeter leads can only be connected one way in order to measure current flow in a single direction. Make sure the positive (+) and negative (−) terminal connections are as described in the test procedures to verify the one-way diode operation.**

In using the meter for making continuity checks, do not be concerned with the actual resistance readings. Zero resistance, or any ohm reading, indicates continuity in the circuit. Infinite resistance indicates an open in the circuit. A high resistance reading where there should be none indicates a problem in the circuit. Checks for short circuits are made in the same manner as checks for open circuits except that the circuit must be isolated from both power and normal ground. Infinite resistance indicates no continuity to ground, while zero resistance indicates a dead short to ground.

Ammeters

An ammeter measures the amount of current flowing through a circuit in units called amperes or amps. Amperes are units of electron flow which indicate how fast the electrons are flowing through the circuit. Since Ohms Law dictates that current flow in a circuit is equal to the circuit voltage divided by the total circuit resistance, increasing voltage also increases the current level (amps). Likewise, any decrease in resistance will increase the amount of amps in a circuit. At normal operating voltage, most circuits have a characteristic amount of amperes, called "current draw" which can be measured using an ammeter. By referring to a specified current draw rating, measuring the amperes, and comparing the two values, one can determine what is happening within the circuit to aid in diagnosis. An open circuit, for example, will not allow any current to flow so the ammeter reading will be zero. More current flows through a heavily loaded circuit or when the charging system is operating.

An ammeter is always connected in series with the circuit being tested. All of the current that normally flows through the circuit must also flow through the ammeter; if there is any other path for the current to follow, the ammeter reading will not be accurate. The ammeter itself has very little resistance to current flow and therefore will not affect the circuit, but it will measure current draw only when the circuit is closed and electricity is flowing. Excessive current draw can blow fuses and drain the battery, while a reduced current draw can cause motors to run slowly, lights to dim and other components to not operate properly. The ammeter can help diagnose these conditions by locating the cause of the high or low reading.

Multimeters

Different combinations of test meters can be built into a single unit designed for specific tests. Some of the more common combination test devices are known as Volt/Amp testers, Tach/Dwell meters, or Digital Multimeters. The Volt/Amp tester is used for charging system, starting system or battery tests and consists of a voltmeter, an ammeter and a variable resistance carbon pile. The voltmeter will usually have at least two ranges for use with 6, 12 and/or 24 volt systems. The ammeter also has more than one range for testing various levels of battery loads and starter current draw. The carbon pile can be adjusted to offer different amounts of resistance. The Volt/Amp tester has heavy leads to carry large amounts of current and many later models have an inductive ammeter pickup that clamps around the wire to simplify test connections. On some models, the ammeter also has a zero-center scale to allow testing of charging and starting systems without switching leads or polarity. A digital multimeter is a voltmeter, ammeter and ohmmeter combined in an instrument which gives a digital readout. These are often used when testing solid state circuits because of their high input impedance (usually 10 megohms or more).

The tach/dwell meter that combines a tachometer and a dwell (cam angle) meter is a specialized kind of voltmeter. The tachometer scale is marked to show engine speed in rpm and the dwell scale is marked to show degrees of distributor shaft rotation. In most electronic ignition systems, dwell is determined by the control unit, but the dwell meter can also be used to check the duty cycle (operation) of some electronic engine control systems. Some tach/dwell meters are powered by an internal battery, while others take their power from the vehicle battery in use. The battery powered testers usually require calibration (much like an ohmmeter) before testing.

TESTING

Open Circuits

To use the self-powered test light or a multimeter to check for open circuits, first isolate the circuit from the vehicle's 12 volt power source by disconnecting the battery or wiring harness connector. Connect the test light or ohmmeter ground clip to a good ground and probe sections of the circuit sequentially with the test light. (start from either end of the circuit). If the light is out/or there is infinite resistance, the open is between the probe and the circuit ground. If the light is on/or the meter shows continuity, the open is between the probe and end of the circuit toward the power source.

Short Circuits

By isolating the circuit both from power and from ground, and using a self-powered test light or multimeter, you can check for shorts to ground in the circuit. Isolate the circuit from power and ground. Connect the test light or ohmmeter ground clip to a good ground and probe any easy-to-reach test point in the circuit. If the light comes on or there is continuity, there is a short somewhere in the circuit. To isolate the short, probe a test point at either end of the isolated circuit (the light should be on/there should be continuity). Leave the test light probe engaged and open connectors, switches, remove parts, etc., sequentially, until the light goes out/continuity is broken. When the light goes out, the short is between the last circuit component opened and the previous circuit opened.

➡**The battery in the test light and does not provide much current. A weak battery may not provide enough power to illuminate the test light even when a complete circuit is made (especially if there are high resistances in the circuit). Always make sure that the test battery is strong. To check the battery, briefly touch the ground clip to the probe; if the light glows brightly the battery is strong enough for testing. Never use a self-powered test light to perform checks for opens or shorts when power is applied to the electrical system under test. The 12 volt vehicle power will quickly burn out the light bulb in the test light.**

Available Voltage Measurement

Set the voltmeter selector switch to the 20V position and connect the meter negative lead to the negative post of the battery. Connect the positive meter lead to the positive post of the battery and turn the ignition switch **ON** to provide a load. Read the voltage on the meter or digital display. A well charged battery should register over 12 volts. If the meter reads below 11.5 volts, the battery power may be insufficient to operate the electrical system properly. This test determines voltage available from the battery and should be the first step in any electrical trouble diagnosis procedure. Many electrical problems, especially on computer controlled systems, can be caused by a low state of charge in the battery. Excessive corrosion at the battery cable terminals can cause a poor contact that will prevent proper charging and full battery current flow.

Normal battery voltage is 12 volts when fully charged. When the battery is supplying current to one or more circuits it is said to be "under load." When everything is off the electrical system is under a "no-load" condition. A fully charged battery may show about 12.5 volts at no load; will drop to 12 volts under medium load; and will drop even lower under heavy load. If the battery is partially discharged the voltage decrease under heavy load may be excessive, even though the battery shows 12 volts or more at no load. When allowed to discharge further, the battery's available voltage under load will decrease more severely. For this reason, it is important that the battery be fully charged during all testing procedures to avoid errors in diagnosis and incorrect test results.

Voltage Drop

When current flows through a resistance, the voltage beyond the resistance is reduced (the larger the current, the greater the reduction in voltage). When no current is flowing, there is no voltage drop because there is no current flow. All points in the circuit which are connected to the power source are at the same voltage as the power source. The total voltage drop always equals the total source voltage. In a long circuit with many connectors, a series of small, unwanted voltage drops due to corrosion at the connectors can add up to a total loss of voltage which impairs the operation of the normal loads in the circuit. The maximum allowable voltage drop under load is critical, especially if there is more than one high resistance problem in a circuit because all voltage drops are cumulative. A small drop is normal due to the resistance of the conductors.

INDIRECT COMPUTATION OF VOLTAGE DROPS

1. Set the voltmeter selector switch to the 20 volt position.
2. Connect the meter negative lead to a good ground.
3. While operating the circuit, probe all loads in the circuit with the positive meter lead and observe the voltage readings. A drop should be noticed after the first load. But, there should be little or no voltage drop before the first load.

DIRECT MEASUREMENT OF VOLTAGE DROPS

1. Set the voltmeter switch to the 20 volt position.
2. Connect the voltmeter negative lead to the ground side of the load to be measured.
3. Connect the positive lead to the positive side of the resistance or load to be measured.
4. Read the voltage drop directly on the 20 volt scale.

Too high a voltage indicates too high a resistance. If, for example, a blower motor runs too slowly, you can determine if perhaps there is too high a resistance in the resistor pack. By taking voltage drop readings in all parts of the circuit, you can isolate the problem. Too low a voltage drop indicates too low a resistance. Take the blower motor for example again. If a blower motor runs too fast in the MED and/or LOW position, the problem might be isolated in the resistor pack by taking voltage drop readings in all parts of the circuit to locate a possibly shorted resistor.

HIGH RESISTANCE TESTING

1. Set the voltmeter selector switch to the 4 volt position.
2. Connect the voltmeter positive lead to the positive post of the battery.
3. Turn on the headlights and heater blower to provide a load.
4. Probe various points in the circuit with the negative voltmeter lead.
5. Read the voltage drop on the 4 volt scale. Some average maximum allowable voltage drops are:
   • FUSE PANEL: 0.7 volts
   • IGNITION SWITCH: 0.5 volts
   • HEADLIGHT SWITCH: 0.7 volts
   • IGNITION COIL (+): 0.5 volts
   • ANY OTHER LOAD: 1.3 volts

➡**Voltage drops are all measured while a load is operating; without current flow, there will be no voltage drop.**

Resistance Measurement

The batteries in an ohmmeter will weaken with age and temperature, so the ohmmeter must be calibrated or "zeroed" before taking measurements. To zero the meter, place the selector switch in its lowest range and touch the two ohmmeter leads together. Turn the calibration knob until the meter needle is exactly on zero.

➡**All analog (needle) type ohmmeters must be zeroed before use, but some digital ohmmeter models are automatically calibrated when the switch is turned on. Self-calibrating digital ohmmeters do not have an adjusting knob, but its a good idea to check for a zero readout before use by touching the leads together. All computer controlled systems require the use of a digital ohmmeter with at least 10 megohms impedance for testing. Before any test procedures are attempted, make sure the ohmmeter used is compatible with the electrical system or damage to the on-board computer could result.**

To measure resistance, first isolate the circuit from the vehicle power source by disconnecting the battery cables or the harness connector. Make sure the key is **OFF** when disconnecting any components or the battery. Where necessary, also isolate at least one side of the circuit to be checked in order to avoid reading parallel resistances. Parallel circuit resistances will always give a lower reading than the actual resistance of either of the branches. When measuring the resistance of parallel circuits, the total resistance will always be lower than the smallest resistance in the circuit. Connect the meter leads to both sides of the circuit (wire or component) and read the actual measured ohms on the meter scale. Make sure the selector switch is set to the proper ohm scale for the circuit being tested to avoid misreading the ohmmeter test value.

✷✷ WARNING

Never use an ohmmeter with power applied to the circuit. Like the self-powered test light, the ohmmeter is designed to operate on its own power supply. The normal 12 volt automotive electrical system current could damage the meter!

Wiring Harnesses

The average automobile contains about ½ mile of wiring, with hundreds of individual connections. To protect the many wires from damage and to keep them from becoming a confusing tangle, they are organized into bundles, enclosed in plastic or taped together and called wiring harnesses. Different harnesses serve different parts of the vehicle. Individual wires are color coded to help trace them through a harness where sections are hidden from view.

Automotive wiring or circuit conductors can be in any one of three forms:

1. Single strand wire
2. Multi-strand wire
3. Printed circuitry

Single strand wire has a solid metal core and is usually used inside such components as alternators, motors, relays and other devices. Multi-strand wire has a core made of many small strands of wire twisted together into a single conductor. Most of the wiring in an automotive electrical system is made up of multi-strand wire, either as a single conductor or grouped together in a harness. All wiring is color coded on the insulator, either as a solid color or as a colored wire with an identification stripe. A printed circuit is a thin film of copper or other conductor that is printed on an insulator backing. Occasionally, a printed circuit is sandwiched between two sheets of plastic for more protection and flexibility. A complete printed circuit, consisting of conductors, insulating material and connectors for lamps or other components is called a printed circuit board. Printed circuitry is used in place of individual wires or harnesses in places where space is limited, such as behind instrument panels.

Since automotive electrical systems are very sensitive to changes in resistance, the selection of properly sized wires is critical when systems are repaired. A loose or corroded connection or a replacement wire that is too small for the circuit will add extra resistance and an additional voltage drop to the circuit. A ten percent voltage drop can result in slow or erratic motor operation, for example, even though the circuit is complete. The wire gauge number is an expression of the cross-section area of the conduc-

tor. The most common system for expressing wire size is the American Wire Gauge (AWG) system.

Gauge numbers are assigned to conductors of various cross-section areas. As gauge number increases, area decreases and the conductor becomes smaller. A 5 gauge conductor is smaller than a 1 gauge conductor and a 10 gauge is smaller than a 5 gauge. As the cross-section area of a conductor decreases, resistance increases and so does the gauge number. A conductor with a higher gauge number will carry less current than a conductor with a lower gauge number.

➡ **Gauge wire size refers to the size of the conductor, not the size of the complete wire. It is possible to have two wires of the same gauge with different diameters because one may have thicker insulation than the other.**

12 volt automotive electrical systems generally use 10, 12, 14, 16 and 18 gauge wire. Main power distribution circuits and larger accessories usually use 10 and 12 gauge wire. Battery cables are usually 4 or 6 gauge, although 1 and 2 gauge wires are occasionally used. Wire length must also be considered when making repairs to a circuit. As conductor length increases, so does resistance. An 18 gauge wire, for example, can carry a 10 amp load for 10 feet without excessive voltage drop; however if a 15 foot wire is required for the same 10 amp load, it must be a 16 gauge wire.

An electrical schematic shows the electrical current paths when a circuit is operating properly. It is essential to understand how a circuit works before trying to figure out why it doesn't. Schematics break the entire electrical system down into individual circuits and show only one particular circuit. In a schematic, no attempt is made to represent wiring and components as they physically appear on the vehicle; switches and other components are shown as simply as possible. Face views of harness connectors show the cavity or terminal locations in all multi-pin connectors to help locate test points.

If you need to backprobe a connector while it is on the component, the order of the terminals must be mentally reversed. The wire color code can help in this situation, as well as a keyway, lock tab or other reference mark.

WIRING REPAIR

Soldering is a quick, efficient method of joining metals permanently. Everyone who has the occasion to make wiring repairs should know how to solder. Electrical connections that are soldered are far less likely to come apart and will conduct electricity much better than connections that are only "pig-tailed" together. The most popular (and preferred) method of soldering is with an electrical soldering gun. Soldering irons are available in many sizes and wattage ratings. Irons with higher wattage ratings deliver higher temperatures and recover lost heat faster. A small soldering iron rated for no more than 50 watts is recommended, especially on electrical systems where excess heat can damage the components being soldered.

There are three ingredients necessary for successful soldering; proper flux, good solder and sufficient heat. A soldering flux is necessary to clean the metal of tarnish, prepare it for soldering and to enable the solder to spread into tiny crevices. When soldering, always use a rosin core solder which is non-corrosive and will not attract moisture once the job is finished. Other types of flux (acid core) will leave a residue that will attract moisture and cause the wires to corrode. Tin is a unique metal with a low melting point. In a molten state, it dissolves and alloys easily with many metals. Solder is made by mixing tin with lead. The most common proportions are 40/60, 50/50 and 60/40, with the percentage of tin listed first. Low priced solders usually contain less tin, making them very difficult for a beginner to use because more heat is required to melt the solder. A common solder is 40/60 which is well suited for all-around general use, but 60/40 melts easier and is preferred for electrical work.

Soldering Techniques

Successful soldering requires that the metals to be joined be heated to a temperature that will melt the solder, usually 360–460°F (182–238°C). Contrary to popular belief, the purpose of the soldering iron is not to melt the solder itself, but to heat the parts being soldered to a temperature high enough to melt the solder when it is touched to the work. Melting flux-cored solder on the soldering iron will usually destroy the effectiveness of the flux.

→**Soldering tips are made of copper for good heat conductivity, but must be "tinned" regularly for quick transference of heat to the project and to prevent the solder from sticking to the iron. To "tin" the iron, simply heat it and touch the flux-cored solder to the tip; the solder will flow over the hot tip. Wipe the excess off with a clean rag, but be careful as the iron will be hot.**

After some use, the tip may become pitted. If so, simply dress the tip smooth with a smooth file and "tin" the tip again. Flux-cored solder will remove oxides but rust, bits of insulation and oil or grease must be removed with a wire brush or emery cloth. For maximum strength in soldered parts, the joint must start off clean and tight. Weak joints will result in gaps too wide for the solder to bridge.

If a separate soldering flux is used, it should be brushed or swabbed on only those areas that are to be soldered. Most solders contain a core of flux and separate fluxing is unnecessary. Hold the work to be soldered firmly. It is best to solder on a wooden board, because a metal vise will only rob the piece to be soldered of heat and make it difficult to melt the solder. Hold the soldering tip with the broadest face against the work to be soldered. Apply solder under the tip close to the work, using enough solder to give a heavy film between the iron and the piece being soldered, while moving slowly and making sure the solder melts properly. Keep the work level or the solder will run to the lowest part and favor the thicker parts, because these require more heat to melt the solder. If the soldering tip overheats (the solder coating on the face of the tip burns up), it should be retinned. Once the soldering is completed, let the soldered joint stand until cool. Tape and seal all soldered wire splices after the repair has cooled.

Wire Harness Connectors

Most connectors in the engine compartment or that are otherwise exposed to the elements are protected against moisture and dirt which could create oxidation and deposits on the terminals.

These special connectors are weather-proof. All repairs require the use of a special terminal and the tool required to service it. This tool is used to remove the pin and sleeve terminals. If removal is attempted with an ordinary pick, there is a good chance that the terminal will be bent or deformed. Unlike standard blade type terminals, these weather-proof terminals cannot be straightened once they are bent. Make certain that the connectors are

properly seated and all of the sealing rings are in place when connecting leads. On some models, a hinge-type flap provides a backup or secondary locking feature for the terminals. Most secondary locks are used to improve connector reliability by retaining the terminals if the small terminal lock tangs are not positioned properly.

Molded-on connectors require complete replacement of the connection. This means splicing a new connector assembly into the harness. All splices should be soldered to insure proper contact. Use care when probing the connections or replacing terminals in them as it is possible to short between opposite terminals. If this happens to the wrong terminal pair, it is possible to damage certain components. Always use jumper wires between connectors for circuit checking and never probe through weatherproof seals.

Open circuits are often difficult to locate by sight because corrosion or terminal misalignment are hidden by the connectors. Merely wiggling a connector on a sensor or in the wiring harness may correct the open circuit condition. This should always be considered when an open circuit or a failed sensor is indicated. Intermittent problems may also be caused by oxidized or loose connections. When using a circuit tester for diagnosis, always probe connections from the wire side. Be careful not to damage sealed connectors with test probes.

All wiring harnesses should be replaced with identical parts, using the same gauge wire and connectors. When signal wires are spliced into a harness, use wire with high temperature insulation only. It is seldom necessary to replace a complete harness. If replacement is necessary, pay close attention to insure proper harness routing. Secure the harness with suitable plastic wire clamps to prevent vibrations from causing the harness to wear in spots or contact any hot components.

→**Weatherproof connectors cannot be replaced with standard connectors. Instructions are provided with replacement connector and terminal packages. Some wire harnesses have mounting indicators (usually pieces of colored tape) to mark where the harness is to be secured.**

In making wiring repairs, its important that you always replace damaged wires with wiring of the same gauge as the wire being replaced. The heavier the wire, the smaller the gauge number. Wires are color-coded to aid in identification and whenever possible the same color coded wire should be used for replacement. A wire stripping and crimping tool is necessary to install solderless terminal connectors. Test all crimps by pulling on the wires; it should not be possible to pull the wires out of a good crimp.

Wires which are open, exposed or otherwise damaged are repaired by simple splicing. Where possible, if the wiring harness is accessible and the damaged place in the wire can be located, it is best to open the harness and check for all possible damage. In an inaccessible harness, the wire must be bypassed with a new insert, usually taped to the outside of the old harness.

When replacing fusible links, be sure to use fusible link wire, NOT ordinary automotive wire. Make sure the fusible segment is of the same gauge and construction as the one being replaced and double the stripped end when crimping the terminal connector for a good contact. The melted (open) fusible link segment of the wiring harness should be cut off as close to the harness as possible, then a new segment spliced in as described. In the case of a damaged fusible link that feeds two harness wires, the harness connections should be replaced with two fusible link wires so that each circuit will have its own separate protection.

➡**Most of the problems caused in the wiring harness are due to bad ground connections. Always check all vehicle ground connections for corrosion or looseness before performing any power feed checks to eliminate the chance of a bad ground affecting the circuit.**

Hard-Shell Connectors

Unlike molded connectors, the terminal contacts in hard-shell connectors can be replaced. Weatherproof hard-shell connectors with the leads molded into the shell have non-replaceable terminal ends. Replacement usually involves the use of a special terminal removal tool that depresses the locking tangs (barbs) on the connector terminal and allows the connector to be removed from the rear of the shell. The connector shell should be replaced if it shows any evidence of burning, melting, cracks, or breaks. Replace individual terminals that are burnt, corroded, distorted or loose.

➡**The insulation crimp must be tight to prevent the insulation from sliding back on the wire when the wire is pulled. The insulation must be visibly compressed under the crimp tabs, and the ends of the crimp should be turned in for a firm grip on the insulation.**

The wire crimp must be made with all wire strands inside the crimp. The terminal must be fully compressed on the wire strands with the ends of the crimp tabs turned in to make a firm grip on the wire. Check all connections with an ohmmeter to insure a good contact. There should be no measurable resistance between the wire and the terminal when connected.

Fusible Links

The fuse link is a short length of special, Hypalon (high temperature) insulated wire, integral with the engine compartment wiring harness and should not be confused with standard wire. It is several wire gauges smaller than the circuit which it protects. Under no circumstances should a fuse link replacement repair be made using a length of standard wire cut from bulk stock or from another wiring harness.

To repair any blown fuse link use the following procedure:

1. Determine which circuit is damaged, its location and the cause of the open fuse link. If the damaged fuse link is one of three fed by a common No. 10 or 12 gauge feed wire, determine the specific affected circuit.

2. Disconnect the negative battery cable.

3. Cut the damaged fuse link from the wiring harness and discard it. If the fuse link is one of three circuits fed by a single feed wire, cut it out of the harness at each splice end and discard it.

4. Identify and procure the proper fuse link with butt connectors for attaching the fuse link to the harness.

➡**Heat shrink tubing must be slipped over the wire before crimping and soldering the connection.**

5. To repair any fuse link in a 3-link group with one feed:

   a. After cutting the open link out of the harness, cut each of the remaining undamaged fuse links close to the feed wire weld.

   b. Strip approximately ½ in. (13mm) of insulation from the detached ends of the two good fuse links. Insert two wire ends into one end of a butt connector, then carefully push one stripped end of the replacement fuse link into the same end of the butt connector and crimp all three firmly together.

➡**Care must be taken when fitting the three fuse links into the butt connector as the internal diameter is a snug fit for three wires. Make sure to use a proper crimping tool. Pliers, side cutters, etc. will not apply the proper crimp to retain the wires and withstand a pull test.**

   c. After crimping the butt connector to the three fuse links, cut the weld portion from the feed wire and strip approximately ½ in. (13mm) of insulation from the cut end. Insert the stripped end into the open end of the butt connector and crimp very firmly.

   d. To attach the remaining end of the replacement fuse link, strip approximately ½ in. (13mm) of insulation from the wire end of the circuit from which the blown fuse link was removed, and firmly crimp a butt connector or equivalent to the stripped wire. Then, insert the end of the replacement link into the other end of the butt connector and crimp firmly.

   e. Using rosin core solder with a consistency of 60 percent tin and 40 percent lead, solder the connectors and the wires at the repairs then insulate with electrical tape or heat shrink tubing.

6. To replace any fuse link on a single circuit in a harness, cut out the damaged portion, strip approximately ½ in. (13mm) of insulation from the two wire ends and attach the appropriate replacement fuse link to the stripped wire ends with two proper size butt connectors. Solder the connectors and wires, then insulate.

7. To repair any fuse link which has an eyelet terminal on one end such as the charging circuit, cut off the open fuse link behind the weld, strip approximately ½ in. (13mm) of insulation from the cut end and attach the appropriate new eyelet fuse link to the cut stripped wire with an appropriate size butt connector. Solder the connectors and wires at the repair, then insulate.

8. Connect the negative battery cable to the battery and test the system for proper operation.

➡**Do not mistake a resistor wire for a fuse link. The resistor wire is generally longer and has print stating, "Resistor-don't cut or splice."**

When attaching a single No. 16, 17, 18 or 20 gauge fuse link to a heavy gauge wire, always double the stripped wire end of the fuse link before inserting and crimping it into the butt connector for positive wire retention.

Add-On Electrical Equipment

The electrical system in your vehicle is designed to perform under reasonable operating conditions without interference between components. Before any additional electrical equipment is installed, it is recommended that you consult your dealer or a reputable repair facility that is familiar with the vehicle and its systems.

If the vehicle is equipped with mobile radio equipment and/or mobile telephone, it may have an effect upon the operation of any on-board computer control modules. Radio Frequency Interference (RFI) from the communications system can be picked up by the vehicle's wiring harnesses and conducted into the control module, giving it the wrong messages at the wrong time. Although well shielded against RFI, the computer should be further protected by taking the following measures:

• Install the antenna as far as possible from the control module. For instance, if the module is located behind the center con-

REMOVE EXISTING VINYL TUBE SHIELDING
REINSTALL OVER FUSE LINK BEFORE CRIMPING
FUSE LINK TO WIRE ENDS

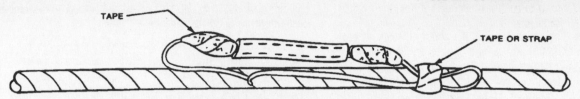

TAPE

TAPE OR STRAP

TYPICAL REPAIR USING THE SPECIAL #17 GA. (9.00" LONG-YELLOW) FUSE LINK REQUIRED FOR THE AIR/COND.
CIRCUITS (2) #687E and #261A LOCATED IN THE ENGINE COMPARTMENT

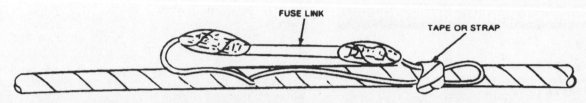

FUSE LINK

TAPE OR STRAP

TYPICAL REPAIR FOR ANY IN-LINE FUSE LINK USING THE SPECIFIED GAUGE FUSE LINK FOR THE SPECIFIC CIRCUIT

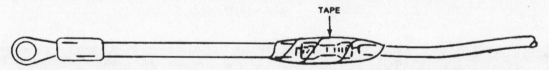

TAPE

TYPICAL REPAIR USING THE EYELET TERMINAL FUSE LINK OF THE SPECIFIED GAUGE FOR ATTACHMENT TO A CIRCUIT WIRE END

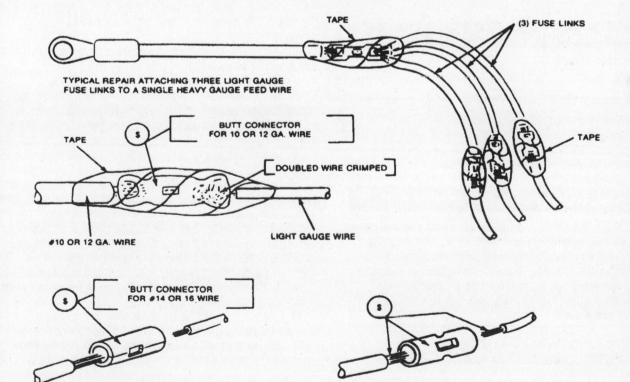

TAPE

(3) FUSE LINKS

TYPICAL REPAIR ATTACHING THREE LIGHT GAUGE
FUSE LINKS TO A SINGLE HEAVY GAUGE FEED WIRE

TAPE

BUTT CONNECTOR
FOR 10 OR 12 GA. WIRE

DOUBLED WIRE CRIMPED

TAPE

#10 OR 12 GA. WIRE

LIGHT GAUGE WIRE

BUTT CONNECTOR
FOR #14 OR 16 WIRE

FUSIBLE LINK REPAIR PROCEDURE

**General fusible link repair—never replace a fusible link with regular wire or a fusible link rated at a higher amperage
than the one being replaced**

sole area, then the antenna should be mounted at the rear of the vehicle.

• Keep the antenna wiring a minimum of eight inches away from any wiring running to control modules and from the module itself. NEVER wind the antenna wire around any other wiring.

• Mount the equipment as far from the control module as possible. Be very careful during installation not to drill through any wires or short a wire harness with a mounting screw.

• Insure that the electrical feed wire(s) to the equipment are properly and tightly connected. Loose connectors can cause interference.

• Make certain that the equipment is properly grounded to the vehicle. Poor grounding can damage expensive equipment.

Mechanical Test Equipment

Vacuum Gauge

Most gauges are graduated in inches of mercury (in. Hg), although a device called a manometer reads vacuum in inches of water (in. H_2O). The normal vacuum reading usually varies between 18 and 22 in. Hg at sea level. To test engine vacuum, the vacuum gauge must be connected to a source of manifold vacuum. Many engines have a plug in the intake manifold which can be removed and replaced with an adapter fitting. Connect the vac-

uum gauge to the fitting with a suitable rubber hose or, if no manifold plug is available, connect the vacuum gauge to any device using manifold vacuum, such as EGR valves, etc. The vacuum gauge can be used to determine if enough vacuum is reaching a component to allow its actuation.

Hand Vacuum Pump

Small, hand-held vacuum pumps come in a variety of designs. Most have a built-in vacuum gauge and allow the component to be tested without removing it from the vehicle. Operate the pump lever or plunger to apply the correct amount of vacuum required for the test specified in the diagnosis routines. The level of vacuum in inches of Mercury (in. Hg) is indicated on the pump gauge. For some testing, an additional vacuum gauge may be necessary.

Intake manifold vacuum is used to operate various systems and devices on late model vehicles. To correctly diagnose and solve problems in vacuum control systems, a vacuum source is necessary for testing. In some cases, vacuum can be taken from the intake manifold when the engine is running, but vacuum is normally provided by a hand vacuum pump. These hand vacuum pumps have a built-in vacuum gauge that allow testing while the device is still attached to the component. For some tests, an additional vacuum gauge may be necessary.

HEATER

Refer to Section 1 for discharging, charging of the air conditioning system.

Heater Assembly

REMOVAL & INSTALLATION

610 and 710
♦ See Figure 1

1. Disconnect the battery ground cable.
2. Drain the coolant.

✳✳ CAUTION

When draining the coolant, keep in mind that cats and dogs are attracted by ethylene glycol antifreeze, and are quite likely to drink any that is left in an uncovered container or in puddles on the ground. This will prove fatal in sufficient quantity. Always drain the coolant into a sealable container. Coolant should be reused unless it is contaminated or several years old.

3. Detach the coolant inlet and outlet hoses.
4. On the 610, remove the center ventilator grille from the bottom of the instrument panel.
5. Remove the heater duct hose from both sides of the heater

unit. Remove the defroster hose or hoses on the 610. On the 710, remove the intake duct and defroster duct from both sides of the heater unit. Remove the console box on the 710 if so equipped.

6. Disconnect the electrical wires of the heater unit (and air conditioner, if so equipped) at their connections.

7. Disconnect and remove the heater control cables.

8. On 710 and 1974–76 610, remove the two bolts on each side of the unit and one on the top. For 1973 610s, remove one attaching bolt from each side and one from the top center of the unit.

9. Remove the unit.

To install:

10. Install the unit in the vehicle with retaining bolts. Connect the heater control cables and the electrical wires of the heater unit (and air conditioner, if so equipped) at their connections.

11. Install the heater duct hose to both sides of the heater unit. Install the defroster hose or hoses on the 610. On the 710, install the intake duct and defroster duct to both sides of the heater unit. Install the console box on the 710 if so equipped.

12. On the 610, install the center ventilator grille to the bottom of the instrument panel.

13. Reconnect the two heater hoses with new hose clamps. Connect the battery ground cable and refill the cooling system.

14. Run the engine for a few minutes with the heater on to make sure the coolant level is correct. Check for any coolant leaks.

15. Check the heater system for proper operation.

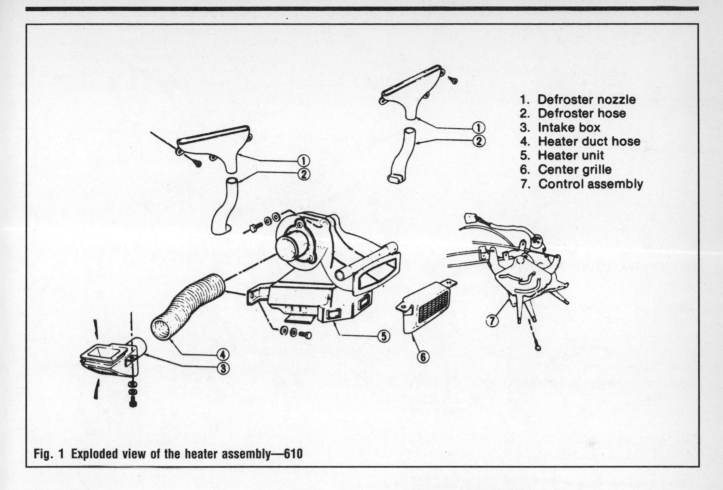

1. Defroster nozzle
2. Defroster hose
3. Intake box
4. Heater duct hose
5. Heater unit
6. Center grille
7. Control assembly

Fig. 1 Exploded view of the heater assembly—610

1977–79 200SX

▶ **See Figure 2**

1. Disconnect the battery cable.
2. Drain the engine coolant and remove the heater hoses from the engine side.

✳✳ CAUTION

When draining the coolant, keep in mind that cats and dogs are attracted by ethylene glycol antifreeze, and are quite likely to drink any that is left in an uncovered container or in puddles on the ground. This will prove fatal in sufficient quantity. Always drain the coolant into a sealable container. Coolant should be reused unless it is contaminated or several years old.

3. Inside the passenger compartment, disconnect the lead wires from the heater unit to the instrument harness.
4. At this point, the instrument panel must be removed in order to remove the heater assembly. To remove the panel proceed as follows:

a. Remove the steering wheel cover.

b. Disconnect the speedometer cable and the radio antenna cable.

c. After noting their position, disconnect the following connectors: instrument harness to body, harness to engine room, transistor ignition unit, and the wiring to the console.

d. Remove the bolts securing the column clamp and lower the steering column.

e. Remove the package tray.

f. Remove the bolts which attach the instrument panel to the mounting bracket on the left and right-hand sides.

g. Remove the trim on the right side windshield pillar, and remove the bolt attaching the instrument panel to the pillar.

h. Remove the trim on the top of the instrument panel.

i. Remove the bolts attaching the instrument panel.

j. Move the instrument panel to the right to remove it.

5. Remove the defroster hoses on both sides of the heater unit.
6. Disconnect the wires to the air conditioner, if so equipped. Disconnect the heater control cables.
7. Remove the three heater retaining bolts and remove the heater assembly.

To install:

8. Install the heater assembly with retaining bolts in the vehicle.
9. Reconnect the wires to the air conditioner if so equipped. Reconnect the heater control cables.
10. Connect the defroster hoses on both sides of the heater unit.
11. Install the instrument panel and all necessary components that were removed to gain access to the instrument panel retaining bolts.
12. Inside the passenger compartment, connect the lead wires to the heater unit from the instrument harness.
13. Reconnect the two heater hoses with new hose clamps. Connect the battery ground cable and refill the cooling system.
14. Run the engine for a few minutes with the heater on to make sure the coolant level is correct. Check for any coolant leaks and the heater system for proper operation.

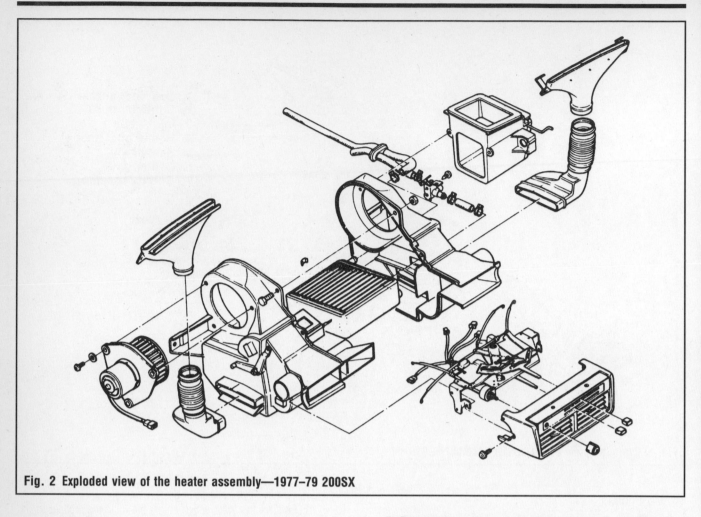

Fig. 2 Exploded view of the heater assembly—1977–79 200SX

1980–81 200SX

▶ **See Figure 3**

1. Set the TEMP lever to the HOT position and drain the coolant.

✳✳ CAUTION

When draining the coolant, keep in mind that cats and dogs are attracted by ethylene glycol antifreeze, and are quite likely to drink any that is left in an uncovered container or in puddles on the ground. This will prove fatal in sufficient quantity. Always drain the coolant into a sealable container. Coolant should be reused unless it is contaminated or several years old.

2. Disconnect the heater hoses from the driver's side of the heater unit.

3. At this point the manufacturer suggests you remove the front seats. To do this, remove the plastic covers over the ends of the seat runners, both front and back, to expose the seat mounting bolts. Remove the bolts and remove the seats.

4. Remove the console box and the floor carpets.

5. Remove the instrument panel lower covers from both the driver's and passenger's sides of the car. Remove the lower cluster lids.

6. Remove the left-hand side ventilator duct.

7. Remove the radio, sound balancer and stereo cassette deck if so equipped.

8. Remove the instrument panel-to-transmission tunnel stay.

9. Remove the rear heater duct from the floor of the vehicle.

10. Remove the center ventilator duct.

11. Remove the left and right-hand side air guides from the lower heater outlets.

12. Disconnect the wire harness connections.

13. Remove the two screws at the bottom sides of the heater unit and the one screw and the top of the unit and remove the unit together with the heater control assembly.

➡On late models the heater control cables and control assembly may have to be removed before the heater unit is removed. Always mark control cables before removing them to ensure correct adjustment and proper operation.

To install:

14. Install the heater assembly with retaining bolts in the vehicle. Reconnect all electrical and heater control cable connections if removed.

15. Install the left and right-hand side air guides to the lower heater outlets.

16. Install the center ventilator duct.

17. Install the rear heater duct to the floor of the vehicle and all components that were removed to gain access to the rear heater duct retaining bolts.

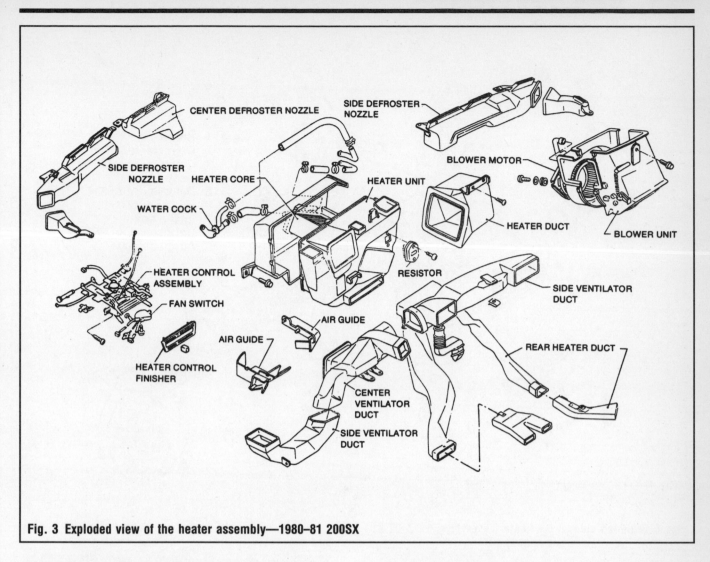

Fig. 3 Exploded view of the heater assembly—1980–81 200SX

18. Install the instrument panel lower covers, floor carpets, console box and seats if removed.

19. Reconnect the two heater hoses with new hose clamps. Connect the battery ground cable and refill the cooling system.

20. Run the engine for a few minutes with the heater on to make sure the coolant level is correct. Check for any coolant leaks and the heater system for proper operation.

➡**You may be able to skip several of the above steps if only certain components of the heater unit need service.**

1977–80 810

▶ **See Figure 4**

1. Disconnect the battery ground cable.
2. Drain the engine coolant.

✳✳ CAUTION

When draining the coolant, keep in mind that cats and dogs are attracted by ethylene glycol antifreeze, and are quite likely to drink any that is left in an uncovered container or in puddles on the ground. This will prove fatal in sufficient quantity. Always drain the coolant into a sealable container. Coolant should be reused unless it is contaminated or several years old.

3. Remove the console box and the console box bracket. Remove the front floor mat.

4. Loosen the screws and remove the rear heater duct.

5. Remove the hose clamps and remove the inlet and outlet hoses.

6. Remove the heater duct and remove the defroster hoses from the assembly.

7. Remove the air intake door control cable.

8. Disconnect the wiring harness to the heater.

9. Remove the retaining bolts and remove the heater unit.

To install:

10. Install the heater unit with retaining bolts in the vehicle.

11. Connect the wiring harness and heater control cables to the heater unit.

12. Reconnect the heater hoses with new hose clamps. Install the rear heater duct.

13. Install the console box assembly and floor mat.

14. Connect the battery ground cable and refill the cooling system. Run the engine for a few minutes with the heater on to make sure the coolant level is correct. Check for any coolant leaks and the heater system for proper operation.

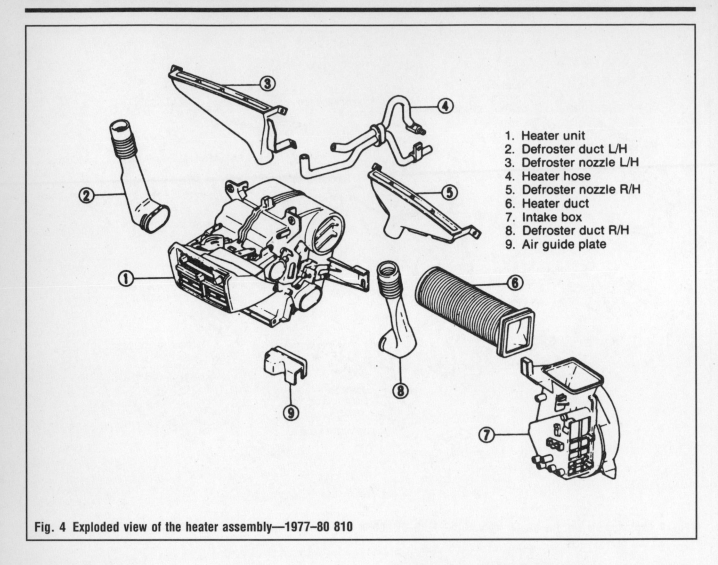

1. Heater unit
2. Defroster duct L/H
3. Defroster nozzle L/H
4. Heater hose
5. Defroster nozzle R/H
6. Heater duct
7. Intake box
8. Defroster duct R/H
9. Air guide plate

Fig. 4 Exploded view of the heater assembly—1977–80 810

1981–84 810/Maxima

▶ See Figures 5 and 6

1. Set the TEMP lever to the HOT position and drain the coolant.

✳✳ CAUTION

When draining the coolant, keep in mind that cats and dogs are attracted by ethylene glycol antifreeze, and are quite likely to drink any that is left in an uncovered container or in puddles on the ground. This will prove fatal in sufficient quantity. Always drain the coolant into a sealable container. Coolant should be reused unless it is contaminated or several years old.

2. Disconnect the heater hoses from the driver's side of the heater unit.

3. At this point the manufacturer suggests that you remove the front seats. To do this, remove the plastic covers over the ends of the seat runners, front and back, to expose the seat mounting bolts. Remove the bolts and lift out the seats.

4. Remove the front floor carpets.

5. Remove the instrument panel lower covers from both the driver's and passenger's sides of the car.

6. Remove the left side ventilator duct.

7. Remove the instrument panel assembly.

8. Remove the rear heater duct from the floor of the car.

9. Tag and disconnect the wire harness connectors.

10. Remove the two screws at the bottom sides of the heater unit and the one screw from the top of the unit. Lift out the heater together with the heater control assembly.

To install:

11. Install the heater assembly with retaining bolts in the vehicle. Reconnect all electrical and heater control cable connections if removed.

12. Install the rear heater duct to the floor of the vehicle and all components that were removed to gain access to the rear heater duct retaining bolts.

13. Install the instrument panel assembly and the left side ventilator duct.

14. Install the instrument panel lower covers, floor carpets and seats if removed.

15. Reconnect the two heater hoses with new hose clamps. Connect the battery ground cable and refill the cooling system.

16. Run the engine for a few minutes with the heater on to make sure the coolant level is correct.

17. Check for any coolant leaks and the heater system for proper operation.

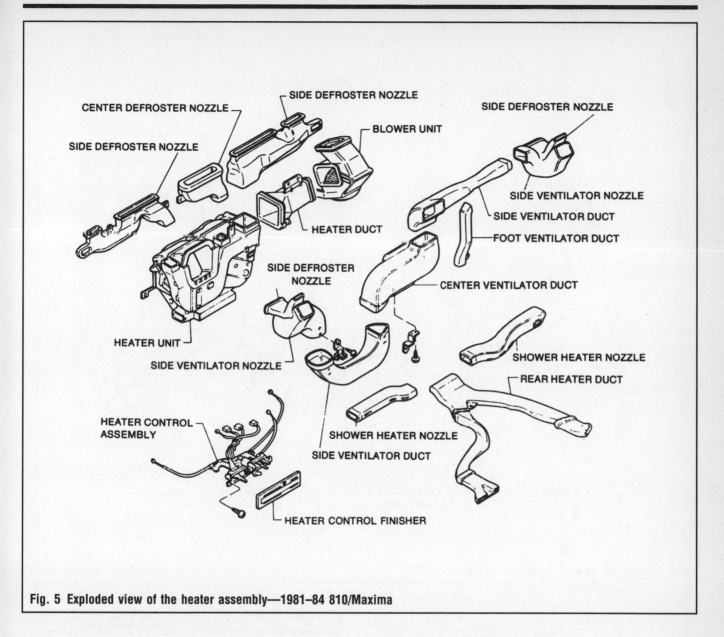

Fig. 5 Exploded view of the heater assembly—1981–84 810/Maxima

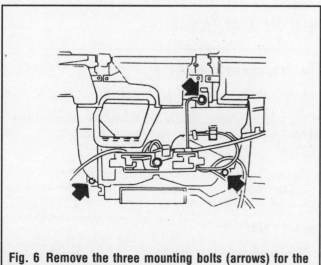

Fig. 6 Remove the three mounting bolts (arrows) for the heater vent—1981–84 810/Maxima

510

▶ See Figure 7

1. Disconnect the ground cable at the battery. Drain the coolant.

✳✳ CAUTION

When draining the coolant, keep in mind that cats and dogs are attracted by ethylene glycol antifreeze, and are quite likely to drink any that is left in an uncovered container or in puddles on the ground. This will prove fatal in sufficient quantity. Always drain the coolant into a sealable container. Coolant should be reused unless it is contaminated or several years old.

2. Remove the console box.
3. Remove the driver's side of the instrument panel.
4. Remove the heater control assembly: remove the defroster ducts, vent door cables at the doors and harness connector.

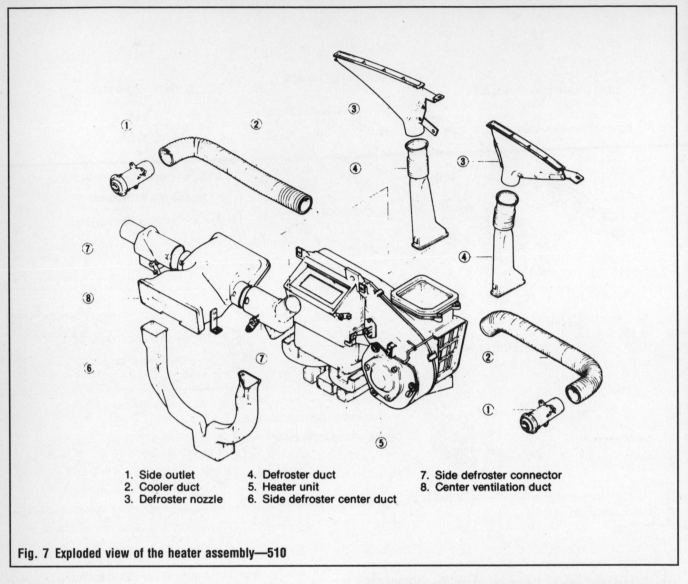

1. Side outlet
2. Cooler duct
3. Defroster nozzle
4. Defroster duct
5. Heater unit
6. Side defroster center duct
7. Side defroster connector
8. Center ventilation duct

Fig. 7 Exploded view of the heater assembly—510

5. Remove the radio.

6. Disconnect the heater ducts, side defrosters and the center vent duct.

7. Remove the screws attaching the defroster nozzle to the unit. Disconnect the blower wiring harness and the heater hoses.

8. Remove the retaining bolts and the heater unit.

To install:

9. Install the heater unit with retaining bolts in the vehicle.

10. Connect the blower wiring harness electrical connection and heater hoses with new hose clamps.

11. Install the defroster nozzle to the heater unit, the heater ducts, side defrosters and the center vent duct.

12. Install the radio and heater control assembly. Install the defroster ducts, vent door cables at the doors and harness electrical connector.

13. Install the driver's side of the instrument panel and console box.

14. Connect the battery ground cable and refill the cooling system.

15. Run the engine for a few minutes with the heater on to make sure the coolant level is correct. Check for any coolant leaks and the heater system for proper operation.

Blower Motor

REMOVAL & INSTALLATION

610, 710, and 1977–79 200SX

1. Remove the heater unit from the vehicle.

➡**You may be able to remove the blower on some models without removing the heater unit from the vehicle.**

2. Remove the three or four screws holding the blower motor in the case and remove the motor with the fan attached.

3. Installation is the reverse of removal. Refer to the exploded view of the heater assembly.

1980–81 200SX

▶ **See Figure 8**

1. Disconnect the battery ground cable. Remove the instrument panel lower cover and cluster lid on the right-hand side.

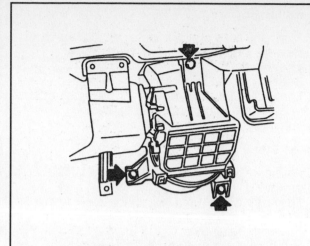

Fig. 8 Remove the bolts retaining the blower assembly—1980–81 200SX

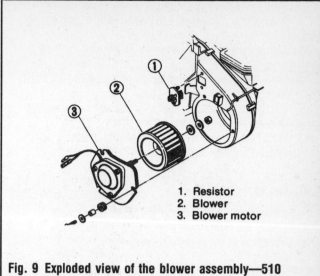

1. Resistor
2. Blower
3. Blower motor

Fig. 9 Exploded view of the blower assembly—510

2. Disconnect the control cable and harness connector from the blower unit.

3. Remove the three bolts and remove the blower unit.

4. Remove the three screws holding the blower motor in the case, unplug the hose running from the rear of the motor into the case and pull the motor together with the fan cage out of the case.

5. Installation is the reverse of removal. Make sure the electrical connection is installed in the correct position.

810 and Maxima

➡**It may be necessary to remove the glove box assembly to gain clearance for heater blower removal and installation. The blower motor is located behind the glove box, facing the floor.**

1. Disconnect the negative battery cable. Remove the heater duct running from the blower case to the heater unit.

2. Disconnect the control cable from the blower case and the harness connector.

3. Remove the screws holding the blower case in place and remove the blower case.

4. Remove the three bolts holding the blower motor in place and remove the blower motor.

5. Installation is the reverse of removal. Make sure the electrical connection is installed in the correct position.

510

◆ **See Figure 9**

1. Disconnect the battery ground cable and the blower motor harness connector.

2. Remove the blower motor by removing the three outer retaining screws and pulling the motor with the fan out of the case.

➡**Make sure you remove the three outer screws and not the three screws holding the motor to the backing plate.**

3. Installation is the reverse of removal. Make sure the electrical connection is installed in the correct position.

Heater Core

REMOVAL & INSTALLATION

610 and 710

➡**The heater unit need not be removed to remove the heater core. It must be removed to remove the blower motor.**

1. Drain the coolant and remove the coolant hoses.

✳✳ CAUTION

When draining the coolant, keep in mind that cats and dogs are attracted by ethylene glycol antifreeze, and are quite likely to drink any that is left in an uncovered container or in puddles on the ground. This will prove fatal in sufficient quantity. Always drain the coolant into a sealable container. Coolant should be reused unless it is contaminated or several years old.

2. Disconnect the control cables on the sides of the heater unit.

3. Remove the clips and the cover from the front of the heater unit. Pull out the core.

4. Reverse the procedure for installation. Run the engine with the heater on for a few minutes to make sure that the system fills with coolant. Always use new heater hose clamps.

1977–79 200SX

1. Remove the heater assembly from the vehicle.

2. Remove the control lever assembly. Remove the knobs, disconnect the lamp wire, remove the center vent (4 screws), disconnect the fan wires, remove the clips and cables, remove the retaining screws and the unit.

3. Disconnect the hose from the heater cock.

4. Remove the connection rod (with bracket) from the air door.

5. Remove the clips on each side of the box, split the box, and remove the core.

6. Install the heater core in the correct location. Reconnect the heater box with the retaining clips.

7. Install the connection rod (with bracket) to the air door.

8. Connect the hose to the heater cock.

9. Install the control lever assembly with attaching parts.

10. Install the heater assembly in the vehicle.

1980 and Later 200SX

1. Remove the heater unit and the heater core hoses.
2. Remove the heater core from the heater unit box.
3. Installation is the reverse of removal.

810 and Maxima

1. Remove the heater assembly. Loosen the clips and screws and remove the center ventilation cover and heater control assembly.

2. Remove the screws securing the door shafts.

3. Remove the clips securing the left and right heater cases, and then separate the cases. Remove the heater core.

4. Installation is in the reverse order of removal.

1978–81 510

1. Remove the heater unit. Loosen the hose clamps and disconnect the inlet and outlet hoses.

2. Remove the clips securing the case halves and separate the cases.

3. Remove the heater core.

4. Installation is in the reverse order of removal.

AIR CONDITIONER

Compressor

➡ **Refer to Section 1 for Charging and Discharging procedures.**

REMOVAL & INSTALLATION

All Models

✳✳ CAUTION

The compressed refrigerant used in the air conditioning system expands into the atmosphere at a temperature of −2°F (−19° C) or lower. This will freeze any surface, including your eyes, that it contacts. In addition, the refrigerant decomposes into a poisonous gas in the presence of a flame. Do not open or disconnect any part of the air conditioning system until you have read the SAFETY WARNINGS section in Section 1.

1. Disconnect the negative battery cables.

2. Remove all the necessary equipment in order to gain access to the compressor mounting bolts.

3. Remove the compressor drive belt.

➡ **To facilitate removal of the compressor belt, remove the idler pulley and bracket as an assembly beforehand from the underside of the car.**

4. Discharge the air conditioning system.

5. Disconnect and plug the refrigerant lines with a clean shop towel.

➡ **Be sure to use 2 wrenches (one to loosen fitting—one to hold fitting in place) when disconnecting the refrigerant lines.**

6. Disconnect and tag all electrical connections.

7. Remove the compressor mounting bolts. Remove the compressor from the vehicle.

8. Install the compressor on the engine and evenly torque all the mounting bolts the same.

9. Connect all the electrical connections and unplug and reconnect all refrigerant lines.

10. Install all the necessary equipment in order to gain access to the compressor mounting bolts.

11. Install and adjust the drive belt.

12. Connect the negative battery cable.

13. Evacuate and charge the system as required. Make sure the oil level is correct for the compressor.

➡ **Do not attempt to the leave the compressor on its side or upside down for more than a couple minutes, as the oil in the compressor will enter the low pressure chambers. Be sure to always replace the O-rings.**

Condenser

➡ **Refer to Section 1 for Charging and Discharging procedures.**

REMOVAL & INSTALLATION

All Models

✳✳ CAUTION

The compressed refrigerant used in the air conditioning system expands into the atmosphere at a temperature of −2°F (−19dg C) or lower. This will freeze any surface, including your eyes, that it contacts. In addition, the refrigerant decomposes into a poisonous gas in the presence of a flame. Do not open or disconnect any part of the air conditioning system until you have read the SAFETY WARNINGS section in Section 1.

1. Disconnect the negative battery cables.

2. Remove the necessary components in order to gain access

to the condenser retaining bolts. If equipped, remove the condenser fan motor, as necessary.

3. Discharge the system. Remove the condenser refrigerant lines and plug them with a clean shop towel.

➡ **On the 200SX models the receiver drier assembly should be removed before removing the condenser.**

4. Remove the condenser retaining bolts. Remove the condenser from the vehicle.

5. Install the condenser in the vehicle and evenly torque all the mounting bolts the same.

➡ **Always use new O-rings in all refrigerant lines.**

6. Reconnect all the refrigerant lines.

7. Install all the necessary equipment in order to gain access to the condenser mounting bolts. If removed, install the condenser fan motor.

8. Connect the negative battery cable.

9. Evacuate and charge the system as required.

Evaporator Core/Cooling Unit

REMOVAL & INSTALLATION

510, 610 and 710 Models
▶ See Figures 10, 11, 12 and 13

➡ **On some models an air filter is installed between the evaporator housing and the air intake housing. This filter should be cleaned once a year. The evaporator housing and cooling unit are the same part.**

1. Disconnect battery ground cable.

2. Discharge air conditioning system, refer to Section 1 for more details.

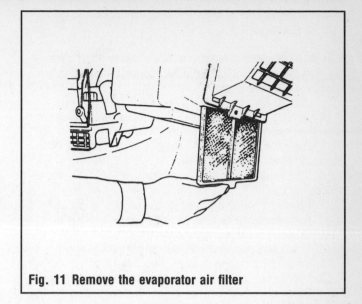

Fig. 11 Remove the evaporator air filter

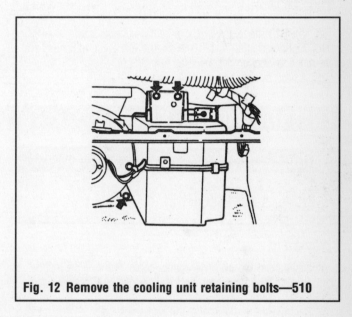

Fig. 12 Remove the cooling unit retaining bolts—510

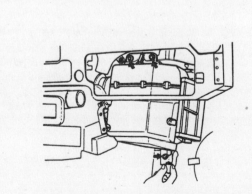

Fig. 10 Remove the evaporator housing retainer bolts—610

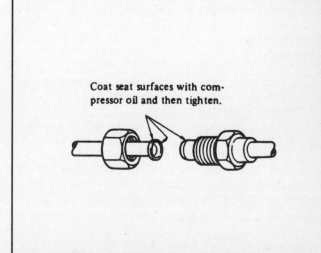

Coat seat surfaces with compressor oil and then tighten.

Fig. 13 Typical A/C fittings—always use new O-rings

3. Loosen flare nuts at each connection of inlet and outlet pipes of evaporator.

➡ **Be sure to use two wrenches when removing or connecting pipe joints. Always plug pipe openings immediately after pipe disconnection.**

4. Remove the instrument cluster lid cover. On 610 models remove the center console box.
5. Disconnect all electrical connections and control cables from cooling unit.
6. Remove the upper and lower attaching bolts and remove the cooling unit.
7. Remove all attaching parts from cooling unit.
8. Remove screws or clips securing upper case to lower case.
9. Separated case and remove the evaporator.
10. Install evaporator core in cooling unit case.
11. Install the attaching parts on the cooling unit.
12. Install the cooling unit with retaining bolts in the vehicle.
13. Connect all electrical connections and control cables. Reconnect the pressure pipes with new O-rings. Install the instrument cluster lid cover.
14. On 610 models, install the center console box.
15. Connect battery cable and charge the air conditioning system. Refer to Section 1 if necessary.
16. Check system for proper operation.

ENTERTAINMENT SYSTEMS

Radio

REMOVAL & INSTALLATION

610 and 710

1. Disconnect the negative battery cable. Remove the instrument cluster. Disconnect all electrical connections, antenna and the speaker connections.
2. Remove the radio knobs and retaining nuts.
3. Remove the rear support bracket and remove the radio.
4. Reverse the procedure for installation.

1977–79 200SX

◆ **See Figure 14**

1. Disconnect the negative battery cable. The instrument panel must be removed in order to remove the radio.
2. Pull out the radio switch knobs.
3. In order to remove the instrument panel, first remove the steering wheel and cover.
4. Remove the control knobs on the instrument panel by pushing in on them and turning them counterclockwise. Once the knobs are removed, remove the nuts.
5. Remove the instrument panel screws. See the illustration for their location.

810 and Maxima; 1977–81 200SX

1. Disconnect battery ground cable.
2. Remove the instrument lower cover and cluster lid cover.
3. Discharge air conditioning system, refer to Section 1 for more details.
4. Disconnect refrigerant lines and electrical harness from the cooling unit.

➡ **Be sure to use two wrenches when removing or connecting pipe joints. Always plug pipe openings immediately after pipe disconnection.**

5. Remove the cooling unit with drain tube.
6. Remove the clips fixing the upper case to lower case.
7. Remove the evaporator core from the cooling unit.
8. Install the evaporator core in the cooling unit. Connect lower and upper case with retaining clips.
9. Install the cooling unit with retaining bolts in the vehicle.
10. Connect all electrical connections. Reconnect the pressure pipes with new O-rings. Install the instrument lower cover and cluster lid cover.
11. Connect battery cable and charge the air conditioning system. Refer to Section 1 if necessary.
12. Check system for proper operation.

6. Disconnect the switch wires (after noting their location) and remove the panel.
7. Loosen the screws and remove the radio from its bracket. Disconnect the wires and pull the radio free.
To install:
8. Install the radio in the radio bracket and connect all electrical connections, speaker wires and antenna.
9. Connect all electrical connections and install the instrument panel and all knobs.
10. Install the steering wheel in the correct position.
11. Reconnect the battery cable. Start the engine and check all components on the instrument panel for proper operation.

1980–81 200SX

1. Disconnect the negative battery cable. Before removing the radio (audio assembly), you must remove the center instrument cluster which holds the heater controls, etc. Remove the two side screws in the cluster. Remove the heater control and the control panel. Remove the two bolts behind the heater control panel and the two bolts at the case of the cluster. Pull the cluster out of the way after disconnecting the lighter wiring and any other control cables.
2. Remove the radio knobs and fronting panel.
3. Remove the five screws holding the radio assembly in place.
4. Remove the radio after unplugging all connections.
5. Installation is the reverse of removal.

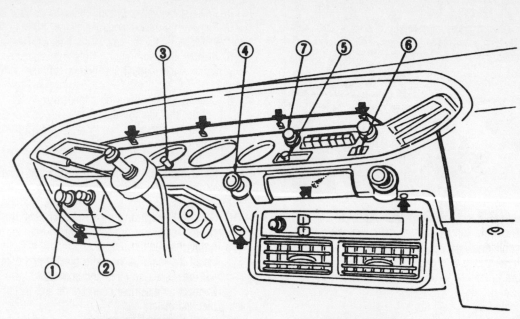

1. Light switch
2. Illumination control knob
3. Trip meter knob
4. Windshield wiper and washer switch knob
5. Hazard switch
6. Rear defogger switch
7. Radio knob

Fig. 14 Instrument panel removal points (arrows)—1977–79 200SX

810 and Maxima

1. Disconnect the battery ground cable. Remove the knobs and nuts on the radio and the choke control wire. Remove the ash tray.

2. If necessary, remove the heater/air conditioning control panel to access the radio's mounting screws.

3. Remove the steering column cover, and disconnect the main harness connectors.

4. Remove the retaining screws and remove the instrument panel cover.

5. Disconnect the wires from the radio and remove the radio from the bracket.

6. Installation is in the reverse order of removal.

To remove the radio from some models, you must first remove the climate control switch panel

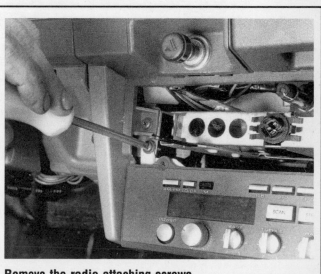

Remove the radio attaching screws

Carefully pull the radio out of its mounting—unplug the wiring harness and antenna cable (arrow)

1978–81 510

▶ **See Figure 15**

➡**Refer to the 1978 510 instrument panel removal points illustration.**

1. Disconnect the battery ground cable.
2. Remove the steering column covers and disconnect the hazard warning switch connector.

3. Loosen the wiper switch attaching screws and remove the wiper switch.
4. Pull out the ash tray and the heater control knobs.
5. Remove the heater control finisher. Insert a screwdriver into the FAN lever slit to remove the finisher. Remove finisher A.
6. Remove the radio knobs, nuts and washers.
7. Remove the manual choke knob and the defroster control knob.
8. Disconnect the following connectors:
   a. center illumination light
   b. cigarette lighter
   c. clock
   d. turn signal switch.
9. Remove the screws from the instrument panel (referred to as cluster lid A in the illustration). The black arrows mark the screws locations.
10. Remove the instrument panel cover. Remove the connections from the radio and remove the radio from its bracket.

To install:

11. Install the radio in the radio bracket and connect all electrical connections, speaker wires and antenna.
12. Connect all electrical connections and install the instrument panel and cover.
13. Install the ashtray assembly, all knobs, heater control finisher and any other electrical connection if necessary.
14. Install the wiper switch assembly. Connect the hazard warning switch connector. Install the steering column covers.
15. Reconnect the battery cable. Start the engine check all components on the instrument panel for proper operation.

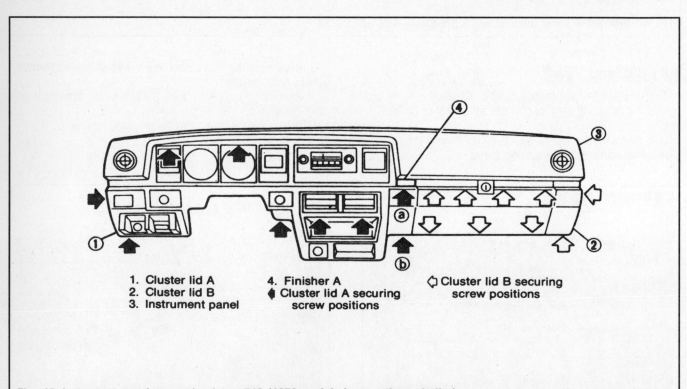

1. Cluster lid A
2. Cluster lid B
3. Instrument panel
4. Finisher A
◀ Cluster lid A securing screw positions
◁ Cluster lid B securing screw positions

Fig. 15 Instrument panel removal points—510 (1978 model shown, others similar)

WINDSHIELD WIPER

Blade and Arm

REMOVAL & INSTALLATION

All Models

1. Pull the wiper arm up.
2. Push the lock pin, then remove the wiper blade.
3. Insert the new wiper blade to the wiper arm until a click sounds.
4. Make sure the wiper blade contacts the glass. Otherwise, the arm may be damaged.
5. To remove the arm assembly lift the end of the wiper arm, which is spring loaded, at the base and remove the attaching nut. On early models just remove the attaching nut at the base of the wiper arm.

Windshield Wiper Motor and Linkage

REMOVAL & INSTALLATION

610, 710, 810, Maxima and 1977–79 200SX

◗ **See Figure 16**

1. Disconnect the battery ground cable. The wiper motor and linkage are accessible from under the hood. Raise the wiper blade from the windshield and remove the retaining nut. Remove the wiper blades and arms.
2. Remove the nuts holding the wiper pivots to the body. Remove the screws holding the wiper motor to the firewall.
3. Disconnect the wiper motor wiring connector and remove the cowl air intake grille.
4. Disconnect the wiper motor from the linkage and remove the linkage assembly through the cowl top.
5. Installation is the reverse of removal.

➡️**If the wipers do not park correctly, adjust the position of the automatic stop cover of the wiper motor, if so equipped.**

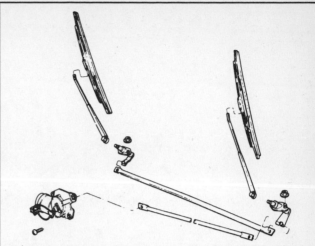

Fig. 16 Exploded view of a common windshield wiper motor and linkage

1978–81 510

1. Disconnect the battery ground cable. Remove the wiper motor.
2. Remove the wiper link inspection cover under the hood.
3. Remove the wiper arms from the pivot shafts by lifting the arms then removing the attaching nuts.
4. Loosen and remove the large nuts securing the pivot shafts to the body. Remove the linkage through the inspection hole.
5. Installation is the reverse of removal.

➡️**Make sure you install the wiper arms in the correct positions by running the system without the arms on, stopping it, then attaching the arms.**

1980–81 200SX

1. Disconnect the battery ground cable.
2. Open the hood and disconnect the motor wiring connection.
3. Unbolt the motor from the body.
4. Disconnect the wiper linkage from the motor and remove the motor.
5. Installation is the reverse of removal.

INSTRUMENTS AND SWITCHES

Instrument Cluster

REMOVAL & INSTALLATION

610 and 710

◗ **See Figure 17**

➡️**It may be necessary to drop the steering column to aid removal. Refer to the exploded view of the 710 instrument cluster removal illustration. Tag all wiring for correct installation.**

1. Disconnect the battery ground cable.
2. Remove the four screws and the steering column cover.
3. Remove the screws which attach the cluster face. Two are just above the steering column, and there is one inside each of the outer instrument recesses.
4. Pull the cluster lid forward.
5. Disconnect the multiple connector.
6. Disconnect the speedometer cable.
7. Disconnect any other wiring.
8. Remove the cluster face.
9. Remove the odometer knob if so equipped.
10. Remove the six screws and the cluster. Instruments may now be readily replaced.

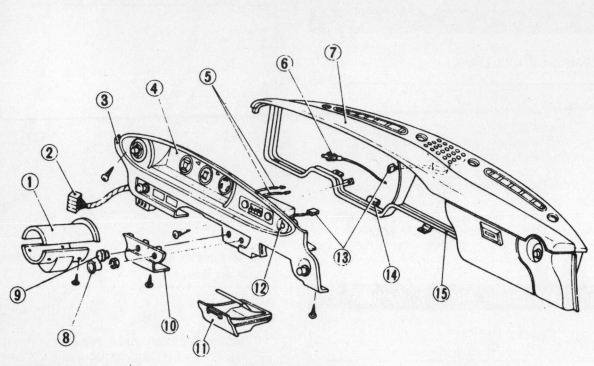

1. Steering column covers
2. Instrument harness
3. Cluster cover
4. Gauges
5. Light monitor
6. Speedometer cable
7. Upper instrument pad
8. Wiper/washer switch knob
9. Light control switch
10. Cluster cover
11. Ash tray
12. Clock
13. Speaker harness
14. Illumination bulb
15. Instrument panel

Fig. 17 Exploded view of the instrument cluster assembly—710

To install:

11. Reconnect all electrical connections and speedometer cable to the instrument cluster. Install the cluster in position with retaining screws.

12. Install the odometer knob if so equipped.

13. Install the cluster face and the steering column cover.

14. Reconnect the battery ground cable.

1977–80 810

1. Disconnect the battery ground cable. Remove the knobs and nuts on the radio and the knob on the choke control wire. Remove the ashtray.

2. Remove the steering column covers.

3. Disconnect the harness connectors after noting their location and marking them.

4. Remove the retaining screws and remove the instrument panel.

5. Installation is in the reverse order of removal.

1977–79 200SX

▶ **See Figure 18**

➡ **This procedure is for instrument panel and cluster. Refer to the exploded view of 1977–79 200SX instrument panel illustration.**

1. Disconnect the battery ground cable.

2. Remove the steering column covers.

3. Disconnect the speedometer cable and the radio antenna.

4. Disconnect all the wires from the back of the panel after noting their location and marking them.

5. Remove the bolts which secure the steering column clamp. Remove the package tray.

6. Unbolt the panel from the brackets on the left and right-hand sides.

7. Remove the right side windshield pillar trim and remove the bolt which attaches the panel to the pillar.

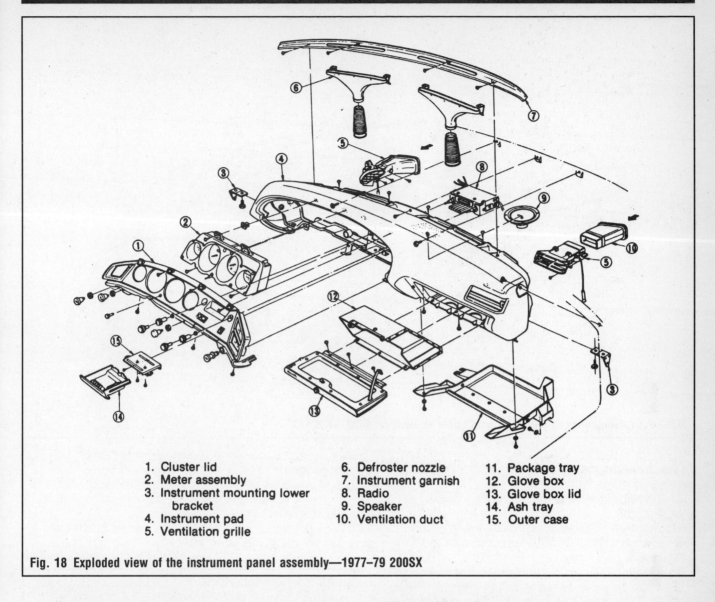

1. Cluster lid
2. Meter assembly
3. Instrument mounting lower bracket
4. Instrument pad
5. Ventilation grille
6. Defroster nozzle
7. Instrument garnish
8. Radio
9. Speaker
10. Ventilation duct
11. Package tray
12. Glove box
13. Glove box lid
14. Ash tray
15. Outer case

Fig. 18 Exploded view of the instrument panel assembly—1977–79 200SX

8. Remove the instrument garnish.

9. Remove the retaining bolts and remove the panel.

To install:

10. Install the panel with retaining bolts in the correct position. Install the instrument garnish.

11. Reconnect all the wires to the back of the panel in the correct location.

12. Connect the speedometer cable, radio antenna and steering column covers.

13. Install the right side windshield pillar trim, steering column clamp and package tray.

14. Reconnect the battery ground cable.

1980–81 200SX

▶ **See Figure 19**

1. Disconnect the battery ground terminal. It may be necessary to remove the steering wheel and covers to remove the instrument cluster.

2. Remove the five bolts holding the cluster in place and pull the cluster out, then remove all connections from its back. Make sure you mark the wiring to avoid confusion during reassembly.

3. Remove the instrument cluster.

4. Installation is the reverse of removal.

1978–81 510

➡**Refer to 1978 510 instrument panel removal points illustration.**

1. Disconnect the battery ground cable.

2. Remove the steering column covers. Disconnect the hazard warning switch connector.

3. Remove the wiper switch. Pull out the ashtray, remove the heater, control knobs, and remove the heater control plate by inserting a screwdriver into the fan lever slit and levering the plate out.

4. Remove the finish plate to the left of the glove compartment.

5. Pull off the radio knobs and remove the nuts and washers.

6. Remove the choke and side defroster knobs.

7. Remove the cluster lid screws.

8. Disconnect the electrical connectors.

9. Remove the cluster lid.

10. Remove the instrument cluster retaining screws. Disconnect

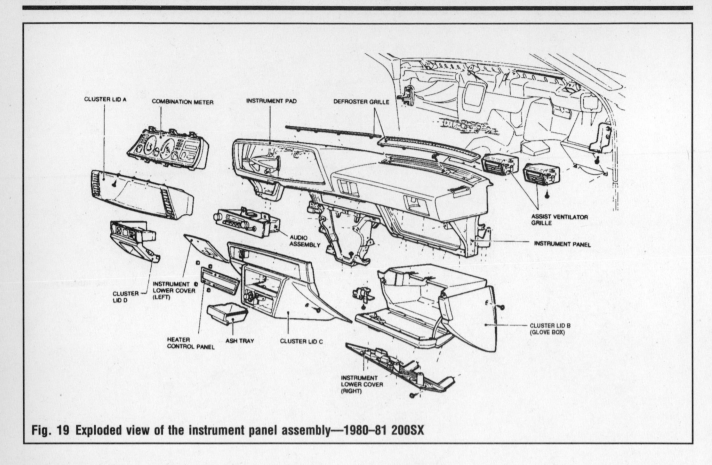

Fig. 19 Exploded view of the instrument panel assembly—1980–81 200SX

the speedometer cable by pushing and turning counterclockwise.

11. Disconnect the instrument cluster wire connectors and remove the cluster.

12. Reconnect all electrical connections and speedometer cable to the instrument cluster. Install the cluster in position with retaining screws.

To install:

13. Install the cluster lid and all knobs.

14. Install the finish plate to the left of the glove compartment.

15. Install the wiper switch, ashtray, heater control knobs and heater control plate.

16. Connect the electrical connection for the hazard warning switch and install the steering column covers.

17. Reconnect the battery ground cable.

1981–84 810/Maxima

▶ **See Figures 20, 21 and 22**

1. Disconnect the negative battery cable. Remove the instrument lower cover.

2. Remove the steering wheel, if necessary.

3. Disconnect the speedometer cable. Remove the six mounting screws and lift out the cluster lid.

4. Unscrew the mounting bolts and lift off the left side instrument pad (this is the hooded part of the dashboard that the instrument cluster sits in).

5. Loosen the instrument cluster mounting screws, pull it out slightly and disconnect all wiring. Remove the cluster.

To install:

6. Reconnect all electrical connections and speedometer cable to the instrument cluster. Install the cluster in position with retaining screws.

7. Install the steering wheel and the instrument lower cover. Reconnect the negative battery cable.

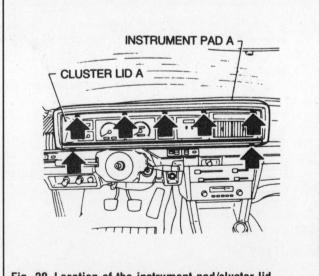

Fig. 20 Location of the instrument pad/cluster lid mounting screws—Maxima

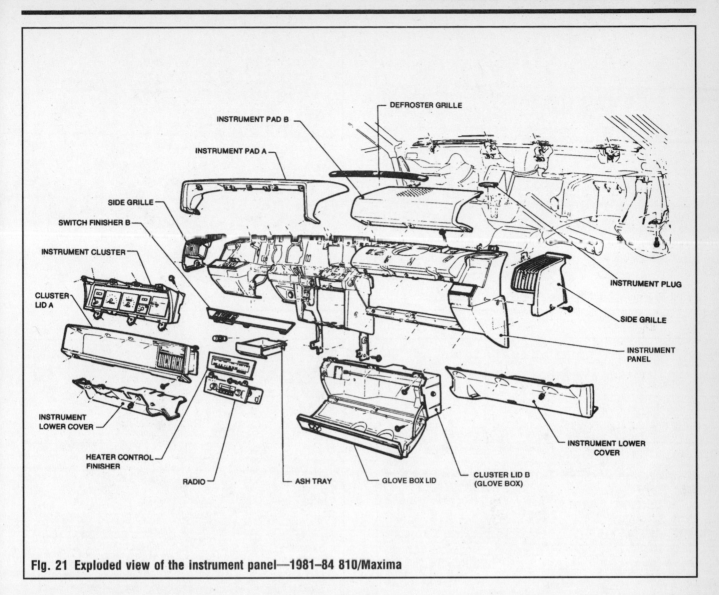

Fig. 21 Exploded view of the instrument panel—1981–84 810/Maxima

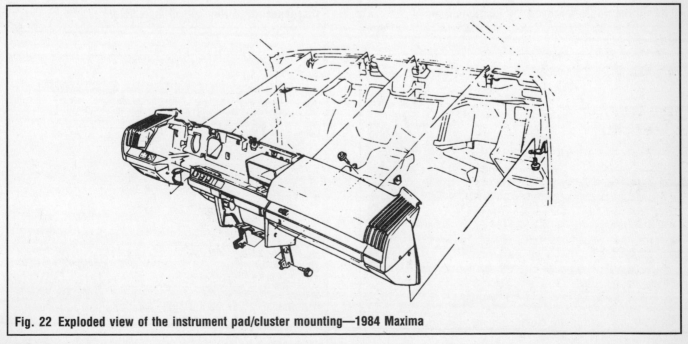

Fig. 22 Exploded view of the instrument pad/cluster mounting—1984 Maxima

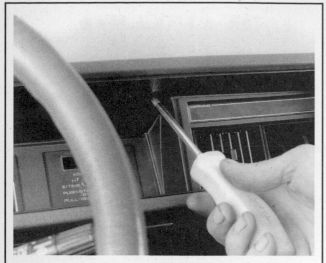

Remove the mounting screws from the cluster lid

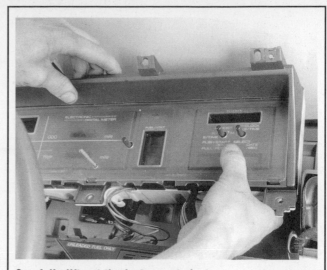

Carefully lift out the instrument cluster

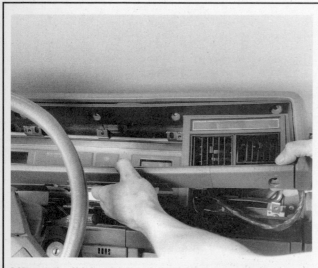

Lift out the lid from around the instrument panel

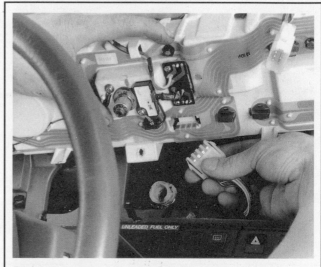

Disconnect all wiring behind the cluster

Remove the instrument cluster mounting screws

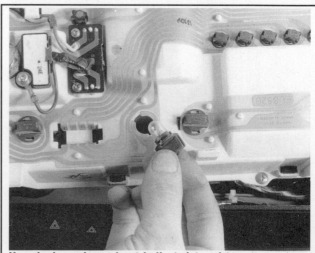

If replacing a burned out bulb, twist and turn to remove it from the printed circuit board

Ignition Switch

Ignition switch removal and installation procedures are covered in Section 8, Suspension and Steering.

Speedometer Cable

REMOVAL & INSTALLATION

1. Remove any lower dash covers that may be in the way and disconnect the speedometer cable from the back of the speedometer.

➡**On some models it may be easier to remove the instrument cluster to gain access to the cable.**

2. Remove the cable from the cable housing. On late models, press the tab at the top of the connector behind the speedometer to release it. If the cable is broken, the other half of the cable will

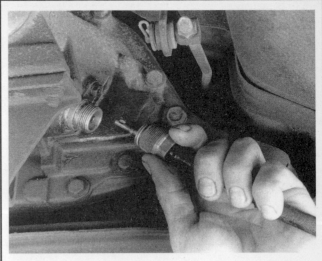

Unscrew, then remove the cable from the transmission

If the speedometer cable is broken, you must remove the other end (arrow) from the transmission

If necessary to remove the cable drive, unfasten the mounting screw . . .

Loosen the locking nut from the speedometer cable at the transmission

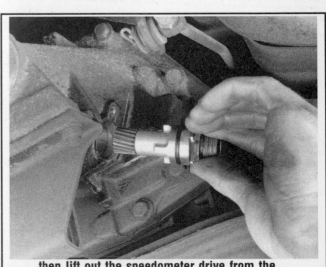

. . . then lift out the speedometer drive from the transmission

have to be removed from the transmission end. Unscrew the retaining knob at the transmission and remove the cable from the transmission extension housing.

To install:

3. Lubricate the cable with graphite power (sold as speedometer cable lubricant) and feed the cable into the housing. It is best to start at the speedometer end and feed the cable down towards the transmission. It is also usually necessary to unscrew the transmission connection and install the cable end to the gear, then reconnect the housing to the transmission. Slip the cable end into the speedometer and reconnect the cable housing.

Seat Belt Warning Buzzer and Light

GENERAL INFORMATION

1973 610

Beginning in 1971, all cars were required to have a warning system which operates a buzzer and warning system light if either of the front seat belts are not fastened when the seats are occupied and the car is in a forward gear. A light with the words Seat Belts, or Fasten Seat Belts is located on the dashboard while a buzzer is located under the dash. They are controlled by pressure sensitive switches hidden in the front bench or bucket seats. A switch in each of the front seat belt retractors turns off the warning system only when the belt or belts are pulled a specified distance out of their retractors.

Two different types of switches are used to control the system, depending upon the type of transmission used.

On manual transmission equipped cars, the transmission neutral switch is used to activate the seat belt warning circuit.

Automatic transmissions use the inhibitor switch to activate the seat belt warning circuit.

When removing the seats, be sure to unplug the pressure sensitive switches at their connections.

Seat Belt/Starter Interlock System

GENERAL INFORMATION

1974–75 Vehicles

As required by law, all 1974 and most 1975 Datsun passenger cars cannot be started until the front seat occupants are seated and have fastened their seat belts. If the proper sequence is not followed, e.g., the occupants fasten the seat belts and then sit on them, the engine cannot be started.

The shoulder harness and lap belt are permanently fastened together, so that they both must be worn. The shoulder harness uses an inertia lock reel to allow freedom of movement under normal driving conditions.

➡**This type of reel locks up when the car decelerates rapidly, as during a crash.**

The switches for the interlock system have been removed from the lap belt retractors and placed in the belt buckles. The seat sensors remain the same as those used in 1973.

For ease of service, the car may be started from outside, by reaching in and turning the key, but without depressing the seat sensors.

In case of system failure, an override switch is located under the hood. This is a one-start switch and it must be reset each time it is used.

LIGHTING

Headlights

REMOVAL & INSTALLATION

◆ **See Figures 23 and 24**

➡**Many Datsuns have radiator grilles which are unit constructed to also serve as headlight frames. In this case, it will be necessary to remove the grille to gain access to the headlights.**

1. Remove the grille, if necessary.
2. Remove the headlight retaining ring screws. These are the three or four short screws in the assembly. There are also two longer screws at the top and side of the headlight which are used to aim the headlight. Do not tamper with these or the headlight will have to be reaimed.
3. Remove the ring on round headlights by turning it clockwise.
4. Pull the headlight bulb from its socket and disconnect the electrical plug.
5. Connect the plug to the new bulb.
6. Position the headlight in the shell. Make sure that the word TOP is, indeed, at the top and that the knobs in the headlight lens engage the slots in the mounting shell.

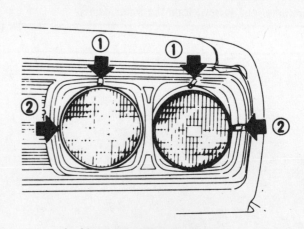

1. Vertical adjustment
2. Horizontal adjustment

Fig. 23 Adjust the headlights by turning the indicated screws—most models similar

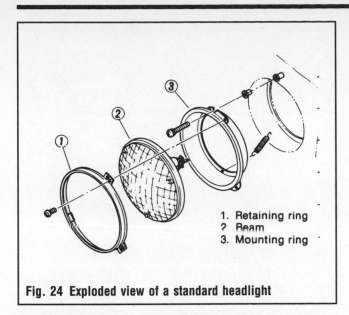

1. Retaining ring
2. Beam
3. Mounting ring

Fig. 24 Exploded view of a standard headlight

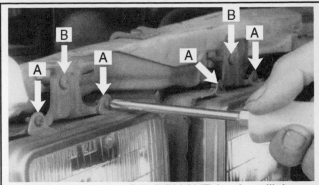

A. Trim ring screw - DO REMOVE for headlight removal and installation
B. Adjuster screw - DO NOT turn unless realigning the lights

DO remove the trim ring screws (A)—DO NOT turn any adjuster screws (B)

Remove the bezel attaching screws . . .

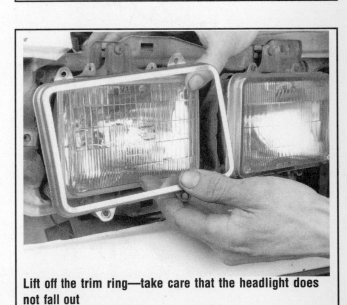

Lift off the trim ring—take care that the headlight does not fall out

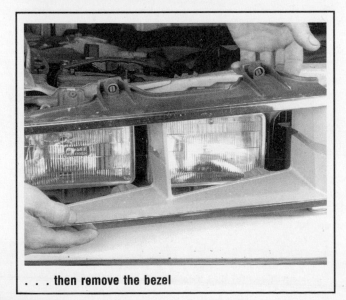

. . . then remove the bezel

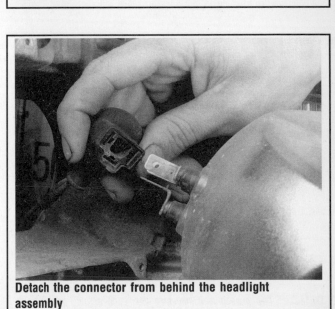

Detach the connector from behind the headlight assembly

7. Place the retaining ring over the bulb and install the screws.
8. Install the grille, if removed.

Signal and Marker Lights

REMOVAL & INSTALLATION

▶ **See Figure 25**

Front Turn Signal and Parking Lights

1. Remove turn signal/parking light lens with retaining screws.
2. Slightly depress the bulb and turn it counterclockwise to release it.

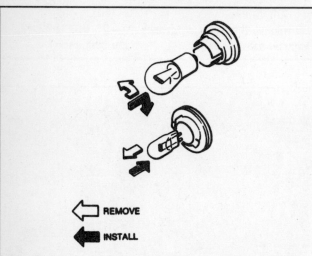

⇦ REMOVE

⬅ INSTALL

Fig. 25 Install or remove the signal or marker light bulb as shown

To install:

3. Carefully push down and turn bulb clockwise at the same time.
4. Install the turn signal/parking light lens with retaining screws.

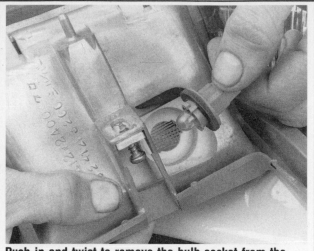

Push in and twist to remove the bulb socket from the turn signal lens

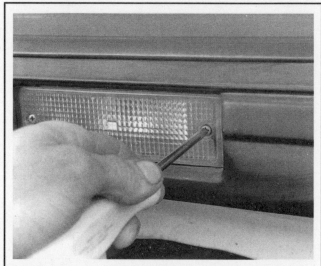

Remove the attaching screws from the parking light lens

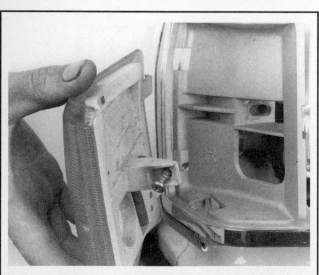

Unfasten the screw and remove the turn signal lens

Push in, twist and turn the parking light bulb

Side Marker Lights

1. Remove side marker light lens with retaining screws.
2. Turn the bulb socket counterclockwise to release it from lens.
3. Pull bulb straight out.

To install:

4. Carefully push the bulb straight in.
5. Turn the bulb socket clockwise to install it in lens.
6. Install side marker light lens with retaining screws.

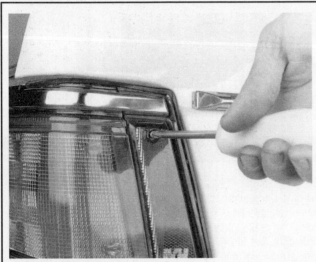

Remove the attaching screws from the side marker light

Lift off the reflective side marker lens

Remove the attaching screw from the bulb socket

Pull the marker light bulb from the socket

Rear Turn Signal, Brake and Parking Lights

1. Remove rear trim panel in rear of vehicle if necessary to gain access to the bulb socket.
2. Slightly depress the bulb and turn it counterclockwise to release it.

To install:

3. To install the bulb carefully push down and turn bulb clockwise at the same time.
4. Install trim panel if necessary.

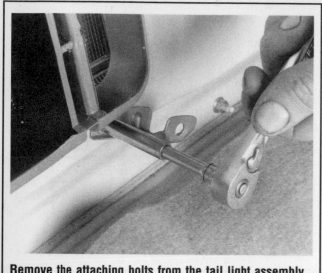

Remove the attaching bolts from the tail light assembly

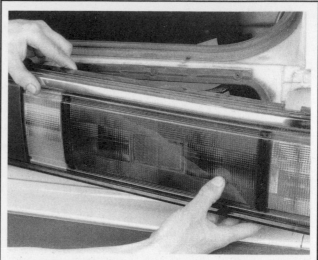

Lift out the tail light assembly from the vehicle

TRAILER WIRING

Wiring the vehicle for towing is fairly easy. There are a number of good wiring kits available and these should be used, rather than trying to design your own.

All trailers will need brake lights and turn signals as well as tail lights and side marker lights. Most areas require extra marker lights for overwide trailers. Also, most areas have recently required back-up lights for trailers, and most trailer manufacturers have been building trailers with back-up lights for several years.

Additionally, some Class I, most Class II and just about all Class III trailers will have electric brakes. Add to this number an accessories wire, to operate trailer internal equipment or to charge the trailer's battery, and you can have as many as seven wires in the harness.

Determine the equipment on your trailer and buy the wiring kit necessary. The kit will contain all the wires needed, plus a plug adapter set which includes the female plug, mounted on the bumper or hitch, and the male plug, wired into, or plugged into the trailer harness.

When installing the kit, follow the manufacturer's instructions.

The color coding of the wires is usually standard throughout the industry. One point to note: some domestic vehicles, and most imported vehicles, have separate turn signals. On most domestic vehicles, the brake lights and rear turn signals operate with the same bulb. For those vehicles with separate turn signals, you can purchase an isolation unit so that the brake lights won't blink whenever the turn signals are operated, or, you can go to your local electronics supply house and buy four diodes to wire in series with the brake and turn signal bulbs. Diodes will isolate the brake and turn signals. The choice is yours. The isolation units are simple and quick to install, but far more expensive than the diodes. The diodes, however, require more work to install properly, since they require the cutting of each bulb's wire and soldering in place of the diode.

One, final point, the best kits are those with a spring loaded cover on the vehicle mounted socket. This cover prevents dirt and moisture from corroding the terminals. Never let the vehicle socket hang loosely; always mount it securely to the bumper or hitch.

CIRCUIT PROTECTION

Fuses

◆ See Figure 26

The fuses can be easily inspected to see if they are blown. Simply pull the fuse from the block, inspect it and replace it with a new one, if necessary.

➡**When replacing a blown fuse, be certain to replace it with one of the correct amperage.**

Fusible Links

◆ See Figure 27

A fusible link(s) is a protective device used in an electrical circuit. When current increases beyond a certain amperage, the fusible metal wire of the link melts, thus breaking the electrical circuit and preventing further damage to the other components and wiring. Whenever a fusible link is melted because of a short circuit, correct the cause before installing a new link. All fusible links are the plug-in kind. To replace them, simply unplug the bad link and insert the new one.

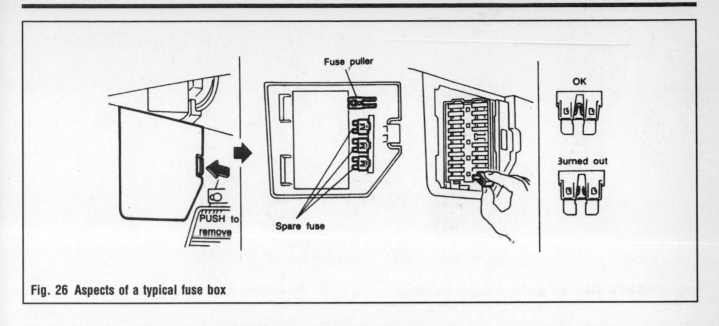

Fig. 26 Aspects of a typical fuse box

Fuse Box and Flasher Location

Year	Model	Fuse Box Location	Flasher Location
1973–77	610, 710	Under instrument panel	Top of pedal assembly ①
1977–80	810	Right side kick panel	Under driver's side of dashboard ①
1981–84	810/Maxima (rear wheel drive)	Underneath glove box	Under driver's side of dashboard, near steering column
1977–79	200SX	Underneath glove box	Turn signal: Behind radio Hazard: Behind glove box
1980–81	200SX	Underneath glove box	Under driver's side dashboard ①
1978–81	510	Under instrument panel, Next to hood release	Under driver's side dashboard ①

① Both the turn signal and the hazard flashers are side by side

NOTE: The original turn signal flasher unit is pink, and larger than the original hazard flasher unit, which is gold.

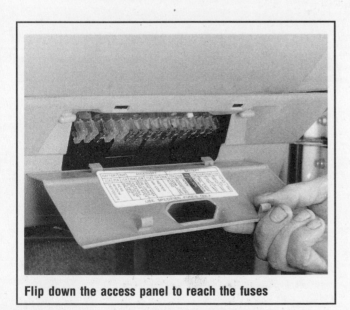

Flip down the access panel to reach the fuses

Remove the blown fuse and replace it with a good one

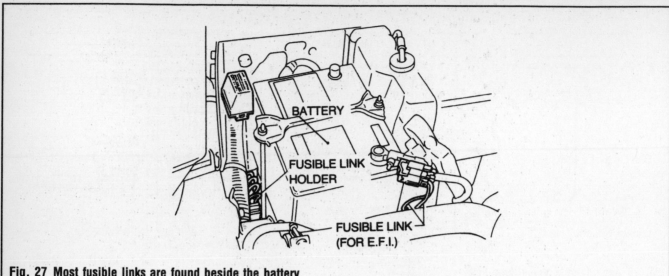

Fig. 27 Most fusible links are found beside the battery

Fusible Links

Year	Model	Number	Location
1973–74	610	2	At positive battery terminal
1976 1974–77	610 710	4	On relay bracket, front right side of engine compartment
1977–84	810/Maxima	6	On relay bracket, in engine compartment ①
1977–79	200SX	2	At positive battery terminal
1980–81	200SX	4	At positive battery terminal
1978–81	510	2	At positive battery terminal

① The fusible links for the fuel injection and the glow plugs (diesel) are located at the positive battery terminal

Circuit Breakers

Circuit breakers are also located in the fuse block. A circuit breaker is an electrical switch which breaks the circuit during an electrical overload. The circuit breaker will remain open until the short or overload condition in the circuit is corrected.

Flashers

To replace the flasher, carefully pull it from the electrical connector. If necessary, remove any component that restricts removal.

Troubleshooting the Heater

Problem	Cause	Solution
Blower motor will not turn at any speed	• Blown fuse • Loose connection • Defective ground • Faulty switch • Faulty motor • Faulty resistor	• Replace fuse • Inspect and tighten • Clean and tighten • Replace switch • Replace motor • Replace resistor
Blower motor turns at one speed only	• Faulty switch • Faulty resistor	• Replace switch • Replace resistor
Blower motor turns but does not circulate air	• Intake blocked • Fan not secured to the motor shaft	• Clean intake • Tighten security
Heater will not heat	• Coolant does not reach proper temperature • Heater core blocked internally • Heater core air-bound • Blend-air door not in proper position	• Check and replace thermostat if necessary • Flush or replace core if necessary • Purge air from core • Adjust cable
Heater will not defrost	• Control cable adjustment incorrect • Defroster hose damaged	• Adjust control cable • Replace defroster hose

Troubleshooting Basic Windshield Wiper Problems

Problem	Cause	Solution
Electric Wipers		
Wipers do not operate— Wiper motor heats up or hums	• Internal motor defect • Bent or damaged linkage • Arms improperly installed on linking pivots	• Replace motor • Repair or replace linkage • Position linkage in park and reinstall wiper arms
Wipers do not operate— No current to motor	• Fuse or circuit breaker blown • Loose, open or broken wiring • Defective switch • Defective or corroded terminals • No ground circuit for motor or switch	• Replace fuse or circuit breaker • Repair wiring and connections • Replace switch • Replace or clean terminals • Repair ground circuits
Wipers do not operate— Motor runs	• Linkage disconnected or broken	• Connect wiper linkage or replace broken linkage
Vacuum Wipers		
Wipers do not operate	• Control switch or cable inoperative • Loss of engine vacuum to wiper motor (broken hoses, low engine vacuum, defective vacuum/fuel pump) • Linkage broken or disconnected • Defective wiper motor	• Repair or replace switch or cable • Check vacuum lines, engine vacuum and fuel pump • Repair linkage • Replace wiper motor
Wipers stop on engine acceleration	• Leaking vacuum hoses • Dry windshield • Oversize wiper blades • Defective vacuum/fuel pump	• Repair or replace hoses • Wet windshield with washers • Replace with proper size wiper blades • Replace pump

Troubleshooting Basic Dash Gauge Problems

Problem	Cause	Solution
Coolant Temperature Gauge		
Gauge reads erratically or not at all	• Loose or dirty connections • Defective sending unit	• Clean/tighten connections • Bi-metal gauge: remove the wire from the sending unit. Ground the wire for an instant. If the gauge registers, replace the sending unit.
	• Defective gauge	• Magnetic gauge: disconnect the wire at the sending unit. With ignition ON gauge should register COLD. Ground the wire; gauge should register HOT.
Ammeter Gauge—Turn Headlights ON (do not start engine). Note reaction		
Ammeter shows charge Ammeter shows discharge Ammeter does not move	• Connections reversed on gauge • Ammeter is OK • Loose connections or faulty wiring • Defective gauge	• Reinstall connections • Nothing • Check/correct wiring • Replace gauge
Oil Pressure Gauge		
Gauge does not register or is inaccurate	• On mechanical gauge, Bourdon tube may be bent or kinked	• Check tube for kinks or bends preventing oil from reaching the gauge
	• Low oil pressure	• Remove sending unit. Idle the engine briefly. If no oil flows from sending unit hole, problem is in engine.
	• Defective gauge	• Remove the wire from the sending unit and ground it for an instant with the ignition ON. A good gauge will go to the top of the scale.
	• Defective wiring	• Check the wiring to the gauge. If it's OK and the gauge doesn't register when grounded, replace the gauge.
	• Defective sending unit	• If the wiring is OK and the gauge functions when grounded, replace the sending unit
All Gauges		
All gauges do not operate	• Blown fuse • Defective instrument regulator	• Replace fuse • Replace instrument voltage regulator
All gauges read low or erratically	• Defective or dirty instrument voltage regulator	• Clean contacts or replace
All gauges pegged	• Loss of ground between instrument voltage regulator and car • Defective instrument regulator	• Check ground • Replace regulator
Warning Lights		
Light(s) do not come on when ignition is ON, but engine is not started	• Defective bulb • Defective wire	• Replace bulb • Check wire from light to sending unit
	• Defective sending unit	• Disconnect the wire from the sending unit and ground it. Replace the sending unit if the light comes on with the ignition ON.
Light comes on with engine running	• Problem in individual system • Defective sending unit	• Check system • Check sending unit (see above)

Troubleshooting Basic Lighting Problems

Problem	Cause	Solution
Lights		
One or more lights don't work, but others do	• Defective bulb(s) • Blown fuse(s) • Dirty fuse clips or light sockets • Poor ground circuit	• Replace bulb(s) • Replace fuse(s) • Clean connections • Run ground wire from light socket housing to car frame
Lights burn out quickly	• Incorrect voltage regulator setting or defective regulator • Poor battery/alternator connections	• Replace voltage regulator • Check battery/alternator connections
Lights go dim	• Low/discharged battery • Alternator not charging • Corroded sockets or connections • Low voltage output	• Check battery • Check drive belt tension; repair or replace alternator • Clean bulb and socket contacts and connections • Replace voltage regulator
Lights flicker	• Loose connection • Poor ground • Circuit breaker operating (short circuit)	• Tighten all connections • Run ground wire from light housing to car frame • Check connections and look for bare wires
Lights "flare"—Some flare is normal on acceleration—if excessive, see "Lights Burn Out Quickly"	• High voltage setting	• Replace voltage regulator
Lights glare—approaching drivers are blinded	• Lights adjusted too high • Rear springs or shocks sagging • Rear tires soft	• Have headlights aimed • Check rear springs/shocks • Check/correct rear tire pressure
Turn Signals		
Turn signals don't work in either direction	• Blown fuse • Defective flasher • Loose connection	• Replace fuse • Replace flasher • Check/tighten all connections
Right (or left) turn signal only won't work	• Bulb burned out • Right (or left) indicator bulb burned out • Short circuit	• Replace bulb • Check/replace indicator bulb • Check/repair wiring
Flasher rate too slow or too fast	• Incorrect wattage bulb • Incorrect flasher	• Flasher bulb • Replace flasher (use a variable load flasher if you pull a trailer)
Indicator lights do not flash (burn steadily)	• Burned out bulb • Defective flasher	• Replace bulb • Replace flasher
Indicator lights do not light at all	• Burned out indicator bulb • Defective flasher	• Replace indicator bulb • Replace flasher

Troubleshooting Basic Turn Signal and Flasher Problems

Most problems in the turn signals or flasher system, can be reduced to defective flashers or bulbs, which are easily replaced. Occasionally, problems in the turn signals are traced to the switch in the steering column, which will require professional service.

F = Front   R = Rear   ● = Lights off   o = Lights on

Problem		Solution
Turn signals light, but do not flash		• Replace the flasher
No turn signals light on either side		• Check the fuse. Replace if defective. • Check the flasher by substitution • Check for open circuit, short circuit or poor ground
Both turn signals on one side don't work		• Check for bad bulbs • Check for bad ground in both housings
One turn signal light on one side doesn't work		• Check and/or replace bulb • Check for corrosion in socket. Clean contacts. • Check for poor ground at socket
Turn signal flashes too fast or too slow		• Check any bulb on the side flashing too fast. A heavy-duty bulb is probably installed in place of a regular bulb. • Check the bulb flashing too slow. A standard bulb was probably installed in place of a heavy-duty bulb. • Check for loose connections or corrosion at the bulb socket
Indicator lights don't work in either direction		• Check if the turn signals are working • Check the dash indicator lights • Check the flasher by substitution
One indicator light doesn't light		• On systems with 1 dash indicator: See if the lights work on the same side. Often the filaments have been reversed in systems combining stoplights with taillights and turn signals. Check the flasher by substitution • On systems with 2 indicators: Check the bulbs on the same side Check the indicator light bulb Check the flasher by substitution

WIRING DIAGRAMS

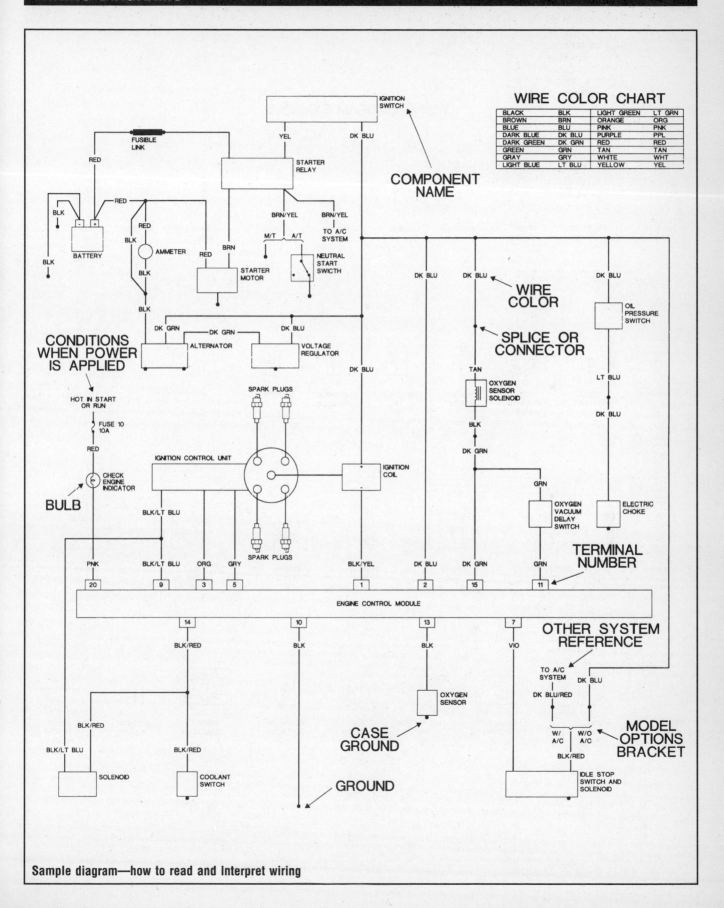

WIRE COLOR CHART

BLACK	BLK	LIGHT GREEN	LT GRN
BROWN	BRN	ORANGE	ORG
BLUE	BLU	PINK	PNK
DARK BLUE	DK BLU	PURPLE	PPL
DARK GREEN	DK GRN	RED	RED
GREEN	GRN	TAN	TAN
GRAY	GRY	WHITE	WHT
LIGHT BLUE	LT BLU	YELLOW	YEL

Sample diagram—how to read and Interpret wiring

WIRING DIAGRAM SYMBOLS

BATTERY	CONNECTOR OR SPLICE	CIRCUIT BREAKER	CAPACITOR	COIL	DIODE	FUSE	FUSIBLE LINK	GROUND	LED

RESISTOR	SINGLE FILAMENT BULB	DUAL FILAMENT BULB	HEATING ELEMENT	SOLENOID OR COIL	VARIABLE RESISTOR	CRYSTAL	POTENTIOMETER	HORN OR SPEAKER

ALTERNATOR	DISTRIBUTOR ASSEMBLY	IGNITION COIL	SPARK PLUG	STEPPER MOTOR	HEAT ACTIVATED SWITCH	RELAY

NORMALLY OPEN SWITCH	NORMALLY CLOSED SWITCH	GANGED SWITCH	3-POSITION SWITCH	REED SWITCH	MOTOR OR ACTUATOR	SPEED SENSOR	JUNCTION BLOCK	MODEL OPTIONS BRACKET

Common wiring diagram symbols

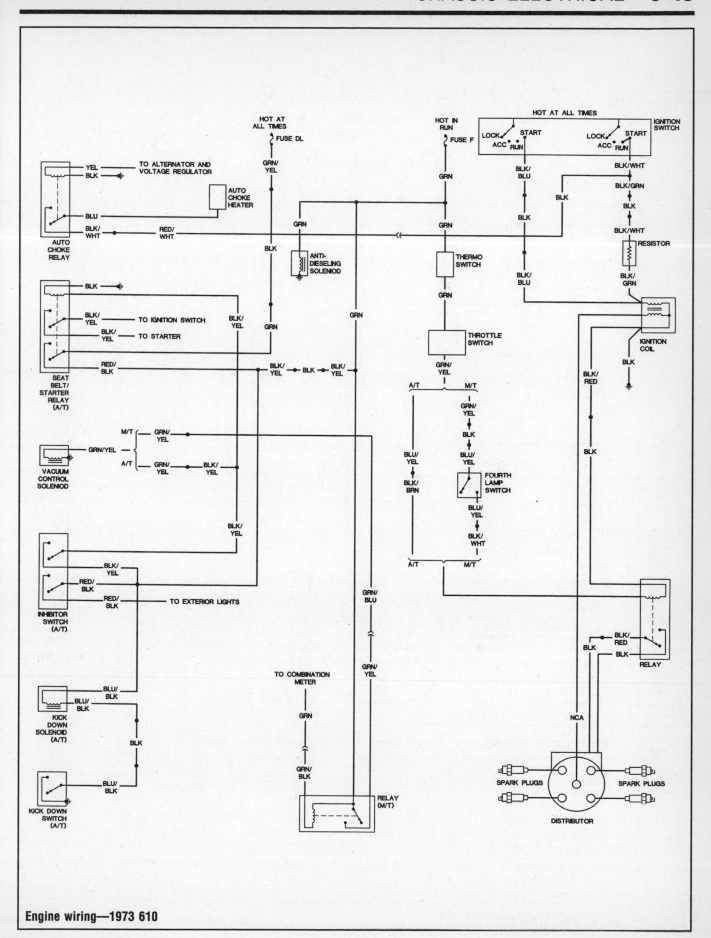

Engine wiring—1973 610

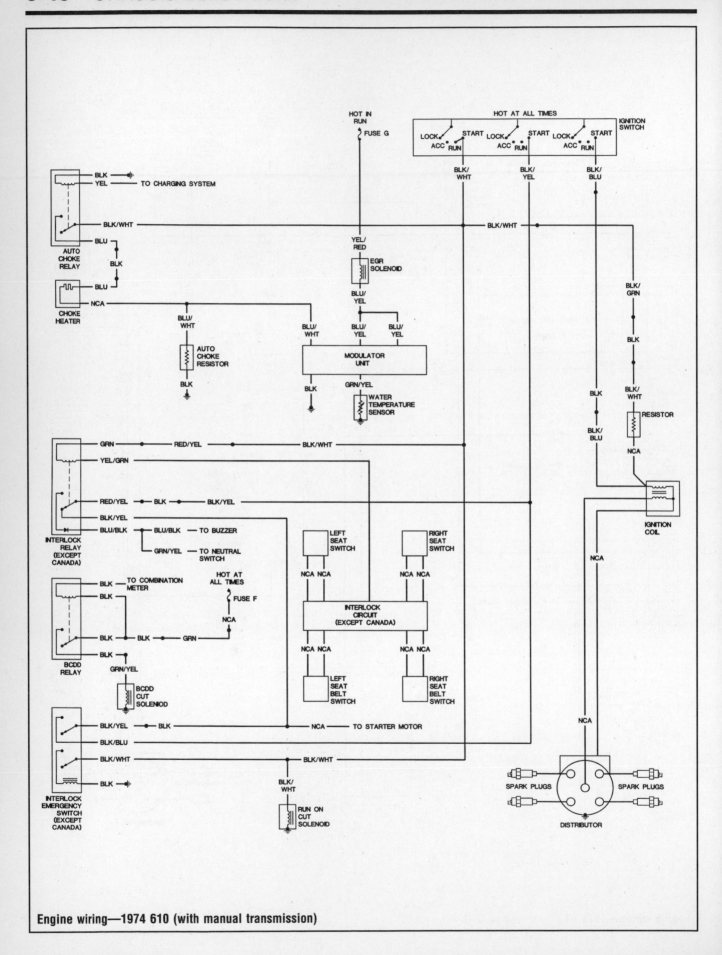

Engine wiring—1974 610 (with manual transmission)

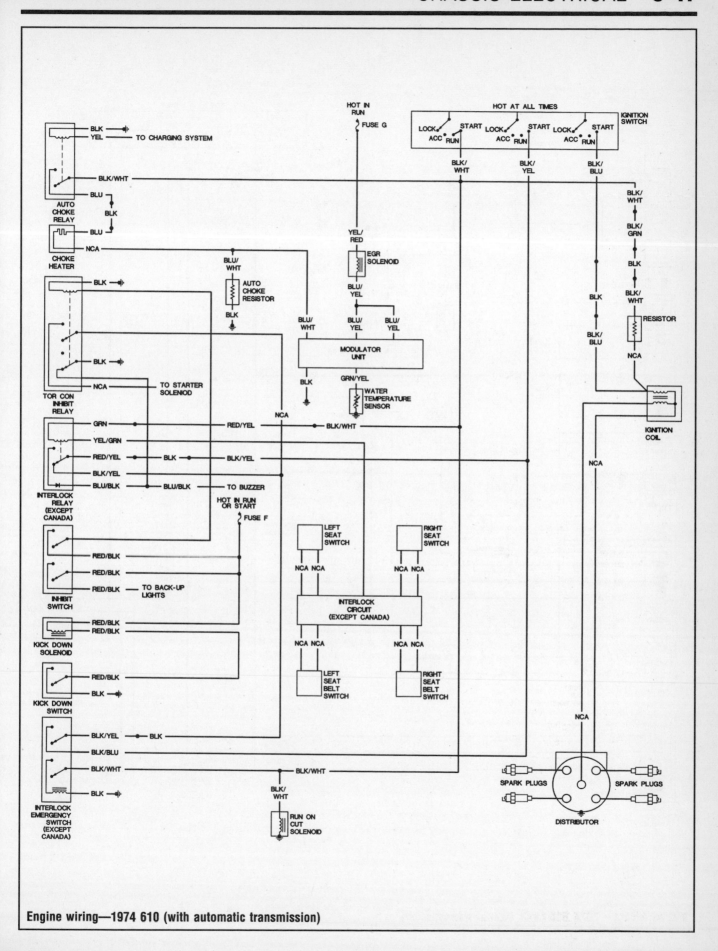

Engine wiring—1974 610 (with automatic transmission)

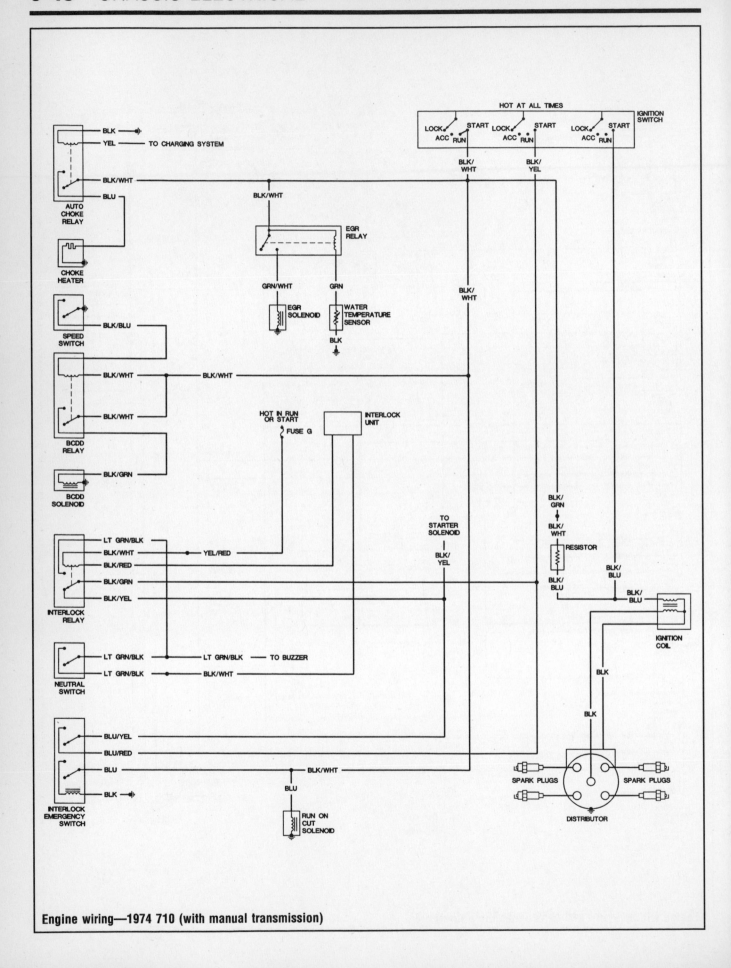

Engine wiring—1974 710 (with manual transmission)

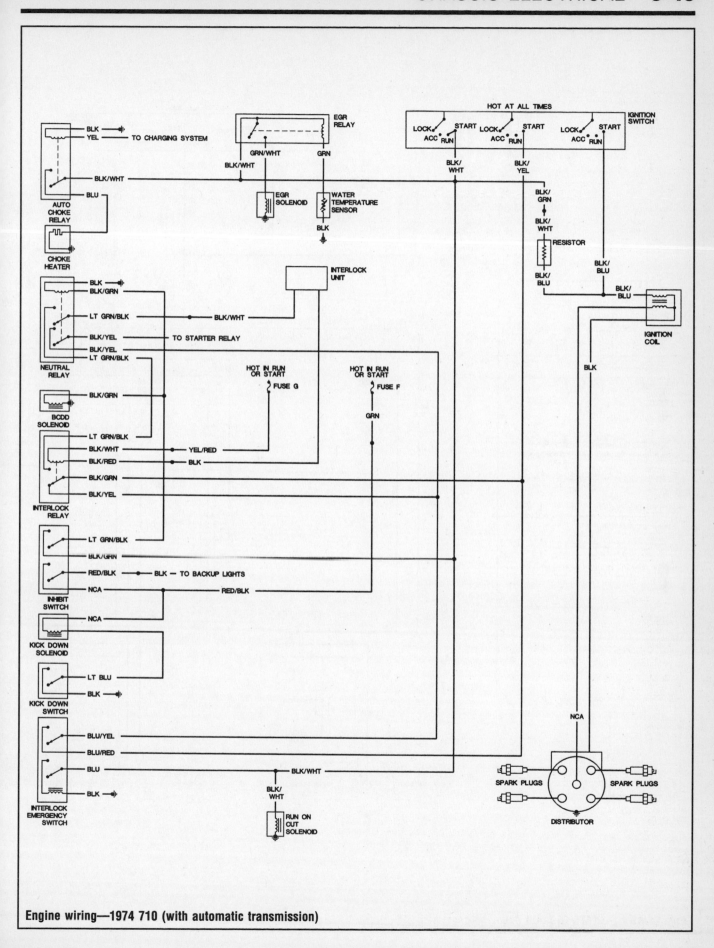

Engine wiring—1974 710 (with automatic transmission)

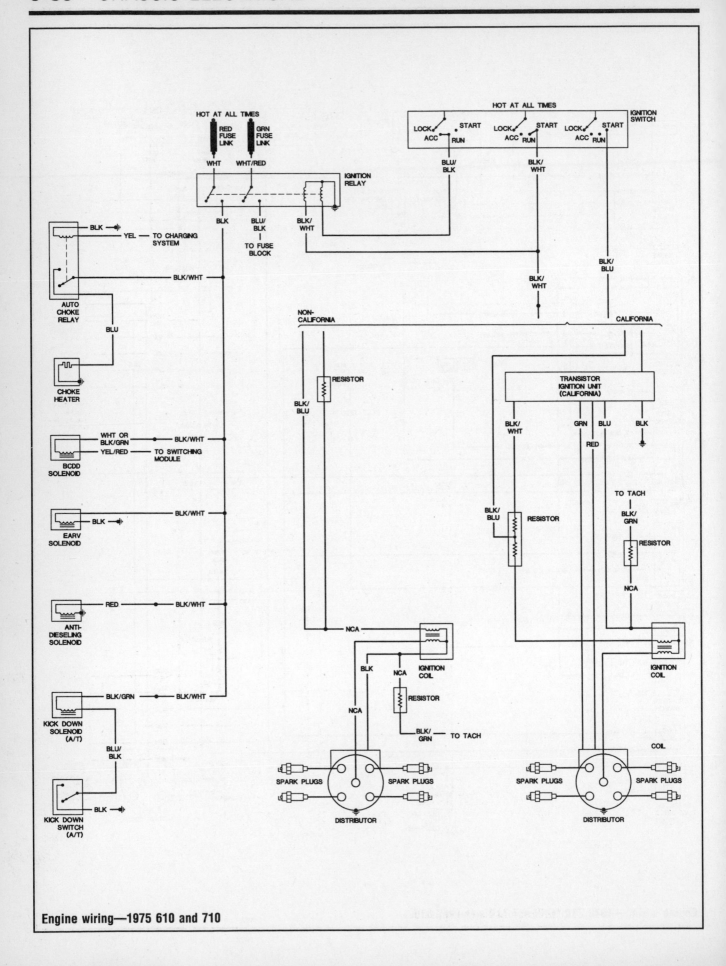

Engine wiring—1975 610 and 710

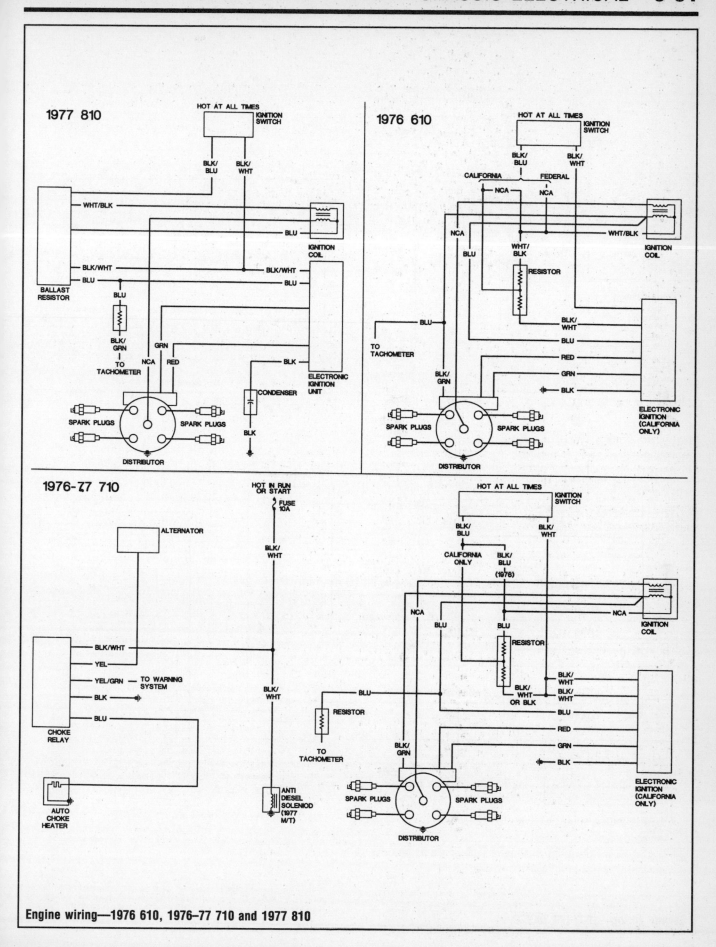

Engine wiring—1976 610, 1976–77 710 and 1977 810

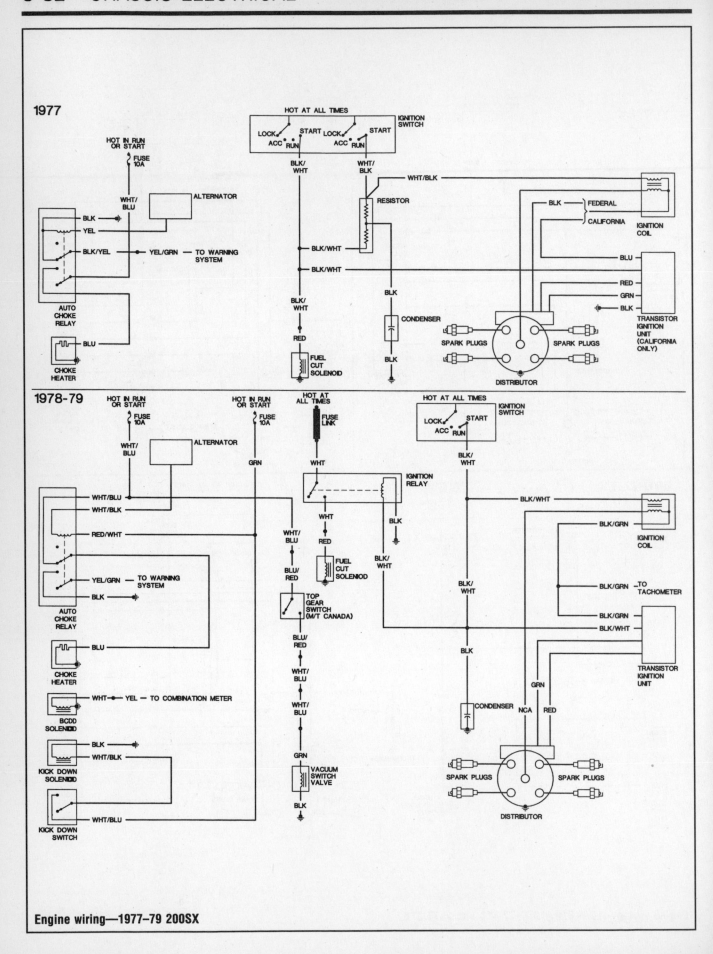

Engine wiring—1977–79 200SX

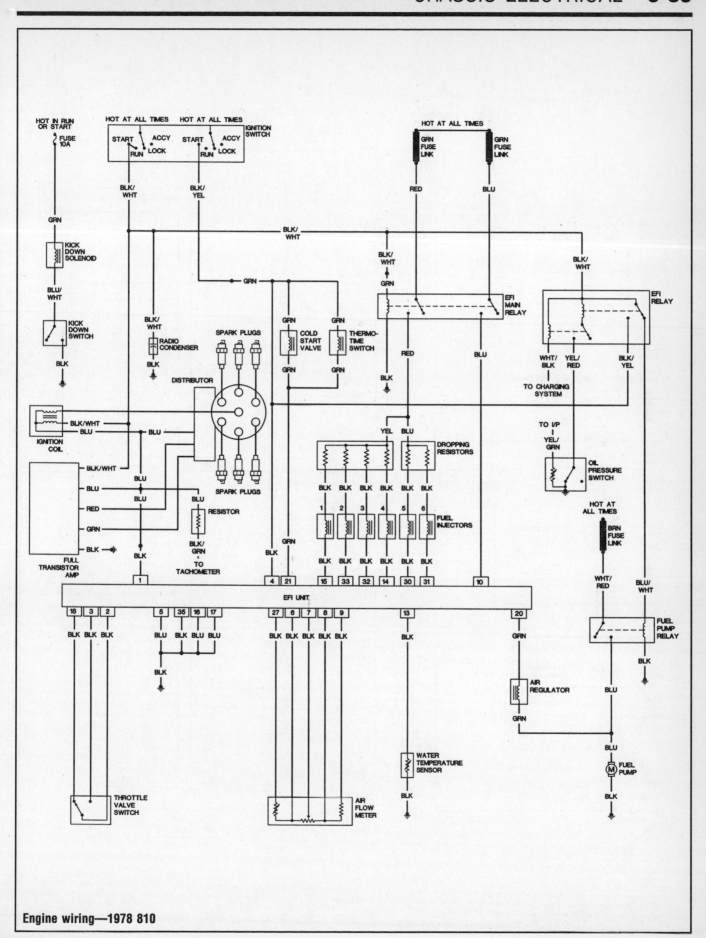

Engine wiring—1978 810

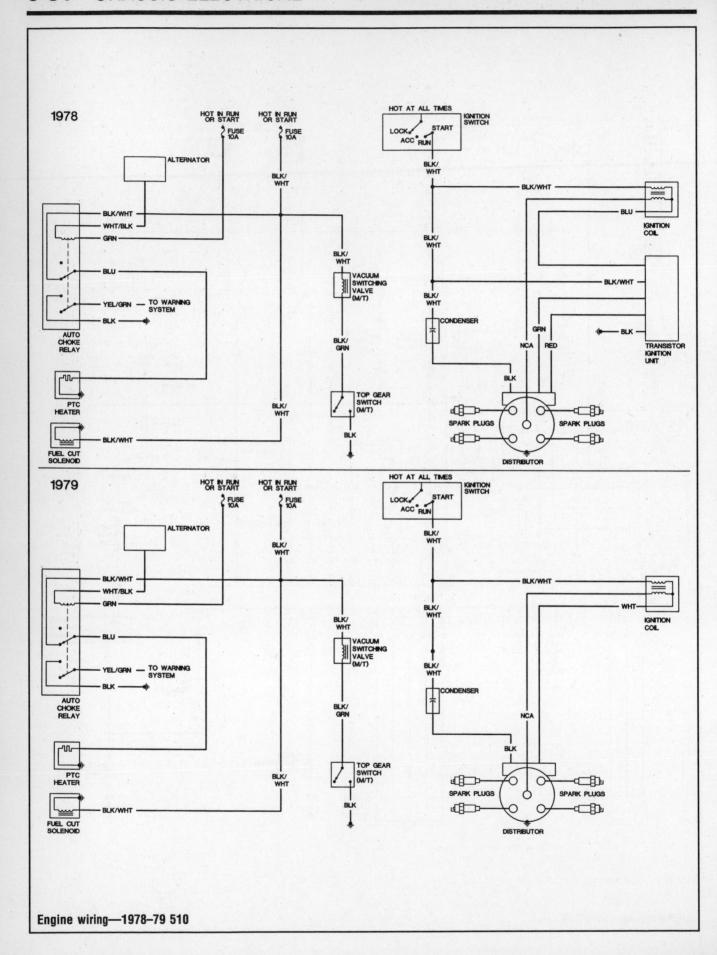

Engine wiring—1978–79 510

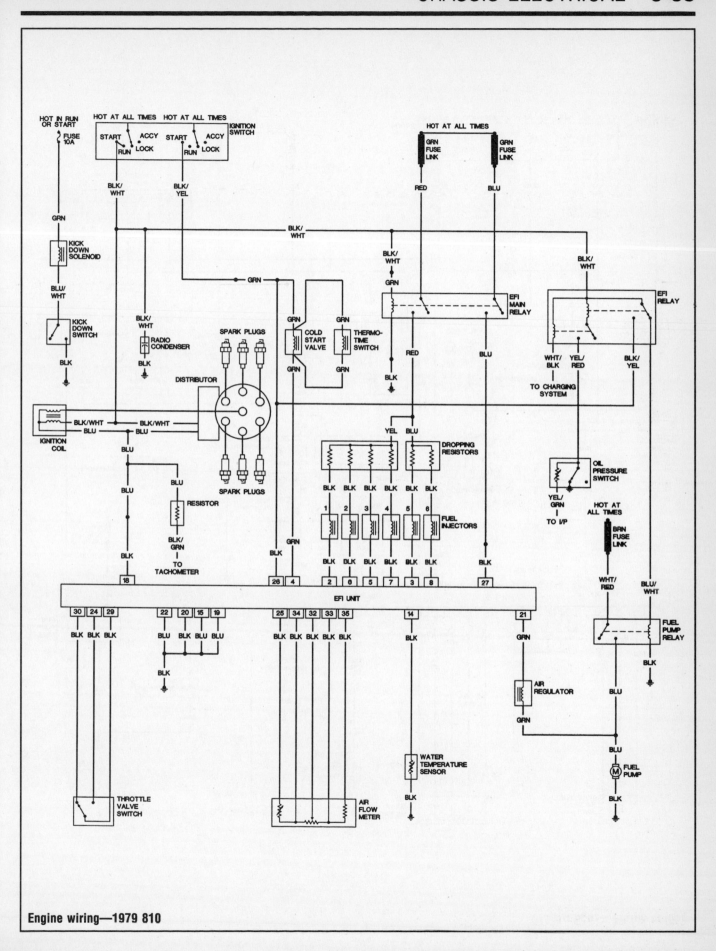

Engine wiring—1979 810

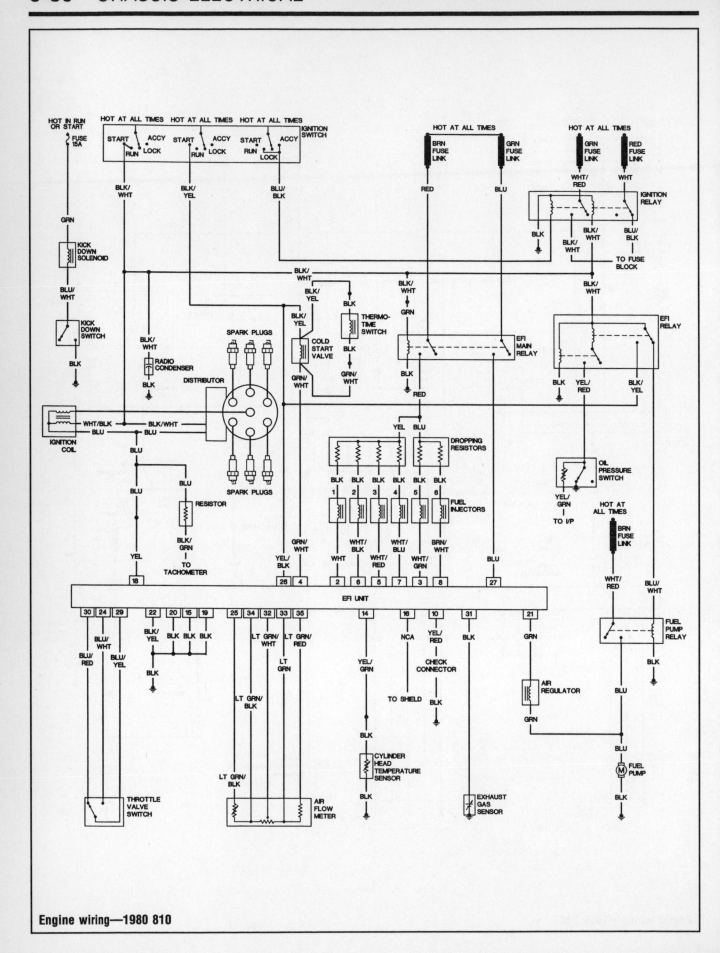

Engine wiring—1980 810

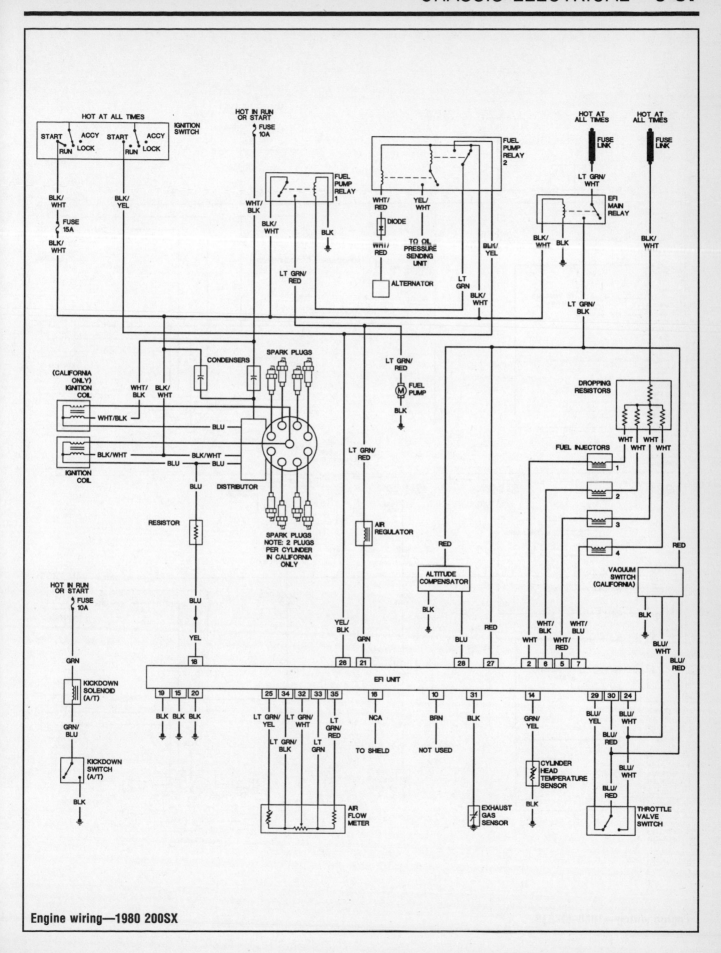

Engine wiring—1980 200SX

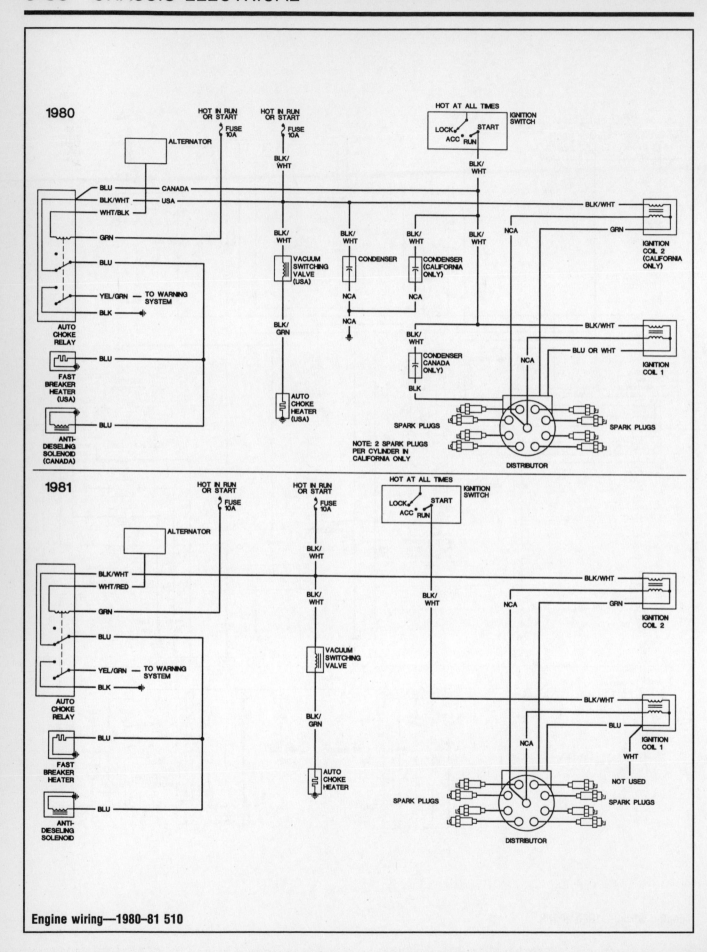

Engine wiring—1980–81 510

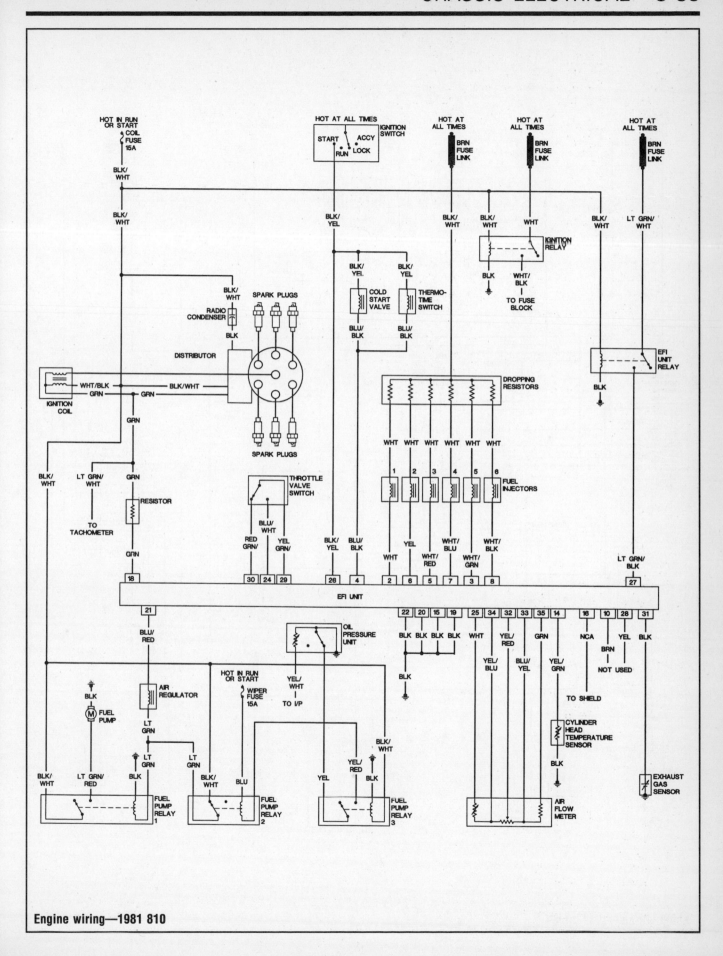

Engine wiring—1981 810

Engine wiring—1981 200SX

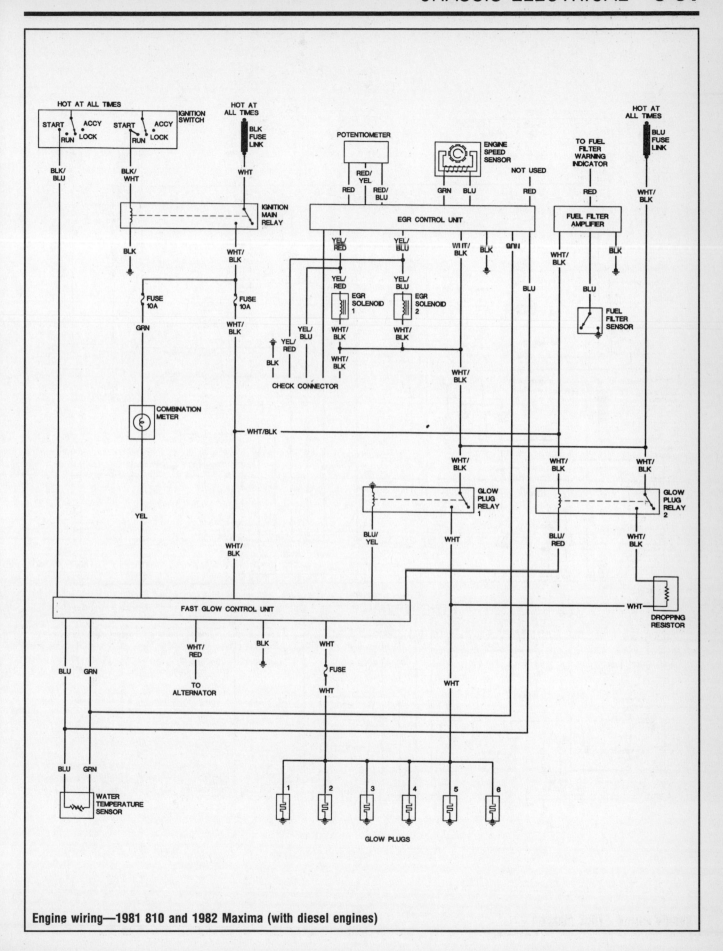

Engine wiring—1981 810 and 1982 Maxima (with diesel engines)

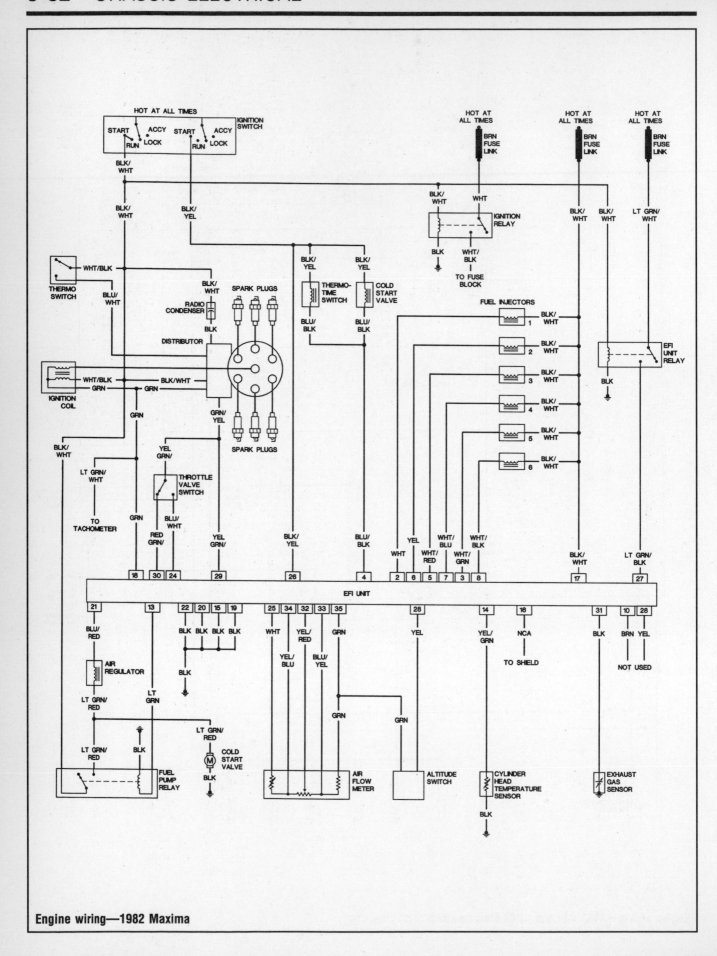

Engine wiring—1982 Maxima

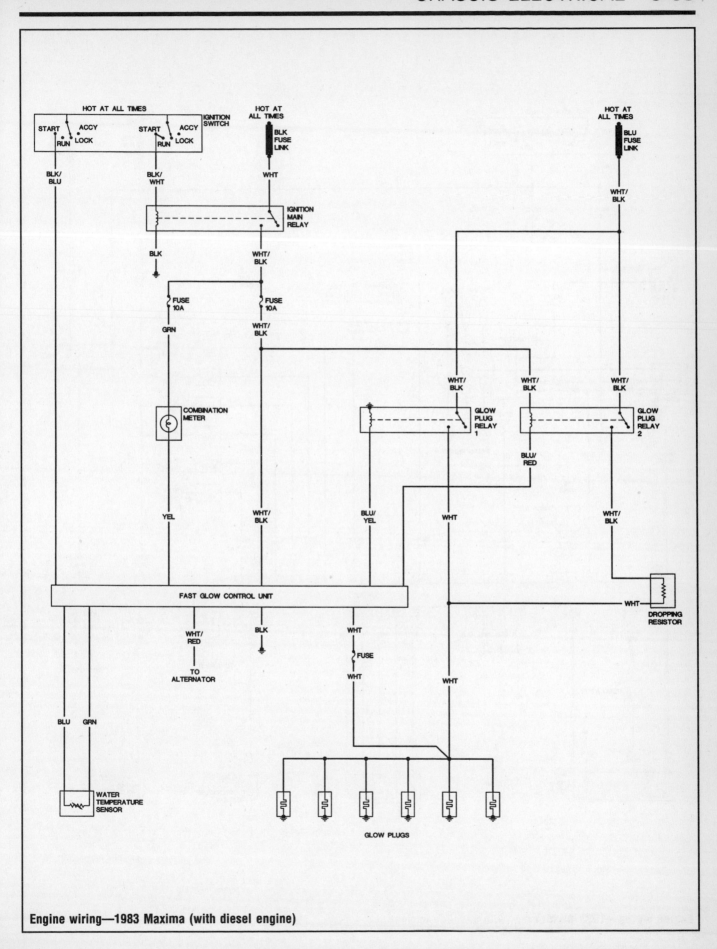

Engine wiring—1983 Maxima (with diesel engine)

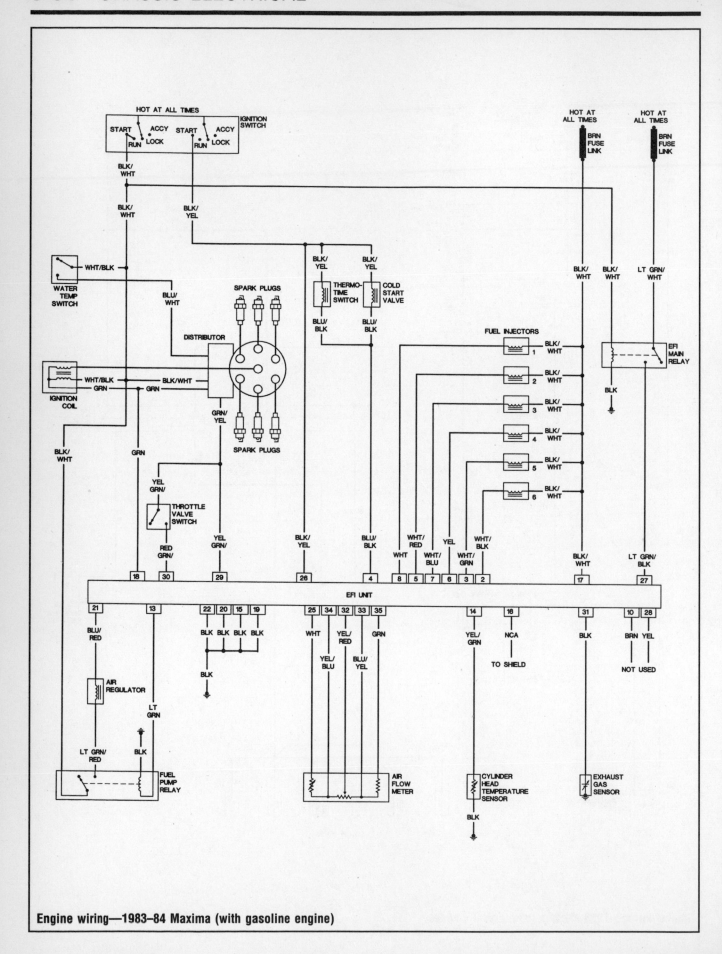

Engine wiring—1983-84 Maxima (with gasoline engine)

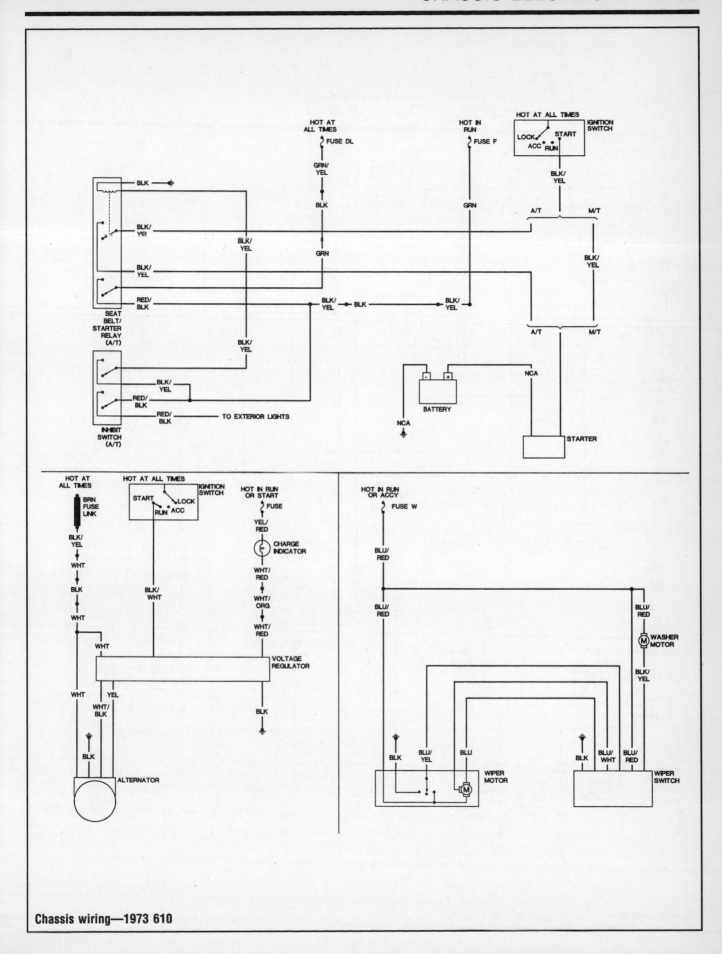

Chassis wiring—1973 610

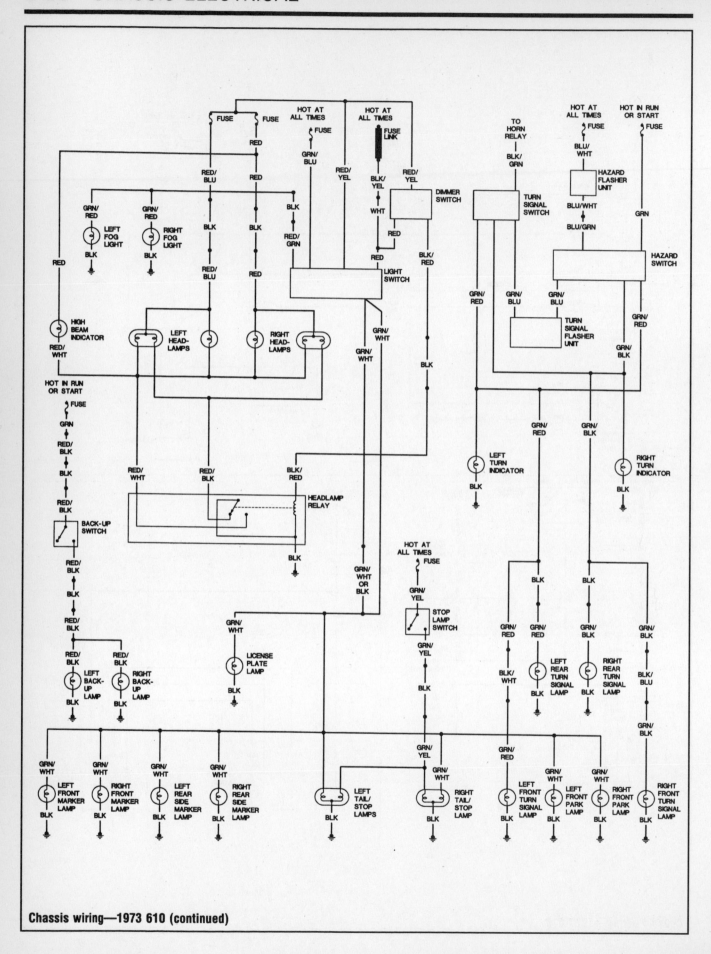

Chassis wiring—1973 610 (continued)

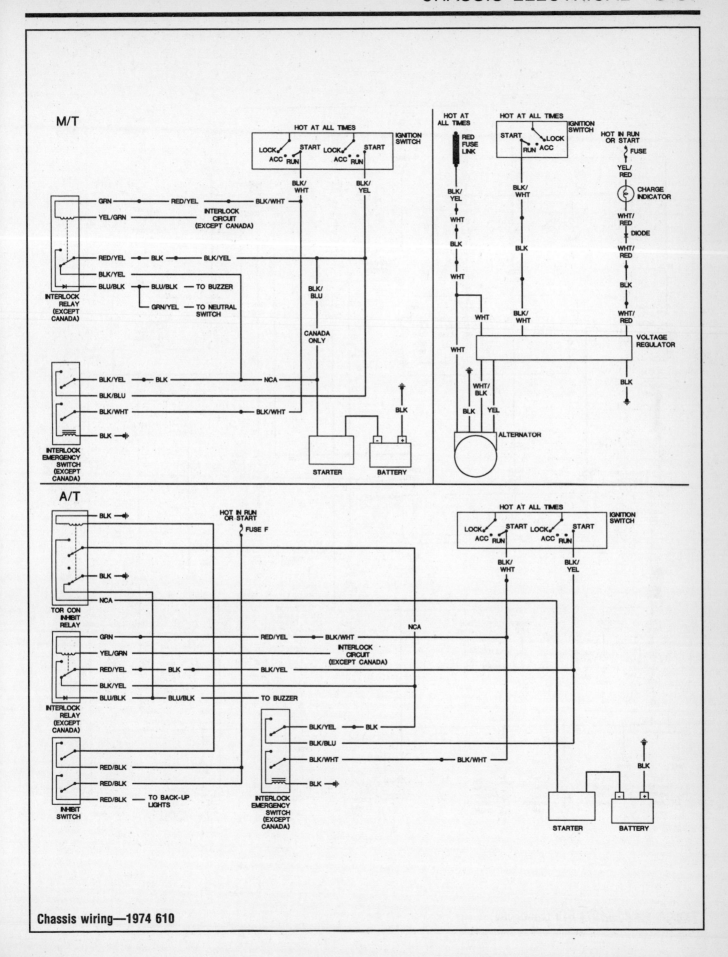

Chassis wiring—1974 610

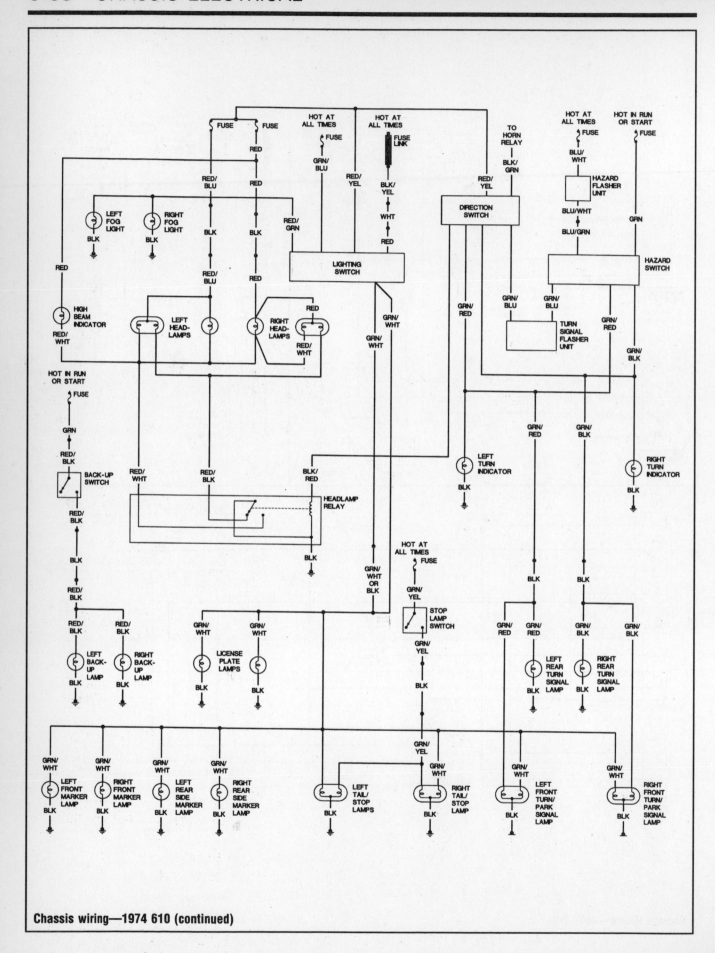

Chassis wiring—1974 610 (continued)

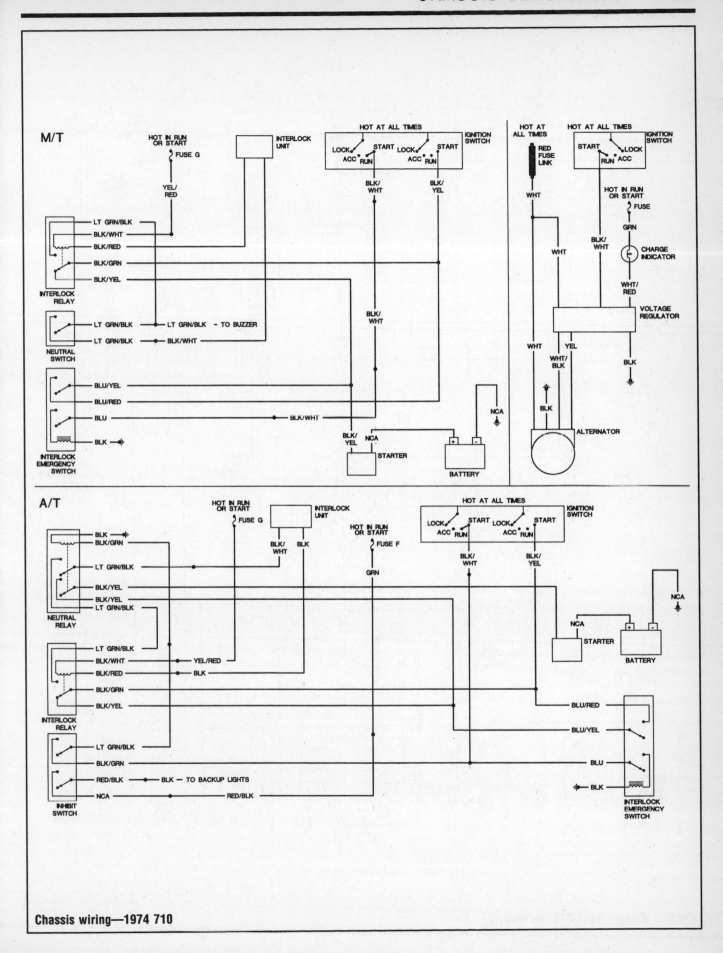

Chassis wiring—1974 710

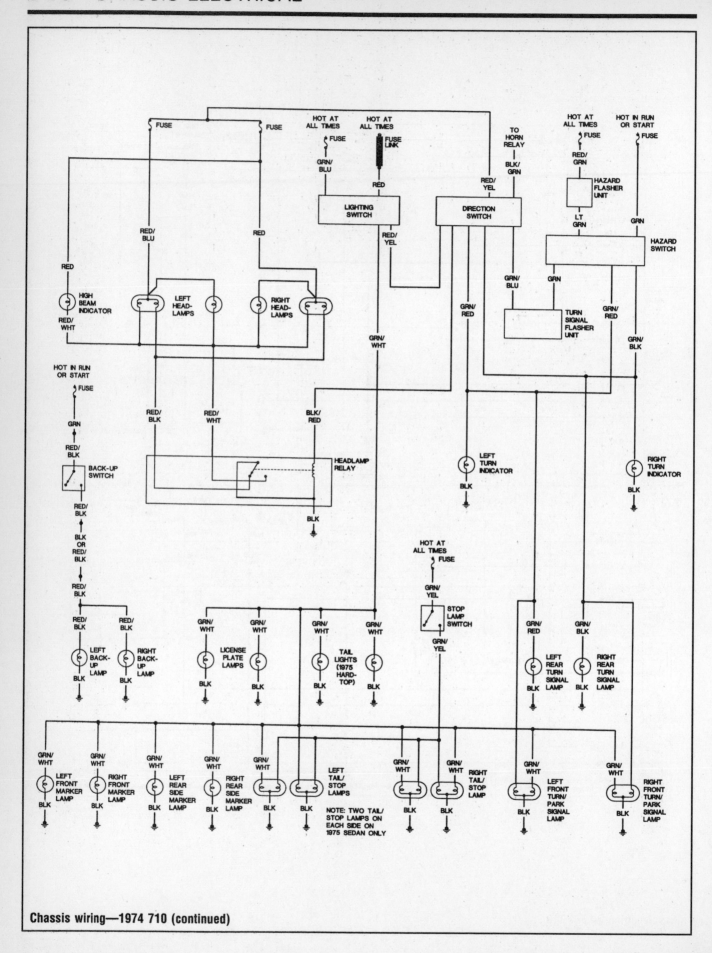

Chassis wiring—1974 710 (continued)

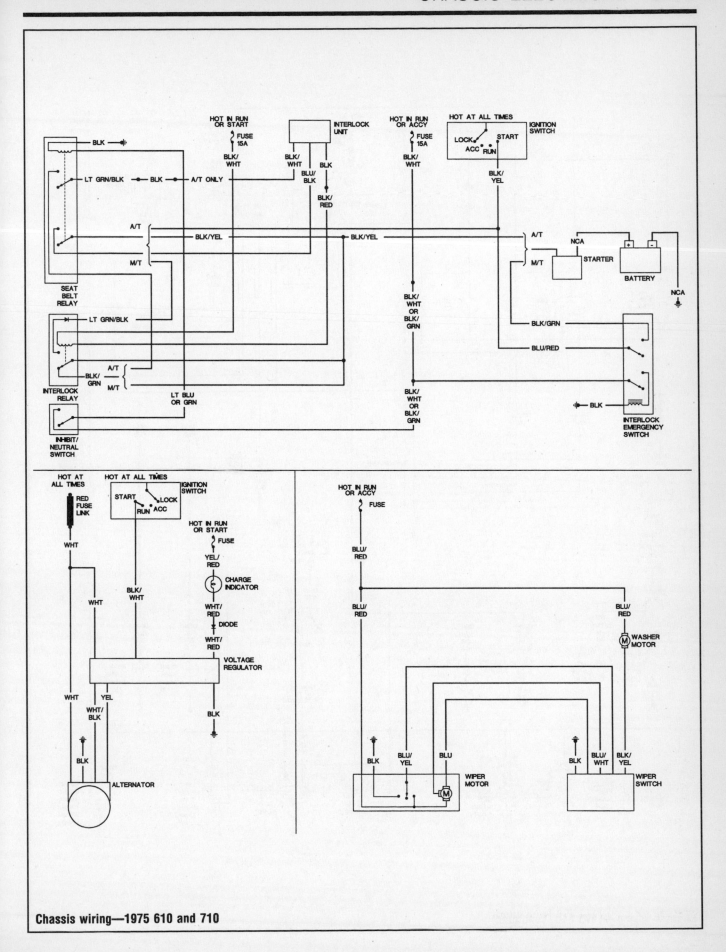

Chassis wiring—1975 610 and 710

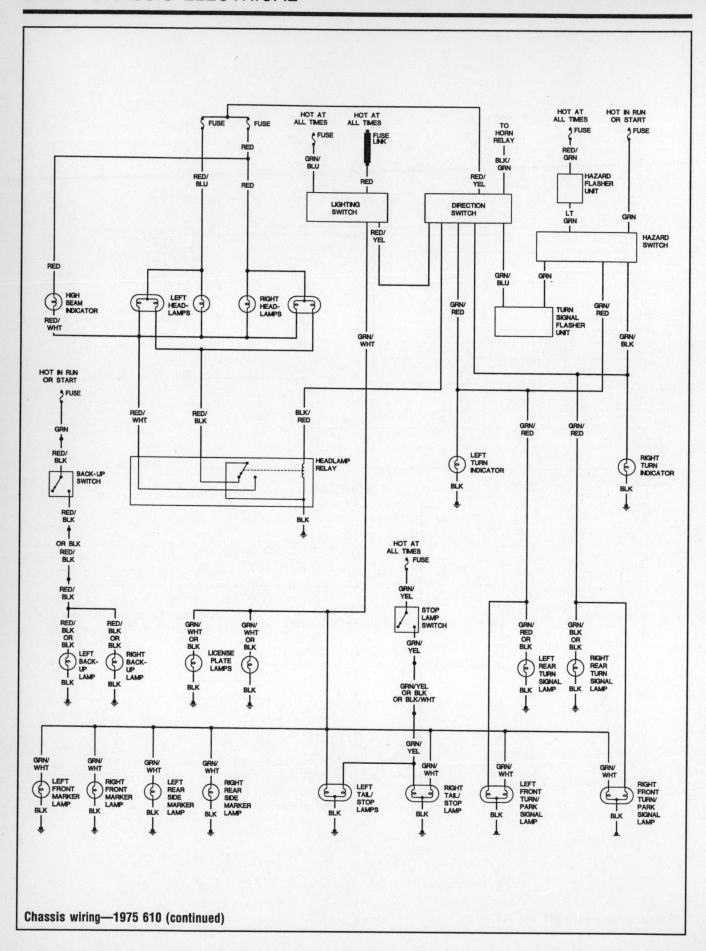

Chassis wiring—1975 610 (continued)

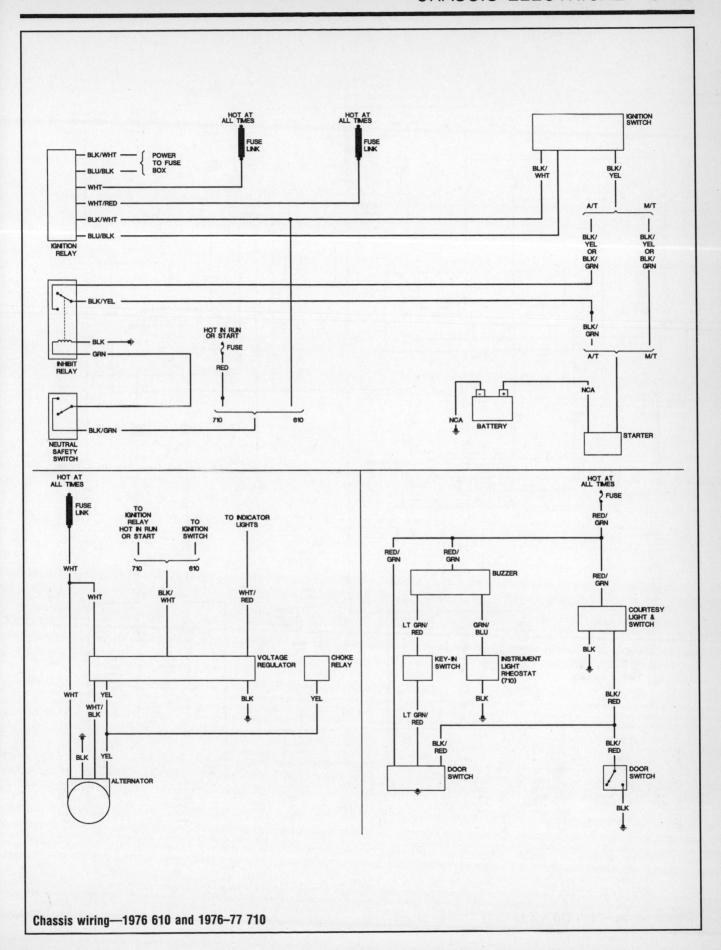

Chassis wiring—1976 610 and 1976–77 710

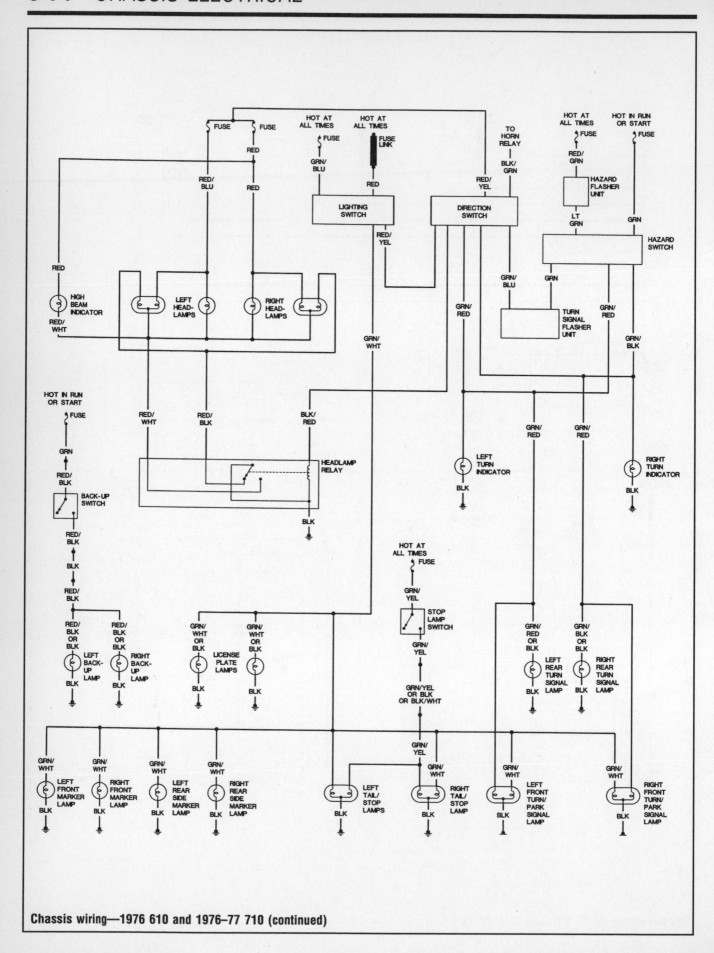

Chassis wiring—1976 610 and 1976-77 710 (continued)

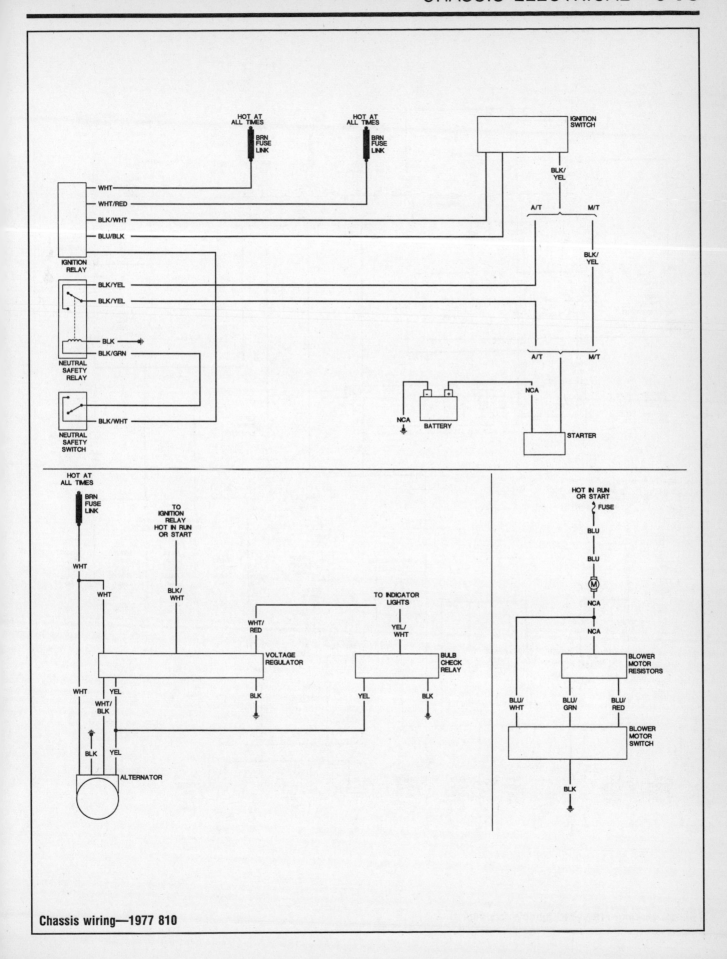

Chassis wiring—1977 810

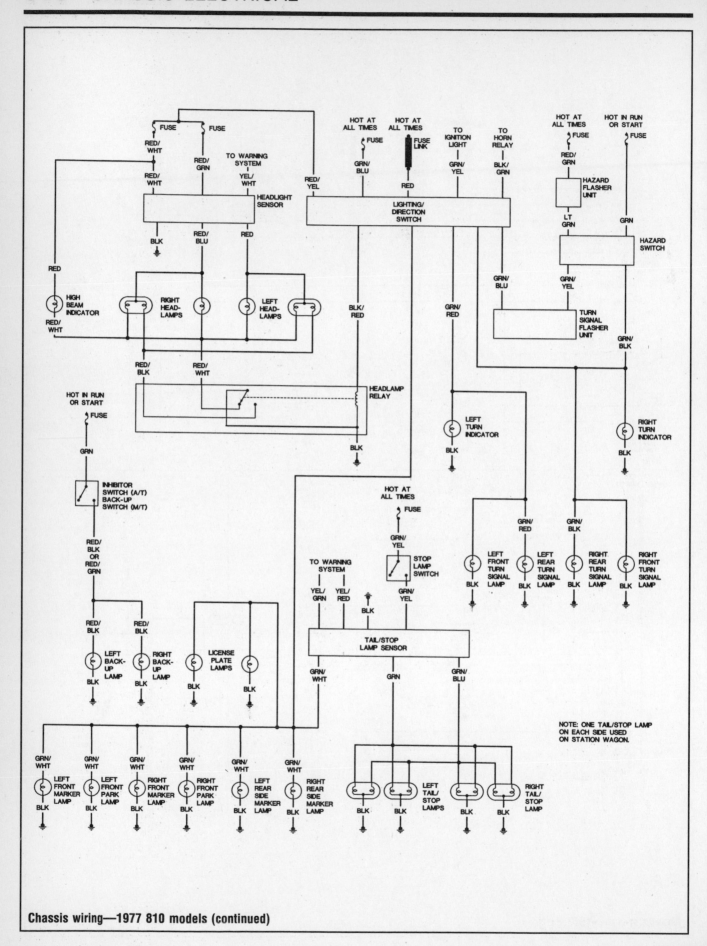

Chassis wiring—1977 810 models (continued)

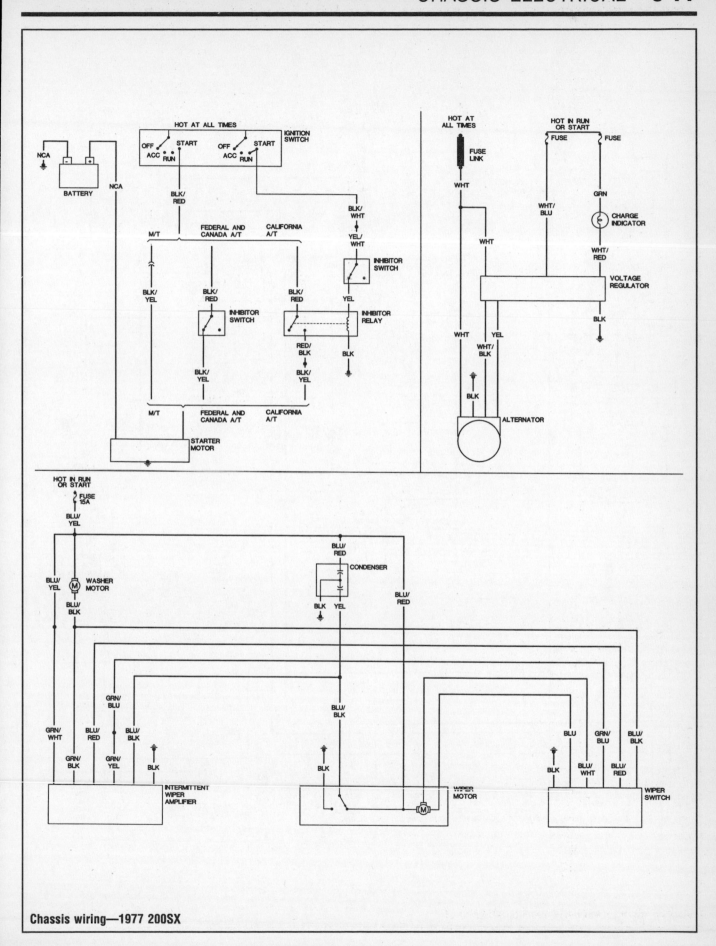

Chassis wiring—1977 200SX

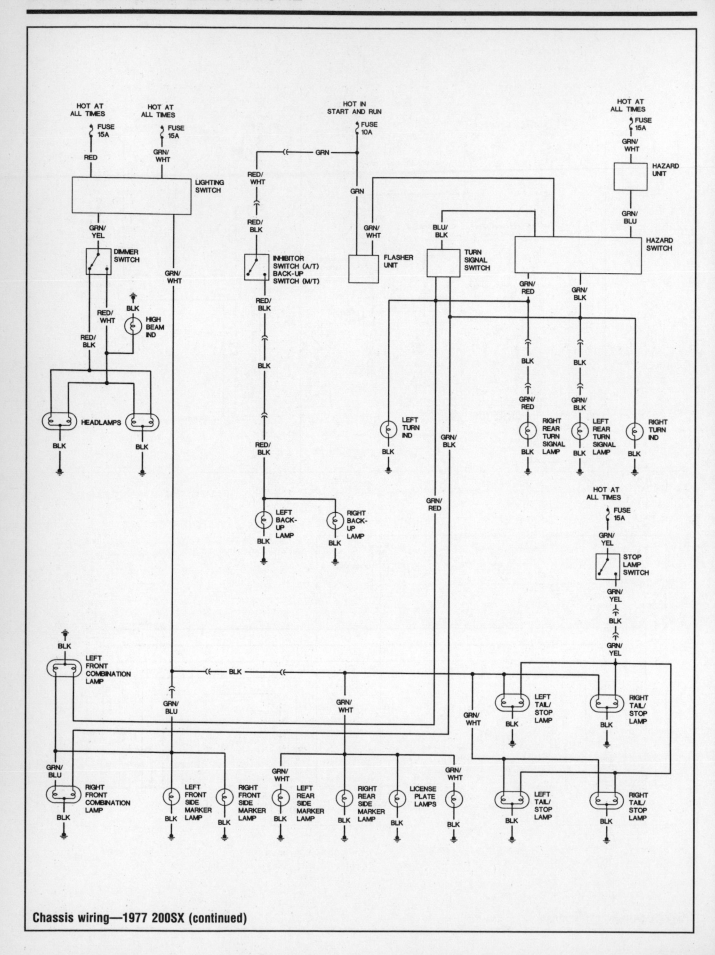

Chassis wiring—1977 200SX (continued)

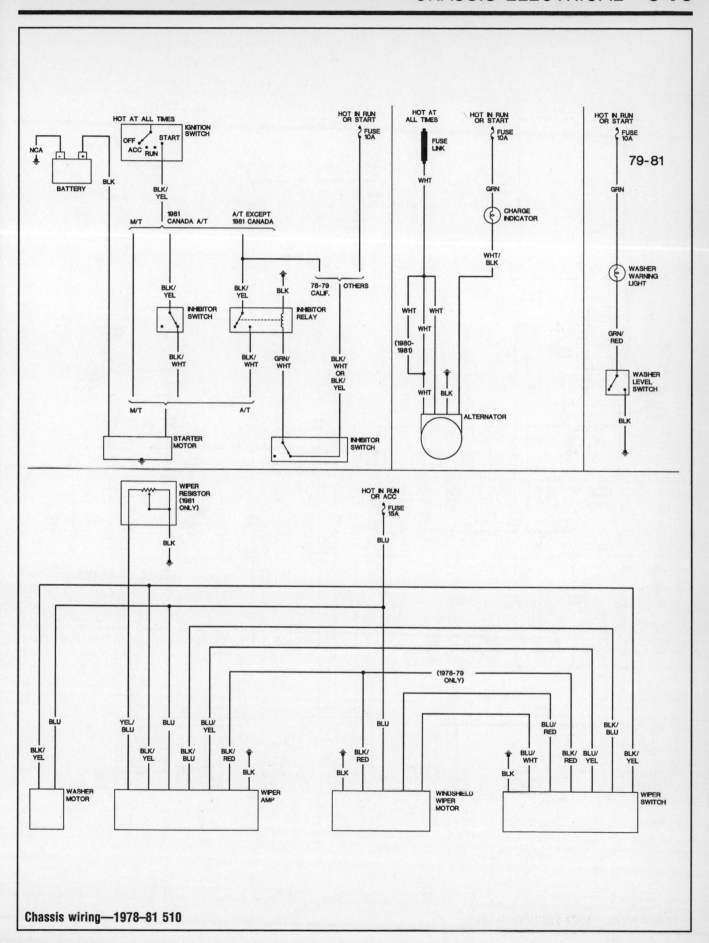

Chassis wiring—1978–81 510

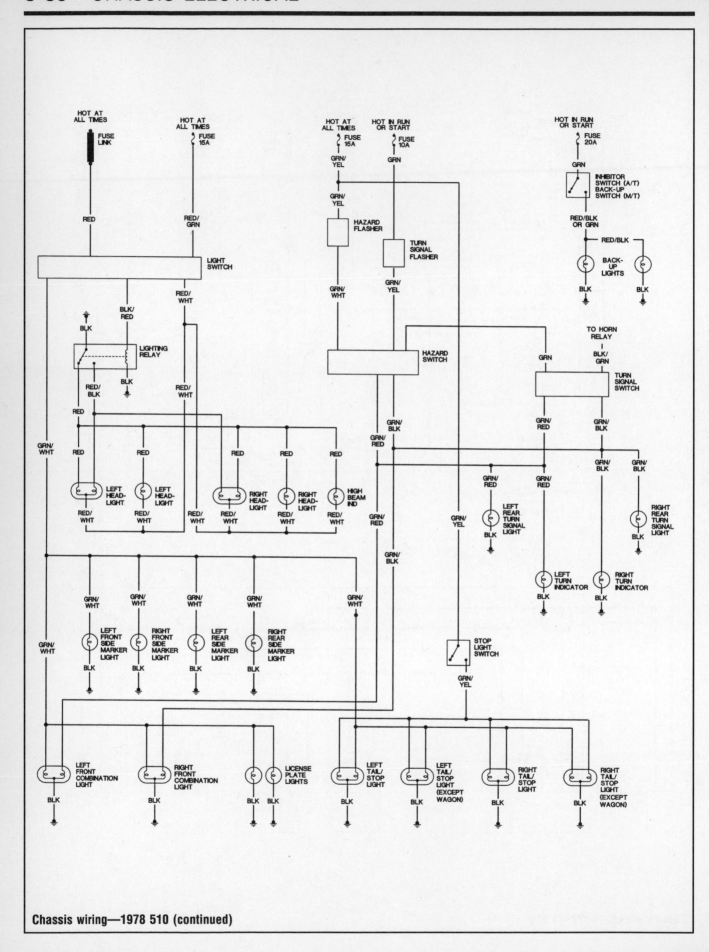

Chassis wiring—1978 510 (continued)

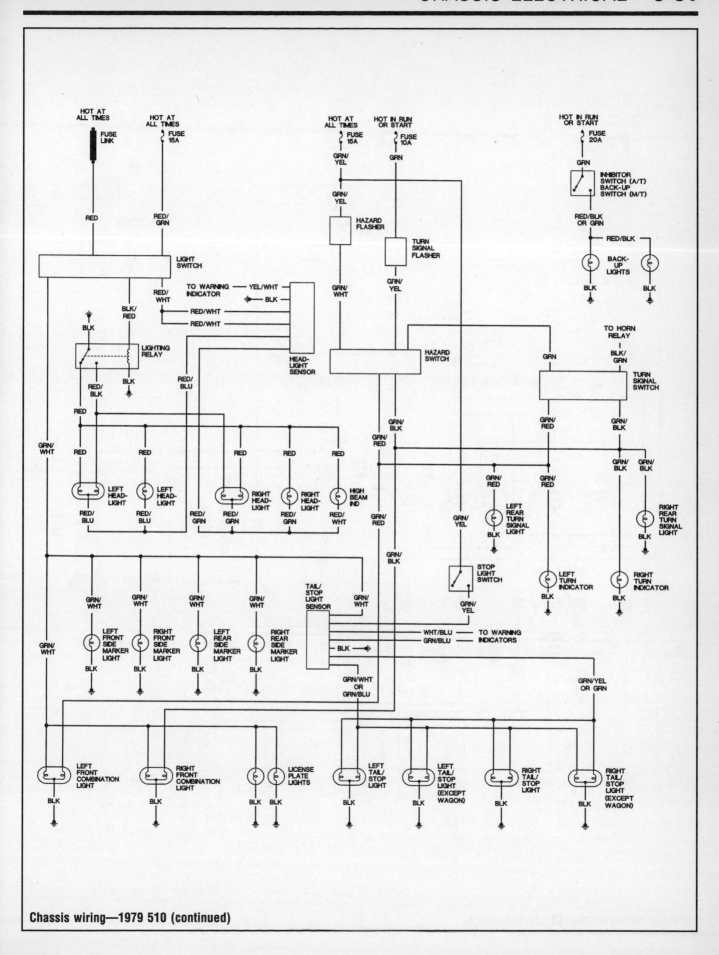

Chassis wiring—1979 510 (continued)

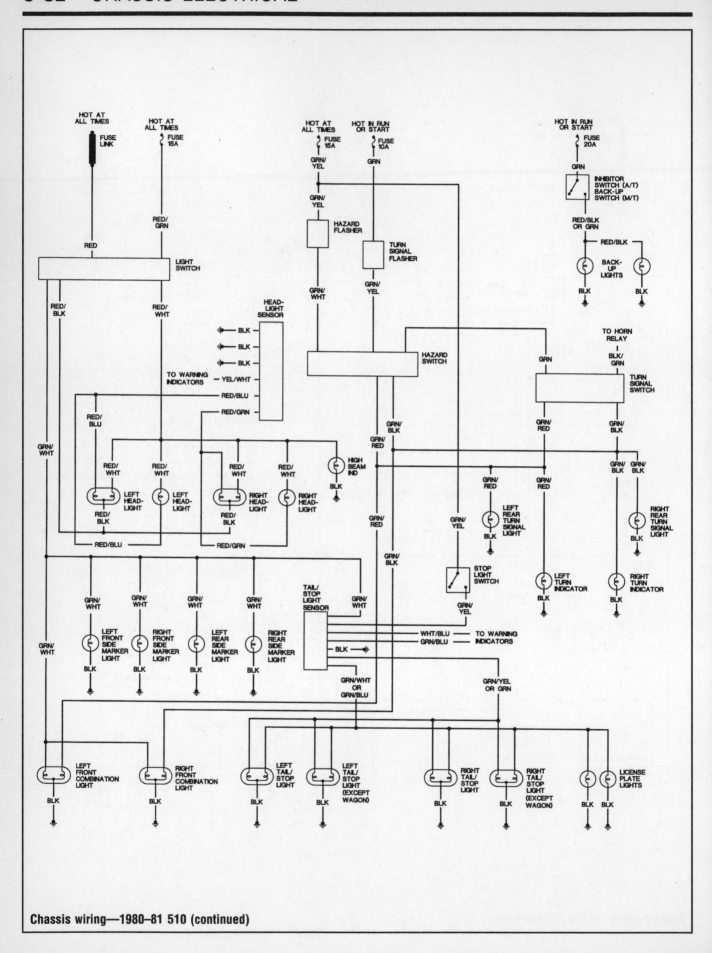

Chassis wiring—1980-81 510 (continued)

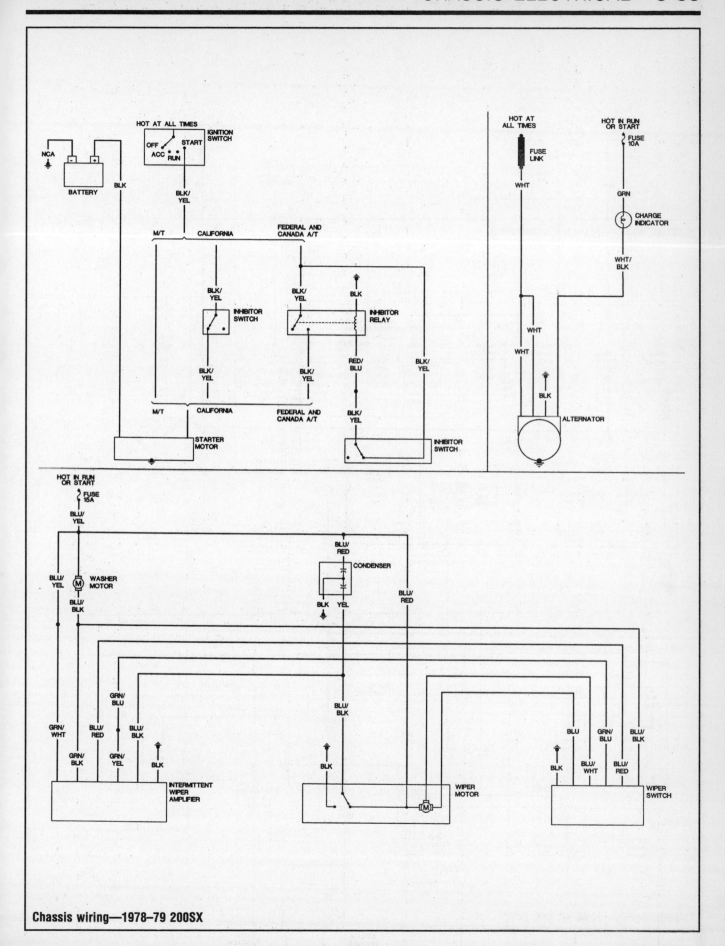

Chassis wiring—1978–79 200SX

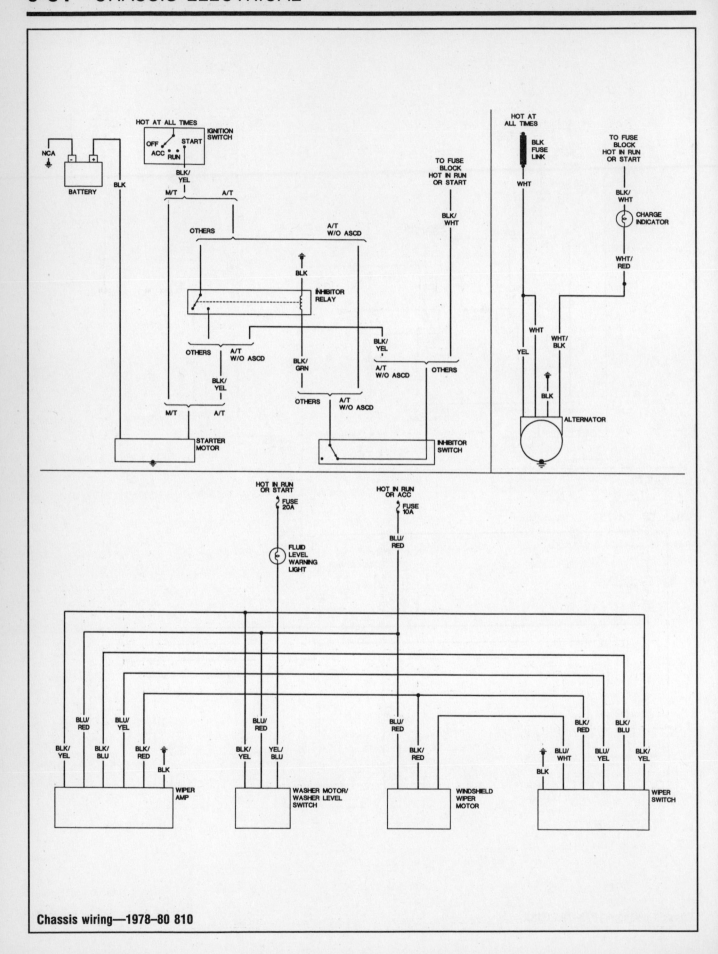

Chassis wiring—1978-80 810

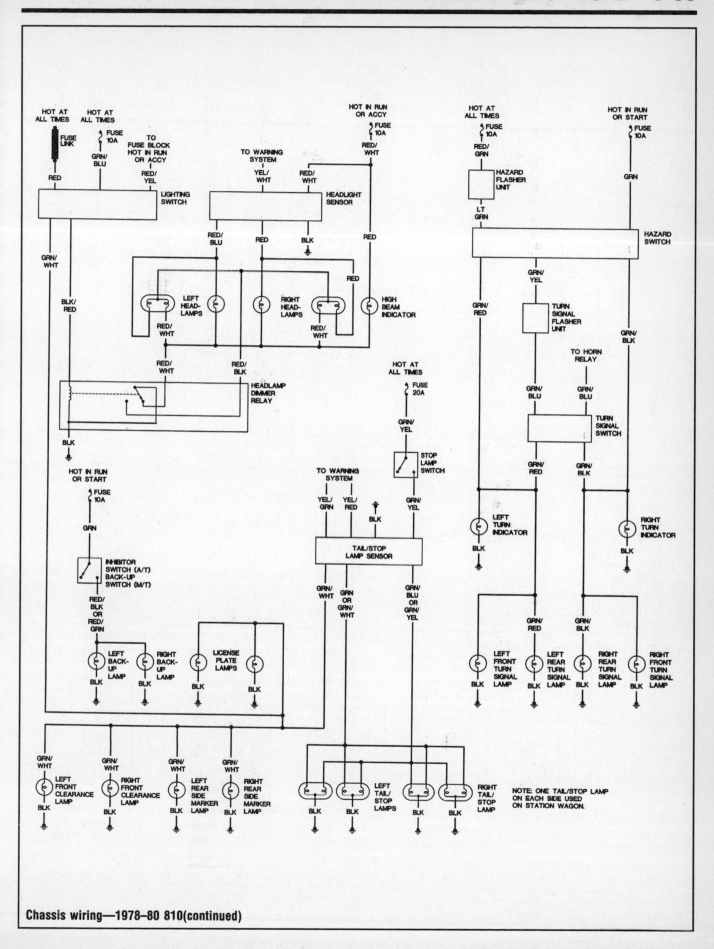

Chassis wiring—1978-80 810(continued)

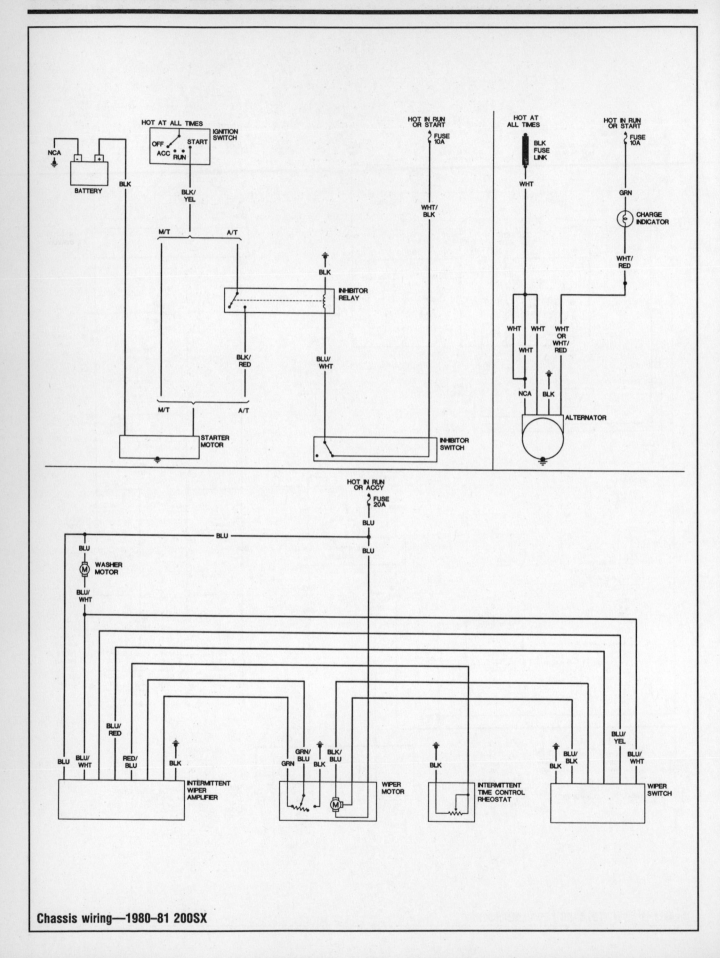

Chassis wiring—1980–81 200SX

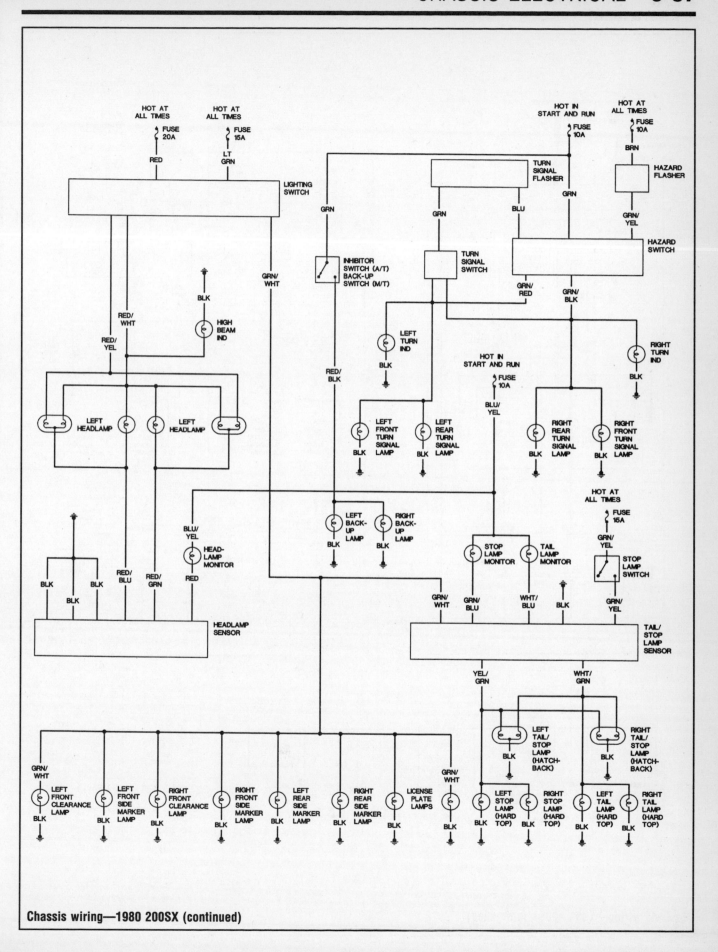

Chassis wiring—1980 200SX (continued)

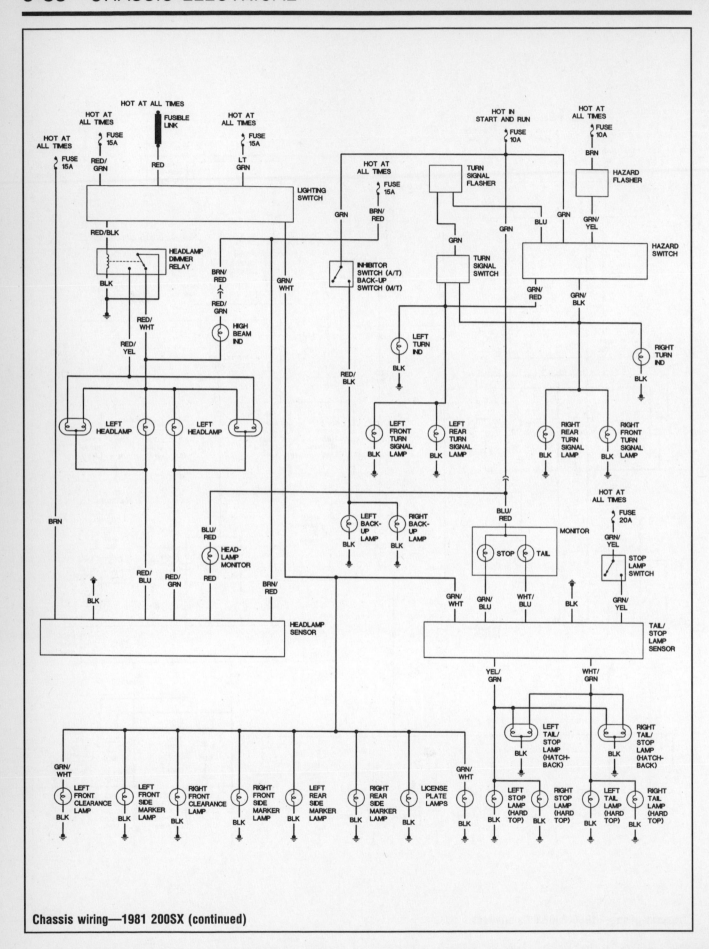

Chassis wiring—1981 200SX (continued)

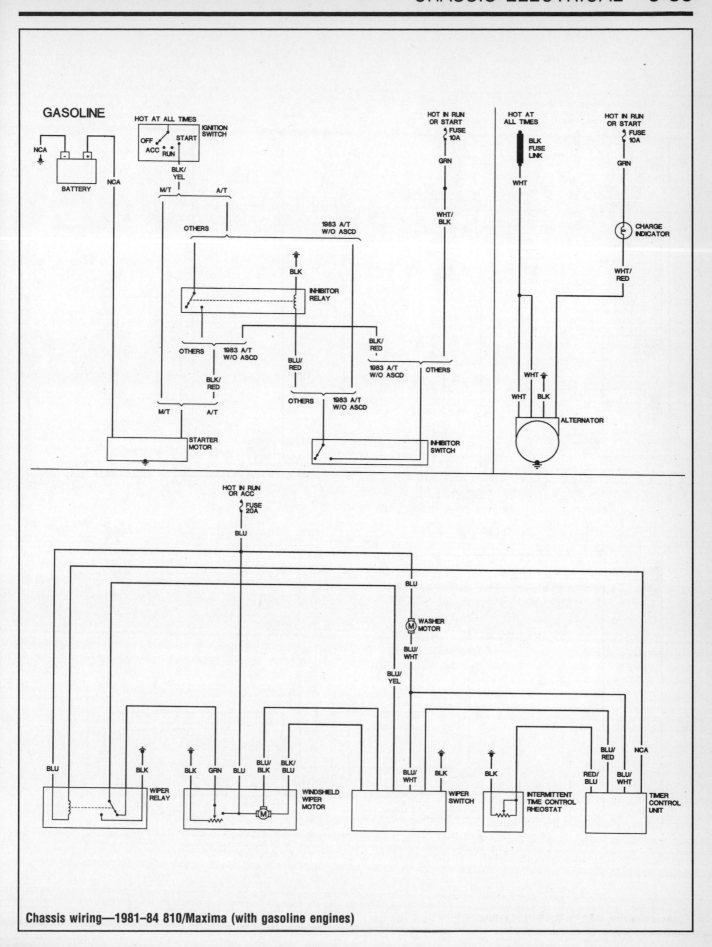

Chassis wiring—1981–84 810/Maxima (with gasoline engines)

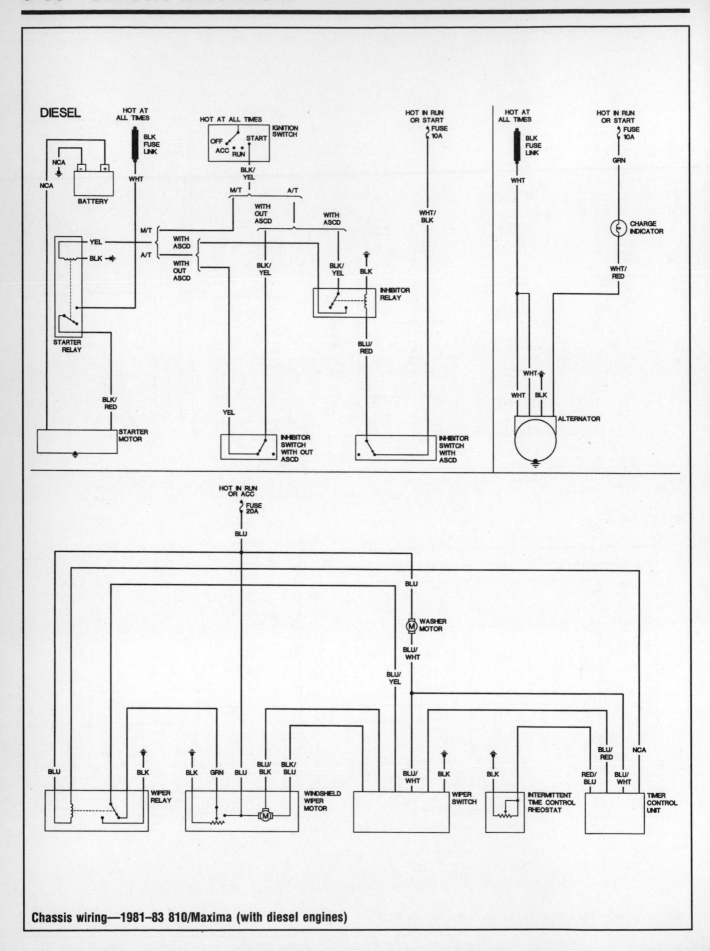

Chassis wiring—1981–83 810/Maxima (with diesel engines)

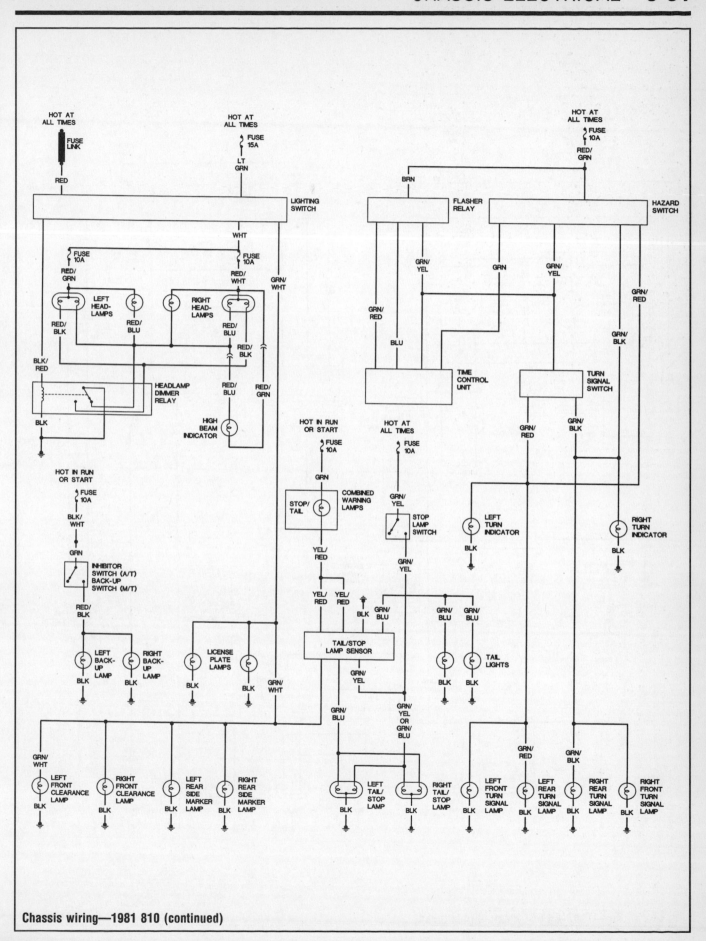

Chassis wiring—1981 810 (continued)

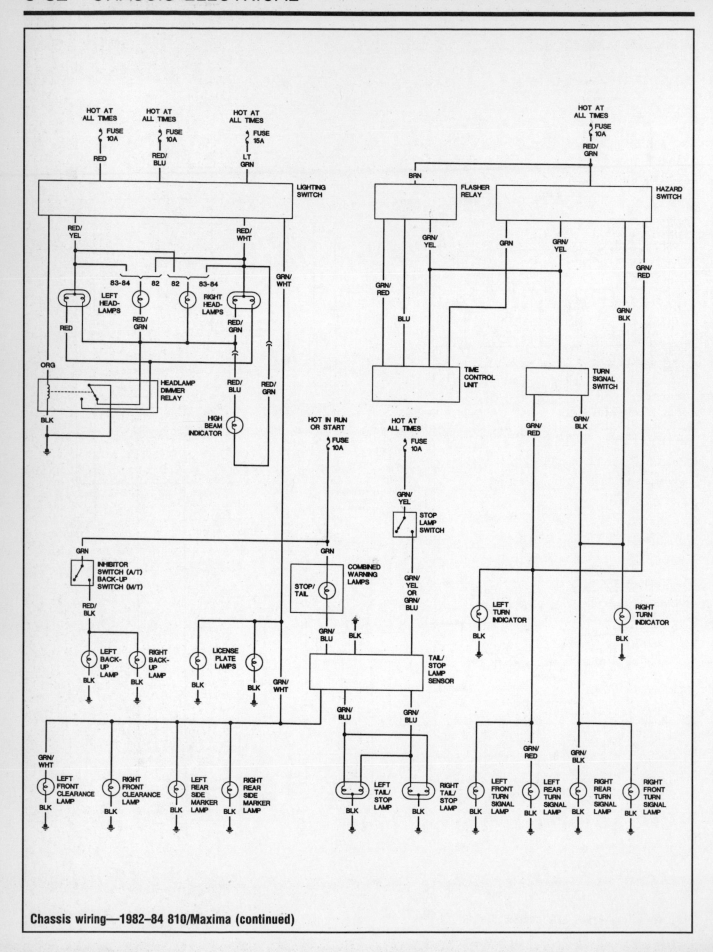

Chassis wiring—1982-84 810/Maxima (continued)

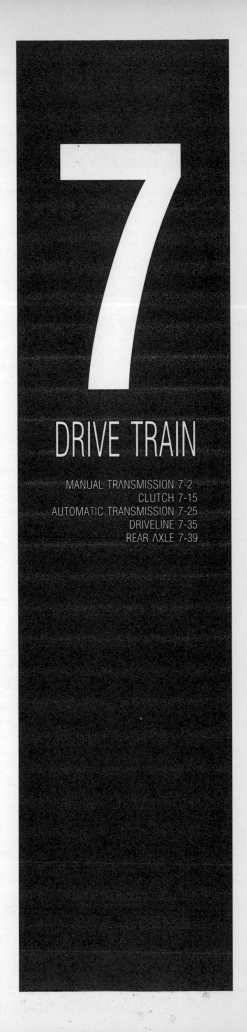

7

DRIVE TRAIN

MANUAL TRANSMISSION

Understanding the Manual Transmission

Because of the way an internal combustion engine breathes, it can produce torque (or twisting force) only within a narrow speed range. Most overhead valve pushrod engines must turn at about 2500 rpm to produce their peak torque. Often by 4500 rpm, they are producing so little torque that continued increases in engine speed produce no power increases.

The torque peak on overhead camshaft engines is, generally, much higher, but much narrower.

The manual transmission and clutch are employed to vary the relationship between engine RPM and the speed of the wheels so that adequate power can be produced under all circumstances. The clutch allows engine torque to be applied to the transmission input shaft gradually, due to mechanical slippage. The vehicle can, consequently, be started smoothly from a full stop.

The transmission changes the ratio between the rotating speeds of the engine and the wheels by the use of gears. 4-speed or 5-speed transmissions are most common. The lower gears allow full engine power to be applied to the rear wheels during acceleration at low speeds.

The clutch driveplate is a thin disc, the center of which is splined to the transmission input shaft. Both sides of the disc are covered with a layer of material which is similar to brake lining and which is capable of allowing slippage without roughness or excessive noise.

The clutch cover is bolted to the engine flywheel and incorporates a diaphragm spring which provides the pressure to engage the clutch. The cover also houses the pressure plate. When the clutch pedal is released, the driven disc is sandwiched between the pressure plate and the smooth surface of the flywheel, thus forcing the disc to turn at the same speed as the engine crankshaft.

The transmission contains a mainshaft which passes all the way through the transmission, from the clutch to the driveshaft. This shaft is separated at one point, so that front and rear portions can turn at different speeds.

Power is transmitted by a countershaft in the lower gears and reverse. The gears of the countershaft mesh with gears on the mainshaft, allowing power to be carried from one to the other. Countershaft gears are often integral with that shaft, while several of the mainshaft gears can either rotate independently of the shaft or be locked to it. Shifting from one gear to the next causes one of the gears to be freed from rotating with the shaft and locks another to it. Gears are locked and unlocked by internal dog clutches which slide between the center of the gear and the shaft. The forward gears usually employ synchronizers; friction members which smoothly bring gear and shaft to the same speed before the toothed dog clutches are engaged.

Identification

▶ See Figure 1

On all models covered in this book the manual transmission serial number is stamped on the front upper face of the transmission case.

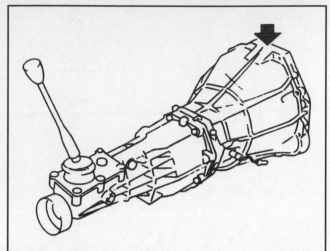

Fig. 1 Look for the manual transmission number on the bell housing

Adjustments

LINKAGE AND SHIFTER

All models are equipped with an integral linkage system. No adjustments are either possible or necessary.

Back-Up Light Switch

REMOVAL & INSTALLATION

All Models

1. Raise the vehicle and support safely with jackstands.
2. Disconnect the electrical connections from the switch.
3. Remove switch from transmission housing, when removing place drain pan under transmission to catch fluid.
4. To install reverse the removal procedures and check the fluid level.

Transmission

REMOVAL & INSTALLATION

▶ See Figures 2 thru 8

1. Disconnect the negative battery cable.
2. Disconnect the accelerator linkage on the 1980–81 200SX, the 1981–83 810 and 1984 Maxima.
3. Raise the car and support it with jackstands.
4. Disconnect the exhaust pipe from the manifold and bracket, if necessary, to gain clearance for transmission removal.
5. Tag and disconnect any switches that are connected to the transmission case (back-up, neutral, top gear or overdrive).

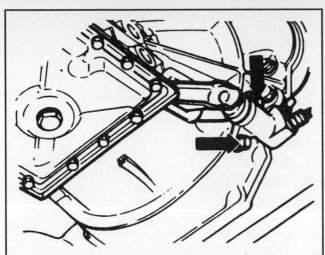

Fig. 2 When removing the transmission, you must remove the clutch slave cylinder

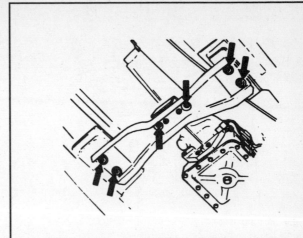

Fig. 5 Remove the crossmember mounting bolts (arrows), then the crossmember—610 and 710

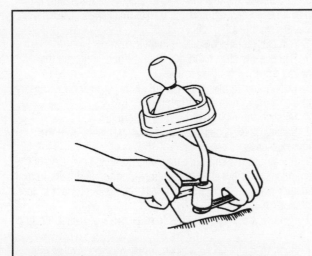

Fig. 3 Most earlier models used nuts to secure the shifter

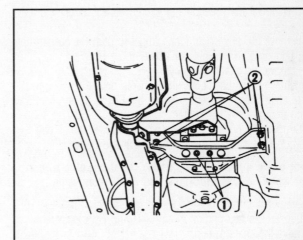

Fig. 6 Rear engine mounting nuts (1), and crossmember mounting nuts (2)—510 models

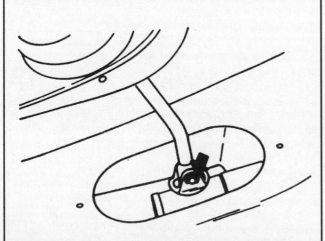

Fig. 4 Most later models used an E-ring to secure the shifter

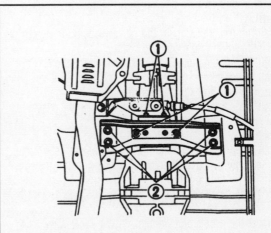

Fig. 7 Rear engine mounting nuts (1), and crossmember mounting nuts (2)—200SX models

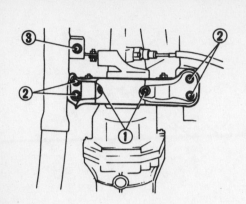

Fig. 8 Rear engine mounting nuts (1), crossmember mounting nuts (2), and exhaust bracket mounting nut (3)—810 models

6. Disconnect the speedometer cable where it attaches to the transmission.

7. Remove the driveshaft. Don't forget to plug the opening in the rear extension so that oil won't flow out.

8. Remove the clutch slave cylinder.

9. Remove the rubber boot and console box (if so equipped). Place the shift lever in neutral, remove the E-ring (later models only) and then remove the shifter.

10. Support the engine by placing a jack under the oil pan with a wooden block used between the jack and the pan.

➡**Do not place a jack directly under the drain plug with a block of wood between the jack and the transmission.**

11. Support the transmission with a transmission jack.

12. Loosen the rear engine mount securing nuts temporarily, then remove the crossmember.

13. Lower the rear of the engine slightly to allow additional clearance.

14. Remove the starter electrical connections and the starter motor.

15. Remove the transmission-to-engine mounting bolts, lower the transmission and remove it toward the rear.

To install:

16. Install the transmission in the correct position. Tighten all the transmission-to-engine mounting bolts.

17. Install the starter motor and electrical connections.

18. Install the crossmember assembly and tighten all retaining nuts to crossmember and rear engine mounts.

19. Install the shifter. Install the rubber boot and console box if so equipped.

20. Install the clutch slave cylinder.

21. Install the driveshaft and connect the speedometer cable.

22. Connect any switches that are connected to the transmission case (back-up, neutral, top gear or overdrive).

23. Connect the exhaust pipe to the manifold and bracket if necessary.

24. Connect the accelerator linkage on the 1980–81 200SX and the 1981–84 810 and Maxima.

25. Connect the negative battery cable. Bleed the clutch hydraulic system if necessary. Road test the vehicle for proper shift pattern operation.

OVERHAUL

4-Speed (Model F4W71B)

DISASSEMBLY

◆ **See Figures 9 thru 15**

This transmission is constructed in three sections: clutch housing, transmission housing and extension housing. There are no case cover plates. There is a cast iron adapter plate between the transmission and extension housings.

1. Remove the clutch housing dust cover. Remove the retaining spring, release bearing sleeve and lever.

2. Remove the backup light/neutral safety switch.

3. Unbolt and remove the clutch housing, rapping with a soft hammer if necessary. Remove the gasket, mainshaft bearing shim, and countershaft bearing shim.

4. Remove the speedometer pinion sleeve.

5. Remove the striker rod pin from the rod. Separate the striker rod from the shift lever bracket.

6. Unbolt and remove the rear extension. It may be necessary to rap the housing with a soft hammer.

7. Remove the mainshaft bearing snapring.

8. Remove the adapter plate and gear assembly from the transmission case.

9. Punch out the shift fork retaining pins. Remove the shift rod snaprings. Remove the detent plugs, springs and balls from the adapter plate. Remove the shift rods, being careful not to lose the interlock balls.

10. Remove the snapring, speedometer drive gear and locating ball.

11. Remove the nut, lockwasher, thrust washer, reverse hub and reverse gear.

12. Remove the snapring and countershaft reverse gear. Remove the snapring, reverse idler gear, thrust washer and needle bearing.

13. Support the gear assembly while rapping on the rear of the mainshaft with a soft hammer.

14. Remove the setscrew from the adapter plate. Remove the shaft nut, spring washer, plain washer and reverse idler shaft.

15. Remove the bearing retainer and the mainshaft rear bushing.

16. To disassemble the mainshaft (rear section), remove the front snapring, 3rd/4th synchronizer assembly, 3rd gear and needle bearing. From the rear, remove the thrust washer, locating ball, 1st gear, needle bearing, 1st gear bushing, 1st/2nd synchronizer assembly, 2nd gear, and needle bearing.

17. To disassemble the clutch shaft, remove the snapring and bearing spacer and press off the bearing.

18. To disassemble the countershaft, press off the front bearing. Press off the rear bearing, press off the gears and remove the keys.

19. Remove the retaining pin, control arm pin and shift control arm from the rear of the extension housing.

ASSEMBLY

1. Place the O-ring in the front cover. Install the front cover to the clutch housing with a press. Put in the front cover oil seal.

2. Install the rear extension oil seal.

3. Assemble the 1st/2nd and 3rd/4th synchronizer assemblies. Make sure that the ring gaps are not both on the same side of the unit.

4. On the rear end of the mainshaft, install the needle bearing, 2nd gear, baulk ring, 1st/2nd synchronizer assembly, baulk ring, 1st gear bushing, needle bearing, 1st gear, locating ball and thrust washer.

5. Drive or press on the mainshaft rear bearing.

6. Install the countershaft rear bearing to the adapter plate. Drive or press the mainshaft rear bearing into the adapter plate until the bearing snapring groove comes through the rear side of the plate. Install the snapring. If it is not tight against the plate, press the bearing back in slightly.

7. Insert the countershaft bearing ring between the countershaft rear bearing and bearing retainer. Install the bearing retainer to the adapter plate. Stake both ends of the screws.

8. Insert the reverse idler shaft from the rear of the adapter plate. Install the spring washer and plain washer to the idler shaft.

9. Place the two keys on the countershaft and oil the shaft lightly. Press on 3rd gear and install a snapring.

10. Install the countershaft into its rear bearing.

11. From the front of the mainshaft, install the needle bearing, 3rd gear, baulk ring, 3rd/4th synchronizer assembly and snapring. Snaprings are available in thicknesses from 1.4–1.6mm to adjust gear end-play.

12. Press the main drive bearing onto the clutch shaft. Install the main drive gear spacer and a snapring. Snaprings are available in thicknesses from 1.8–2.0mm to adjust gear end-play.

13. Insert a key into the countershaft drive gear with 4th gear and drive on the countershaft 4th gear with a drift. The rear end of the countershaft should be held steady while driving on the gear, to prevent rear bearing damage.

14. Install the reverse hub, reverse gear, thrust washer, and lock tab on the rear of the mainshaft. Install the shaft nut temporarily.

15. Install the needle bearing, reverse idler gear, thrust washer, and snapring.

16. Place the countershaft reverse gear and snapring on the rear of the countershaft. Snaprings are available in thicknesses from 1.0–1.5mm to adjust gear end-play.

17. Engage both 1st and 2nd gears to lock the shaft.

18. On the rear of the mainshaft, install the snapring, locating ball, speedometer drive gear, and snapring. Snaprings are available in thicknesses from 1.0–1.5mm.

19. Recheck end-play and backlash of all gears.

20. Place the reverse shift fork on the reverse gear and install the reverse shift rod. Install the detent ball, spring and plug. Install the fork retaining pin. Place two interlock balls between the reverse shift rod and the 3rd/4th shift rod location. Install the 3rd/4th shift fork and rod. Install the detent ball, spring and plug. This plug is shorter than the other two. Install the fork retaining pin. Place two interlock balls between the 1st/2nd shift rod location and the 3rd/4th shift rod. Install the 1st/2nd shift fork and rod. Install the detent ball, spring and plug.

21. Install the shift rod snaprings.

22. Apply sealant sparingly to the adapter plate and transmission housing. Install the transmission housing to the adapter plate and bolt it down temporarily.

23. Drive in the countershaft front bearing with a drift. Place the snapring in the mainshaft front bearing.

24. Apply sealant sparingly to the adapter plate and extension housing. Align the shift rods in the neutral positions. Position the striker rod to the shift rods and bolt down the extension housing.

25. Insert the striker rod pin, connect the rod to the shift lever bracket and install the striker rod pin retaining ring. Replace the shift control arm.

26. To select the proper mainshaft bearing shim, first measure the amount the bearing protrudes from the front of the transmission case. Then measure the depth of the bearing recess in the rear of the clutch housing. Required shim thickness is found by subtracting, the difference is required shim size. Shims are available in thicknesses of 1.4mm and 1.6mm.

27. To select the proper countershaft front bearing shim, measure the amount that the bearing is recessed into the transmission case. Shim thickness should equal this measurement. Shims are available in thicknesses from 0.04mm to 1.0mm.

28. Apply sealant sparingly to the clutch and transmission housing mating surfaces.

29. Replace the clutch operating mechanism.

30. Install the shift lever temporarily and check shifting action.

5-Speed (Models FS5W71B and FS5W71C)
▶ **See Figures 9 thru 15**

This transmission is similar to the 4-speed transmission (Model F4W71B). The overhaul can be accomplished by following the outline for the disassembly and assembly of the 4-speed.

Servo type synchromesh is used, instead of the Borg Warner type in the four speed. Shift linkage and interlock arrangements are the same, except the reverse shift rod also operates 5th gear. Most service procedures are identical to those for the four speed unit.

Those procedures that are unique to the 5-speed follow:

DISASSEMBLY

To disassemble the synchronizers, remove the circlip, synchronizer ring, thrust block, brake band, and anchor block. Be careful not to mix parts of the different synchronizer assemblies.

ASSEMBLY

1. The synchronizer assemblies for 2nd, 3rd, and 4th are identical. When assembling the 1st gear synchronizer, be sure to install the 2.2mm thick brake band at the bottom.

2. When assembling the mainshaft, select a 3rd gear synchronizer hub snapring to minimize hub end-play. snaprings are available in thicknesses of 1.5–1.6mm, 1.50–1.55mm and 1.45–1.50mm. The synchronizer hub must be installed with the longer boss to the rear.

3. When reassembling the gear train, install the mainshaft, countershaft, and gears to the adapter plate. Hold the rear nut and force the front nut against it to a torque of 217 ft. lbs. for 1979 models and 123 ft. lbs. for 1980–84 models. Select a snapring to minimize end-play of the 5th gear bearing at the rear of the mainshaft. Snaprings are available in thicknesses from 1.0–1.5mm.

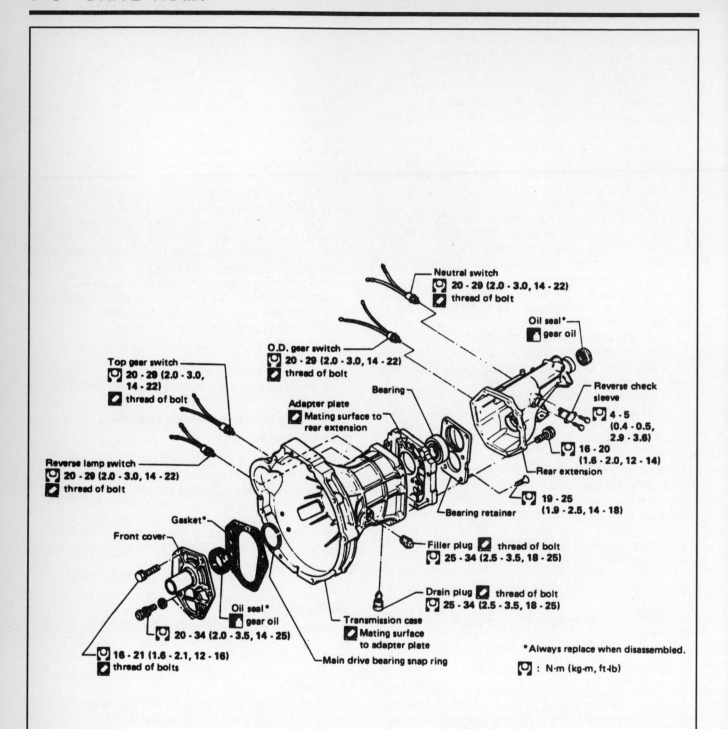

Fig. 9 Exploded view of the case components—FS5W71B transmission shown, 4-speed transmissions similar

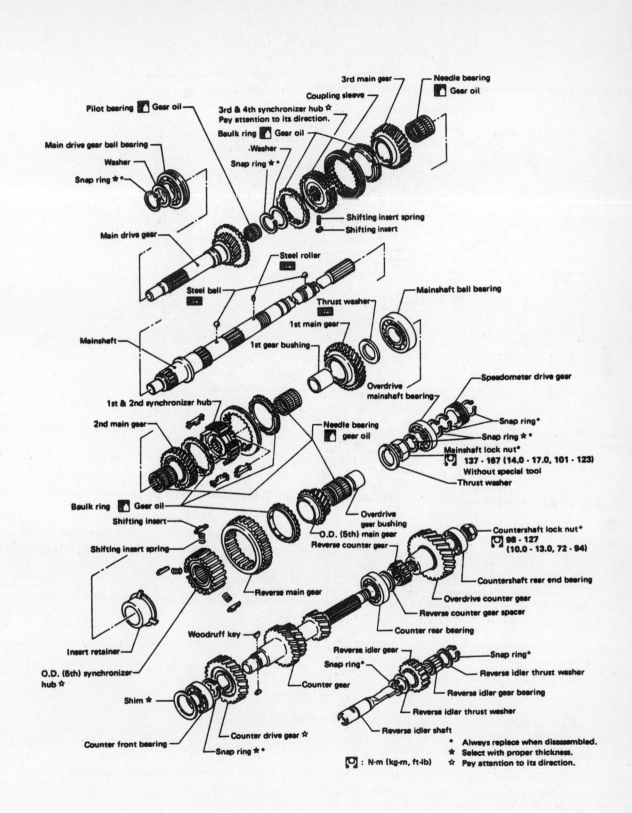

Fig. 10 Exploded view of the gear components—FS5W71B transmission shown, 4-speed transmissions similar

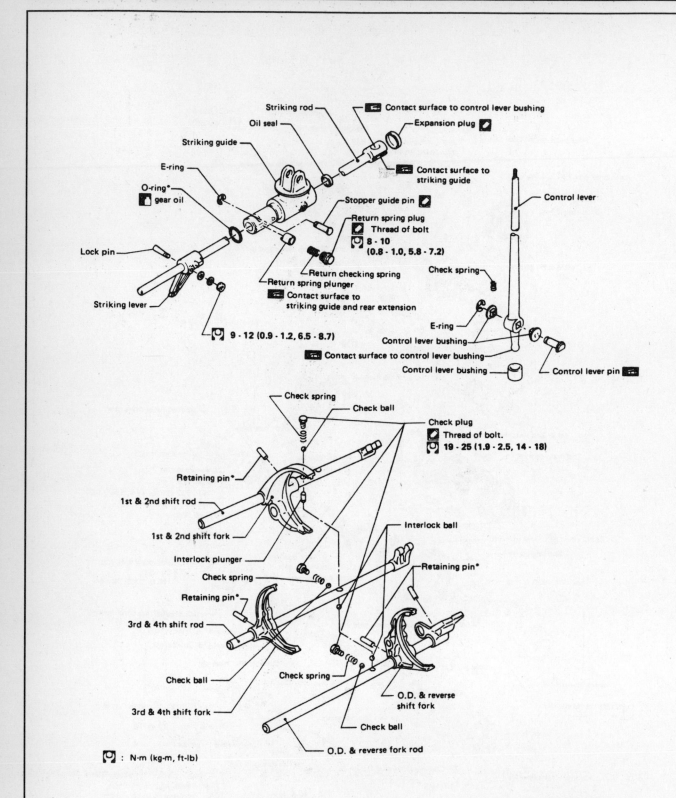

Fig. 11 Exploded view of the shift control components—FS5W71B transmission shown, 4-speed transmissions similar

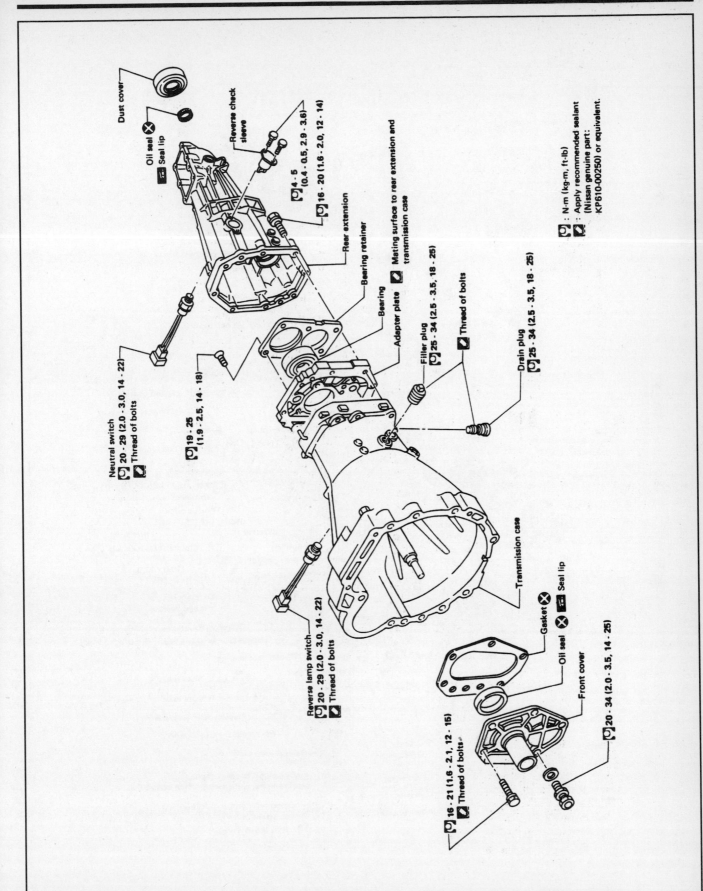

Fig. 12 Exploded view of the case components—FS5W71C transmission shown, 4-speed transmissions similar

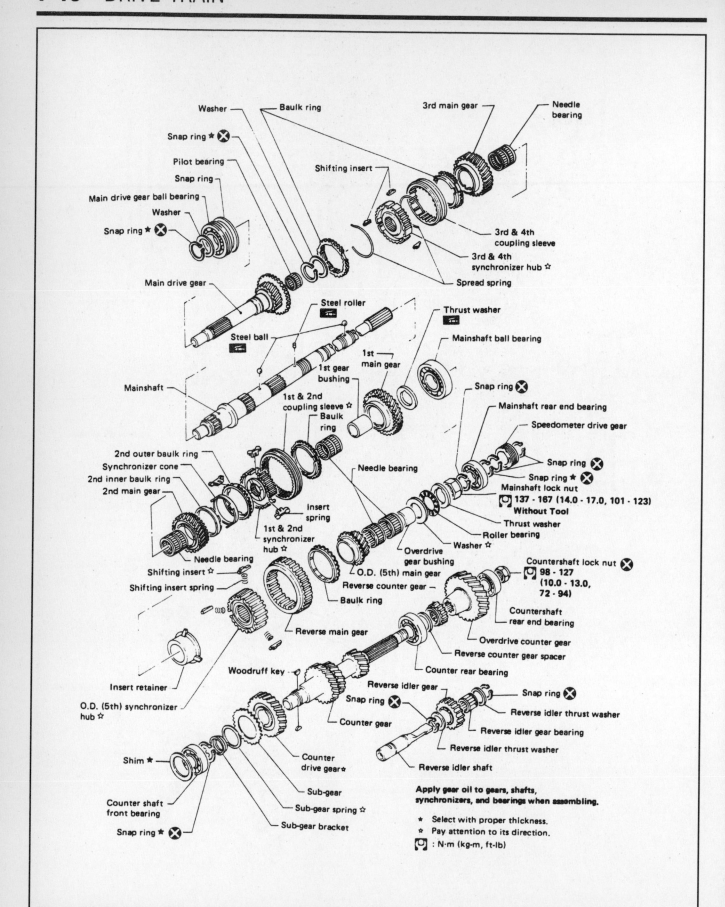

Fig. 13 Exploded view of the gear components—FS5W71C transmission shown, 4-speed transmissions similar

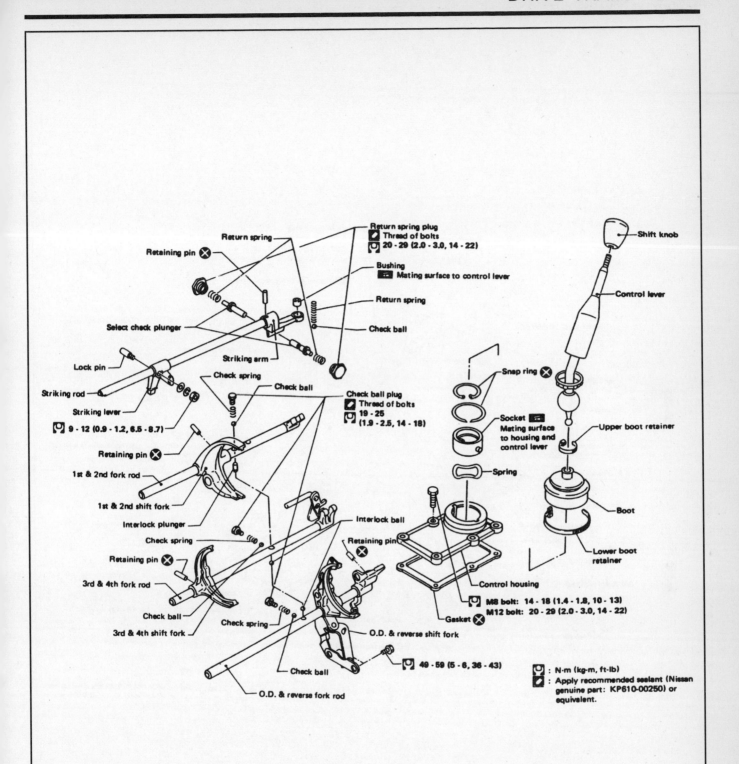

Return spring

Retaining pin ⊗

Return spring plug
Thread of bolts
20 - 29 (2.0 - 3.0, 14 - 22)

Bushing
Mating surface to control lever

Return spring

Select check plunger

Check ball

Striking arm

Lock pin

Striking rod

Striking lever

Check spring

Check ball

Check ball plug
Thread of bolts
19 - 25
(1.9 - 2.5, 14 - 18)

9 - 12 (0.9 - 1.2, 6.5 - 8.7)

Retaining pin ⊗

1st & 2nd fork rod

1st & 2nd shift fork

Interlock plunger

Interlock ball

Check spring

Retaining pin

Retaining pin ⊗

3rd & 4th fork rod

Check ball

3rd & 4th shift fork

Check spring

O.D. & reverse shift fork

Gasket

Check ball

O.D. & reverse fork rod

Shift knob

Control lever

Snap ring ⊗

Socket
Mating surface
to housing and
control lever

Spring

Upper boot retainer

Boot

Lower boot retainer

Control housing

M8 bolt: 14 - 18 (1.4 - 1.8, 10 - 13)
M12 bolt: 20 - 29 (2.0 - 3.0, 14 - 22)

49 - 59 (5 - 6, 36 - 43)

: N·m (kg-m, ft-lb)

: Apply recommended sealant (Nissan
genuine part: KP610-00250) or
equivalent.

Fig. 14 Exploded view of the shift control components—FS5W71C transmission (with mainshaft braking mechanism) shown, 4-speed transmissions similar

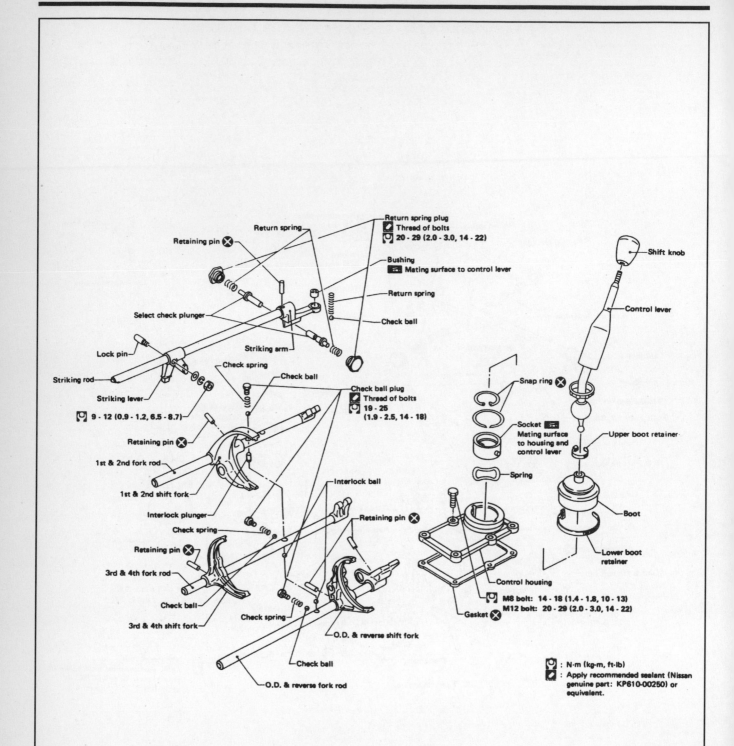

Fig. 15 Exploded view of the shift control components—FS5W71C transmission (without mainshaft braking mechanism) shown, 4-speed transmissions similar

Troubleshooting the Manual Transmission

Problem	Cause	Solution
Transmission shifts hard	• Clutch adjustment incorrect • Clutch linkage or cable binding • Shift rail binding	• Adjust clutch • Lubricate or repair as necessary • Check for mispositioned selector arm roll pin, loose cover bolts, worn shift rail bores, worn shift rail, distorted oil seal, or extension housing not aligned with case. Repair as necessary.
	• Internal bind in transmission caused by shift forks, selector plates, or synchronizer assemblies • Clutch housing misalignment • Incorrect lubricant • Block rings and/or cone seats worn	• Remove, dissemble and inspect transmission. Replace worn or damaged components as necessary. • Check runout at rear face of clutch housing • Drain and refill transmission • Blocking ring to gear clutch tooth face clearance must be 0.030 inch or greater. If clearance is correct it may still be necessary to inspect blocking rings and cone seats for excessive wear. Repair as necessary.
Gear clash when shifting from one gear to another	• Clutch adjustment incorrect • Clutch linkage or cable binding • Clutch housing misalignment • Lubricant level low or incorrect lubricant • Gearshift components, or synchronizer assemblies worn or damaged	• Adjust clutch • Lubricate or repair as necessary • Check runout at rear of clutch housing • Drain and refill transmission and check for lubricant leaks if level was low. Repair as necessary. • Remove, disassemble and inspect transmission. Replace worn or damaged components as necessary.
Transmission noisy	• Lubricant level low or incorrect lubricant • Clutch housing-to-engine, or transmission-to-clutch housing bolts loose • Dirt, chips, foreign material in transmission • Gearshift mechanism, transmission gears, or bearing components worn or damaged • Clutch housing misalignment	• Drain and refill transmission. If lubricant level was low, check for leaks and repair as necessary. • Check and correct bolt torque as necessary • Drain, flush, and refill transmission • Remove, disassemble and inspect transmission. Replace worn or damaged components as necessary. • Check runout at rear face of clutch housing
Jumps out of gear	• Clutch housing misalignment • Gearshift lever loose • Offset lever nylon insert worn or lever attaching nut loose • Gearshift mechanism, shift forks, selector plates, interlock plate, selector arm, shift rail, detent plugs, springs or shift cover worn or damaged • Clutch shaft or roller bearings worn or damaged	• Check runout at rear face of clutch housing • Check lever for worn fork. Tighten loose attaching bolts. • Remove gearshift lever and check for loose offset lever nut or worn insert. Repair or replace as necessary. • Remove, disassemble and inspect transmission cover assembly. Replace worn or damaged components as necessary. • Replace clutch shaft or roller bearings as necessary

Troubleshooting the Manual Transmission (cont.)

Problem	Cause	Solution
Jumps out of gear (cont.)	• Gear teeth worn or tapered, synchronizer assemblies worn or damaged, excessive end play caused by worn thrust washers or output shaft gears	• Remove, disassemble, and inspect transmission. Replace worn or damaged components as necessary.
	• Pilot bushing worn	• Replace pilot bushing
Will not shift into one gear	• Gearshift selector plates, interlock plate, or selector arm, worn, damaged, or incorrectly assembled	• Remove, disassemble, and inspect transmission cover assembly. Repair or replace components as necessary.
	• Shift rail detent plunger worn, spring broken, or plug loose	• Tighten plug or replace worn or damaged components as necessary
	• Gearshift lever worn or damaged	• Replace gearshift lever
	• Synchronizer sleeves or hubs, damaged or worn	• Remove, disassemble and inspect transmission. Replace worn or damaged components.
Locked in one gear—cannot be shifted out	• Shift rail(s) worn or broken, shifter fork bent, setscrew loose, center detent plug missing or worn	• Inspect and replace worn or damaged parts
	• Broken gear teeth on countershaft gear, clutch shaft, or reverse idler gear	• Inspect and replace damaged part
	Gearshift lever broken or worn, shift mechanism in cover incorrectly assembled or broken, worn damaged gear train components	• Disassemble transmission. Replace damaged parts or assemble correctly.
Transfer case difficult to shift or will not shift into desired range	• Vehicle speed too great to permit shifting	• Stop vehicle and shift into desired range. Or reduce speed to 3–4 km/h (2–3 mph) before attempting to shift.
	• If vehicle was operated for extended period in 4H mode on dry paved surface, driveline torque load may cause difficult shifting	• Stop vehicle, shift transmission to neutral, shift transfer case to 2H mode and operate vehicle in 2H on dry paved surfaces
	• Transfer case external shift linkage binding	• Lubricate or repair or replace linkage, or tighten loose components as necessary
	• Insufficient or incorrect lubricant	• Drain and refill to edge of fill hole with SAE 85W-90 gear lubricant only
	• Internal components binding, worn, or damaged	• Disassemble unit and replace worn or damaged components as necessary
Transfer case noisy in all drive modes	• Insufficient or incorrect lubricant	• Drain and refill to edge of fill hole with SAE 85W-90 gear lubricant only. Check for leaks and repair if necessary. Note: If unit is still noisy after drain and refill, disassembly and inspection may be required to locate source of noise.
Noisy in—or jumps out of four wheel drive low range	• Transfer case not completely engaged in 4L position	• Stop vehicle, shift transfer case in Neutral, then shift back into 4L position
	• Shift linkage loose or binding	• Tighten, lubricate, or repair linkage as necessary
	• Shift fork cracked, inserts worn, or fork is binding on shift rail	• Disassemble unit and repair as necessary
Lubricant leaking from output shaft seals or from vent	• Transfer case overfilled	• Drain to correct level
	• Vent closed or restricted	• Clear or replace vent if necessary

Troubleshooting the Manual Transmission (cont.)

Problem	Cause	Solution
Lubricant leaking from output shaft seals or from vent (cont.)	• Output shaft seals damaged or installed incorrectly	• Replace seals. Be sure seal lip faces interior of case when installed. Also be sure yoke seal surfaces are not scored or nicked. Remove scores, nicks with fine sandpaper or replace yoke(s) if necessary.
Abnormal tire wear	• Extended operation on dry hard surface (paved) roads in 4H range	• Operate in 2H on hard surface (paved) roads

CLUTCH

Understanding the Clutch

◆ See Figure 16

✳✳ CAUTION

The clutch driven disc contains asbestos, which has been determined to be a cancer causing agent. Never clean clutch surface with compressed air! Avoid inhaling any dust from any clutch surface! When cleaning clutch surfaces, use a commercially available brake cleaning fluid.

The purpose of the clutch is to disconnect and connect engine power at the transmission. A vehicle at rest requires a lot of engine torque to get all that weight moving. An internal combustion engine does not develop a high starting torque (unlike steam engines) so it must be allowed to operate without any load until it builds up enough torque to move the vehicle. To a point, torque increases with engine rpm. The clutch allows the engine to build up torque by physically disconnecting the engine from the transmission, relieving the engine of any load or resistance.

The transfer of engine power to the transmission (the load) must be smooth and gradual; if it weren't, drive line components would wear out or break quickly. This gradual power transfer is made possible by gradually releasing the clutch pedal. The clutch disc and pressure plate are the connecting link between the engine and transmission. When the clutch pedal is released, the disc and plate contact each other (the clutch is engaged) physically joining the engine and transmission. When the pedal is pushed in, the disc and plate separate (the clutch is disengaged) disconnecting the engine from the transmission.

Most clutch assemblies consists of the flywheel, the clutch disc, the clutch pressure plate, the throw out bearing and fork, the actuating linkage and the pedal. The flywheel and clutch pressure plate (driving members) are connected to the engine crankshaft and rotate with it. The clutch disc is located between the flywheel and pressure plate, and is splined to the transmission shaft. A driving member is one that is attached to the engine and transfers engine power to a driven member (clutch disc) on the transmission shaft. A driving member (pressure plate) rotates (drives) a driven member (clutch disc) on contact and, in so doing, turns the transmission shaft.

There is a circular diaphragm spring within the pressure plate cover (transmission side). In a relaxed state (when the clutch pedal is fully released) this spring is convex; that is, it is dished outward toward the transmission. Pushing in the clutch pedal actuates the attached linkage. Connected to the other end of this is the throw out fork, which hold the throw out bearing. When the clutch pedal is depressed, the clutch linkage pushes the fork and bearing forward to contact the diaphragm spring of the pressure plate. The outer edges of the spring are secured to the pressure plate and are pivoted on rings so that when the center of the spring is compressed by the throw out bearing, the outer edges bow outward and, by so doing, pull the pressure plate in the same direction away from the clutch disc. This action separates the disc from the plate, disengaging the clutch and allowing the transmission to be shifted into another gear. A coil type clutch return spring attached to the clutch pedal arm permits full release of the pedal. Releasing the pedal pulls the throw out bearing away from the diaphragm spring resulting in a reversal of spring position. As bearing pressure is gradually released from the spring center, the outer edges of the spring bow outward, pushing the pressure plate into closer contact with the clutch disc. As the disc and plate move closer together, friction between the two increases and slippage is reduced until, when full spring pressure is applied (by fully releasing the pedal) the speed of the disc and plate are the same. This stops all slipping, creating a direct connection between the plate and disc which results in the transfer of power from the engine to the transmission. The clutch disc is now rotating with the pressure plate at engine speed and, because it is splined to the transmission shaft, the shaft now turns at the same engine speed.

The clutch is operating properly if:

1. It will stall the engine when released with the vehicle held stationary.

2. The shift lever can be moved freely between 1st and reverse gears when the vehicle is stationary and the clutch disengaged.

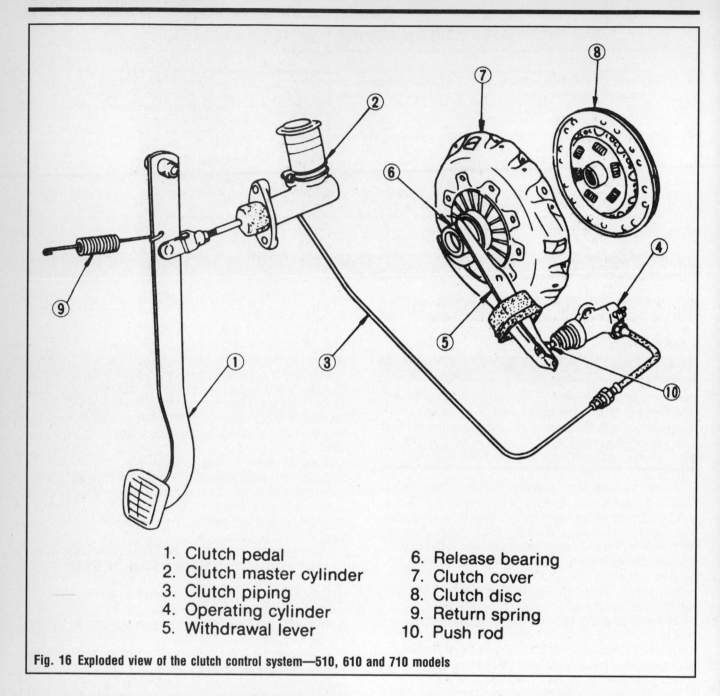

1. Clutch pedal
2. Clutch master cylinder
3. Clutch piping
4. Operating cylinder
5. Withdrawal lever
6. Release bearing
7. Clutch cover
8. Clutch disc
9. Return spring
10. Push rod

Fig. 16 Exploded view of the clutch control system—510, 610 and 710 models

Adjustments

PEDAL HEIGHT & FREE PLAY

◆ See Figure 17

Refer to the Clutch Specifications Chart for clutch pedal height above floor and pedal free-play.

All models have a hydraulically operated clutch. Pedal height is usually adjusted with a stopper limiting the upward travel of the pedal. Pedal free-play is adjusted at the master cylinder pushrod. If the pushrod is nonadjustable, free-play is adjusted by placing shims between the master cylinder and the firewall.

Clutch Specifications

Model	Pedal Height Above Floor (in.)	Pedal Free-Play (in.)
510	6.5	0.04–0.20
610	6.9	0.04–0.12
710	7.09	0.04–0.20
1977–80 810	6.9	0.04–0.20
1981–83 810, Maxima	7.25	0.04–0.20
1977–79 200SX	7.60	0.04–0.12
1980–81 200SX	6.70	0.04–0.20
1984 Maxima	6.9	0.04–0.20

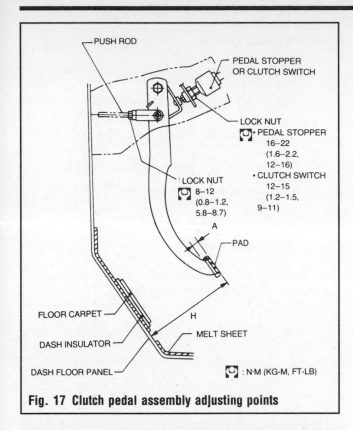

Fig. 17 Clutch pedal assembly adjusting points

Driven Disc and Pressure Plate

REMOVAL & INSTALLATION

▶ **See Figures 18 thru 25**

1. Remove the transmission or transaxle from the engine as detailed earlier in this section.

2. Insert a clutch aligning bar or similar tool all the way into the clutch disc hub. This must be done so as to support the weight of the clutch disc during removal. Mark the clutch assem-

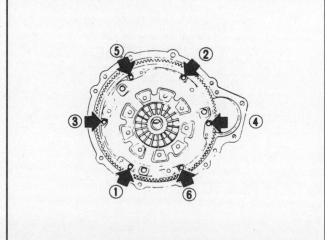

Fig. 18 Loosen the bolts to the clutch assembly one turn at a time, in the sequence provided

Typical clutch alignment tool, note how the splines match the transmission's input shaft

Loosen and remove the clutch and pressure plate bolts evenly, a little at a time . . .

. . . then carefully remove the clutch and pressure plate assembly from the flywheel

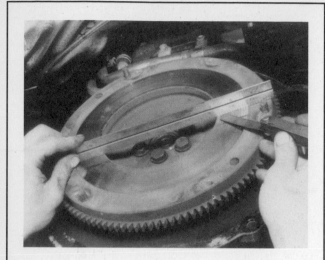

Check across the flywheel surface, it should be flat

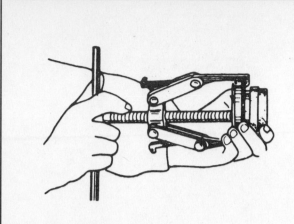

Fig. 19 Use a universal puller and adapter to pull the release bearing out of the bearing sleeve

If necessary, lock the flywheel in place and remove the retaining bolts . . .

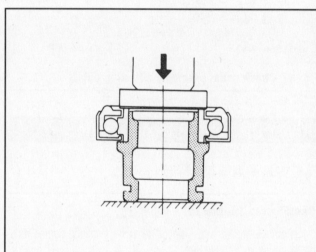

Fig. 20 Install the release bearing on the sleeve using a press as shown

. . . then remove the flywheel from the crankshaft in order replace it or have it machined

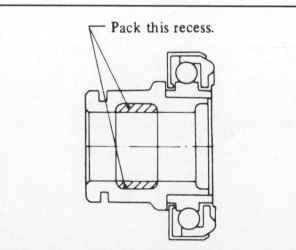

Pack this recess.

Fig. 21 Apply grease to the release bearing bore where indicated

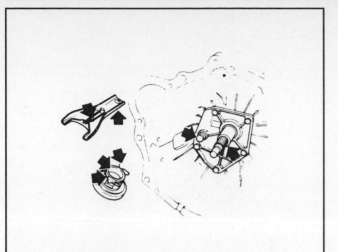

Fig. 22 Grease the points indicated (arrows) prior to installing the clutch

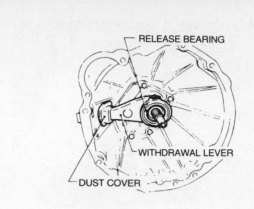

Fig. 23 Use this illustration to restore the correct withdrawal lever-to-release bearing relationship upon installation

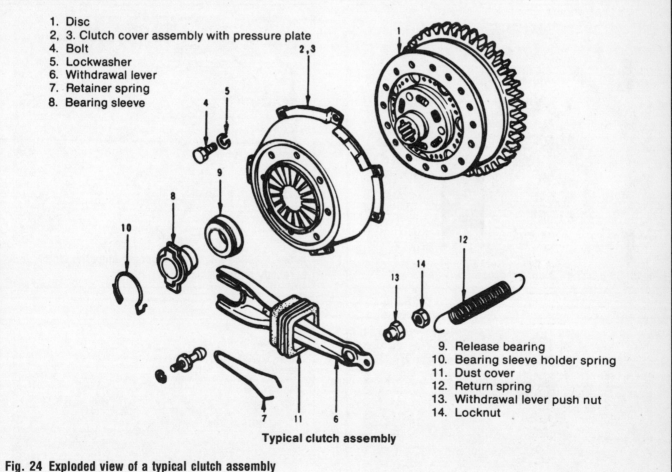

1. Disc
2, 3. Clutch cover assembly with pressure plate
4. Bolt
5. Lockwasher
6. Withdrawal lever
7. Retainer spring
8. Bearing sleeve

9. Release bearing
10. Bearing sleeve holder spring
11. Dust cover
12. Return spring
13. Withdrawal lever push nut
14. Locknut

Typical clutch assembly

Fig. 24 Exploded view of a typical clutch assembly

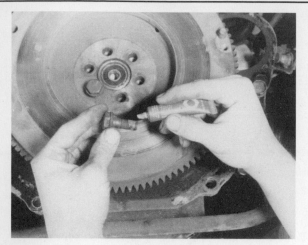

Upon installation, it is usually a good idea to apply a thread-locking compound to the flywheel bolts

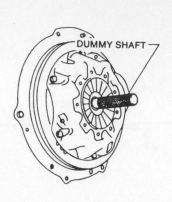

Fig. 25 Use a splined clutch alignment tool (dummy shaft) as shown, when installing the clutch assembly

Check the pressure plate for excessive wear

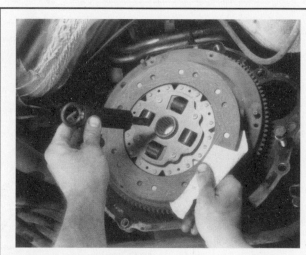

Install a clutch alignment arbor, to align the clutch assembly during installation

Be sure that the flywheel surface is clean, before installing the clutch

Clutch plate installed with the arbor in place

Clutch plate and pressure plate installed with the alignment arbor in place

Install the clutch assembly bolts and tighten in steps, using an X pattern

Pressure plate-to-flywheel bolt holes should align

Be sure to use a torque wrench to tighten all bolts

You may want to use a thread locking compound on the clutch assembly bolts

bly-to-flywheel relationship with paint or a center punch so that the clutch assembly can be assembled in the same position from which it is removed.

3. Loosen the bolts in sequence, a turn at a time. Remove the bolts.

4. Remove the pressure plate and clutch disc.

5. Remove the release mechanism from the transmission housing. Apply lithium based molybdenum disulfide grease to the bearing sleeve inside groove, the contact point of the withdrawal lever and bearing sleeve, the contact surface of the lever ball pin and lever. Replace the release mechanism.

6. Inspect the pressure plate and flywheel for wear, scoring, etc., using a straightedge and feeler gauge and reface or replace as necessary. Inspect the release bearing and replace as necessary. Apply a small amount of grease to the transmission splines. Install the disc on the splines and slide back and forth a few times. Remove the disc and remove excess grease on hub. Be sure no grease contacts the disc or pressure plate.

To install:

7. Install the disc, aligning it with a splined dummy shaft.

8. Install the pressure plate and tighten the bolts to 11–16 ft. lbs.

9. Remove the dummy shaft.

10. Replace the transmission or transaxle.

Clutch Master Cylinder

REMOVAL & INSTALLATION

1. Disconnect the clutch pedal arm from the pushrod.

2. Disconnect the clutch hydraulic line from the master cylinder.

➡**Take precautions to keep brake fluid from coming in contact with any painted surfaces.**

3. Remove the nuts attaching the master cylinder and remove the master cylinder and pushrod toward the engine compartment side.

4. Install the master cylinder in the reverse order of removal and bleed the clutch hydraulic system.

OVERHAUL

▶ **See Figure 26**

1. Remove the master cylinder from the vehicle.

2. Drain the clutch fluid from the master cylinder reservoir.

3. Remove the boot and circlip and remove the pushrod.

4. Remove the stopper, piston, cup and return spring.

5. Clean all of the parts in clean brake fluid.

6. Check the master cylinder and piston for wear, corrosion and scores and replace the parts as necessary. Light scoring and glaze can be removed with crocus cloth soaked in brake fluid.

7. Generally, the cup seal should be replaced each time the master cylinder is disassembled. Check the cup and replace it if it is worn, fatigued, or damaged.

8. Check the clutch fluid reservoir, filler cap, dust cover and the pipe for distortion and damage and replace the parts as necessary.

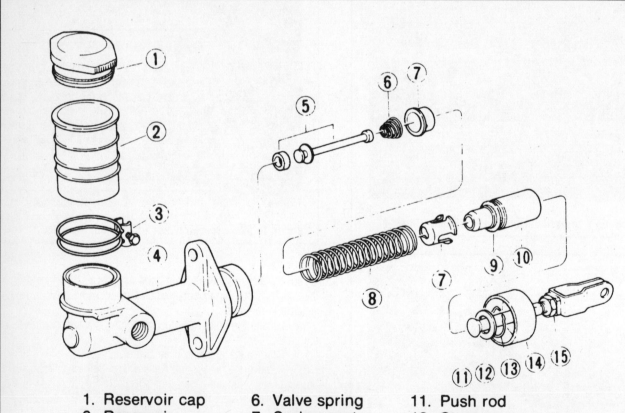

1. Reservoir cap	6. Valve spring	11. Push rod
2. Reservoir	7. Spring seat	12. Stopper
3. Reservoir band	8. Return spring	13. Stopper ring
4. Cylinder body	9. Piston cup	14. Dust cover
5. Valve assembly	10. Piston	15. Nut

Fig. 26 Exploded view of a typical clutch master cylinder

9. Lubricate all new parts with clean brake fluid.

10. Reassemble the master cylinder parts in the reverse order of disassembly, taking note of the following:

a. Reinstall the cup seal carefully to prevent damaging the lipped portions.

b. Adjust the height of the clutch pedal after installing the master cylinder in position on the vehicle.

c. Fill the master cylinder and clutch fluid reservoir and then bleed the clutch hydraulic system.

Clutch Slave Cylinder

REMOVAL & INSTALLATION

1. Remove the slave cylinder attaching bolts and the pushrod from the shift fork.

2. Disconnect the flexible fluid hose from the slave cylinder and remove the unit from the vehicle.

3. Install the slave cylinder in the reverse order of removal and bleed the clutch hydraulic system.

OVERHAUL

▶ **See Figure 27**

1. Remove the slave cylinder from the vehicle.

2. Remove the pushrod and boot.

3. Force out the piston by blowing compressed air into the slave cylinder at the hose connection.

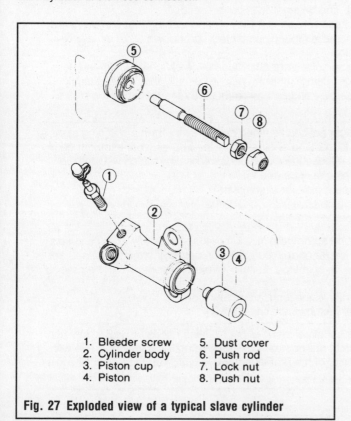

1. Bleeder screw
2. Cylinder body
3. Piston cup
4. Piston
5. Dust cover
6. Push rod
7. Lock nut
8. Push nut

Fig. 27 Exploded view of a typical slave cylinder

✳✳ CAUTION

Be careful not to apply excess air pressure to avoid possible injury.

4. Clean all of the parts in clean brake fluid.

5. Check and replace the slave cylinder bore and piston if wear or severe scoring exists. Light scoring and glaze can be removed with crocus cloth soaked in brake fluid.

6. Normally the piston cup should be replaced when the slave cylinder is disassembled. Check the piston cup and replace it if it is found to be worn, fatigued or scored.

7. Replace the rubber boot if it is cracked or broken.

8. Lubricate all of the new parts in clean brake fluid and reassemble in the reverse order of disassembly, taking note of the following:

a. Use care when reassembling the piston cup to prevent damaging the lipped portion of the piston cup.

b. Fill the master cylinder with brake fluid and bleed the clutch hydraulic system.

c. Adjust the clearance between the pushrod and the shift fork to $5/64''$.

BLEEDING THE CLUTCH HYDRAULIC SYSTEM

▶ **See Figures 28 and 29**

1. Check and fill the clutch fluid reservoir to the specified level as necessary. During the bleeding process, continue to check and replenish the reservoir to prevent the fluid level from getting lower than ½ the specified level.

2. Remove the dust cap from the bleeder screw on the clutch slave cylinder and connect a tube to the bleeder screw and insert the other end of the tube into a clean glass or metal container.

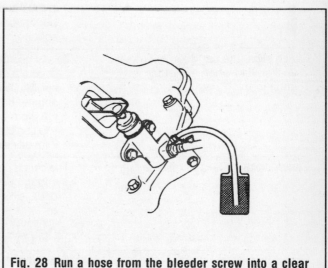

Fig. 28 Run a hose from the bleeder screw into a clear container filled with brake fluid

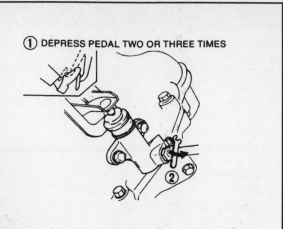

① DEPRESS PEDAL TWO OR THREE TIMES

Fig. 29 Pump the clutch pedal several times, release the clutch pedal, then open the bleeder screw—repeat as necessary

➡**Take precautionary measures to prevent the brake fluid from getting on any painted surfaces.**

3. Pump the clutch pedal SLOWLY several times, hold it down and loosen the bleeder screw.

4. Tighten the bleeder screw and release the clutch pedal gradually. Repeat this operation until air bubbles disappear from the brake fluid being expelled out through the bleeder screw.

5. Repeat until all evidence of air bubbles completely disappears from the brake fluid being pumped out through the tube.

6. When the air is completely removed, securely tighten the bleeder screw and replace the dust cap.

7. Check and refill the master cylinder reservoir as necessary.

8. Depress the clutch pedal several times to check the operation of the clutch and check for leaks.

Troubleshooting Basic Clutch Problems

Problem	Cause
Excessive clutch noise	Throwout bearing noises are more audible at the lower end of pedal travel. The usual causes are: • Riding the clutch • Too little pedal free-play • Lack of bearing lubrication A bad clutch shaft pilot bearing will make a high pitched squeal, when the clutch is disengaged and the transmission is in gear or within the first 2″ of pedal travel. The bearing must be replaced. Noise from the clutch linkage is a clicking or snapping that can be heard or felt as the pedal is moved completely up or down. This usually requires lubrication. Transmitted engine noises are amplified by the clutch housing and heard in the passenger compartment. They are usually the result of insufficient pedal free-play and can be changed by manipulating the clutch pedal.
Clutch slips (the car does not move as it should when the clutch is engaged)	This is usually most noticeable when pulling away from a standing start. A severe test is to start the engine, apply the brakes, shift into high gear and SLOWLY release the clutch pedal. A healthy clutch will stall the engine. If it slips it may be due to: • A worn pressure plate or clutch plate • Oil soaked clutch plate • Insufficient pedal free-play
Clutch drags or fails to release	The clutch disc and some transmission gears spin briefly after clutch disengagement. Under normal conditions in average temperatures, 3 seconds is maximum spin-time. Failure to release properly can be caused by: • Too light transmission lubricant or low lubricant level • Improperly adjusted clutch linkage
Low clutch life	Low clutch life is usually a result of poor driving habits or heavy duty use. Riding the clutch, pulling heavy loads, holding the car on a grade with the clutch instead of the brakes and rapid clutch engagement all contribute to low clutch life.

AUTOMATIC TRANSMISSION

Understanding Automatic Transmissions

The automatic transmission allows engine torque and power to be transmitted to the rear wheels within a narrow range of engine operating speeds. It will allow the engine to turn fast enough to produce plenty of power and torque at very low speeds, while keeping it at a sensible rpm at high vehicle speeds (and it does this job without driver assistance). The transmission uses a light fluid as the medium for the transmission of power. This fluid also works in the operation of various hydraulic control circuits and as a lubricant. Because the transmission fluid performs all of these functions, trouble within the unit can easily travel from one part to another. For this reason, and because of the complexity and unusual operating principles of the transmission, a very sound understanding of the basic principles of operation will simplify troubleshooting.

TORQUE CONVERTER

The torque converter replaces the conventional clutch. It has three functions:

1. It allows the engine to idle with the vehicle at a standstill, even with the transmission in gear.

2. It allows the transmission to shift from range-to-range smoothly, without requiring that the driver close the throttle during the shift.

3. It multiplies engine torque to an increasing extent as vehicle speed drops and throttle opening is increased. This has the effect of making the transmission more responsive and reduces the amount of shifting required.

The torque converter is a metal case which is shaped like a sphere that has been flattened on opposite sides. It is bolted to the rear end of the engine's crankshaft. Generally, the entire metal case rotates at engine speed and serves as the engine's flywheel.

The case contains three sets of blades. One set is attached directly to the case. This set forms the torus or pump. Another set is directly connected to the output shaft, and forms the turbine. The third set is mounted on a hub which, in turn, is mounted on a stationary shaft through a one-way clutch. This third set is known as the stator.

A pump, which is driven by the converter hub at engine speed, keeps the torque converter full of transmission fluid at all times. Fluid flows continuously through the unit to provide cooling.

Under low speed acceleration, the torque converter functions as follows:

The torus is turning faster than the turbine. It picks up fluid at the center of the converter and, through centrifugal force, slings it outward. Since the outer edge of the converter moves faster than the portions at the center, the fluid picks up speed.

The fluid then enters the outer edge of the turbine blades. It then travels back toward the center of the converter case along the turbine blades. In impinging upon the turbine blades, the fluid loses the energy picked up in the torus.

If the fluid was now returned directly into the torus, both halves of the converter would have to turn at approximately the same speed at all times, and torque input and output would both be the same.

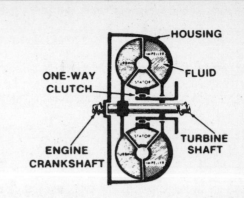

The torque converter housing is rotated by the engine's crankshaft, and turns the impeller—The impeller then spins the turbine, which gives motion to the turbine shaft, driving the gears

In flowing through the torus and turbine, the fluid picks up two types of flow, or flow in two separate directions. It flows through the turbine blades, and it spins with the engine. The stator, whose blades are stationary when the vehicle is being accelerated at low speeds, converts one type of flow into another. Instead of allowing the fluid to flow straight back into the torus, the stator's curved blades turn the fluid almost 90° toward the direction of rotation of the engine. Thus the fluid does not flow as fast toward the torus, but is already spinning when the torus picks it up. This has the effect of allowing the torus to turn much faster than the turbine. This difference in speed may be compared to the difference in speed between the smaller and larger gears in any gear train. The result is that engine power output is higher, and engine torque is multiplied.

As the speed of the turbine increases, the fluid spins faster and faster in the direction of engine rotation. As a result, the ability of the stator to redirect the fluid flow is reduced. Under cruising conditions, the stator is eventually forced to rotate on its one-way clutch in the direction of engine rotation. Under these conditions, the torque converter begins to behave almost like a solid shaft, with the torus and turbine speeds being almost equal.

PLANETARY GEARBOX

The ability of the torque converter to multiply engine torque is limited. Also, the unit tends to be more efficient when the turbine is rotating at relatively high speeds. Therefore, a planetary gearbox is used to carry the power output of the turbine to the driveshaft.

Planetary gears function very similarly to conventional transmission gears. However, their construction is different in that three elements make up one gear system, and, in that all three elements are different from one another. The three elements are: an outer gear that is shaped like a hoop, with teeth cut into the inner surface; a sun gear, mounted on a shaft and located at the very center of the outer gear; and a set of three planet gears, held by pins in a ring-like planet carrier, meshing with both the sun gear and the outer gear. Either the outer gear or the sun gear may be held stationary, providing more than one possible torque multiplication factor for each set of gears. Also, if all three gears are forced to rotate at the same speed, the gearset forms, in effect, a solid shaft.

Most automatics use the planetary gears to provide various reductions ratios. Bands and clutches are used to hold various portions of the gearsets to the transmission case or to the shaft on which they are mounted. Shifting is accomplished, then, by changing the portion of each planetary gearset which is held to the transmission case or to the shaft.

SERVOS & ACCUMULATORS

The servos are hydraulic pistons and cylinders. They resemble the hydraulic actuators used on many other machines, such as bulldozers. Hydraulic fluid enters the cylinder, under pressure, and forces the piston to move to engage the band or clutches.

The accumulators are used to cushion the engagement of the servos. The transmission fluid must pass through the accumulator

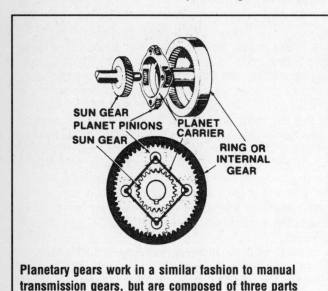

Planetary gears work in a similar fashion to manual transmission gears, but are composed of three parts

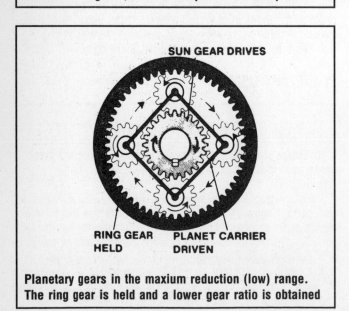

Planetary gears in the maxium reduction (low) range. The ring gear is held and a lower gear ratio is obtained

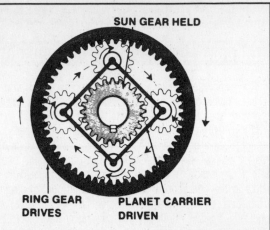

Planetary gears in the minimum reduction (drive) range. The ring gear is allowed to revolve, providing a higher gear ratio

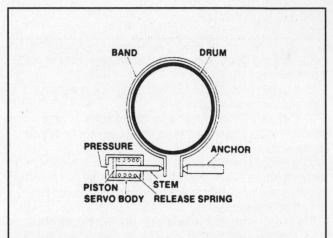

Servos, operated by pressure, are used to apply or release the bands, to either hold the ring gear or allow it to rotate

on the way to the servo. The accumulator housing contains a thin piston which is sprung away from the discharge passage of the accumulator. When fluid passes through the accumulator on the way to the servo, it must move the piston against spring pressure, and this action smooths out the action of the servo.

HYDRAULIC CONTROL SYSTEM

The hydraulic pressure used to operate the servos comes from the main transmission oil pump. This fluid is channeled to the various servos through the shift valves. There is generally a manual shift valve which is operated by the transmission selector lever and an automatic shift valve for each automatic upshift the transmission provides.

➡**Many new transmissions are electronically controlled. On these models, electrical solenoids are used to better control the hydraulic fluid. Usually, the solenoids are regulated by an electronic control module.**

There are two pressures which affect the operation of these valves. One is the governor pressure which is effected by vehicle speed. The other is the modulator pressure which is effected by intake manifold vacuum or throttle position. Governor pressure rises with an increase in vehicle speed, and modulator pressure rises as the throttle is opened wider. By responding to these two pressures, the shift valves cause the upshift points to be delayed with increased throttle opening to make the best use of the engine's power output.

Most transmissions also make use of an auxiliary circuit for downshifting. This circuit may be actuated by the throttle linkage the vacuum line which actuates the modulator, by a cable or by a solenoid. It applies pressure to a special downshift surface on the shift valve or valves.

The transmission modulator also governs the line pressure, used to actuate the servos. In this way, the clutches and bands will be actuated with a force matching the torque output of the engine.

Identification

▶ **See Figure 30**

The automatic transmission serial number label is attached to the side of the transmission housing on all models.

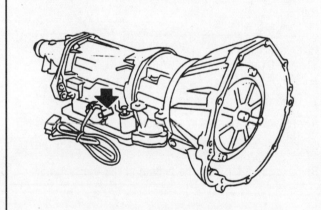

Fig. 30 Look for the automatic transmission serial number on the transmission case where indicated (arrow)—200SX transmission shown, others similar

Fluid Pan and Filter

REMOVAL & INSTALLATION

▶ **See Figure 31**

1. Jack up the front of the car and support it safely on jackstands.

2. Slide a drain pan under the transmission. Loosen the rear oil pan bolts first, to allow most of the fluid to drain off without making a mess on your garage floor.

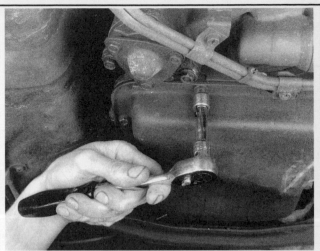

To remove the automatic transmission fluid pan and filter, first loosen the pan bolts

With all the bolts loosened, and most removed, drain the fluid pan from one end

Once the bulk of the fluid is drained, remove the pan and drain the rest

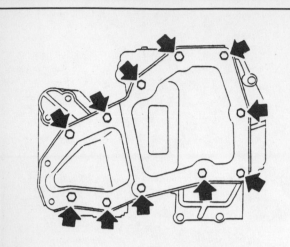

Fig. 31 Remove the automatic transmission filter bolts (indicated), then the filter

More fluid may begin to come out (arrow) once you have begun to remove the filter bolts

Wipe off the excess fluid with a lint-free cloth before removing the filter from the transmission

Remove the filter from the bottom of the transmission

Remove the attaching mounting bolts from the filter

3. Remove the remaining bolts and drop the pan. Remove the 11 transmission filter retaining bolts and remove the filter from the transmission. Install a new filter in the correct position and tighten the transmission filter retaining bolts to 2–3 ft. lbs.

To install:

4. Discard the old gasket, clean the pan, and reinstall the pan with a new gasket.

5. Tighten the retaining bolts in a crisscross pattern starting at the center.

➡**The transmission case is aluminum, so don't exert too much force on the bolts. Tighten the bolts to 3.6–5.1 ft. lbs.**

6. Refill the transmission through the dipstick tube and check the fluid level.

Adjustments

SHIFT LINKAGE

1973–78 Models
▶ **See Figure 32**

1. Loosen the trunnion locknuts at the lower end of the control level. Remove the selector level knob and console.

2. Put the transmission selector in N and put the transmission shift level in the Neutral position by pushing it all the way back, then moving it forward two stops.

3. Check the vertical clearance between the top of the shift level pin and transmission control bracket (A in the illustration). It should be 0.5–1.5mm. Adjust the nut at the lower end of the selector lever compression rod, as necessary.

4. Check the horizontal clearance (B) between the shift lever pin and transmission control bracket. It should be 0.5mm. Adjust the trunnion locknuts as necessary to get this clearance.

5. Replace the console with the shift pointer correctly aligned. Install the shift knob.

1979–84 Models
▶ **See Figure 33**

Adjustment is made at the locknuts at the base of the shifter, which control the length of the shift control rod.

1. Place the shift lever in D.

2. Loosen the locknuts and move the shift lever until it is firmly in the D range, the pointer is aligned, and the transmission is in D range.

3. Tighten the locknuts.

4. Check the adjustment. Start the car and apply the parking brake. Shift through all the ranges, starting in P. As the lever is moved from P to 1, you should be able to feel the detents in each range. If proper adjustment is not possible, the grommets are probably worn and should be replaced.

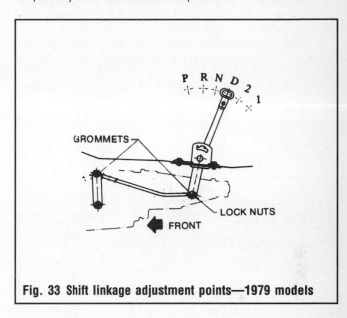

Fig. 33 Shift linkage adjustment points—1979 models

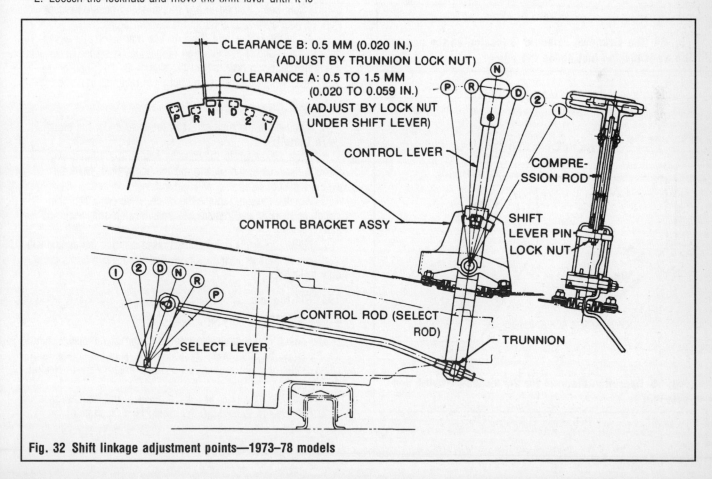

Fig. 32 Shift linkage adjustment points—1973–78 models

CHECKING KICKDOWN SWITCH & SOLENOID

♦ **See Figures 34, 35 and 36**

1. Turn the key to the normal **ON** position, and depress the accelerator all the way. The solenoid in the transmission should make an audible click.

2. If the solenoid does not work, inspect the wiring, and test it electrically to determine whether the problem is in the wiring, the kickdown switch, or the solenoid.

3. If the solenoid requires replacement, drain a little over 2 pts (1 liter) of fluid from the transmission before removing it.

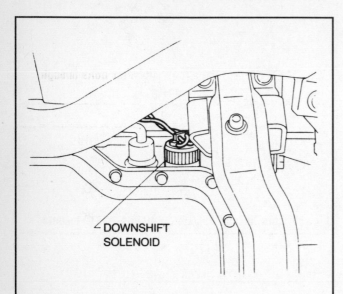

Fig. 34 The kickdown solenoid is located on the side of the transmission just above the pan

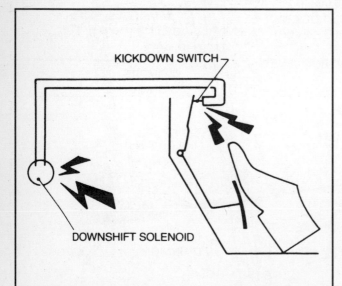

Fig. 35 Operation diagram for the kickdown switch and solenoid

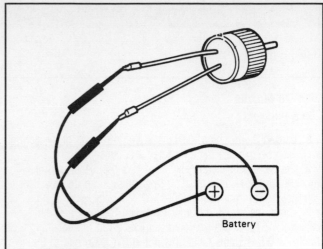

Fig. 36 Check the kickdown solenoid by applylying battery voltage—it should make an audible "click"

Neutral Safety Switch

REMOVAL, INSTALLATION & ADJUSTMENT

1973–80 Models

The switch unit is bolted to the left side of the transmission case, behind the transmission shift lever. The switch prevents the engine from being started in any transmission position except Park or Neutral. It also controls the backup lights.

1. Apply the brakes and check to see that the starter works only in the P and N transmission ranges. If the starter works with the transmission in gear, adjust the switch as described below.

2. Remove the transmission shift level retaining nut and the lever.

3. Remove the switch.

4. Remove the machine screw in the case under the switch.

To install:

5. Align the switch to the case by inserting a 1.5mm pin, through the hole in the switch into the screw hole. Mark the switch location.

6. Remove the pin, replace the machine screw, install the switch as marked, and replace the transmission shift lever and retaining nut.

7. Make sure while holding the brakes on, that the engine will start only in Park or Neutral. Check that the backup lights go on only in Reverse.

1981–84 Models

♦ **See Figures 37 and 38**

The switch unit is bolted to the the transmission case, behind the transmission shift lever. The switch prevents the engine from being started in any transmission position except Park or Neutral. It also controls the backup lights.

1. Place the transmission selector lever in the Neutral range.

2. Remove the screw from the switch (see illustration).

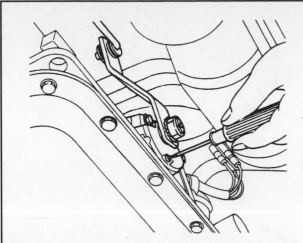

Fig. 37 Remove the screw from the inhibitor switch as shown

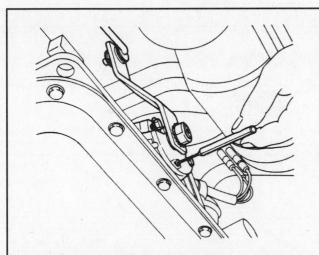

Fig. 38 Adjust the inhibitor switch with an aligning pin, as shown

3. Loosen the attaching bolts. With a aligning pin (2.0mm diameter) move the switch until the pin falls into the hole in the rotor.

4. Tighten the attaching bolts equally.

5. Make sure while holding the brakes on, that the engine will start only in Park or Neutral. Check that the backup lights go on only in Reverse.

Transmission

REMOVAL & INSTALLATION

◆ **See Figures 39, 40, 41, 42 and 43**

1. Disconnect the negative battery cable.

➡ **Take care not to damage any adjacent parts when dismounting transmission.**

2. Remove the accelerator linkage.
3. Detach the shift linkage.

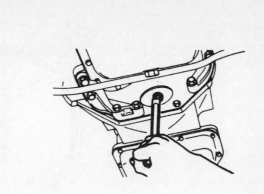

Fig. 39 Disconnect the torque converter bolts through the access hole

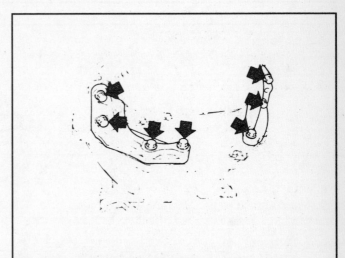

Fig. 40 Loosen the bolts indicated (arrows), then remove the transmission gussets

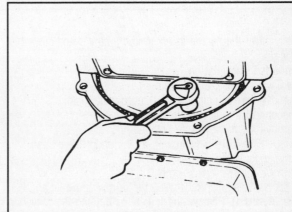

Fig. 41 Remove the bolts securing the torque converter to the driveplate

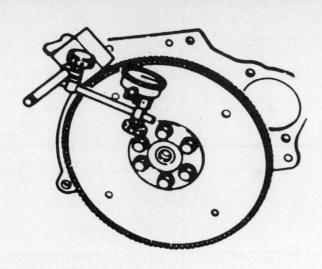

Fig. 42 Check the driveplate (flywheel) run-out with a dial gauge

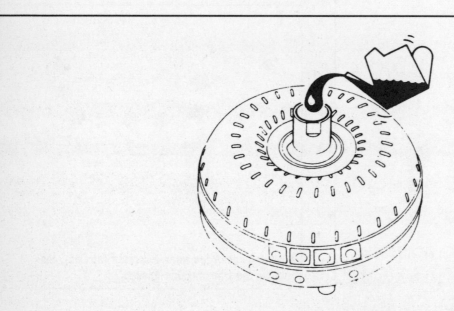

Fig. 43 Refill the torque converter with the correct type and quantity of fluid before installation

4. Disconnect the neutral safety switch/inhibitor and downshift solenoid wiring.

5. Drain the transmission.

6. Remove the front exhaust pipe.

7. Remove the vacuum tube and speedometer cable.

8. Disconnect the fluid cooler tubes.

9. Remove the driveshaft and starter.

10. Support the transmission with a jack under the oil pan. Support the engine also.

11. Remove the rear crossmember.

12. Mark the relationship between the torque converter and the drive plate (flywheel). Remove the four bolts holding the converter to the drive plate through the hole at the front, under the engine. Unbolt the transmission from the engine.

To install:

13. Install the transmission to the engine and the crossmember in the correct position. Tighten the drive plate to crankshaft bolts 101–116 ft lbs. Tighten the drive plate to torque converter and converter housing to engine bolts 29–36 ft. lbs. Tighten the transmission to crossmember bolts to 23–31 ft. lbs. and the crossmember to body frame mounting bolts to 43–58 ft. lbs.

14. Connect the driveshaft and install the starter with the electrical connections.

15. Connect the fluid cooler tubes and the speedometer cable.

16. Install the exhaust system and reconnect all the linkage, electrical connections and hoses if they were removed.

17. Reconnect the battery cable. Refill the transmission and check the fluid level.

18. After the fluid level is correct and no leaks are present, road test the vehicle for proper operation.

Lockup Torque Converter Service Diagnosis

Problem	Cause	Solution

No lockup	• Faulty oil pump
	• Sticking governor valve
	• Valve body malfunction
	    (a) Stuck switch valve
	    (b) Stuck lockup valve
	    (c) Stuck fail-safe valve
	• Failed locking clutch
	• Leaking turbine hub seal
	• Faulty input shaft or seal ring
		• Replace oil pump
		• Repair or replace as necessary
		• Repair or replace valve body or its internal components as necessary
		
		• Replace torque converter
		• Replace torque converter
		• Repair or replace as necessary

Will not unlock	• Sticking governor valve
	• Valve body malfunction
	    (a) Stuck switch valve
	    (b) Stuck lockup valve
	    (c) Stuck fail-safe valve
		• Repair or replace as necessary
		• Repair or replace valve body or its internal components as necessary

Stays locked up at too low a speed in direct	• Sticking governor valve
	• Valve body malfunction
	    (a) Stuck switch valve
	    (b) Stuck lockup valve
	    (c) Stuck fail-safe valve
		• Repair or replace as necessary
		• Repair or replace valve body or its internal components as necessary

Locks up or drags in low or second	• Faulty oil pump
	• Valve body malfunction
	    (a) Stuck switch valve
	    (b) Stuck fail-safe valve
		• Replace oil pump
		• Repair or replace valve body or its internal components as necessary

Sluggish or stalls in reverse	• Faulty oil pump
	• Plugged cooler, cooler lines or fittings
	• Valve body malfunction
	    (a) Stuck switch valve
	    (b) Faulty input shaft or seal ring
		• Replace oil pump as necessary
		• Flush or replace cooler and flush lines and fittings
		• Repair or replace valve body or its internal components as necessary

Loud chatter during lockup engagement (cold)	• Faulty torque converter • Failed locking clutch • Leaking turbine hub seal	• Replace torque converter • Replace torque converter • Replace torque converter
Vibration or shudder during lockup engagement	• Faulty oil pump • Valve body malfunction • Faulty torque converter • Engine needs tune-up	• Repair or replace oil pump as necessary • Repair or replace valve body or its internal components as necessary • Replace torque converter • Tune engine
Vibration after lockup engagement	• Faulty torque converter • Exhaust system strikes underbody • Engine needs tune-up • Throttle linkage misadjusted	• Replace torque converter • Align exhaust system • Tune engine • Adjust throttle linkage
Vibration when revved in neutral Overheating: oil blows out of dip stick tube or pump seal	• Torque converter out of balance • Plugged cooler, cooler lines or fittings • Stuck switch valve	• Replace torque converter • Flush or replace cooler and flush lines and fittings • Repair switch valve in valve body or replace valve body
Shudder after lockup engagement	• Faulty oil pump • Plugged cooler, cooler lines or fittings • Valve body malfunction • Faulty torque converter • Fail locking clutch • Exhaust system strikes underbody • Engine needs tune-up • Throttle linkage misadjusted	• Replace oil pump • Flush or replace cooler and flush lines and fittings • Repair or replace valve body or its internal components as necessary • Replace torque converter • Replace torque converter • Align exhaust system • Tune engine • Adjust throttle linkage

Troubleshooting Basic Automatic Transmission Problems

Problem	Cause	Solution
Fluid leakage	• Defective pan gasket	• Replace gasket or tighten pan bolts
	• Loose filler tube	• Tighten tube nut
	• Loose extension housing to transmission case	• Tighten bolts
	• Converter housing area leakage	• Have transmission checked professionally
Fluid flows out the oil filler tube	• High fluid level	• Check and correct fluid level
	• Breather vent clogged	• Open breather vent
	• Clogged oil filter or screen	• Replace filter or clean screen (change fluid also)
	• Internal fluid leakage	• Have transmission checked professionally
Transmission overheats (this is usually accompanied by a strong burned odor to the fluid)	• Low fluid level	• Check and correct fluid level
	• Fluid cooler lines clogged	• Drain and refill transmission. If this doesn't cure the problem, have cooler lines cleared or replaced.
	• Heavy pulling or hauling with insufficient cooling	• Install a transmission oil cooler
	• Faulty oil pump, internal slippage	• Have transmission checked professionally
Buzzing or whining noise	• Low fluid level	• Check and correct fluid level
	• Defective torque converter, scored gears	• Have transmission checked professionally
No forward or reverse gears or slippage in one or more gears	• Low fluid level	• Check and correct fluid level
	• Defective vacuum or linkage controls, internal clutch or band failure	• Have unit checked professionally
Delayed or erratic shift	• Low fluid level	• Check and correct fluid level
	• Broken vacuum lines	• Repair or replace lines
	• Internal malfunction	• Have transmission checked professionally

Transmission Fluid Indications

The appearance and odor of the transmission fluid can give valuable clues to the overall condition of the transmission. Always note the appearance of the fluid when you check the fluid level or change the fluid. Rub a small amount of fluid between your fingers to feel for grit and smell the fluid on the dipstick.

If the fluid appears:	It indicates:
Clear and red colored	• Normal operation
Discolored (extremely dark red or brownish) or smells burned	• Band or clutch pack failure, usually caused by an overheated transmission. Hauling very heavy loads with insufficient power or failure to change the fluid, often result in overheating. Do not confuse this appearance with newer fluids that have a darker red color and a strong odor (though not a burned odor).
Foamy or aerated (light in color and full of bubbles)	• The level is too high (gear train is churning oil) • An internal air leak (air is mixing with the fluid). Have the transmission checked professionally.
Solid residue in the fluid	• Defective bands, clutch pack or bearings. Bits of band material or metal abrasives are clinging to the dipstick. Have the transmission checked professionally.
Varnish coating on the dipstick	• The transmission fluid is overheating

DRIVELINE

Driveshaft and Universal Joints

▶ **See Figures 44 and 45**

The driveshaft transfers power from the engine and transmission to the differential and rear axles and then to the rear wheels to drive the car. All of the models covered in this book utilize a conventional driveshaft. Except on the 610 wagon, the 810/Maxima, the 1977–79 200SX with manual transmission only and all 1980–81 200SX models, the driveshaft assembly has two universal joints—one at each end— and a slip yoke at the front of the assembly which fits into the back of the transmission. The 610, 810/Maxima, and 200SX incorporate an additional universal joint at the center of the driveshaft with a support bearing.

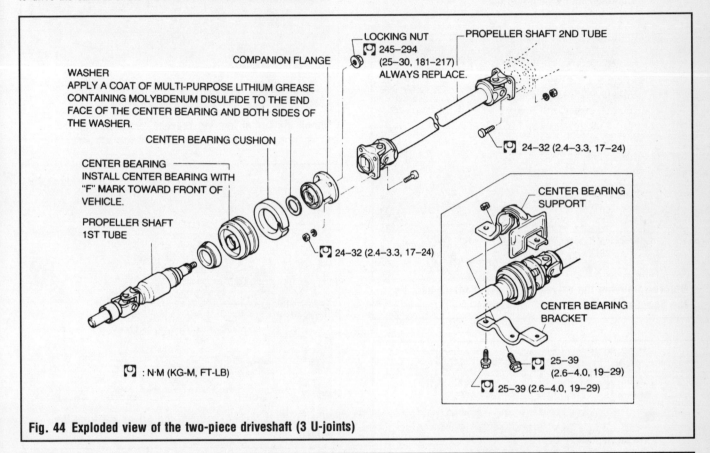

Fig. 44 Exploded view of the two-piece driveshaft (3 U-joints)

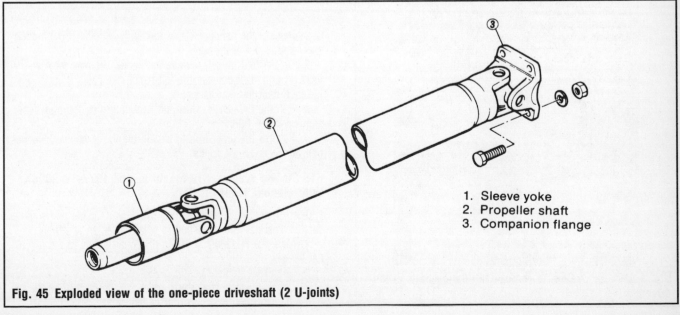

1. Sleeve yoke
2. Propeller shaft
3. Companion flange

Fig. 45 Exploded view of the one-piece driveshaft (2 U-joints)

REMOVAL & INSTALLATION

510, 610 (Except Station Wagon), 710, 1977–79 200SX With Automatic Transmission

These driveshafts are the one piece type with a U-joint and flange at the rear, and a U-joint and a splined sleeve yoke which fits into the rear of the transmission, at the front. The U-joints must be disassembled for lubrication at 24,000 mile intervals. The splines are lubricated by transmission oil.

Before removing the driveshaft, make a matchmark on the flanges (arrow)

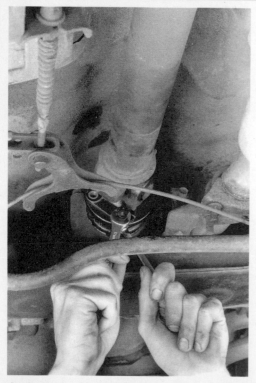

Use a back-up wrench to remove the flange bolts at the driveshaft

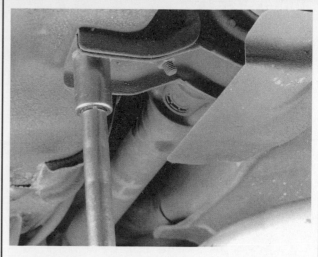

Unbolt the center bearing bracket

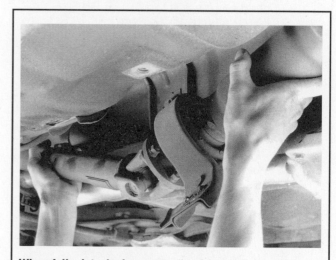

When fully detached, remove the driveshaft from the vehicle

1. Release the handbrake and loosen the muffler (510 model) and rotate it out of the way.

2. On the 510 model, remove the handbrake rear cable adjusting nut and disconnect the left-handbrake cable from the adjuster. Unbolt the rear flange.

3. Pull the driveshaft down and back and plug the transmission extension housing.

4. Reverse the procedure to install, oiling the splines. Flange bolt torque is 15–24 ft. lbs.

610 Station Wagon, 810/Maxima, and 1977–79 200SX With Manual Transmission

These models use a driveshaft with three U-joints and a center support bearing. The driveshaft is balanced as an assembly.

1. Mark the relationship of the driveshaft flange to the differential flange.

2. Unbolt the center bearing bracket.

3. Unbolt the driveshaft back under the rear axle. Plug the rear of the transmission to prevent oil or fluid loss.

4. On installation, align the marks made in Step 1. Tighten the flange bolts to 15–24 ft. lbs.

U-JOINT OVERHAUL

Disassembly

1. Mark the relationship of all components for reassembly.
2. Remove the snaprings. On early units, the snaprings are seated in the yokes. On later units, the snaprings seat in the needle bearing races.
3. Tap the yoke with brass or rubber mallet to release one bearing cap. Be careful not to lose the needle rollers.
4. Remove the other bearing caps. Remove the U-joint spiders from the yokes.

Inspection

1. Spline backlash should not exceed 0.5mm.
2. Driveshaft runout should not exceed 0.4mm.
3. On later model with snaprings seated in the needle bearing races, different thicknesses of snaprings are available for U-joint adjustment. Play should not exceed 0.02mm.
4. U-joint spiders must be replaced if the bearing journals are worn more than 0.15mm from their original diameter.

Assembly

1. Place the needle rollers in the races and hold them in place with grease.
2. Put the spider into place in its yokes.
3. Replace all seals.
4. Tap the races into position and secure them with snaprings.

CENTER BEARING REPLACEMENT

◆ **See Figures 46, 47 and 48**

The center bearing is a sealed unit which must be replaced as an assembly if defective.
1. Remove the driveshaft.
2. Paint a matchmark across where the flanges behind the cen-

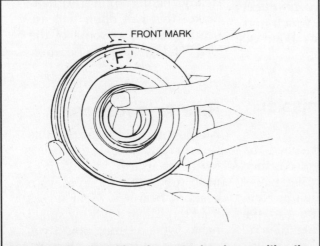

Fig. 46 Before installing the center bearing, position the (F) mark so it is facing the front of the car

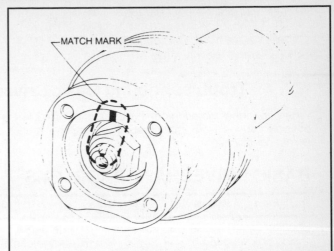

Fig. 47 Paint a matchmark where the companion flange is aligned with the shaft prior to removing the nut

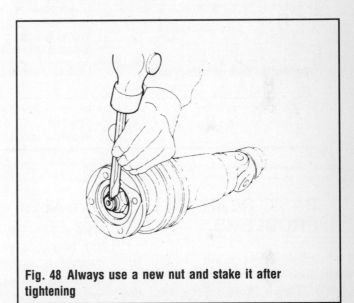

Fig. 48 Always use a new nut and stake it after tightening

ter yoke are joined. This is for assembly purposes. If you don't paint or somehow mark the relationship between the two shafts, they may be out of balance when you put them back together.
3. Remove the bolts and separate the shafts. Make a matchmark on the front driveshaft half which lines up with the mark you made on the flange half.
4. You must devise a way to hold the driveshaft while unbolting the companion flange from the front driveshaft. Do not place the front driveshaft tube in a vise, because the chances are it will get crushed. The best way is to grip the flange somehow while loosening the nut. It is going to require some strength to remove.
5. Press the companion flange off the front driveshaft and press the center bearing from its mount.
6. The new bearing is already lubricated. Install it into the mount, making sure that the seals and so on are facing the same way as when removed. Also make sure the F mark is facing the front of the car.
7. Slide the companion flange on to the front driveshaft, aligning the marks made during removal. Install the washer and

locknut. If the washer and locknut are separate pieces, tighten them to 145–175 ft. lbs. If they were a unit, tighten to 180–217 ft. lbs. Check that the bearing rotates freely around the driveshaft. Stake the nut (always use a new nut).

8. Connect the companion flange to the other half of the driveshaft, aligning the marks made during removal. Tighten the bolts securely.
9. Install the driveshaft.

Troubleshooting Basic Driveshaft and Rear Axle Problems

When abnormal vibrations or noises are detected in the driveshaft area, this chart can be used to help diagnose possible causes. Remember that other components such as wheels, tires, rear axle and suspension can also produce similar conditions.

BASIC DRIVESHAFT PROBLEMS

Problem	Cause	Solution
Shudder as car accelerates from stop or low speed	• Loose U-joint • Defective center bearing	• Replace U-joint • Replace center bearing
Loud clunk in driveshaft when shifting gears	• Worn U-joints	• Replace U-joints
Roughness or vibration at any speed	• Out-of-balance, bent or dented driveshaft • Worn U-joints • U-joint clamp bolts loose	• Balance or replace driveshaft • Replace U-joints • Tighten U-joint clamp bolts
Squeaking noise at low speeds	• Lack of U-joint lubrication	• Lubricate U-joint; if problem persists, replace U-joint
Knock or clicking noise	• U-joint or driveshaft hitting frame tunnel • Worn CV joint	• Correct overloaded condition • Replace CV joint

BASIC REAR AXLE PROBLEMS

First, determine when the noise is most noticeable.

Drive Noise: Produced under vehicle acceleration.

Coast Noise: Produced while the car coasts with a closed throttle.

Float Noise: Occurs while maintaining constant car speed (just enough to keep speed constant) on a level road.

Road Noise

Brick or rough surfaced concrete roads produce noises that seem to come from the rear axle. Road noise is usually identical in Drive or Coast and driving on a different type of road will tell whether the road is the problem.

Tire Noise

Tire noises are often mistaken for rear axle problems. Snow treads or unevenly worn tires produce vibrations seeming to originate elsewhere. **Temporarily** inflating the tires to 40 lbs will significantly alter tire noise, but will have no effect on rear axle noises (which normally cease below about 30 mph).

Engine/Transmission Noise

Determine at what speed the noise is most pronounced, then stop the car in a quiet place. With the transmission in Neutral, run the engine through speeds corresponding to road speeds where the noise was noticed. Noises produced with the car standing still are coming from the engine or transmission.

Front Wheel Bearings

While holding the car speed steady, lightly apply the footbrake; this will often decease bearing noise, as some of the load is taken from the bearing.

Rear Axle Noises

Eliminating other possible sources can narrow the cause to the rear axle, which normally produces noise from worn gears or bearings. Gear noises tend to peak in a narrow speed range, while bearing noises will usually vary in pitch with engine speeds.

NOISE DIAGNOSIS

The Noise Is	Most Probably Produced By
• Identical under Drive or Coast	• Road surface, tires or front wheel bearings
• Different depending on road surface	• Road surface or tires
• Lower as the car speed is lowered	• Tires
• Similar with car standing or moving	• Engine or transmission
• A vibration	• Unbalanced tires, rear wheel bearing, unbalanced driveshaft or worn U-joint
• A knock or click about every 2 tire revolutions	• Rear wheel bearing
• Most pronounced on turns	• Damaged differential gears
• A steady low-pitched whirring or scraping, starting at low speeds	• Damaged or worn pinion bearing
• A chattering vibration on turns	• Wrong differential lubricant or worn clutch plates (limited slip rear axle)
• Noticed only in Drive, Coast or Float conditions	• Worn ring gear and/or pinion gear

REAR AXLE

Identification

There are a few different types of rear axles used on the cars covered in this guide. A solid rear axle is used on 1977–81 200SX, 710, and all station wagon models. The 1978–81 510 uses a solid rear axle with either coil springs or leaf springs, depending on whether it is a sedan or a wagon. Independent rear suspension (IRS) is used on the 610 sedans, 810/Maxima sedan (some models use solid rear axle). In this (IRS) design separate axle driveshafts are used to transmit power from the differential to the wheels.

Determining Axle Ratio

The drive axle is said to have a certain axle ratio. This number (usually a whole number and a decimal fraction) is actually a comparison of the number of gear teeth on the ring gear and the pinion gear. For example, a 4.11 rear means that theoretically, there are 4.11 teeth on the ring gear and one tooth on the pinion gear or, put another way, the driveshaft must turn 4.11 times to turn the wheels once. Actually, on a 4.11 rear, there might be 37 teeth on the ring gear and 9 teeth on the pinion gear. By dividing the number of teeth on the pinion gear into the number of teeth on the ring gear, the numerical axle ratio (4.11) is obtained. This also provides a good method of ascertaining exactly what axle ratio one is dealing with.

Another method of determining gear ratio is to jack up and support the car so that both rear wheels are off the ground. Make a chalk mark on the rear wheel and the driveshaft. Put the transmission in neutral. Turn the rear wheel one complete turn and count the number of turns that the driveshaft makes. The number of turns that the driveshaft makes in one complete revolution of the rear wheel is an approximation of the rear axle ratio.

Axle Shaft (Solid Rear Axle)

REMOVAL & INSTALLATION

▶ **See Figures 49 thru 54**

➡**Bearings must be pressed on and off the shaft with an arbor press. Unless you have access to one, it is inadvisable to attempt any repair work on the axle shaft and bearing assemblies.**

1. Remove the hub cap or wheel cover. Loosen the lug nuts.
2. Raise the rear of the car and support it safely on stands.
3. Remove the rear wheel. Remove the four brake backing plate retaining nuts. Detach the parking brake linkage from the brake backing plate.
4. Attach a slide hammer to the axle shaft and remove it. Use a slide hammer and a two pronged puller to remove the oil seal from the housing.

➡**If a slide hammer is not available, the axle can sometimes be pried out using prybars on opposing sides of the hub.**

If end-play is found to be excessive, the bearing should be replaced. Shimming the bearing is not recommended as this ignores end-play of the bearing itself and could result in improper seating of the bearing.

5. Using a chisel, carefully nick the bearing retainer in three or four places. The retainer does not have to be cut, only collapsed enough to allow the bearing retainer to be slid off the shaft.
6. Pull or press the old bearing off.
7. Install a new bearing by pressing it into position.

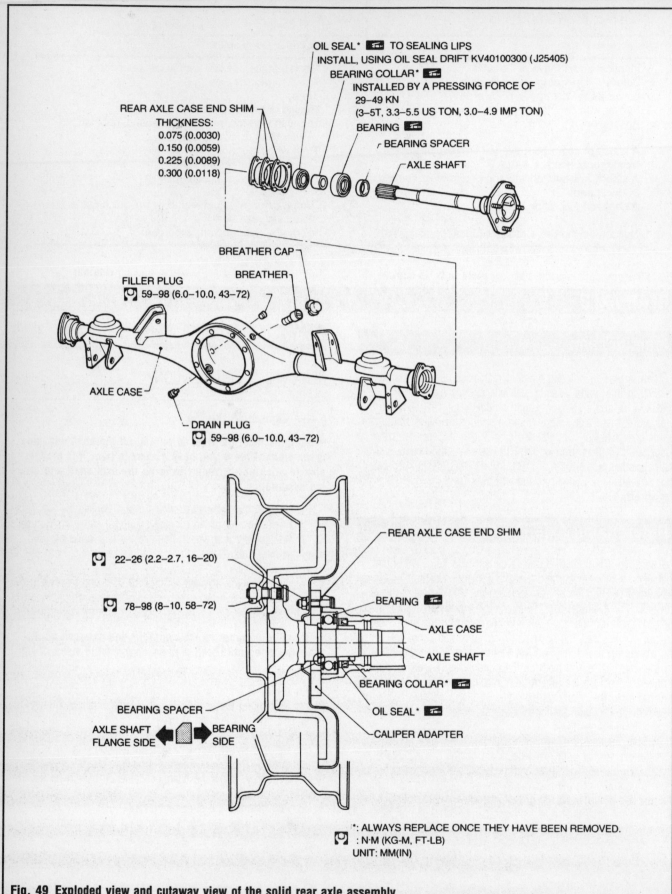

Fig. 49 Exploded view and cutaway view of the solid rear axle assembly

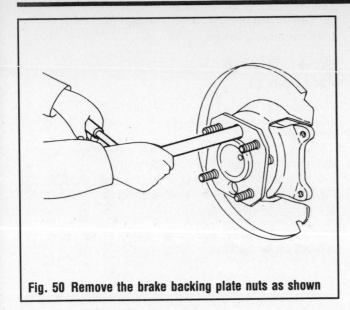

Fig. 50 Remove the brake backing plate nuts as shown

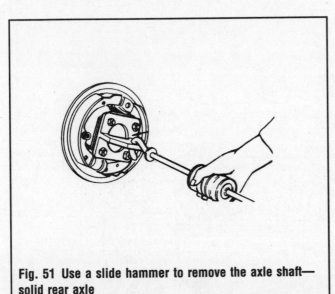

Fig. 51 Use a slide hammer to remove the axle shaft—solid rear axle

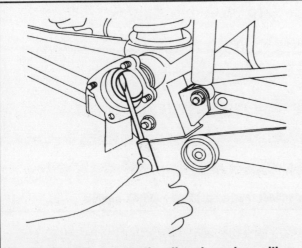

Fig. 52 Carefully remove the oil seal—replace with a new one before axle shaft installation

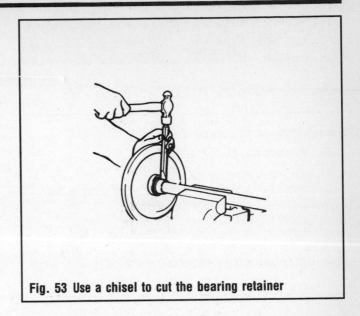

Fig. 53 Use a chisel to cut the bearing retainer

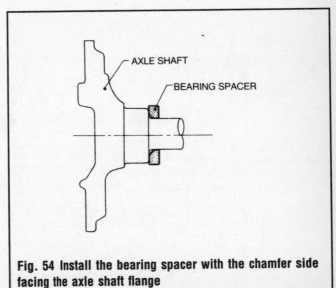

AXLE SHAFT

BEARING SPACER

Fig. 54 Install the bearing spacer with the chamfer side facing the axle shaft flange

To install:

8. Install the outer bearing retainer with its raised surface facing the wheel hub, and then install the bearing and the inner bearing retainer in that order on the axle shaft.

9. With the smaller chamfered side of the inner bearing retainer facing the bearing, press on the retainer. The edge of the retainer should fully touch the bearing.

10. Clean the oil seal seat in the rear axle housing. Apply a thin coat of chassis grease.

11. Using a seal installation tool, drive the oil seal into the rear axle housing. Wipe a thin coat of bearing grease on the lips of the seal.

12. Determine the number of retainer gaskets which will give the correct bearing-to-outer retainer clearance of 0.25mm.

13. Insert the axle shaft assembly into the axle housing, being careful not to damage the seal. Ensure that the shaft splines engage those of the differential pinion. Align the vent holes of the gasket and the outer bearing retainer. Install the retaining bolts.

14. Install the nuts on the bolts and tighten them evenly, and in a criss-cross pattern, to 20 ft. lbs.

Halfshaft (Independent Rear Suspension)

REMOVAL & INSTALLATION

Except 1982–84 810/Maxima
▶ **See Figures 55, 56, 57 and 58**

1. Raise and support the car.
2. Remove the U-joint yoke flange bolts at the outside. Remove the U-joint center bolt at the differential.
3. Remove the axle shaft.
4. Installation is the reverse. Tighten the outside flange bolts to 36–43 ft. lbs. Tighten the four differential side flange bolts to 36–43 ft. lbs. On axle shafts retained to the differential with a single center bolt, tighten the bolt to 17–23 ft. lbs., 1973–77, or 23–31 ft. lbs. for 1978–81 models.

1982–84 810 and Maxima
▶ **See Figure 59**

1. Raise and support the rear of the car.
2. Disconnect the halfshaft on the wheel side by removing the four flange bolts.
3. Grasp the halfshaft at the center and extract it from the differential carrier by prying it with a suitable prybar.
4. Installation is in the reverse order of removal. Install the differential end first and then the wheel end. Tighten the four flange bolts to 20–27 ft. lbs.

➡**Take care not to damage the oil seal or either end of the halfshaft during installation.**

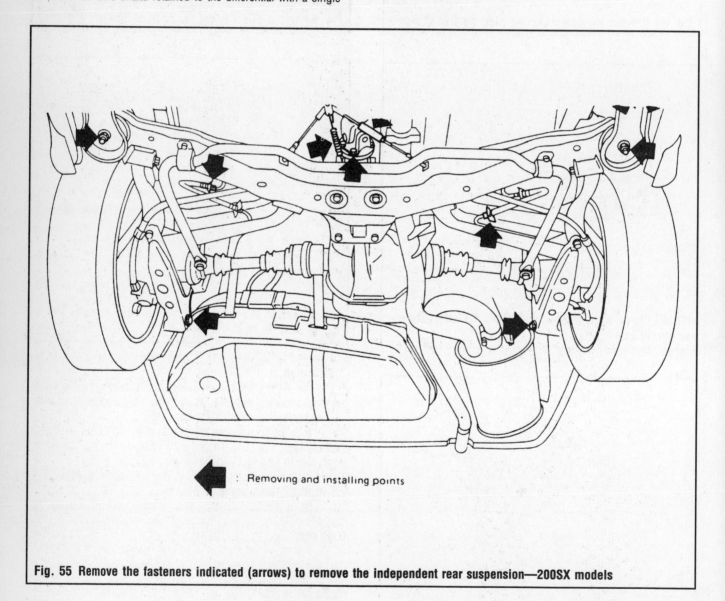

◀ : Removing and installing points

Fig. 55 Remove the fasteners indicated (arrows) to remove the independent rear suspension—200SX models

Wheel alignment
- Camber cannot be adjusted.
- Vehicle requires only toe-in adjustment.
  −2 to 0 mm (−0.08 to 0 in), (−12' to 0)
  Refer to section MA for checking wheel alignment.

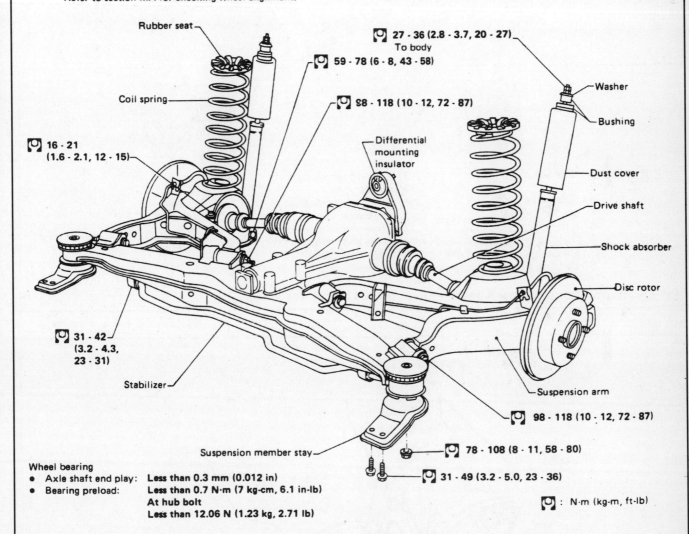

Rubber seat

Coil spring

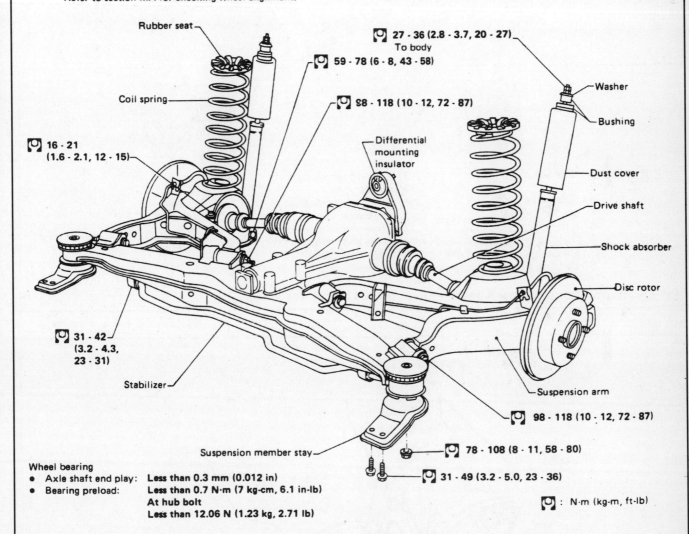 27 - 36 (2.8 - 3.7, 20 - 27)
To body

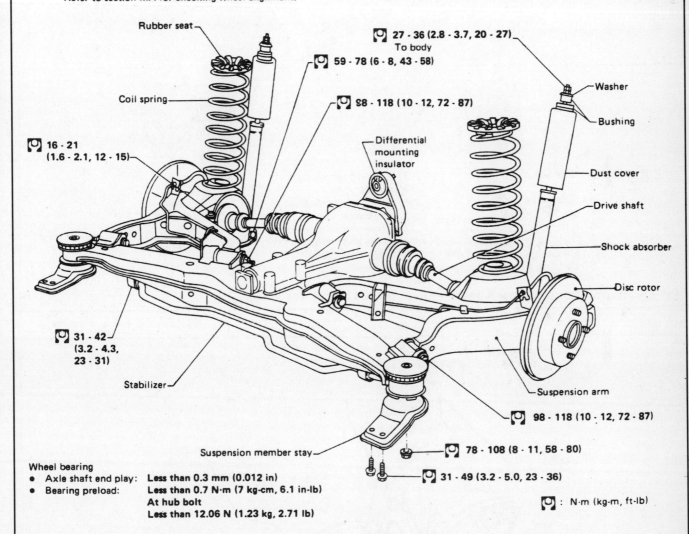 59 - 78 (6 - 8, 43 - 58)

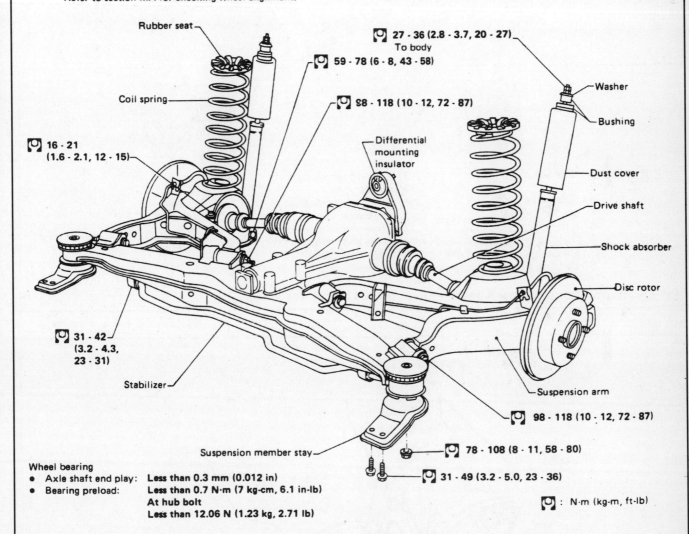 98 - 118 (10 - 12, 72 - 87)

Differential mounting insulator

Washer

Bushing

Dust cover

Drive shaft

Shock absorber

Disc rotor

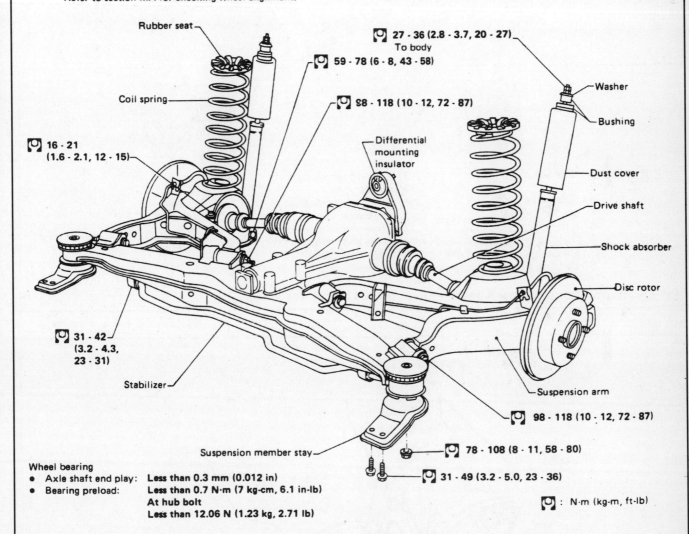 16 - 21
(1.6 - 2.1, 12 - 15)

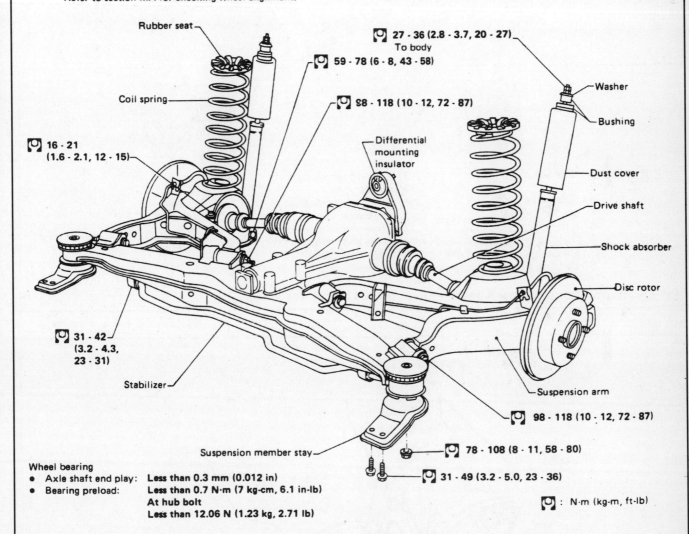 31 - 42
(3.2 - 4.3, 23 - 31)

Stabilizer

Suspension member stay

Suspension arm

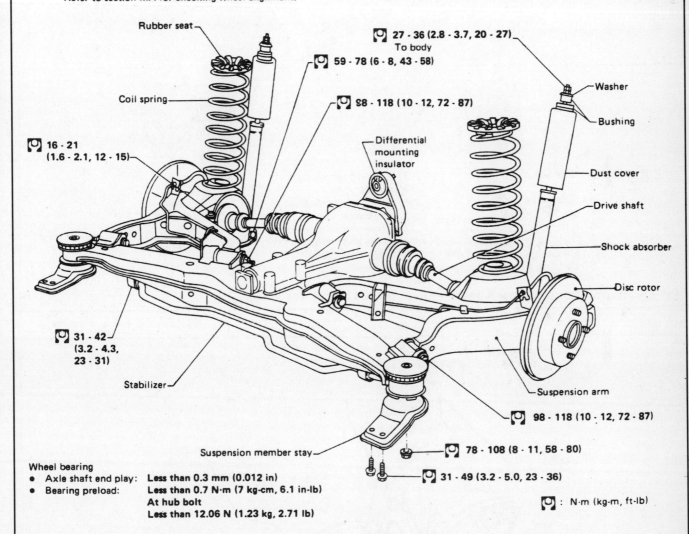 98 - 118 (10 - 12, 72 - 87)

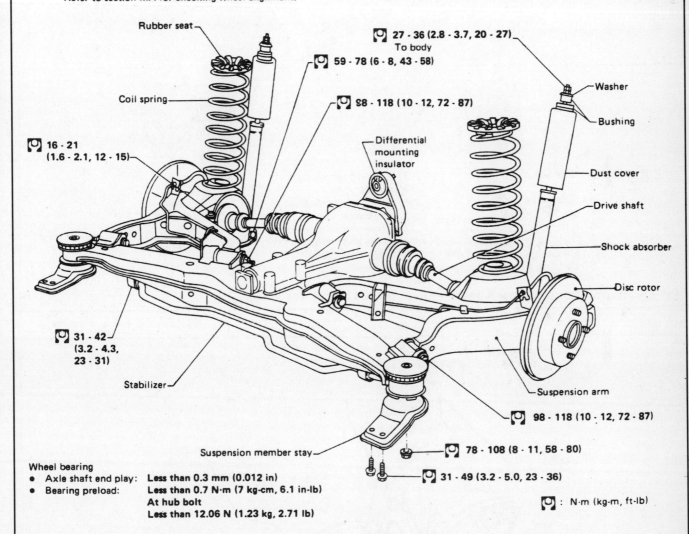 78 - 108 (8 - 11, 58 - 80)

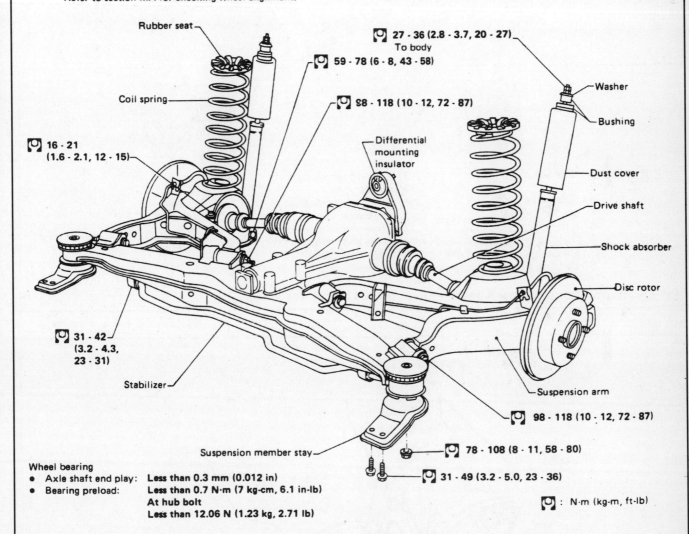 31 - 49 (3.2 - 5.0, 23 - 36)

 : N·m (kg-m, ft-lb)

Wheel bearing
- Axle shaft end play: **Less than 0.3 mm (0.012 in)**
- Bearing preload: **Less than 0.7 N·m (7 kg-cm, 6.1 in-lb)**
  At hub bolt
  Less than 12.06 N (1.23 kg, 2.71 lb)

Fig. 56 Components of the rear axle and rear suspension—independent rear suspension—200SX models

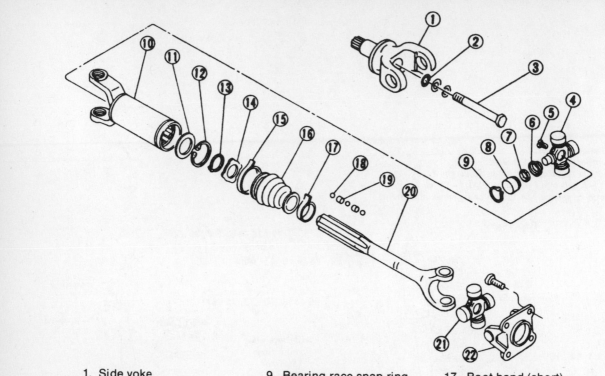

1. Side yoke
2. O-ring
3. Side yoke bolt
4. Spider journal
5. Filler plug
6. Dust cover
7. Oil seal
8. Bearing race assembly
9. Bearing race snap ring
10. Sleeve yoke
11. Sleeve yoke stopper
12. Snap ring
13. Drive shaft snap ring
14. Drive shaft stopper
15. Boot band (long)
16. Rubber boot
17. Boot band (short)
18. Ball
19. Ball spacer
20. Driveshaft
21. Spider assembly
22. Flange yoke

Fig. 57 Exploded view of the rear halfshaft—except 1982–84 810/Maxima models

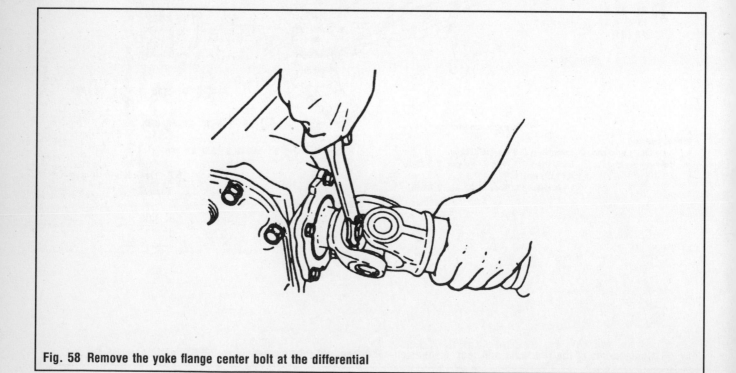

Fig. 58 Remove the yoke flange center bolt at the differential

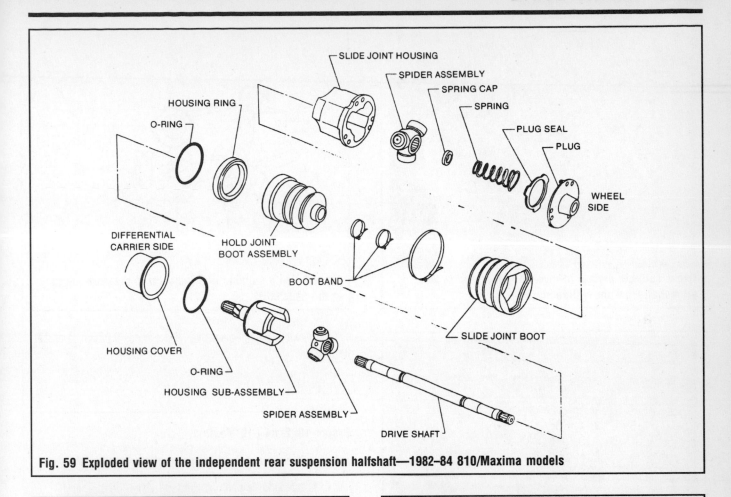

Fig. 59 Exploded view of the independent rear suspension halfshaft—1982–84 810/Maxima models

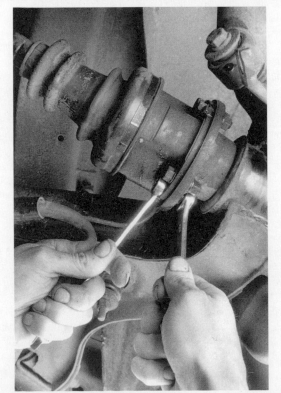

To detach the halfshaft, use a back-up wrench to remove the wheel side flange bolts

Once detached, lower the wheel side of the driveshaft so you can free the differential side

Use a suitable prytool to lever the inner end of the driveshaft from the differential

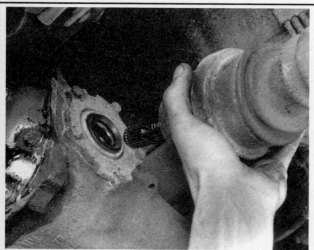

Once it is free of the differential, lower the driveshaft from the vehicle

INSPECTION

Except 1982–84 810/Maxima
▶ See Figure 60

Before disassembling the axle shaft, inspect it as follows:

1. Check the parts for wear or damage. Replace the shaft as an assembly if defects are found.

2. Extend and compress the axle shaft (full stroke). Check the action for smoothness.

3. Check the play in the axle shaft. Fully compress the shaft and check the play with a dial indicator. If play exceeds 0.1mm for models through 1978, or 0.2mm, for 1979–80 models, the shaft must be replaced. The sleeve yoke, balls, spacers and outer shaft are not available as service parts.

4. Check the U-joints for smoothness. If movement is notchy or loose, overhaul the U-joints.

Fig. 60 Use a suitable dial indicator to measure the play in the halfshaft

5. Check the U-joint axial play. If it exceeds 0.02mm, overhaul the U-joints.

OVERHAUL

Except 1982–84 810/Maxima

➡You will need a pair of snapring pliers for this job.

1. Matchmark the parts across the U-joint journals, and across the sliding yoke (outer shaft to sleeve yoke). The axle shaft was balanced as a unit and must be rebuilt as originally assembled.

2. Remove the snap spring from the U-joints and disassemble them as outlined in the U-joint Overhaul procedure in this chapter.

3. Cut the boot band and remove the boot from the sleeve yoke.

4. Remove the snapring from the sleeve yoke at the boot end.

5. Remove the outer shaft carefully. Do not lose any of the balls or spacers.

6. It is not necessary to remove the snapring and sleeve yoke plug at the differential end of the sleeve yoke, because the parts are not available for service. If any damage is present, the entire axle shaft must be replaced.

7. Clean the spacers, balls, and sleeve yoke and outer shaft grooves in solvent. Check the parts for wear, distortion, cracks, straightness, etc. If there is any question as to the integrity of the part, replace the axle shaft.

8. Check the snapring, grease seal, and dust seal for wear or damage. These parts are available for service and should be replaced as necessary.

9. Apply a fairly generous amount of grease to the yoke and shaft grooves. Install the balls and spacers onto the shaft. The grease will retain them. Be sure they are in the correct sequence.

10. Before assembling the shaft and sleeve yoke, apply a large glob of grease to the inner end of the sleeve yoke. You can put a blob of grease on the end of the shaft, too.

11. Align the parts according to the matchmarks made in Step 1. Slide the shaft into the sleeve yoke, making sure none of the balls or spacers is displaced.

12. Compress the shaft and check the play again. Refer to the inspections procedure. Replace the shaft if necessary.

13. Install the boot onto the sleeve yoke and retain with a new boot band.

14. Clean, repack, and assemble the U-joints. Select snaprings which will yield 0.02mm of axial play. Be certain to use the same thickness snapring on opposite sides of the journals to retain driveline balance, and to keep the stresses evenly distributed.

15. Install the axle shaft.

1982–84 810 and Maxima Rear Wheel Drive

◗ **See Figures 61 thru 66**

1. Clamp the halfshaft in a vise using soft jaws.

2. Using pliers, pry the plug from the wheel side of the half-shaft.

3. Remove the plug seal, spring, spring cap and the boot bands.

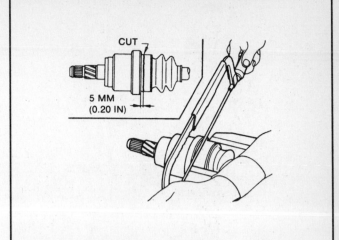

Fig. 63 Use a hacksaw to cut off the hold joint band, then remove the housing subassembly

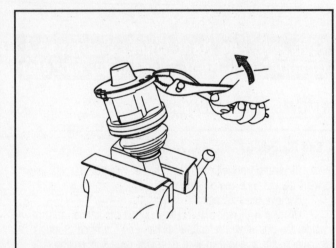

Fig. 61 Use pliers to remove the plug from the wheel side of the rear halfshaft as shown

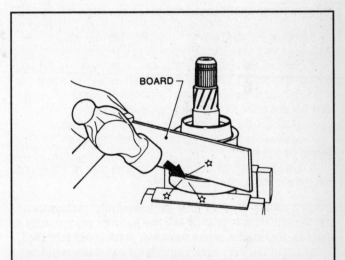

Fig. 64 Use a board and mallet to bend the housing cover

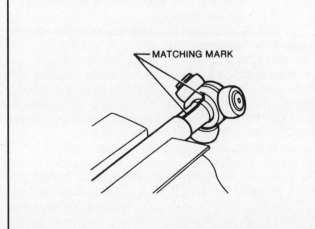

Fig. 62 Matchmark the spider assembly to the halfshaft

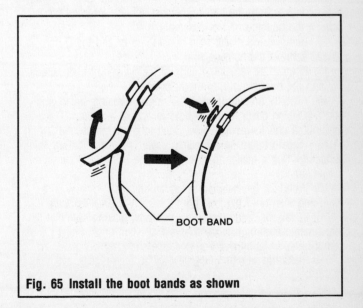

Fig. 65 Install the boot bands as shown

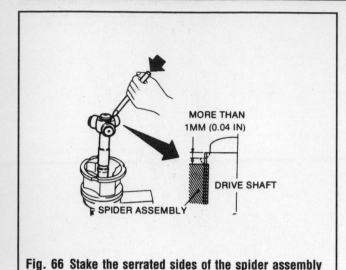

Fig. 66 Stake the serrated sides of the spider assembly upon installation

➡**Never reuse boot bands once they have been removed.**

4. Scribe a matchmark on the spider assembly and the half-shaft.

5. Remove the spider assembly with a press. Do not attempt to touch the contact surface of the halfshaft end at the spring cap or housing subassembly. Always support the halfshaft with your hand while you are removing the spider assembly.

6. Draw out the slide joint boot and the boot bands.

7. Loosen the vise and turn the halfshaft around so that the differential end is up.

8. Using a hacksaw, cut off the hold joint boot assembly and then remove the housing subassembly.

➡**When cutting the hold joint boot assembly, make sure that the halfshaft is pushed into the housing subassembly in order to prevent the spider assembly from being scratched. Never reuse the boot assembly after it has been removed.**

9. Remove and discard the boot band and then remove the spider assembly as detailed in Steps 4–5.

10. Cut off the remaining part of the hold joint boot assembly and remove it from the housing subassembly. Be careful not to scratch the housing ring or assembly.

11. Remove and discard the housing cover and the O-ring.

12. Remove the housing ring.

13. Remove all remaining parts of the hold joint boot assembly and the boot band from the halfshaft.

14. Attach a housing ring, an O-ring, a housing subassembly and a housing cover to a new hold joint boot assembly. Place the assembled unit flange in a vise. Don't forget to grease the O-ring.

15. Place a board on a housing cover to prevent it from being scratched. Use a mallet and bend the edge over along the entire circumference.

16. Withdraw the housing subassembly, install a new boot band and then hold the joint boot assembly on the halfshaft.

17. Install the spider assembly securely, making sure that the matchmarks are aligned. Make sure that when press fitting the assembly, the serration chamfer faces the shaft.

18. Stake the serration sides evenly at three places, avoiding

areas that have been previously staked. Always stake two or three teeth in an area where the staked gap is more than 0.1mm.

19. Pack with grease.

20. Install the greased O-ring to the housing assembly and then place the hold joint boot assembly so that its flange is in the vise. Be sure that no other part of the assembly is in the vise.

21. Insert the housing subassembly into place and then bend the edge as detailed in Step 2 for the housing cover.

22. Apply sealant. Set the boot and install the boot bands.

23. Turn the halfshaft in the vise so that the wheel side is up.

24. Install the new boot bands, slide joint boot and slide joint housing on the halfshaft. Be careful not to scratch the boot with the end of the shaft.

25. Install the spider assembly as previously detailed.

26. Install the large diameter boot band and then pack with grease.

27. Install the spring cap, spring and plug seal. Install the plug and secure with dummy bolts. Lock the plug by bending it and then remove the dummy bolts.

28. Install the small diameter boot band and replace the half-shaft.

Stub Axle and Rear Wheel Bearings (Independent Rear Suspension Models)

REMOVAL & INSTALLATION

◆ **See Figures 67, 68, 69, 70 and 71**

1. Block the front wheels. Loosen the wheel nuts, raise and support the car, and remove the wheel.

2. Remove the halfshaft.

3. On cars with rear disc brakes, unbolt the caliper and move it aside. Do not allow the caliper to hang by the hose. Support the caliper with a length of wire or rest it on a suspension member.

4. Remove the brake disc on models with rear disc brakes. Remove the brake drum on cars with drum brakes.

5. Remove the stub axle nut. You will have to hold the sub axle at the outside while removing the nut from the axle shaft side. The nut will require a good deal of force to remove, so be sure to hold the stub axle firmly.

6. Remove the stub axle with a slide hammer and an adapter. The outer wheel bearing will come off with the stub axle.

7. Remove the companion flange from the lower arm.

8. Remove and discard the grease seal and inner bearing from the lower arm using a drift made for the purpose or a length of pipe of the proper diameter. The outer bearing can be removed from the stub axle with a puller. If the grease seal or the bearings are removed, new parts must be used on assembly.

9. Clean all the parts to be reused in solvent.

To install:

10. Sealed type bearings are used. When the new bearings are installed, the sealed side must face out. Install the sealed side of the outer bearing facing the wheel, and the sealed side of the inner bearing facing the differential.

11. Press the outer bearing onto the stub axle.

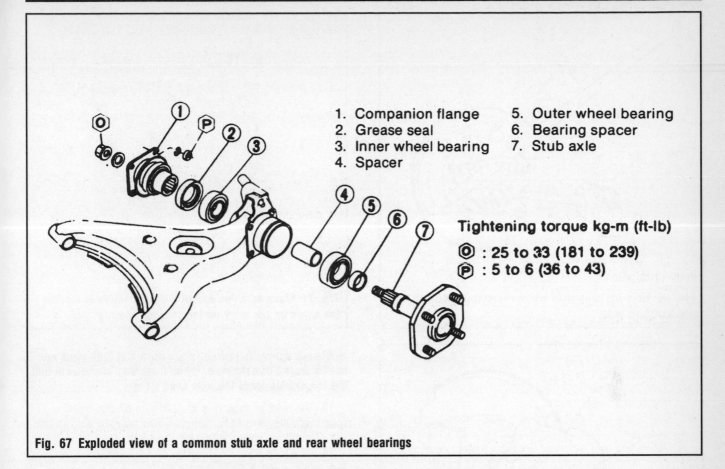

1. Companion flange
2. Grease seal
3. Inner wheel bearing
4. Spacer
5. Outer wheel bearing
6. Bearing spacer
7. Stub axle

Tightening torque kg-m (ft-lb)

◎ : 25 to 33 (181 to 239)
Ⓟ : 5 to 6 (36 to 43)

Fig. 67 Exploded view of a common stub axle and rear wheel bearings

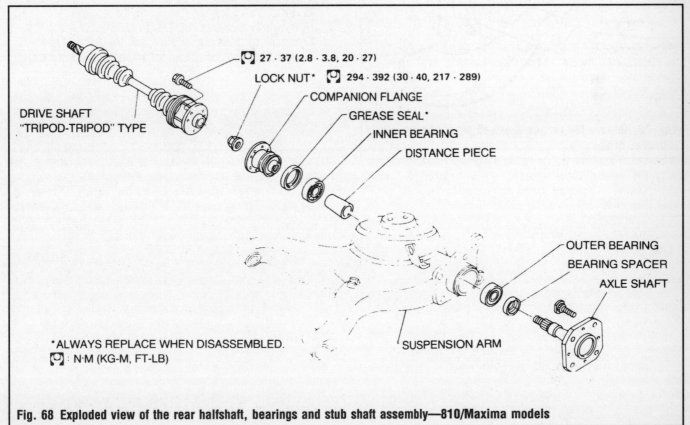

DRIVE SHAFT
"TRIPOD-TRIPOD" TYPE

27 - 37 (2.8 - 3.8, 20 - 27)
LOCK NUT * 294 - 392 (30 - 40, 217 - 289)
COMPANION FLANGE
GREASE SEAL*
INNER BEARING
DISTANCE PIECE

OUTER BEARING
BEARING SPACER
AXLE SHAFT

SUSPENSION ARM

*ALWAYS REPLACE WHEN DISASSEMBLED.
: N·M (KG-M, FT-LB)

Fig. 68 Exploded view of the rear halfshaft, bearings and stub shaft assembly—810/Maxima models

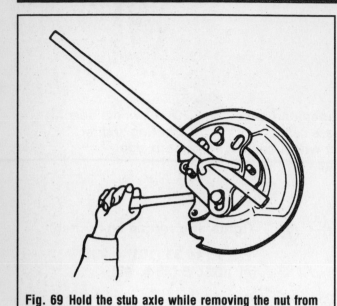

Fig. 69 Hold the stub axle while removing the nut from the halfshaft side

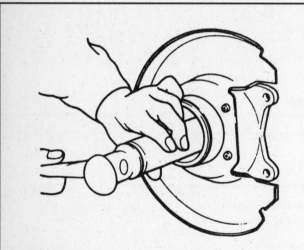

Fig. 70 Remove the grease seal and inner bearing with a drift or driver

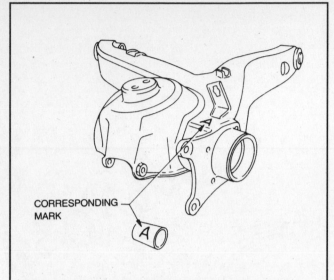

CORRESPONDING MARK

Fig. 71 Make sure you install a spacer which is marked the same as the mark on the bearing housing

➡**When a spacer is reused, make sure that both ends are not collapsed or deformed. When installing, make sure that the larger side faces the axle shaft flange.**

12. The bearing housing is stamped with a letter. Select a spacer with the same marking. Install the spacer on the stub axle.

13. Install the stub axle into the lower arm.

14. Install the new inner bearing into the lower arm with the stub axle in place. Install a new grease seal.

15. Install the companion flange onto the stub axle.

16. Install the stub axle nut. Tighten to 181–239 ft. lbs.

17. Install the brake disc or drum, and the caliper if removed.

18. Install the halfshaft. Install the wheel and lower the car.

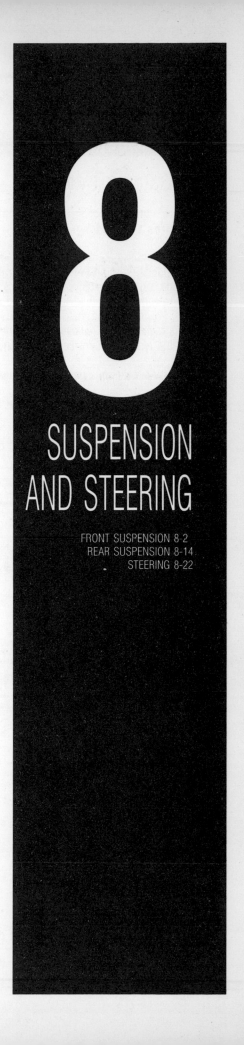

8

SUSPENSION AND STEERING

FRONT SUSPENSION

MacPherson Strut

REMOVAL & INSTALLATION

♦ **See Figures 1, 2 and 3**

All strut assemblies are precision parts and retain the springs under tremendous pressure even when removed from the car. For these reasons, several expensive special tools and substantial specialized knowledge are required to safely and effectively work on these parts. We recommend that if spring or shock absorber repair work is required, you remove the strut or struts involved and take them to a repair facility which is fully equipped and familiar with the car.

1. Jack up the car and support it safely with jackstands. Remove the wheel.
2. Remove the brake caliper. Remove the disc and hub assembly.

3. Disconnect the tension rod and stabilizer bar from the transverse link.
4. Unbolt the steering arm. If applicable, remove the lower strut mounting bolts from the control arm. Pry the control arm down to detach it from the strut.
5. Place a jack under the bottom of the strut.
6. Open the hood and remove the nuts holding the top of the strut.
7. Lower the jack slowly and cautiously until the strut assembly can be removed.

To install:

8. Install the strut assembly on the vehicle and tighten the strut-to-knuckle arm to 53–72 ft. lbs. Tighten the tension rod to transverse link to 33–40 ft. lbs. and the strut to hoodledge bolts to 23–31 ft. lbs.

➡**The self-locking nuts holding the top of the strut must always be replaced when removed.**

9. Bleed the brakes.
10. Install the wheel.

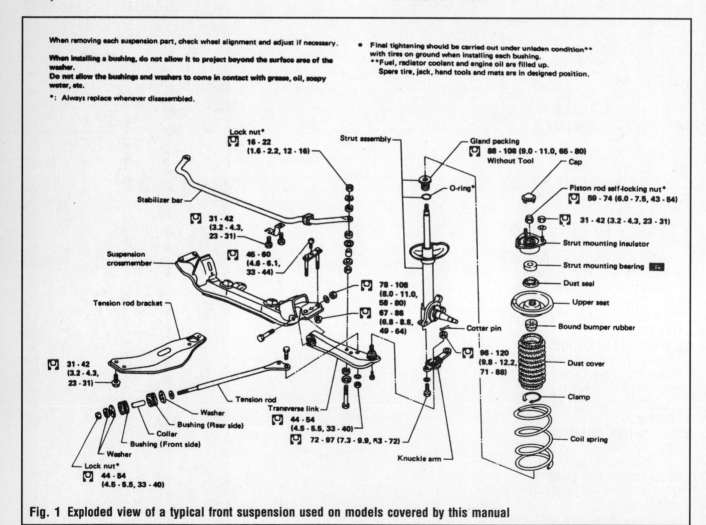

Fig. 1 Exploded view of a typical front suspension used on models covered by this manual

COMMON FRONT SUSPENSION & STEERING COMPONENTS

1. Ball joint mounting nuts
2. Tie rod
3. Strut rod
4. Stabilizer bar
5. A-arm pivot
6. Power steering lines
7. Suspension crossmember
8. Power steering rack boot
9. Lower A-arm
10. MacPherson strut
11. Steering knuckle

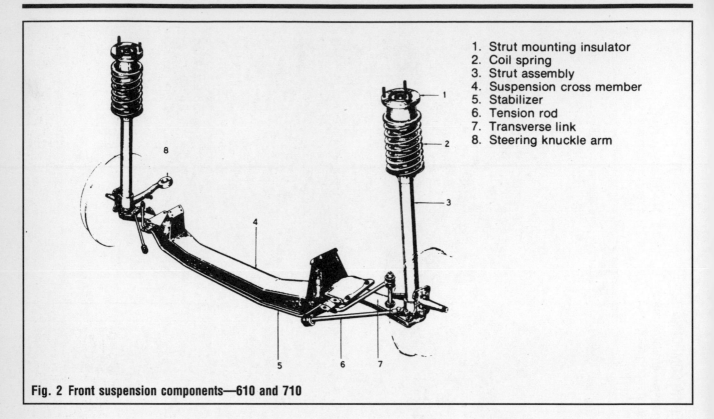

1. Strut mounting insulator
2. Coil spring
3. Strut assembly
4. Suspension cross member
5. Stabilizer
6. Tension rod
7. Transverse link
8. Steering knuckle arm

Fig. 2 Front suspension components—610 and 710

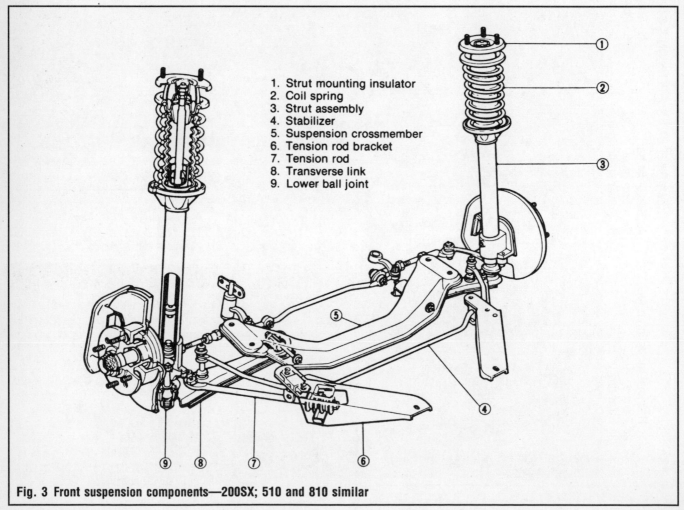

1. Strut mounting insulator
2. Coil spring
3. Strut assembly
4. Stabilizer
5. Suspension crossmember
6. Tension rod bracket
7. Tension rod
8. Transverse link
9. Lower ball joint

Fig. 3 Front suspension components—200SX; 510 and 810 similar

To remove the front MacPherson strut, you must remove the steering arm

Remove the upper strut mounting nuts at the shock tower

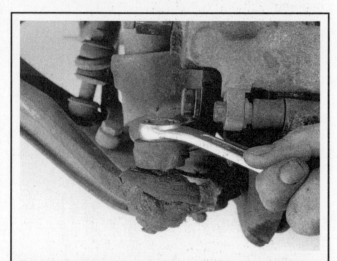

Once the cotter pin is removed, remove the castellated nut at the steering arm

Lower the strut assembly, then safely remove the spring or take it to a repair facility for service

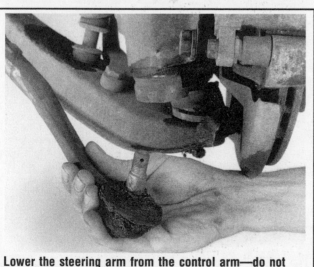

Lower the steering arm from the control arm—do not hammer on the threaded end

OVERHAUL (STRUT CARTRIDGE REPLACEMENT)

▶ See Figures 4 thru 11

✳✳ CAUTION

The coil springs are under considerable tension, and can exert enough force to cause serious injury. Disassemble the struts only using the proper tools, and use extreme caution.

Coil springs on all models must be removed with the aid of a coil spring compressor. If you don't have one, don't try to improvise by using something else: you could risk injury. The Datsun/Nissan coil spring compressor is Special Tool ST3565S001 or variations of that number. Basically, they are all the same tool, except for the 1980–81 200SX and the 1981–83 810 and Maxima spring compressor, Special Tool HT71730000, which is totally different unit. These are the recommended compressors, although they are probably not the only spring compressors which will work. Always follow manufacturer's instructions when operating a spring compressor. You can now buy cartridge type shock absorbers for many Datsun/Nissan: installation procedures are not the same as those given here. In this case, follow the instructions that come with the shock absorbers.

To remove the coil spring, you must first remove the strut assembly from the vehicle.

1. Secure the strut assembly in a vise.

2. Attach the spring compressor to the spring, leaving the top few coils free.

3. Remove the dust cap from the top of the strut to expose the center nut, if a dust cap is provided.

4. Compress the spring just far enough to permit the strut insulator to be turned by hand. Remove the self locking center nut.

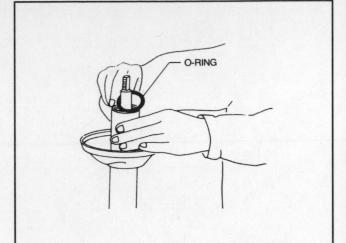

Fig. 6 Remove the O-ring from the top of the piston guide rod

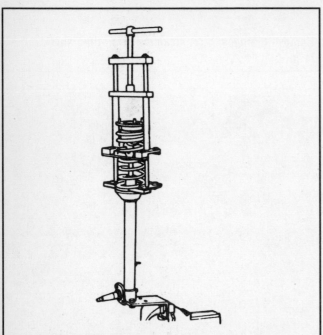

Fig. 4 Install a suitable spring compressor to remove the coil spring from the strut

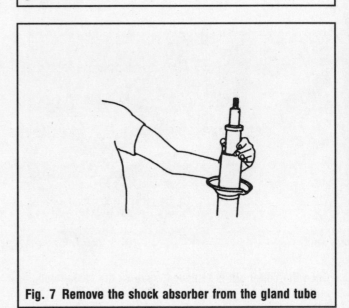

Fig. 7 Remove the shock absorber from the gland tube

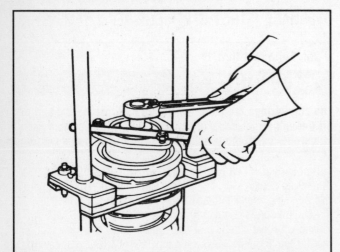

Fig. 5 Hold the upper mount with a rod to unscrew the piston rod nut

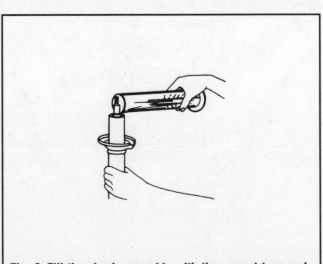

Fig. 8 Fill the shock assembly with the correct type and amount of oil

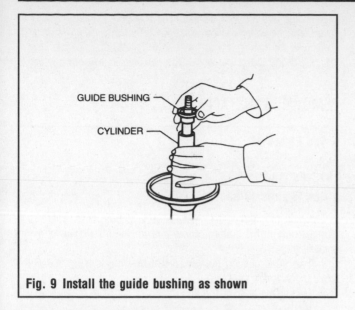

Fig. 9 Install the guide bushing as shown

5. Take out the strut insulator, strut bearing, oil seal, upper spring seat and bound bumper rubber from the top of the strut. Note their sequence of removal and be sure to assemble them in the same order.

6. Remove the spring with the spring compressor still attached.

7. To remove the shock absorber: Remove the dust cap, if so equipped, and push the piston rod down until it bottoms. With the piston in this position, loosen and remove the gland packing shock absorber retainer. This calls for Datsun/Nissan Special Tool ST35500001, but you should be able to loosen it either with a pipe wrench or by tapping it around with a drift.

➡️**If the gland tube is dirty, clean it before removing it to prevent dirt from contaminating the fluid inside the strut tube.**

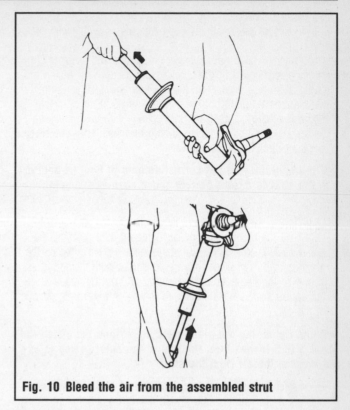

Fig. 10 Bleed the air from the assembled strut

8. Remove the O-ring from the top of the piston rod guide and lift out the piston rod together with the cylinder. Drain all of the fluid from the strut and shock components into a suitable container. Clean all parts.

➡️**The piston rod, piston rod guide and cylinder are a matched set: single parts of this shock assembly should not be exchanged with parts of other assemblies.**

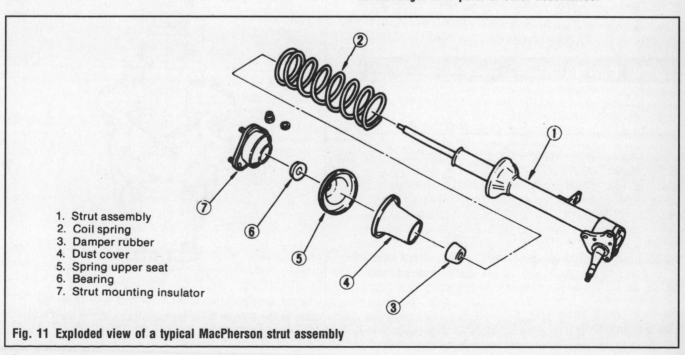

1. Strut assembly
2. Coil spring
3. Damper rubber
4. Dust cover
5. Spring upper seat
6. Bearing
7. Strut mounting insulator

Fig. 11 Exploded view of a typical MacPherson strut assembly

To install:

9. Assemble the shock absorber into the assembly with the following notes:

a. After installing the cylinder and piston rod assembly (the shock absorber kit) in the outer casing, remove the piston rod guide, if so equipped, from the cylinder and pour the correct amount of new fluid into the cylinder and strut outer casing. To find this amount consult the instructions with your shock absorber kit. The amount of oil should be listed. Use only Nissan Genuine Strut Oil or its equivalent.

➡**It is important that the correct amount of fluid be poured into the strut to assure correct shock absorber damping force.**

b. Install the O-ring, fluid and any other cylinder components. Fit the gland packing and tighten it after greasing the gland packing-to-piston rod mating surfaces. Note that on the Maxima with front wheel drive, you must install the spring as shown in the illustration. Also, make sure on this model that the spring seat is positioned with the notch toward the outside of the car.

➡**When tightening the gland packing, extend the piston rod about 3 to 5 inches from the end of the outer casing to expel most of the air from the strut.**

c. After the kit is installed, bleed the air from the system in the following manner: hold the strut with its bottom end facing down. Pull the piston rod out as far as it will go. Turn the strut upside down and push the piston in as far as it will go. Repeat this procedure several times until an equal pressure is felt on both the pull out and the push in strokes of the piston rods. The remaining assembly is the reverse of disassembly.

10. When reassembling the strut assembly, observe the following:

a. Make sure you assemble the unit with the shock absorber piston rod fully extended.

b. When assembling, take care that the rubber spring seats, both top and bottom, and the spring are positioned in their grooves before releasing the spring.

Lower Ball Joint

INSPECTION

The lower ball joint should be replaced when play becomes excessive. Nissan/Datsun does not publish specifications on just what constitutes excessive play, relying instead on a method of determining the force (in inch pounds) required to keep the ball joint turning. This method is not very helpful to the backyard mechanic since it involves removing the ball joint, which is what we are trying to avoid in the first place. An effective way to determine ball joint play is to jack up the car until the wheel is just a couple of inches off the ground and the ball joint is unloaded (meaning you can't jack directly underneath the ball joint). Place a long bar under the tire and move the wheel and tire assembly up and down. Keep one hand on top of the tire while you are doing this. If there is over ¼" of play at the top of the tire, the ball joint is probably bad. This is assuming that the wheel bearings are in

good shape and properly adjusted. As a double check on this, have someone watch the ball joint while you move the tire up and down with the bar. If you can see considerable play, besides feeling play at the top of the wheel, the ball joint needs replacing.

REMOVAL & INSTALLATION

◆ **See Figure 12**

1973–80 Models
◆ **See Figures 13 and 14**

The ball joint should be greased every 30,000 miles. There is a plugged hole in the bottom of the joint for the installation of a grease fitting.

1. Raise and support the car so that the wheels hang free. Remove the wheel.

2. Unbolt the tension rod and stabilizer bar from transverse link.

3. Unbolt the strut from the steering arm.

4. Remove the cotter pin and ball joint stud nut. Separate the ball joint and steering arm.

5. Unbolt the ball joint from the transverse link.

To install:

6. Install the ball joint to the transverse link. Grease the joint after installation.

7. Reconnect the steering arm and the ball joint. Install a new cotter pin and ball joint stud nut.

8. Connect the strut to the steering arm.

9. Bolt the tension rod and stabilizer bar to the transverse link. Install the wheel.

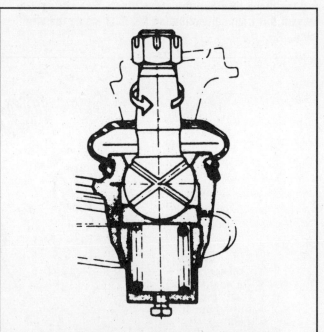

Fig. 12 Cross-section of a typical ball joint. Note the plug at the bottom for a grease nipple. Make sure the rubber boot is in good condition; if not, replace it

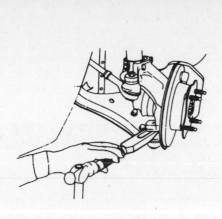

Fig. 13 A pickle fork can be used to separate the ball joint from the knuckle

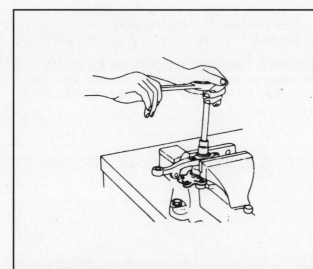

Fig. 14 Remove the ball joint from the knuckle as shown

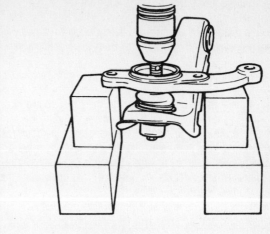

Fig. 15 The ball joint must be pressed out of the knuckle—1981–84 models

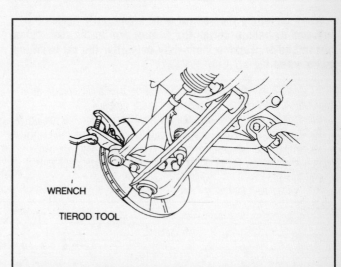

WRENCH

TIEROD TOOL

Fig. 16 Separate the knuckle from the tie rod using a suitable removal tool

1981–84 Models
▶ See Figure 15

The ball joints on these models are a press fit into the knuckle arm. Follow the Lower Control Arm removal and installation procedure. After Step 8 is completed, the knuckle arm ball joint must be pressed out of the knuckle arm using a special press. Most suspension specialists have this equipment.

Lower Control Arm (Transverse Link) and Ball Joint

REMOVAL & INSTALLATION

▶ See Figures 16 and 17

You'll need a ball joint remover for this operation.
1. Jack up the vehicle and support it with jackstands. Remove the wheel.

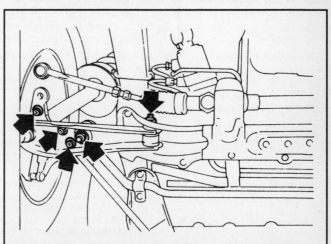

Fig. 17 Remove the knuckle arm from the strut (left arrows) and the control arm (transverse link) from the vehicle

2. Remove the splash board, if so equipped.

3. Remove the cotter pin and castle nut from the tie rod (steering arm) ball joint and separate the ball joint from the side rod. You'll need either a fork-type or puller-type joint remover.

4. Separate the steering knuckle arm from the MacPherson strut.

5. Remove the tension rod and stabilizer bar from the lower arm.

6. Remove the nuts or bolts connecting the lower control arm (transverse link) to the suspension crossmember on all models.

7. On the 810/Maxima, to remove the transverse link (control arm) on the steering gear side, separate the gear arm from the sector shaft and lower steering linkage. To remove the transverse link on the idler arm side, detach the idler arm assembly from the body frame and lower steering linkage.

8. Remove the lower control arm (transverse link) with the suspension ball joint and knuckle arm still attached.

To install:

9. Install the lower control arm (transverse link) with the ball joint and knuckle arm attached.

➡**When installing the control arm, temporarily tighten the nuts and/or bolts securing the control arm to the suspension crossmember. Tighten them fully only after the car is sitting on its wheels.**

10. Install the nuts or bolts connecting the lower control arm (transverse link) to the suspension crossmember.

11. Connect the steering knuckle arm to the MacPherson strut.

12. Install the tension rod and stabilizer bar to the lower arm.

13. Install the (steering arm) ball joint to the side rod and tighten the locknut to 58–72 ft. lbs. Install the castle nut with a new cotter pin.

14. Install the wheel and lower the vehicle always tighten all bolts and nuts to correct specifications. Tighten the lower control arm to the suspension crossmember bolts to 58–80 ft. lbs. Tighten the tension rod to transverse link to 33–40 ft. lbs. and the stabilizer bar to transverse link to 12–16 ft. lbs. Tighten the knuckle arm to knuckle spindle to 53–72 ft. lbs.

15. Install the splash board, if so equipped. Lubricate the ball joints after the complete installation.

Front Wheel Bearings

REPLACEMENT

◆ **See Figures 18 thru 24**

➡**After the wheel bearings have been removed or replaced or the front axle has been reassembled be sure to adjust wheel bearing preload. Refer to the Adjustment procedure in this section.**

1. Raise and support the vehicle safely.
2. Remove the front wheels and the brake caliper assemblies.

➡**Brake hoses do not need to be disconnected from the brake caliper assemblies. Make sure the brake hoses are secure and do not let caliper assemblies hang unsupported from the vehicle.**

3. Work off center hub cap by using thin tool. If necessary tap around it with a soft hammer while removing.

4. Pry off cotter pin and take out adjusting cap and wheel bearing locknut.

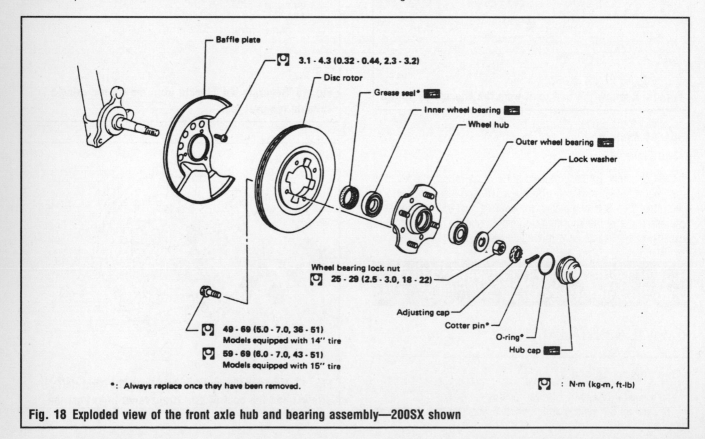

Fig. 18 Exploded view of the front axle hub and bearing assembly—200SX shown

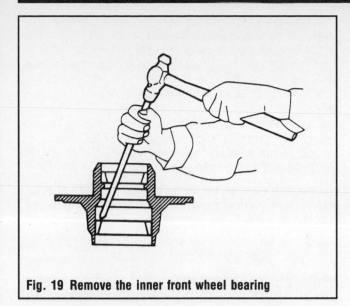

Fig. 19 Remove the inner front wheel bearing

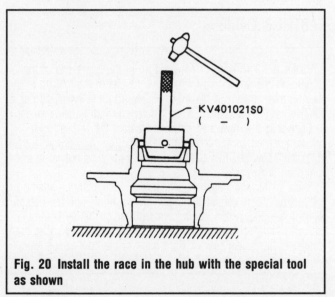

Fig. 20 Install the race in the hub with the special tool as shown

KV401021S0
(–)

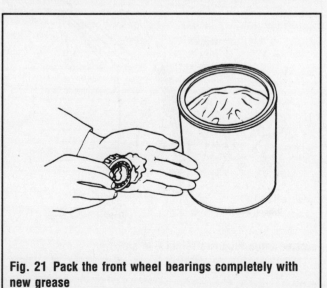

Fig. 21 Pack the front wheel bearings completely with new grease

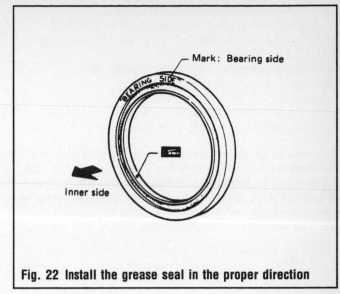

Mark: Bearing side

Inner side

Fig. 22 Install the grease seal in the proper direction

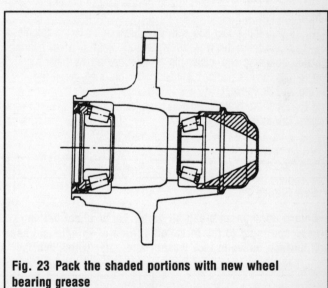

Fig. 23 Pack the shaded portions with new wheel bearing grease

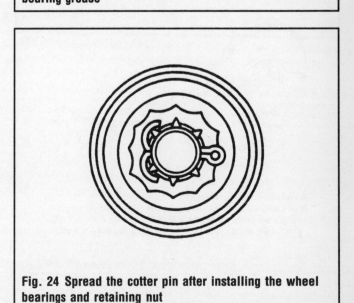

Fig. 24 Spread the cotter pin after installing the wheel bearings and retaining nut

5. Remove wheel hub with disc brake rotor from spindle with bearings installed. Remove the outer bearing from the hub.

6. Remove inner bearing and grease seal from hub using long brass drift pin or equivalent.

7. If it is necessary to replace the bearing outer races, drive them out of the hub with a brass drift pin and mallet.

To install:

8. Install the outer bearing race with a tool (KV401021S0 special tool number) until it seats in the hub flush.

➡**Place a large glob of grease into the palm of one hand and push the bearing through it with a sliding motion. The grease must be forced through the side of the bearing and in between each roller. Continue until the grease begins to ooze out the other side through the gaps between the rollers. The bearing must be completely packed with grease.**

9. Pack each wheel bearing with high temperature wheel bearing grease. Pack hub and hub cap with the recommended wheel bearing grease up to shaded portions. Refer to the illustration.

10. Install the inner bearing and grease seal in the proper position in the hub.

11. Install the wheel hub with disc brake rotor to the spindle.

12. Install the outer wheel bearing, lock washer, wheel bearing locknut, adjusting cap, cotter pin (always use a new cotter pin and O-ring for installation), spread cotter pin then install the O-ring and dust cap.

13. Install the brake caliper assemblies and bleed brakes if necessary. Install the front wheels.

ADJUSTMENT

♦ **See Figure 25**

➡**Before adjustment clean all parts. Apply wheel bearing grease sparingly to the threaded portion of spindle and contact surface between lock washer and outer wheel bearing.**

1. Raise and support the vehicle safely, remove the front wheels and the brake caliper assemblies.

2. Torque wheel bearing locknut to 18–22 ft. lbs.

3. Turn the wheel hub several times in both directions to seat wheel bearing correctly.

4. Again tighten wheel bearing nut to specification 18–22 ft. lbs.

5. Loosen locknut approximately 60°. Install adjusting cap and align groove of nut with hole in spindle. If alignment cannot be obtained, change position of adjusting cap. Also, if alignment cannot be obtained, loosen locknut slightly but not more than 15°.

➡**If possible measure the wheel bearing preload and axial play. Repeat above procedures until correct starting torque is obtained. Refer to the illustration.**

6. Spread the cotter pin and install hub cap with a new O-ring.

7. Install caliper assemblies and front wheels.

Front End Alignment

CASTER & CAMBER

Caster is the forward or rearward tilt of the upper end of the kingpin, or the upper ball joint, which results in a slight tilt of the steering axis forward or backward. Rearward tilt is referred to as a positive caster, while forward tilt is referred to as negative caster.

Camber is the inward or outward tilt from the vertical, measured in degrees of the front wheels at the top. An outward tilt gives the wheel positive camber. Proper camber is critical to assure even tire wear.

Since caster and camber are adjusted traditionally by adding or subtracting shims behind the upper control arms, and the Datsun/Nissans covered in this guide have replaced the upper control arm with the MacPherson strut, the only way to adjust caster and camber is to replace bent or worn parts of the front suspension.

Axial play: 0 mm (0 in)
When bearing preload (As measured at wheel hub bolt):
With new parts   6.9 - 14.7 N (0.7 - 1.5 kg, 1.5 - 3.3 lb)
With used parts 2.0 - 7.8 N (0.2 - 0.8 kg, 0.4 - 1.8 lb)

Fig. 25 Measure wheel bearing preload and axial play

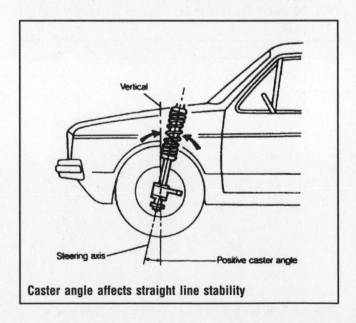

Caster angle affects straight line stability

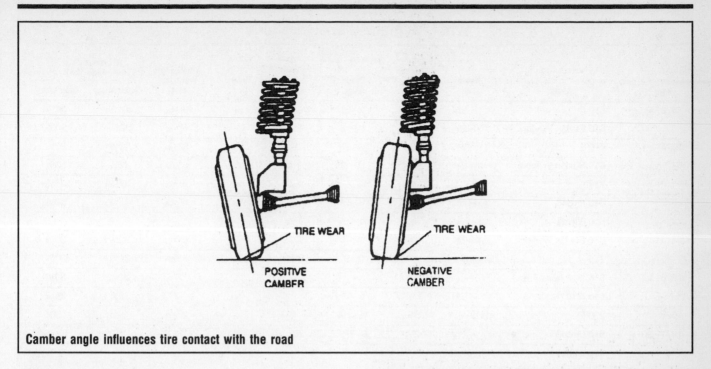

Camber angle influences tire contact with the road

TOE

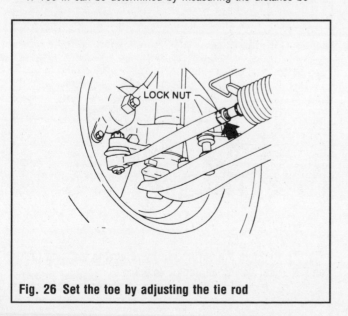

Fig. 26 Set the toe by adjusting the tie rod

♦ See Figure 26

Toe is the amount, measured in a fraction of an inch, that the wheels are closer together at one end than the other. Toe-in means that the front wheels are closer together at the front than the rear. Toe-out means the rears are closer than the front. Datsun/Nissans are adjusted to have a slight amount of toe-in. Toe-in is adjusted by turning the tie rod, which has a righthand thread on one end and a left-hand thread on the other.

You can check your vehicle's toe-in yourself without special equipment if you make careful measurements. The wheels must be straight ahead.

1. Toe-in can be determined by measuring the distance between the center of the tire treads, at the front of the tire and at the rear. If the tread pattern of your car's tires makes this impossible, you can measure between the edges of the wheel rims, but make sure to move the car forward and measure in a couple of places to avoid errors caused by bent rims or wheel runout.

2. If the measurement is not within specifications, loosen the locknuts at both ends of the tie rod (the driver's side locknut is left-hand threaded).

3. Turn the top of the tie rod toward the front of the car to reduce toe-in, or toward the rear to increase it. When the correct dimension is reached, tighten the locknuts and check the adjustment.

➡ **The length of the tie rods must always be equal to each other.**

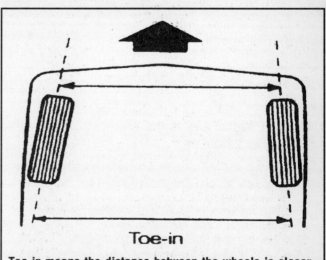

Toe-in means the distance between the wheels is closer at the front than at the rear of the wheels

Wheel Alignment Specifications

Year	Model	Caster Range (deg)	Caster Preferred Setting (deg)	Camber Range (deg)	Camber Preferred Setting (deg)	Toe-In (in.)	Steering Axis Inclination (deg)	Wheel Pivot Ratio (deg) Inner Wheel	Wheel Pivot Ratio (deg) Outer Wheel
1973	610	1¼–2¾	2	1½–2¾	2	½	6 21/32	32½+	30½
	610 Station Wagon	1¼–2¾	2	1½–3	2¼	½	6 21/32	32½+	30½
1974	610	1¼–2¾	2	1¼–2¾	2	½	6 21/32	32½+	30½
	610 Station Wagon	1¼–2¾	2	1½–3	2¼	½	6 21/32	32½+	30½
	710	1 3/16–2 11/16	1 15/16	1 7/16–2 15/16	1⅛	⅝	6 13/32	37½+	31 27/32
1975	610 (Front)	1¼–2¾	2	1¼–2¾	2	½	6 21/32	32½+	30½
	610 (Rear)	—	—	¾–2¼	1½	5/16	—	—	—
	610 Station Wagon	1¼–2¾	2	1½–3	2¼	½	6 21/32	32½+	30½
	710	1 3/16–2 11/16	1 15/16	2 15/16	2 15/16	⅜	6 13/32	32½+	30½
1976–77	610, 710 (Bias Tires)	—	—	—	—	¼	7	32½+	30½
	610, 710 (Radials)	1 1/16–2 9/16	1 13/16	1¼–2¾	2	7/32	7	32½+	30½
1977	200SX	1 1/32–2¼	1 21/32	½–1½	1	⅛	7 13/16	35	30
1977–80	810 (Front)	1 3/16–2 11/16	2¼	0–1½	¾	⅛	7 29/32	20	18 20/32
	810 (Rear)	—	—	—	—	3/16	—	—	—
1978–79	200SX	1 1/16–2 9/16	1 13/16	5/16–1 13/16	17/16	⅛	7 13/16	35	30
1978–81	510 Station Wagon	15/16–2 7/16	1 9/16	1/16–1 9/16	¾	1/16	8 5/32	20	19½
1979–81	510	1 1/16–2 9/16	1 13/16	−¼–1¼	½	1/16	8 27/32	20	19½
1981–83	810 (Front)	1 15/16–4 7/16	3 11/16	−5/16–1 3/16	7/16	1/32	12⅛	20	18 11/16
	810 (Rear)	—	—	15/16–2 7/16	1 11/16	7/32	—	—	—
1980–81	200SX	1¾–3¼	2½	−1 1/16–13/16	1/16	3/64	8 5/32	20	18 45/64
1984	Maxima (Front)	2 15/16–4 7/16	3 11/16	−1 5/16–1 3/16	7/16	1/32	12⅛	20	18 11/16
	Maxima (Rear)	—	—	1¼–2¾	2	5/32	—	—	—

REAR SUSPENSION

Leaf Springs

REMOVAL & INSTALLATION

▶ See Figure 27

610 Station Wagon, All 710 and 1977–79 200SX Models

▶ See Figures 28 and 29

1. Raise the rear axle until the wheels hang free. Support the car on jackstands. Support the rear axle with a floor jack.
2. Remove the spare tire.
3. Unbolt the bottom end of the shock absorber.
4. Unbolt the axle from the spring leaves.
5. Unbolt the front spring bracket from the body. Lower the spring end and bracket to the floor.
6. Unbolt and remove the rear shackle.

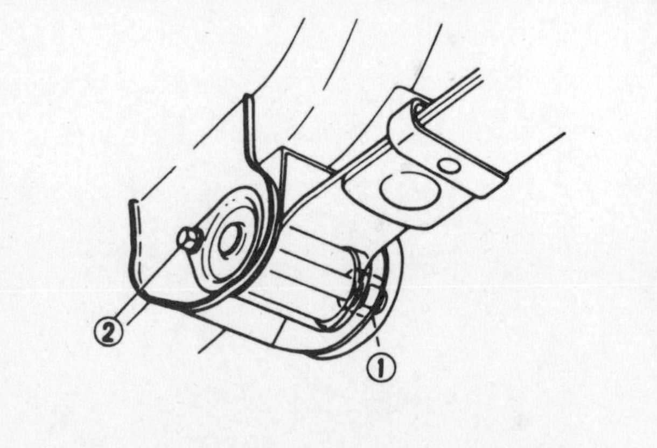

Fig. 27 Remove the spring pin by removing the nuts (1 and 2)—leaf spring-equipped vehicles

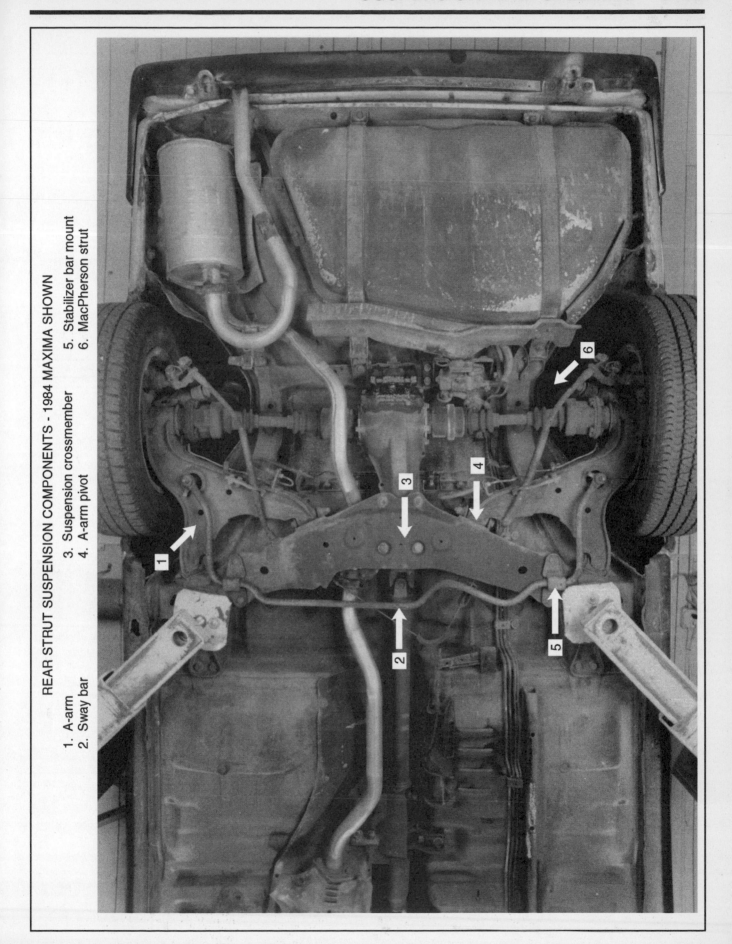

REAR STRUT SUSPENSION COMPONENTS - 1984 MAXIMA SHOWN

1. A-arm
2. Sway bar
3. Suspension crossmember
4. A-arm pivot
5. Stabilizer bar mount
6. MacPherson strut

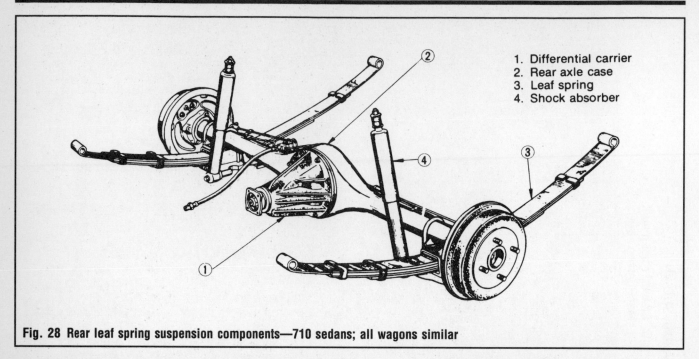

1. Differential carrier
2. Rear axle case
3. Leaf spring
4. Shock absorber

Fig. 28 Rear leaf spring suspension components—710 sedans; all wagons similar

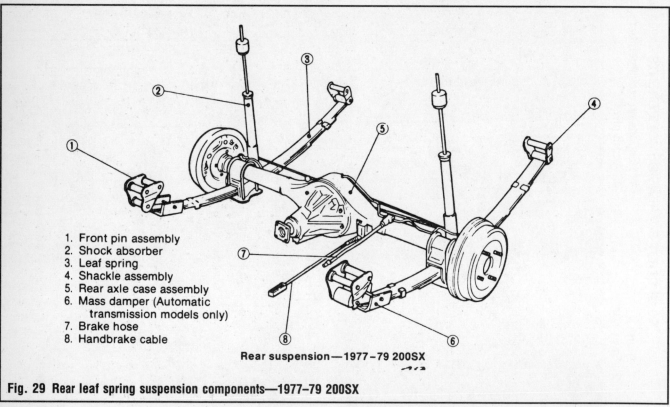

1. Front pin assembly
2. Shock absorber
3. Leaf spring
4. Shackle assembly
5. Rear axle case assembly
6. Mass damper (Automatic transmission models only)
7. Brake hose
8. Handbrake cable

Rear suspension—1977–79 200SX

Fig. 29 Rear leaf spring suspension components—1977–79 200SX

7. Unbolt the bracket from the spring.

8. Before reinstallation, coat the front bracket pin and bushing, and the shackle pin and bushing with a soap solution.

9. Install the spring and shackle in the correct position to the vehicle. Connect the axle housing to the spring leaves. The front pin nut and the shock absorber mounting should be tightened after the vehicle is lowered to the floor. Make sure that the elon-gated flange of the rubber bumper is to the rear.

10. Remove the floor jack and install the spare tire.

510 and 810 Station Wagon Models

1. Raise the rear of the car and support it with jackstands.

2. Remove the wheels and tires.

3. Disconnect the lower end of the shock absorber and remove the U-bolt nuts.

4. Place a jack under the rear axle.

5. Disconnect the spring shackle bolts at the front and rear of the spring.

6. Lower the jack slowly and remove the spring.

7. Installation is in the reverse order of removal.

Coil Springs

REMOVAL & INSTALLATION

610 Sedan Model
▶ **See Figure 30**

1. Raise the rear of the vehicle and support it on jackstands.
2. Remove the wheels.
3. Disconnect the handbrake linkage and return spring.
4. Unbolt the axle driveshaft flange at the wheel end.
5. Unbolt the rubber bumper inside the bottom of the coil spring.

6. Jack up the suspension arm and unbolt the shock absorber lower mounting.

7. Lower the jack slowly and cautiously. Remove the coil spring, spring seat, and rubber bumper.

8. Install the spring assembly in the correct position, making sure that the flat face of the spring is at the top.

9. Jack up the suspension arm and bolt the shock absorber to the lower mounting.

10. Bolt the rubber bumper inside the bottom of the coil spring and connect the axle driveshaft flange at the wheel end.

11. Connect the handbrake linkage and return spring and install the wheels.

510 Sedan and Hatchback and 1980–81 200SX Models
▶ **See Figure 31**

1. Raise the car and support it with jackstands.
2. Support the center of the differential with a jack or other suitable tool.
3. Remove the rear wheels.
4. Remove the bolts securing the lower ends of the shock absorbers.
5. Lower the jack under the differential slowly and carefully and remove the coil springs after they are fully extended.
6. Installation is in the reverse order of removal.

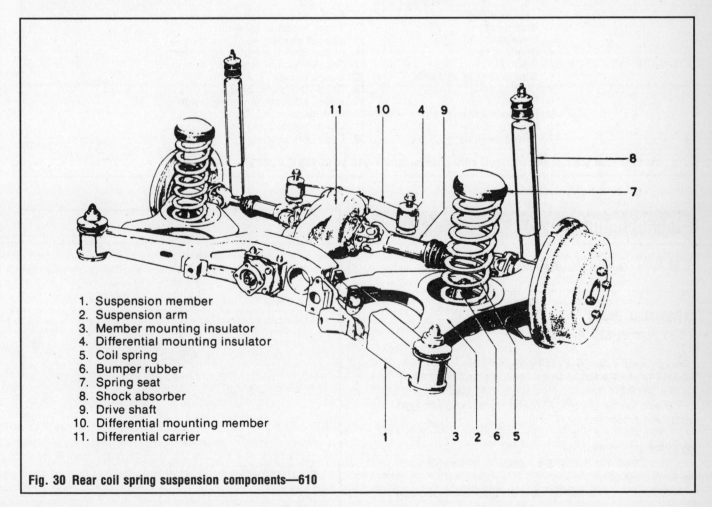

1. Suspension member
2. Suspension arm
3. Member mounting insulator
4. Differential mounting insulator
5. Coil spring
6. Bumper rubber
7. Spring seat
8. Shock absorber
9. Drive shaft
10. Differential mounting member
11. Differential carrier

Fig. 30 Rear coil spring suspension components—610

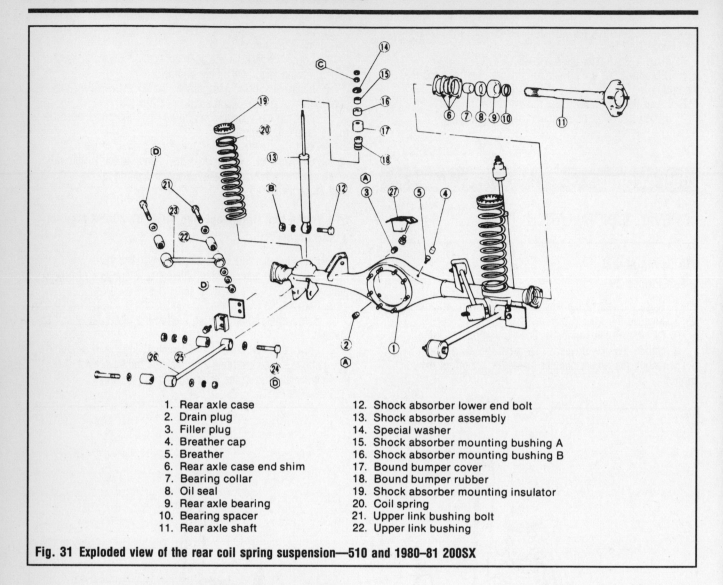

1. Rear axle case
2. Drain plug
3. Filler plug
4. Breather cap
5. Breather
6. Rear axle case end shim
7. Bearing collar
8. Oil seal
9. Rear axle bearing
10. Bearing spacer
11. Rear axle shaft
12. Shock absorber lower end bolt
13. Shock absorber assembly
14. Special washer
15. Shock absorber mounting bushing A
16. Shock absorber mounting bushing B
17. Bound bumper cover
18. Bound bumper rubber
19. Shock absorber mounting insulator
20. Coil spring
21. Upper link bushing bolt
22. Upper link bushing

Fig. 31 Exploded view of the rear coil spring suspension—510 and 1980–81 200SX

MacPherson Strut

REMOVAL & INSTALLATION

810/Maxima Sedan

▶ **See Figures 32, 33 and 34**

The struts and spring are removed as a unit. Disassembly of the strut requires a spring compressor. For strut disassembly, follow the procedure given for front suspension MacPherson struts.

1. Raise the car and safely support the rear end with jackstands and a floor jack.

2. Open the trunk and remove the three nuts which secure the top of the strut to the body.

3. Disconnect the strut at the bottom by removing the bolt at the suspension arm.

4. Service the strut as detailed under the Front Suspension procedures.

5. Installation is the reverse of removal. Install the strut so that the larger hole on the lower end faces out.

Fig. 32 The three upper strut bolts are accessible through the trunk—810/Maxima

To remove the rear MacPherson strut, remove the lower mounting bolt after disconnecting the top

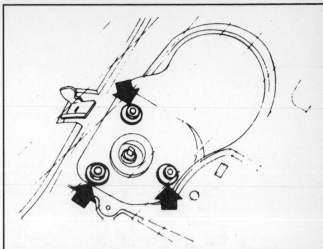
Fig. 33 The lower end of the strut is secured by a single bolt (arrow)—810/Maxima

Remove the lower strut bolt and set it in a safe place, or replace it if it is worn or damaged

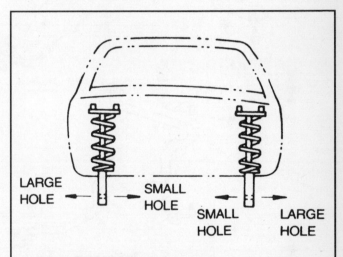
LARGE HOLE — SMALL HOLE SMALL HOLE — LARGE HOLE

Fig. 34 Install the rear struts so that the larger hole on the lower end faces out—810/Maxima

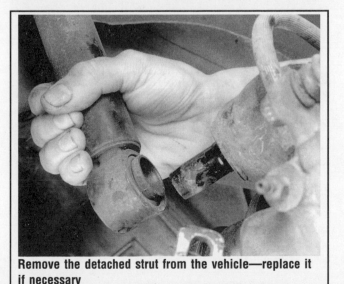
Remove the detached strut from the vehicle—replace it if necessary

OVERHAUL

◗ See Figures 35 and 36

➥It is necessary throughout strut work to keep all parts absolutely clean. This procedure is for when a shock absorber kit-cartridge is not used.

1. Matchmark the strut mounting insulator for reassembly at the same angle.
2. Install a spring compressor and compress the spring until the spring insulator can be turned by hand.
3. Remove the rebound stop locknut so the threads on the piston rod will not be damaged. Use a tool such as ST35490000 (J26083) or equivalent to remove the packing. Then, force the piston rod downward until it bottoms.
4. Withdraw the piston rod and guide from the strut cylinder.
5. Pour the correct amount of an approved strut fluid into the strut. Use 11.2 fl. oz. for non-adjustable struts and 11.0 fl. oz. for adjustable struts.

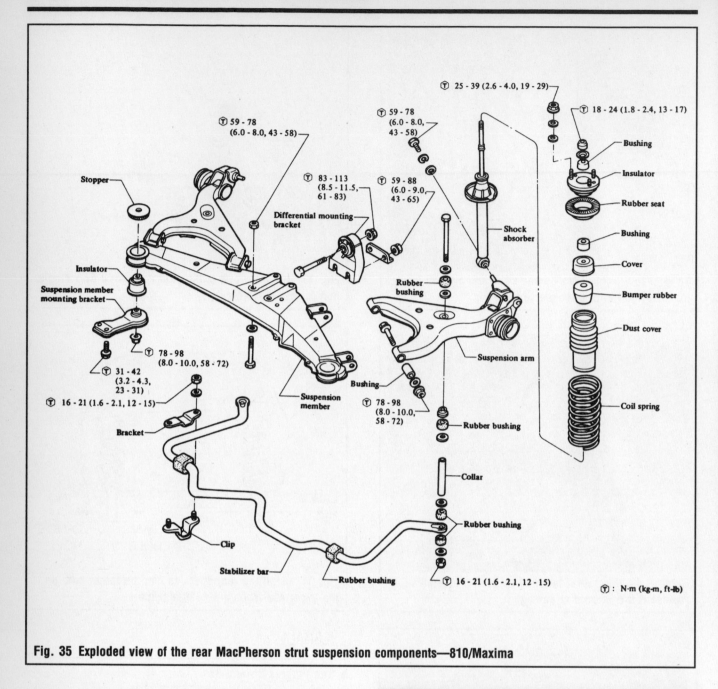

Fig. 35 Exploded view of the rear MacPherson strut suspension components—810/Maxima

6. Then, lubricate the sealing lip of the gland packing. Tape over the strut rod threads and then install the gland packing. Tighten it with the special wrench. Torque to 65–80 ft. lbs.

7. Pump the strut rod up and down several times with it in its normal vertical position and upside down to remove airbubbles.

8. Install the upper spring seat and mounting insulator. Make sure the matchmark on the insulator corresponds with the location hole on the upper spring seat.

9. Position the spring so its end rests against the stop on the lower seat. Install the remaining spring retaining parts including the piston rod self locking nut (torque to 43–58 ft. lbs.) and the upper nut that retains the flexible washer (torque to 26–35 ft. lbs.).

Shock Absorber

REMOVAL & INSTALLATION

♦ See Figures 37, 38 and 39

200SX, 510, 610 and 710 Sedans

1. Open the trunk and remove the cover panel, if necessary, to expose the shock mounts. Pry off the mount covers, if so equipped. On leaf spring models, jack up the rear of the vehicle and support the rear axle on stands.

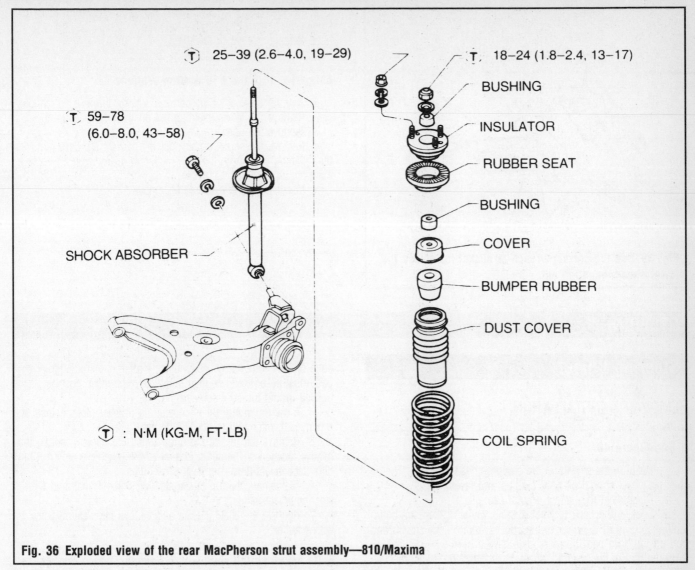

T 25–39 (2.6–4.0, 19–29)

T 18–24 (1.8–2.4, 13–17)

T 59–78
(6.0–8.0, 43–58)

BUSHING

INSULATOR

RUBBER SEAT

BUSHING

COVER

BUMPER RUBBER

DUST COVER

SHOCK ABSORBER

COIL SPRING

T : N·M (KG-M, FT-LB)

Fig. 36 Exploded view of the rear MacPherson strut assembly—810/Maxima

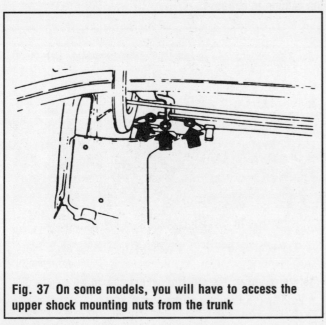

Fig. 37 On some models, you will have to access the upper shock mounting nuts from the trunk

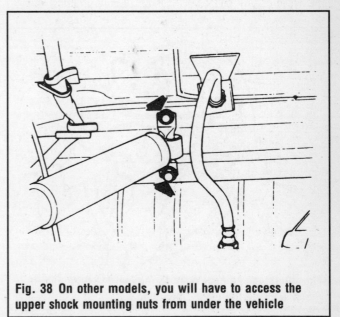

Fig. 38 On other models, you will have to access the upper shock mounting nuts from under the vehicle

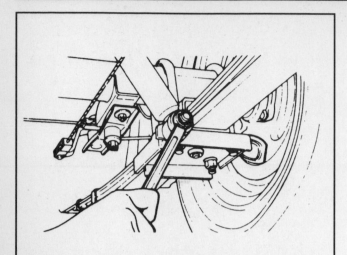

Fig. 39 Use the correct wrench or socket to remove the lower shock mounting nut

2. Remove the two nuts holding the top of the shock absorber. Unbolt the bottom of the shock absorber.

3. Remove the shock absorber.

4. Installation is the reverse of removal.

510, 610, 710 and 810 Station Wagons

1. Jack up the rear of the car and support the axle on stands.

2. Remove the lower retaining nut on the shock absorber.

3. Remove the upper retaining bolt(s).

4. Remove the shock from under the car. On the 610, remove the retaining strap from the old shock and install it on the replacement shock.

5. Installation is the reverse of removal.

STEERING

Steering Wheel

REMOVAL & INSTALLATION

♦ **See Figure 40**

1. Position the wheels in the straight-ahead direction. The steering wheel should be right side up and level.

2. Disconnect the battery ground cable.

3. Look at the back of your steering wheel. If there are countersunk screws in the back of the spokes, remove the screws and pull off the horn pad. Some models have a horn wire running from the pad to the steering wheel. Disconnect it. There are three other types of horn buttons or rings on Datsuns. The first simply pulls off. The second, which is usually a large, semitriangular pad, must be pushed up, then pulled off. The third must be pushed in and turned clockwise.

4. If the mounting nut is covered by a cover plate instead of a horn pad, remove it to access the nut.

5. Remove the rest of the horn switch mechanism, noting the relative location of the parts. Remove the mechanism only if it hinders subsequent wheel removal procedures.

6. Matchmark the top of the steering column shaft and the steering wheel flange.

7. Remove the attaching nut and remove the steering wheel with a puller.

➡**Do not strike the shaft with a hammer, which may cause the column to collapse.**

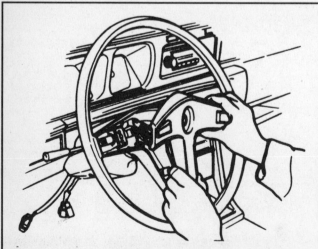

Fig. 40 It will be necessary to remove the horn pad to reach the steering wheel mounting nut

Before removal, the steering wheel should be centered, with the tires pointing straight ahead

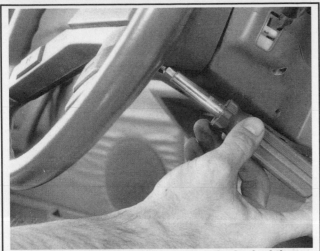

If necessary, remove the screws from the back of the steering wheel spokes

After it is loosened, remove the nut securing the wheel

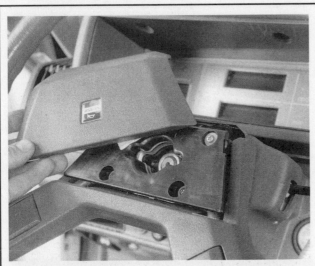

Remove the cover plate—1984 Maxima wheel shown

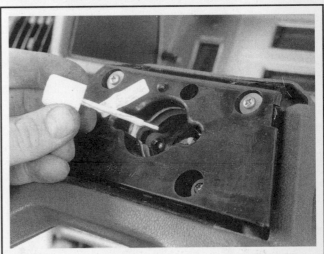

Matchmark the top of the steering column shaft to the wheel

With a suitable socket and driver, remove the mounting nut from the steering wheel

Mount a suitable steering wheel puller, then turn the puller's screw to extract the wheel

To install:

8. Install the steering wheel in the reverse order of removal, aligning the punch marks. Do not drive or hammer the wheel into place, or you may cause the collapsible steering column to collapse, in which case you'll have to buy a whole new steering column unit.

9. Tighten the steering wheel nut to 22–25 ft. lbs. on the 1977–79 200SX and front wheel drive Maximas. Tighten all other steering wheel nuts to 28–36 ft. lbs.

10. Reinstall the horn button, pad, ring, or cover plate.

Turn Signal/Combination Switch

REMOVAL & INSTALLATION

▶ **See Figure 41**

On some models, the turn signal switch is part of a combination switch. The whole unit is removed together.

1. Disconnect the battery ground cable.

2. Remove the steering wheel as previously outlined. Observe the caution on the collapsible steering column.

3. Remove the steering column covers.

4. Remove the switch retaining screws.

5. Disconnect the electrical plugs from the switch, then remove the switch.

➡**On some vehicles the control (lighting, wiper and washer, hazzard and cruise control set) switches can be replaced without removing the combination base.**

To install:

6. Install the switch in the proper position. Many models have turn signal switches that have a tab which must fit into a hole in the steering shaft in order for the system to return the switch to the neutral position after the turn has been made. Be sure to align the tab and the hole when installing.

7. Install the steering column covers and steering wheel.

8. Reconnect the battery cable. Turn key to the ON position

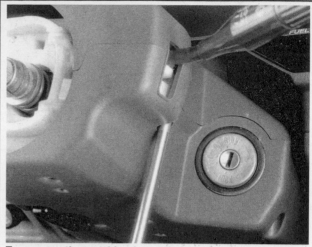

To remove the combination switch, remove the screws holding the column cover halves

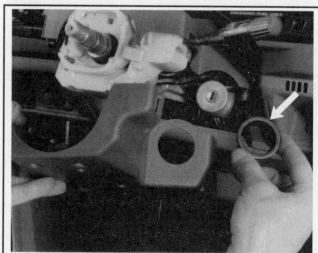

When detached, remove the lower cover—note the trim ring also removed (arrow)

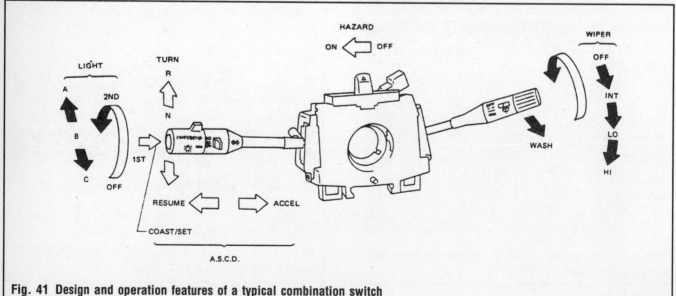

Fig. 41 Design and operation features of a typical combination switch

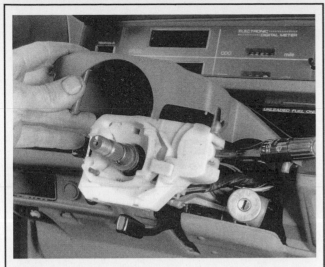

Remove the upper column cover

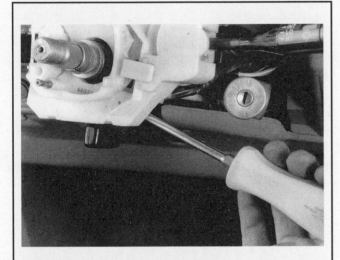

Remove the switch retaining screws

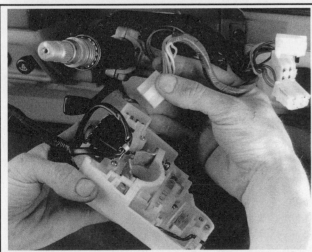

Disconnect the electrical harness plug, then remove the switch

and check system for proper operation. Make sure that the turn signals will cancel after the vehicle has made a turn.

➡**On many models, the individual stalk assemblies can be removed without removing the combination switch base assembly. Simply disconnect the electrical lead and remove the 2 stalk-to-base mounting screws.**

Steering Lock

REMOVAL & INSTALLATION

▶ **See Figure 42**

The steering lock/ignition switch/warning buzzer assembly is attached to the steering column by special screws whose heads shear off on installation. The screws must be drilled out to remove the assembly. The ignition switch or warning switch can be replaced without removing the assembly. The ignition switch is on the back of the assembly, and the warning switch on the side. The warning buzzer, which sounds when the driver's door is opened with the steering unlocked, is located behind the instrument panel. Install shear type screws and then cut off the screw heads.

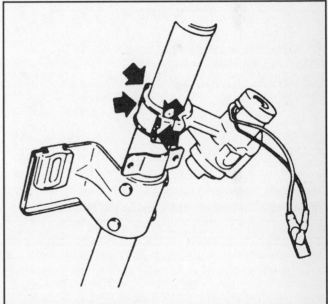

Fig. 42 Remove the steering lock securing screws (arrows)—1977–79 200SX shown

Tie Rod Ends (Steering Side Rods)

REMOVAL & INSTALLATION

▶ **See Figure 43**

You will need a ball joint remover for this operation.
1. Jack up the front of the vehicle and support it on jackstands.

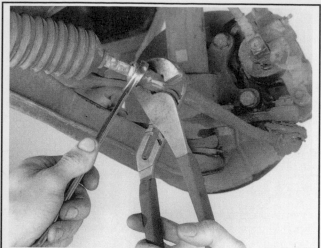

To remove the locknut, hold the tie rod so the torque is applied to the nut, not the ball joint

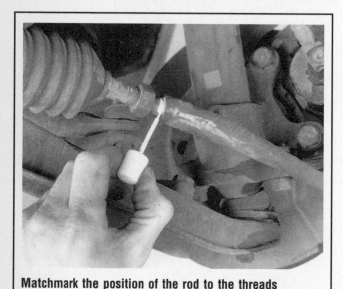

Matchmark the position of the rod to the threads

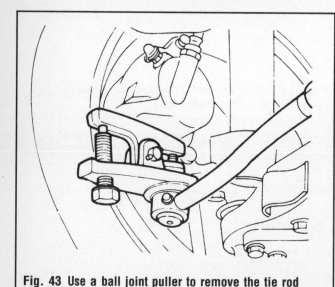

Fig. 43 Use a ball joint puller to remove the tie rod

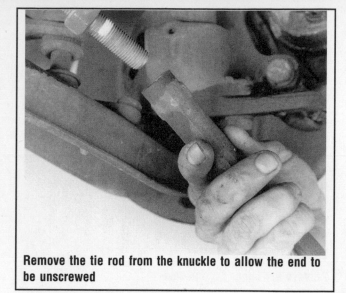

Remove the tie rod from the knuckle to allow the end to be unscrewed

2. Locate the faulty tie rod end. It will have a lot of play in it and the dust cover will probably be ripped.

3. Remove the cotter key and nut from the tie rod stud. Note the position of the tie rod end in relation to the rest of the steering linkage.

➡ **After loosening the locknut or removing the tie rod end, matchmark the threads with paint or white correction fluid to ensure correct installation length.**

4. Loosen the locknut holding the tie rod to the rest of the steering linkage.

5. Free the tie rod ball joint from either the relay rod or steering knuckle by using a ball joint remover.

6. Unscrew and remove the tie rod end, counting the number of turns it takes to completely free it.

To install:

7. Install the new tie rod end, turning it in exactly as far as you screwed out the old one. Make sure it is correctly positioned in relation to the rest of the steering linkage and aligns with the matchmarks made previously.

8. Fit the ball joint and nut, tighten them and install a new cotter pin. Before finally tightening the tie rod locknut or clamp, adjust the toe-in of the vehicle.

Manual Steering Gear

REMOVAL & INSTALLATION

▶ **See Figures 44 and 45**

1977–86 200SX Models

1. Disconnect the exhaust pipe from the exhaust manifold, if necessary, and remove the bolt securing the exhaust pipe to the transmission mounting insulator.

2. Remove the bolt holding the worm shaft to the rubber coupling.

3. Remove the nut holding the pitman arm to the sector shaft and remove the pitman arm.

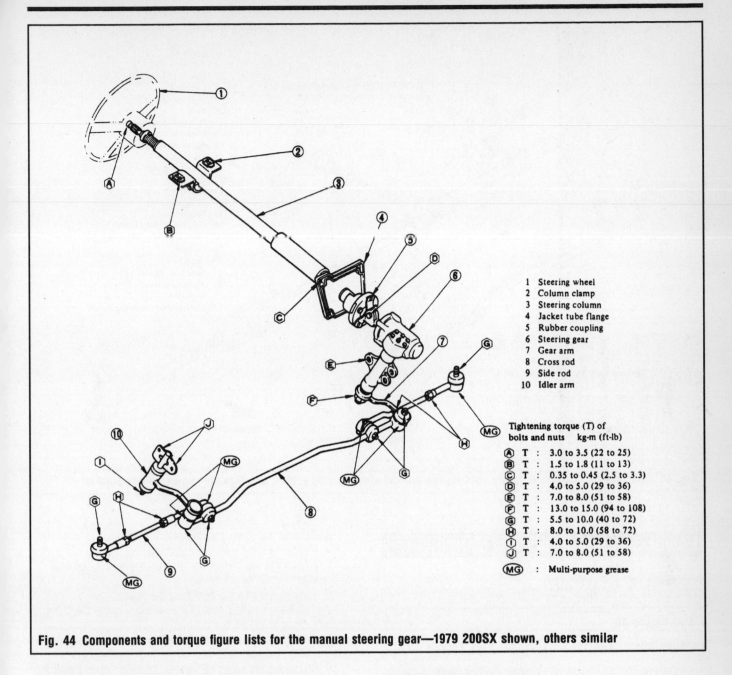

1   Steering wheel
2   Column clamp
3   Steering column
4   Jacket tube flange
5   Rubber coupling
6   Steering gear
7   Gear arm
8   Cross rod
9   Side rod
10 Idler arm

**Tightening torque (T) of
bolts and nuts   kg-m (ft-lb)**

(A) T : 3.0 to 3.5 (22 to 25)
(B) T : 1.5 to 1.8 (11 to 13)
(C) T : 0.35 to 0.45 (2.5 to 3.3)
(D) T : 4.0 to 5.0 (29 to 36)
(E) T : 7.0 to 8.0 (51 to 58)
(F) T : 13.0 to 15.0 (94 to 108)
(G) T : 5.5 to 10.0 (40 to 72)
(H) T : 8.0 to 10.0 (58 to 72)
(I) T : 4.0 to 5.0 (29 to 36)
(J) T : 7.0 to 8.0 (51 to 58)

(MG) : Multi-purpose grease

Fig. 44 Components and torque figure lists for the manual steering gear—1979 200SX shown, others similar

4. Remove the steering gear attaching bolts and then remove the steering gear from the vehicle.

To install:

5. Install the steering gear with attaching bolts to the vehicle.
6. Install the pitman arm assembly to the selector shaft.
7. Connect the worm shaft to the rubber coupling.
8. Reconnect the exhaust system if necessary. Check the wheel alignment after installation.

1977–81 810 Model

Refer to the procedure above as a guide for Removal and Installation of the manual steering gear. The front steering (non rack and pinion) gear used in these vehicles is very similar as the above.

1982–84 810/Maxima Models

➡ **These vehicles use a rack and pinion steering gear type.**

1. Raise and support the front of the vehicle safely and remove the front wheels.
2. Remove the lower joint from the steering column at the rubber coupling.
3. Remove the lower joint assembly from the pinion.
4. Remove the side rod studs from the steering knuckles.
5. Remove the gear housing-to-crossmember bolts and then remove the steering gear from the vehicle.
6. Installation is the reverse order of the removal procedure.

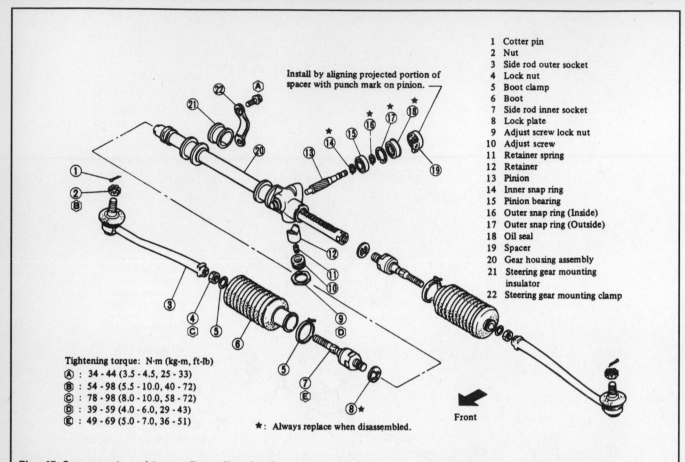

Install by aligning projected portion of spacer with punch mark on pinion.

1 Cotter pin
2 Nut
3 Side rod outer socket
4 Lock nut
5 Boot clamp
6 Boot
7 Side rod inner socket
8 Lock plate
9 Adjust screw lock nut
10 Adjust screw
11 Retainer spring
12 Retainer
13 Pinion
14 Inner snap ring
15 Pinion bearing
16 Outer snap ring (Inside)
17 Outer snap ring (Outside)
18 Oil seal
19 Spacer
20 Gear housing assembly
21 Steering gear mounting insulator
22 Steering gear mounting clamp

Tightening torque: N·m (kg-m, ft-lb)
(A) : 34 - 44 (3.5 - 4.5, 25 - 33)
(B) : 54 - 98 (5.5 - 10.0, 40 - 72)
(C) : 78 - 98 (8.0 - 10.0, 58 - 72)
(D) : 39 - 59 (4.0 - 6.0, 29 - 43)
(E) : 49 - 69 (5.0 - 7.0, 36 - 51)

★ : Always replace when disassembled.

Front

Fig. 45 Components and torque figure lists for the manual steering gear—1982 810/Maxima shown, others similar

Power Steering Gear

REMOVAL & ADJUSTMENT

♦ **See Figure 46**

1980–81 200SX and 1982–84 810/Maxima Models

1. Remove the air cleaner and remove the bolt securing the U-joint to the worm shaft.
2. Disconnect and plug the hoses from the power steering gear.
3. Remove the pitman arm from the sector shaft, using a suitable puller.
4. Remove the steering gear securing bolts and remove the steering gear from the vehicle.
5. Installation is the reverse order of the removal procedure.

1982–84 810/Maxima Models

➡**These vehicles use a rack and pinion type power steering gear.**

1. Remove the bolt securing the lower shaft to power steering gear assembly.
2. Disconnect the hoses from the power steering gear and plug the hoses to prevent leakage.

3. Remove the power steering gear mounting bolts.
4. Remove the exhaust pipe mounting nut.
5. Disconnect the control cable or linkage for the transmission and position it out of the way.
6. Remove the steering gear from the vehicle.
7. Install the steering gear to the vehicle. Tighten the clamp retaining bolts to 29–36 ft. lbs.
8. Connect the control cable or linkage to the transmission and install the exhaust system.
9. Reconnect the hoses to the power steering gear. Install the bolt securing the lower shaft to power steering gear assembly.
10. Check the fluid level. Start the engine check for leaks and for proper operation of the system.

Power Steering Pump

REMOVAL & INSTALLATION

1. Remove the hoses at the pump and plug the openings shut to prevent contamination. Position the disconnected lines in a raised attitude to prevent leakage.
2. Remove the pump belt.
3. Loosen the retaining bolts and any braces, and remove the pump.
4. Installation is the reverse of removal. Adjust the belt tension

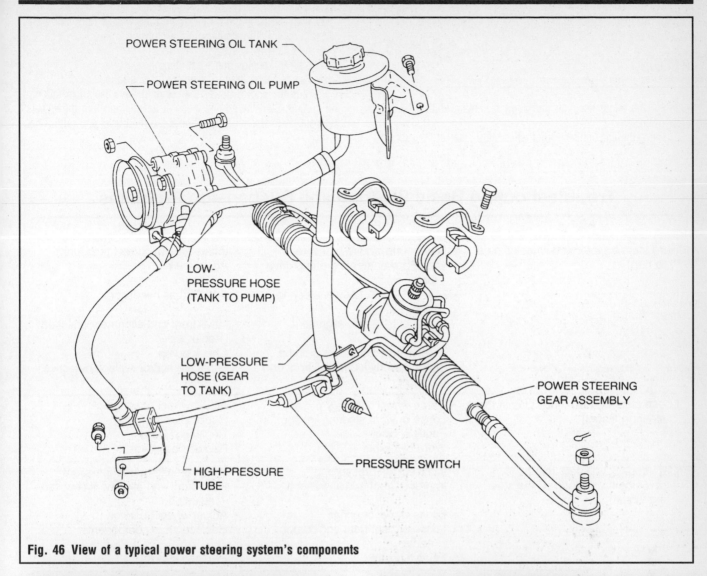

POWER STEERING OIL TANK

POWER STEERING OIL PUMP

LOW-PRESSURE HOSE (TANK TO PUMP)

LOW-PRESSURE HOSE (GEAR TO TANK)

HIGH-PRESSURE TUBE

PRESSURE SWITCH

POWER STEERING GEAR ASSEMBLY

Fig. 46 View of a typical power steering system's components

To remove the power steering pump, disconnect the pump from the brackets

When detached, remove the power steering pump from the vehicle by referring to the Belts section in Section 1, General Information and Maintenance. Bleed the system.

BLEEDING

1. Fill the pump reservoir and allow to remain undisturbed for a few minutes.
2. Raise the car until the front wheels are clear of the ground.
3. With the engine off, quickly turn the wheels right and left several times, lightly contacting the stops.
4. Add fluid if necessary.
5. Start the engine and let it idle.
6. Repeat Steps 3 and 4 with the engine idling.
7. Stop the engine, lower the car until the wheels just touch the ground. Start the engine, allow it to idle, and turn the wheels back and forth several times. Check the fluid level and refill if necessary.

Troubleshooting Basic Steering and Suspension Problems

Problem	Cause	Solution
Hard steering (steering wheel is hard to turn)	• Low or uneven tire pressure • Loose power steering pump drive belt • Low or incorrect power steering fluid • Incorrect front end alignment • Defective power steering pump • Bent or poorly lubricated front end parts	• Inflate tires to correct pressure • Adjust belt • Add fluid as necessary • Have front end alignment checked/ adjusted • Check pump • Lubricate and/or replace defective parts
Loose steering (too much play in the steering wheel)	• Loose wheel bearings • Loose or worn steering linkage • Faulty shocks • Worn ball joints	• Adjust wheel bearings • Replace worn parts • Replace shocks • Replace ball joints
Car veers or wanders (car pulls to one side with hands off the steering wheel)	• Incorrect tire pressure • Improper front end alignment • Loose wheel bearings • Loose or bent front end components • Faulty shocks	• Inflate tires to correct pressure • Have front end alignment checked/ adjusted • Adjust wheel bearings • Replace worn components • Replace shocks
Wheel oscillation or vibration transmitted through steering wheel	• Improper tire pressures • Tires out of balance • Loose wheel bearings • Improper front end alignment • Worn or bent front end components	• Inflate tires to correct pressure • Have tires balanced • Adjust wheel bearings • Have front end alignment checked/ adjusted • Replace worn parts
Uneven tire wear	• Incorrect tire pressure • Front end out of alignment • Tires out of balance	• Inflate tires to correct pressure • Have front end alignment checked/ adjusted • Have tires balanced

Troubleshooting the Steering Column

Problem	Cause	Solution
Will not lock	• Lockbolt spring broken or defective	• Replace lock bolt spring
High effort (required to turn ignition key and lock cylinder)	• Lock cylinder defective	• Replace lock cylinder
	• Ignition switch defective	• Replace ignition switch
	• Rack preload spring broken or deformed	• Replace preload spring
	• Burr on lock sector, lock rack, housing, support or remote rod coupling	• Remove burr
	• Bent sector shaft	• Replace shaft
	• Defective lock rack	• Replace lock rack
	• Remote rod bent, deformed	• Replace rod
	• Ignition switch mounting bracket bent	• Straighten or replace
	• Distorted coupling slot in lock rack (tilt column)	• Replace lock rack
Will stick in "start"	• Remote rod deformed	• Straighten or replace
	• Ignition switch mounting bracket bent	• Straighten or replace
Key cannot be removed in "off-lock"	• Ignition switch is not adjusted correctly	• Adjust switch
	• Defective lock cylinder	• Replace lock cylinder
Lock cylinder can be removed without depressing retainer	• Lock cylinder with defective retainer	• Replace lock cylinder
	• Burr over retainer slot in housing cover or on cylinder retainer	• Remove burr
High effort on lock cylinder between "off" and "off-lock"	• Distorted lock rack	• Replace lock rack
	• Burr on tang of shift gate (automatic column)	• Remove burr
	• Gearshift linkage not adjusted	• Adjust linkage
Noise in column	• One click when in "off-lock" position and the steering wheel is moved (all except automatic column)	• Normal—lock bolt is seating
	• Coupling bolts not tightened	• Tighten pinch bolts
	• Lack of grease on bearings or bearing surfaces	• Lubricate with chassis grease
	• Upper shaft bearing worn or broken	• Replace bearing assembly
	• Lower shaft bearing worn or broken	• Replace bearing. Check shaft and replace if scored.
	• Column not correctly aligned	• Align column
	• Coupling pulled apart	• Replace coupling
	• Broken coupling lower joint	• Repair or replace joint and align column
	• Steering shaft snap ring not seated	• Replace ring. Check for proper seating in groove.
	• Shroud loose on shift bowl. Housing loose on jacket—will be noticed with ignition in "off-lock" and when torque is applied to steering wheel.	• Position shroud over lugs on shift bowl. Tighten mounting screws.
High steering shaft effort	• Column misaligned	• Align column
	• Defective upper or lower bearing	• Replace as required
	• Tight steering shaft universal joint	• Repair or replace
	• Flash on I.D. of shift tube at plastic joint (tilt column only)	• Replace shift tube
	• Upper or lower bearing seized	• Replace bearings
Lash in mounted column assembly	• Column mounting bracket bolts loose	• Tighten bolts
	• Broken weld nuts on column jacket	• Replace column jacket
	• Column capsule bracket sheared	• Replace bracket assembly

Troubleshooting the Steering Column (cont.)

Problem	Cause	Solution
Lash in mounted column assembly (cont.)	· Column bracket to column jacket mounting bolts loose	· Tighten to specified torque
	· Loose lock shoes in housing (tilt column only)	· Replace shoes
	· Loose pivot pins (tilt column only)	· Replace pivot pins and support
	· Loose lock shoe pin (tilt column only)	· Replace pin and housing
	· Loose support screws (tilt column only)	· Tighten screws
Housing loose (tilt column only)	· Excessive clearance between holes in support or housing and pivot pin diameters	· Replace pivot pins and support
	· Housing support-screws loose	· Tighten screws
Steering wheel loose—every other tilt position (tilt column only)	· Loose fit between lock shoe and lock shoe pivot pin	· Replace lock shoes and pivot pin
Steering column not locking in any tilt position (tilt column only)	· Lock shoe seized on pivot pin	· Replace lock shoes and pin
	· Lock shoe grooves have burrs or are filled with foreign material	· Clean or replace lock shoes
	· Lock shoe springs weak or broken	· Replace springs
Noise when tilting column (tilt column only)	· Upper tilt bumpers worn	· Replace tilt bumper
	· Tilt spring rubbing in housing	· Lubricate with chassis grease
One click when in "off-lock" position and the steering wheel is moved	· Seating of lock bolt	· None. Click is normal characteristic sound produced by lock bolt as it seats.
High shift effort (automatic and tilt column only)	· Column not correctly aligned	· Align column
	· Lower bearing not aligned correctly	· Assemble correctly
	· Lack of grease on seal or lower bearing areas	· Lubricate with chassis grease
Improper transmission shifting—automatic and tilt column only	· Sheared shift tube joint	· Replace shift tube
	· Improper transmission gearshift linkage adjustment	· Adjust linkage
	· Loose lower shift lever	· Replace shift tube

Troubleshooting the Ignition Switch

Problem	Cause	Solution
Ignition switch electrically inoperative	· Loose or defective switch connector	· Tighten or replace connector
	· Feed wire open (fusible link)	· Repair or replace
	· Defective ignition switch	· Replace ignition switch
Engine will not crank	· Ignition switch not adjusted properly	· Adjust switch
Ignition switch will not actuate mechanically	· Defective ignition switch	· Replace switch
	· Defective lock sector	· Replace lock sector
	· Defective remote rod	· Replace remote rod
Ignition switch cannot be adjusted correctly	· Remote rod deformed	· Repair, straighten or replace

Troubleshooting the Turn Signal Switch

Problem	Cause	Solution
Turn signal will not cancel	• Loose switch mounting screws • Switch or anchor bosses broken • Broken, missing or out of position detent, or cancelling spring	• Tighten screws • Replace switch • Reposition springs or replace switch as required
Turn signal difficult to operate	• Turn signal lever loose • Switch yoke broken or distorted • Loose or misplaced springs • Foreign parts and/or materials in switch • Switch mounted loosely	• Tighten mounting screws • Replace switch • Reposition springs or replace switch • Remove foreign parts and/or material • Tighten mounting screws
Turn signal will not indicate lane change	• Broken lane change pressure pad or spring hanger • Broken, missing or misplaced lane change spring • Jammed wires	• Replace switch • Replace or reposition as required • Loosen mounting screws, reposition wires and retighten screws
Turn signal will not stay in turn position	• Foreign material or loose parts impeding movement of switch yoke • Defective switch	• Remove material and/or parts • Replace switch
Hazard switch cannot be pulled out	• Foreign material between hazard support cancelling leg and yoke	• Remove foreign material. No foreign material impeding function of hazard switch—replace turn signal switch.
No turn signal lights	• Inoperative turn signal flasher • Defective or blown fuse • Loose chassis to column harness connector • Disconnect column to chassis connector. Connect new switch to chassis and operate switch by hand. If vehicle lights now operate normally, signal switch is inoperative • If vehicle lights do not operate, check chassis wiring for opens, grounds, etc.	• Replace turn signal flasher • Replace fuse • Connect securely • Replace signal switch • Repair chassis wiring as required
Instrument panel turn indicator lights on but not flashing	• Burned out or damaged front or rear turn signal bulb • If vehicle lights do not operate, check light sockets for high resistance connections, the chassis wiring for opens, grounds, etc. • Inoperative flasher • Loose chassis to column harness connection • Inoperative turn signal switch • To determine if turn signal switch is defective, substitute new switch into circuit and operate switch by hand. If the vehicle's lights operate normally, signal switch is inoperative.	• Replace bulb • Repair chassis wiring as required • Replace flasher • Connect securely • Replace turn signal switch • Replace turn signal switch
Stop light not on when turn indicated	• Loose column to chassis connection • Disconnect column to chassis connector. Connect new switch into system without removing old.	• Connect securely • Replace signal switch

Troubleshooting the Turn Signal Switch (cont.)

Problem	Cause	Solution
Stop light not on when turn indicated (cont.)	Operate switch by hand. If brake lights work with switch in the turn position, signal switch is defective.	
	• If brake lights do not work, check connector to stop light sockets for grounds, opens, etc.	• Repair connector to stop light circuits using service manual as guide
Turn indicator panel lights not flashing	• Burned out bulbs	• Replace bulbs
	• High resistance to ground at bulb socket	• Replace socket
	• Opens, ground in wiring harness from front turn signal bulb socket to indicator lights	• Locate and repair as required
Turn signal lights flash very slowly	• High resistance ground at light sockets	• Repair high resistance grounds at light sockets
	• Incorrect capacity turn signal flasher or bulb	• Replace turn signal flasher or bulb
	• If flashing rate is still extremely slow, check chassis wiring harness from the connector to light sockets for high resistance	• Locate and repair as required
	• Loose chassis to column harness connection	• Connect securely
	• Disconnect column to chassis connector. Connect new switch into system without removing old. Operate switch by hand. If flashing occurs at normal rate, the signal switch is defective.	• Replace turn signal switch
Hazard signal lights will not flash—turn signal functions normally	• Blow fuse	• Replace fuse
	• Inoperative hazard warning flasher	• Replace hazard warning flasher in fuse panel
	• Loose chassis-to-column harness connection	• Conect securely
	• Disconnect column to chassis connector. Connect new switch into system without removing old. Depress the hazard warning lights. If they now work normally, turn signal switch is defective.	• Replace turn signal switch
	• If lights do not flash, check wiring harness "K" lead for open between hazard flasher and connector. If open, fuse block is defective	• Repair or replace brown wire or connector as required

Troubleshooting the Manual Steering Gear

Problem	Cause	Solution
Play or looseness in steering	• Steering wheel loose	• Inspect shaft spines and repair as necessary. Tighten attaching nut and stake in place.
	• Steering linkage or attaching parts loose or worn	• Tighten, adjust, or replace faulty components
	• Pitman arm loose	• Inspect shaft splines and repair as necessary. Tighten attaching nut and stake in place
	• Steering gear attaching bolts loose	• Tighten bolts
	• Loose or worn wheel bearings	• Adjust or replace bearings
	• Steering gear adjustment incorrect or parts badly worn	• Adjust gear or replace defective parts
Wheel shimmy or tramp	• Improper tire pressure	• Inflate tires to recommended pressures
	• Wheels, tires, or brake rotors out-of-balance or out-of-round	• Inspect and replace or balance parts
	• Inoperative, worn, or loose shock absorbers or mounting parts	• Repair or replace shocks or mountings
	• Loose or worn steering or suspension parts	• Tighten or replace as necessary
	• Loose or worn wheel bearings	• Adjust or replace bearings
	• Incorrect steering gear adjustments	• Adjust steering gear
	• Incorrect front wheel alignment	• Correct front wheel alignment
Tire wear	• Improper tire pressure	• Inflate tires to recommended pressures
	• Failure to rotate tires	• Rotate tires
	• Brakes grabbing	• Adjust or repair brakes
	• Incorrect front wheel alignment	• Align incorrect angles
	• Broken or damaged steering and suspension parts	• Repair or replace defective parts
	• Wheel runout	• Replace faulty wheel
	• Excessive speed on turns	• Make driver aware of conditions
Vehicle leads to one side	• Improper tire pressures	• Inflate tires to recommended pressures
	• Front tires with uneven tread depth, wear pattern, or different cord design (i.e., one bias ply and one belted or radial tire on front wheels)	• Install tires of same cord construction and reasonably even tread depth, design, and wear pattern
	• Incorrect front wheel alignment	• Align incorrect angles
	• Brakes dragging	• Adjust or repair brakes
	• Pulling due to uneven tire construction	• Replace faulty tire
Hard or erratic steering	• Incorrect tire pressure	• Inflate tires to recommended pressures
	• Insufficient or incorrect lubrication	• Lubricate as required (refer to Maintenance Section)
	• Suspension, or steering linkage parts damaged or misaligned	• Repair or replace parts as necessary
	• Improper front wheel alignment	• Adjust incorrect wheel alignment angles
	• Incorrect steering gear adjustment	• Adjust steering gear
	• Sagging springs	• Replace springs

Troubleshooting the Turn Signal Switch

Problem	Cause	Solution
Hissing noise in steering gear	• There is some noise in all power steering systems. One of the most common is a hissing sound most evident at standstill parking. There is no relationship between this noise and performance of the steering. Hiss may be expected when steering wheel is at end of travel or when slowly turning at standstill.	• Slight hiss is normal and in no way affects steering. Do not replace valve unless hiss is extremely objectionable. A replacement valve will also exhibit slight noise and is not always a cure. Investigate clearance around flexible coupling rivets. Be sure steering shaft and gear are aligned so flexible coupling rotates in a flat plane and is not distorted as
Stop light not on when turn indicated (cont.)	Operate switch by hand. If brake lights work with switch in the turn position, signal switch is defective. • If brake lights do not work, check connector to stop light sockets for grounds, opens, etc.	• Repair connector to stop light circuits using service manual as guide
Turn indicator panel lights not flashing	• Burned out bulbs • High resistance to ground at bulb socket • Opens, ground in wiring harness from front turn signal bulb socket to indicator lights	• Replace bulbs • Replace socket • Locate and repair as required
Turn signal lights flash very slowly	• High resistance ground at light sockets • Incorrect capacity turn signal flasher or bulb • If flashing rate is still extremely slow, check chassis wiring harness from the connector to light sockets for high resistance • Loose chassis to column harness connection • Disconnect column to chassis connector. Connect new switch into system without removing old. Operate switch by hand. If flashing occurs at normal rate, the signal switch is defective.	• Repair high resistance grounds at light sockets • Replace turn signal flasher or bulb • Locate and repair as required • Connect securely • Replace turn signal switch
Hazard signal lights will not flash— turn signal functions normally	• Blow fuse • Inoperative hazard warning flasher • Loose chassis-to-column harness connection • Disconnect column to chassis connector. Connect new switch into system without removing old. Depress the hazard warning lights. If they now work normally, turn signal switch is defective. • If lights do not flash, check wiring harness "K" lead for open between hazard flasher and connector. If open, fuse block is defective	• Replace fuse • Replace hazard warning flasher in fuse panel • Conect securely • Replace turn signal switch • Repair or replace brown wire or connector as required

Troubleshooting the Power Steering Gear (cont.)

Problem	Cause	Solution
Steering wheel surges or jerks when turning with engine running especially during parking	• Low oil level • Loose pump belt • Steering linkage hitting engine oil pan at full turn • Insufficient pump pressure • Pump flow control valve sticking	• Fill as required • Adjust tension to specification • Correct clearance • Check pump pressure. (See pressure test). Replace relief valve if defective. • Inspect for varnish or damage, replace if necessary
Excessive wheel kickback or loose steering	• Air in system • Steering gear loose on frame • Steering linkage joints worn enough to be loose • Worn poppet valve • Loose thrust bearing preload adjustment • Excessive overcenter lash	• Add oil to pump reservoir and bleed by operating steering. Check hose connectors for proper torque and adjust as required. • Tighten attaching screws to specified torque • Replace loose pivots • Replace poppet valve • Adjust to specification with gear out of vehicle • Adjust to specification with gear out of car
Hard steering or lack of assist	• Loose pump belt • Low oil level **NOTE:** Low oil level will also result in excessive pump noise • Steering gear to column misalignment • Lower coupling flange rubbing against steering gear adjuster plug • Tires not properly inflated	• Adjust belt tension to specification • Fill to proper level. If excessively low, check all lines and joints for evidence of external leakage. Tighten loose connectors. • Align steering column • Loosen pinch bolt and assemble properly • Inflate to recommended pressure
Foamy milky power steering fluid, low fluid level and possible low pressure	• Air in the fluid, and loss of fluid due to internal pump leakage causing overflow	• Check for leak and correct. Bleed system. Extremely cold temperatures will cause system aeriation should the oil level be low. If oil level is correct and pump still foams, remove pump from vehicle and separate reservoir from housing. Check welsh plug and housing for cracks. If plug is loose or housing is cracked, replace housing.
Low pressure due to steering pump	• Flow control valve stuck or inoperative • Pressure plate not flat against cam ring	• Remove burrs or dirt or replace. Flush system. • Correct
Low pressure due to steering gear	• Pressure loss in cylinder due to worn piston ring or badly worn housing bore • Leakage at valve rings, valve body-to-worm seal	• Remove gear from car for disassembly and inspection of ring and housing bore • Remove gear from car for disassembly and replace seals

Troubleshooting the Power Steering Pump

Problem	Cause	Solution
Chirp noise in steering pump	• Loose belt	• Adjust belt tension to specification
Belt squeal (particularly noticeable at full wheel travel and stand still parking)	• Loose belt	• Adjust belt tension to specification
Growl noise in steering pump	• Excessive back pressure in hoses or steering gear caused by restriction	• Locate restriction and correct. Replace part if necessary.
Growl noise in steering pump (particularly noticeable at stand still parking)	• Scored pressure plates, thrust plate or rotor • Extreme wear of cam ring	• Replace parts and flush system • Replace parts
Groan noise in steering pump	• Low oil level • Air in the oil. Poor pressure hose connection.	• Fill reservoir to proper level • Tighten connector to specified torque. Bleed system by operating steering from right to left—full turn.
Rattle noise in steering pump	• Vanes not installed properly • Vanes sticking in rotor slots	• Install properly • Free up by removing burrs, varnish, or dirt
Swish noise in steering pump	• Defective flow control valve	• Replace part
Whine noise in steering pump	• Pump shaft bearing scored	• Replace housing and shaft. Flush system.
Hard steering or lack of assist	• Loose pump belt • Low oil level in reservoir **NOTE:** Low oil level will also result in excessive pump noise • Steering gear to column misalignment • Lower coupling flange rubbing against steering gear adjuster plug • Tires not properly inflated	• Adjust belt tension to specification • Fill to proper level. If excessively low, check all lines and joints for evidence of external leakage. Tighten loose connectors. • Align steering column • Loosen pinch bolt and assemble properly • Inflate to recommended pressure
Foaming milky power steering fluid, low fluid level and possible low pressure	• Air in the fluid, and loss of fluid due to internal pump leakage causing overflow	• Check for leaks and correct. Bleed system. Extremely cold temperatures will cause system aeration should the oil level be low. If oil level is correct and pump still foams, remove pump from vehicle and separate reservoir from body. Check welsh plug and body for cracks. If plug is loose or body is cracked, replace body.
Low pump pressure	• Flow control valve stuck or inoperative • Pressure plate not flat against cam ring	• Remove burrs or dirt or replace. Flush system. • Correct
Momentary increase in effort when turning wheel fast to right or left	• Low oil level in pump • Pump belt slipping • High internal leakage	• Add power steering fluid as required • Tighten or replace belt • Check pump pressure. (See pressure test)
Steering wheel surges or jerks when turning with engine running especially during parking	• Low oil level • Loose pump belt • Steering linkage hitting engine oil pan at full turn • Insufficient pump pressure	• Fill as required • Adjust tension to specification • Correct clearance • Check pump pressure. (See pressure test). Replace flow control valve if defective.

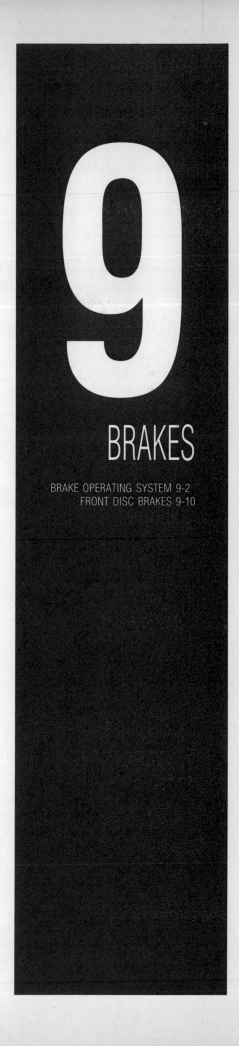

9

BRAKES

BRAKE OPERATING SYSTEM

✳ CAUTION

Brake shoes may contain asbestos, which has been determined to be a cancer causing agent. Never clean the brake surfaces with compressed air! Avoid inhaling any dust from any brake surface! When cleaning brake surfaces, use a commercially available brake cleaning fluid.

Basic Operating Principles

Hydraulic systems are used to actuate the brakes of all modern automobiles. The system transports the power required to force the frictional surfaces of the braking system together from the pedal to the individual brake units at each wheel. A hydraulic system is used for two reasons.

First, fluid under pressure can be carried to all parts of an automobile by small pipes and flexible hoses without taking up a significant amount of room or posing routing problems.

Second, a great mechanical advantage can be given to the brake pedal end of the system, and the foot pressure required to actuate the brakes can be reduced by making the surface area of the master cylinder pistons smaller than that of any of the pistons in the wheel cylinders or calipers.

The master cylinder consists of a fluid reservoir along with a double cylinder and piston assembly. Double type master cylinders are designed to separate the front and rear braking systems hydraulically in case of a leak. The master cylinder coverts mechanical motion from the pedal into hydraulic pressure within the lines. This pressure is translated back into mechanical motion at the wheels by either the wheel cylinder (drum brakes) or the caliper (disc brakes).

Steel lines carry the brake fluid to a point on the vehicle's frame near each of the vehicle's wheels. The fluid is then carried to the calipers and wheel cylinders by flexible tubes in order to allow for suspension and steering movements.

In drum brake systems, each wheel cylinder contains two pistons, one at either end, which push outward in opposite directions and force the brake shoe into contact with the drum.

In disc brake systems, the cylinders are part of the calipers. At least one cylinder in each caliper is used to force the brake pads against the disc.

All pistons employ some type of seal, usually made of rubber, to minimize fluid leakage. A rubber dust boot seals the outer end of the cylinder against dust and dirt. The boot fits around the outer end of the piston on disc brake calipers, and around the brake actuating rod on wheel cylinders.

The hydraulic system operates as follows: When at rest, the entire system, from the piston(s) in the master cylinder to those in the wheel cylinders or calipers, is full of brake fluid. Upon application of the brake pedal, fluid trapped in front of the master cylinder piston(s) is forced through the lines to the wheel cylinders. Here, it forces the pistons outward, in the case of drum brakes, and inward toward the disc, in the case of disc brakes. The motion of the pistons is opposed by return springs mounted outside the cylinders in drum brakes, and by spring seals, in disc brakes.

Upon release of the brake pedal, a spring located inside the master cylinder immediately returns the master cylinder pistons to the normal position. The pistons contain check valves and the master cylinder has compensating ports drilled in it. These are uncovered as the pistons reach their normal position. The piston check valves allow fluid to flow toward the wheel cylinders or calipers as the pistons withdraw. Then, as the return springs force the brake pads or shoes into the released position, the excess fluid reservoir through the compensating ports. It is during the time the pedal is in the released position that any fluid that has leaked out of the system will be replaced through the compensating ports.

Dual circuit master cylinders employ two pistons, located one behind the other, in the same cylinder. The primary piston is actuated directly by mechanical linkage from the brake pedal through the power booster. The secondary piston is actuated by fluid trapped between the two pistons. If a leak develops in front of the secondary piston, it moves forward until it bottoms against the front of the master cylinder, and the fluid trapped between the pistons will operate the rear brakes. If the rear brakes develop a leak, the primary piston will move forward until direct contact with the secondary piston takes place, and it will force the secondary piston to actuate the front brakes. In either case, the brake pedal moves farther when the brakes are applied, and less braking power is available.

All dual circuit systems use a switch to warn the driver when only half of the brake system is operational. This switch is usually located in a valve body which is mounted on the firewall or the frame below the master cylinder. A hydraulic piston receives pressure from both circuits, each circuit's pressure being applied to one end of the piston. When the pressures are in balance, the piston remains stationary. When one circuit has a leak, however, the greater pressure in that circuit during application of the brakes will push the piston to one side, closing the switch and activating the brake warning light.

In disc brake systems, this valve body also contains a metering valve and, in some cases, a proportioning valve. The metering valve keeps pressure from traveling to the disc brakes on the front wheels until the brake shoes on the rear wheels have contacted the drums, ensuring that the front brakes will never be used alone. The proportioning valve controls the pressure to the rear brakes to lessen the chance of rear wheel lock-up during very hard braking.

Warning lights may be tested by depressing the brake pedal and holding it while opening one of the wheel cylinder bleeder screws. If this does not cause the light to go on, substitute a new lamp, make continuity checks, and, finally, replace the switch as necessary.

The hydraulic system may be checked for leaks by applying pressure to the pedal gradually and steadily. If the pedal sinks very slowly to the floor, the system has a leak. This is not to be confused with a springy or spongy feel due to the compression of air within the lines. If the system leaks, there will be a gradual change in the position of the pedal with a constant pressure.

Check for leaks along all lines and at wheel cylinders. If no external leaks are apparent, the problem is inside the master cylinder.

DISC BRAKES

Instead of the traditional expanding brakes that press outward against a circular drum, disc brake systems utilize a disc (rotor) with brake pads positioned on either side of it. An easily-seen analogy is the hand brake arrangement on a bicycle. The pads squeeze onto the rim of the bike wheel, slowing its motion. Automobile disc brakes use the identical principle but apply the braking effort to a separate disc instead of the wheel.

The disc (rotor) is a casting, usually equipped with cooling fins between the two braking surfaces. This enables air to circulate between the braking surfaces making them less sensitive to heat buildup and more resistant to fade. Dirt and water do not drastically affect braking action since contaminants are thrown off by the centrifugal action of the rotor or scraped off the by the pads. Also, the equal clamping action of the two brake pads tends to ensure uniform, straight line stops. Disc brakes are inherently self-adjusting. There are three general types of disc brake:

1. A fixed caliper.
2. A floating caliper.
3. A sliding caliper.

The fixed caliper design uses two pistons mounted on either side of the rotor (in each side of the caliper). The caliper is mounted rigidly and does not move.

The sliding and floating designs are quite similar. In fact, these two types are often lumped together. In both designs, the pad on the inside of the rotor is moved into contact with the rotor by hydraulic force. The caliper, which is not held in a fixed position, moves slightly, bringing the outside pad into contact with the rotor. There are various methods of attaching floating calipers. Some pivot at the bottom or top, and some slide on mounting bolts. In any event, the end result is the same.

DRUM BRAKES

Drum brakes employ two brake shoes mounted on a stationary backing plate. These shoes are positioned inside a circular drum which rotates with the wheel assembly. The shoes are held in place by springs. This allows them to slide toward the drums (when they are applied) while keeping the linings and drums in alignment. The shoes are actuated by a wheel cylinder which is mounted at the top of the backing plate. When the brakes are applied, hydraulic pressure forces the wheel cylinder's actuating links outward. Since these links bear directly against the top of the brake shoes, the tops of the shoes are then forced against the inner side of the drum. This action forces the bottoms of the two shoes to contact the brake drum by rotating the entire assembly slightly (known as servo action). When pressure within the wheel cylinder is relaxed, return springs pull the shoes back away from the drum.

Most modern drum brakes are designed to self-adjust themselves during application when the vehicle is moving in reverse. This motion causes both shoes to rotate very slightly with the drum, rocking an adjusting lever, thereby causing rotation of the adjusting screw. Some drum brake systems are designed to self-adjust during application whenever the brakes are applied. This on-board adjustment system reduces the need for maintenance adjustments and keeps both the brake function and pedal feel satisfactory.

POWER BOOSTERS

Virtually all modern vehicles use a vacuum assisted power brake system to multiply the braking force and reduce pedal effort. Since vacuum is always available when the engine is operating, the system is simple and efficient. A vacuum diaphragm is located on the front of the master cylinder and assists the driver in applying the brakes, reducing both the effort and travel he must put into moving the brake pedal.

The vacuum diaphragm housing is normally connected to the intake manifold by a vacuum hose. A check valve is placed at the point where the hose enters the diaphragm housing, so that during periods of low manifold vacuum brakes assist will not be lost.

Depressing the brake pedal closes off the vacuum source and allows atmospheric pressure to enter on one side of the diaphragm. This causes the master cylinder pistons to move and apply the brakes. When the brake pedal is released, vacuum is applied to both sides of the diaphragm and springs return the diaphragm and master cylinder pistons to the released position.

If the vacuum supply fails, the brake pedal rod will contact the end of the master cylinder actuator rod and the system will apply the brakes without any power assistance. The driver will notice that much higher pedal effort is needed to stop the car and that the pedal feels harder than usual.

Vacuum Leak Test

1. Operate the engine at idle without touching the brake pedal for at least one minute.
2. Turn off the engine and wait one minute.
3. Test for the presence of assist vacuum by depressing the brake pedal and releasing it several times. If vacuum is present in the system, light application will produce less and less pedal travel. If there is no vacuum, air is leaking into the system.

System Operation Test

1. With the engine **OFF**, pump the brake pedal until the supply vacuum is entirely gone.
2. Put light, steady pressure on the brake pedal.
3. Start the engine and let it idle. If the system is operating correctly, the brake pedal should fall toward the floor if the constant pressure is maintained.

Power brake systems may be tested for hydraulic leaks just as ordinary systems are tested.

Adjustments

Front disc brakes are used on all Datsun/Nissans covered in this manual. All models are equipped with independent front and rear hydraulic systems with a warning light to indicate loss of pressure in either system. Most early models have rear drum brakes.

The 1980–81 200SX is equipped with rear disc brakes with the parking brake system activating the main brake pads via a mechanical lever assembly. All models have a vacuum booster system to lessen the required pedal pressure. The parking brake on all models operates the rear brakes through a cable system.

➡Only certain types of drum brakes require adjustment. Some drum brakes are automatically adjusted when the parking brake is applied. No disc brakes need adjustment. They are self adjusting.

To adjust the brakes, raise the wheels, disconnect the parking brake linkage from the rear wheels, apply the brakes hard a few times to center the drums, and proceed as follows:

DRUM BRAKES

Bolt Type Adjuster

◆ **See Figure 1**

Turn the adjuster bolt on the backing plate until the wheel can no longer be turned, then back off until the wheel is free of drag. Repeat the procedure on the other adjuster bolt on the same wheel. Some models may have only one adjuster bolt per wheel.

Some models incorporate a click arrangement with the bolt adjuster. The adjustment proceeds in clicks or notches. The wheel will often be locked temporarily as the adjuster passes over the center for each click. Thus, the adjuster is alternately hard and easy to turn. When the wheel is fully locked, back off 1–3 clicks.

Toothed Adjusting Nut

Remove the rubber cover from the backing plate. Align the hole in the brake backing plate with the adjusting nut. To spread the brake shoes, turn the toothed adjusting nut with a tool. Stop turning when a considerable drag is felt. Back off the nut a few notches so that the correct clearance is reached between the brake drum and the brake shoes. Make sure that the wheel rotates freely.

Automatic Adjusters

No manual adjustment is necessary. The self-adjuster operates whenever the hand or foot brakes (on some models) are used.

After Adjustment

After adjusting the brakes, reconnect the handbrake linkage. Make sure that there is no rear wheel drag with the handbrake released. Loosen the handbrake adjustment if necessary.

BRAKE PEDAL

◆ **See Figure 2**

Before adjusting the pedal, make sure that the brakes are correctly adjusted. Adjust the pedal free-play by means of the adjustable pushrod or by replacing shims between the master cylinder and the brake booster or firewall. Free-play should be approximately 1–5mm on all models through 1984.

Adjust the pedal height by means of the adjustable pedal arm stop pad in the driver's compartment on models through 1984.

The pedal height (floorboard-to-pedal pad) should be approximately 152mm for all 510s and the 1980–81 200SX.

Pedal height should be about 165mm for the 1981–84 810/Maxima; 178mm for all 1977–79 200SX, 610s, 710s and the 1977–80 810.

Brake Light Switch

REMOVAL & INSTALLATION

1. Disconnect the negative battery cable.
2. Disconnect the wiring connector at the switch.
3. Remove the switch locknut.
4. Remove the switch.
5. Install the switch and adjust it so the brake lights are not on unless the brake pedal is depressed.

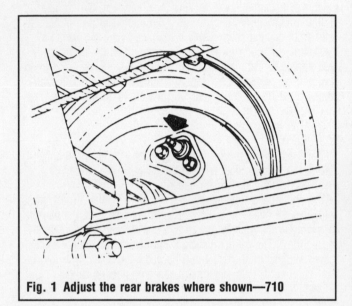

Fig. 1 Adjust the rear brakes where shown—710

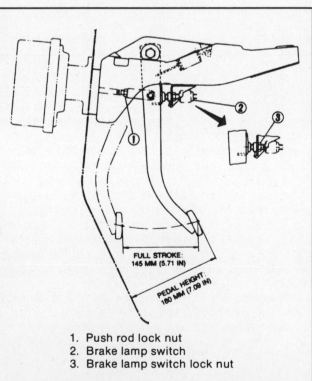

1. Push rod lock nut
2. Brake lamp switch
3. Brake lamp switch lock nut

Fig. 2 Adjust the brake pedal within the specifications shown—all models similar

Master Cylinder

REMOVAL & INSTALLATION

1. Clean the outside of the master cylinder thoroughly, particularly around the cap and fluid lines. Disconnect the fluid lines and cap them to exclude dirt.

2. If equipped with a fluid level sensor, disconnect the wiring harness from the master cylinder.

3. Disconnect the brake fluid tubes, then plug the openings to prevent dirt from entering the system.

4. Remove the mounting bolts at the firewall or the brake booster (if equipped) and remove the master cylinder from the vehicle.

To install:

5. Install the master cylinder to the vehicle. Connect all brake lines and fluid level sensor wiring if so equipped. Refill the reservoir with brake fluid and bleed the system.

➡**Ordinary brake fluid will boil and cause brake failure under the high temperatures developed in disc brake systems; use DOT 3 brake fluid in the brake systems. The adjustable pushrod is used to adjust brake pedal free-play. If the pushrod is not adjustable, there will be shims between the cylinder and the mount. These shims, or the adjustable pushrod, are used to adjust brake pedal free-play.**

OVERHAUL

◗ **See Figures 3 and 4**

➡ **Master cylinders are supplied to Datsun/Nissan by two manufacturers: Nabco and Tokico. Parts between these manufacturers are not interchangeable. Be sure you obtain the correct rebuilding kit for your master cylinder.**

The master cylinder can be disassembled using the illustrations as a guide. Clean all parts in clean brake fluid. Replace the cylin-

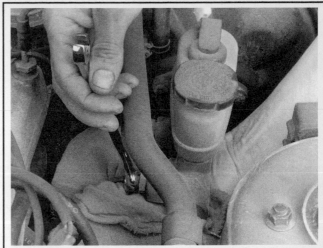

Preferably with a flare wrench, disconnect the lines from the master cylinder ports

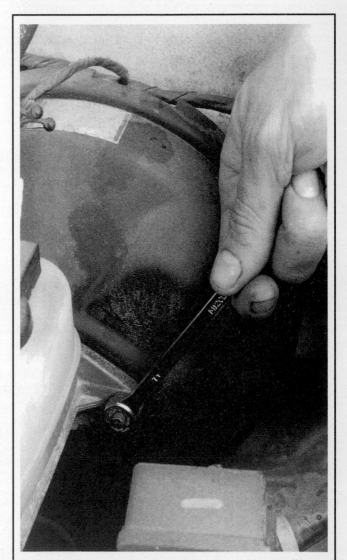

Remove the mounting nuts at the vacuum booster (if equipped)—1984 Maxima shown

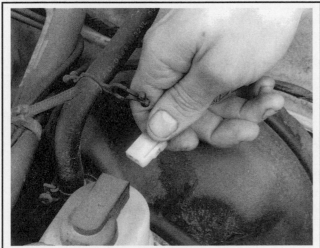

To remove the master cylinder, you will have to disconnect the fluid level sensor (if equipped)

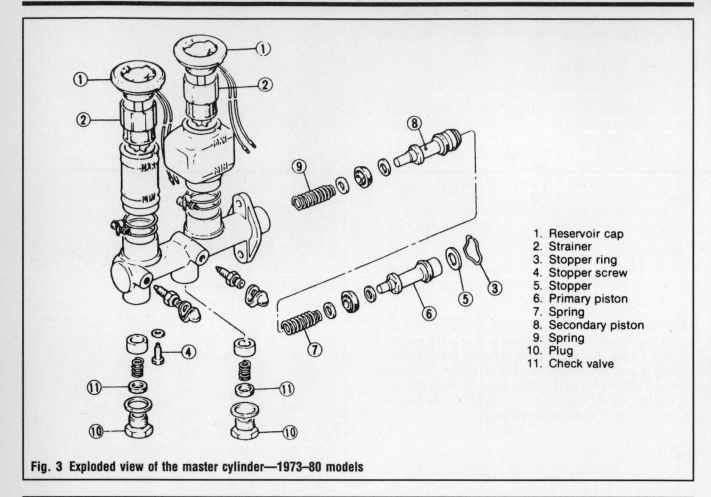

1. Reservoir cap
2. Strainer
3. Stopper ring
4. Stopper screw
5. Stopper
6. Primary piston
7. Spring
8. Secondary piston
9. Spring
10. Plug
11. Check valve

Fig. 3 Exploded view of the master cylinder—1973–80 models

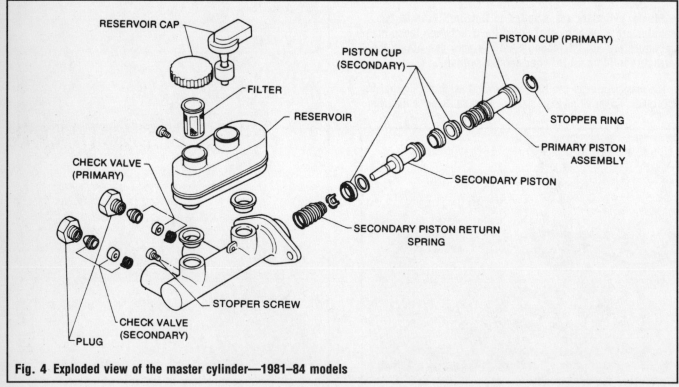

Fig. 4 Exploded view of the master cylinder—1981–84 models

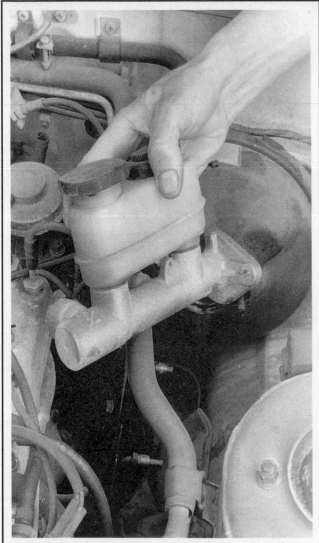

Once fully detached, remove the master cylinder from the vehicle

der or piston as necessary if clearance between the two exceed 0.15mm. Lubricate all parts with clean brake fluid on assembly. Master cylinder rebuilding kits, containing all the wearing parts may be available to simplify overhaul. In many cases, however, it is more time and cost effective to replace a faulty master cylinder with a new or aftermarket rebuilt one.

Power Brake Booster

REMOVAL & INSTALLATION

▶ **See Figures 5 and 6**

➡**Make sure all vacuum lines and connectors are in good condition. A small vacuum leak will cause a big problem in the power brake system.**

1. Remove the master cylinder mounting nuts and pull the master cylinder assembly (brake lines connected) away from the power booster.
2. Detach the vacuum lines from the booster.
3. Detach the booster pushrod at the pedal clevis.
4. Unbolt the booster from under the dash and lift it out of the engine compartment.

To install:

5. Install the brake booster assembly in the vehicle. Tighten the master cylinder-to-booster nuts to 72–96 inch lbs.; the booster-to-firewall nuts to 72–96 inch lbs.
6. Connect the booster pushrod to the pedal clevis. Connect the vacuum lines to brake booster.
7. Start the engine and check brake operation.

Brake Proportioning Valve

▶ **See Figure 7**

All Datsun/Nissans covered in this guide are equipped with brake proportioning valves of several different types. The valves all do the same job, which is to separate the front and rear brake lines, allowing them to function independently, and preventing the rear brakes from locking before the front brakes. Damage, such as brake line leakage, in either the front or rear brake system will not affect the normal operation of the unaffected system. If, in the event of a panic stop, the rear brakes lock up before the front brakes, it could mean the proportioning valve is defective. In that case, replace the entire proportioning valve.

REMOVAL & INSTALLATION

1. Disconnect and plug the brake lines at the valve.
2. Unscrew the mounting bolt(s) and remove the valve.

➡**Do not disassemble the valve.**

3. Installation is in the reverse order of removal. Bleed the system.

Bleeding the Brake System

▶ **See Figure 8**

The purpose of bleeding the brakes is to expel air trapped in the hydraulic system. The system must be bled whenever the pedal feels spongy, indicating that air, which is compressible, has entered the system. It must also be bled whenever the system has been opened or repaired. You will need a helper for this job.

Never reuse brake fluid which has been bled from the system.

The sequence for bleeding is right rear, left rear, right front, left front. The usual procedure is to bleed at the points farthest from the master cylinder first.

1. Clean all dirt from around the master cylinder reservoir caps. Remove the caps and fill the master cylinder to the proper level with clean, fresh brake fluid meeting DOT 3 specifications.

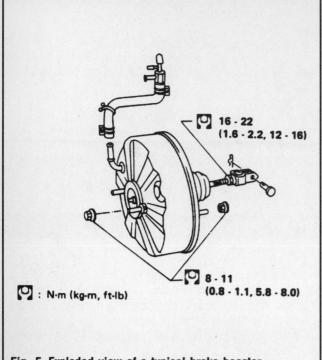

16 - 22
(1.6 - 2.2, 12 - 16)

8 - 11
(0.8 - 1.1, 5.8 - 8.0)

: N·m (kg-m, ft-lb)

Fig. 5 Exploded view of a typical brake booster assembly

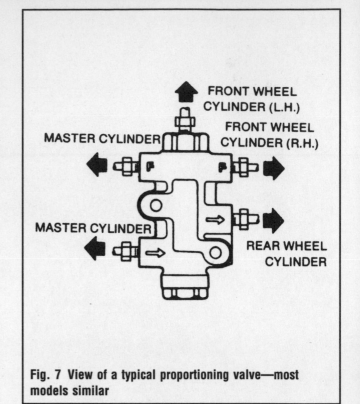

MASTER CYLINDER

FRONT WHEEL CYLINDER (L.H.)

FRONT WHEEL CYLINDER (R.H.)

MASTER CYLINDER

REAR WHEEL CYLINDER

Fig. 7 View of a typical proportioning valve—most models similar

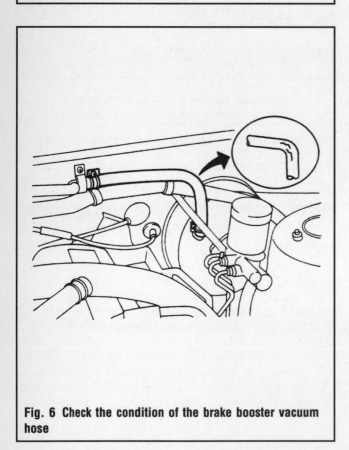

Fig. 6 Check the condition of the brake booster vacuum hose

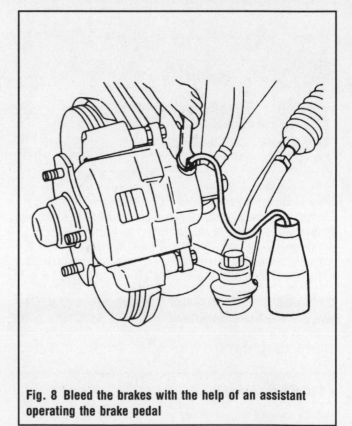

Fig. 8 Bleed the brakes with the help of an assistant operating the brake pedal

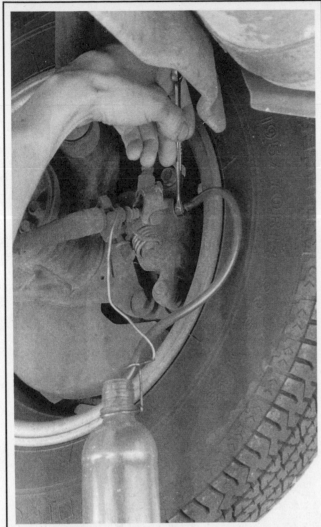

To bleed the brakes, use a flare wrench to loosen the bleeder valve with a tube attached

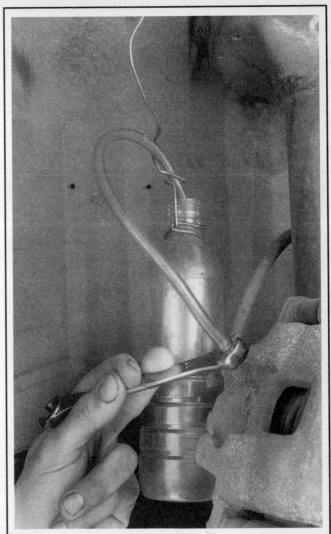

Use a basic plastic jar or bottle like the one shown as a container for collecting the fluid

➡Brake fluid picks up moisture from the air, which reduces its effectiveness and causes brake line corrosion. Don't leave the master cylinder or the fluid container open any longer than necessary. Be careful not to spill brake fluid on painted surfaces. Wipe up any spilled fluid immediately and rinse the area with clear water.

2. Clean all the bleeder screws. You may want to give each one a shot of penetrating solvent to loosen it up. Seizure is a common problem with bleeder screws, which then break off, sometimes requiring replacement of the part to which they are attached (e.g., calipers, etc.).

3. Attach a length of clear vinyl tubing to the bleeder screw on the wheel cylinder. Insert the other end of the tube into a clear, clean plastic jar half filled with brake fluid.

4. Have your helper slowly depress the brake pedal. As this is done, open the bleeder screw 1/3–1/2 of a turn, and allow the fluid to run through the tube. Close the bleeder screw before the pedal reaches the end of its travel. Have your assistant slowly release the pedal. Repeat this process until no air bubbles appear in the expelled fluid.

➡Some front drum brakes have two hydraulic cylinders and two bleeder screws. Both cylinders must be bled.

5. Repeat the procedure on the other three brakes, checking the fluid level in the master cylinder reservoirs often. Do not allow the reservoirs to run dry, or the bleeding process will have to be repeated.

FRONT DISC BRAKES

✳✳✳ CAUTION

Brake shoes may contain asbestos, which has been determined to be a cancer causing agent. Never clean the brake surfaces with compressed air! Avoid inhaling any dust from any brake surface! When cleaning brake surfaces, use a commercially available brake cleaning fluid.

Brake Pads

REMOVAL & INSTALLATION

▶ **See Figures 9 and 10**

Types N20, N22, N22A, N32 and N34L Caliper

▶ **See Figure 11**

1. Raise and support the front of the car. Remove the wheels.
2. Remove the retaining clip from the outboard pad.
3. Remove the pad pins retaining the anti-squeal springs.
4. Remove the pads.

To install:

5. Open the bleeder screw slightly and push the outer piston into the cylinder until the dust seal groove aligns with the end of the seal retaining ring, then close the bleed screw. Be careful because the piston can be pushed too far, requiring disassembly of the caliper to repair. Install the inner pad.

6. Pull the yoke to push the inner piston into place. Install the outer pad.

7. Lightly coat the areas where the pins touch the pads, and where the pads touch the caliper (at the top) with grease. Do not allow grease to get on the pad friction surfaces.

8. Install the anti-squeal springs and pad pins. Install the clip.

9. Apply the brakes a few times to seat the pads. Check the master cylinder level. Add fluid if necessary. Bleed the brakes if necessary.

1. Bleeder valve
2. Hydraulic hose
3. Caliper pin
4. Caliper carrier
5. Dust shield
6. Caliper
7. Outer brake pad
8. Anti-rattle clip
9. Brake disc (rotor)

Typical front brake system components

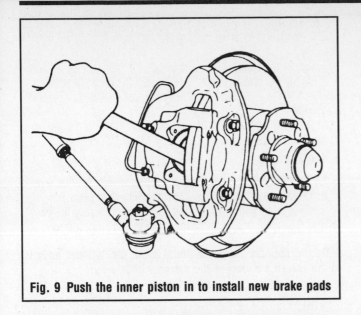

Fig. 9 Push the inner piston in to install new brake pads

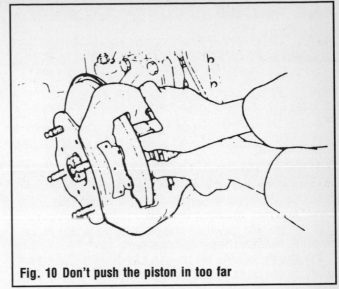

Fig. 10 Don't push the piston in too far

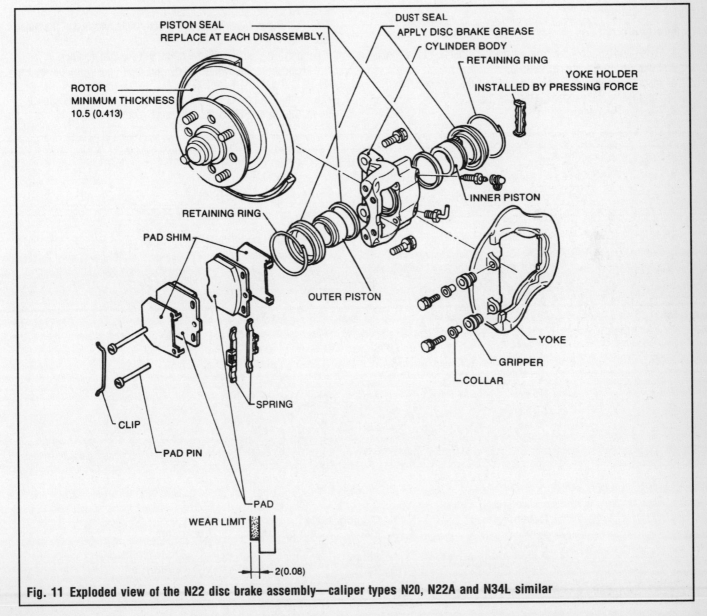

PISTON SEAL
REPLACE AT EACH DISASSEMBLY.

DUST SEAL
APPLY DISC BRAKE GREASE
CYLINDER BODY
RETAINING RING

YOKE HOLDER
INSTALLED BY PRESSING FORCE

ROTOR
MINIMUM THICKNESS
10.5 (0.413)

INNER PISTON

RETAINING RING

PAD SHIM

OUTER PISTON

YOKE

GRIPPER

COLLAR

SPRING

CLIP

PAD PIN

PAD

WEAR LIMIT

2(0.08)

Fig. 11 Exploded view of the N22 disc brake assembly—caliper types N20, N22A and N34L similar

Annette Type Caliper

▶ **See Figure 12**

1. Raise and support the front of the car. Remove the wheels.
2. Remove the clip, pull out the pins, and remove the pad springs.
3. Remove the pads by pulling them out with pliers.

To install:

4. To install, first lightly coat the yoke groove and end surface of the piston with grease. Do not allow grease to contact the pads or rotor.
5. Open the bleeder screw slightly and push the outer piston into the cylinder until its end aligns with the end of the boot retaining ring. Do not push too far, which will require caliper disassembly to correct. Install the inner pad.
6. Pull the yoke toward the outside of the car to push the inner piston into place. Install the outer pad.
7. Apply the brakes a few times to seat the pads. Check the master cylinder and add fluid if necessary. Bleed the brakes if necessary.

Type SC Caliper

▶ **See Figure 13**

1. Raise and support the front of the car. Remove the wheels.
2. Push up on the clip to remove.
3. Insert a small prybar into the back of the pad opposite the piston and move the caliper all the way out.
4. Remove the pads.

To install:

5. Open the bleeder screw slightly and press the piston into the caliper.
6. Install the pads, shims, and clips.
7. Apply the brakes a few times to seat the pads. Check the master cylinder level and add fluid if necessary. Bleed the brakes as required.

Type CL22V Caliper

▶ **See Figure 14**

1. Raise the front of the car and support it with safety stands.
2. Unscrew and remove the lower pin bolt (sub pin).
3. Swing the cylinder body upward and then remove the pad retainer, the inner and outer shims and the pads themselves.

➡**Do not depress the brake pedal when the cylinder body is in the raised position or the piston will pop out.**

To install:

4. Clean the piston end of the cylinder body and the pin bolt holes. Be careful not to get oil on the rotor.
5. Pull the cylinder body to the outer side and install the inner pad.
6. Install the outer pad, the shim and the pad retainer.
7. Reposition the cylinder body and then tighten the pin bolt to 12–15 ft. lbs. (16–21 Nm).
8. Apply the brakes a few times to seat the new pads. Check the fluid level and bleed the brakes as required.

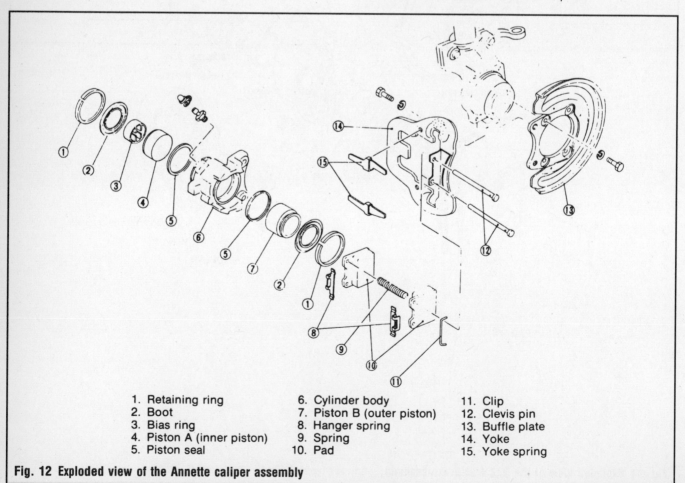

1. Retaining ring	6. Cylinder body	11. Clip
2. Boot	7. Piston B (outer piston)	12. Clevis pin
3. Bias ring	8. Hanger spring	13. Buffle plate
4. Piston A (inner piston)	9. Spring	14. Yoke
5. Piston seal	10. Pad	15. Yoke spring

Fig. 12 Exploded view of the Annette caliper assembly

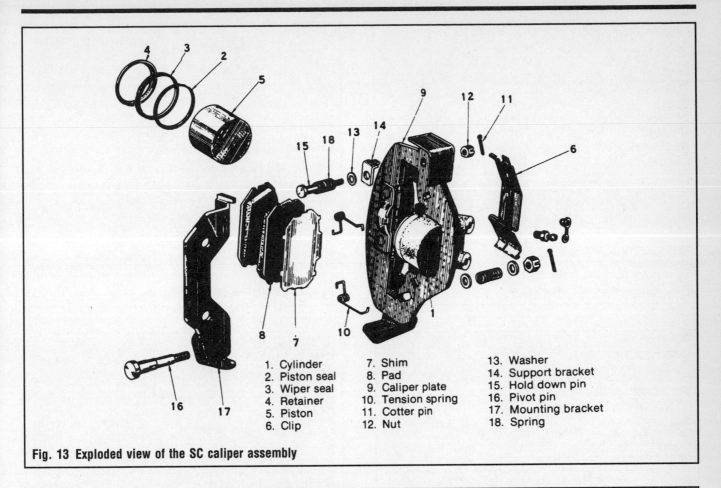

1. Cylinder
2. Piston seal
3. Wiper seal
4. Retainer
5. Piston
6. Clip
7. Shim
8. Pad
9. Caliper plate
10. Tension spring
11. Cotter pin
12. Nut
13. Washer
14. Support bracket
15. Hold down pin
16. Pivot pin
17. Mounting bracket
18. Spring

Fig. 13 Exploded view of the SC caliper assembly

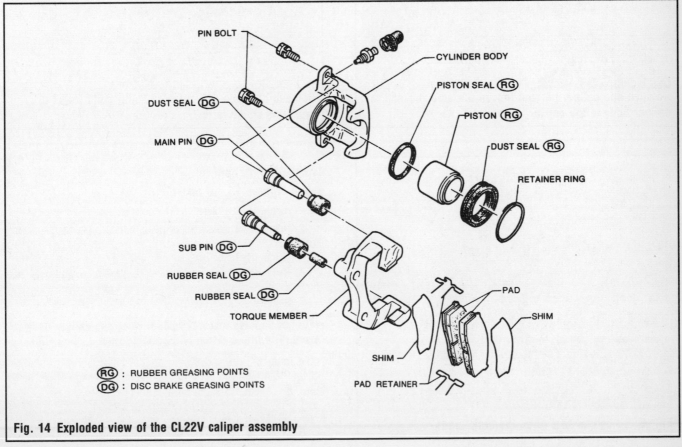

PIN BOLT
CYLINDER BODY
DUST SEAL (DG)
MAIN PIN (DG)
PISTON SEAL (RG)
PISTON (RG)
DUST SEAL (RG)
RETAINER RING
SUB PIN (DG)
RUBBER SEAL (DG)
RUBBER SEAL (DG)
TORQUE MEMBER
PAD
SHIM
SHIM
PAD RETAINER

(RG) : RUBBER GREASING POINTS
(DG) : DISC BRAKE GREASING POINTS

Fig. 14 Exploded view of the CL22V caliper assembly

To remove the front brake pads, safely raise the vehicle, then remove the front wheel(s)

Remove the anti-rattle clips from the pads

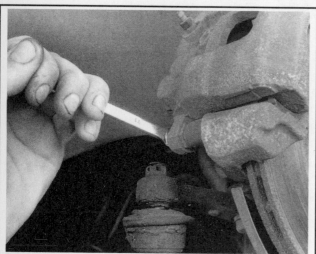

Remove one caliper pin and loosen the other holding the caliper body to the carrier

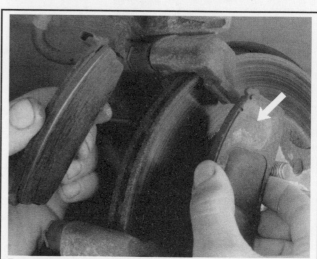

Remove the pads—if replacing them, don't forget to reuse the shims (arrow)

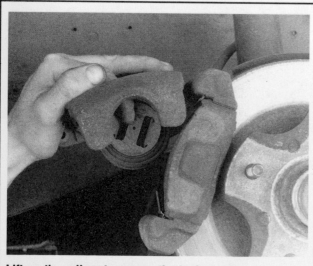

Lift up the caliper to expose the brake pads

Type AD22V Caliper

▶ **See Figures 15, 16 and 17**

    1. Remove the wheel.

    2. Remove the lower caliper guide pin. See the accompanying illustration.

    3. Rotate the brake caliper body upward.

    4. Remove the brake pad retainer and the inner and outer pad shims.

    5. Remove the brake pads.

➡**Do not depress the brake pedal when the caliper body is raised. The brake piston will be forced out of the caliper.**

  To install:

    6. Clean the piston end of the caliper body and the pin bolt holes. Be careful not to get oil on the brake rotor.

    7. Pull the caliper body to the outer side and install the inner brake pad. Make sure both new pads are kept clean!

    8. Install the outer pad, shim and pad retainer.

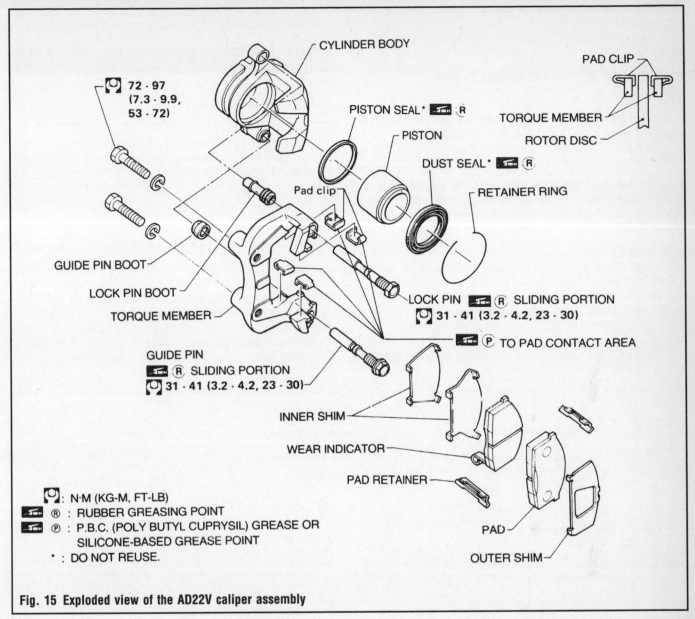

CYLINDER BODY

PAD CLIP

72 - 97
(7.3 - 9.9,
53 - 72)

PISTON SEAL* ⬛R

TORQUE MEMBER

ROTOR DISC

PISTON

DUST SEAL* ⬛R

Pad clip

RETAINER RING

GUIDE PIN BOOT

LOCK PIN BOOT

TORQUE MEMBER

LOCK PIN ⬛R SLIDING PORTION
31 - 41 (3.2 - 4.2, 23 - 30)

⬛P TO PAD CONTACT AREA

GUIDE PIN
⬛R SLIDING PORTION
31 - 41 (3.2 - 4.2, 23 - 30)

INNER SHIM

WEAR INDICATOR

PAD RETAINER

⬛ : N·M (KG-M, FT-LB)
⬛R : RUBBER GREASING POINT
⬛P : P.B.C. (POLY BUTYL CUPRYSIL) GREASE OR
SILICONE-BASED GREASE POINT
* : DO NOT REUSE.

PAD

OUTER SHIM

Fig. 15 Exploded view of the AD22V caliper assembly

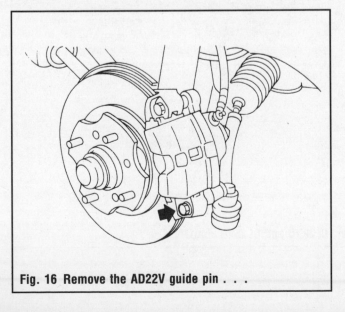

Fig. 16 Remove the AD22V guide pin . . .

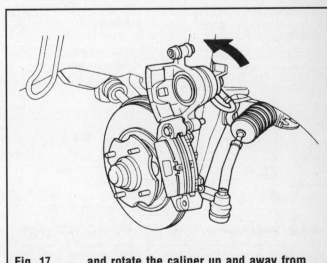

Fig. 17 . . . and rotate the caliper up and away from the rotor

9. Reposition the caliper body and then tighten the guide pin bolt to 23–30 ft. lbs.

10. Apply the brakes a few times to seat the pads before driving out on the road.

Types CL28VB, CL22VB and CL25VB Caliper

▶ See Figure 18

1. Raise the vehicle and support it securely. Remove the front wheel. Remove the pin (lower) bolt from the caliper.

2. Swing the caliper body upward on the upper bolt. Remove the pad retainers (springs) and inner and outer shims.

➡**Do not depress the brake pedal when the cylinder body is in the raised position or the piston will pop out. Avoid damaging the piston seal when removing/installing the pads and retainers.**

To install:

3. Check the level of fluid in the master cylinder. If the fluid is near the maximum level, use a clean syringe to remove fluid until the level is down well below the lip of the reservoir. Then, use a large C-clamp to press the caliper piston back into the caliper, to allow room for the installation of the thicker new pads.

4. Install the new pads, utilizing new shims, in reverse order.

Tighten the lower retaining bolt to 16–23 ft. lbs. Make sure you pump the brakes and get a hard pedal before driving the car!

Brake Caliper

REMOVAL & INSTALLATION

Refer to Brake Pads Removal and Installation procedure in this section. Remove both guide pins, torque member fixing bolts and brake hose connector. The brake system must be bled refer to the necessary procedure.

INSPECTION

You should be able to check the pad lining thickness without removing the pads. Check the Brake Specifications chart at the end of this section to find the manufacturer's pad wear limit. However, this measurement may disagree with your state inspection laws. When replacing pads, always check the surface of the rotors for scoring or wear. The rotors should be removed for resurfacing if badly scored.

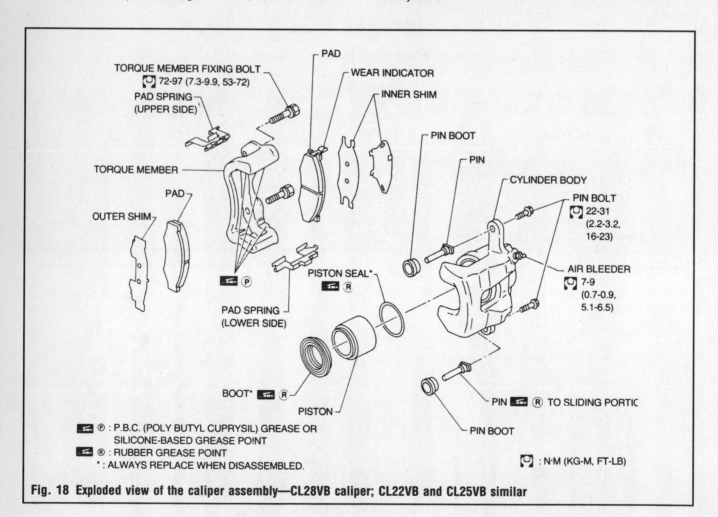

Fig. 18 Exploded view of the caliper assembly—CL28VB caliper; CL22VB and CL25VB similar

OVERHAUL

Types N20, N22, N22A, N32 and N34L Caliper
▶ **See Figure 19**

1. With the vehicle supported safely and the front wheels off, remove the brake fluid tube from the caliper assembly.

2. Remove the caliper from the knuckle assembly by removing the mounting bolts, located at the rear of the caliper, and lifting the caliper from the rotor.

3. Remove the pads from the caliper (refer to the pad removal procedure).

4. Remove the gripper pin attaching nuts and separate the yoke from the cylinder body.

5. Remove the yoke holder from the piston and remove the retaining rings and dust seals from the ends of both pistons.

6. Apply air pressure gradually into the fluid chamber of the caliper, to force the pistons from the cylinders.

7. Remove the piston seals.

8. Inspect the components for damage or excessive wear. Replace or repair as needed.

9. To assemble, install the piston seals in the cylinder bore. Lubricate seals and pistons.

10. Slide the A piston into the cylinder, followed by the B piston so that its yoke groove coincides with the yoke groove of the cylinder.

11. Install the dust seal and clamp tightly with the retaining ring.

12. Install the yoke holder on the A piston and install the gripper to yoke.

➡ **The use of soapy water will aid in the installation of the gripper pins.**

13. Support the end of B piston and press the yoke into the yoke holder.

14. Install the pads, anti squeal springs, pad pins and retain with the clip.

15. Tighten the gripper pin attaching nuts to 12–15 ft. lbs. and install the caliper on the spindle knuckle. Tighten the caliper mounting bolts to 53–72 ft. lbs.

16. Bleed the system, check the fluid level, install the wheels and lower the vehicle.

Annette Type Caliper
▶ **See Figures 20 and 21**

1. Remove the pads.
2. Disconnect the brake tube.
3. Remove the two bottom strut assembly installation bolts to provide clearance.
4. Remove the caliper assembly mounting bolts.
5. Loosen the bleeder screw and press the pistons into their bores.
6. Clamp the yoke in a vise and tap the yoke head with a hammer to loosen the cylinder. Be careful that the primary piston does not fall out.
7. Remove the bias ring from the primary piston. Remove the retaining rings and boots from both pistons. Depress and remove the pistons from the cylinder. Remove the piston seal from the cylinder carefully with the fingers so as not to mar the cylinder wall.
8. Remove the yoke springs from the yoke.

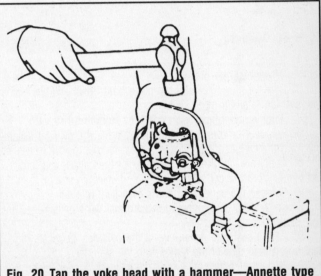

Fig. 20 Tap the yoke head with a hammer—Annette type

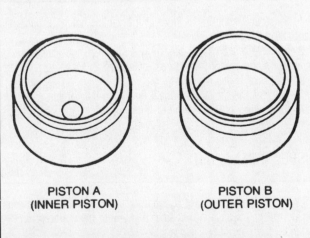

Fig. 19 Comparison of the inner (A) and outer (B) pistons—caliper types N20, N22, N32 and N34L

PISTON A
(INNER PISTON)

PISTON B
(OUTER PISTON)

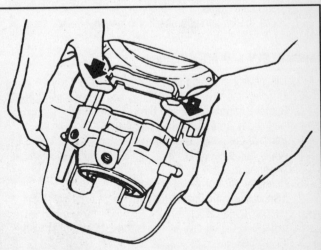

Fig. 21 Assemble the yoke and cylinder as shown—Annette type

9. Wash all parts with clean brake fluid.

10. If the piston or cylinder is badly worn or scored, replace both. The piston surface is plated and must not be polished with emery paper. Replace all seals. The rotor can be removed and machined if scored, but final thickness must be at least 8.5mm. Runout must not exceed 0.025mm.

11. Lubricate the cylinder bore with clean brake fluid and install the piston seal.

12. Insert the bias ring into primary piston so that the rounded ring portion comes to the bottom of the piston. Primary piston has a small depression inside, while secondary does not.

13. Lubricate the pistons with clean brake fluid and insert into the cylinder. Install the boot and retaining ring. The yoke groove of the bias ring of primary piston must align with the yoke groove of the cylinder.

14. Install the yoke springs to the yoke so the projecting portion faces to the disc (rotor).

15. Lubricate the sliding portion of the cylinder and yoke. Assemble the cylinder and yoke by tapping the yoke lightly.

16. Replace the caliper assembly and pads. Tighten the mounting bolts to 33–41 ft. lbs. Rotor bolt torque is 20–27 ft. lbs. Strut bolt torque is 33–44 ft. lbs. Bleed the system of air.

Type SC Caliper

1. Remove the brake pads.
2. Disconnect the brake hose.
3. Remove the cotter pins from the hold-down and pivot pins. Remove the retaining nuts.
4. Remove the caliper plate from its mounting bracket.
5. Remove the torsion spring and remove the cylinder assembly from the caliper plate.
6. Apply air into the fluid chamber of the caliper and force the piston from the cylinder.
7. Remove the wiper seal and piston seal retainer.
8. Inspect the components for abnormal wear or damage. Repair or replace as necessary.
9. Fit the seal into its groove in the cylinder. Lubricate the seal and piston. Install the piston into the cylinder.
10. Place the caliper plate over the cylinder assembly and install the torsion spring.
11. Install the caliper plate on the mounting bracket and install the nuts and cotter pins.
12. Bleed the system and check the reservoir level.

Types CL22V and AD2V Caliper

1. Disconnect and plug the brake line.
2. Unscrew the two mounting bolts and remove the caliper.
3. Remove the main pin and the sub pin and then separate the cylinder body from the torque member.
4. Remove the piston dust cover.
5. Apply compressed air gradually to the fluid chamber until the piston pops out.
6. Carefully pry out the piston seal.
7. Inspect the components for damage or excessive wear. Replace or repair as necessary.
8. Install the piston seal in the cylinder bore. Lubricate the seals and pistons.

9. Fit the dust seal onto the piston, insert the dust seal into the groove on the cylinder body and then install the piston.

10. Place the cylinder body and torque member together, grease the main and sub pins, install the pins and tighten them to 12–15 ft. lbs. (16–21 Nm) on the CL22V, and 23–30 ft. lbs. on the AD22V.

11. Install the caliper and tighten the mounting bolts to 36–51 ft. lbs. (46–69 Nm) on the CL22V, and 53–72 ft. lbs. on the AD22V. Reconnect the brake line and install the wheels.

12. Bleed the system, check the fluid level and lower the vehicle.

Types CL28VB, CL22VB and CL25VB Caliper

1. Remove the brake pads. Disconnect the brake hose and plug the open end of the hose. Remove the two caliper mounting bolts and remove the caliper.

2. Place a wooden block between the caliper piston and the pad retainer opposite it. Then, gently apply compressed air to the brake hose connection. This will remove the piston and dust seal. Note the direction in which the piston seal is installed.

3. Clean all parts in clean brake fluid. Inspect the inner cylinder bore for rust, scoring, or mechanical wear. Remove minor imperfections with emery paper. Replace the caliper body if these imperfections cannot be removed. Inspect the piston for such imperfections. If they exist, it must be replaced, as the surface is polished!

4. Inspect the lockpins, bolts, piston seal, bushings, and pin seals for damage and replace all parts as necessary.

5. Insert the piston seal into the groove on the caliper body. Install the inner edge of the rubber boot into the piston groove and then install the piston. Work the edge of the rubber boot into the groove in the caliper body.

6. Perform the remaining procedures in the reverse of removal. Tighten the caliper mounting pins to 53–72 ft. lbs. Refill the system with clean brake fluid and bleed it thoroughly. Make sure you pump the brakes and get a hard pedal before operating the car.

Brake Disc (Rotor)

REMOVAL & INSTALLATION

1. Raise and support the front of the vehicle safely on jackstands and remove the wheels.

2. Remove brake caliper assembly and wheel hub assembly. Refer to the necessary procedures in Section 8. Make sure not to twist the brake hose.

3. Remove the brake disc/wheel hub from the vehicle.

4. Installation is the reverse of removal. Adjust the wheel bearings.

INSPECTION

Check the brake rotor for roughness, cracks or chips. The rotor can be machined on a brake lathe; many auto parts stores have complete machine shop service.

To remove the brake disc (rotor), safely raise the vehicle, then remove the wheel

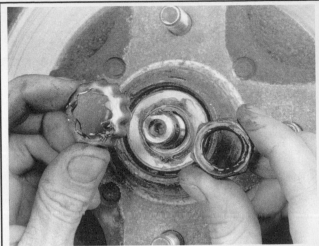

Remove the nut and nut cap to expose the wheel bearings

Once the caliper is removed, pry off the wheel bearing dust cap

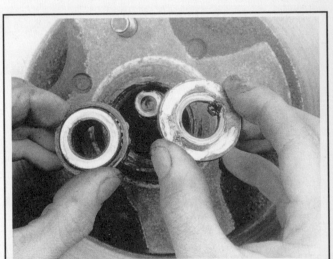

Remove the large washer and wheel bearing from the spindle

Remove the cotter pin at the castellated nut, then discard the pin—replace with a new one

With the outer wheel bearings removed, pull off the rotor from the spindle

In most cases, you will have to remove the inner wheel bearings (arrow)

The bearing seal must be pried out—these damage often and must be replaced

REAR DRUM BRAKES

✳✳ CAUTION

Brake shoes may contain asbestos, which has been determined to be a cancer causing agent. Never clean the brake surfaces with compressed air! Avoid inhaling any dust from any brake surface! When cleaning brake surfaces, use a commercially available brake cleaning fluid.

Brake Drums

REMOVAL & INSTALLATION

▶ See Figures 22 and 23

1. Raise the rear of the vehicle and support it on jackstands.
2. Remove the wheels.
3. Release the parking brake.
4. Pull off the brake drums. On some models there are two threaded service holes in each brake drum. If the drum will not come off, fit two correct size bolts in the service holes and screw them in: this will force the drum away from the axle.
5. If the drum cannot be easily removed, back off the brake adjustment.

➡**Never depress the brake pedal while the brake drum is removed.**

6. Installation is the reverse of removal.

INSPECTION

After removing the brake drum, wipe out the accumulated dust with a damp cloth.

✳✳ CAUTION

Do not blow the brake dust out of the drums with compressed air or lung power. Brake linings may contain asbestos, a known cancer causing substance. Dispose of the cloth after use.

Inspect the drum for cracks, deep grooves, roughness, scoring, or out-of-roundness. Replace any brake drum which is cracked.

Smooth any slight scores by polishing the friction surface with the fine emery cloth or have the drum machined (trued) at a machine shop. Heavy or extensive scoring will cause excessive brake lining wear and should be removed from the brake drum through resurfacing.

Brake Shoes

REMOVAL & INSTALLATION

1. Raise the vehicle and support it on jackstands. Remove the wheels.
2. Release the parking brake. Disconnect the cross rod from the lever of the brake cylinder. Remove the brake drum. Place a heavy rubber band around the cylinder to prevent the piston from coming out.
3. Remove the return springs and shoes.
4. Clean the backing plate and check the wheel cylinder for leaks. To remove the wheel cylinder, remove the brake line, dust cover, securing nuts or plates and adjusting shims. Clearance between the cylinder and the piston should not exceed 0.015mm.
5. The drums must be machined if scored or out of round more than 0.05mm. The drum inside diameter should not be machined beyond 229.5mm. Minimum safe lining thickness is 1.5mm.

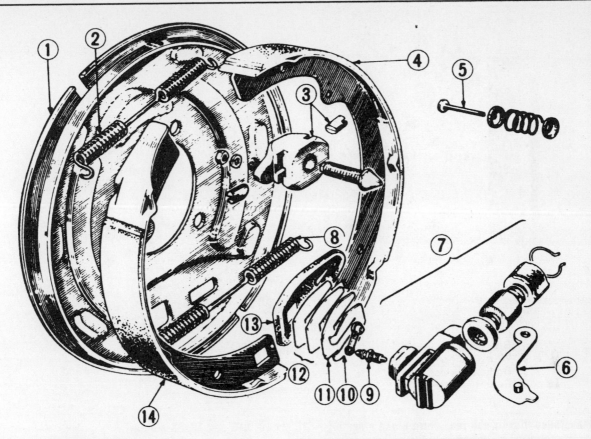

1. Brake disc
2. Return spring adjuster side
3. Brake shoe adjuster
4. Brake shoe assembly-fore
5. Anti-rattler pin
6. Lever
7. Rear wheel cylinder.
8. Return spring cylinder side
9. Bleeder
10. Lock plate A
11. Lock plate B
12. Lock plate C and D
13. Dust cover
14. Brake shoe assembly-after

Fig. 22 Exploded view of the rear drum brake assembly—610 and 710

To install:

6. Hook the return springs into the new shoes. The springs should be between the shoes and the backing plate. The longer return spring must be adjacent to the wheel cylinder. A very thin film of grease may be applied to the pivot points at the ends of the brake shoes. Grease the shoe locating buttons on the backing plate, also. Be careful not to get grease on the linings or drums.

7. Place one shoe in the adjuster and piston slots, and pry the other shoe into position.

8. Replace the drums and wheels. Adjust the brakes. Bleed the hydraulic system of air if the brake lines were disconnected.

9. Reconnect the handbrake, making sure that it does not cause the shoes to drag when it is released.

Wheel Cylinder

REMOVAL, INSTALLATION AND OVERHAUL

➡Datsun/Nissan obtains parts from two manufacturers: **Nabco and Tokico. Parts are not interchangeable. The name of the manufacturer is usually on the wheel cylinder.**

1. Raise and support the vehicle on jackstands. Remove the wheel.

2. Remove the wheel cylinder from the backing plate.

3. Remove the dust boot and take out the piston. Discard the piston cup. The dust boot can be reused, if necessary, but it is better to replace it.

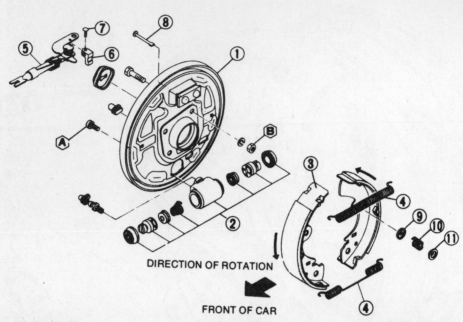

1. Brake disc
2. Wheel cylinder assembly
3. Brake shoe assembly
4. Return spring
5. Adjuster assembly
6. Stopper
7. Stopper pin
8. Anti-rattle pin
9. Spring seat
10. Anti-rattle spring
11. Retainer

DIRECTION OF ROTATION

FRONT OF CAR

Fig. 23 Exploded view of the rear drum brake assembly—510 shown, 810 and 200SX similar

4. Wash all of the components in clean brake fluid.
5. Inspect the piston and piston bore. Replace any components which are severely corroded, scored, or worn. The piston and piston bore can be polished lightly with crocus cloth.
6. Wash the wheel cylinder and piston thoroughly in clean brake fluid, allowing them to remain lubricated for assembly.

7. Coat all of the new components to be installed in the wheel cylinder with clean brake fluid prior to assembly.
8. Assemble the wheel cylinder and install it in the reverse order of removal. Assemble the remaining components and bleed the brake hydraulic system.

REAR DISC BRAKES

❊❊ CAUTION

Brake shoes may contain asbestos, which has been determined to be a cancer causing agent. Never clean the brake surfaces with compressed air! Avoid inhaling any dust from any brake surface! When cleaning brake surfaces, use a commercially available brake cleaning fluid.

Brake Pads

REMOVAL & INSTALLATION

Type AN12H Caliper

1. Raise and support the rear of the car with jackstands. Remove the wheel.
2. Remove the clip at the outside of the pad pins.

3. Remove the pad pins. Hold the anti-squeal springs in place with your finger.
4. Remove the pads.
To install:
5. First clean the end of the piston with clean brake fluid.
6. Lightly coat the caliper-to-pad, the yoke-to-pad, retaining pin-to-pad, and retaining pin-to-bracket surfaces with grease. Do not allow grease to get on the rotor or pad surfaces.
7. Push the piston into place with a prytool by pushing in on the piston while at the same time turning it clockwise into the bore. Then, with a lever between the rotor and yoke, push the yoke over until the clearance to install the pads is equal.
8. Install the shims and pads, anti-squeal springs and pins. Install the clip. Note that the inner pad has a tab which must fit into the piston notch. Therefore, be sure that the piston notch is centered to allow proper pad installation.
9. Apply the brake a few times to center the pads. Check the master cylinder fluid level and add if necessary.

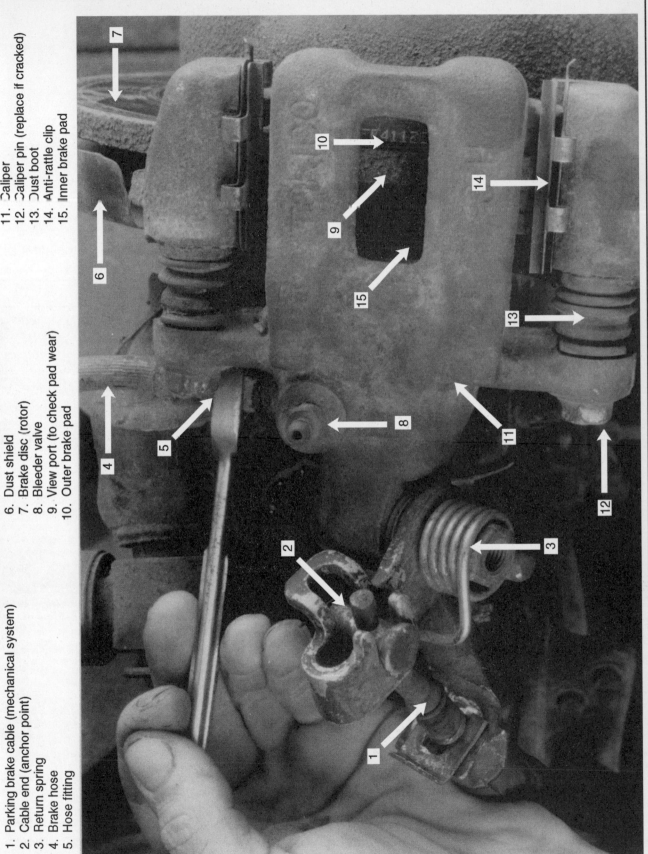

REAR DISC BRAKE SYSTEM COMPONENTS

1. Parking brake cable (mechanical system)
2. Cable end (anchor point)
3. Return spring
4. Brake hose
5. Hose fitting
6. Dust shield
7. Brake disc (rotor)
8. Bleeder valve
9. View port (to check pad wear)
10. Outer brake pad
11. Caliper
12. Caliper pin (replace if cracked)
13. Dust boot
14. Anti-rattle clip
15. Inner brake pad

Types CL11H and CL9H Caliper
♦ **See Figure 24**

1. Raise the rear of the car and support it with jackstands. Remove the wheel.
2. Remove the pin bolts and lift off the caliper body.
3. Pull out the pad springs and then remove the pads and their shims.
4. Clean the piston end of the caliper body and the area around the pin holes. Be careful not to get oil on the rotor.
5. Using a pair of needle nosed pliers, carefully turn the piston clockwise back into the caliper body. Take care not to damage the piston boot.
6. Coat the pad contact area on the mounting support with a silicone based grease.
7. Install the pads, shims and the pad springs.

➡**Always use new shims.**

8. Position the caliper body in the mounting support and tighten the pin bolts to 16–23 ft. lbs. (22–31 Nm.).
9. Replace the wheel, lower the car and bleed the system.

Types CL11HB and CL14B Caliper

1. Raise the vehicle and support it on jackstands. Remove the rear wheel.
2. Remove the two pin bolts and the lock spring. Remove the caliper, suspending it above the disc so as to avoid putting any strain on the hose.
3. Remove the pad retainers, pads, and shims.

➡**Do not depress the brake pedal when the cylinder body is in the raised position or the piston will pop out. Avoid damaging the piston seal when removing/installing the pads and retainers.**

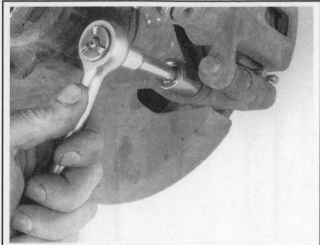

To remove the rear brake pads, unbolt the caliper and remove it

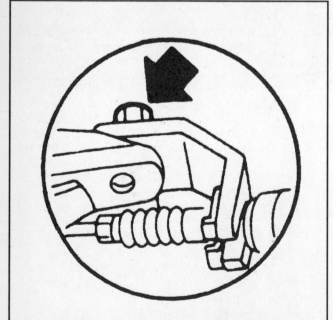

Fig. 24 Remove the parking brake cable mounting brace bolt where indicated (arrow)—type CL11H caliper

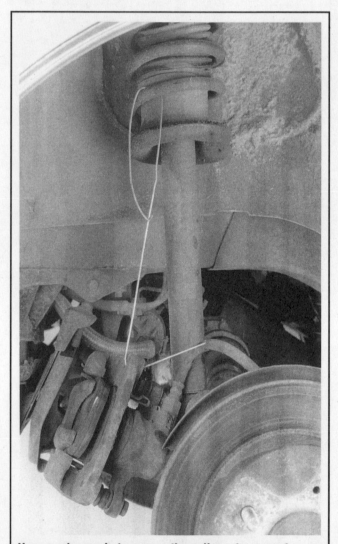

Have a wire ready to secure the caliper, to prevent strain on the hydraulic brake hose

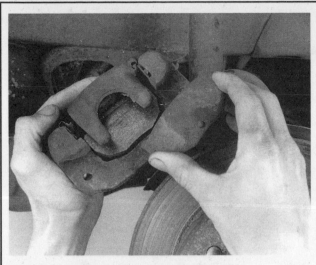

Remove the outer brake pads from the caliper

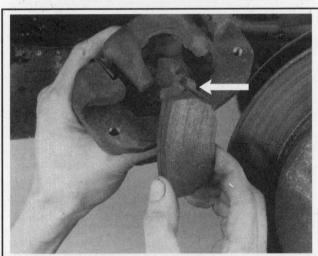

Remove the inner brake pads from the caliper—note the wear indicator location (arrow)

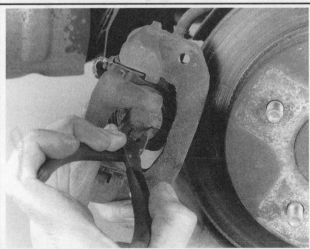

Pliers work to turn in the piston—you may also buy an inexpensive, specialized tool to do this

4. Check the level of fluid in the master cylinder. If the fluid is near the maximum level, use a clean syringe to remove fluid until the level is down well below the lip of the reservoir. Then, press the caliper piston back into the caliper by turning it clockwise (it has a helical groove on the outer diameter). This will allow room for the installation of the thicker new pads.

5. Install the new pads using new shims in reverse order of the removal procedure. Tighten the caliper pin bolts to 16–23 ft. lbs. Make sure you pump the brakes and get a hard pedal before driving the car!

Brake Caliper

REMOVAL, INSTALLATION & OVERHAUL

Type AN12H Caliper
▶ **See Figures 25, 26 and 27**

1. Raise and support the vehicle on jackstands.
2. Disconnect the brake hose from the caliper. Plug the hose and caliper to prevent fluid loss.
3. Disconnect the parking brake cable.
4. Remove the mounting bolts and remove the caliper from the suspension arm.
5. Remove the pads.
6. Stand the caliper assembly on end, large end down, and push on the caliper to separate it from the yoke.
7. Remove the retaining rings and dust seals from both pistons.
8. Push in on the outer piston to force out the piston assembly. Remove the piston seals.
9. Remove the yoke spring from the yoke.
10. Disengage the piston assembly by turning the outer piston counterclockwise.
11. Disassemble the outer piston by removing the snapring.
12. Disassemble the inner piston by removing the snapring. This will allow the spring cover, spring, and spring seat to come out. Remove the inner snapring to remove the key plate, pushrod, and strut.
   To install:
13. Assemble the pistons in reverse order of disassembly. Apply a thin coat of grease to the groove in the pushrod, its O-ring, the strut ends, oil seal, piston seal, and the inside of the dust seal.
14. Install the piston seals. Apply a thin coat of grease to the sliding surfaces of the piston and caliper bore. Install the pistons into the caliper. Install the retainers onto the dust seals.
15. Install the yoke springs on the yoke.
16. Lightly coat the yoke and caliper body contact surfaces, and the pad pin hole, with silicone grease. Assemble the yoke to the caliper.
17. Install the pads.
18. Install the caliper to the suspension arm (28–38 ft. lbs.). Connect the parking brake cable. Connect the brake hose. Apply the brakes a few times to center the pads. Bleed the system.
19. Lower the vehicle.

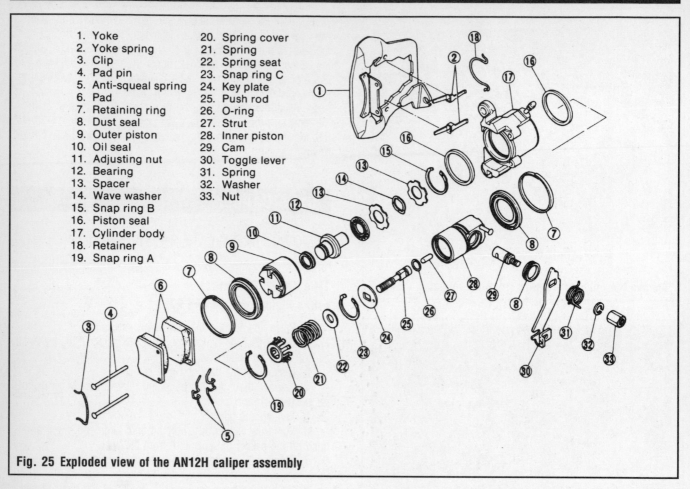

1. Yoke
2. Yoke spring
3. Clip
4. Pad pin
5. Anti-squeal spring
6. Pad
7. Retaining ring
8. Dust seal
9. Outer piston
10. Oil seal
11. Adjusting nut
12. Bearing
13. Spacer
14. Wave washer
15. Snap ring B
16. Piston seal
17. Cylinder body
18. Retainer
19. Snap ring A
20. Spring cover
21. Spring
22. Spring seat
23. Snap ring C
24. Key plate
25. Push rod
26. O-ring
27. Strut
28. Inner piston
29. Cam
30. Toggle lever
31. Spring
32. Washer
33. Nut

Fig. 25 Exploded view of the AN12H caliper assembly

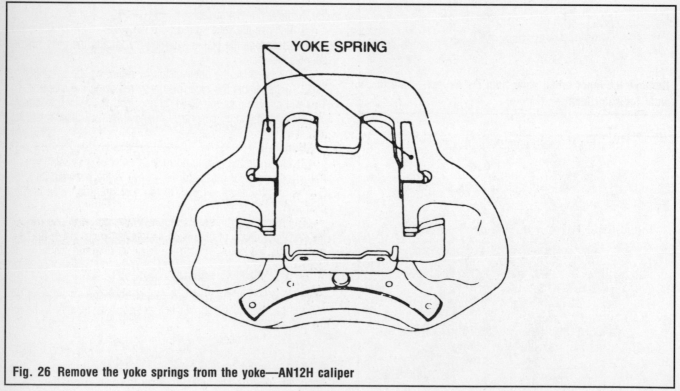

YOKE SPRING

Fig. 26 Remove the yoke springs from the yoke—AN12H caliper

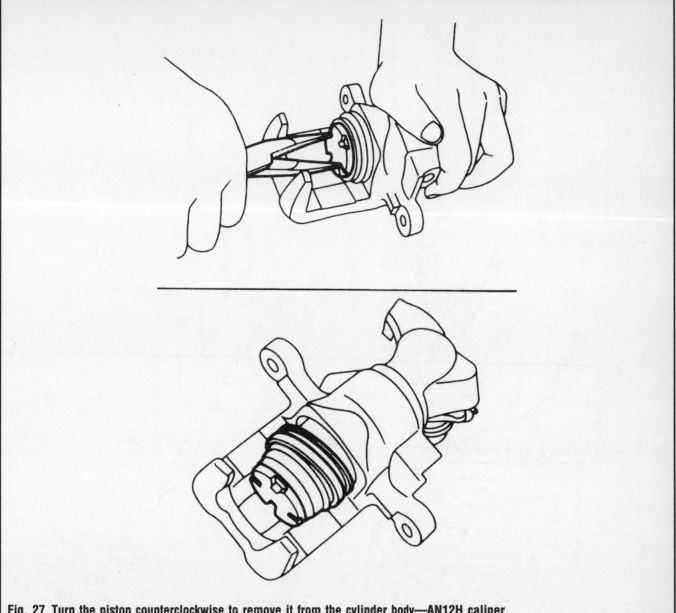

Fig. 27 Turn the piston counterclockwise to remove it from the cylinder body—AN12H caliper

Types CL11H, CL11HB, CL14B and CL9H Caliper

▶ **See Figures 28 thru 37**

1. Remove the brake pads.
2. Unscrew the mounting bolts and remove the caliper assembly.
3. Remove the pin bolts and separate the caliper body from the mounting support.
4. Using needlenose pliers, turn the piston counterclockwise and remove it.
5. Pry out the ring from inside the piston. You can now remove the adjusting nut, the ball bearing, the wave washer and the spacers.

6. Installation is in the reverse order of removal. Tighten the caliper mounting bolts to 28–38 ft. lbs. (38–52 Nm.).

Brake Disc (Rotor)

REMOVAL & INSTALLATION

1. Raise and support the rear of the vehicle safely and remove the wheels.
2. Remove brake caliper assembly. Refer to the necessary procedure. Make sure not to twist the brake hose.

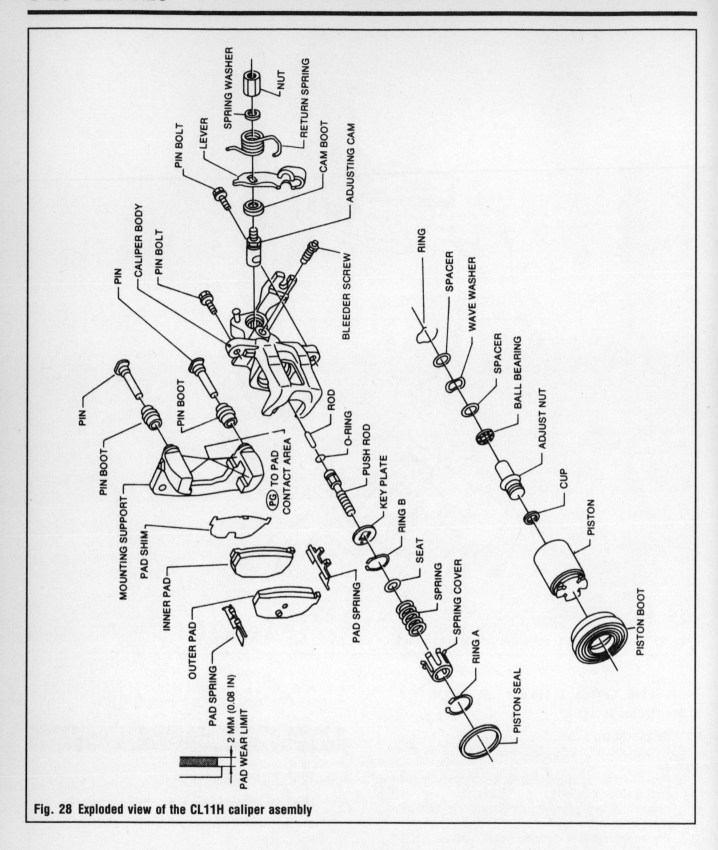

Fig. 28 Exploded view of the CL11H caliper asembly

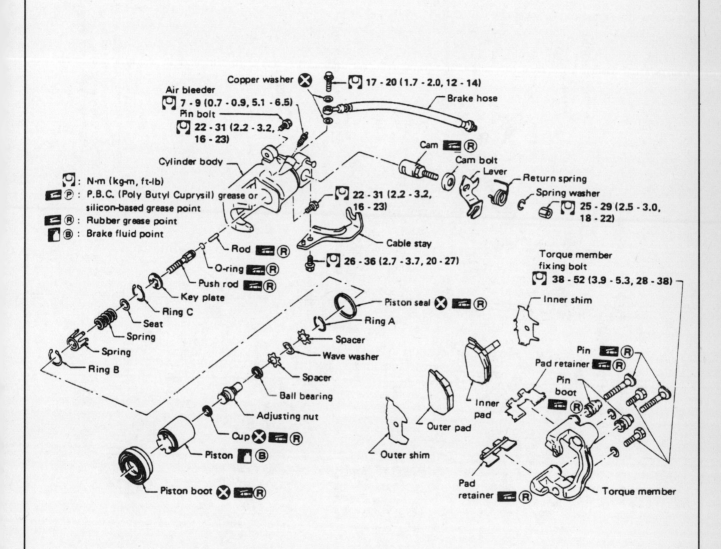

Fig. 29 Exploded view of the CL11HB caliper assembly

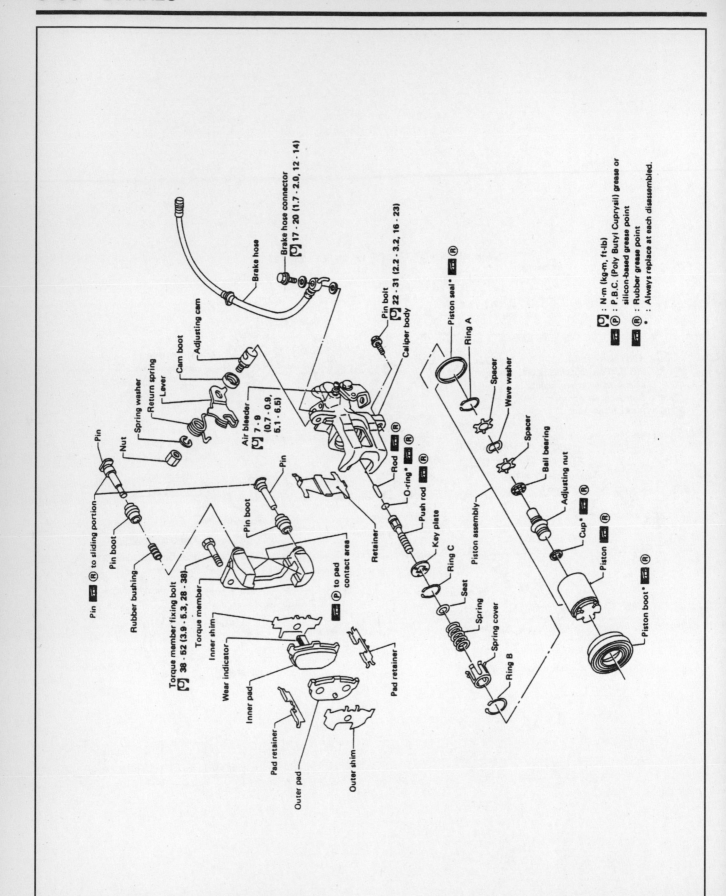

Fig. 30 Exploded view of the CL9H caliper assembly

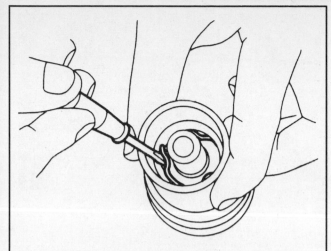

Fig. 31 Pry out the ring from inside the piston (some may be snapring types)—CL11H caliper

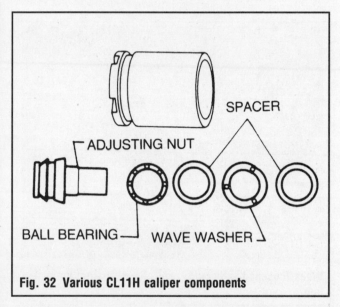

Fig. 32 Various CL11H caliper components

SPACER

ADJUSTING NUT

BALL BEARING   WAVE WASHER

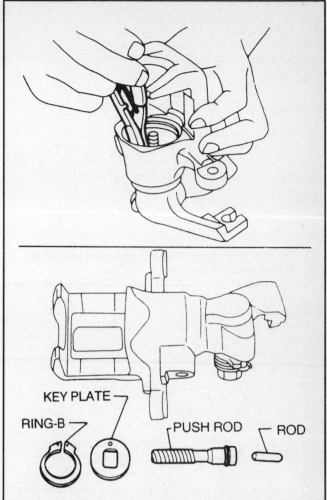

KEY PLATE

RING-B   PUSH ROD   ROD

Fig. 34 Remove the ring (B) with snapring pliers, then the key plate, pushrod and rod—CL11H caliper

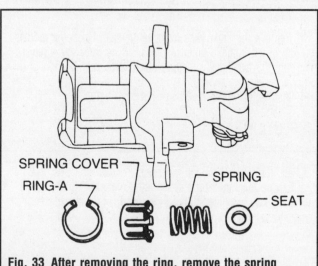

SPRING COVER

RING-A   SPRING

SEAT

Fig. 33 After removing the ring, remove the spring cover, spring and seat—CL11H caliper

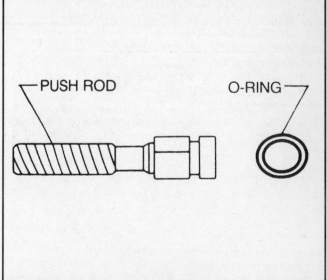

PUSH ROD   O-RING

Fig. 35 Remove the O-ring from the pushrod (use a new O-ring for installation)—CL11H caliper

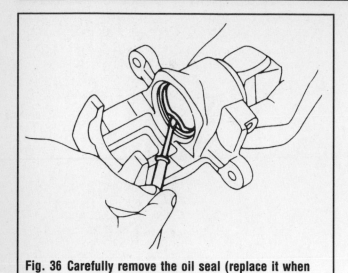

Fig. 36 Carefully remove the oil seal (replace it when reassembling)—CL11H caliper

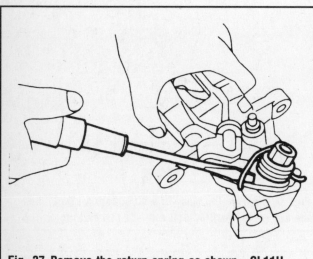

Fig. 37 Remove the return spring as shown—CL11H caliper

To remove the rear brake disc (rotor), raise and support the vehicle, then remove the wheel

Using correctly threaded bolts, screw them in alternately to press off the rotor

When loosened sufficiently, pull the rotor from the wheel hub

3. Remove the brake disc from the vehicle. On some models you can use 2 suitable bolts to press off the rotor, by screwing them into the two holes provided on the "top hat" portion of the rotor.

4. Installation is the reverse of removal.

INSPECTION

Check the brake rotor for roughness, cracks or chips. The rotor can be machined on a brake lathe most auto parts stores have complete machine shop service. The rotors should be machined or replaced during every rear disc brake pad replacement.

PARKING BRAKE

ADJUSTMENT

Handbrake adjustments are generally not needed, unless the cables have stretched.

All Models
▶ **See Figure 38**

There is an adjusting nut on the cable under the car, usually at the end of the front cable and near the point at which the two cables from the rear wheels come together (the equalizer). Some models also have a turnbuckle in the rear cable to compensate for cable stretching.

1. Adjust the rear brakes with the parking brake fully released.
2. Apply the hand brake lever so that it is approximately 3–3¼" from its fully released position.
3. Adjust the parking brake turnbuckle, locknuts, or equalizer so that the rear brakes are locked.
4. Release the parking brake. The wheels should turn freely. If not, loosen the parking brake adjuster until the wheels turn with no drag.

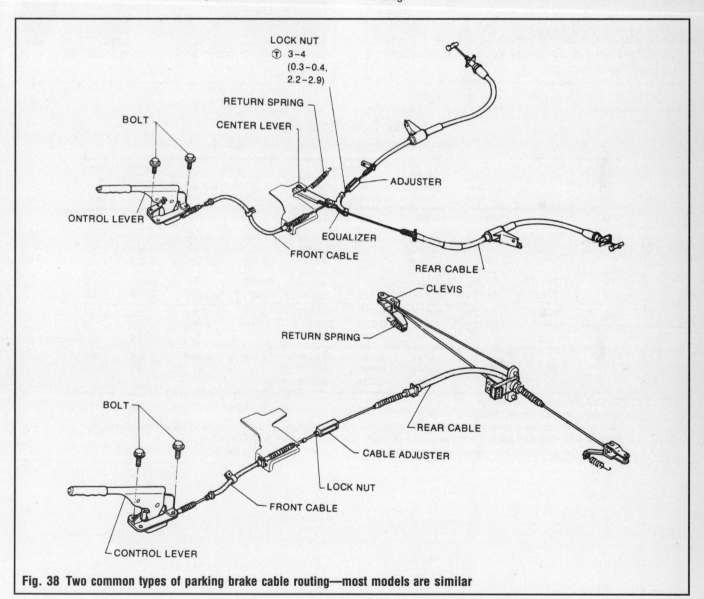

Fig. 38 Two common types of parking brake cable routing—most models are similar

You will not need to remove the cable adjuster unless replacing the cables

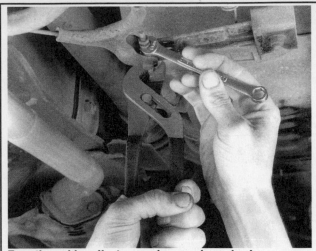

Turn the cable adjuster as shown using a back-up wrench

Brake Specifications
All measurements given are in inches unless noted

Model	Year	Lug Nut Torque (ft. lbs.)	Master Cylinder Bore	Brake Disc●		Drum		Minimum Lining Thickness●	
				Minimum Thickness	Maximum Run-Out	Diameter	Max. Wear Limit	Front	Rear
510	1978–81	58–72	0.8125	0.331	0.0047	9.000	9.060	0.080	0.059
610	1973–74	58–65	0.750	0.331	0.0048	9.000	9.055	0.039	0.059
	1975	58–65	0.750	0.331	0.0048	9.000	9.055	0.063	0.059
	1976–77	58–65	0.750	0.331	0.0048	9.000	9.055	0.079	0.059
710	1974–75	58–65	0.750	0.331	0.0047	9.000	9.055	0.039	0.059
	1976–77	58–65	0.750	0.331	0.0047	9.000	9.055	0.079	0.059
810/ Maxima	1977–80	58–72	0.8125	0.413	0.0059	9.000	9.060	0.080	0.059
	1981–84	58–72	0.8125	0.630/ 0.339	0.0059/① 0.0059	9.000	9.060	0.079/ 0.079	0.059
200SX	1977–79	58–65	0.750	0.331	0.0047	9.000	9.060	0.059	0.059
	1980–81	58–72	0.8750	0.413/ 0.339	0.0047/ 0.0059	—	—	0.079	0.079

—Not Applicable
●Second figure is for rear disc
NOTE: Minimum lining thickness is as recommended by the manufacturer. Due to variation in state inspection regulations, the minimum allowable thickness may be different than recommended by the manufacturer.
① 0.0028 in. on 1983-84 models, on front and rear

Troubleshooting the Brake System

Problem	Cause	Solution
Low brake pedal (excessive pedal travel required for braking action.)	• Excessive clearance between rear linings and drums caused by inoperative automatic adjusters	• Make 10 to 15 alternate forward and reverse brake stops to adjust brakes. If brake pedal does not come up, repair or replace adjuster parts as necessary.
	• Worn rear brakelining	• Inspect and replace lining if worn beyond minimum thickness specification
	• Bent, distorted brakeshoes, front or rear	• Replace brakeshoes in axle sets
	• Air in hydraulic system	• Remove air from system. Refer to Brake Bleeding.
Low brake pedal (pedal may go to floor with steady pressure applied.)	• Fluid leak in hydraulic system	• Fill master cylinder to fill line; have helper apply brakes and check calipers, wheel cylinders, differential valve tubes, hoses and fittings for leaks. Repair or replace as necessary.
	• Air in hydraulic system	• Remove air from system. Refer to Brake Bleeding.
	• Incorrect or non-recommended brake fluid (fluid evaporates at below normal temp).	• Flush hydraulic system with clean brake fluid. Refill with correct-type fluid.
	• Master cylinder piston seals worn, or master cylinder bore is scored, worn or corroded	• Repair or replace master cylinder
Low brake pedal (pedal goes to floor on first application—o.k. on subsequent applications.)	• Disc brake pads sticking on abutment surfaces of anchor plate. Caused by a build-up of dirt, rust, or corrosion on abutment surfaces	• Clean abutment surfaces
Fading brake pedal (pedal height decreases with steady pressure applied.)	• Fluid leak in hydraulic system	• Fill master cylinder reservoirs to fill mark, have helper apply brakes, check calipers, wheel cylinders, differential valve, tubes, hoses, and fittings for fluid leaks. Repair or replace parts as necessary.
	• Master cylinder piston seals worn, or master cylinder bore is scored, worn or corroded	• Repair or replace master cylinder
Decreasing brake pedal travel (pedal travel required for braking action decreases and may be accompanied by a hard pedal.)	• Caliper or wheel cylinder pistons sticking or seized	• Repair or replace the calipers, or wheel cylinders
	• Master cylinder compensator ports blocked (preventing fluid return to reservoirs) or pistons sticking or seized in master cylinder bore	• Repair or replace the master cylinder
	• Power brake unit binding internally	• Test unit according to the following procedure: (a) Shift transmission into neutral and start engine (b) Increase engine speed to 1500 rpm, close throttle and fully depress brake pedal (c) Slow release brake pedal and stop engine (d) Have helper remove vacuum check valve and hose from power unit. Observe for backward movement of brake pedal. (e) If the pedal moves backward, the power unit has an internal bind—replace power unit

Troubleshooting the Brake System (cont.)

Problem	Cause	Solution
Spongy brake pedal (pedal has abnormally soft, springy, spongy feel when depressed.)	• Air in hydraulic system	• Remove air from system. Refer to Brake Bleeding.
	• Brakeshoes bent or distorted	• Replace brakeshoes
	• Brakelining not yet seated with drums and rotors	• Burnish brakes
	• Rear drum brakes not properly adjusted	• Adjust brakes
Hard brake pedal (excessive pedal pressure required to stop vehicle. May be accompanied by brake fade.)	• Loose or leaking power brake unit vacuum hose	• Tighten connections or replace leaking hose
	• Incorrect or poor quality brakelining	• Replace with lining in axle sets
	• Bent, broken, distorted brakeshoes	• Replace brakeshoes
	• Calipers binding or dragging on mounting pins. Rear brakeshoes dragging on support plate.	• Replace mounting pins and bushings. Clean rust or burrs from rear brake support plate ledges and lubricate ledges with molydisulfide grease. **NOTE:** If ledges are deeply grooved or scored, do not attempt to sand or grind them smooth—replace support plate.
	• Caliper, wheel cylinder, or master cylinder pistons sticking or seized	• Repair or replace parts as necessary
	• Power brake unit vacuum check valve malfunction	• Test valve according to the following procedure: (a) Start engine, increase engine speed to 1500 rpm, close throttle and immediately stop engine (b) Wait at least 90 seconds then depress brake pedal (c) If brakes are not vacuum assisted for 2 or more applications, check valve is faulty
	• Power brake unit has internal bind	• Test unit according to the following procedure: (a) With engine stopped, apply brakes several times to exhaust all vacuum in system (b) Shift transmission into neutral, depress brake pedal and start engine (c) If pedal height decreases with foot pressure and less pressure is required to hold pedal in applied position, power unit vacuum system is operating normally. Test power unit. If power unit exhibits a bind condition, replace the power unit.
	• Master cylinder compensator ports (at bottom of reservoirs) blocked by dirt, scale, rust, or have small burrs (blocked ports prevent fluid return to reservoirs).	• Repair or replace master cylinder **CAUTION:** Do not attempt to clean blocked ports with wire, pencils, or similar implements. Use compressed air only.
	• Brake hoses, tubes, fittings clogged or restricted	• Use compressed air to check or unclog parts. Replace any damaged parts.
	• Brake fluid contaminated with improper fluids (motor oil, transmission fluid, causing rubber components to swell and stick in bores	• Replace all rubber components, combination valve and hoses. Flush entire brake system with DOT 3 brake fluid or equivalent.
	• Low engine vacuum	• Adjust or repair engine

Troubleshooting the Brake System (cont.)

Problem	Cause	Solution
Grabbing brakes (severe reaction to brake pedal pressure.)	• Brakelining(s) contaminated by grease or brake fluid	• Determine and correct cause of contamination and replace brakeshoes in axle sets
	• Parking brake cables incorrectly adjusted or seized	• Adjust cables. Replace seized cables.
	• Incorrect brakelining or lining loose on brakeshoes	• Replace brakeshoes in axle sets
	• Caliper anchor plate bolts loose	• Tighten bolts
	• Rear brakeshoes binding on support plate ledges	• Clean and lubricate ledges. Replace support plate(s) if ledges are deeply grooved. Do not attempt to smooth ledges by grinding.
	• Incorrect or missing power brake reaction disc	• Install correct disc
	• Rear brake support plates loose	• Tighten mounting bolts
Dragging brakes (slow or incomplete release of brakes)	• Brake pedal binding at pivot	• Loosen and lubricate
	• Power brake unit has internal bind	• Inspect for internal bind. Replace unit if internal bind exists.
	• Parking brake cables incorrrectly adjusted or seized	• Adjust cables. Replace seized cables.
	• Rear brakeshoe return springs weak or broken	• Replace return springs. Replace brakeshoe if necessary in axle sets.
	• Automatic adjusters malfunctioning	• Repair or replace adjuster parts as required
	• Caliper, wheel cylinder or master cylinder pistons sticking or seized	• Repair or replace parts as necessary
	• Master cylinder compensating ports blocked (fluid does not return to reservoirs).	• Use compressed air to clear ports. Do not use wire, pencils, or similar objects to open blocked ports.
Vehicle moves to one side when brakes are applied	• Incorrect front tire pressure	• Inflate to recommended cold (reduced load) inflation pressure
	• Worn or damaged wheel bearings	• Replace worn or damaged bearings
	• Brakelining on one side contaminated	• Determine and correct cause of contamination and replace brakelining in axle sets
	• Brakeshoes on one side bent, distorted, or lining loose on shoe	• Replace brakeshoes in axle sets
	• Support plate bent or loose on one side	• Tighten or replace support plate
	• Brakelining not yet seated with drums or rotors	• Burnish brakelining
	• Caliper anchor plate loose on one side	• Tighten anchor plate bolts
	• Caliper piston sticking or seized	• Repair or replace caliper
	• Brakelinings water soaked	• Drive vehicle with brakes lightly applied to dry linings
	• Loose suspension component attaching or mounting bolts	• Tighten suspension bolts. Replace worn suspension components.
	• Brake combination valve failure	• Replace combination valve
Chatter or shudder when brakes are applied (pedal pulsation and roughness may also occur.)	• Brakeshoes distorted, bent, contaminated, or worn	• Replace brakeshoes in axle sets
	• Caliper anchor plate or support plate loose	• Tighten mounting bolts
	• Excessive thickness variation of rotor(s)	• Refinish or replace rotors in axle sets
Noisy brakes (squealing, clicking, scraping sound when brakes are applied.)	• Bent, broken, distorted brakeshoes	• Replace brakeshoes in axle sets
	• Excessive rust on outer edge of rotor braking surface	• Remove rust

Troubleshooting the Brake System (cont.)

Problem	Cause	Solution
Noisy brakes (squealing, clicking, scraping sound when brakes are applied.) (cont.)	• Brakelining worn out—shoes contacting drum of rotor	• Replace brakeshoes and lining in axle sets. Refinish or replace drums or rotors.
	• Broken or loose holdown or return springs	• Replace parts as necessary
	• Rough or dry drum brake support plate ledges	• Lubricate support plate ledges
	• Cracked, grooved, or scored rotor(s) or drum(s)	• Replace rotor(s) or drum(s). Replace brakeshoes and lining in axle sets if necessary.
	• Incorrect brakelining and/or shoes (front or rear).	• Install specified shoe and lining assemblies
Pulsating brake pedal	• Out of round drums or excessive lateral runout in disc brake rotor(s)	• Refinish or replace drums, re-index rotors or replace

10

BODY

EXTERIOR

Doors

REMOVAL & INSTALLATION

Front or Rear

▶ **See Figure 1**

1. Place a jack or stand beneath the door to support its weight.

➡ **Place a rag between the lower edge of the door and jack or stand to prevent damage to painted surface.**

2. Remove door without hinge.
3. Remove the door hinge.
4. Installation is the reverse order of removal.

➡ **When installing hinge, coat the hinge link with recommended multipurpose grease.**

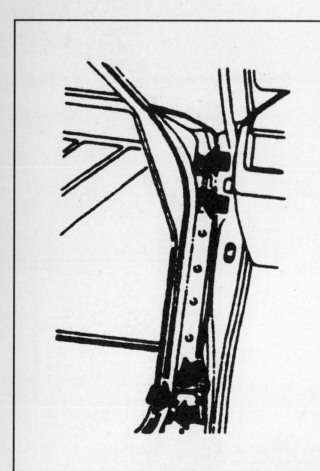

Fig. 1 To remove the door, remove the mounting bolts indicated

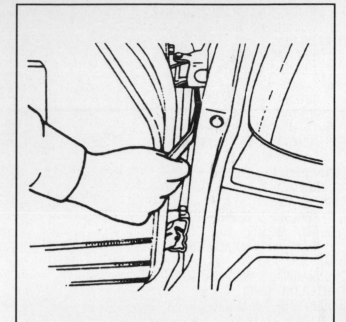

Fig. 2 A special tool may be available to aid with the adjustment of the hinge, if needed

ADJUSTMENT

Front or Rear

▶ **See Figures 2, 3 and 4**

Proper door alignment can be obtained by adjusting the door hinge and door lock striker. The door hinge and striker can be moved up and down fore and aft in enlarged holes by loosening the attaching bolts.

➡ **The door should be adjusted for an even and parallel fit for the door opening and surrounding body panels.**

Hood

REMOVAL & INSTALLATION

1. Open the hood and protect the body with covers to protect the painted surfaces.
2. Mark the hood hinge locations on the hood for proper reinstallation.
3. Holding both sides of the hood, unscrew the bolts securing the hinge to the hood. This operation requires a helper.
4. Installation is the reverse of removal.

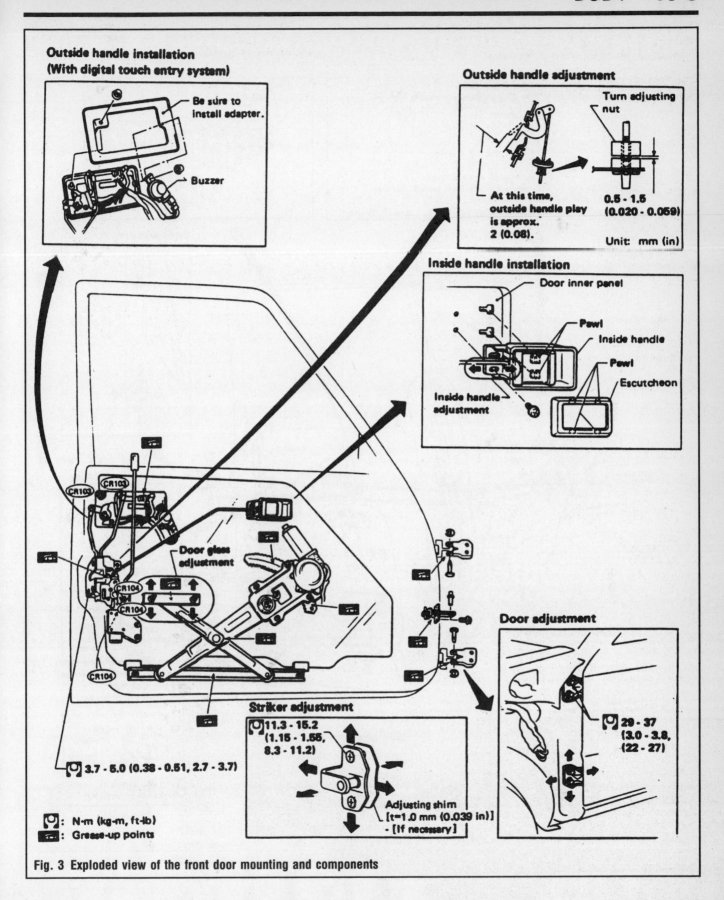

**Outside handle installation
(With digital touch entry system)**

Be sure to install adapter.

Buzzer

Outside handle adjustment

Turn adjusting nut

At this time, outside handle play is approx. 2 (0.08).

0.5 - 1.5 (0.020 - 0.059)

Unit: mm (in)

Inside handle installation

Door inner panel

Pawl

Inside handle

Pawl

Escutcheon

Inside handle adjustment

CR103

CR103

CR104

CR104

CR104

Door glass adjustment

Door adjustment

29 - 37 (3.0 - 3.8, (22 - 27)

3.7 - 5.0 (0.38 - 0.51, 2.7 - 3.7)

Striker adjustment

11.3 - 15.2 (1.15 - 1.55, 8.3 - 11.2)

Adjusting shim [t=1.0 mm (0.039 in)] - [If necessary]

: N·m (kg-m, ft-lb)

: Grease-up points

Fig. 3 Exploded view of the front door mounting and components

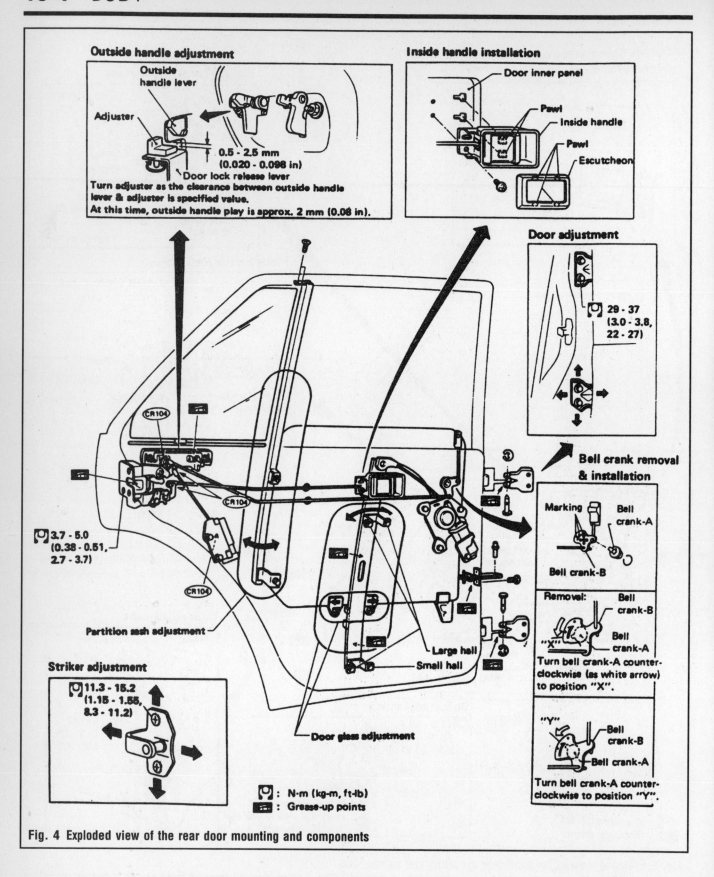

Outside handle adjustment

Outside handle lever

Adjuster

0.5 - 2.5 mm
(0.020 - 0.098 in)

Door lock release lever

Turn adjuster as the clearance between outside handle lever & adjuster is specified value.
At this time, outside handle play is approx. 2 mm (0.08 in).

Inside handle installation

Door inner panel

Pawl

Inside handle

Pawl

Escutcheon

Door adjustment

29 - 37
(3.0 - 3.8, 22 - 27)

Bell crank removal & installation

Marking

Bell crank-A

Bell crank-B

Removal:

Bell crank-B

Bell crank-A

"X"

Turn bell crank-A counter-clockwise (as white arrow) to position "X".

"Y"

Bell crank-B

Bell crank-A

Turn bell crank-A counter-clockwise to position "Y".

CR104

3.7 - 5.0
(0.38 - 0.51, 2.7 - 3.7)

CR104

CR104

Partition sash adjustment

Striker adjustment

11.3 - 15.2
(1.15 - 1.55, 8.3 - 11.2)

Large hall

Small hall

Door glass adjustment

: N·m (kg-m, ft-lb)

: Grease-up points

Fig. 4 Exploded view of the rear door mounting and components

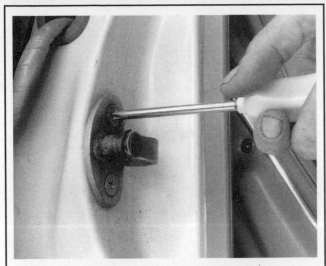

To help align the door, adjust the door lock striker

Take the opportunity to lubricate the lock mechanism with a suitable lubricant when adjusting the door

ALIGNMENT

▶ **See Figures 5, 6 and 7**

The hood can be adjusted with bolts attaching the hood to the hood hinges, hood lock mechanism and hood bumpers. Adjust the hood for an even fit between the front fenders.

1. Adjust the hood fore and aft by loosening the bolts attaching the hood to the hinge and repositioning hood.

2. Loosen the hood bumper locknuts and lower bumpers until they do not contact the front of the hood when the hood is closed.

3. Set the striker at the center of the hood lock, and tighten the hood lock securing bolts temporarily.

4. Raise the two hood bumpers until the hood is flush with the fenders.

5. Tighten the hood lock securing bolts after the proper adjustment has been obtained.

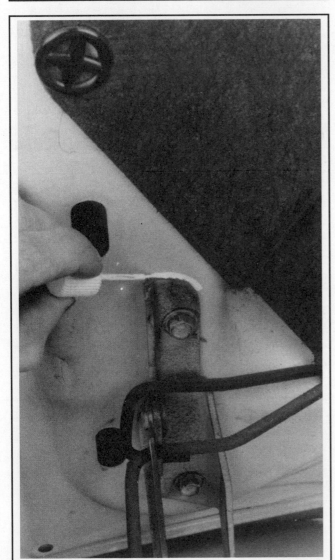

Prior to removing the hood, trace a line around the hood hinge to gain room to work

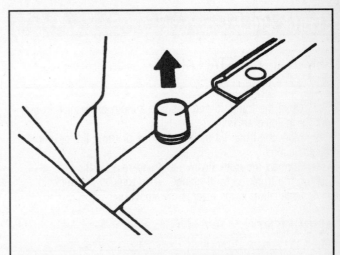

Fig. 5 If necessary to make the hood fit squarely in place, adjust the hood at the rubber bumper

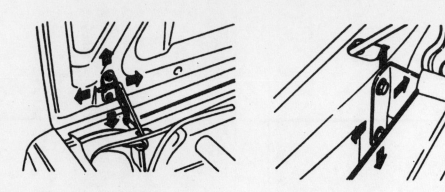

Fig. 6 Adjust the hood at the hinges so the gaps on all sides are matched and it fits symmetrically

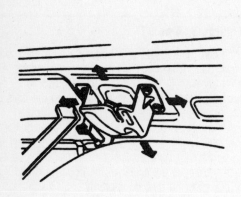

Fig. 7 Adjust the hood at the hood lock so that it latches with light effort

Trunk Lid

REMOVAL & INSTALLATION

1. Open the trunk lid and position a cloth or cushion to protect the painted areas.
2. Mark the trunk lid hinge locations or trunk lid for proper reinstallation.
3. Support the trunk lid by hand and remove the bolts attaching the trunk lid to the hinge. Then remove the trunk lid.
4. Installation is the reverse of removal.

ALIGNMENT

1. Loosen the trunk lid hinge attaching bolts until they are just loose enough to move the trunk lid.
2. Move the trunk lid for and aft to obtain a flush fit between the trunk lid and the rear fender.

3. To obtain a snug fit between the trunk lid and weatherstrip, loosen the trunk lid lock striker attaching bolts enough to move the lid, working the striker up and down and from side to side as required.
4. After the adjustment is made tighten the striker bolts securely.

Hatchback or Tailgate Lid

REMOVAL & INSTALLATION

1. Open the lid and disconnect the rear defogger harness if so equipped.
2. Mark the hinge locations on the lid for proper relocation.
3. Position rags between the roof and the upper end of the lid to prevent scratching the paint.
4. Support the lid and remove the support bolts the hinge retaining bolts and remove the lid.
5. Installation is the reverse of removal.

➡ **Be careful not to scratch the lift support rods. A scratched rod may cause oil or gas leakage.**

ALIGNMENT

◗ **See Figure 8**

1. Open the hatchback lid.
2. Loosen the lid hinge to body attaching bolts until they are just loose enough to move the lid.
3. Move the lid up and down to obtain a flush fit between the lid and the roof.
4. After adjustment is completed tighten the hinge attaching bolts securely.

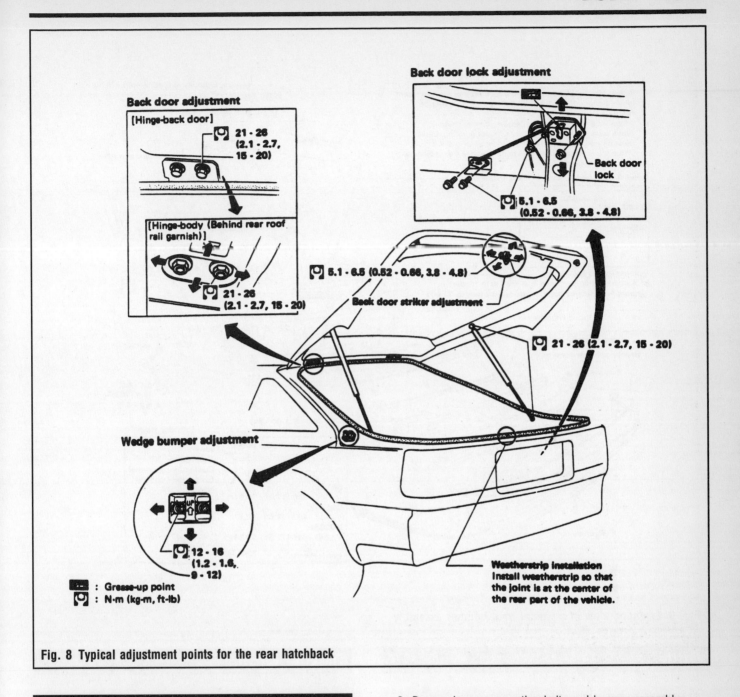

Back door adjustment

[Hinge-back door]

21 - 26
(2.1 - 2.7,
15 - 20)

[Hinge-body (Behind rear roof rail garnish)]

21 - 26
(2.1 - 2.7, 15 - 20)

Back door lock adjustment

Back door lock

5.1 - 6.5
(0.52 - 0.66, 3.8 - 4.8)

5.1 - 6.5 (0.52 - 0.66, 3.8 - 4.8)

Back door striker adjustment

21 - 26 (2.1 - 2.7, 15 - 20)

Wedge bumper adjustment

12 - 16
(1.2 - 1.6,
9 - 12)

■ : Grease-up point

☐ : N·m (kg-m, ft-lb)

Weatherstrip installation
Install weatherstrip so that the joint is at the center of the rear part of the vehicle.

Fig. 8 Typical adjustment points for the rear hatchback

Bumpers

REMOVAL & INSTALLATION

Front or Rear

♦ See Figure 9

➥Refer to the exploded view of Body Front and Rear End Assembly.

1. Disconnect all electrical connectors at bumper assembly if so equipped.

2. Remove bumper mounting bolts and bumper assembly.
3. Remove shock absorbers from bumper.

✳✳ CAUTION

The shock absorber is filled with a high pressure gas and should not be disassembled, drilled or exposed to an open flame.

4. Install shock absorbers and bumper in reverse order of removal.

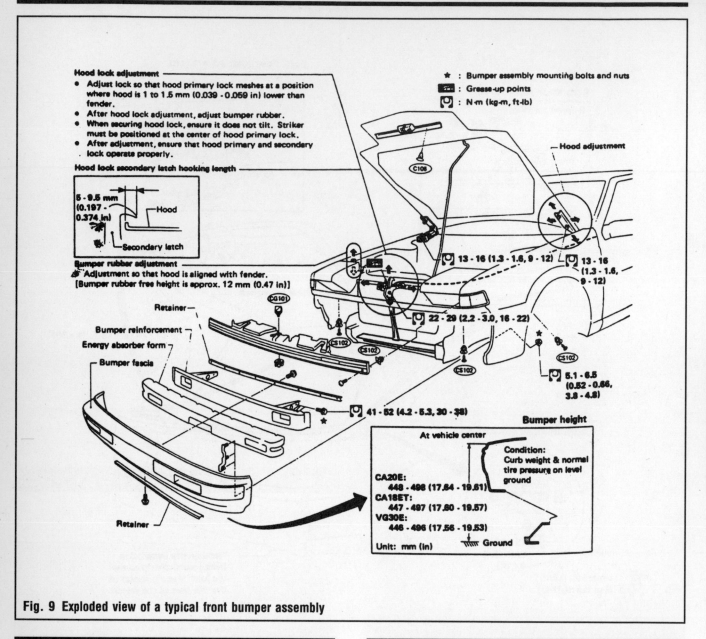

Fig. 9 Exploded view of a typical front bumper assembly

Grille

REMOVAL & INSTALLATION

1. Remove radiator grille bracket bolts.

➡**Refer to the exploded view of Body Front End Assembly. The radiator grille assembly is made of plastic, thus never use excessive force to remove it.**

2. Remove radiator grille from the vehicle.
3. To install, reverse the removal procedures.

Outside Mirrors

REMOVAL & INSTALLATION

Manually Adjustable

◆ **See Figures 10, 11 and 12**

1. Remove control knob handle.
2. Remove door corner finisher panel.
3. Remove mirror body attaching screws, and then remove mirror body.
4. Installation is in the reverse order of removal.

➡**Apply sealer to the rear surface of the door corner finisher panel during installation to prevent water leak.**

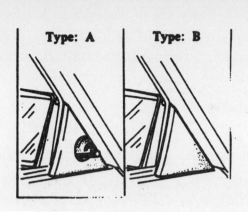

Fig. 10 Design features of two common door finisher panels

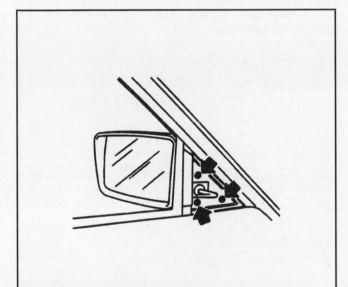

Fig. 11 Remove the mirror mounting screws where indicated (arrows)

Fig. 12 Upon installation, apply sealer to the rear surface of the finisher panel

Power Adjustable
♦ **See Figure 13**

1. Remove door corner finisher panel.
2. Remove mirror body attaching screws, and then remove mirror body.
3. Disconnect the electrical connection.

➡**It may be necessary to remove the door trim panel to gain access to the electrical connection.**

4. Installation is in the reverse order of removal.

Antenna

REMOVAL & INSTALLATION

1. Remove antenna mounting nut.
2. Disconnect the antenna lead at the radio.
3. Remove antenna from vehicle.
4. Installation is in the reverse order of removal.

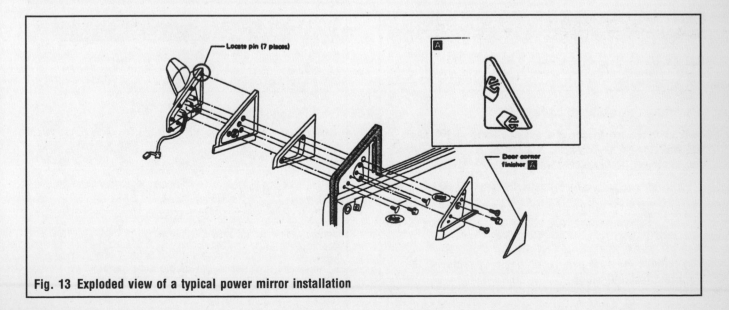

Fig. 13 Exploded view of a typical power mirror installation

INTERIOR

Door Panel, Glass and Regulator

REMOVAL & INSTALLATION

Front or Rear

◆ See Figures 14, 15, 16 and 17

➡️Refer to the exploded view of Front and Rear Door Assembly.

1. Remove the regulator handle by pushing the set pin spring off.

2. Remove the arm rest, door inside handle escutcheon and door lock.

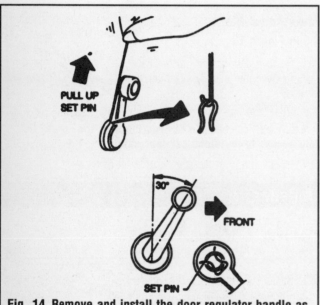

Fig. 14 Remove and install the door regulator handle as shown

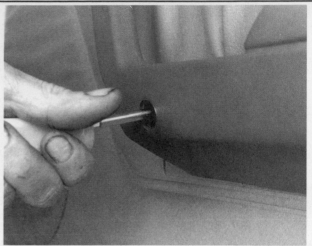

After removing the cover plug(s), use a screwdriver to remove the fasteners

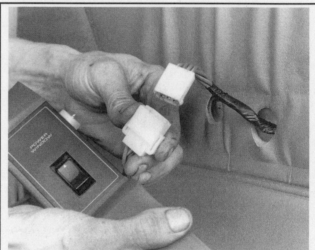

If equipped, disconnect the harness plug for the power window switch on the armrest

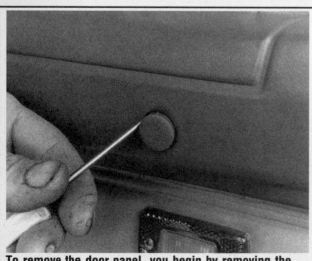

To remove the door panel, you begin by removing the armrest fastener plugs

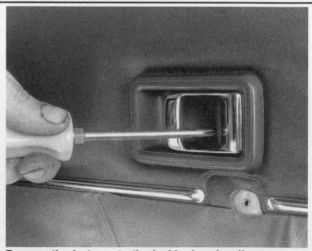

Remove the fastener to the inside door handle escutcheon

Lift out the escutcheon and place it with the other parts

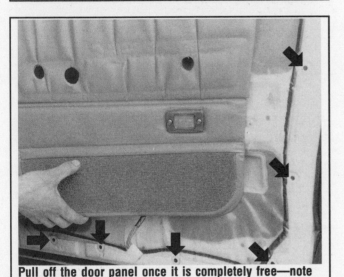

Pull off the door panel once it is completely free—note the plug holes (arrows)

3. Remove the door finisher and sealing screen.

4. On some models it may be necessary to remove the outer door moulding.

5. Lower the door glass with the regulator handle until the regulator-to-glass attaching bolts appear at the access holes in the door inside panel.

6. Raise the door glass and draw it upwards.

7. Remove the regulator attaching bolts and remove the regulator assembly through the large access hole in the door panel.

To install:

8. Install the window regulator assembly in the door.

9. Connect all mounting bolts and check for proper operation.

10. Adjust the window if necessary and install the door trim panel.

11. Install all the attaching components to the door panel.

12. Install the window regulator handle.

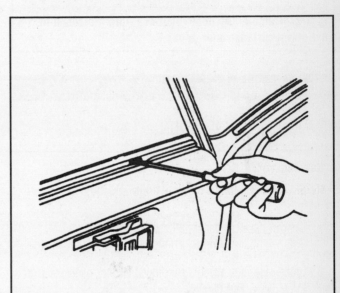

Fig. 15 Remove the outer door moulding using a suitable prytool

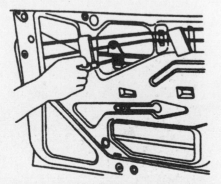
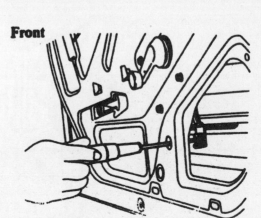

Rear

Front

Fig. 16 Remove the glass attaching bolts as shown

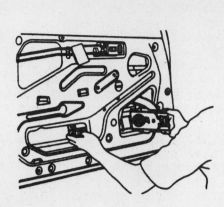

Fig. 17 Remove the door regulator from the cutout in the stamped inner door panel

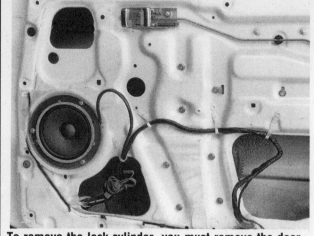

To remove the lock cylinder, you must remove the door panel and sealing screen

Door Locks

REMOVAL & INSTALLATION

▶ **See Figure 18**

➡**Refer to the exploded view of Front and Rear Door Assembly.**

1. Remove the door panel and sealing screen.
2. Remove the lock cylinder from the rod by turning the resin clip.
3. Loosen the nuts attaching the outside door handle and remove the outside door handle.
4. Remove the screws retaining the inside door handle and door lock, and remove the door lock assembly from the hole in the inside of the door.

5. Remove the lock cylinder by removing the retaining clip.
To install:
6. Install the lock cylinder and clip to the door.
7. Install the door lock assembly and handles.
8. Install door panel and all attaching parts.

Electrical Window Motor

REMOVAL & INSTALLATION

➡**Refer to the exploded view of Front and Rear Door Assembly.**

1. Remove the door panel and sealing screen.
2. Remove the power window motor mounting bolts.
3. Remove all electrical connections and cable connection.

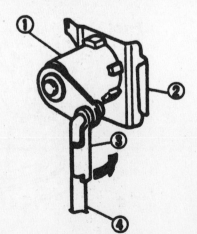

1. Door lock cylinder
2. Retaining clip
3. Resin clip
4. Lock cylinder rod

Fig. 18 Design features of a typical lock cylinder assembly

4. Remove the power window motor from the vehicle.
5. Installation is in the reverse order of removal.

Inside Rear View Mirror

REMOVAL & INSTALLATION

1. Remove rear view mirror mounting bolt or screw cover.
2. Remove rear view mirror mounting bolt(s)/screw(s).
3. Remove mirror.
4. Installation is in the reverse order of removal.

Remove the mirror—note the square base that aids proper installation (arrow)

To remove the mirror, unfasten the screw securing it

Seats

REMOVAL & INSTALLATION

Front
▶ **See Figure 19**

➡**On power seat models remove the seat then remove the power seat motor assembly and drive cable.**

1. Remove front seat mounting bolts.
2. Remove front seat assembly.
3. Installation is in the reverse order of removal.

Rear
▶ **See Figure 20**

1. Remove rear seat cushion mounting bolts.
2. Remove screw attaching luggage floor carpet.
3. Remove rear seat back by tilting forward and pulling straight up.

➡**On hatchback models the rear seat back is removed similar to the front seat.**

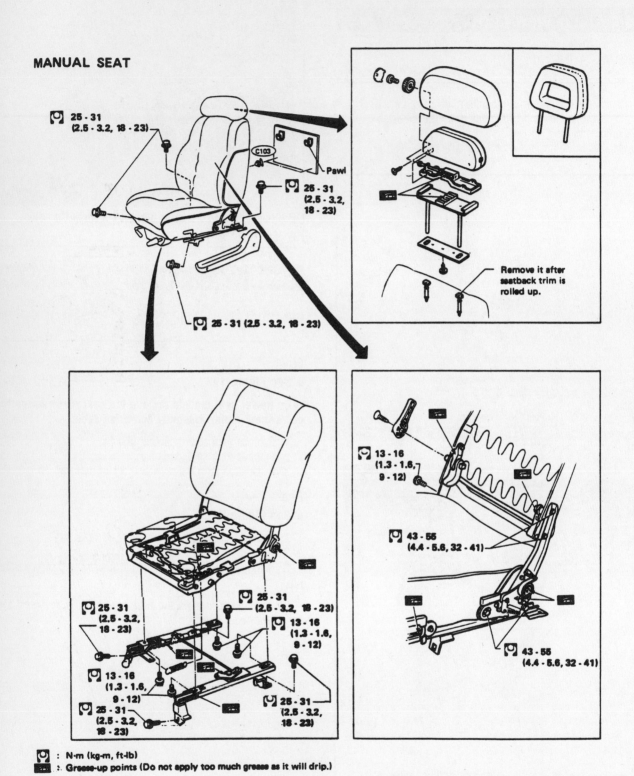

MANUAL SEAT

25 - 31
(2.5 - 3.2, 18 - 23)

C103

Pawl

25 - 31
(2.5 - 3.2,
18 - 23)

Remove it after
seatback trim is
rolled up.

25 - 31 (2.5 - 3.2, 18 - 23)

13 - 16
(1.3 - 1.6,
9 - 12)

43 - 55
(4.4 - 5.6, 32 - 41)

25 - 31
(2.5 - 3.2,
18 - 23)

25 - 31
(2.5 - 3.2, 18 - 23)

13 - 16
(1.3 - 1.6,
9 - 12)

43 - 55
(4.4 - 5.6, 32 - 41)

13 - 16
(1.3 - 1.6,
9 - 12)

25 - 31
(2.5 - 3.2,
18 - 23)

25 - 31
(2.5 - 3.2,
18 - 23)

: N·m (kg-m, ft-lb)

: Grease-up points (Do not apply too much grease as it will drip.)

Fig. 19 Exploded view of various manual front seat components

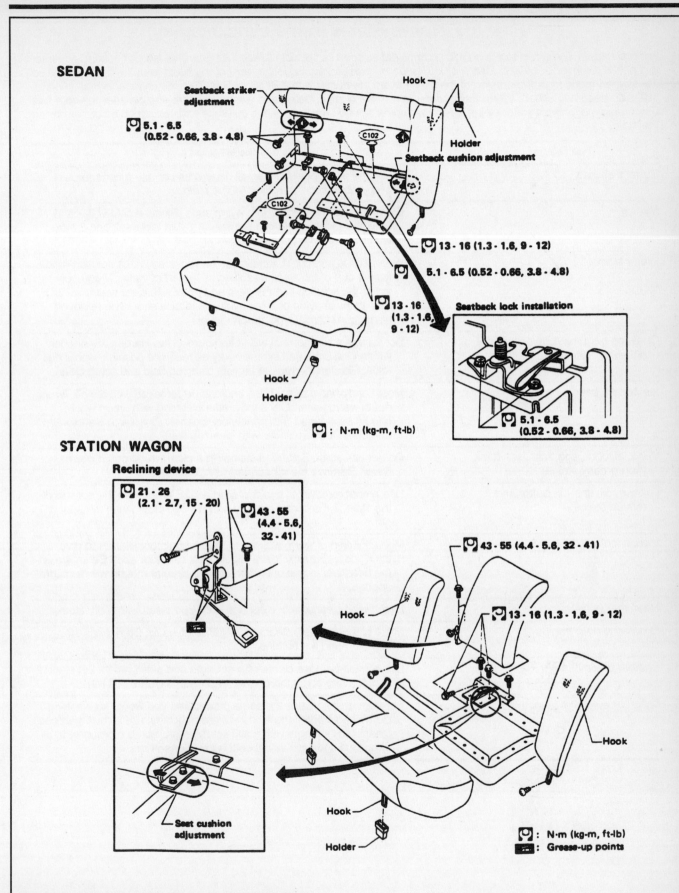

SEDAN

Seatback striker adjustment

5.1 - 6.5 (0.52 - 0.66, 3.8 - 4.8)

C102

Hook

Holder

Seatback cushion adjustment

C102

13 - 16 (1.3 - 1.6, 9 - 12)

5.1 - 6.5 (0.52 - 0.66, 3.8 - 4.8)

13 - 16 (1.3 - 1.6, 9 - 12)

Seatback lock installation

5.1 - 6.5 (0.52 - 0.66, 3.8 - 4.8)

Hook

Holder

: N·m (kg-m, ft-lb)

STATION WAGON

Reclining device

21 - 26 (2.1 - 2.7, 15 - 20)

43 - 55 (4.4 - 5.6, 32 - 41)

43 - 55 (4.4 - 5.6, 32 - 41)

13 - 16 (1.3 - 1.6, 9 - 12)

Hook

Hook

Seat cushion adjustment

Hook

Holder

: N·m (kg-m, ft-lb)

: Grease-up points

Fig. 20 Exploded view of various rear seat components

How to Remove Stains from Fabric Interior

For rest results, spots and stains should be removed as soon as possible. Never use gasoline, lacquer thinner, acetone, nail polish remover or bleach. Use a 3' x 3" piece of cheesecloth. Squeeze most of the liquid from the fabric and wipe the stained fabric from the outside of the stain toward the center with a lifting motion. Turn the cheesecloth as soon as one side becomes soiled. When using water to remove a stain, be sure to wash the entire section after the spot has been removed to avoid water stains. Encrusted spots can be broken up with a dull knife and vacuumed before removing the stain.

Type of Stain	How to Remove It
Surface spots	Brush the spots out with a small hand brush or use a commercial preparation such as K2R to lift the stain.
Mildew	Clean around the mildew with warm suds. Rinse in cold water and soak the mildew area in a solution of 1 part table salt and 2 parts water. Wash with upholstery cleaner.
Water stains	Water stains in fabric materials can be removed with a solution made from 1 cup of table salt dissolved in 1 quart of water. Vigorously scrub the solution into the stain and rinse with clear water. Water stains in nylon or other synthetic fabrics should be removed with a commercial type spot remover.
Chewing gum, tar, crayons, shoe polish (greasy stains)	Do not use a cleaner that will soften gum or tar. Harden the deposit with an ice cube and scrape away as much as possible with a dull knife. Moisten the remainder with cleaning fluid and scrub clean.
Ice cream, candy	Most candy has a sugar base and can be removed with a cloth wrung out in warm water. Oily candy, after cleaning with warm water, should be cleaned with upholstery cleaner. Rinse with warm water and clean the remainder with cleaning fluid.
Wine, alcohol, egg, milk, soft drink (non-greasy stains)	Do not use soap. Scrub the stain with a cloth wrung out in warm water. Remove the remainder with cleaning fluid.
Grease, oil, lipstick, butter and related stains	Use a spot remover to avoid leaving a ring. Work from the outisde of the stain to the center and dry with a clean cloth when the spot is gone.
Headliners (cloth)	Mix a solution of warm water and foam upholstery cleaner to give thick suds. Use only foam—liquid may streak or spot. Clean the entire headliner in one operation using a circular motion with a natural sponge.
Headliner (vinyl)	Use a vinyl cleaner with a sponge and wipe clean with a dry cloth.
Seats and door panels	Mix 1 pint upholstery cleaner in 1 gallon of water. Do not soak the fabric around the buttons.
Leather or vinyl fabric	Use a multi-purpose cleaner full strength and a stiff brush. Let stand 2 minutes and scrub thoroughly. Wipe with a clean, soft rag.
Nylon or synthetic fabrics	For normal stains, use the same procedures you would for washing cloth upholstery. If the fabric is extremely dirty, use a multi-purpose cleaner full strength with a stiff scrub brush. Scrub thoroughly in all directions and wipe with a cotton towel or soft rag.

GLOSSARY

AIR/FUEL RATIO: The ratio of air-to-gasoline by weight in the fuel mixture drawn into the engine.

AIR INJECTION: One method of reducing harmful exhaust emissions by injecting air into each of the exhaust ports of an engine. The fresh air entering the hot exhaust manifold causes any remaining fuel to be burned before it can exit the tailpipe.

ALTERNATOR: A device used for converting mechanical energy into electrical energy.

AMMETER: An instrument, calibrated in amperes, used to measure the flow of an electrical current in a circuit. Ammeters are always connected in series with the circuit being tested.

AMPERE: The rate of flow of electrical current present when one volt of electrical pressure is applied against one ohm of electrical resistance.

ANALOG COMPUTER: Any microprocessor that uses similar (analogous) electrical signals to make its calculations.

ARMATURE: A laminated, soft iron core wrapped by a wire that converts electrical energy to mechanical energy as in a motor or relay. When rotated in a magnetic field, it changes mechanical energy into electrical energy as in a generator.

ATMOSPHERIC PRESSURE: The pressure on the Earth's surface caused by the weight of the air in the atmosphere. At sea level, this pressure is 14.7 psi at 32°F (101 kPa at 0°C).

ATOMIZATION: The breaking down of a liquid into a fine mist that can be suspended in air.

AXIAL PLAY: Movement parallel to a shaft or bearing bore.

BACKFIRE: The sudden combustion of gases in the intake or exhaust system that results in a loud explosion.

BACKLASH: The clearance or play between two parts, such as meshed gears.

BACKPRESSURE: Restrictions in the exhaust system that slow the exit of exhaust gases from the combustion chamber.

BAKELITE: A heat resistant, plastic insulator material commonly used in printed circuit boards and transistorized components.

BALL BEARING: A bearing made up of hardened inner and outer races between which hardened steel balls roll.

BALLAST RESISTOR: A resistor in the primary ignition circuit that lowers voltage after the engine is started to reduce wear on ignition components.

BEARING: A friction reducing, supportive device usually located between a stationary part and a moving part.

BIMETAL TEMPERATURE SENSOR: Any sensor or switch made of two dissimilar types of metal that bend when heated or cooled due to the different expansion rates of the alloys. These types of sensors usually function as an on/off switch.

BLOWBY: Combustion gases, composed of water vapor and unburned fuel, that leak past the piston rings into the crankcase during normal engine operation. These gases are removed by the PCV system to prevent the buildup of harmful acids in the crankcase.

BRAKE PAD: A brake shoe and lining assembly used with disc brakes.

BRAKE SHOE: The backing for the brake lining. The term is, however, usually applied to the assembly of the brake backing and lining.

BUSHING: A liner, usually removable, for a bearing; an anti-friction liner used in place of a bearing.

CALIPER: A hydraulically activated device in a disc brake system, which is mounted straddling the brake rotor (disc). The caliper contains at least one piston and two brake pads. Hydraulic pressure on the piston(s) forces the pads against the rotor.

CAMSHAFT: A shaft in the engine on which are the lobes (cams) which operate the valves. The camshaft is driven by the crankshaft, via a belt, chain or gears, at one half the crankshaft speed.

CAPACITOR: A device which stores an electrical charge.

CARBON MONOXIDE (CO): A colorless, odorless gas given off as a normal byproduct of combustion. It is poisonous and extremely dangerous in confined areas, building up slowly to toxic levels without warning if adequate ventilation is not available.

CARBURETOR: A device, usually mounted on the intake manifold of an engine, which mixes the air and fuel in the proper proportion to allow even combustion.

CATALYTIC CONVERTER: A device installed in the exhaust system, like a muffler, that converts harmful byproducts of combustion into carbon dioxide and water vapor by means of a heat-producing chemical reaction.

CENTRIFUGAL ADVANCE: A mechanical method of advancing the spark timing by using flyweights in the distributor that react to centrifugal force generated by the distributor shaft rotation.

CHECK VALVE: Any one-way valve installed to permit the flow of air, fuel or vacuum in one direction only.

CHOKE: A device, usually a moveable valve, placed in the intake path of a carburetor to restrict the flow of air.

CIRCUIT: Any unbroken path through which an electrical current can flow. Also used to describe fuel flow in some instances.

CIRCUIT BREAKER: A switch which protects an electrical circuit from overload by opening the circuit when the current flow exceeds a predetermined level. Some circuit breakers must be reset manually, while most reset automatically.

COIL (IGNITION): A transformer in the ignition circuit which steps up the voltage provided to the spark plugs.

COMBINATION MANIFOLD: An assembly which includes both the intake and exhaust manifolds in one casting.

COMBINATION VALVE: A device used in some fuel systems that routes fuel vapors to a charcoal storage canister instead of venting them into the atmosphere. The valve relieves fuel tank pressure and allows fresh air into the tank as the fuel level drops to prevent a vapor lock situation.

COMPRESSION RATIO: The comparison of the total volume of the cylinder and combustion chamber with the piston at BDC and the piston at TDC.

CONDENSER: 1. An electrical device which acts to store an electrical charge, preventing voltage surges. 2. A radiator-like device in the air conditioning system in which refrigerant gas condenses into a liquid, giving off heat.

CONDUCTOR: Any material through which an electrical current can be transmitted easily.

CONTINUITY: Continuous or complete circuit. Can be checked with an ohmmeter.

COUNTERSHAFT: An intermediate shaft which is rotated by a mainshaft and transmits, in turn, that rotation to a working part.

CRANKCASE: The lower part of an engine in which the crankshaft and related parts operate.

CRANKSHAFT: The main driving shaft of an engine which receives reciprocating motion from the pistons and converts it to rotary motion.

CYLINDER: In an engine, the round hole in the engine block in which the piston(s) ride.

CYLINDER BLOCK: The main structural member of an engine in which is found the cylinders, crankshaft and other principal parts.

CYLINDER HEAD: The detachable portion of the engine, usually fastened to the top of the cylinder block and containing all or most of the combustion chambers. On overhead valve engines, it contains the valves and their operating parts. On overhead cam engines, it contains the camshaft as well.

DEAD CENTER: The extreme top or bottom of the piston stroke.

DETONATION: An unwanted explosion of the air/fuel mixture in the combustion chamber caused by excess heat and compression, advanced timing, or an overly lean mixture. Also referred to as "ping".

DIAPHRAGM: A thin, flexible wall separating two cavities, such as in a vacuum advance unit.

DIESELING: A condition in which hot spots in the combustion chamber cause the engine to run on after the key is turned off.

DIFFERENTIAL: A geared assembly which allows the transmission of motion between drive axles, giving one axle the ability to turn faster than the other.

DIODE: An electrical device that will allow current to flow in one direction only.

DISC BRAKE: A hydraulic braking assembly consisting of a brake disc, or rotor, mounted on an axle, and a caliper assembly containing, usually two brake pads which are activated by hydraulic pressure. The pads are forced against the sides of the disc, creating friction which slows the vehicle.

DISTRIBUTOR: A mechanically driven device on an engine which is responsible for electrically firing the spark plug at a predetermined point of the piston stroke.

DOWEL PIN: A pin, inserted in mating holes in two different parts allowing those parts to maintain a fixed relationship.

DRUM BRAKE: A braking system which consists of two brake shoes and one or two wheel cylinders, mounted on a fixed backing plate, and a brake drum, mounted on an axle, which revolves around the assembly.

DWELL: The rate, measured in degrees of shaft rotation, at which an electrical circuit cycles on and off.

ELECTRONIC CONTROL UNIT (ECU): Ignition module, module, amplifier or igniter. See Module for definition.

ELECTRONIC IGNITION: A system in which the timing and firing of the spark plugs is controlled by an electronic control unit, usually called a module. These systems have no points or condenser.

END-PLAY: The measured amount of axial movement in a shaft.

ENGINE: A device that converts heat into mechanical energy.

EXHAUST MANIFOLD: A set of cast passages or pipes which conduct exhaust gases from the engine.

FEELER GAUGE: A blade, usually metal, of precisely predetermined thickness, used to measure the clearance between two parts.

FIRING ORDER: The order in which combustion occurs in the cylinders of an engine. Also the order in which spark is distributed to the plugs by the distributor.

FLOODING: The presence of too much fuel in the intake manifold and combustion chamber which prevents the air/fuel mixture from firing, thereby causing a no-start situation.

FLYWHEEL: A disc shaped part bolted to the rear end of the crankshaft. Around the outer perimeter is affixed the ring gear. The starter drive engages the ring gear, turning the flywheel, which rotates the crankshaft, imparting the initial starting motion to the engine.

FOOT POUND (ft. lbs. or sometimes, ft.lb.): The amount of energy or work needed to raise an item weighing one pound, a distance of one foot.

FUSE: A protective device in a circuit which prevents circuit overload by breaking the circuit when a specific amperage is present. The device is constructed around a strip or wire of a lower amperage rating than the circuit it is designed to protect. When an amperage higher than that stamped on the fuse is present in the circuit, the strip or wire melts, opening the circuit.

GEAR RATIO: The ratio between the number of teeth on meshing gears.

GENERATOR: A device which converts mechanical energy into electrical energy.

HEAT RANGE: The measure of a spark plug's ability to dissipate heat from its firing end. The higher the heat range, the hotter the plug fires.

HUB: The center part of a wheel or gear.

HYDROCARBON (HC): Any chemical compound made up of hydrogen and carbon. A major pollutant formed by the engine as a byproduct of combustion.

HYDROMETER: An instrument used to measure the specific gravity of a solution.

INCH POUND (inch lbs.; sometimes in.lb. or in. lbs.): One twelfth of a foot pound.

INDUCTION: A means of transferring electrical energy in the form of a magnetic field. Principle used in the ignition coil to increase voltage.

INJECTOR: A device which receives metered fuel under relatively low pressure and is activated to inject the fuel into the engine under relatively high pressure at a predetermined time.

INPUT SHAFT: The shaft to which torque is applied, usually carrying the driving gear or gears.

INTAKE MANIFOLD: A casting of passages or pipes used to conduct air or a fuel/air mixture to the cylinders.

JOURNAL: The bearing surface within which a shaft operates.

KEY: A small block usually fitted in a notch between a shaft and a hub to prevent slippage of the two parts.

MANIFOLD: A casting of passages or set of pipes which connect the cylinders to an inlet or outlet source.

MANIFOLD VACUUM: Low pressure in an engine intake manifold formed just below the throttle plates. Manifold vacuum is highest at idle and drops under acceleration.

MASTER CYLINDER: The primary fluid pressurizing device in a hydraulic system. In automotive use, it is found in brake and hydraulic clutch systems and is pedal activated, either directly or, in a power brake system, through the power booster.

MODULE: Electronic control unit, amplifier or igniter of solid state or integrated design which controls the current flow in the ignition primary circuit based on input from the pick-up coil. When the module opens the primary circuit, high secondary voltage is induced in the coil.

NEEDLE BEARING: A bearing which consists of a number (usually a large number) of long, thin rollers.

OHM: (Ω) The unit used to measure the resistance of conductor-to-electrical flow. One ohm is the amount of resistance that limits current flow to one ampere in a circuit with one volt of pressure.

OHMMETER: An instrument used for measuring the resistance, in ohms, in an electrical circuit.

OUTPUT SHAFT: The shaft which transmits torque from a device, such as a transmission.

OVERDRIVE: A gear assembly which produces more shaft revolutions than that transmitted to it.

OVERHEAD CAMSHAFT (OHC): An engine configuration in which the camshaft is mounted on top of the cylinder head and operates the valve either directly or by means of rocker arms.

OVERHEAD VALVE (OHV): An engine configuration in which all of the valves are located in the cylinder head and the camshaft is located in the cylinder block. The camshaft operates the valves via lifters and pushrods.

OXIDES OF NITROGEN (NOx): Chemical compounds of nitrogen produced as a byproduct of combustion. They combine with hydrocarbons to produce smog.

OXYGEN SENSOR: Used with the feedback system to sense the presence of oxygen in the exhaust gas and signal the computer which can reference the voltage signal to an air/fuel ratio.

PINION: The smaller of two meshing gears.

PISTON RING: An open-ended ring which fits into a groove on the outer diameter of the piston. Its chief function is to form a seal between the piston and cylinder wall. Most automotive pistons have three rings: two for compression sealing; one for oil sealing.

PRELOAD: A predetermined load placed on a bearing during assembly or by adjustment.

PRIMARY CIRCUIT: The low voltage side of the ignition system which consists of the ignition switch, ballast resistor or resistance wire, bypass, coil, electronic control unit and pick-up coil as well as the connecting wires and harnesses.

PRESS FIT: The mating of two parts under pressure, due to the inner diameter of one being smaller than the outer diameter of the other, or vice versa; an interference fit.

RACE: The surface on the inner or outer ring of a bearing on which the balls, needles or rollers move.

REGULATOR: A device which maintains the amperage and/or voltage levels of a circuit at predetermined values.

RELAY: A switch which automatically opens and/or closes a circuit.

RESISTANCE: The opposition to the flow of current through a circuit or electrical device, and is measured in ohms. Resistance is equal to the voltage divided by the amperage.

RESISTOR: A device, usually made of wire, which offers a preset amount of resistance in an electrical circuit.

RING GEAR: The name given to a ring-shaped gear attached to a differential case, or affixed to a flywheel or as part of a planetary gear set.

ROLLER BEARING: A bearing made up of hardened inner and outer races between which hardened steel rollers move.

ROTOR: 1. The disc-shaped part of a disc brake assembly, upon which the brake pads bear; also called, brake disc. 2. The device mounted atop the distributor shaft, which passes current to the distributor cap tower contacts.

SECONDARY CIRCUIT: The high voltage side of the ignition system, usually above 20,000 volts. The secondary includes the ignition coil, coil wire, distributor cap and rotor, spark plug wires and spark plugs.

SENDING UNIT: A mechanical, electrical, hydraulic or electromagnetic device which transmits information to a gauge.

SENSOR: Any device designed to measure engine operating conditions or ambient pressures and temperatures. Usually electronic in nature and designed to send a voltage signal to an on-board computer, some sensors may operate as a simple on/off switch or they may provide a variable voltage signal (like a potentiometer) as conditions or measured parameters change.

SHIM: Spacers of precise, predetermined thickness used between parts to establish a proper working relationship.

SLAVE CYLINDER: In automotive use, a device in the hydraulic clutch system which is activated by hydraulic force, disengaging the clutch.

SOLENOID: A coil used to produce a magnetic field, the effect of which is to produce work.

SPARK PLUG: A device screwed into the combustion chamber of a spark ignition engine. The basic construction is a conductive core inside of a ceramic insulator, mounted in an outer conductive base. An electrical charge from the spark plug wire travels along the conductive core and jumps a preset air gap to a grounding point or points at the end of the conductive base. The resultant spark ignites the fuel/air mixture in the combustion chamber.

SPLINES: Ridges machined or cast onto the outer diameter of a shaft or inner diameter of a bore to enable parts to mate without rotation.

TACHOMETER: A device used to measure the rotary speed of an engine, shaft, gear, etc., usually in rotations per minute.

THERMOSTAT: A valve, located in the cooling system of an engine, which is closed when cold and opens gradually in response to engine heating, controlling the temperature of the coolant and rate of coolant flow.

TOP DEAD CENTER (TDC): The point at which the piston reaches the top of its travel on the compression stroke.

TORQUE: The twisting force applied to an object.

TORQUE CONVERTER: A turbine used to transmit power from a driving member to a driven member via hydraulic action, providing changes in drive ratio and torque. In automotive use, it links the driveplate at the rear of the engine to the automatic transmission.

TRANSDUCER: A device used to change a force into an electrical signal.

TRANSISTOR: A semi-conductor component which can be actuated by a small voltage to perform an electrical switching function.

TUNE-UP: A regular maintenance function, usually associated with the replacement and adjustment of parts and components in the electrical and fuel systems of a vehicle for the purpose of attaining optimum performance.

TURBOCHARGER: An exhaust driven pump which compresses intake air and forces it into the combustion chambers at higher than atmospheric pressures. The increased air pressure allows more fuel to be burned and results in increased horsepower being produced.

VACUUM ADVANCE: A device which advances the ignition timing in response to increased engine vacuum.

VACUUM GAUGE: An instrument used to measure the presence of vacuum in a chamber.

VALVE: A device which control the pressure, direction of flow or rate of flow of a liquid or gas.

VALVE CLEARANCE: The measured gap between the end of the valve stem and the rocker arm, cam lobe or follower that activates the valve.

VISCOSITY: The rating of a liquid's internal resistance to flow.

VOLTMETER: An instrument used for measuring electrical force in units called volts. Voltmeters are always connected parallel with the circuit being tested.

WHEEL CYLINDER: Found in the automotive drum brake assembly, it is a device, actuated by hydraulic pressure, which, through internal pistons, pushes the brake shoes outward against the drums.

MASTER

INDEX